YOUNG CHARLES SUMNER
AND THE LEGACY OF
THE AMERICAN ENLIGHTENMENT, 1811–1851

DATE DUE

Charles Sumner in 1846 by Eastman Johnson. *Courtesy National Park Service, Longfellow National Historic Site.*

YOUNG
CHARLES SUMNER

AND THE LEGACY OF THE
AMERICAN ENLIGHTENMENT, 1811–1851

Anne-Marie Taylor

UNIVERSITY OF MASSACHUSETTS PRESS
Amherst

Copyright © 2001 by University of Massachusetts Press
All rights reserved
Printed in the United States of America

LC 2001035600
ISBN 1-55849-300-X

Designed by Milenda Nan Ok Lee
Set in Adobe Garamond by Graphic Composition, Inc.
Printed and bound by Thomson-Shore, Inc.

Library of Congress Cataloging-in-Publication Data
Taylor, Anne-Marie, 1964–
Young Charles Sumner and the legacy of the American Enlightenment,
1811–1851 / Anne-Marie Taylor.
p. cm.
Based on the author's dissertation.
Includes bibliographical references and index.
ISBN 1-55849-300-X (alk. paper)
1. Sumner, Charles, 1811–1874. 2. Sumner, Charles, 1811–1874—Childhood
and youth. 3. Legislators—United States—Biography. 4. United States. Congress.
Senate—Biography. 5. Free Soil Party (U.S.). 6. United States—Politics and
government—1815–1861. 7. Antislavery movements—United States—History.
8. Sumner, Charles, 1811–1874—Political and social views. 9. Enlightenment—
United States. 10. Boston (Mass.)—Intellectual life—19th century. I. Title.
E415.9.S9 T39 2001
973.5'092—dc21 2001035600

British Library Cataloguing in Publication data are available.

To My Parents

"The Duties of Life are more than Life."
—Francis Bacon

CONTENTS

ACKNOWLEDGMENTS

LET ME FIRST thank Charles Sumner himself. No one could have taken me on an odyssey of quite the compelling richness and variety—from art, letters, and philosophy to reform and politics, through America and Europe—that he has. A professor once advised me against devoting a term paper to Sumner because it would simply require too much time and research. It is the only advice, considerate as it was, that I am glad I did not follow. In all other cases, it is to my own stubbornness that I must credit all the faults that remain in this book. But I know full well how much I have learned and benefited from the generosity among lovers of history in the sharing of ideas, information, encouragement, and, yes, advice. The discovery of all their kindness has been perhaps the most rewarding thing of all.

I owe my greatest debt to Leonard L. Richards, who guided me through every version of this book from its earliest inception with a wise and critical eye, deftly aimed questions, and a constant, infectious enthusiasm. Winfred E. A. Bernhard and Stephen B. Oates likewise, through many versions, helped hone my understanding of the subject by reminding me to keep my attention on the overarching ideas, the point behind the story, and on telling that story as well as possible. David Paroissien also read the whole manuscript, offering both good counsel and good countenance. The scholarship and humanism of these gentlemen has been a constant example to me. To their expertise and encouragement I owe more than I can ever say.

It is with great pleasure that I thank Clark Dougan, senior editor of the University of Massachusetts Press, for his faith in my work and his ever patient helpfulness; Carol Betsch, managing editor, for her perfect combination of professionalism and graciousness; and Kay Scheuer, without whose painstaking copyediting this book would have been the poorer.

The staffs of the following libraries deserve my thanks for all their kind assistance during my visits to them: The Andover-Harvard Theological Library—especially Malcolm C. Hamilton, Interim Librarian; the American Antiquarian Society; the Bostonian Society; the Government Documents and Microforms Departments of the Boston Public Library—in particular Charles S. Longley, Curator of Microtexts and Newspapers; The Houghton Library, Harvard University; the Harvard University Archives; the Harvard Law School Library—

especially David Warrington, Head of Special Collections, and David de Lorenzo, then Curator of Manuscripts; the Massachusetts Historical Society— in particular Virginia Smith, Reference Librarian, and Anne E. Bentley, Curator of the Art Collection; and the W.E.B. Du Bois Library of the University of Massachusetts at Amherst—especially the reference librarians, Linda Seidman, Head of Special Collections and Archives, and most particularly Edla Holm and the staff of the Interlibrary Loan Office, who saw me through countless reels of microfilm with a despatch and cheerfulness which made my visits to them a social as well as an academic pleasure.

For their gracious permission to quote from letters in their possession I am most grateful to the Harvard Law School Library, the Harvard University Archives, the Houghton Library of Harvard University, and the Massachusetts Historical Society.

Nor can I fail to express my appreciation to all those people and libraries who took part in the microfilming of the papers of Charles Sumner. Making this vast correspondence readily available is a great boon to all students of Sumner and of countless aspects of nineteenth-century American and European history. It can only encourage a better and wider understanding of the man and his time. The originals of the letters I have so happily been able to use from this compilation may be found in the following repositories: the Adams Papers at the Massachusetts Historical Society (from the microfilm edition of which come all the correspondence with the Adams family reproduced on the Sumner microfilm); the Boston Public Library; the Department of Special Collections, Boston University; the Manuscripts Division, John Hay Library, Brown University; Trinity College Library, Cambridge; the Clarke Historical Library, Central Michigan University; the Cincinnati Museum Center; the Rare Book and Manuscript Library, Columbia University; Rare and Manuscript Collections, Cornell University; the Rare Book, Manuscript, and Special Collections Library, Duke University; the Free Library of Philadelphia; Special Collections, Harvard Law School Library; the Houghton Library, Harvard University; the Huntington Library; the Library of Congress; the Maine Historical Society; the Massachusetts Historical Society; the Rare Books and Special Collections Division, McGill University Libraries; William L. Clements Library, University of Michigan; the National Park Service, Longfellow National Historic Site, Cambridge, Mass.; the New England Historic Genealogical Society; the New-York Historical Society; the Henry W. and Albert A. Berg Collection of English and American Literature, and the Manuscripts and Archives Division, The New York Public Library; Archives Library Division, Ohio Historical Society; the Codrington Library, All Souls College, Oxford; the Peabody Essex Museum, Salem, Mass.; the Historical Society of Pennsylvania; the Arthur and Elizabeth Schlesinger Library, Radcliffe College; the Rhode Island Historical Society; the Department of Rare

Books and Special Collections, Rush Rhees Library, University of Rochester; the Sophia Smith Collection, Smith College; the Archives of American Art, Smithsonian Institution; the Harry Ransom Humanities Research Center, The University of Texas at Austin; Department of Manuscripts and Rare Books, Library of University College London; the West Sussex Records Office; Special Collections, Wichita State University Library; the Beinecke Rare Book and Manuscript Library, Yale University; Special Collections, Bailey/Howe Library, University of Vermont.

It is not only historians and librarians, however, who have helped me. Many friends, too, have put up with my fixation on Charles Sumner and the events of "a hundred and fifty years ago" with endless patience and wholesome reminders to get out once in a while for fresh air or good talk. And when I could not take their advice, my puppy Toby slept by my feet as I worked.

My deepest thanks must go to my parents. They first taught me to love books, admire virtue, and seek to do my duty—as they first taught me the meaning of selfless love. Throughout this project, as through all the projects of my life, they have been my teachers, research assistants, first readers and critics, inspiration, comforters, and warmest supporters. To them I dedicate this book with love and gratitude.

A.-M. T.

NOTE ON TYPOGRAPHY

In order to preserve as much as possible of the flavor of the original letters which form the backbone of this book, I have tried faithfully to reproduce their original characteristics—multiple underlinings, frequent abbreviations, even simple misspellings—when they did not seem to detract from the meaning. The number of underlinings has been indicated typographically as follows.

italics   *freedom*

reflects one underline in the original letter;

italics + underline   <u>*freedom*</u>

reflects two underlines;

italic small caps   *FREEDOM*

reflects three underlines;

italic small caps + underline   <u>*FREEDOM*</u>

reflects four underlines.

YOUNG CHARLES SUMNER
AND THE LEGACY OF
THE AMERICAN ENLIGHTENMENT, 1811–1851

INTRODUCTION

CHARLES SUMNER is one of America's greatest yet most neglected statesmen. To the profound moral questions and rapid social change that faced the nineteenth century, he sought to bring the experience of history, a broad philosophical understanding of man and society, and the goals of a humanitarian idealism. As both his philosophical outlook and the antislavery movement in which he made his most famous contributions came into discredit in the more conservative and cynical late nineteenth and twentieth centuries, however, Sumner came to be defined narrowly as an antislavery senator, typecast as an arrogant fanatic, and too often reduced to a stock character in the historical literature. His stature too great for him to be set completely aside, no history of the American Civil War and Reconstruction could fail to mention him, but the intellectual outlook and cultural values that gave him that stature were generally ignored or belittled. As a result of this misunderstanding of Sumner, in both his intellectual and personal character, America has been robbed of one of her most appealing leaders and inspiring voices, of a man whom, even before he entered the United States Senate where he would do his greatest service, an English public man and political thinker praised as "an Orator"—which meant not only a literary man but a moral leader—"& nearly a Philosopher."[1]

Long before entering the Senate, the young Sumner had had an international reputation as a promising jurist at a time when, unlike any other intellectual or artistic production, American and European jurisprudence were accepted on equal footing by European intellectuals. He participated actively in the cultural flowering that became known as the American Renaissance, and was a friend of such as Longfellow, Emerson, and Whittier. Outside New England he was a valued correspondent of such as Francis Lieber, Richard Cobden, and Alexis de Tocqueville. As a much admired and beloved orator, he was himself acknowledged as one of America's most important rising men of letters. He had also begun a career as one of the nation's most influential art patrons. At the same time, Sumner had achieved wide renown and provoked heated controversy as an outspoken champion of legal reform, international peace, education reform, and the reform of prison discipline at a time when the American debate on the latter subject was held the most productive in the Western world. He had become one of

New England's most prominent antislavery activists as well as a founder of the antislavery Free Soil party.

In 1851, at the age of forty, Sumner was elected to the United States Senate, where he would serve the last twenty-three years of his life. It was there that he helped found the Republican party, which would go on to conduct the Civil War and abolish slavery. In 1856, for his outspokenness against slavery, Sumner would be brutally assaulted on the floor of the Senate by a congressman from South Carolina, but he would return to the institution to become the foremost senatorial leader of emancipation, of the concept of equality before the law, and of full civil and political rights for all Americans regardless of color. Sumner would also be considered Washington's greatest expert on international affairs. As Chairman of the Foreign Relations Committee from 1861 to 1871, he would keep the United States from adding foreign war to her domestic war, prevent her threatened takeovers of Caribbean nations, further the principle of arbitration, and uphold and help to expand the dictates of international law. The hatred against him felt by the supporters of slavery is still remembered, but he was at least as deeply beloved by humanitarians, literary men, and ordinary people across the North. They reacted to the news of Sumner's death at the age of sixty-three in 1874 with such an outpouring of feeling that, in the history of the Republic, only President Lincoln's assassination had been met with greater public mourning.

Popular interest in Sumner at the time of his death inspired a flood of biographies to recount, celebrate and, as time went on, to criticize his life and accomplishments. The rejection of the philosophical concerns of the first part of the nineteenth century by very different assumptions about human nature and society after the end of Reconstruction and especially in the twentieth century has meant, by contrast, that since 1911 there have appeared just two biographies of Sumner, only one of them of full length. An unfortunate phenomenon has resulted. The one biography of Sumner that stands out for its richness of detail and of source material, for its understanding of its subject, and for its general fairness and reliability has been relatively little used by recent historians because it was written by a friend of Sumner's. Instead they have relied upon the one full-length twentieth-century scholarly biography, which, however, is fatally flawed by its misuse of sources, and by a pervasive and distorting bias.

When Edward Pierce published his memoir of Sumner in 1877 and 1893, he had been not only a friend of Sumner's for twenty-five years, but also a close observer of the antislavery movement, and had known all its leaders, especially in Massachusetts, very well. Though he went into law rather than politics, he took part in the early Reconstruction efforts at Port Royal, South Carolina, during the Civil War. In the effervescence of his first youthful attachment to Sumner he began collecting documents for a future biography, and he continued to do so as his friendship and his own judgment matured. He was one of three friends to whom Sumner would will his papers—those same papers that now form the bulk of the collection at Harvard's Houghton Library—while, through requests for information, Pierce put together another impressive collection of his own. Pierce did not hide his political orientation—when he agreed as well as when he disagreed with Sumner,—but he took a lawyerly care in his use of sources and in his documentation, and tried to be fair to Sumner, his friends, and his antagonists alike. Pierce was writing a memoir, however, not a study. He did not neglect the important effect of Boston's society on its politics, but it was not his role to analyze New England culture; nor did he attempt an analysis of Sumner's ideas. It is sometimes apparent, too, that a difference of just eighteen years between his age and Sumner's was enough, in a period of rapid change, to make some of the cultural forces that had made a deep impression on Sumner seem obscure to Pierce.

The study of those cultural forces and of their influence on Sumner's thought might well have been the province of a twentieth-century historian, but apparently the cultural forces of the twentieth century itself got in the way. For most of the century, until the effects of another civil rights movement began to be widely felt, the historical profession, especially with regard to the Civil War and Reconstruction, was dominated by an hostility to the antislavery movement and the aim of civil and political equality for blacks. Sumner's very prominence in the movement, his early support for such equality, guaranteed that, after having achieved popularity in his own time, Sumner would once again in the twentieth century be portrayed more as he had been by nineteenth-century slave owners—as a narrow, arrogant dogmatist, or indeed a reckless fanatic, blindly seeking the ill of the nation.[2]

Along with this anti-intellectual bias, much of twentieth-century historiography was written under the shadow of World War I. Disillusioned by the realities of the Great War, the so-called revisionist historians, who would long dominate the profession, thought that war was too horrible ever to admit of any true ideological cause, that it could come about only by a kind of mass insanity or a failure of leadership. It followed that the debate over slavery could not explain the Civil War, the coming of which was ascribed rather to a "blundering generation" of self-seeking politicians who failed to accept necessary compromises. Such assumptions were not likely to encourage careful analysis of the ideas of a man like Charles Sumner.[3]

The fact that, in 1960 and 1970, David Donald published a heavily researched two-volume biography of Sumner showed that he wished to go beyond early twentieth-century historiography's partisan and dismissive attitude toward the antislavery movement. Subsequent studies of Sumner's career must confront the wealth of material contained in these volumes. Donald was not able, however, to escape the traditional anti-abolitionist and anti–New England bias. As Paul

Goodman has pointed out, Donald was also deeply influenced by revisionist writing. At about the same time that his biography of Sumner first appeared, Donald published articles arguing, for example, that the growth of abolitionism could be explained not by any opposition to slavery, but by the desire of the sons of former Federalists to recover their family status lost to the growth of industrialism, and by the loneliness of their daughters, deprived of suitable husbands. The public was willing to support such irresponsible and self-absorbed leaders, argued Donald in a companion piece, because the expansion of the suffrage in the early nineteenth century had admitted to the vote an ill-informed generation.[4]

Under these historiographical influences, Donald wrote his biography of Sumner, portraying him as the quintessential "revisionist" antislavery man. Sumner, Donald alleged, was a man intellectually shallow, imitative, but obstinate, reckless, and fanatical in his crusading for those positions that he borrowed from others. The man pictured by Donald was cold of temperament, weak and devious, concealing his personal ambition behind the façade of antislavery out of a combination of hypocrisy and self-delusion, and was thus justly mistrusted by conservative statesmen and the leaders of his community. Having achieved great power by the late 1850's and eager for more, this person played an important role in bringing on the tragic and needless Civil War, but without ever achieving enough intellectual maturity to understand what folly he had committed. ·

This is the portrait given in Donald's biography; it is not a portrait of the real Charles Sumner. In order to achieve it, Donald must consistently misuse his sources. He disregards evidence of the evolution of Sumner's ideas and openly belittles what ideas he cannot deny. He misrepresents Sumner's relationships with others. He assumes that the judgments of enemies are generally more perspicacious or simply more interesting than those of friends because they are hostile. He edits quotations to eliminate parts that conflict with his interpretation, or implies that quotations support his interpretation when the supporting evidence is supplied only by his own additions. He takes quotations out of context in such a way as to change their meaning. Beyond this, he never seriously considers the cultural and intellectual history of New England, of the legal profession, of America's artistic and literary awakening, or of the reform movements, all of which, however, had a profound effect on Sumner's thinking and career. Donald's own lack of sympathy, even frank hostility, toward Sumner and toward reformers in general seems to permit him to take such liberties unawares. Representative examples of these practices will be discussed in the notes of the present book, but David Donald himself has recently and candidly admitted a fundamental reason for his failure to draw a convincing portrait of Sumner: "Though I have spent much of my life studying the history of agitators," he writes, "I have never grown to like them, or even particularly to sympathize with them. There is something about the reformist temperament, with its zealotry, its absolute certainty of goals and its indifference to means, that I have never found congenial. It is easier for me to understand a pragmatist like Lincoln than an ideologue like Charles Sumner."[5]

It has been all too common to base explanations of Sumner's motivation and outlook on interpretations of his later career, on politicians' and historians' subsequent reactions to the controversies in which he took part, and especially on unsympathetic interpretations of the antislavery movement as a whole. This is a mistake. To understand Charles Sumner one must begin at the beginning. This biography will thus focus on Sumner's background, education, and young manhood, on his life before he took public office. The work that would make him most famous lies beyond the scope of the present volume, but to appreciate that work, one must first understand the development of Sumner's own mind and character in the culture that nursed him, and the philosophical and moral dilemmas that propelled him to question his proper role in society. It was only as a result of these things that Sumner entered public life, slowly and late, and with already carefully thought out and well-established views on human nature, on the development of human history, and on the future to which society should tend.

These were burning questions as Sumner grew up and came to manhood. When he was born, the new nation was only thirty-five years old. The brash, hopeful Jacksonian nation so often portrayed was also full of concerns about America's lingering colonial and emerging democratic shortcomings. David Donald suggests, in the preface to his second volume, that the concept of civilization was fundamental to Sumner's thinking. Unfortunately, he did not follow up his remark; it would have been fruitful to do so. In the early decades of the country's history, many Americans were vitally concerned about American civilization or the lack thereof. They saw about them a society as yet unformed, full of vitality but in danger of remaining permanently crude and selfish. These Americans were anxious to establish a firm intellectual and artistic foundation from which the United States might grow to share equally in the richness of Western culture and be deservedly respected by the elder nations. Growing up among educated Bostonians, Sumner imbibed such concerns from earliest youth and responded to them with the fullness of a soul that itself craved education and culture. Whether promoting American law, letters, sculpture, or social reform, Sumner considered that he was striving for the richest fulfillment of American culture.

Literary and social reform did not consistently go together in the United States; more American reformers of the first half of the nineteenth century were motivated by evangelical religion than by cultural fulfillment. For Sumner, however, that fulfillment required social as well as literary improvement, the improvement of mankind as well as of art, for Sumner took his intellectual spirit and motivation from the American Enlightenment. Like its European counterpart, in its own generally less skeptical and anti-institutional way, the American Age of Light debated about the nature of man, about his perfectibility, about the perfectibility of his society and the progress of human history, and about the ties that bind men and their nations together. Though the popular, nationalistic, and material concerns of the nineteenth century would soon replace the cosmopolitan humanism of the Enlightenment, the movement that had overseen the founding of the nation was still alive as Sumner grew up, and nowhere did it retain its old vibrancy more than in the educated circles of Boston and Cambridge and in the hearts of Sumner's own family.

Though politics would gnaw at it, Sumner would never abandon the hopeful understanding of human nature and its potential that formed the basis of American Moral Philosophy—that philosophy, deeply influenced by the Scottish Enlightenment, in which late eighteenth- and early nineteenth-century American higher education was grounded. For Sumner, as for the moral philosophers, that human potential came from man's ability, with application, to balance his own animal, intellectual, and ethical faculties, striving to place his whole being under the guidance of his reason and his conscience. Steeped in the legal tradition spurred by the Enlightenment's emphasis on the rule of law over that of men, Sumner likewise early responded to the principles of Natural Law—which, though of ancient origin, was at the heart of the debates over the relationship of man and society in the Age of Light—and its modern offspring the ideal of natural rights. From such foundations, Sumner took his passionate belief in civilization, that is, in a society both cultivated and just.

Nor could a child of New England and of the American Revolution ignore the implications of such beliefs for his own role in society. The obligation of the individual to work, according to his ability, for the public good, had been stressed by both Puritanism and Revolutionary republicanism. Though by the early nineteenth century the former existed only in its cultural legacy and the latter was already waning, those who had grown up during the Revolution continued to feel that call to duty. So did many of their children, spurred on perhaps by the feeling that their noble creed was already dying with the rise of mass democracy, industrialism and corporate capitalism, and the very success of the American experiment. "The duties of life are more than life," Sumner's father had believed and taught his children. Much of the energy and poignancy of Sumner's own story, much of its triumph and tragedy, comes from his own effort to live up to the creed of his fathers.

It is this double creed—that the humanistic ideals of the Enlightenment represented the best foundation for the public good, and that the individual had a duty to work for that good—that pushed Sumner gradually into reform and politics. He had, indeed, always felt a natural attraction to politics. So long as they seemed to him a mere personal temptation, however, he set them aside; it was only when he felt his conscience enlisted that he relented and accepted what had then become in his eyes a duty. His political apprenticeship of the 1840's would, in turn, cause him his first serious disillusionment. A similar disillusionment had once caused his father to abandon a political career. A combination of disappointment in politicians and his own essential continuing idealism about the future of man instead drove Sumner into political life.

The children and grandchildren of the Revolution had been raised to cherish the Union as both a political and a moral entity. As great ethical questions arose over matters of public policy, however, Americans divided in their loyalties between the moral Union envisioned by Enlightenment idealism and the political Union. Sumner was pained to see the leaders of the community—men who by tradition should have been moral as well as political leaders—abandon the Enlightenment principles once shared by all in favor of the security and self-interest of the material Union and increasingly of their class. To Sumner this was not only the overthrow of a noble tradition, it was an abnegation of that duty that each generation owed to the ones that would follow; it was selfishness throwing down the gauntlet to progress. This was a challenge that Sumner in his idealism could not forgo.

PART I

"O! For Some Retreat Where The *Mind* &
Not Its Appetites Can Be Fed"

FATHER AND SON

WHEN Charles Sumner looked back, he rarely spoke of the day-to-day realities of his childhood, remembering primarily the days of constant study, the humbleness of his family's circumstances, and their unhappiness. His whole life would bear testimony, however, to the values he had inherited from his family and his birthplace. He was born in Boston in 1811, a grandson of the American Revolution and a son of the final glow of the Enlightenment. John Adams had been accustomed to say that his generation had devoted itself to war and politics so that the next generation could study the sciences and the generation after that, the arts. It was such an aspiration, such a vision of civilization and of humanitarian idealism, such a sense of duty that would continue to drive Charles Sumner.[1]

Boston in 1811 was a bustling town of over 30,000 people, still small enough for everyone to mind everyone else's affairs, already big enough to be outgrowing its town meeting. It was a commercial port where ships bearing exotic fruits and Chinese silks crowded together at the wharves and sent their bowsprits jutting over the streets, and where the press of population was beginning to spread both humble frame houses and elegant brick mansions over the still green hills that dominated the little peninsula. Like the rest of the new country, but in its own proud and independent, some said parochial manner, Boston was debating with itself over the meaning of the Revolution in which it had played such a prominent role. Jeffersonian Republicans challenged the dominant Federalists. Unitarians challenged Trinitarians, and religious dissenters challenged both. Arguments over the French Revolution mingled with debates over our relationship with the mother country.

Heeding John Adams' call, Bostonian sons of the Revolution were striving to create scientific and cultural institutions to transform the busy mercantile port into the Athens of America, or perhaps more specifically into a second Liverpool, the culturally active port city of the admired scholar William Roscoe. Adams himself began the process in 1780 with the foundation of the American Academy of Arts and Sciences, inspired by Philadelphia's American Philosophical Society. The state's young history would soon receive a repository in the Massachusetts Historical Society, and in the first decade of the new century Boston would follow in the footsteps of the great British literary reviews with the new *Monthly*

Anthology and of the great British libraries with the Boston Athenæum, hoping thus to lay the foundations in the New World of a literary tradition worthy of the Old World. Meanwhile lawyers were attempting to professionalize themselves like their English brethren while trying to distinguish an American common law tradition. Massachusetts was proud of her already old educational traditions, which stretched back to her founding, but the sons and grandsons of the Revolution would repeatedly work to improve the cultural and educational standards of the Boston Latin School and of Harvard College (already calling itself a university) to bring them up to a level with the great schools of Europe. Everywhere Massachusetts, with her own particular earnestness, was striving for a cultural coming of age.

So was the Sumner family. Their struggle was most obviously economic, but in their hearts it was even more cultural. Charles Sumner's parents, Charles Pinckney and Relief (Jacob) Sumner, had neither of them been born in Boston. They both came from villages south of the city, he from Milton and she from Hanover. Both families had come to Massachusetts Bay in the 1630's and had been consistently respectable farming families, conscious of their civic duty, generally comfortable in means and prolific. Through his mother's family Charles Sumner was distantly related to Governor William Bradford, and through his father's family to the Massachusetts chief justice and popular Federalist governor Increase Sumner. His maternal great-grandfather was a well-to-do landowner and member of the Revolutionary Committee of Public Safety, while his paternal grandfather was a Revolutionary war hero. But the family fortunes changed during and just after the Revolution. The gate to their past was closed to them, and young Charles Pinckney and Relief would seek to build a better future in New England's capital.[2]

Everything changed for the Jacob children in 1799. At the beginning of August, David Jacob, their father, died at the age of thirty-six. Within a few weeks he was followed by their little sister Matilda, and then, a few days later, by their mother. The remaining six children, ranging in age from seventeen to two, were orphans. It is likely that they were divided up among relatives or neighbors to be cared for, but this was an added burden in difficult times. After a period of post-Revolutionary prosperity the New England economy was becoming strained as the rising population ran up against the long-brewing shortage of farmland. Young people from all over eastern New England began to leave home in record numbers to find land farther west or work in the cities. The two eldest Jacob children soon left, too, but it was more than money that sent Hannah and Relief to Boston. Relief had been only fourteen when she lost her parents, Hannah three years older. Neither had more than a common-school education, yet both grew to be respected for their intelligence and interest in learning. Hannah had a long career ahead of her as a schoolteacher. It is perhaps no surprise that neither of them found a husband to her taste in little Hanover and that they preferred to seek a better life in the city. Conditions were not easy, and the young women, now in their twenties, lodged in a boardinghouse on South Russell Street, on the poorer northern slope of Beacon Hill, where they took in needlework. But Relief and a fellow-boarder caught each other's eye and respect. He was nine years older than she, a Harvard graduate and a lawyer. His name was Charles Pinckney Sumner, and on 25 April 1810 hers became Mrs. Sumner.[3]

Money was tight, and the new couple set up their first household only a block away from the boardinghouse where they had met, moving into a little rented frame house on the corner of May and Buttolph, now Revere and Irving Streets, looking north and west down the steep hill. Perched on the edge of the poor black section of town, an area of crime and brothels, it was not an elegant address, but from the first, Mr. Sumner and his bride were the sort of couple people noticed. "'She was tall and stately,' said one who knew her well, 'with the old-school dignity of manner; and, if thought distant, you soon forgot, in her genial friendliness and evident superiority of mind, every thing except that she was one of the most admirable of women.'" He was literary, warm and even sentimental with friends, punctilious in the discharge of duty, noted for his old-fashioned courtliness. It was to these high-minded parents in their humble house that Charles Sumner and his twin sister Matilda were born on 6 January 1811. The babies brought with them double joy and, especially for their father, double worry for a future to which no new grounds of happiness could restore a luster long since faded.[4]

Charles Pinckney Sumner had had dreams. From the start his parents had encouraged in him the republican values of the Revolution and the aspirations of education. His father Job Sumner had been, in his happy-go-lucky way, an idealist. He had impatiently thrown off his family's farming ways to seek a better life through education and then, in the immediate aftermath of the battles of Lexington and Concord, had abandoned Harvard for the Continental Army. Charles Pinckney, his only child, could hardly have been more completely a son of the Revolution, born on 20 January in the very year 1776, when his father, having already fought at Bunker Hill, was off invading Canada on a career that would keep him active through the war and raise him to the rank of Major. As second-in-command during the evacuation of New York at the end of the war, it was he who ordered the salute to the departing General Washington that became "the last military salute of the Revolutionary army."[5]

It was not all glory. The spontaneous, ebullient, adventurous Major had failed to solemnize his tie to Esther Holmes, his son's mother, thus giving ammunition to future scandalmongers and denying his son and grandchildren the full pleasure of their pride in his accomplishments. He thus also denied them their grandmother, who, apart from a few details, became a ghost in the historical record. Perhaps his father's imperfect responsibility encouraged Charles Pinckney's own penetrating sense of duty, but it did not diminish the boy's admiration for him, nor, it seems, Esther's. Having originally named the child Job after his father, she then doubly honored her beloved by obeying his desires and changing his son's name. The boy would thus carry through life the name of his father's democratic- and cultural-minded South Carolinian comrade-at-arms, as well as the pride his mother must have cultivated in him for his father's heroism in the cause of independence and republican government.[6]

In the end there was nothing but pride. The Major's death in September 1789 at the age of thirty-five ended any dreams Esther and her little boy might have had of their all becoming a family. For a brief moment it had seemed things might work out. Congress had been so slow to pay members of the Continental Army that some of its officers had contemplated mutiny in 1783, and Major Sumner, the ninth of thirteen children of a widowed mother, had no money of his own. But when in 1785 Congress appointed him commissioner to settle the accounts between Georgia and the Confederation government, he thought he had struck it rich. He was so well received in Georgia that he set up a fine household and responded with immediate grateful generosity to his new hosts as well as family members back home. He was too trusting. Within three years he lamented: "I have been robbed by almost every man I have put any confidence in. They have taken all." Friends saw his once robust health decline. Hardly more than a year later, struck by food poisoning on a journey north, he died in New York. His thirteen-year-old son was left with mingled grief and pride to scour the newspaper accounts of the hero's funeral given his father. He read how it had been attended by the Society of the Cincinnati, Vice President John Adams, Secretary of War Henry Knox, and the entire Massachusetts delegation to the first Congress meeting under the new Constitution. In later life Charles Pinckney Sumner would write out long accounts of his father's life, would defend in the papers the namesake his father had given him, would follow his father into the Society of the Cincinnati, would always make sure his grave was tended, and would feel increasing regret over what seemed to him his own generation's failure to honor the political and cultural legacy for which his father's generation had fought.[7]

Major Sumner's desires that his son educate himself and become the gentleman and scholar he himself had always wished to be were realized. Before his death, Major Sumner had given whatever money he could earn or borrow to keep his son in school. With no financial guarantees for the future, Major Sumner nonetheless urged the thirteen-year-old's schoolmaster that he wanted the boy to learn Latin "as though he was destined for college," and he encouraged his son to "be a studious, good boy, and learn eloquence and manners, as well as wisdom and the languages, at the academy." Though, through those early and lonely years growing up, Charles Pinckney had to alternate between school and the farm chores he hated, he eventually fulfilled his father's dream, being graduated from Harvard, Phi Beta Kappa, in 1796.[8]

The boys whose first memories in life were of their fathers' fighting the Revolution arrived at college age when American fervor for its sister revolution in France was at its peak in 1792 and early 1793. No class was more affected than Charles Pinckney Sumner's. Voltaire, Rousseau, and d'Alembert were the heroes of the day—and the boys' favorite nicknames for each other. Tom Paine was so idolized that the college authorities presented each student with a copy, gratis, of Richard Watson's *Apology for the Bible* to counteract the spread of deism and insubordination. But during the year 1793 the execution of Louis XVI, the onset of the Terror, and the arrogance of Edmond Genêt, France's minister to the United States, turned the tide of popular sympathy especially at a Harvard controlled by the clergy. Relations declined till in 1798, with a "quasi-war" raging between France and the United States, Harvard had to drop from its Commencement exercises the French dialogue customarily performed by students for fear of the audience's anger at the now hated language.[9]

But Charles Pinckney Sumner's devotion to the Revolution for which his father had fought had evolved into a deep belief in the most liberal ideals of the Enlightenment—peace, equality, human brotherhood. His original interest in Tom Paine was not unusual; more so was his continued loyalty to Paine in 1795, when, in a valedictory poem, he portrayed God frowning upon the country's injustices, including its efforts to

> With slavish boldness prosecute the plan,
> To make a libel of the rights of man.

Lest his reader should miss the point, the nineteen-year-old advocate added a footnote to explain that the line referred indeed to Tom Paine's book.[10]

That same year, in a poem entitled "The Compass," Sumner offered a more complete statement of his Enlightenment idealism. The poem sings the benefits to technology, to commerce, to peace, to man brought by the advancement of learning and science symbolized by the compass. None of these benefits is greater than those which promote the happiness and "the *mutual good* of all mankind" through free trade and justice:

> More true inspir'd, we antedate the time,
> When futile war shall cease thru' every clime;
> No sanction'd slavery AFRIC's sons degrade,
> But equal rights shall equal earth pervade.[11]

The young man had the courage of his convictions. The year after he was graduated from college he embarked upon a voyage through the West Indies, despite the recent hostility between the United States and England and the present hostility prevailing there with France. In February 1798 his ship landed at Port-au-Prince on a Saint-Domingue torn by revolution. It had begun as a series of slave uprisings at the start of the decade as the black slaves of France's richest colony, inspired partly by the ideals of France's own Revolution, rose up against their white French masters. Rebellion soon became full-fledged revolution despite the National Convention's belated 1793 vote of emancipation. When Charles Pinckney Sumner arrived in 1798, the Revolution was midway in its career, with the great Dominican general Toussaint Louverture trying to gain control of the island by playing off its former French owners against the present British occupiers in what had become an international war.[12]

The events on Saint-Domingue had long since spread terror, not only among the island's whites, but among slaveholders in the United States who feared their own slaves might revolt. Even non-slaveholders and whites in those northern states that had already abolished slavery were horrified by the lurid stories in the newspapers of the brutality and blood-letting that characterized the Revolution. Atrocities were committed on all sides, but it was the blacks who took the full blame in the press, especially after white refugees from the island began pouring into the United States in 1793. Rumors of slave revolts swept across the South, followed by swift and often brutal repression. To be sure, some isolated individuals defended the Revolution in what would become the nation of Haiti on the grounds of the universal human rights proclaimed by the French Revolution and the American Declaration of Independence alike. None of these was more famous than Charles Pinckney Sumner's hero Tom Paine, now living in France. Even the American antislavery societies were afraid to join them, however, agreeing only in urging what the Americans usually called San Domingo as an illustration of the consequences of slaveholding. Long before Charles Pinckney Sumner left on his trip, virtually all expression of sympathy for the Haitian Revolution had been stifled. The once flourishing antislavery societies had begun a sharp decline in the face of the nervous horror of public opinion—a horror that long outlived the actual events and became a living ember in the debate over slavery in the United States that would itself culminate in civil war.[13]

Charles Pinckney Sumner's idealism was not frightened by the press or the opinions of his neighbors, however, nor by the more present dangers of an ongoing war. He was pleased to put in at Port-au-Prince and gladly accepted the invitation tendered by the Haitian authorities to all Americans present to join in their celebration of Washington's birthday. He collected a store of observations with which one day to impress upon his children the importance of freedom and human rights, but he did not wait to express his sympathy to the Revolution then under way. At the public dinner to which he had been invited, Sumner raised his glass to toast "Liberty, Equality, and Happiness, to all men." General Jean-Pierre Boyer, later President of the Haitian Republic, was so pleased with his words "that he sent one of his aids-de-camp to invite the young American to take the seat of honor by his side at the feast."[14]

Charles Pinckney Sumner would remain faithful all his life to the ideals of human brotherhood that had inspired him from youth. The equality he wished for Haiti he wished also for his own country, and he wished it in all aspects of human relations, believing it not only intrinsically right, but the only possible basis for a republic. Finding religious prejudice as unacceptable as racial prejudice, he deeply regretted the common American intolerance of Catholics. He often noted the inconsistency of the Puritans' leaving home to escape religious persecution only to persecute the Quakers. In contrast, he defended the religious tolerance of the Romans who, he once chastised Reverend John Sylvester John Gardiner of Trinity Church for forgetting, had never persecuted the Christians for their religion but only prosecuted them for repeatedly breaking the laws. In small but frequent and public ways, Sumner expressed his disapproval of present-day prejudice—pointedly accepting, against his usual rule, an invitation to a public dinner offered by the Irish Charitable Society in 1830 and offering a toast to Lord Baltimore, writing a public letter to cancel his subscription to a newspaper in protest against its anti-Catholic attacks, or giving thirty dollars to help the victims of the 1834 mob-burning of the Ursuline convent in Charlestown, an event that deeply depressed him.[15]

As he dreamt of a society without religious prejudice, so Charles Pinckney Sumner dreamt of a society blind to color. Though he never joined any abolitionist organization, he remained antislavery all his life and always had cordial relations with abolitionists. He was always ready to tell sad stories about the effects of slavery as he had witnessed them in the West Indies and also in the United States, while on his way to Georgia in late 1802 and early 1803 to settle unfinished business from his father's estate. He resented the arrogance of slaveholders' trying to dictate federal policy to their own advantage and telling Northerners "that we have no right to open our lips on the subject of slavery" even in the common national capital, which he labeled "a slave market." Nor did he spare Northern complicity in the peculiar institution through its commerce and shipping. Even more than religious prejudice, Sumner feared the effect of slavery on the future of the whole nation, lamenting in 1820 to a neighbor: "Our children's heads will some day be broken on a cannon-ball on this question."[16]

Beyond the institution of slavery, Charles Pinckney Sumner saw racism and the spirit of caste as the real danger: "To allow any class of persons [such as blacks & other persons under the ban of the law] to stand on an unequal footing for any thing short of crime, tends to obliterate in our minds & affections that love of equality on which our Commonwealth is based." Thus he felt that "[t]he best thing the Abolitionists can do for the people of color is to make their freedom a blessing to them in the states where they are free." Sumner himself insisted "he should be entirely willing to sit on the bench with a negro judge," and later, as Sheriff of Suffolk County, he took especial pains to make sure black prisoners got fair trials. He attacked racial segregation in the schools and spoke out against the legal ban on interracial marriage. In the street he gave "his customary bow" to all he met, whatever their complexion. In all of this he fully justified his eldest son's later appraisal of him as "a person [. . .] of remarkable independence."[17]

Such an idealism could not survive unsaddened by the realities of society. Nor could the personal hopes and dreams of such an idealistic young man bereft of family and financial support survive the realities of life untarnished and intact. At least as early as college, Charles Pinckney Sumner wanted to be a poet—not an occasional poet in his spare time like so many literary gentlemen with other careers; he wanted to live a life devoted to literature, writing polished and thoughtful verses on the human condition and the rights of man like another Pope or Cowper. He delighted in writing versified college themes, even using such occasions to lament the difficulties imposed by schoolwork on the student "Who tempts the steep of literary fame!", and he was very proud that his Vale-dictory Poem was "requested by his class." For his college friends he chose similarly literary-minded young men. Leonard Woods would become a professor of theology at Andover Seminary and, despite his political conservatism, would take a warm paternal pride in the decision of Charles Pinckney Sumner's eldest son to devote himself to moral reform, while John Pickering, future philologist and specialist in the North American Indian languages, would one day be eulogized by the young Charles Sumner, just then beginning his oratorical career, as the consummate scholar. To none was Charles Pinckney Sumner closer than to Joseph Story, two years his junior but his alter ego in attachment to the ideals of the French Revolution and in his poetical ambition. Separated after college, the two shared a correspondence full of books, poetry, and the dreams of noble fame their Revolutionary fathers had taught them to aspire to—as well as a sentimental warmth that, on Sumner's part, approached gratitude for having, after such a lonely youth, found a soulmate to respond to his innermost thoughts.[18]

Poetry was a respectable pastime for such cultivated young men, but it could not be a career and offered no hope of a livelihood. The first American poet to make a living from his art would be Henry Wadsworth Longfellow, future best friend of Charles Pinckney Sumner's eldest son. Sumner and Story shared the realization that they would have to give up their beloved literature for the law, the profession considered most noble and at least traditionally associated with the private cultivation of letters. Joseph Story, future Supreme Court Justice, made the transition more easily as he gradually discovered a congenial pursuit in the law. But young Sumner was wounded by the necessity of abandoning his more deeply cherished literary visions in favor of a profession his liberal ideals could not respect. Knowing in his heart his fate, he spent the year after college teaching and filling a commonplace book with quoted strictures on the dishonesty of lawyers "Who . . . prepare / For clients' wretched fate the legal snare," those "dark insidious men" who work "to perplex the truth / And lengthen simple justice into trade." His year of escape into the West Indies could not change the inevitable.

> Hence forth farewell then feverish thirst of pan
> Farewell the longings for a poet's name
> Perish my muse![19]

By the fall of 1798 both Sumner and Story were at work studying law and consoling each other. Story said that only the "hope of 'immortality'" kept up his courage, and wrote: "Charles, I flatter myself your heart is not unknown to me; *I have seen your spirit rise above your situation;* I have seen your ambition engaged in pursuits which ennoble by the impartation of excellence." Modestly brushing this aside as flattery, Sumner responded with similar encouragement: "Go on my Dear Friend perseveringly, inspired & buoy'd up by the hope of 'Immortality.' You pant for virtuous Fame & you will most assuredly attain it."[20]

Charles Pinckney Sumner studied law with the well-respected Judge George Richards Minot and then served in the office of Josiah Quincy, later Mayor of Boston and President of Harvard, who would remain a good friend despite their political differences. In 1801 Sumner passed the bar and set up in practice for himself in Boston. But he could not reconcile himself to his new profession. Instead he spent the next ten years and more searching elsewhere for the moral satisfaction he felt he had given up with literature, unable to keep his practice from languishing in the meantime.[21]

First he sought intellectual companionship and instruction with the Masons, whom he joined immediately in 1801. It was not unusual for young men like Sumner, newly set up in the city and in a profession, to come together in the Masonic Order. Through its veil of secrecy it gave off the promise of sociability and mutual encouragement in lonely and changing times. More than this, though he admitted to knowing little or nothing about Masonry before he joined, young Sumner was attracted by its pretensions to Enlightenment ideals and its claim to be "a 'Noble Science founded on Geometry,'" a subject in which he had always felt weak. He rose to the third degree, the most common, but soon became dissatisfied with the Masons' greater emphasis upon conviviality and good food and drink than on intellectual discussion and learning, and after a few years Sumner let his involvement drop.[22]

More sustained was Charles Pinckney Sumner's search for a satisfying religious home. Religiously tolerant and nontheological, what he really desired was a religious community that would give moral satisfaction based on the humanitarian ideals he cherished equally in the secular world. Perhaps this is what led him to prefer an Episcopalianism more tolerant of human frailty to New England's dominant but pessimistic Congregationalism. Upon his first settling in Boston he became a member of Trinity Church, the largest and most important Episcopal parish in the city. At first he tried to participate fully in Trinity's worship, even serving as clerk and "after the English style," reading responses from "an elevated seat near the chancel." But over time he may have become frustrated by the long-serving Reverend Gardiner's religious and social conservatism. Though he would cautiously remain a member of Trinity Church into the mid-1820's, by the opening years of the century Sumner was already beginning to inquire into the still controversial Unitarianism.[23]

It was during his year of teaching after college that Sumner met Henry Ware, in whose private school at Hingham he tutored for a time. Henry Ware was then still a decade away from his momentous installation in 1805 as Hollis Professor of Divinity at Harvard, an event symbolic of the capture of the state's foremost school by the rising Unitarians and one that fed the growing feud between them and their parent Congregationalists. Personally, however, Henry Ware was a gentle, benevolent individual, who seemed almost "colorless" compared to the controversies that would swirl about him, and Charles Pinckney Sumner formed a lifelong friendship with him. Charles Sumner would later remember the pleasure with which often, from a very small boy, "I have sat at his table on Sunday Evng, & walked and played afterwards in the garden"—undoubtedly while the Reverend and his father sat and talked.[24] Soon Charles Pinckney Sumner had formed another lifelong friendship—shared by the whole Sumner family—with the liberal-minded, meek, and kindly Ezra Stiles Gannett, soon to become assistant to William Ellery Channing at the prestigious Federal Street Church and first president of the American Unitarian Association. In 1822 the young Gannett, not yet ordained, baptized the Sumners' seventh child, Mary. Within three years Charles Pinckney Sumner would move his family from Trinity to the Unitarian King's Chapel. He was pleased by Unitarianism's rejection of the Congregationalists' traditional doctrine of the innate depravity of man in favor of an Enlightenment belief in man's potential goodness. Yet he remained unsatisfied and would keep his reservations about any particular sect. When in 1832 the Unitarian minister and budding Transcendentalist Ralph Waldo Emerson broke with his church by his refusal to offer the sacrament and left the ministry, Charles

Pinckney Sumner privately applauded him: "If I were a minister, & had sufficient courage, I would do the same."[25]

In his search for moral satisfaction no domain was more significant to Sumner than politics. Politics allowed him to take part in the ongoing work of establishing and maintaining the sound republican society for which his father's generation had fought. Thus Charles Pinckney Sumner always saw politics in national terms, upholding "*our UNION* as the ark of safety." The young Sumner shared his countrymen's admiration for Washington and in 1800, at the invitation of his hometown of Milton, eulogized him as a man of humanity and selflessness who had devoted his life to the good of his fellow countrymen and whose reward should be a corresponding republican virtue in the new American nation. In a world of monarchies and failed republican experiments, Sumner agreed with the prevailing celebration of true republicanism as the rule of the "omnipotent majority," where the great body of the people elected their rulers and the minority acquiesced in the choice and eschewed mere party politics or factionalism. The distrust of parties had a long tradition in Anglo-American thought, and it seemed to Sumner especially reasonable here where party divisions mirrored sectional divisions.[26]

Despite his rejection of the idea of party politics, it was Jefferson and the Democratic-Republican party that inspired Sumner to do more than acquiesce in his country's leaders. Privately he had deplored the high-handed disregard for the spirit of the law that he saw in such legislation as the 1798 Alien and Sedition Acts, and he attacked the New England Federalists' increasing tendency to sectionalist, anti-Southern rhetoric and the talk of the most conservative among them as early as 1804 for a separate New England nation. That this sectional talk was justified by evocation of Washington's name angered Sumner, who admired Washington precisely for his nationalism. So long as the Federalists were in power Sumner did not speak his minority views publicly and, though he was then of age, he did not vote in the election of 1800, but he felt freer when Jefferson became President. The liberal Enlightenment ideals that Jefferson represented much more closely matched his own, and Sumner was clearly sympathetic to the policy of greater diffusion of political authority and of religious tolerance called for by the Republicans. In Massachusetts Jefferson's party was also the party of nationalism and, thus it seemed to Sumner, of antipartyism, which, for him, gave it its most urgent appeal.[27]

By the campaign season of 1803–1804 Sumner felt moved to make his private feelings public and to take an active part in the effort to reëlect Jefferson. It was a critical and exciting moment for Bay State Republicans in particular. Massachusetts had long been dominated by the Federalists of Boston and the eastern seaboard, but the especially crushing Republican defeat of 1803, one year before the presidential contest, had energized the dissenters to strenuous action. Sumner could follow all these developments from the inside through his dear friend Joseph Story, who had become an important member of the state party. In 1804 Sumner delivered an address at Milton to urge the reëlection of Jefferson, and he eagerly threw back at the Federalists their talk of majority rule and energetic government, now superseded by complaints "of the fickle breath of popular applause"—fickle only to those whose "indiscretion has worn out" the people's tolerance for their authority.[28]

Jefferson won reëlection with the help of Massachusetts, which gave its first Republican majority that year. The party made big gains within the state as well, starting a trend of some years in the Republicans' favor. In his pleasure at the outcome, Sumner wrote a deferential letter in his best hand to Jefferson himself, expressing his heartfelt admiration and enclosing some of his writings. It would have been entirely natural for him at the same time to hope for some little recognition of his efforts—the time he had given to politics and undoubtedly his open attachment to the less powerful and less well-to-do Republicans had further undermined his struggling law practice—but he asked for none and none was immediately forthcoming. Still, Sumner continued his involvement despite the practical difficulties, and in 1806 he was rewarded with the post of clerk of the Massachusetts House. He held the post for most of the next five years, serving the last two under the speakership of Joseph Story. Story tried unsuccessfully to tempt his friend to take on the editorship of a Republican newspaper during the presidential contest of 1808—a position Sumner may well have thought too stridently partisan—but Sumner did continue to make campaign speeches for the Republicans, upholding their strong stand to defend the nation against the arrogant aggressions of England, the "leviathan of the day," and of France, for whom he insisted our gratitude should not become servitude. Always his arguments turned on keeping the nation together, united in its devotion to the republican ideal.[29]

If politics were most meaningful to Charles Pinckney Sumner's search for intellectual fulfillment, they also caused him his greatest disillusionment. He had dreamt of contributing to the success of the republican nation for which his father had fought. Instead he watched Americans veer ever further from both their republican virtues and their attachment to the Union, at the same time that he found himself increasingly isolated for his own republican independence. It started the very year he became clerk of the Massachusetts House. On 3 June 1806 someone lodged a complaint that Sumner had been politically partial in his duties as official record-keeper. Sumner's personal integrity was already well known, and when he complained of this ill treatment the House refused to give the charge official consideration or to have it entered into the record. Still, the charge itself stung.[30]

There would be no more such efforts to attach scandal to his name through official channels, but in 1811 Sumner found himself attacked in the newspapers. In that year the Republicans enjoyed their zenith of power in Massachusetts, the crest of the wave they had been riding since 1804. In 1811 the Republicans won both the state House and Senate as well as the governorship, and they immediately passed their strongest measures, including the Universal Suffrage Law and the especially controversial Religious Liberty Law. Both their success and their agenda angered the Federalists, who waged a newspaper campaign against their rivals and would rally as the Republicans had eight years earlier and return to power starting in 1812, undoing the Republicans' legislation. That summer of 1811 the Federalist *Boston Gazette* charged that the Republicans' most extreme legislation was really the work of "apostate Federalists" who had infiltrated the Republican party in order to undermine it. The writer was thus able to attack the men themselves for their "consummate baseness" toward both parties, as well as the Republican party for not realizing that its most talented representatives and officers were really Federalists. Among these "rogues" the attacker listed both Story and Sumner.[31]

Sumner felt moved to respond in a letter to the editors, but it was the sort of defense that must have displeased both Federalists and Republicans. Fundamentally rejecting the legitimacy of both political parties in accordance with traditional philosophy as expressed in Washington's Farewell Address, and ignoring state policies in favor of national affairs, Sumner defended himself on the grounds of political independence. He could not be qualified as a Federalist because he had been too young to vote for either Washington or Adams, and had not seen fit to vote before 1804 for Jefferson's reëlection. But, in point of fact, he could not give "unqualified praise or censure" to the course of any of the nation's first four presidents, and taking their point of view as his own he wrote: "The thousand circumstances that daily *try their souls,* must often have disgusted them with their painful pre-eminence, and led them to view public life as a labarinth in which great men are sometimes bewildered, and small men are lost; where the thread of wisdom is scarcely perceptible to the touch, and those who tread at random come out as well as those who step with care." Charles Pinckney Sumner concluded that he chose "to be in solitude . . . rather than be crowded into any company, however respectable." It was more than a response to an attack; it was a farewell to politics.[32]

The year 1811 should have been a happy one for Charles Pinckney Sumner. His young marriage was a good one, founded in compatible tastes and mutual respect, and the year began with the birth of their first two children. Even the political attack he suffered that summer listed him as one of the principal talents of the Republican party. Instead, 1811 was the year of Sumner's greatest disillusionment, the start of a new path in life that seemed to him to lead nowhere but down. Having chosen a profession he could not respect, he had sought intellectual and moral satisfaction in other company and other domains. Most especially he had hoped to play some role in the building of the Great Republic. Instead, he found himself politically isolated, distrusted by politicians for the very independence he believed to be a republican duty. For a time he had had the sympathy of his friend Joseph Story, who had also become a Republican from a combination of liberal views of social justice and a commitment to strong nationalism. Story and Sumner had shared their gradual disillusionment at the petty bickering of mere politicians and the weakness of the Republican administrations in their defense of the nation against the European powers. But Story had not sacrificed his profession to politics. He had come to love the law, indeed to believe the legal profession more important to the future of the Republic than the political arena, and was now a highly respected and well-to-do lawyer who in 1810 had even argued before the Supreme Court. In 1811 Story joined the Supreme Court. He was not President Madison's first choice to be sure, for Jefferson—Madison's good friend as well as ideological head of the party—distrusted this "pseudo-republican" as much as Story had come to distrust the third President, but Story thus became the youngest man ever elevated to the Court, and it was just the start of a remarkable career.[33]

Sumner was proud of his friend and correspondingly humiliated by what seemed to him his own failure. Politics had brought him only bitterness. He now found himself with no political future, little legal practice to fall back on, and a new family to care for. If that were not enough, little Charles and Matilda were born premature, weighing only three and a half pounds each, and for a time it was not certain they would make it. "I have now passed more than half the age of man," the thirty-five-year-old Sumner wrote that summer, even before the newspaper attacks, "and the ambition of youth is in me now checked by the . . . cautious, and sober thoughts of age." With the end of the 1811 term he withdrew from all political activity. By 1812, angrily rejecting both the Republicans' decision to go to war against England without sufficient cause and the New England Federalists' moves toward secession in protest, he gave up on both parties and even stopped voting. For the next two years, for the first time since his unhappy year after college, Sumner kept a private journal in which to pour out his political thoughts and misgivings. Then he switched to writing newspaper articles on all kinds of cultural and social questions. But, mostly, he returned full-time to his legal practice and devoted himself to the support of his family and the future of his children.[34]

Even now, however, professional success eluded Charles Pinckney Sumner. Perhaps prospective clients were turned away by a lack of enthusiasm he could not hide, or by his public ties to the Republican party. In any case, the law was then a difficult career from which to make a good living. A few well-connected lawyers dominated the arena and did well for themselves, while the vast majority, with less talent or help, had to compete for what business was left over. Sumner brought to his work the same conscientiousness he had previously put into his search for moral satisfaction, but, though he read widely through the legal literature and kept abreast of intellectual and professional trends in the law, his actual business rarely went beyond such work as the collection of bills. He probably made well under the average lawyer's income of $1,000.[35]

If money had already been a worry for Charles Pinckney Sumner when he was alone, it became a preoccupation now that he had a family to feed—a growing family. Within just the next six years the twins would be joined by three more boys, and eventually there would be nine children in all. Their father always credited the family's ability to live within his income to his wife Relief's good sense and frugality. But while his respect for her only increased, his respect for himself slipped further. His correspondence with Joseph Story, who was rapidly gaining national attention for his work as Associate Justice, slackened. When, in 1815, Sumner wrote to encourage Story in the professional work of starting a course of law lectures at Cambridge, it was without the easy confidence of old. "I do not, & I cannot, see you quite so often & so familiarly as I was once accustomed to. The more a man is elevated by the just award of his country, tho' his admirers are to be found every where, his friends must be looked for almost exclusively in the circle of the great, and I bow to the unalterable nature of things." Thus Charles Pinckney Sumner apologized for his "cowardly bashfulness," and could not be turned from it even by Story's sensitive reply and his gracious reminder of how unusual it had been in their college days for an upperclassman like Sumner to befriend a younger student: "I shall always remember the kind notice with which you honored me at college." Their feelings would remain warm, but the two men would see little of each other over the years to come. In 1819 Sumner gave up his practice for good, and accepted a post as deputy sheriff. This held out at least the hope of a better income in the future, though the immediate improvement was disappointing. For a man who had dreamt from a boy of being a gentleman and a scholar, the self-imposed demotion cut to the heart. One of the first things he did upon accepting the job was to write to Josiah Quincy, the early law teacher he still called "master," to apologize.[36]

Little Charles and his siblings knew nothing of all this. Of their father's disappointments they saw and felt only the results. He had become sad, unsmiling, even forbidding. A little over average height he had never been handsome, and now had become thin & worn, "an emaciated, attenuated figure." From the start his children were used to seeing him always studiously working, reading, writing articles, and they early respected him for his integrity, his sense of duty, his learning and cultivation. They saw in him a man who cared deeply about important public issues, but who seemed withdrawn from the bosom of his family. These realities weighed on their mother as well. All his life, Charles would show a marked sensitivity to the difficulties of a woman's life—a sensitivity that must have been first awakened as he watched his mother worry about her husband, raise her nine children, scrimp and save to make ends meet, and encourage the education of all her children while being unable to spare the time to further her own. From his mother Charles learned also to keep such troubles private. Unlike her husband—who could not help but dwell upon his misfortunes to friends and even to strangers—she proudly bore family disappointments and financial worries with a patience or resignation that gave her a reputation for imperturbability. Within the family, however, when the children were unhappy or sick, it was "the enduring love and watchfulness of Mother" that comforted them with a quiet but steady warmth that their father could no longer bring himself to express.[37]

Charles was an affectionate child who felt keenly the cloud that hung over the household. He found his father difficult to know and very demanding, but no one admired his father more or wanted more to follow in his footsteps to be a scholar and a gentleman. Charles was encouraged to believe in education by the whole household, his mother's intelligence and well-spokenness seconding his father's learning. Nor did he have to go far to take his first academic steps, for his Aunt Hannah, his mother's elder sister, had set up her Dame School on the top floor of their own house, and there Charles and Matilda learned their ABC's. With the rudiments of education, the children also learned the liberal principles of the Enlightenment so prized by their father, of tolerance and antislavery, values that were reinforced by such popular school books as Caleb Bingham's *Columbian Orator,* which Charles particularly enjoyed. Soon Charles was reading all the time, and his mother would remember him always with book in hand from the earliest age. Like his father, he soon discovered history, "often rising before day-light to read Hume & Gibbon." This, he later remembered, was "my first passion."[38]

But to be accepted as a gentleman required a classical education and that required money, something in short supply in the Sumner household. Charles' father worried about this more than his son knew. As his eldest children approached school age, Charles Pinckney Sumner joined the debate then raging over Boston's schools and fired off a series of articles to the Boston *Yankee* condemning the poor educational and health conditions of the public schools compared to the vaunted Latin School. The School Committee hardly cared whether the former were better off than slave ships or British prison hulks, he exclaimed. Education is "*the poor man's best birthright,*" he urged, and he denounced the "invidious" distinctions made between the schools of the rich and those of the poor. In the end, all he could do was to take the step down to deputy sheriff with its meager financial improvement.[39]

Little Charles saw the problem in more personal terms. He felt that if only he could sufficiently impress upon his father his own earnestness and seriousness of purpose he would get his classical education. Diligently saving what coins he could, Charles bought copies of the first-year Latin books from students who no longer needed them and, unbeknownst to his parents, studied the books all on his own. Years later he still remembered the swell of pride he had felt as he "came down to his father one morning as he was shaving, & astonished him by reciting & reading in Latin." His reward was the Latin School, which he entered at the age of ten with his next youngest brother Albert in August 1821.[40]

Charles was tall for his age, a rather gangling, awkward child. The other boys called him "gawky Sumner" because his long limbs seemed always to get in the way of their childish games; adults liked the boy for his quiet seriousness, his intelligence and modesty. This was all right with Charles, who never took particular interest in games but was proud of his youthful cultivation, his already unusual familiarity with literature and history, and the respect it earned him among serious people. It was in other ways that the Latin School would hurt his pride. In the elegant three-story brick building on ancient School Street, Charles was thrown together with the sons of Boston's most prestigious families. Robert C. Winthrop, a direct descendant of John Winthrop and himself a future congressman, was there at the time. Little Wendell Phillips, the future reformer whose father was about to become Boston's first mayor and who was descended from a fellow *Arbella* passenger and close associate of John Winthrop, refused even to speak to the Sumner boy who came from the wrong slope of Beacon Hill. Charles now felt ashamed of the rough shoes and homemade clothes of cheap satinette— "never a nice fitting or handsomely appearing suit"—that were the best his mother could do for him. He became aware of the humbleness of their household, the iron forks and knives that were all they could afford. Later in life he would be very sensitive to the false criticism that he had been "born in affluence and bred in elegance."[41]

Charles had been taught to value education more than class, however—indeed, to think of education as class. For all of its class consciousness Boston still agreed with that principle. To have an entrée into Boston's best society a young man at the time did not need an impressive pedigree, but did have to show himself a cultivated gentleman. Many of the new leaders of Boston society in this period of dynamic growth had come from unpretentious backgrounds themselves, but proved themselves social leaders by devoting themselves to education and the arts and the advancement of younger men of intellectual promise. The headmaster of the Latin School, the kindly and cultivated Benjamin Apthorp Gould, was anxious that his boys, whatever their social background, should be well trained in the gentlemanly arts. He continued the traditional stress on memorization and recitation as a foundation of public speaking, and he strengthened the classical curriculum, which included Cæsar, Sallust, Cicero, Ovid, Virgil and others, as well as a good introduction to Greek. But Gould added to this, and to mathematics, the innovation of composition and recitation in English to prepare the boys for the public expression expected of the leaders of a republican community.[42]

Charles did not achieve the first rank at the Latin School, perhaps in part because his reading was so much self-motivated and wider than it was focused, but also because, from the start, his literary mind found mathematics bewildering. But he impressed teachers and fellow-pupils alike by his extensive reading, his accurate memory, and his apparent self-possession, especially in recitations. He received many prizes for both Latin and English composition and was awarded the coveted Franklin medal at the completion of his studies, with President John Quincy Adams presiding at the festivities. No prize meant so much, however, to the fifteen-year-old graduate as his father's approval. In August 1826 the Latin School boys went to Faneuil Hall to hear the "god-like" Daniel Webster deliver his oration in commemoration of the lives of John Adams and Thomas Jefferson who had died within hours of each other that Fourth of July. The slender Charles pushed his way eagerly behind the dignitaries into the crowded hall, and, despairing of seeing anything through the sea of heads, he took desperate action: "I dived—I dived, and began working my way along upon my hands and knees among the legs of the men." He emerged at the front of the hall just in time to hear Webster pronounce of Jefferson: "'Felix, non vitae tantum claritate, sed etiam opportunitate mortis.'" The boy felt a thrill. "Then I felt proud," he later recounted, "for I understood the sentence; and I felt that I too belonged to the brotherhood of scholars." He rushed home to share the moment with his father who pulled Tacitus' *Agricola* from the shelf to see whether Charles had remembered the line accurately. "We were both pleased to find that I had; he showed the words to me then, in their original application."[43]

The next step had to be Harvard, but for a long time that had seemed unattainable. While the Latin School represented a financial sacrifice justified by the boy's intelligence and desire to learn, Harvard was simply a financial impossibility so long as Charles Pinckney Sumner, as deputy sheriff, was still making less than $900 a year and had, as he now did, eight children to consider. For a time Charles set his heart upon West Point. It offered the possibility of a respectable education without the necessity of tuition. Perhaps it also teased his nostalgic admiration for his grandfather the Major. Charles and his father shared both a hatred of war and a little taste for the military. The elder Sumner, though he complained it was "a piece of empty nonsense," regularly attended the annual meetings of the Ancient and Honorable Artillery Company and could be seen drilling in his uniform on the Common. Charles may well have already felt the admiration for Napoleon for which he became known in the coming years.[44]

But on 6 September 1825 the family fortunes finally changed. Governor Levi Lincoln, son of Jefferson's Attorney General, appointed Charles Pinckney Sumner High Sheriff of Suffolk County, which contains Boston, thus in an instant more than doubling his salary with the added promise of lucrative fees. This was not the position that the budding poet or even the young lawyer had dreamt of rising to, but the new Sheriff put all his integrity and conscientiousness into his post. He had long since accepted the necessity of mortifying his own pride to fulfill his obligations to others. It became his habit to quote Lord Bacon: "The duties of life are more than life." The new position meant he could rent a larger brick house on more respectable Hancock Street for his crowded family and offer better prospects to his children. What mattered more than anything was that his eldest son could now go to Harvard. For this the father was penetrated with gratitude. For years he would remember Levi Lincoln with gifts, including an inscribed twelve-volume set of the Diplomatic Correspondence of the American Revolution. In 1834 he again thanked Governor Lincoln for being "my greatest earthly benefactor. Without your favor I should probably not have sent a son to College or emerged from that humility of station from which at the age of forty nine you saw fit to draw me." Charles was grateful, too. Though he briefly clung to his first idea of West Point, he soon realized that a military academy could lead only to a life of soldiering or of business that would leave little room for his cultural tastes and aspirations. He entered Harvard with high hopes and would retain all his life a truly filial devotion to the alma mater that had made everything possible.[45]

To young Sumner Harvard represented first of all the culmination of that classical education that would enable him to follow the ideal of the scholar and the gentleman that he had inherited from his father and his grandfather. In this sense, he entered Harvard at just the right moment. The struggles between Unitarians and Congregationalists had long since been settled, in the college and the community at large, in favor of the liberal religionists and their more hopeful philosophy. A decade of student unrest and rebellion in protest against the meager, dry curriculum and teaching methods had also just ended by the mid-1820's. Still in the future lay the great period of educational reform under the presidency of Charles Pinckney Sumner's old master Josiah Quincy. His accession as the school's first lay president in 1829 during Charles' senior year symbolized and capped the twenty-year-long shift in the faculty and administration from the control of Unitarian ministers to that of the lawyers and businessmen of the first circles of Boston and Cambridge society. President Quincy's reforms would aim to strengthen the school's educational standards, but also to create a closer and more exclusive tie between Harvard and Boston's religiously liberal but politically conservative upper class, a trend that would culminate in Harvard's being turned into a private college in 1865. But in the last years of the presidency of the cultivated and benevolent Reverend John T. Kirkland there was a more gentle period of reform that combined some educational experimentation with the traditional ideal of making gentlemen through education, rather than educating exclusively the sons of gentlemen.[46]

In keeping with this ideal the Reverend Kirkland had promoted the beautification of the campus. To the venerable—and many thought dowdy—brick colonial structures such as Harvard and Massachusetts Halls, the college had added the more modern granite University Hall, which was designed in 1815 by Charles Bulfinch to close the circle of buildings and create the secluded enclave of Harvard Yard. Former mud tracks had been turned into neat gravel paths with elm saplings planted along their borders. In the same way the Reverend Kirkland had introduced fencing and gymnastics to give the boys gentlemanly grace and elegance. Like his protégé at the Latin School, Benjamin Gould, he had also added to the classical curriculum composition and declamation in English to train the boys in the art of public expression expected of the leaders of a republic. Meanwhile, faculty and students were discussing cosmopolitan educational reforms. Though the older faculty, displeased, blocked substantial change, the students were excited by new teachers like George Ticknor—fresh from the University of Göttingen—who tried to introduce such European teaching methods as the class lecture to replace the traditional recitations and bring American instruction up to European standards. Sumner's father looked approvingly upon these new trends and, upon Charles' matriculation, admonished his son to take full advantage of the opportunity given him—to cultivate "a delight & veneration" for the "academic shades" "surrounded by enclosures & gravelled walks, adorned with thick set shrubery & ornamental trees" and "which could not easily be excelled in the favored climate of Athens in the grove of Academus." Most importantly, he enjoined his son to remember as he passed into these shades that "[g]ood learning & good behavior are commonly companions. They ought never to be disjoined."[47]

Sumner tried hard to live up to his father's expectations and his own hopes. If he generally did not find recitations challenging, he used the college resources to challenge himself. He made warm, intellectually lively, and stimulating friendships. He enjoyed his relative freedom from home, and prided himself on his ability to use it responsibly. To be sure, he had his disappointments. His old nemeses from the Latin School only got worse. Put on the spot one day by a physics professor, Sumner frankly admitted: "I don't know; you know I don't pretend to know any thing about mathematics." He gave up even cutting the pages of his algebra textbook, and made it through exams only by the grace of his re-markable memory. Because mathematics made up half the consideration for class rank, Sumner had reluctantly to give up his dreams of getting into the top third of his class and, therefore, of being considered for Phi Beta Kappa.[48]

In anything having to do with literature or history, modern or ancient, how-ever, Sumner flourished, and he most enjoyed and most impressed the most de-manding and modern of his professors. Professor Ticknor, who had a reputation for making his students care about literature by bringing the authors of the past to life in his lectures, was so impressed by Sumner's meticulous notes from his course on French literature that he wrote the youth's father: "If your son contin-ues as diligent as he has been, he will go far in the ways of reputation and suc-cess." Edward Tyrell Channing, younger brother of the Unitarian divine William Ellery Channing, was a formidable figure whose chilling sarcasm frightened mediocre students in his course on rhetoric and oratory, and he was a stickler in both speaking and writing style. But "Ned" Channing opened up to his bright students, inviting them to his rooms for after-class discussions about literature. Sumner particularly enjoyed his courses, and was "among the best in forensics." His speaking was noted for its "great degree of earnestness, with an entire free-dom from any effort to make a *dash*." Other students, who trembled at the thought of having to speak publicly, stood in awe of Sumner's seeming ease and self-possession on declamation days, and thought it only natural that, at his jun-ior exhibition in 1829, Sumner should choose the part of the Orator in a Greek dialogue and defend his superiority over other professions with great rhetorical gusto.[49]

Sumner was not so much interested in oratory, however, as he was in reading. He was proud that his native facility allowed him to finish his assignments in short order and thus have extra time, not to rewrite and perfect his themes, but hungrily to acquire new knowledge. He took out more books from the library than any other student in his freshman year, and, by the time of graduation, "[n]o student . . . had read as widely." He read miscellaneous history, and liter-ary classics like *Don Quixote*, went through the works of Sir Walter Scott—then all the rage,—Sir Edmund Burke, and the American Washington Irving, and, al-ways his favorites, Milton and Shakespeare. He read regularly through such re-spected literary journals as the London *Retrospective Review* and the *Edinburgh Review*, starting a commonplace book in which to record not only admired quo-tations but information on the lives and works of authors who interested him. He discovered a particular fondness for—and began to undergo the influence of—the lesser-known Elizabethan and Jacobean poets and dramatists such as Beaumont and Fletcher, Sir John Suckling, and John Marston, and he wrote their tribute in language that would describe his own mature writing style: "I admire the old English authors. In them is to be found the pure well of English undefiled. There is a richness of expression with them to which we moderns are strangers; but, above all, there is a force and directness which constitute their chief merit. They are copious without being diffuse, and concise without being obscure. [. . .] They did not write till the spirit within forced them to; and when they did, they wrote with all that energy and expansion of thought which sincerity and earnestness could not fail to give." What Sumner read, he remembered. To the repertoire of choice Latin quotations started at the Latin School and always growing, he now added innumerable passages from his native literature, from which he would be able to quote easily all his life, and many of which would find their way into his later writings. At the time his fellow students relied upon him in history as "a repertory of facts to which we might always resort," and joked that his letters were so encrusted with literary allusions and quotations that he should accompany them by a Lemprière.[50]

Reading was an old pleasure that Sumner had discovered at home, but, in his father's house intellectual pursuits and, indeed, all aspects of life were clothed in an earnestness uniformly stern and somber. The fun and carefree society of a college campus was to Sumner a breath of fresh air. Here, for the first time, he tasted real friendship which became to him a necessity, and he would keep in touch through life with some of that first circle of college friends. Barzillai Frost and Jonathan French Stearns would later become ministers, Stearns being also the grandson of the Reverend Jonathan French, a beloved professor and guardian of Sumner's father as he had been preparing for college at Andover. John White Browne, later a liberal-minded and mild-mannered lawyer, was at college an admirer of Byron and a fiery partisan. Steady and responsible Charlemagne Tower would later leave the law for teaching and business to care for his family. Thomas Hopkinson, "Hop," would take top honors in the class; he was six years older than Sumner, having returned to college after working for a time, while Sumner himself was one of the youngest members of his class.[51]

With these friends and others, Sumner's natural good humor and sociability blossomed. In an age that relished good talk, Sumner discovered a talent for conversation that earned him the nickname "Chatterbox." Together with his friends, he laughed and punned and made good fun of dull textbooks and classes, of "Mathematics piled on Mathematics! Metaphysics murdered and mangled! Prayer-bells after prayer bells! but worse than all, Commons upon Commons! clean, handsome plates, & poor food!" School was made fun of—and public speaking practiced—in Harvard's lively clubs, too, many of which Sumner joined. At one of the Hasty Pudding Club's popular moot courts, he used "not only the formidable engine of legal argument, but the two edged sword of satire, the poisoned darts of irony, and the barbed shafts of ridicule" to prosecute that "notorious felon alias Mr. Blackboard." All of these clubs were devoted to discussing good books and presenting essays, and Sumner relished their serious debates "upon vexed questions of literature and history, and sometimes pressed his view aggressively." He was learning to present it publicly, too. On 2 November 1829 before "the Nine," a secret literary club he had formed with some friends, Sumner read an article of his on the universities of Oxford and Cambridge. It was the first article he had ever published in a newspaper.[52]

Sumner's fun was thus nearly all intellectual, and his father need not have enjoined Charles quite so heavily to honor "the learning that can be acquired at College" and to shun the company and manners that might lead one "reluctantly [to] gain matriculation at Houses of Correction, County Jails & State Prisons." All through his college years Sumner dutifully returned home every Saturday— the students' day off,—making the five-mile trek from Harvard to Hancock Street on foot. Sensitive to his father's financial worries—so deeply ingrained that they survived his change of fortune—Sumner lived frugally, as close as possible to the minimum spending levels described by the college catalogue. Once or twice he did play hooky to escape a dull recitation, and had his conscience scolded by his father for it: "It is of little avail to have expensive and learned professorships established at college if a scholar does not devote his whole time to the duties prescribed." Sumner never had the least association with rowdy or dissolute elements. He was always amiable and polite, and "quick to beg pardon when he found that he had unconsciously wounded" any feelings. He took no interest in sports as such, though he did like an occasional swim or a long walk— including one strenuous summer-long walking tour of New England and New York with his friends—and he did love the thrill of racing the stagecoach down Massachusetts Avenue on his velocipede. His deepest pleasure, however, was always the company of books and friends.[53]

Indeed Sumner was proud of his own studiousness and gentlemanly conduct, and consciously maintained high standards for both. Untempted by youthful rebellion, he tended to be respectful of authorities—whether his father, a great orator like Daniel Webster, or the literary classics and respected critics he read so much. He tried to model himself after them, but also, with a degree of youthful absolutism, required that they live up to the highest standards themselves. Not even the famed oratory of the distinguished Concord lawyer Samuel Hoar could win Sumner's praise when once he slipped. When Hoar quoted the famous line, "Tempora mutantur, nos et mutantur in illis," and mistakenly said "cum illis" instead, Sumner, disturbed, turned to his companion and complained: "A man ought to be ashamed who quotes an author and does not quote correctly." It was some time before Sumner, himself famous for the accuracy of his memory, would trust Samuel Hoar again. While others were impressed by Sumner's apparent confidence and self-possession, however, Sumner himself lived with the constant and painful sense of falling short of his own goals.[54]

The only thing in himself Sumner did not doubt was the integrity and uprightness of his own character, his mature sense of responsibility. His desire to have this appreciated by others led to the one act of apparent insubordination on his college record. During his first two years at Harvard Sumner conformed to the mandatory dress code that had been established only a few years earlier as one of George Ticknor's reforms to stamp out the spirit of rebellion of the early 1820's. The code required that the students wear a black or "black-mixed" coat and pantaloons, along with a black-mixed or white waistcoat. One day, in his junior year, Sumner came to class wearing a buff-colored waistcoat. He was, accordingly, summoned before the Parietal Board. He denied guilt, instead calmly maintaining that the vest was really white. It "might need the manipulations of a laundress," he said, "but it was worn for the lawful color." This time he got off with a warning, but when the Parietal Board learned that he was persisting in his misbehavior he was again summoned and, this time, officially admonished on his record for "illegal dress." He made no change. In the end it was the Parietal Board that blinked. They closed the matter by voting "that hereafter Mr. Sumner's vest be considered by this Board white."[55]

Sumner was not launching upon a career of social reform or trying to anticipate Théophile Gauthier's rebelliously defiant rose-colored vest. Buff itself was a color of highly respectable significance. Blue and buff were the colors of the patriots in the American Revolution. Edmund Burke had chosen a buff-colored waistcoat in which to deliver his greatest oratorical efforts, and the great Daniel Webster was now doing the same. Instead of undermining the purpose of the Harvard dress code, Sumner believed he was upholding it. What was its purpose but to instill a sense of responsibility into the students? But Sumner knew that he would be responsible and adult without the imposition of outside rules and, in the small community that was Harvard, he proudly thought professors and students alike should know that, and trust him.[56]

Sumner's deep sense of personal dignity brought to life for him the ideal of the dignity of mankind so fundamental to that Moral Philosophy that he had first learned from his father, and which was the dominant intellectual creed not only of Harvard and the Latin School, but of American higher education and philosophical life generally. Derived in great part from the Common Sense school of the Scottish Enlightenment and its reaction against the more skeptical and cynical tendencies of eighteenth-century thinking exemplified by David Hume, American Moral Philosophy tried to reconcile Enlightenment Humanism with traditional Protestantism by stressing man's moral nature. It had a special meaning to the Unitarians who dominated the intellectual world of Boston and Cambridge. Just as the Enlightenment and the Erasmian Renaissance before it had championed human potential and endeavor over the old mediæval stress upon faith and theology, New England Unitarians championed human nature's capacity for self-control and goodness over the traditional Calvinist belief in pre-destination and human depravity. Without giving up the traditional Puritan and Revolutionary insistence upon duty, they stressed the Humanist belief in free will.[57]

Sumner, lacking any hint of Calvinism in his own background, found such a philosophy only natural. He felt the appropriateness of the three spheres into which Moral Philosophy divided human nature. The animal was not inherently evil and was necessary to man's survival, as Harvard professors taught, but the intellectual, governed by the faculty of reason, was infinitely higher, and was surpassed in nobility and duty only by the ethical, man's moral sense, ruled by the conscience. The emotions likewise were divided into reckless, selfish, and indefensible "passions," or those "sentiments" and "benevolent affections" that attached people to the path of reason and conscience. All Harvard professors, whatever their subject, taught that the individual's greatest duty was to develop all his faculties to their fullest, to achieve a harmonious balance among them, and to follow the path of Right, for they believed that the true purpose of education was to build young people's characters.[58]

Nor was it incompatible with Sumner's own sensibility that the years when he was at college were precisely those in which Harvard's Moral Philosophy course took its own most hopeful view of human nature. In the late 1820's and early 1830's, perhaps more than at any other period in its history, Harvard deëmphasized the teachings of utilitarians like William Paley and sensualists like John Locke in favor of the Scottish philosophers Dugald Stewart and Thomas Brown—the latter a favorite of Sumner's father—who both stressed man's innate moral nature, his native capacity to, in the words of New England's own Cotton Mather, "Do Good," and the happiness that that duty would bring. As children of the classical tradition, Harvard professors did not fail to put also before their students the reward of fame—that esteem bestowed by worthy people upon those who practice virtue. When Sumner, throughout life, spoke of doing good, of the mathematical certainty of the Right— which, along with all fundamental concepts, he would always capitalize,—of the desire to cultivate a society wise and just, of the obligation to strive for the highest standard even if unattainable, of the necessity of bending one's life to a habit of duty, he spoke with the voice of that American Moral Philosophy that he had imbibed from earliest childhood, studied through school, and met with in the world of New England's intellectual life.[59]

Believing in the ability of man to improve both himself and his society, full of the satisfaction of learning and the pleasures of warm friendships, Sumner looked forward with great expectations. How strange, almost immoral, a Calvinistic pessimism seemed to him. He was appalled in his senior year when a student two years younger than himself took it into his head "that he was fated to be dissipated" and "fated to commit suicide" and then suddenly fulfilled his own prophecy. Sumner could not conceive of such a hopeless and destructive "*Fatalism,*"—"That a young man of but 17 should *voluntarily* cut asunder the thread of life & give up the present ills, for 'those we know not of' would be *any where* a melancholy subject of reflection & thought; but how much more so in *College,* where he was pleasantly situated among those of his own age & where one might suppose the inducements to cling to life were the strongest." When later that year a second student tried to do the same thing, Sumner wrote reprovingly: "I always fill my cups to overflowing—I drink pity to those who have to swallow their bitter waters."[60]

Though he agreed with Moral Philosophy's ultimate stress upon the conscience, Sumner was still most intoxicated by the pleasures of intellectual improvement. This seemed to him the most striking side of man's potential. He expressed his sentiments publicly when, for their senior exhibition, he and three other students were assigned to write and perform a "conference" consisting in "A Comparative Estimate of Alexander, Cæsar, Cromwell, and Bonaparte as Statesmen and Warriors." New England generally held the Frenchman in low esteem, and just a couple of years earlier the greatly respected Reverend William Ellery Channing had published an article using him as an object lesson of moral failure and tyranny, as opposed to Sumner's own hero Milton. Without denying his moral imperfections, Sumner rejected the derogatory name "Bonaparte," and wrote a spirited defense of the Emperor who had, more than anyone before him, realized the objectives of the French Revolution:

> It is too much in fashion to depreciate the abilities & to misrepresent the actions of Napoleon. All the criminalities & missteps of a life of great temptation & power have been raked up against him, while the innumerable benefits he conferred upon his country & the glorious actions he performed have all been forgotten [. . .].
>
> Yet this man who could lead an army on to victory, organise the government of a great nation, form & digest the *Code Napoleon*—this man whose works are not written upon leaves, which can be scattered by the winds, but indelibly stamped on the whole face of Europe & of the age in which he lived—this man has been denied the possession of high intellectual powers!

Sumner admitted that he was tempted into his enthusiasm for Napoleon in part because "[p]ublic opinion, we think, has wronged him." But he was thus also expressing his faith in the capacity of the human intellect and his affection for the liberal humanitarian ideals of the Enlightenment.[61]

Sumner combined his admiration for history with his hope in the future and in human achievement likewise during his walking tour of New England and

New York in the summer of 1829. It was an occasion of much pleasure, but Sumner also carefully noted all he saw. Once home he published extracts of his journals celebrating history in the Revolutionary Battle of Bennington, whose field he had gone carefully over, and the future in the newly opened Erie Canal, which he praised as "a new road to wealth" for New York and a monument to the daring and modern thinking of Governor De Witt Clinton. And in a similar spirit Sumner used his Commencement exercises in 1830 to make a statement of religious tolerance. Assigned a part on "the Superstition of the American Indians" he changed the title to "The Religious Notions of the North American Indians," and proceeded to defend the essential humanity and nobility of the Indian religions, comparing them to Roman dignity and contrasting them pointedly with the narrow and bigoted sectarianism of the Puritans. Privately, Sumner began his college commonplace book in 1827 with this quote from his father's favorite author: "I believe in one God & no more; and I hope for happiness beyond this life. I believe [in] the equality of man & I believe that religious duties consist in doing justice, loving mercy & endeavoring to make our fellow-citizens happy."[62]

Difficult as he found it to express, Sumner's father was proud of his eldest son. When Charles admitted his reluctance to accept his Commencement part because, reflecting his class rank, it seemed too insignificant, his father made it clear that duty required his acceptance. But this time he added: "You have gained credit by the parts you have performed; and I do not doubt you could sustain your reputation amid any competition. You have never been associated with any but honorable compeers on exhibition days, and the esteem in which the Faculty hold you is to me a source of satisfaction."[63]

Sumner left Harvard full of ideas and hopes and uncertainty. His college years had been the happiest he had known, full of expanding horizons and new friends, but now he had to face that first momentous decision of any young man's life—the choice of a profession. The difficulty was not so much that he did not know what choice to make, but rather that from the start, deep down, he knew that there was only one possible choice, and, like his father before him, he found his duty and his inclination to be incompatible. Sumner thus decided to put off the decision. The family's new financial situation made it possible for him to indulge in the luxury of a year off at home. At the same time the nineteen-year-old's increasing maturity pushed him to try to make the most of that year. He felt dissatisfied with his own accomplishments at college. He had read widely, to be sure, but without discipline. He had spent much time studying the things he liked, but he began to feel that he had been too willing to sidestep those he did not.

Now Sumner planned an extensive study list to flesh out the work already done at college and to patch up what he felt were its deficiencies. He did not omit mathematics. And at first he was pleased to find it generally easier than it had been in college, though he continued to find the "roots of algebra" to be "but bitter," as he joked to Jonathan Stearns. He was no philosophical sectarian, but, inspired by the basic faith of the Enlightenment as he had learned it through Moral Philosophy, Sumner included on his list further reading in Dugald Stewart, and other writers on philosophy and political economy. Then of course there were great historical works from Thucydides to Hallam, including Robertson's *Charles V,* and Roscoe's *Leo* and *Lorenzo.* He continued classical literature with such as Juvenal, Cicero, and Horace, and could never give up Milton, Shakespeare, and the British poets.[64]

Sumner studied outside the house, too. He attended a series of winter lectures given by the popular Society for the Diffusion of Useful Knowledge on natural history, the history of Massachusetts, and "on Useful Knowledge, as an ally of Religion," taking careful notes on them all. Nor did he miss any important oratorical event. He enjoyed former Mayor Josiah Quincy's address in the Old South Meeting House on the occasion of Boston's bicentennial, and he and John Browne went together to hear a number of efforts, both political and legal, by Daniel Webster, then at the height of his fame. Sumner embarked on this broad plan of self-improvement with determination and enthusiasm, and vowed to Stearns: "I have doomed myself for this year at least to hard labor—I intend to diet on study—go to bed late & get up early & leave none of my time unemployed."[65]

For all his good intentions, Sumner found the year after college to be more difficult than he had imagined. He read a good deal, but still found his favorite subjects too beguiling, fell short of his goals, and felt dissatisfied. The atmosphere in his father's house was less than inspiring, and may have seemed even gloomier than before in comparison to the pleasures and warm friendships of college. "You and I, I believe," he wrote to Tower just a month after their graduation, "had some sympathies with one another on departure; we both of us looked upon Cambridge with rather warmer feelings than most, and dreaded to sunder ourselves from so many kindly associations. One month 'hath not a whit altered *me;*' my mind is still full of those feelings of affection which bound me to the place and the friends I there enjoyed. I find it hard to untie the spell that knits me so strongly to college life." Sumner would keep up those ties with a frank and frequent correspondence. He and his friends shared their experiences, encouraged each other in their first post-collegiate work, helped each other to improve their writing styles, and shared their reading. Books were their favorite presents to each other. Sumner, remaining in Boston, filled many commissions for the others in seeking out desired books in new and used bookstores as well as the old college library—a task he delighted in, for "a bookstore or a library is my paradise."[66]

A greater distraction came in November when the family moved a third time.

They did not go far—moving from close to the top of Hancock Street down its steep incline to Number 20, a simple brick Greek Revival house with a little columned porch—but, for the first time, this house they would own. For a while things were in a tumble—and must have been great good fun to the younger members of the family. There were nine children now, five boys and four girls, of whom the last was little Julia, born in 1827—all just the right age to make life difficult for their serious eldest brother who was trying his best to study in the parlor. Playfully he complained to Tower: "My study! *mehercle!* it would require the graphic pencil of Hogarth to set it before you,—children and chairs, boxes and books, andirons and paper, sunlight and Sumner; in short, a common rest-ing-place for all the family. I often think of you and your neat premises when I am sitting, like Chance amidst the little chaos around."[67]

It was the feeling of purposelessness that most pained Sumner. At college he had felt himself stirred by the acquisition of knowledge and, more than that, by contact with great and inspiriting ideas. Feeling isolated at home, he continued instinctively to search for something intellectually and morally stimulating. Set-tling on a profession was his duty, but Sumner's idealism, his faith in human na-ture, and the hope for the future that they sustained were also searching for an outlet. Though he could not yet see it as a possible career, he had, in fact, already found the cause that would in time change his life. It was just "shortly after [he] left college" that Sumner attended a lecture at Cambridge by William Ladd. Ladd had devoted his life to the cause of ending war, and had just had a signal victory in the creation of the American Peace Society in 1828, bringing together different local groups with different approaches into one national organization. It was not the first time that Sumner was moved by the idea of international peace. When "scarcely nine years old" he had attended an address before the Massachusetts Peace Society by Josiah Quincy, famous for his oratory, that had "made a deep and lasting impression on my mind." It had not destroyed his boy-hood pleasure with "the illusion of battles & wars," but it had instilled a latent sense of dissatisfaction with them that gradually came to the surface. Though he could not yet conquer his admiration for Napoleon, already in college Sumner had come to believe, intellectually at least, in the "wickedness & woe" of warfare. Ladd's lecture and his desire for a congress of nations to regulate international re-lations peacefully would help build the foundation of Sumner's future commit-ment to international law, and inspire his first published writing and public words in the cause of reform.[68] For the time being, however, Sumner's idealism had attached itself to what he saw as a yet greater—because even more exciting—distraction from his true responsibility,—politics.

Sumner had for some time kept himself well informed on the issues of the day. In college he had shown himself willing to debate and defend positions literary and ideological that he believed in, even if unpopular. His natural enthusiasm had already caused concern to his now antipolitical father. As the presidential contest of 1828 between John Quincy Adams and Andrew Jackson heated up, Sheriff Sumner warned his son against engaging in any political discussion on this emotional topic, even with the elderly uncle he was visiting for the summer. "Charles, upon your discretion & good deportment, the happiness of my life will in no trifling degree depend." But it was not until the following year that Sumner's interest in politics became exceptional, for it was only then that he felt touched in his heart and conscience.[69]

Sumner was in his senior year when the Anti-Masonic fervor spread into Massachusetts. It had started in upstate New York three years earlier with the kidnapping of an obscure Batavia stonemason named William Morgan by a group—apparently a network—of Masons, after he had published an exposé of the Masonic Order's often irreverent- and gruesome-sounding secret oaths and rituals. When he failed to return, there seemed no doubt that the Masons had indeed, as rumored, thrown him into the Niagara River to silence him forever. Evidence of the kidnapping was overwhelming, though the murder was never actually proven. It took up to twenty trials and the appointment of three special prosecutors by the state to achieve only a scattering of minor convictions. The ineptitude and long-drawn-out ineffectiveness of the proceedings to investigate and try the case, and the fact that most of the officials in charge as well as the jurors turned out to be Masons themselves, inflamed the traditional republican fear of conspiracies against liberty, especially by powerful oligarchies.[70]

What began as a grassroots ideological movement of moral outrage against the Masonic threat to republican values quickly became politicized in the fluid state of political parties in the late 1820's and early 1830's, and through it many young men who would later play prominent roles in American history got their first taste of politics. In New York the Anti-Masons filled the need for a popular political opposition to the dominant aristocratic Clinton wing of the Jacksonian party and launched the careers of political manager Thurlow Weed and his protégé William Henry Seward, later a fellow Republican senator of Sumner's and later still his nemesis as Lincoln's Secretary of State. In Pennsylvania Anti-Masonry was likewise the political springboard for Thaddeus Stevens, later to become leader of the Radical Republicans in the House of Representatives during the Civil War and Reconstruction. In Massachusetts, the decision of Sumner's own future friend and mentor John Quincy Adams to join the Anti-Masons in 1831 brought his son Charles Francis fervently into the cause that would lead him into antislavery politics and a close collaboration with Charles Sumner. This politicization within a movement that prided itself on its moral tone was controversial, and arguments over the formation of a political party and over possible coalitions with other political groups were fierce—harbingers of similar arguments within the antislavery movement. Even those who accepted the creation of a political party, however, retained a strong sense of their own ethical motivation, and large numbers of the young men who joined the Anti-Masonic party went on to become antislavery Whigs, Free Soilers, and Republicans.[71]

Charles Pinckney Sumner was personally horrified at what he considered the certain murder of Morgan, especially because he himself, however long before, had for a time been a Mason. In the furor over William Morgan's disappearance, many Masons became "seceders" from the organization, contributing to the massive though temporary decimation of the Order's strength, and they often claimed that their secession had been undertaken at great personal danger. Sheriff Sumner's deep concern for law and order, spurred by his new professional awareness of lawlessness and disorder, gave deep personal meaning to his outrage, and throughout 1829 he watched with great interest the growth of the Anti-Masonic organization in and around Boston. So long removed from the Masons, however, he felt neither attachment to the Order nor fear of it, and his remarks against the society were moderate in tone. When the zealous Anti-Masonic Suffolk Committee asked the Sheriff to share his opinions, he wrote and published a tract that, plainly but calmly, condemned Masonry for undermining the duty of young men to their own education, to religion, to their families. He rejected the common Anti-Masonic charge that Masonry controlled Massachusetts' political and legal structure, but he did warn of the potential danger of a secret society with its own political hierarchy and private law: "Masonic obligations of some sort have probably led wicked and foolish men to the belief that those who take them, are thereby placed superior to all law except Masonic law; that a Mason, in becoming such, absolves himself from the laws of his country; and that owing allegiance to Masonry, he may surrender himself exclusively to its protection. This is a horrible belief, congenial to the heart of a pirate, and totally at war with that benevolence to which the fraternity have in times past made undisputed claim."[72]

The Masons, angered by the force of the growing movement against them, lashed out against this attack from the popularly respected Sheriff with hysterical vigor, and vilified him in a three-month-long weekly barrage in the Boston *Masonic Mirror*. They attacked him for partisanship, hypocrisy, selfishness, dishonesty, and "malignity," as well as antirepublicanism, and for taking out his frustrations at his own professional disappointments on the Masons; insinuations were even made of indecent behavior on his part. This unforeseen attack ended Sheriff Sumner's tendency to downplay the dangers of speaking out against the Masons. Like many other "seceders" he came over the coming years to feel that his outspokenness on this issue was the motivation behind all the professional enmity he encountered. Even when his unpopular views on slavery and race seemed more likely causes of resentment, he blamed Masons for trying to destroy his career.[73]

Charles was stunned by the viciousness of these attacks against his father. As the controversy unfolded during his senior year, he had to struggle against the temptation to devote too much of his time to reading the newspapers instead of studying. The temptation was only harder to resist during his year off. As the year wore on, he gave over more and more of his time to the newspapers, keeping up with both sides of the debate. He sent his friends piles of clippings from Benjamin Hallett's *Free Press* and other Anti-Masonic papers, and it was even said that he contributed articles of his own to Hallett's paper. As his involvement grew, so too did his motivation, from the loyal defense of his injured father to the arousal of his conscience against the sort of organization that could sanction a systematic and cruel attack against a man of unquestioned integrity, the sort of organization that seemed fully to justify his father's concerns for republican society. "I have been scourged into my present opinions," Sumner explained to his friend Stearns, "by the abuse which my Father has met with—viz—my mind was bro't by this to see *what Masonry did; & to enquire what it could do*."[74]

Sumner's was not a popular position for the son of a lawyer and sheriff, nor for a Harvard alumnus. Anti-Masonry tended to appeal most to rural and working-class people who felt shut out by the propertied classes or threatened by the growing power of commerce and industry. The Masonic Order appealed most to those men who filled the upper commercial and civic circles, or who desired to, which generally included both lawyers and Harvard students. In addition, though a second party system was in the process of forming around the differing popular reactions to President Jackson, traditional antiparty feeling remained strong. Americans continued to believe that parties were really just factions, by definition personal and selfish, and therefore dangerously antithetical to a republic. This feeling, which would in later years give the Anti-Masons a popular reputation for exceptional virtue, at first worked against them, even as they shared it. Sumner's acceptance not only of the Anti-Masons but of the Anti-Masonic party thus set him apart from the friends and society he generally mingled in. Unlike that of many of his future political colleagues, too, his interest in Anti-Masonry would not be a stepping stone to antislavery. The son of Charles Pinckney Sumner needed no such outside influence. Nor would it be a stepping stone to politics, for Sumner would long resist such a choice.[75]

To Sumner Anti-Masonry, and therefore Anti-Masonic politics, remained a question of conscience. So he defended it to his friends when, with one voice, they peppered him with earnest letters urging him to give over his involvement in such a zealous and uncouth movement. "Some there are with more zeal than knowledge," Sumner admitted of the Anti-Masons to Stearns, "& whose rabid philosophy will not suffer them to judge ~~between~~ in ca[n]dour & truth. They strain the principles of their party to such a tension that they almost crack (as in the case you instanced); but pray set this down to the infirmity of man. They—

poor men—have their consciences on their side; & with that ally need we admire that they are insensible to those feelings which would make them stop? For myself—my mind is made up. I shall never give back. Yet may this hand forget its cunning if ever aught shall come from me savouring of intolerance or unwarrantable exclusion."[76]

John Browne playfully mocked his friend's motivation as "knight-errantry" and addressed him as "Don Carlos," but Sumner's argument had a practical side to it as well. His defense of the Anti-Masons revealed a full, and modern, acceptance of the legitimacy of opposition parties. He even justified the excesses of the movement on the grounds that they were natural to political parties: "What party ever showed uniform placidness? And especially what young party? The blood is too warm to beat slowly or healthfully. Sores & Ulcers show themselves."[77] Having accepted the legitimacy of parties, Sumner forcefully defended their right to use plainly political means to advance their cause. When Charlemagne Tower took his turn at trying to bring his friend to his senses, he objected to what seemed the essential intolerance of the Anti-Masons' refusal to vote for any Masons. Sumner shot back: "You ask if the course of Antimasons is not proscriptive? No. No. Is the course of the Nat[ional] Republicans in not voting for a Jackson-man & of a Jack-man in not voting for a Nat Rep *proscriptive*? Was the course of Democrats & Federalists—of Whigs & Tories *proscriptive*? No. Neither of these parties would put into office a man who did not accord with them in sentiment, deeming that the welfare of the state hinged upon *their* creed—& just so it is with Antimasons, they will put no man in power, to whom they cannot look for a reflection of their own sentiments." There was no prejudice involved, he insisted, for men are Masons by choice and may at any time give up their Lodges. Frustrated to be consistently misunderstood in what seemed so clearly right to him, Sumner confessed to his friend: "My opinion is so strongly made up upon this point that I am worried by any contradiction."[78]

Charles initially joined the Anti-Masonic cause out of concern for his father, and his father objected to his involvement out of concern for his son. Instead of bringing the two closer together, their mutual concern formed a little seed of disagreement between them. Sheriff Sumner had also been much hurt by the Masonic attacks against him. In his 1829 letter to the Suffolk Committee he had denied the possibility of the kind of Masonic takeover of legislatures and the judiciary that many Anti-Masons believed had already happened, but in the years after the attacks he became increasingly willing to believe in the existence of such a conspiracy against liberty, and he began to fill a new series of private political notebooks with strictures on the Masonic oligarchy, which he came to compare in power and ruthlessness to the Slave Power he had already long condemned. As in his old Jeffersonian days, Sheriff Sumner again felt himself in an independent-minded but hopeless minority, powerless against an evil oligarchy that was able to sway or lull the too-apathetic majority. He had long felt pessimistic about the future of the country; he began now to despair. But he could not accept his eldest son's willingness to enlist in the fight. As he had warned Charles in 1828 and would often again: "The leading principle of a republican government is that the majority must rule, & the minority must obey; & whether I am in a small or large minority I never mean to join the standard of rebellion." If the majority could not govern wisely, then there could by definition be no hope for a republic. The wiser Anti-Masonic minority must stoically learn "'[t]he threats of pain & ruin to despise.'" He taught his children "to bow to the powers that be," and "never rebel against the Government either state or national: rather quit the territory than stay & be a malcontent. But try to stick to your country; be fond of the enjoyment of domestic life & mind your own business." From painful personal experience he insisted to his sons: "Plough not in the field of faction. It yields thorns & thistles & weeds & briars in rank abundance."[79]

Sumner's own ideas about politics were not untouched by the tradition that influenced his father and friends. Though he accepted political parties, he retained an admiration for a true statesmanship that shunned factions and devoted itself to the higher good of the whole community. He enjoyed defending Napoleon for his intellect and the great institutions he had founded, but Sumner frankly admitted that Napoleon's greatest fault was precisely one of statesmanship. Napoleon had perhaps sincerely wished to do good to his countrymen, but the Emperor had gradually confused France and Napoleon Bonaparte in his own mind. Lorenzo de' Medici, in Roscoe's beloved portrait, showed a much nobler sense of statesmanship, as Sumner wrote admiringly in his commonplace book: "The character of *Lorenzo de Medici* appears to be one of the most estimable History records. A man with so great an ambition, & yet with one so well controulled & directed—with so much power in his hands & so little disposition to increase it by any infringements of the rights of his countrymen—with so many temptations in his path & so firm & Hercules-like always in his choice—so great a statesman & magistrate—so strict a scholar—& so fine a poet—so great a friend to the ingenious & patron of talent in every shape, the Annals of no country but Florence can show. In him seemed to centre all those talents, which Heaven scatters *singly* so sparcely; & these were moulded & directed by a temper, soft & amiable."[80]

Thus, Sumner could not fully respect politics, especially as an interest for a young man like himself with no profession. Conscience had motivated his engagement in Anti-Masonry, but his conscience also told him that politics appealed strongly to his emotions, that he found them exciting, exhilarating, and that they thus constituted a temptation away from the more serious intellectual and ethical pursuits that he prized above all. As the time passed, Sumner became more and more worried about the danger of such a temptation. He agreed with his friend Tower about "the din of business & politics. My *reason* loathes them;—my feelings, despite my reason, love them. O! for some retreat where the *mind* & not its appetites can be fed. Politics have been the upsetter of many a student. There is a Circean witchery in them which keeps their votaries enchained 'unconscious of their foul disfigurement'. My *reason* has enlisted me in Anti-Masonry—my *feelings* have nearly run away with my reason, not that I ever will disclaim Anti-M; but I feel that it has engrossed too much of my thoughts." Sumner could not, however, accept his father's entire withdrawal from politics, his belief that when the majority does wrong the minority must learn abnegation. Republican government rather engaged every individual citizen in the nation's political life. An American cannot keep "his mind wholly aloof from politics," Sumner insisted. "He must be on some side or other."[81]

The more newspapers Sumner read and the more he worried about the presidential election coming in 1832—the first for the Anti-Masons—the more anxious he felt about the choice of a profession that still hung over him. Like their fathers, Sumner and his generation had been taught to cultivate a higher aspiration for that noble fame that had been sung by great republicans from Cicero to Milton to the American Founding Fathers. Sumner's own father had grown up with the same vision inherited from his Revolutionary father and had felt deeply his inability to reach it. Harvard had taught the lesson over and over in its classes from rhetoric and oratory, which encouraged the boys to dream of useful and eminent professions, to Moral Philosophy, and to its parting shaft to the class of 1830—a final theme on "Bread and Fame." Sumner's friends thought he was particularly motivated by this vision. To Stearns, Browne proudly admired Sumner's "pervading ambition,—not an intermittent gust of an affair, blowing a hurricane at one time, then subsiding to a calm, but a strong steady breeze, which will bear him well on in the track of honor."[82]

To his friends Sumner privately admitted to being "guilty" of such an ambition. He was inspired by the dream of that higher usefulness to one's fellow man that could be grounded only in a deep understanding of literature, history, and human nature, but to which literature alone, he realized, offered no professional path. He felt the republican duty of enlightened service to one's fellow citizens, from which mere vulgar politics could be only a harmful distraction. The only secular profession society offered that was traditionally bound to these ideals, and that pointed also to the path not only of worldly success but of achieving eminence and the elevated recognition of one's peers and countrymen, was the law. Sumner carefully investigated this possibility. As early as March 1830 he and Hopkinson, who had already studied a little law, were invited to attend one of Sheriff Sumner's semi-annual dinners for members of the Massachusetts bench and bar. During his year off Sumner and Browne, who had himself settled on the law, attended together in Boston and Salem, Browne's hometown, a series of trials featuring Daniel Webster in his legal capacity. And Sumner began to read about the lives of the great jurists of history, referring to them admiringly in his letters and keeping notes in his commonplace book.[83]

The law's reputation of being dry as dust was no more inspiring to Sumner personally than his own father's experience with it was encouraging, and he longed to find some more agreeable alternative, but the longer he put off the final decision the harder it seemed to be and the more his conscience plagued him. "There is no railway to fame," he wrote to Tower that winter, trying to encourage himself as well as his friend. "Labor, labor must be before our eyes; nay, more, its necessity must sink deep in our hearts." But he felt that he was not being laborious enough, while his friends were all taking their first steps toward their future professions. The heavy atmosphere of home and his father's unbending definition of duty added to his gloom. He felt guilty to be standing "all the day idle, dependent upon my Father for support & a profession." Considering various professional possibilities, Sumner tried schoolteaching, but developed "a natural hydrophobia" to a job that had more to do with disciplining wild children than with intellectual and moral stimulation. "My age begins to tell me I ought to stand on my own legs & loosens the chain which has ever held me to ho[m]e. I see no m[eans] of making *money* or reputation any where, wi[th the] exception of the *former* as a school-master, & can I eat garlic & wormwood & bitterness for the sake of a few paltry farthings?"[84]

Under these pressures, Sumner felt ever more "distrustful of myself." His letters grew more serious, and he wondered with some dismay whether he were "becoming a melancholy man." As his friends praised him for taking a year off to deepen his education and prepare himself fully for a noble profession, Sumner sadly made fun of his inactivity and the return of his old "indecision of character." For advice, Sumner turned most to Hopkinson because he was six years older and had been more in the world. "Hop" encouraged Sumner not to be so gloomy, for "if you do not make a strong man of yourself, on you rests the sin of throwing away talents and education which I might envy, and which might make your name familiar in men's mouths." But he rebuked his young friend precisely for setting his ideals too high: "That vague ambition which looks at ends and overlooks means is the cause of half your troubles, and is caused by your overmuch reading and ignorance of men. Your thoughts have conversed only with kings, generals, and poets. Come down to this tame world and this tame reality of things."[85]

Sumner would never be able to follow Hopkinson's suggestion to lower his aims; he felt too deeply the duty to strive not only for improvement but for greatness. Instead, it was precisely under the impetus of his higher ideals, braced by

(top) The Boston Latin School as it was when young Sumner attended and dreamt of becoming a scholar and gentleman like his father. Engraving in the *Memorial History of Boston* after a watercolor by Epes Sargent Dixwell.

(bottom) The house bought by Sheriff Sumner in 1830 for his family would remain his eldest son's home for most of the next thirty-seven years, but in Charles' mind it could never quite be dissevered from the unhappiness of his relationship with his father. Engraving from Elias Nason's *Life and Times of Charles Sumner.*

(above left) This bust by Thomas Crawford would remain for Sumner a life-long souvenir of his Grand Tour of Europe and especially of his golden summer in Rome. Modeled originally in plaster in 1839, this marble copy would be Crawford's thank you in 1843 for Sumner's decisive help with his career. Bequest of Charles Sumner. *Courtesy, Museum of Fine Arts, Boston. Reproduced with permission.* © 2000 *Museum of Fine Arts, Boston. All Rights Reserved.*

(above right) It was Sumner's ability to convince the Boston Athenæum to buy Crawford's *Orpheus and Cerberus* (1843) that launched the sculptor's career and Sumner's own budding reputation as one of the foremost American art patrons of his generation. Gift of Mr. and Mrs. Cornelius C. Vermeule III. *Courtesy, Museum of Fine Arts, Boston. Reproduced with permission.* © 2000 *Museum of Fine Arts, Boston. All Rights Reserved.*

(top, opposite page) This 1833 engraving of Harvard for Benjamin Pierce's history of the college shows on the right the Law School's then brand-new Dane Hall where Sumner remembered spending "the happiest time of my life." *Courtesy, Harvard University Archives.*

(bottom, opposite page) Sumner's "more than parent" Joseph Story inspired him with the nobility of the Natural Law. Oil by Charles Osgood in 1837. *Courtesy, Peabody Essex Museum.*

(above) The delicate Reverend William Ellery Channing, whose moral courage helped to focus Sumner's own sensitivity to Moral Philosophy and to the dictates of conscience. Oil by Spiradone Gambardella in 1838. *Courtesy, Harvard University Portrait Collection, Gift of Frederick A. Eustis, Class of 1835, in accordance with the will of Mary Channing Eustis.*

(left, opposite page) Cornelius Conway Felton in 1846 by Eastman Johnson. *Courtesy, National Park Service, Longfellow National Historic Site. (right, opposite page)* George Stillman Hillard in the 1850's. *Courtesy, The Bostonian Society / Old State House. (bottom, opposite page)* Samuel Gridley Howe. *Courtesy, Massachusetts Historical Society.*

Together Charley Sumner, his literary law partner George Hillard, the professor of languages and budding poet Henry Longfellow, the jolly Greek professor Corny Felton, and Sumner's "alter ego" the philanthropic and dashing "Chevalier" Howe banded together as the inseparable Five of Clubs.

(opposite page) Henry Wadsworth Longfellow in 1846 by Eastman Johnson. Fanny Appleton in early 1834 by G. P. A. Healy. *Both Courtesy, National Park Service, Longfellow National Historic Site.*

Longfellow had to wait seven long years for his beloved Fanny's hand, but their marriage was one of singular harmony, as was their friendship with Sumner to whom they were a chosen brother and sister and the warmest solace of a lonely life.

The Longfellows' Craigie House has changed little since Sumner spent his happy weekends with Longfellow and Fanny and their friends sharing good food and drink, free conversation about everything from art and politics to the unhappinesses of life, and ever truest sympathy. A contemporary engraving by an unknown artist. *Courtesy, National Park Service, Longfellow National Historic Site.*

growing unhappiness and maturity, that he made his final decision to return to Harvard that autumn to study the law. The decision gave some relief, but, as he confided to Stearns with a hint of pain, the lifting of the old burden uncovered a new one: "I think of hitching upon the law at Cam[bridge]. this coming Comm[encemen]t. I am grateful for the encouraging word you give me. I am rather despondent & I meet from none of my family those vivifying expressions, which a young mind always heartily accepts. My Father says nought by way of encouragement. He seems determined to let me shape my own course; so that if I am wise I shall be wise for myself & if I ~~sink~~ am foolish I alone shall bear it. It may be well that it is so. I do not revolt from taking my fate into my own hands. I shall go to Camb. with a cartload of *resolves* & I believe with enough of the firmness of a *man* to abide by a 500th part." His father may have been thinking less of encouraging his son's independence than remembering the pain with which, so many years earlier, he himself had made the same decision for the same reasons and with the same regrets. He would be anxious lest his son were making the same mistake. But this he could not say. Thus another seed of misunderstanding and disappointment slipped between father and son.[86]

As autumn approached, so Sumner's enthusiasm to renew his studies increased. It was not love for his chosen field that drove him on, but frustration at the "unprofitableness" of the latter part of his year off. He berated himself for having given so much of his time to "newspapers and politics . . . No more of this though." Once again, as he had one year before, but with a new sense of purpose, he made a "bushell full of *resolves*" about his coming course of study, in which he included not only the full course of legal studies, but Greek and history, Moral Philosophy and literature as well. "All empty company & association I shall eschew; & seek in the solitariness of my own mind the best (because the least seducing from my studies) companion. Can I hold fast to these good determinations? I fear much the rebellious spirit of the *mortal*. However, '*I will try.*'" His taste and his conscience pulling in other directions, Sumner chose the rational path of duty, hoping it might also lead to happiness. He swore to Tower that he was determined to "leave all the little associations, which turned my mind from its true course."[87]

THE JURIST

"A NEW CURTAIN has risen," wrote Sumner excitedly in September 1831 from his room at Harvard. "I have left Boston & the profitless thoughts which its streets, its inhabitants, its politics & its newspapers ever excite. I find myself again in loved Cam. where is sociality & retirement . . ." It felt good to turn from the "frittering cares" of politics and the somberness of home to the intellectual stimulation and companionship of school, and to feel a renewed sense of purpose. To his delight, Sumner found his new studies engaging: "[I] have read a Vol & a half of Blackstone & am enamoured of the Law." What he found at Harvard Law School was a deepening of the world view, of the philosophical ideas, the ethical concerns, and the cultivated life that he had already encountered at home and in college. More than this, for the first time he found the means of doing that duty that he had been raised to prepare himself for. He did not yet see just how it would influence his thinking, nor to what degree it would deceive his expectations.[1]

Those expectations were high. The high standards his father had taught his children, his own long-cherished dream of becoming a scholar and gentleman like his father,—all this Sumner had naturally associated with his father's profession. Charles Pinckney Sumner may not have known great success in the law, but he had always treated it as a literary and scholarly field, one that should be viewed in the combined light of Enlightenment Humanism's respect for law, of Revolutionary republicanism's stress upon civic duty in a government of laws, and of the highest literary and ethical standards of the classical tradition symbolized by the great advocate and moralist of antiquity, Cicero himself.

This belonged to a new view of the legal profession. Well into the eighteenth century, lawyers had continued to be thought of as tradesmen only, not professionals at all. By the Revolutionary period, however, a significant number of lawyers was anxious to achieve the professional status traditionally reserved to ministers. Intellectually-minded, they wished to elevate the caliber of lawyers, and, accustomed to dealing with landed or commercial gentlemen, they wished to be considered gentlemen themselves. If Charles Pinckney Sumner's financial standing was not typical of this generally well-to-do group, his cultural aspirations were. Here he made all his closest personal and professional associations.

With them he shared in the efforts that had by the 1820's, and with the help of the constitutional and governmental preoccupations of the Revolution, brought lawyers general acceptance as professionals—though without yet conquering the traditional popular distrust of lawyers as shysters.[2]

Having inherited his father's literary and idealistic nature, Sumner imbibed from childhood this Ciceronian ideal of the lawyer as cultivated and civic-minded scholar embodied in his father, his father's closest colleagues, and the distinguished and cultivated leaders of the Massachusetts bench and bar who came to dine semi-annually at the Sheriff's house. Nor was Sumner insensitive to the urgent sense of purpose these early nineteenth-century jurists felt in their half-won battle for public approval. In his choice of a career, he could not fail to be inspired by such an ennobling vision. "The fact is I look upon a *mere* lawyer, a reader of cases & cases alone, as one of the veriest wretches in the world. Dry items & facts, argumentative reports & details of pleadings must incrust the mind with somewhat of their own rust. A lawyer must be a man of polish—with an *omnium gatherum* of knowledge. There is no branch of study or thought, but what he can betimes summon to his aid, if his resources allow it. What is the retailer of law-facts by the side of the man who invests his legal acquisitions in the fair garments [of] an elegantly-informed mind?"[3]

The same Ciceronian ideal that determined Sumner's choice of the law also determined his choice of Harvard Law School. The very idea of a school of law was new, born of the jurists' desire to raise the academic standards of the profession and divorce it from the tradesmanlike associations of the traditional apprenticeship. There was opposition to such schools at first by those fearful that professionalization might mean a restriction in the overall number of lawyers, by struggling lawyers who feared losing their livelihood, by those who wanted to keep the income brought in by apprenticeships. The Massachusetts legislature even put into place disabilities for those students who chose the new law schools, requiring them, despite their studies, to complete a year's apprenticeship before they could pass the bar. Such considerations did not weigh heavily for Sumner when he considered the ideals he saw in the new schools and the caliber of the men who stood behind them. These included such nationally renowned jurists as New York's Chancellor James Kent who had established a pioneering series of law lectures as far back as the 1790's, and Charles Pinckney Sumner's dear friend, now perhaps the most influential associate justice of the Supreme Court, Joseph Story.[4]

It was Story himself who gave the young and struggling Harvard Law School a new burst of idealism and purpose when he became its head in 1829. Charles Pinckney Sumner had wanted to see his friend in this post as early as 1815 when the idea of a series of law lectures in Cambridge had first been discussed. When Joseph Story finally took the post at the appointment of his friend the new

President of Harvard College, Josiah Quincy, Sheriff Sumner was one of the invited guests at the inauguration and offered his thoughtful benediction in the form of a toast:

> The Law just as 'tis "wrong or rightly understood,—
> Our greatest evil or our greatest good."[5]

The toast seemed prophetic. The school's transformation was immediate. The younger Sumner would say that through Story's influence "the Law School, which had been a sickly branch, became the golden mistletoe of our ancient oak." The Law School's three rooms in the old brick gambrel-roofed "College House No. 2," next to the Middlesex County Court House, had echoed with the footsteps of its sole remaining student before Story arrived. But soon there were a good dozen young men there listening eagerly to their new professor. Story brought to his post not only his vast scholarship and the experience and prestige of his eighteen years on the Supreme Court, but also an irresistible personal dynamism and a guiding vision that made him for the next fifteen years a delight and an inspiration to his students. He seemed a second Cicero—"[h]e was in himself a whole triumvirate," marveled Sumner—as he divided his time among the classroom, the Supreme Court, and a third career as writer. His numerous treatises on American law—nearly a library in themselves—were produced "as fast as Sir Walter Scott produced novels," said Sumner, and immediately became the standard reference works for lawyers all over the country. Once settled at Harvard Law School, Story always insisted that he loved teaching best. Indeed, Sumner would have to coax him hard to allow himself to be identified as Justice of the Supreme Court rather than just "Professor Story" on the title pages of his legal commentaries. With his students Story conversed about the law with an infectious mixture of personal warmth, intellectual exuberance, playful humor, and deep conviction. He loved his students, calling them always "'my boys' and felt towards them as if they were all members of one family with him." He made Sumner and his fellow students feel proud by treating them not as inferiors but "as gentlemen," encouraging them to follow in the Ciceronian ideal and to feel that they were already entering the brotherhood of lawyers.[6]

Sumner entered into this atmosphere with delight and enthusiasm. His early worries about the difficulties of the law were soothed by Story's "always ready and profuse [. . .] instructions" and his anticipation of the students' questions, so that he left "no stone unturned by which the rugged paths of the law might be made smoother and the steep ascents be more easily passed." Sumner would later fondly remember how "[t]he law, which is sometimes supposed to be harsh and crabbed, became inviting under his instructions." And as the graduate of Harvard Law School looked back from his new law office upon the advantages of his legal education, it was with deepest appreciation for all that Story's instructions had given him that he would compare the new law schools "with the feeble lights, afforded to students a quarter of a century ago, when the priceless time of legal pupilage was sacrificed and lost, so far as a knowledge of the principles of the profession and of the science of the law was concerned, in a devotion to the daily routine of duties in an office, to the copying of contracts, the making of writs, and the drawing of deeds—the mere handicraft of the profession—without finding opportunity for study, or an instructor to render more than nominal assistance."[7]

Joseph Story taught law according to the Enlightenment tradition with its faith in the rational and universal character of the natural world. He stressed not individual cases and precedents, but legal history and philosophy, suffusing his classroom discussions of the apparently illogical vagaries of the Anglo-American common law with the spirit of legal science that would, in the words of Story's own idol the great English Lord Chief Justice William Mansfield, bring "order out of chaos." In this, Story followed the great jurists of the Age of Reason, who believed that law could be approached as a true science and that "[t]he duty of legal scientists, like that of such great natural scientists as Blumenbach, Buffon, and Lamarck, was to discover regularity and symmetry in nature's confusion and complexity." This desire to classify and to organize the law inspired the comprehensive legal treatises from Sir William Blackstone's *Commentaries on the Laws of England* to Joseph Story's own *Commentaries on the Constitution*, which he was writing while Sumner was a student. Sumner felt a new intellectual excitement as he saw how the concept of legal science, the Ciceronian ideal, and the new professionalism of the law reinforced one another. Story showed that to be a true jurist in the Enlightenment tradition a lawyer must be scientist, moralist, even philosopher, and always scholar, with a broad familiarity with the great legal authorities of all times, and a deep understanding of the historical development of the law: "He should addict himself to the study of philosophy, of rhetoric, of history, and of human nature. It is from the want of this enlarged view of duty, that the profession has sometimes been reproached with a sordid narrowness, with a low chicane, with a cunning avarice, and with a deficiency in liberal and enlightened policy. [. . .] The perfect lawyer, like the perfect orator, must accomplish himself for his duties by familiarity with every study. It may be truly said, that to him nothing, that concerns human nature or human art, is indifferent or useless."[8]

The Enlightenment's universalism and cosmopolitanism did not stop at the water's edge, nor did Story's teaching. Story himself was an expert in comparative law, being well versed in the European Roman or civil law tradition as well as the Anglo-American common law, in ancient as well as modern law. Though his ultimate preference was for the common law, Story urged upon his students the study of comparative law among their own states as well as among nations. As Story's disciple and colleague at the Law School, Simon Greenleaf, explained: "In this science, as in the comparative anatomy of a sister profession, we best understand our own system of laws by comparing it with those of other nations." Or, as Story himself once advised a student, local law is important and should never be neglected, but "you should ever remember that real, solid permanent fame belongs to higher attainments, to the knowledge of principles, & to that noble jurisprudence, of which Lord Mansfield, quoting Cicero, said that nature was not one law at Rome & another at Athens."[9]

Just as the Enlightenment's universalist spirit encouraged knowledge of other systems of law, so it urged the use of that knowledge in the service of developing civilized bonds among nations, and held in high esteem those branches of law that regulated those bonds. The Supreme Court assumed that its member from New England would be an expert in maritime and admiralty law. Story, a native of the seaport of Marblehead, Massachusetts, did not disappoint them, and he brought these specialties back to his classrooms in Cambridge, along with the most universal and cosmopolitan of them all, international law, than which no field of knowledge could "give so high a finish, or so brilliant an ornament, or so extensive an instruction [. . .] to a professional education," and which, moreover, "is at all times the duty, and ought to be the pride, of all who aspire to be statesmen."[10]

Sumner admired this systematic, historical, cultivated approach, but, more than anything else, he felt himself inspired by what in Story's hands became the pinnacle of the ancient tradition of Natural Law as understood by the Age of Reason: "The law of nature is nothing more than those rules which human reason deduces from the various relations of man, to form his character, and regulate his conduct, and thereby insure his permanent happiness. . . . It is, therefore, in the largest sense, the philosophy of morals. . . . It seems to concentrate all morality in the simple precept of love to God and love to man." Thus Story in his inaugural address, and over and over again in his classroom for the next fifteen years, planted the study of law upon a foundation inherited from Aristotle and Cicero and Burke, which conjoined law and ethics, subordinating human laws to the dictates of a higher universal moral law, for, as the great Blackstone taught, "all positive law is an endeavor to enact universal natural law."[11]

The Natural Law tradition rejected the rule of might by holding every man to the obligations toward his fellow men and toward society enjoined by the moral law, by promoting the ideal of a society founded on the twin dictates of virtue and duty. The Natural Law tradition had been of fundamental inspiration to republican thinkers from Cicero to the American Founding Fathers for its constraint of law, and therefore of law-givers, to a higher standard and to the promotion of the public good. In the seventeenth and eighteenth centuries the Natural Law tradition was joined by the complementary natural rights philosophy, which, as a corrective to Natural Law's stress upon duties and the public welfare, emphasized individual rights and freedoms and looked to the equality of all men, not only in their moral obligations but in their political rights as well. Together the two philosophies, seen at the time as conservative and liberal poles of the same tradition, had inspired the authors of the Declaration of Independence and the Constitution, and the republican tradition that Joseph Story passed on to his students.[12]

More than this, Story used the tradition of the Law of Nature to merge law with Moral Philosophy. He taught law, as other Harvard professors taught oratory or literature, as a means to elevate his students' consciences and their sense of responsibility toward their fellow men. Following William Paley, Story taught the young citizens in his classes that Natural Law is "the science, which teaches men their duty and the reasons of it," showing how it "comprehends man's duties to God, to himself, to other men, and as a member of political society." Like the moral philosophers, Story insisted that these duties are impressed upon man by his own "conscience [. . .] under a sense of religious responsibility," for conscience is the God-given human faculty for seeking and understanding the moral law. A society based upon such principles would be well ordered and happy.[13]

Already deeply attached to the principles of virtue and duty, Sumner warmed to such a vision. His belief in religious tolerance and faith in the goodness of man heard here their echo. His conscience, which had already been inflamed against Masonic immorality and lawlessness, found inspiration in this philosophy that made law the servant of morals and duty, ideally "the temple in which the majesty of right has taken its abode." At the same time Sumner was struck by both the responsibility and the eminence of the lawyer who must serve mankind through those laws: "A lawyer is one of the best or worst of men according as he shapes his course," said Sumner, echoing the sentiment of his father's toast at Story's inaugural. "He may breed strife; & he may settle the dissentions of years." This gave the lawyer the duty of being a moral leader in society, a position deeply respected in Puritan and New England thinking but traditionally reserved for ministers, as Sumner exclaimed to his friend: "Tower, we have struck the true profession—the one, in which the mind is the most sharpened & quickened; & the duties of which, properly discharged, are most vital to the interests of the country; for religion exists independent of its ministers—every breast feels it; but the *Law* lives only in the Honesty & learning of Lawyers. Let us feel conscious, then, of our responsibility; &, by as much as our profession excells in interest & importance, give to it a corresponding dedication of our abilities."[14]

A fellow Harvardian who went on to become a minister remembered that in law school Sumner "talked much of ethics and international law. He had a great strength of conviction on ethical subjects and decided religious principle; yet he was little theological, much less ecclesiastical." Sumner was most concerned not with the kingdom of heaven, not with what he called "the aridness of Theology," but with what could be done on earth, with "the embowered truths of History." When his old friend Jonathan Stearns, whom he had once playfully hailed as "the flag-staff of Unitarianism," tried to convert Sumner in the winter of 1833 to a more active religiosity, Sumner declined. Treading gently so as not to offend a dear friend, Sumner nonetheless personally rejected basic tenets even of the liberal theology of Unitarianism: "I remained & still remain unconvinced that Christ was divinely commissioned to preach a revelation to men & that he was entrusted with the power of working miracles." More than this, Sumner candidly admitted that "I do not think that I have a basis for faith to build upon. I am without religious feeling. I seldom refer my happiness or acquisitions to ye Great Father from whose mercy they are derived." But Sumner was not without a faith of his own, one that harkened back, as did his legal ideals, to the Enlightenment. Referring to himself as a "conscientious unbeliever," he rejected the divinity of Christ but not his teachings: "I believe [. . .] that my love to my neighbor viz my anxiety that my fellow-creatures shld be happy & disposition to serve them in their honest endeavors, is pure & strong. Certainly I do feel an affection for every thing that God created & *this feeling is my religion.*" With this idealism Sumner sometimes "astonished" his comrades. One day he and a group of fellow law students were chatting together about what they would do after graduation to achieve that "*greatness*" they all dreamt of, "which we," one of them later remembered, "understood as being—wealth—power—place[—]fame." There was a general flush of incredulity, he reminded Sumner, when "[y]ou proclaimed *your* object to be that of doing the greatest amount of *good* to mankind." In the law, Sumner believed he had found the means to that end.[15]

Thus devoted, as he once recommended to another, to "reading law for a *purpose & an end,* other than ye bare getting of information," Sumner felt "every spur & ambition exciting" him and plunged into his studies. Pained at the "[d]ays of idleness" of the year before law school, he now read from morning till late at night, seldom going to bed before two and sometimes not till dawn. He familiarized himself not only with the regular course reading, but with all the standard legal works and beyond into the source books, making "myself acquainted more or less with every work of the common law, from the Year Books in uncouth Norman down to the latest reports." To this he added great works in continental and international law, never forgetting his favorite reading in English literature. Such a course had at first seemed daunting to him, but a new sense of discipline carried him through the reading and began to infuse his writing, which became tauter and more energetic. As at college, but with more control, he aimed at "the highest standard." He later advised a younger student about his method: "If you place a low standard at which to aim, you will not surely rise above it, even if you reach it. Whereas, failing to reach a higher mark may be full of honor." Sumner's friends were amazed at how much he was acquiring. His old college friend and now fellow law student John Browne, joking that he himself was much more lax in his reading, wrote: "We often laugh together in speaking of the time to come, when I tell him I will send to him for law when I have a case to look up. He is to the law what he used to be to history,—a repertory of facts to which we might all resort." Professor Story marveled likewise to President Quincy's family at his student's "wonderful memory; he keeps all his knowledge in order, and can put his hand on it in a moment. This is a great gift."[16]

As at college, Sumner became devoted to the library. As the second student appointed by Story to be law librarian and as the author of the law collection's first catalogue, Sumner soon came to know the new library so well that "if every vol. was in its place, [I] could find any vol. desired in the dark." As librarian he was also the first student to have a room in the now growing Law School's new building. The little Greek temple was called Dane Hall after the school's benefactor Nathan Dane, and among its professors and students gave Harvard Law School its affectionate names of Dane Law School or Dane College. It stood at the southern end of the campus below Massachusetts Hall, and from his second-story window under its pediment Sumner looked out through the temple's columns and the trees toward the center of the still rural town. He thought it "the pleasantest room in Cambridge." Inside it was always "piled with books," remembered William Wetmore Story, Joseph Story's young son— "the shelves overflowed and the floor was littered with them." Miss Peters, a daughter of Supreme Court Reporter Richard Peters, recalled how, when she was a little girl, the "slender, bright-eyed" young Sumner gave her and her father a tour of the law library "with what seemed to me an adoring reverence for the hallowed spot, so that his voice was subdued and his touch rested tenderly on the dear books as he stood showing them to my father."[17]

Sumner worked so hard at the Law School that he worried his family and friends. He had by now reached his full height of six feet two inches, but at 120 pounds he was little more than bones, with ever blood-shot eyes and a "harsh, constant cough." His friends could not help but fear that he might meet the same fate as his twin sister Matilda, who was just then dying of consumption. To his friends' concerns, Sumner replied with a touch of irony that: "I never was better." His father's fears mingled perhaps with uncharacteristic astonishment at just how much his son was reading: "Charles, while you study law, be not too discursive. Study your prescribed course well. That is enough to make you a lawyer. You may bewilder your mind by taking too wide a range." But Sumner was insistent upon his new course, as he informed his friend Stearns: "Who can have spoken to you of me such flattering words, as should imply that I was hurting my health with study?—*Contra*—I reprove myself for lack of study. I am well-determined, though, that if health is continued to me, *lack of study* shall not be laid to my charge. *Study* is the talisman." Study was the way not only to the knowledge and scholarship that he prized so much, but to the usefulness and eminence that might come from them. "In these days, more than of old, *labor* makes the man. The improved means of knowledge place us all on a level—it is *labor*, backed indeed by talents, which spurns that level."[18]

Sumner prized that love of study and desire for knowledge in others as well and, with the sense of duty belonging to the eldest brother, urged them upon his younger siblings. It was for her intelligence that he already felt an especial affection for his little sister Mary, not yet ten years old when he was graduated from law school. Their father, who admired poise and gentleness and patience—his wife's qualities—was closest to his eldest daughters. He deeply esteemed his already elegant and "docile" middle daughter Jane, and when his quiet and "beloved" Matilda passed away at just twenty-one in March 1832, his eldest son was struck at the sight of their normally undemonstrative father in tears. Little Mary was very different from her sisters. She found the discipline of regular study hard, but she constantly asked questions about everything and, when she did not get satisfactory answers, she would sit down and cry. Though he agreed that she needed to learn a little patience, Charles from the start warmed to her active mind: "She has fine intelligence & an *inquisitiveness,* which I think a good omen. I hope she will not abandon any of that; though, I wish, she wld try to bear her little disappointments in not being able to have her questions answered, *with more nerve.*"[19]

If family and friends worried about Sumner's own diligence and health, his professors delighted in his enthusiasm and ability, and soon considered him a friend as well. Sumner quickly became close to Joseph Story's first colleague at the Law School, John Ashmun, and in 1831 it was Sumner who watched alone at the young man's premature deathbed. When Simon Greenleaf, a Maine lawyer and court reporter, became Story's second colleague, he too was soon drawn into a warm friendship with his student. But Sumner's closest tie of all was soon to Joseph Story himself. The fact that Sumner was the son of Story's old college friend would have been enough to bring professor and student to each other's notice. As Story once jested to the young man, he had "a heritable right to your friendship." But soon Judge Story, as his friends called him—never Justice,—and the younger Sumner developed their own close friendship based on their shared taste for literature and scholarship as well as the law, and warmed by each man's natural affectionateness. They were both famous for their love of conversation as well—though even Sumner could not outtalk Joseph Story—and the two would sit by the fireside long into the night while Sumner, a natural-born student, "plied [Story] with an ever-flowing stream of questions" that the professor delighted to answer. Before long Sumner was a guest at the Storys' house "two or three evenings in the week," where Story "always received him with a beaming face, and treated him almost as if he were a son." Nor did Mrs. Story feel differently, or their son, William Wetmore, then in college, who awaited Sumner's visits "with eager pleasure" and thought of him as an older brother. For Sumner, all of this naturally contributed to making the years at the Law School, "the happiest of my life."[20]

Sumner's devotion to the law had also helped to dull the attraction of politics that had been so strong in the year or two before he entered Dane College. He still found politics intriguing, but he believed that he now had weightier matters to engage his mind and that he could set politics aside as a childish game. These feelings were strengthened by the month-and-a-half-long sojourn that Sumner, as all young lawyers were urged to do, made in Washington in the early spring of 1834 at the end of his Harvard studies. The capital city was a shock to Sumner, who had grown up in a Boston that prided itself on its intellectual heritage and was, during his youth, proudly revitalizing and beautifying its streets and building new institutions. Washington was unformed at best, "the City of great design" but design only, with sparsely laid out "poor stinted brick houses" like the worst buildings of the port areas surrounding Boston. The "spacious & far-reaching streets" were empty and all of dust, "horridly full of dust," an aspect truly uncivilized compared to the elegant brick townhouses, the paved and landscaped streets of Boston.[21]

But it was the politicians themselves who most disappointed Sumner. He had set out to Washington hoping against hope to "see the *men* of the land," that is, hoping to find true statesmen, the counterparts of the Ciceronian jurists he admired, despite the warnings of those back home that the city was no better than a "great political Sodom." What he found were legislative halls in which the members hardly listened to one another, preferring to catch up on their correspondence or their reading rather than hear each other's speeches. Halls intended for serious discussion were instead devoid of all spirit of debate. Even the Senate, which, given its Roman, indeed Ciceronian, evocations, should have aimed for a higher standard, was disappointing. Listening approvingly to one senator, Sumner regretted that, though the public would surely be convinced when it read the speech: "The Senate do not listen." It was only downstairs in the Supreme Court that he found men seriously and soberly debating great issues together. "Every day's attendance in the *political part* of the Capitol shows me clearly that all speeches are delivered to the people beyond, and not to the Senators or Representatives present. In the Supreme Court, the object of speaking is to convince. The more I see of *politics* the more I learn to love *law*."[22]

To his father and Story and Greenleaf, all of whom were watching him with close concern, anxious lest his youthful interest in politics prove too strong, Sumner wrote in turn with self-conscious emphasis that he felt no temptation for political life. To his father he insisted that he had no desire to return to Washington and that politics served only to wed him more to the law, "which, I feel, will give me an honorable livelihood." He reassured Greenleaf: "Notwithstanding the attraction afforded by the Senate & the newspaper fame which I see the politicians there acquire, I feel no envy therefor & no disposition to enter the unweeded garden in which they are laboring—even if its gates were wide open to me; in plain language, I see no political condition that I shld be willing to desire—even if I thought it within my reach,—which, indeed, I do not think of the humblest." And to the Judge he wrote that after he heard John C. Calhoun's next speech he would leave town, and that "he probably will be ye last man I shall hear in Washington—*ever.* I shall never come here again. No inducement, I think,—at least none that my most flighty ambition can look forward to, will take me away from the study & calm pursuit of my profession, wherever I shall determine to pitch my tent. Politics are my loathing." Perhaps Sumner's insistence was intended partly to steel himself against lingering temptation. When it came time to go he admitted candidly: "I feel a little melancholy at leaving, as I have become almost a denizen here—have habituated myself to ye hours & style of living here, so that I shall feel ye change. And yet there is nothing that I have met—either in ye Senate or ye Ct or in ye well-furnished tables of ye richest hotels—that I wld take in exchange for ye calm enjoyts. & employmts. to which I have bin accustomed. I feel in an unnatural state & I shall have joy in once more resuming my constant labors."[23]

Sumner's condemnation of politics was as real as his attachment to them. He found politics exciting, but that meant to him that they adhered to the animal in man, to his appetites and passions, too often the lowest ones, rather than to his intellect and conscience. They represented the selfish turmoil of competing states and interests, rather than the coöperation of disinterested men for the good of the whole nation. Sumner had found in the law a pursuit based upon reason and ethics, a pursuit based upon "those everlasting principles which are at the bottom of all society and order," that worked through study and scholarship toward the goal of universal justice. Politics could not even live up to its own ideal of statesmanship. Politics seemed to degrade civilization; law worked to elevate it. Sumner found politics indeed at once repellent and beguiling, but the law had earned his respect. When he returned to Boston to take up his practice he intended it to be for good.[24]

Judge Story, fully seconded by his friend and colleague Simon Greenleaf, hoped it would be for good, too. He had come to think so highly of Sumner that he had singled him out as the young man he wanted for his successor as head of the Dane Law School, and even, he hoped, on the Supreme Court. Story thus took special pains to help Sumner in his professional course. It was Story who had encouraged Sumner to stay on an extra term at the Law School after he had completed his coursework in May 1833. Story managed to have this time counted as the first six months of the apprenticeship Sumner was still legally required to undergo. The next six months of the apprenticeship Sumner spent in the office of the cultivated Bostonian lawyer Benjamin Rand. Nor did he pass his time in the usual menial chores of copying documents and writing writs, but rather in reading through Rand's extensive library and discussing law with his master. A month and a half of this apprenticeship was taken up by the trip to Washington—learning about the workings of the Supreme Court on location as Story's guest. Sumner's apprenticeship was thus rendered as untradesmanlike as possible. Before it was over, Judge Story had offered his former student a teaching position at Harvard Law School.[25]

Sumner was torn by the offer. He loved the scholarly glow of Cambridge and its promise of association with such distinguished and agreeable colleagues. He was both honored and tempted. At the same time he was afraid, if he went early into teaching, that he might never achieve the worldly success he hoped for. He could not forget his own family's struggle with hardship. He had long dreamt of traveling abroad to complete his education and of someday having a family of his own, but these things required the kind of money he was more likely to earn in practice than teaching. Nor was the little regarded profession of teaching likely to lead to eminence and fame. Joseph Story had dignified his professorship with the considerable reputation he had already won on the Supreme Court, not the other way around. As he weighed these considerations in his mind in that summer of 1834, Sumner shared his worries with his old friend John Browne, who had by now set up in practice in his native Salem. Browne had also worried about the future of his friend who preferred to write "learned" and "speculative" rather than "practical" articles, but he had no hesitation about the Judge's offer, and reproved his friend for his unhappiness: "All your inclinations (I do not see through a glass darkly) and all your habits set you on with a strong tendency toward a green eminence of fame and emolument in your profession; but you are not destined to reach it by travelling through the ordinary business of a young lawyer in the courts. You see that yourself, and you affect to be sad thereat. Instead of looking back with regret to the practice which you are to leave to other spirits touched less finely, and to far less fine issues, you should reserve both your eyes to look forward and see the reasons of rejoicing. By all means take up the offer of the judge, and never think of opening an office in the city."[26]

Sumner could not give up so easily. He declined Story's offer and, not even waiting for the Boston courts to reopen after their summer holidays, he rushed off to Worcester to pass the bar. By October he had argued his first case as junior counsel to a friend from the Law School, George Stillman Hillard. Their efforts were noticed in Boston's leading newspaper: "The defence was conducted with much ability by Messrs. G. S. Hillard and Charles Sumner. This was the first essay of the latter gentleman, who is said to be more deeply read in the law than any other individual of similar age." Hillard had been just one year ahead of Sumner at the Law School and was second only to Sumner himself in Judge Story's esteem and affections. The two friends complemented each other well, Sumner's excessive generosity in helping others being balanced by Hillard's better business sense, while Sumner's energy and capacity for work balanced Hillard's more delicate constitution. They also shared a deep love of literature and of art, as well as an inclination to melancholy springing for Sumner from the loneliness of bachelorhood and for Hillard from the loneliness of an ill-assorted marriage. Within the month, Hillard and Sumner had set up in practice as partners on the second floor of the new building at Number Four Court Street in the heart of Boston, a place that became not only their offices, but the center of their social world, and Sumner's lodgings.[27]

If Sumner had chosen an active practice over the philosophical retirement of the academy, he nonetheless did everything he could to suffuse his professional career with the intellectual and idealistic spirit he had loved at Cambridge. His choice of a partnership with the cultivated and congenial Hillard, despite flattering and much more lucrative offers, was proof of this. Not only the friend of Joseph Story, Sumner now became his assistant in the editing and publication of his voluminous and internationally respected works, and he gratefully cultivated the intellectual ties initially opened to him as Story's protégé and quickly strengthened by his own striking ability and warmth. The "indefatigable student" with the demeanor "of a shy and modest maiden," charmed everyone he met.[28] Though the demanding young Sumner tried to hide his own disappointment at Chancellor James Kent's "grossly ungrammatical" conversation and at his vanity, he deeply impressed the New York jurist, whose *Commentaries on American Law* had been the country's most comprehensive legal treatise until Story undertook his literary labors in the 1830's, and who now came to share Story's hopes that Sumner would one day succeed to their position as leader of the American legal profession and advocate of the Ciceronian tradition. In Washington, Sumner quickly made a friend of Supreme Court Reporter Richard Peters, who asked his help on legal points as early as 1834, while, on the same trip to Washington, Sumner prepared a brief for the Senate Judiciary Committee.[29]

Through Richard Peters, Sumner made another acquaintance that would last a lifetime. During that Washington spring of 1834 Peters gave Francis Lieber a letter of introduction to the young Boston attorney. At nineteen Sumner had received a copy of Lieber's highly popular *Encyclopædia Americana* from the Boston Society for the Diffusion of Useful Knowledge as first prize for his essay on commerce; now Lieber was so impressed by their first meeting that he immediately wrote to his friend Joseph Story to learn the young man's Christian name and address that he might write him, and thus initiated what Lieber's biographer would call "an incredibly voluminous correspondence."[30]

Francis Lieber was nearly thirteen years older than Sumner and had already more than a lifetime of experience. His first memories were of Napoleon's troops marching into his native Berlin. He saw the battle of Waterloo with his own eyes, and was wounded at Namur. For his young liberal idealism he had been harassed and jailed by Prussia's autocratic order, and had finally left Europe for America in 1827. Now Sumner would quickly become one of his closest collaborators, along with Hillard and Story himself, in what Lieber hoped would be his *magnum opus*. The *Political Ethics*—Story suggested the title—was to add the techniques of German social science to the spirit of American Moral Philosophy in order to analyze American republicanism. His plan, explained Sumner in the review of a later work, "comprehends the subject of morality, and of the rights and duties of citizens, with regard to the various institutions, which enter into the great element, the State; in brief, it comprehends that vast body of political relations, which cannot be determined by strict law, and which have never before been classified and considered as a whole."[31]

Sumner, whose energy if not his free time, matched Lieber's own, responded generously to Lieber's constant calls for assistance in the research for his book, and he relished the chance to probe into the implications of republican society and government. Lieber, his mind always teeming with ideas, could be very demanding of his appointed research assistants, setting them, as a later friend of Sumner's put it, "to tasks which it was not easy to perform, and sometimes put their good nature to a strain." They all had cause to complain at one time or another, but Sumner, too much interested in the work and too anxious to help a friend, allowed himself to be put upon more than any, and not only helped with the research but became what friends called Lieber's "standing committee of vigilance" to watch over the publication and advertisement of his works in the North, while Lieber suffered in his Southern exile as professor of political science at the University of South Carolina. No wonder that when Sumner was preparing to leave the country in 1837, Story joked: "What poor Lieber will do without you I know not. He will die, I fear, for want of a rapid, voluminous, never ending correspondence." As Lieber wrote enthusiastically to his wife: "Sumner is one of the finest men I know [. . .] he has the true [inspiration of knowledge], studies hard & *deep*, and is withal enthusiastically devoted to me.

He verily loves me. He loves literature, fine arts and is a noble piece of God's creation."[32]

Despite all these flattering attentions and stimulating ties, Sumner was from the first disappointed in his profession and felt his dreams for the future slipping away. Having given up a post at the Law School in order to achieve position and fame while benefitting his fellow man through his practice, he thus felt divided against himself. His friends grew worried to see him overworked and depressed. To them he seemed to be doing well. He himself later recalled that in those first years he had a "considerable" practice for one of his age, and that his "income [had been] larger than that of any other person at the time so young in his profession." That did not mean a great deal of money, but it did reflect his reputation.[33]

Sumner simply could not warm to the day-to-day drudgeries of a legal office, however—the mechanical duties of writing writs and trading in technicalities that he had managed to avoid so well as a student. Nor could he hide his displeasure at "the long and grotesque retinue of forms and appendages" of the common law, making fun of some of them even before setting up in practice: "The most ardent supporter of the common law would not venture to claim, for the trial of a writ of right, the extraordinary jury, called the grand assize, or great jury, composed of four knights, 'girt with swords,' and who chose twelve other persons to be joined with them; though so long a time has elapsed since this jury has sat upon a cause in England, that the number of which it is composed, as well as their character, and the solemnities of their sitting, seem quite a matter of doubt." More serious for a young advocate, Sumner felt uncomfortable and unsure of himself in the courtroom. He knew the legal authorities and their history inside out. As his old college friend Hopkinson had once before warned him, however, he was so used to conversing in person and in books with the greatest authorities, that he was afraid to trust his own judgment in the fray. At his editor's desk he could speak with authority, but as soon as he stepped in front of a jury he distrusted his own resources and, instead of thrusting and parrying with the opposing side, he fell back on learned but often remote discussions of legal history. Juries were not always convinced.[34]

More than this, Sumner disliked the direction the whole legal profession was taking. As the nineteenth century came into its own, fewer and fewer young men, even of his own generation, looked up to the Ciceronian ideal that had inspired Sumner. Instead of aspiring to positions of moral leadership as learned gentlemen, the new generation in an age of emerging corporate capitalism seemed more commonly to aspire to lucrative jobs as entrepreneurs. Young lawyers, too, increasingly conceived of their profession as one not of scholarship so much as of technical expertise, not of gentlemanliness so much as of business.

As Sumner looked out in imagination over the future, he realized that he had pre-pared himself, by training and taste, for a world that was vanishing before his eyes. He had been inspired by the visions of the Enlightenment, by the ideals of the century that was dying, and he was irked by the values now replacing them. He had envisioned taking his place in a society founded on reason and the order that comes from devotion to duty and virtue. But the new century coming into its own was striving to escape from all restraints and upheld not order but laissez-faire, not mutual obligation but unbridled individualism. Sumner had dreamt of rising up by scholarship to achieve eminence and fame and take his place in an aristocracy of merit, but the new century distrusted intellectuals and rejected any kind of traditional aristocracy, including one of merit, replacing them with new heroes, the self-made businessman and the common man whose integrity had not been corrupted by too much education. After 1835 even the Supreme Court seemed to be following this new but narrow path. Two years later Sumner was disappointed by his first interview with the new Democratic Chief Justice Roger B. Taney, whose Baltimore study was "a raw ill-furnished apart-ment, with a paltry collection of books, which seem to be very seldom used." The highest lawyer in the land appeared to be "without any signs of the jurist about him."[35]

Sumner blamed this change on a reckless and anti-intellectual spirit taking over American culture. As he corresponded with more and more jurists from Eu-rope as well as his own country, he was pained at the comparison between the es-teem with which scholarly pursuits were hailed in the Old World and the in-creasing scorn for them among Americans. In both England and the United States there was then much discussion as to whether there should be an amalga-mation between the system of common law courts and the system of the courts of equity, created to deal with legal cases which could not fairly be determined on the basis of statute law alone. Sumner was very much interested in this ques-tion, which seemed to bear so much upon how well a nation could do justice. But when the English jurist Arthur James Johnes asked Sumner about the prospects of having an edition of his work on the subject published here, Sum-ner had to respond sadly that, though he would be delighted to promote it,

> I am afraid there is not interest enough felt generally in my country in any thing that is not directly *practical* to induce a publisher to undertake an edition here at present. We make great changes often in our laws; but they are made too of-ten with more zeal than knowledge, & without much reference to foreign stud-ies or theoretical discussions. Thus in Massachusetts, the Legislature at its last session, by one short enactment, not preceded by any enquiry or the report of a committee, abolished Special Pleading. The copious report of yr Commis-sioners on this subject was neglected, or more probably was unknown to the

promoters of the measure. Such rash & experimental legislation is our curse. If we sometimes lop off an abuse, we as often tear away a vigorous branch & mar the form & beauty of the goodly tree—of our jurisprudence.[36]

In both his own writings and his conversation and correspondence with students, Sumner tried actively to uphold and teach the Ciceronian ideal and its moral standards. The reports of Judge Story's decisions that Sumner published in the late 1830's and early 'forties as Reporter of the First Judicial Circuit were hailed by American and English jurists alike for their precision and scholarly fullness. Even before passing the bar, Sumner had accepted a post as assistant editor of *The American Jurist and Law Magazine,* the most prestigious American law journal here or in Europe. Founded in 1829, the very year of Harvard's rededication, the *Jurist* was the premier voice of the Ciceronian lawyers. Devoted to "law as a liberal study," it opened its first issue with an address on the natural link between legal science and republicanism by Joseph Story himself. Sumner and his friends Hillard and fellow Number-Four colleague Luther Cushing, as assistant editors and then editors-in-chief as of 1836, carried on in full the *Jurist's* tradition—whether in defending the elegance and humility of older editorial forms now being attacked by the Jacksonian journals that preferred the bolder *I* to the traditional *we,* or in upholding the Ciceronian connection among law, philosophy, and morality, and the conservative values of nationalism and of the active use of government for the public good being assailed by Jacksonian individualism and states' rights.[37]

"There are few I flatter myself," wrote Sumner significantly to a student, "who are more disposed than I am to view the law as a coherent collection of principles, rather than a bundle of cases." In this spirit he wrote his own articles for the *Jurist,* focusing on legal principles and the accomplishments of great liberal-minded jurists like Sir James Mackintosh, whom he praised for his elegant literary abilities: "We respect and admire the learned lawyer, but we love and would take to our bosoms the elegant scholar and man of literature." This was the example he constantly urged on students, "knowing, from my experience with law-students, that ye whisperings of their indolence & the suggestions of practitioners, with more business than knowledge, lead them to consider that all proper professional attainments may be stored up with very light study. I know, from observation, that great learning is not necessary in order to make money at the bar; & that, indeed, the most ignorant are often among the wealthiest lawyers; but I would not dignify their pursuit with ye name of a profession; it is in nothing better than a trade."[38]

Instead, Sumner stressed the importance of education, frequently reviewing and extolling the collections of important libraries, and urging every county and bar to establish its own library that no lawyer be forced by the expense to do without its crucial benefits. Even when Sumner dealt with more technical questions, it was usually in the context of comparative or international law, and he never failed to point up the underlying principles of all law: "Can the intelligent student of law, and especially the enlightened jurist, whose heart and time are proverbially devoted, beyond the measure by which love of other pursuits is regulated, to the deep mysteries of his profession, fail to survey with equal delight the laws which regulate the rights and protect the property of the inhabitants of other countries—to observe the variety of systems which prevail, and to detect the general principles, which, being found equally in all, are most properly to be referred to the great parent of law—the inborn promptings of nature and omnipresent truth?"[39]

Everywhere, in law and life, Sumner upheld the highest possible standards and devotion to scholarship and ethics, to the intellect and conscience. When his younger brother George got to be of an age to think of choosing a profession himself, Charles told him that it did not matter what profession he chose so long as he followed it in a scientific and philanthropic spirit. If he should decide for the law, Charles urged him to "follow law, & become a thorough & liberal jurist & advocate, who sees & regards mankind, as much as ye special interests of his client. Follow, my dear boy, an honorable calling, which shall engross yr time & give you position & fame, besides which shall enable you to benefit yr fellowmen."[40]

Feeling painfully the discrepancy between his own ideal and the prevailing trends of the new age, Sumner naturally drifted back toward the Law School, where he could be closest to the scholarly work he loved best and the spirit of the law he most respected. Though he had declined the Judge's offer to join the Law School in 1834, by 1835 Sumner had become the standing choice as substitute whenever Story was on Supreme Court duty in Washington or when he occasionally fell ill. Sumner thus found himself teaching law for some weeks or months of each year through the mid-1830's and early 'forties. For a time in 1837 while Story and Greenleaf were both in Washington, the one judging and the other arguing the celebrated Charles River Bridge case, Sumner had "sole charge of the school." Judge Story was delighted, his hopes unabated. When Sumner first took his place at their beloved "Dane College," the Judge wrote his young friend: "I hope that this is but the beginning & that one day you may fill the Chair which [Professor Greenleaf] or I occupy, if he or I, like Aristocrats, can hope to appoint our successors." Soon Sumner came to share this dream himself, without yet realizing that his vision of Harvard Law School was not quite the same as Story's.[41]

Judge Story had set his hopes on Sumner less even for the young man's expertise than for his intellectual and ethical approach to the law. Story feared for the future as he watched the cultural changes of the new century reaching among his students. The changes were so rapid that the next generation would no longer even comprehend the intellectual outlook of the Ciceronians. Just twenty years' difference between the dates of their graduation from Harvard Law School would be enough to make it impossible for Sumner's future friend Edward Pierce to understand the nature of Story's confidence in Sumner. When Pierce described Sumner as a lawyer he concluded that he was indeed more suited for a place "as author or teacher," rather than in practice: "His intellect lacked subtlety; it was generally repelled by abstruse and technical questions, and, led by Story's example, sought the more congenial domains of international and commercial law. Some of his surviving fellow-students recall that he was not thought to have what is called 'a legal mind;' though Story and Greenleaf, each of whom counted on him as colleague or successor, do not appear to have observed this defect." Story and Greenleaf did not observe this defect for the good reason that they perceived it rather as Sumner's principal strength. This was no difference between a good legal mind and a nonlegal mind, but rather between two different definitions of a legal mind. The Judge admired young Sumner precisely because he embodied the Ciceronian ideal and could carry into the next generation Story's own war against the narrow legal instrumentalism and the emerging business mentality that threatened to plunge the law back into the character of a trade.[42]

The mission of Story at the Law School, the mission he wanted Sumner to succeed to, went much further than saving the legal profession from modern anti-intellectualism. Story was fighting to save the Republic itself, and for that he believed a legal profession devoted to the social and moral principles of the Enlightenment to be crucial. Story blamed the present rise of divisiveness and violence in American life on a decline of republican values which he, like his friend Charles Pinckney Sumner, associated with the growth of party politics and their offspring, political demagogues like Andrew Jackson. By the 1820's Story thus watched the final demise of his old enemy the Federalist party with dismay, convinced that the disorderly trends in American culture were the result of a "crisis of leadership." He could well have agreed with Henry Adams who later wrote that "it was the old Ciceronian idea of government by *the best* that produced the long line of New England statesmen." Like the Federalists, Story believed America needed the guidance of men above party, of ethical and disinterested statesmen, "men, in short, who may safely be entrusted with public affairs, because they have high talents and solid acquirements, and unite with these a liberal spirit, a thorough acquaintance with the details, as well as with the principles of government, and a lofty ambition, as well as an honest purpose, to serve their country, and to give permanence to its institutions and interests. Such men, and no other men, are entitled to the character of statesmen."[43]

To reinvigorate republican ideals Story devoted himself to training a new generation of such statesmen. Working privately but closely with other New England conservatives to recreate the old Federalist party—and thus helping to bring together what in the 1830's would become the conservative wing of the new Whig party—Story fostered the political careers of such conservative leaders as Edward Everett and the young Boston aristocrat Robert C. Winthrop, who had been just a few years ahead of Sumner at the Latin School and at Harvard, and who would play such an ironically painful part in Sumner's own future political career. For twenty years Story maintained a veritable partnership with Daniel Webster himself, collaborating with him on Supreme Court arguments and Senate bills alike. Story saw his most important contribution to this movement, however, in his teaching post at Harvard Law School. He had come to believe, as his biographer put it, "that law treated as a science, administered by lawyers and judges, was a corrective to party government and possibly even an alternative to it—one uniquely compatible with republican principles."[44] In his inaugural address at the Law School he had lamented the modern democratic notion "that men are born legislators; that no qualifications beyond plain sense and common honesty are necessary for the management of the intricate machine of government; and, above all, of that most delicate and interesting of all machines, a republican government." It was Story's mission to train the wise new leadership America needed. This was the mission to which he hoped Charles Sumner would succeed.[45]

Sumner's and Story's shared devotion to Ciceronian and republican ideals, to the Natural Law tradition against modern self-serving instrumentalism, their common belief in the importance of scholarship, in the country's need for educated leaders, and in the duty of government to support the country's cultural as well as material progress and to work for the common good—all these things had led them together into the Whig party and into the shared hope that Sumner would one day take over Dane College and follow in the Judge's footsteps. Neither had as yet any idea to what degree those same ideals would become an insuperable barrier between them, and make it impossible for Sumner to take over Story's mission.

Prominent among the fellow conservatives whom Story supported as the best men upon whose authority a responsible republic must rest were the conservative manufacturers who, by the 1830's had become some of the most powerful men in New England, especially in and around Boston. Believing, as a basic faith of the Enlightenment, that commerce was an agent of civilization—"the nurse of the arts; the genial friend of liberty, justice and order"—a spreader of education and "philanthropy" in a republic and of understanding among peoples, Story thus, in the name of republicanism, put the law solidly behind capitalism in his classroom lectures and his judicial decisions. He did not fully appreciate how different was the emerging nineteenth-century corporate capitalism in scale and social orientation from eighteenth-century commercialism, nor foresee the big business and the robber barons of the Gilded Age. Story's faith in law and his conviction of its place in a republican society was too great for him to imagine its becoming the servant rather than the master of capitalism, and prevented him from realizing that the relationship he thus furthered would, in time, help capitalism to flourish at the expense of the legal profession's belief in the universal principles of Natural Law, as well as at the expense of republican values.[46]

Sumner also believed in the duty of the best men to exert their authority on civic affairs. Even in college he had been unable to accept his father's more democratic view that the majority have the right to their way whether wise or not. Sumner also naturally associated the best men with the conservative political and business leaders of whom Story was one; he shared the Enlightenment's view of commerce with both Story and his father. But business as such did not interest Sumner any more than mathematics had in school. Rather than out of any deep conviction in the benefits of capitalism, Sumner was attached to these social leaders because they were the educated and cultivated class. Their business acumen meant nothing to him, but he admired their support of the arts and of educational institutions. It was "gratifying" to think that in the spirit of that true Renaissance man Lorenzo de' Medici, for whom they proclaimed their admiration, the New England merchants were beginning to share in "[t]he spirit of chivalry, which once possessed a single class of society," and which, in the present enlightened and democratic age, "is now diffused, with considerable uniformity, through all sorts of men." Their equal support of humanitarian institutions gave Sumner confidence that their social ideas could not be far behind their ideas on culture. He did not yet dream that the conservative business and political leadership of Massachusetts, strengthened in part by the efforts of Judge Story, would one day appear to him as the greatest obstacle to progressive ethical change.[47]

Already Sumner's sense of the public good, and of how much social change was acceptable in its name, was fundamentally different from theirs and from Story's. In the famed Charles River Bridge case of 1837, which brought a Bostonian dispute to the Supreme Court, Sumner thought the good of the community rode on the victory of the new bridge's right to serve the people over the old bridge's right to maintain its corporate monopoly, while Story argued that that same public good required the honoring of the old corporation's contract. This conclusion seemed so unacceptable to Sumner that at first he even admitted his fear that Story's support for the old bridge might be unconsciously influenced by his close ties to the corporation. When he read the final decision, Sumner had to confess himself almost "irresistibly carried away by the rushing current"—and the sound scholarship—of Story's argument, which seemed to him like "champagne" compared to the "hog-wash" of Chief Justice Taney's weak reasoning. Yet Sumner remained uncomfortable. The disjunction between the intellectual quality of scholarship and the ethical question of right, as Sumner saw it, troubled a young man who had always so closely associated the two, and despite his respect for Story's reasoning, Sumner could not bring himself to accept the Judge's conclusion. Story's anxiety for the social order was strengthening his tie to the Natural Law principles of authority and duty, while Sumner was starting down the path that would lead him to see his inescapable moral duty in the protection of natural human rights.[48]

Sumner's adherence to the Whig party was thus built upon a different foundation from Story's. He certainly agreed with Story and Greenleaf in deploring the laissez-faire policies and anti-intellectualism of the Democratic party. Together they denounced the violence and states' rights pretensions of Democratic South Carolina's threats to nullify federal law. Though they rejoiced in his "glorious" Nullification Proclamation, they condemned President Jackson for general lawlessness and deplored his disregard for the Supreme Court's ruling protecting the rights of the Cherokees to land coveted for its gold by their Georgian neighbors. Always they agreed in upholding nationalism and the rule of law, basic tenets of the Whig party, and they always would. Yet Sumner's dislike for the Jacksonians did not translate into an entire rejection of the Democratic party. He admired the Jeffersonian ideal of abstract and universal human rights that was still a cornerstone of Democratic rhetoric, even though Sumner faulted the party for not living up to it. His support of the Whigs was as much for their promotion of voluntary and government programs to support the arts, education, and benevolence as it was for their nationalism and emphasis on law. Sumner's younger brother George—sharing many of the same principles inherited from their father, but with greater bravado—would himself be an active adherent of the Democratic party for twenty years.[49]

The Whig party was in the mid-1830's only newly formed and was welded together by its common opposition to Jacksonian policies. Already, however, it combined those who disapproved of the direction of change in the new century, or who frankly feared it, with those who looked forward to change but wished to see it effected through legal and governmental institutions rather than outside them. Story, though he considered himself a progressive, was increasingly of the former, while Sumner, who considered himself a conservative, was of the latter. Together they represented the fault line on which the Whig party would, only a decade later, be torn apart.[50]

Sumner's professors, actively encouraging a conservative political revival out of fear for the social order, sometimes worried that their chosen successor was too much tempted by a liberal idealism they thought could lead to social chaos. They kept a cautious eye on Sumner's youthful admiration for Napoleon's efforts to establish order on the principles of the French Revolution, as well as his too ready acceptance of the abolitionists they themselves were coming to consider a threat to society. For the time being, Story and Greenleaf said, or at least wrote nothing plainly of their fears concerning the direction in which this liberal idealism might lead their protégé. Story himself was inclined to be indulgent. After all, Sumner was only in his twenties, and was it not natural for young men to entertain liberal visions? Story himself at that age had loved Rousseau and supported the French Revolution. Conservatism, he thought, came naturally with age and wisdom. Still, he and his colleague kept a close watch on the young man. Greenleaf later confessed to Sumner that "your friends in Dane Hall had once begun to mingle their sorrowful bodings lest your freedom of spirit & love of liberty might lead you at least to sympathize with views of men whose pastime is endless change under the name of reformation—or rather might tend to give them an *apparent* title to your name & countenance."[51]

Sumner did not consider his love of liberty to be an impediment to conservatism but rather an integral part of it. Conservatism was to him as much opposed to the spirit of "endless change" as it was to reaction, and he rejected both, as he believed did Story and Greenleaf. True conservatism meant to him the pursuit of progress through responsible means, the pursuit of the cultural and humanitarian improvement of society through the means of established legal and political institutions, the accomplishment of meaningful change to build a wholesome and progressive nation. It was for his theory of evolutionary progress as opposed to violent revolution that Sumner would all his life admire Edmund Burke, the idol of conservative-minded Americans, including Joseph Story. Sumner's attraction to scholarship and cultivation further attached him to the self-consciously conservative families who made up most of his social circle in these years—especially men like Story and Greenleaf, Harvard's President and the old friend of both law professors as well as of his own father, Josiah Quincy, his fellow jurist and friend Judge William Prescott and his family, and the cultivated cotton manufacturer Samuel Lawrence.[52]

At the same time, Sumner's sense of liberty made him naturally more anxious for change than his older friends and drew him closer and closer to the benevolent reform movements that were flourishing in the 1830's, when the meeting of evangelicalism with the Enlightenment produced in America, as in Europe, what Howard Mumford Jones would call a "decade of the worship of humanity." It was not immediately clear that Sumner's budding sympathy with the reform movements would pull him away from his professors. Story's conservatism was not reaction. A belief in progress still remained a cornerstone of his thinking. Story had spoken out strongly and publicly against the slave trade in his 1822 circuit court decision in the case of the slave ship *La Jeune Eugénie,* and he had been one of several eminent conservatives including Daniel Webster to judge an essay contest sponsored by the American Peace Society in 1833 on the establishment of a congress of nations to bring about international peace—a contest Sumner had taken great interest in. But while Story's tolerance for such movements and for the men involved in them was cooling, Sumner's was only just awakening.[53]

Unlike Story's, Sumner's attachment to the law stimulated and directed his first involvement in reform. The reforming spirit of the 1830's had not spared the legal profession, and from the very start of his professional life Sumner filled his reading and correspondence with inquiries into ways to improve the legal system or mitigate social problems associated in one way or another with law. Most explosive of all within the profession was the raging and sometimes "ugly" debate over the codification of the laws. The young Sumner seemed to follow Story's lead into the battle, and when in 1836 Story was appointed to head a state commission to settle the question he wanted Sumner as his "assistant." Sumner did not serve, convinced by friends that he should "seem to *hold back* rather than *press forward*," to disarm those tongues that wagged that his rapid advancement was due to Story's "friendship & favour." It was more than delicacy, however, that would separate Sumner and Story on the issue of codification.[54]

The debate was very much fed by the traditional distrust of lawyers now fanned by the Jacksonian ethic of the common man. Jacksonian lawyers attacked the common law's reliance upon precedent and the power it gave élite judges rather than democratic legislatures in the formation of the law. Robert Rantoul, Jr., leader of the Massachusetts codificationists, declared that "[j]udge-made law is *ex post facto* law." Surrounded by outspoken reformers in the tumultuous 1830's, Ciceronian admirers of the common law tradition feared that the radicals' crusade to replace English law with a continental-style code derived from the democratic rhetoric of natural rights was only the opening wedge of an assault upon the whole social fabric. Story himself was not so categorical. A student of comparative law, he was perfectly aware of imperfections in the common law. His own *Commentaries* were an effort to systematize American law. He stood rather with the moderates who favored a degree of reform while maintaining the overall system as it was.[55]

Sumner's natural inclination drew him to Story's position, for it combined a recognition of the need for change with a cautious and institutional approach. In Burkean manner, Sumner disagreed with the radicals' belief that they could successfully "frame a *new* system from *new* materials, without consulting the previous customs, habits & history of the country." The disagreement of the young man who admired Napoleon's law code was untinged, however, by the fear common to conservatives. When Story was faced with the radicals' persistence and democratic fervor, he grew worried. Though he told Sumner he had "no interest in the fate of the project," he nonetheless accepted the chairmanship of the commission out of what he confided to fellow conservative George Ticknor was "an anxious desire to moderate the movement, & to report a very qualified system of codification, principally though not exclusively, of our common civil law."[56] Sumner was unaware of any change in the Judge and continued to believe that they stood on the same ground, pleased that Story wanted "no *Anti-Codists*" on the commission. While Story was engaged in preparing a report that would be so lukewarm that no reform would ever result, Sumner confidently expected a report that would "aim to show that Codification is at once expedient & practicable. It will make an era, perhaps, in the history of the law in our country, for, coming with the authority of Judge Story's name, & with the cogency of his learning & reasons, it will be calculated to have a very great influence throughout the country, & perhaps, to flow back with a strong tide upon Law Reform in England."[57]

Sumner never lost interest in the codification movement. At the close of the Civil War, after years of trying, he would finally prevail upon the United States Senate to undertake an investigation of the practicability of codifying federal law—though by then his understanding of where he stood in the currents of conservatism and reform had long since changed. In 1852 he eulogized the radical Robert Rantoul, whose interest in reform had gone beyond codification to temperance, free trade, abolition of capital punishment, and antislavery among other causes, as "a *Reforming Conservative* and a *Conservative Reformer*"—his highest praise.[58]

Thinking it natural that, as a lawyer, he should take an interest in other reforms within the legal system, Sumner could not fail to be attracted by the important debate then raging over prison discipline. American experiments with the improvement of prisons put the United States at the head of an international inquiry and brought such distinguished observers to our shores as Alexis de Tocqueville and Judge Frédéric A. Demetz from France and Dr. Nicolaus H. Julius from Prussia. It was Lieber who introduced Sumner to the multifaceted Julius—who had also translated George Ticknor's history of Spanish literature into German—during his stay in Boston in 1835, and their discussion of prison discipline and other reforms would fill their correspondence for many years. Sumner's closest discussions, however, were with his new friend Francis Lieber who, as a social scientist, was fascinated by the causes of crime and speculated that much, though not all, of it resulted from "bad environment" rather than any inherent trait of human nature. And, of course, Sumner argued the question back and forth with his likeminded partner Hillard who gave Lieber's pamphlet *A Popular Essay on Penal Law* a very friendly review in the backyard of the Boston Prison Discipline Society, whose twelfth annual report Lieber's pamphlet directly attacked. It would be some years before Sumner would feel comfortable about speaking up in what was to become an increasingly bitter debate, but he would very soon become a member of the Boston Prison Discipline Society. Though inclined to place even more emphasis on the role of education, Sumner agreed essentially with Lieber about the causes of crime, and with much enlightened international opinion that a more liberal prison discipline system was needed than what the Boston Prison Discipline Society's present president Louis Dwight was inclined to support.[59]

Given his belief that education and social influences were important in crime and given his natural hatred of violence, Sumner could not approve of the most extreme legal penalty, capital punishment. That, too, was being heatedly discussed in the General Court, Massachusetts' state legislature, in the mid-1830's, under the leadership of the same Robert Rantoul, Jr., who was so prominent in the codification debate. Interested American and European friends alike kept in touch with the course of the debates through their correspondence with Sumner. As with all social questions, Sumner enjoyed arguing about this issue with Lieber, but the strength of his own opposition to the death penalty was closer to the position of Robert Rantoul than to that of his German friend. He found full support at Number Four Court Street, however, where he, Hillard, and Cushing, as editors of the *Jurist*, agreed in condemning capital punishment not only as ineffective in deterring crime but as contrary to the progress of civilization.[60]

Sumner's long-standing interest in the movement to end war likewise found encouragement in his new profession. Without discussing the issue, he would, when occasion arose, quote peace-minded lawyers with approval in the *Jurist*, including Sir James Mackintosh's statement: "No war is just which is not defensive"—a sentiment that would find its echo in Sumner's first oration, ten years later. Francis Lieber, whose youth in war-torn Europe had encouraged a romantic taste for the military, was inclined to think his young friend rather naïve on this point. Sumner nonetheless found evidence of the enduring beauty of human nature in Lieber's sketches of his own experience in war. Of Lieber's account of his meeting his future wife in a hospital after the battle of Namur, Sumner exclaimed: "Oh! human nature! War did not choke the delicate sensibilities, which glow in either sex, or alter the nature of man, which, indeed, is indestructible." Sumner found Lieber's account of the battle of Waterloo a most effective denunciation of war, and more than once insisted to him that it should be "published as a *Peace* Tract or as an Essay in some Journal of the Peace Soc—perhaps I shall write some introductory remarks." Sumner was not yet ready to go that far, but it was the subject of peace that would elicit his first mature writings on a topic other than law, and within five years he would become a member of the American Peace Society.[61]

For the time being, Sumner's interest in reform questions remained purely personal. He had not yet come to think that his duty to do good could not be performed by honorably following his profession. Uncertain of himself, of his ability to speak effectively and meaningfully, he passed up even those opportunities to speak that it was expected a young man of his promise and connections should take. When in 1835 Hillard did his civic duty by pronouncing his Fourth of July oration—the young republican's coming out—and then being elected to the General Court, Sumner applauded enthusiastically from the sidelines, but did not follow. And yet, privately discussing the nature of republicanism that Lieber was analyzing in his great work then in progress, the *Political Ethics,* Sumner showed his deep concern about the duties of citizenship and wondered aloud whether the right to vote might not entail the obligation to do so. "If voting be a duty, & not a privilege, should not the duty be enforced by law?" Implicit in the inquiry was the question of his own duty that Sumner was beginning to ask himself with new seriousness. It was a question that would always be associated in his mind with both the law that was his profession and the reforms that were awakening his conscience.[62] Of all the reforms in which Sumner took an interest in the 1830's, none would force him to think about the meaning of that duty more than the struggle against slavery.

There was no moment when Sumner first came to believe in the evil of slavery. Given his father's strong and independent feelings on this subject, dating back far before his son's birth, Sumner could well call his antislavery feelings "almost autochtonous." He and his siblings could remember from childhood their father's stories about slavery and its effects in Georgia and the West Indies, stories about Southern poverty and about the Haitian Revolution. Sumner inherited a lifelong concern for the fate of Haiti from his father, whose "stories of the people there are among my earliest memories." There were stories, too, of the magnanimous decisions of men like the Virginian Edward Coles who sold his estate to take his slaves to Illinois, there to give them all farms and freedom. Closer to home, Sumner became naturally and early familiar with Boston's black community. The western slope of Beacon Hill, at the top of which Sumner himself had been born, was ungraciously known as "Nigger Hill." Belknap, now Joy Street, one block over from Hancock Street, was the cultural center of Boston's black community, and Sumner's father had cordial relations with its inhabitants. As young Charles walked down the street with his father, he learned that the color of the people one passed and spoke to had no effect on a gentleman's demeanor.[63]

Boston and the social relations he knew there offered little evidence of the realities of slavery, however, and could not prepare Sumner for what he would see when he first went South. Traveling out of Baltimore on the last leg of his 1834 trip to Washington, he was shocked: "The distance is but 38 miles—yet we were till night laboring over ye road—the worst I ever was upon. The whole country was barren & cheerless—houses were sprinkled very thinly on ye road & when they did appear, they were little better than hovels—were log-huts, which Father will remember, though none else of ye Family may be able to conceive them. For ye 1st time, I saw slaves—& my worst pre-conception of their appearance & ignorance did not fall as low as their actual stupidity. They appear to be nothing more than moving masses of flesh, unendowed with any thing of intelligence above ye brutes. I have now an idea of ye blight upon that part of our country in which they live." For a young man so hopeful about human nature, believing so deeply in the importance of education, and having an almost religious devotion to the dignity of man, there could be no worse an indictment of a system or society than that it lowered men to the level of brute beasts. It was after this sight that Sumner began to study the issue of slavery more intently.[64]

Antislavery had never before been so explosive an issue as in the 1830's. The fears touched off by the Missouri Crisis and the Nullification Controversy were suddenly inflamed by a barrage of abolitionist publicity in mid-decade. This was made possible by the creation of more effective abolitionist organizations and by a veritable revolution in printing, spawned by a combination of low postal rates and the new availability of cheaper and more efficient steam presses. Thus armed, the abolitionists swamped the country with an unprecedented flood of inexpensive pamphlets and newspapers denouncing the South's peculiar institution. A wave of mob violence, committed mainly by "gentlemen of property and standing" against abolitionists— but almost universally blamed on the abolitionists—heightened fears of civil dissolution. Conservative leaders and ordinary citizens everywhere were appalled at what they considered the abolitionists' reckless threat to the Union. Sumner was not afraid of such a stigmatized subject, any more than his father had been to support the Haitian Revolution—an event still horrifying Bostonians thirty years after the fact—but he was careful about what he said, especially with the older conservative men with whom he corresponded most. Lieber's residence in South Carolina made Sumner cautious, and, though Judge Story had spoken out against the slave trade, Sumner could not help but be aware of Story's increasing discomfort in the face of abolitionist agitation, a discomfort that over the next decade would begin to express itself in open condemnation in his classroom of the Garrisonians. Sumner's corresponding discretion left little direct evidence of exactly what he read and when he read it, but it is clear that his interest was active and sustained, and that he looked to the law as the natural solution.[65]

For the two or three years following his trip to Washington, Sumner studied the problem of slavery carefully. It was likely soon after his return that he read Lydia Maria Child's *Appeal in Favor of that Class of Americans Called Africans,* which had first appeared in 1833, "the first anti-slavery work ever printed in America in book form," recalled abolitionist Thomas Wentworth Higginson. In the *Appeal* Mrs. Child gave a detailed historical indictment of slavery and of its effect upon Southern society, as well as of its baleful influence on American politics, and took no prisoners in the process either among Southerners or their Northern sympathizers. Utterly rejecting the genteel American Colonization Society as a racist organization, Mrs. Child urged immediate emancipation. The book earned her an important place in the abolitionist movement at the expense of excommunication from Boston's respectable society. George Ticknor, who had commanding influence in Boston's upper class and who had gained her admittance to the Athenæum library where she had done her research, slammed his door in the hitherto popular and esteemed author's face, as did the Athenæum. Massachusetts' future Attorney General James T. Austin "hurled the *Appeal* out the window with a pair of tongs." Sumner, by contrast, found the book deeply absorbing and convincing, and even twenty years later remembered to Mrs. Child—who had by then become a friend—what a persuasive influence her book had had on his mind at that time.[66]

It was probably not long after that that Sumner read the Reverend William Ellery Channing's book *Slavery,* which came out in November 1835, and to the writing of which Channing himself said Mrs. Child's example had urged him. Mrs. Child's book was historical and richly factual. The Reverend Channing instead offered a philosophical argument in the tradition of that American Moral Philosophy of which he was one of the greatest spokesmen. Channing's work was more conservative than Mrs. Child's, refusing to cast blame upon the slaveholders who were themselves victims of their own culture. Sumner must have felt deep sympathy with the Reverend's conviction that the greatest evil of slavery was its degradation of the human spirit, for by it "[t]he most sacred right of human nature, that of developing his best faculties, is denied." Channing also took up the republican question of the relative weight of duties and rights in civil society. He maintained the traditional harmony between the two, but his emphasis was all upon individual rights, even conflating the two so that one man's rights became another's duty. Sumner must have nodded his agreement when Channing insisted that, though it was not always so in fact, "Right is older than human law. Law ought to be its voice." Soon, if not already by this time, Sumner could count Channing a friend as well, with whom he delighted in discussing the dilemma of slavery and Moral Philosophy.[67]

In that same year Sumner took an even more unusual step. He began to read William Lloyd Garrison's antislavery newspaper, the *Liberator.* Unlike Mrs. Child and the Reverend Channing, the Newburyport printer had never had any place in Boston's cultivated society. At its best, his newspaper had a circulation of around fifteen hundred people, all but a few of them from Boston's black community. The *Liberator*'s violent and uncompromising rhetoric was immediately branded as "incendiary" and considered far beyond the pale of respectability. Sumner—like Channing—did not like its language. "I have never been satisfied with its tone," he later stated. "It has seemed to me often vindictive, bitter & unchristian." Nonetheless, he soon began to subscribe to it, and would continue to take it until it ceased publication in 1865: "It was the first paper I ever subscribed for. I did it in the sincerity of my early opposition to Slavery."[68]

There were events, too, to complement Sumner's reading, to some of which he had personal ties through his father. The country plunged into violence in 1835 as the number of riots and especially of anti-abolitionist mobs rose to a peak. On 21 October Boston was hit by one of the most notorious. The mob that gathered that Wednesday afternoon had been long in preparation, and when they found that their intended target, the visiting English abolitionist George Thompson, had left town, they attacked Garrison himself. The outspoken editor but mild-mannered man soon found himself roughly enveloped by angry rioters, stripped of his outer clothing, his glasses smashed, and a rope put about his body. He was saved from greater violence only because a few men cried out: "Don't hurt him! He is an American!" and rushed him to the City Hall, then in the Old State House. There the Mayor and county officials, in the absence of an organized police force, may have saved his life by taking him into custody and transferring him to jail, wrote Garrison with gleeful irony, "as a disturber of the peace!!"[69]

What precise role Sheriff Sumner played is not recorded, but Garrison thanked him both publicly and privately. Sheriff Sumner deplored the decade's rise in violence and saw it as evidence of the decline of the American Republic. Unlike almost everyone else but the abolitionists themselves, however, he did not blame the abolitionists but saw them as innocent victims of public prejudice. Very likely Charles Pinckney Sumner also encouraged or took pride in some act of kindness by his eldest living daughter Jane toward Garrison, for which Garrison thanked her as well. Her father admired the then fifteen-year-old girl as "a defender of all who in her judgment were unjustly accused." Garrison visited the whole family at home shortly after the mobbing. "The Sumners were, as usual, quite polite and chatty," he wrote his wife; "—they inquired particularly after Mrs. Garrison, and hoped she would visit them—declared that I was too good a man to be mobbed—&c. &c. Am I?" Charles probably did not meet Garrison at the time as he was still living in town, but he must have heard many stories from all the family, and he agreed completely both in deploring the present wave of violence and in laying the blame squarely on the abolitionists' opponents.[70]

The following summer, for his role in a case growing out of slavery, Sheriff Sumner himself was the object of verbal attacks. Late in July 1836 a ship arrived from Baltimore carrying two black women who were claimed as fugitive slaves by a constable on behalf of a Maryland slaveholder. On request of several black Bostonians, the young abolitionist lawyer Samuel E. Sewall got "a habeas corpus to bring the women before" Massachusetts Chief Justice Lemuel Shaw. Sewall described the hearing that took place on 1 August in a courtroom packed by

Boston's black community: "After the chief justice this morning had given his opinion that they must be discharged, but before actually giving the order for their discharge, the agent of the owner asked if he could take them without a warrant. Upon this all the colored people rushed to the door with the women, thinking probably that they were actually discharged and no time was to be lost. They were soon placed in a carriage and conveyed out of town." The authorities followed them, but the two women disappeared without a trace.[71]

Back in Boston, this turn left some people, and not just the slaveholder's agent, very angry. Sewall was, of course, widely blamed and suspected of having intentionally allowed the two women to escape. Also widely and bitterly attacked was the High Sheriff of Suffolk County. Charles Pinckney Sumner had not actually been in the courtroom. After having conferred with Sewall and some deputies to make sure all was in order, he had gone about other business. But this left deep suspicions in many minds that he, too, was guilty of collusion. The Democratic papers complained that his "alleged negligence and lack of energy" were "the chief topic of conversation in all public places." Several newspapers found proof of his dereliction of duty in the fact that, just before the hearing, he was seen to take Sewall "by the hand and said to him—'I wish you success in your cause, sir.'" Chiding the eavesdroppers, Sheriff Sumner defended himself in his own article: "Whether I addressed Mr. Sewall, as it is said, I cannot tell; but, I should be ashamed of myself, if I did not wish that every person claimed as a slave, might be *proved* to be a freeman; which is the purport of the words attributed to me." In the privacy of his notebooks, Sheriff Sumner commented:

> There are some persons in Boston whom it would not shock to see two colored women seized in the Court House, in the presence of a Judge, to be adjudged as slaves; & forcibly borne away as such.
> "My soul turn from them."[72]

His eldest son did not turn from him, but felt proud. To their common friend the prominent Portland attorney Charles S. Daveis, Sumner wrote of his and his father's thanks for his expressions of sympathy and support, adding: "The public will have a victim, & his situation seemed to present him as the fit offering." He was the fit offering because of his official position as High Sheriff, but perhaps also because of his long-standing reputation for radically unpopular views on the explosive subject of slavery. Charles Sumner was learning not only about the evils of slavery, but about the dangers of antislavery.[73]

In the main, however, Sumner was optimistic about the future. The growing strength of the abolitionists, the wave of mob violence spreading across the country, the efforts of the federal government to hold back the tide of change by stopping abolitionist mailings to the South and by instituting a gag rule against anti-slavery petitions in Congress, the unmeasured ravings of Southern politicians against the abolitionists—all this seemed to be grounds for a new public sympathy for the antislavery argument. In hopes of contributing to the general revolution of opinion, Sumner was eager to speak out on such an issue, especially among the young and, because they tended to follow the conservative political opinions of Boston's upper class, particularly to Harvard students. In this he was fully seconded by a good friend of his, the widow Mrs. Judge Howe who took well-behaved undergraduates into her Cambridge home as boarders. She was a woman of spirited intelligence and conversation, and Sumner enjoyed regular luncheons at her table where discussion about art, literature, history, and current events flowed freely between them for their own pleasure, but also consciously for the benefit of the undergraduates who sat and listened attentively. The subject of slavery did not fail to come up. One of the undergraduates later remembered "how Sumner used to hurl his thunders against the opponents of Free Mails and Free Petitions, and how enthusiastically Mrs. Howe used to back him up when she thought the youngsters were becoming too much excited on the other side."[74]

By 1835 Lieber was enduring these difficulties personally in South Carolina. More delicate with older friends than with students, Sumner gently though quickly quizzed his friend about his new perspective on the institution from within the most outspoken state of the slave South. "What think you of it? Shld it longer exist? Is not emancipation practicable?" he urged. And he added his hopefulness about Northern opinion: "We are becoming abolitionists at the North fast—the riots, the attempts to abridge the freedom of discussion, Gov. McDuffie's message & the conduct of the South generally have caused many to think favorably of immediate emancipation who never before inclined to it." Sumner hated slavery first for the degradation it imposed on human nature. As a scholar he hated it also for the restrictions it placed upon the mind, through the abridgment of the freedom of speech and of thought. He felt sorry for Lieber, whose endless efforts to find a more congenial position in the North seemed doomed to failure: "I wonder that your free spirit can endure the bondage to which opinion at the South must subject you—tying your tongue & taming all your expressions." But, not fully sure of Lieber's own opinions, Sumner hesitated to push too far and asked "pardon for this language, for, perhaps, I mistake your views & situation."[75]

At the same time, Sumner was getting to know a growing number of people in the North who shared his feelings. He may not yet have known Garrison, but he was well enough acquainted with the Reverend Samuel May, Jr., then Secretary of the Massachusetts Anti-Slavery Society and, incidentally, a cousin of Samuel E. Sewall, to introduce to him the Frenchman Charles Poyen, who was visiting Boston. He thought May would be glad to know Poyen, for he "has had remarkable opportunities of observing the condition of the slaves in the West Indies, & has prepared a little work on the subject of emancipation." That winter of 1835–1836 Sumner also met for the first time the English writer Harriet Martineau, then visiting Boston herself and preparing her own volume on American society. She found Sumner and his partner Hillard "glorious fellows," and they began a friendship that would last for life. When her book appeared the following year, Sumner knew it would "make the feathers fly," but he hoped "her castigation will do good," even in the South: "Her comments on slavery are said to be scorching. I do not regret this. I hope that through her some truths may reach the South. Perhaps, her book may be burned by the hangman—certainly it will be placed on the *Index Expurgatorius* of the South."[76]

Sumner's closest antislavery contacts, however, were right inside his own office at Number Four Court Street. His partner George Hillard agreed with him fully. Soon Sumner had contributed to making a convert of another old friend, Wendell Phillips. The same Phillips who, at the age of nine, had refused to speak to the humbly born Sumner, had maintained his reputation as a snob into college—a weakness hard to resist for the son of John Phillips and the only Harvard student to be taken home on weekends in a coach with liveried servants. He grew up quickly at Harvard Law School, however, where he studied at the same time though with much less enthusiasm than Sumner, and the two young men, thrown close together, gradually became friends. Phillips had his own office a few doors down Court Street, but, making no pretense of loving the law, he did not attract many clients—a condition more upsetting to his ego than his pocketbook—and, with time hanging heavy on his hands, he spent a good deal of it in the offices of Hillard and Sumner.[77]

Coming from an aristocratic and orthodox Congregationalist family, Phillips had not before been exposed to antislavery. But one day in November 1835 he and Sumner were invited to accompany James Alvord, a friend of Sumner's, on a stagecoach ride to Greenfield in order to keep a certain young lady busy while Alvord romanced her companion, his fiancée. At the last minute Sumner begged out, probably struck with shyness at the thought of having thus to occupy a marriageable girl. It turned out well for Phillips who, during that long ride and conversation, found the love of his life and his future wife in Ann Terry Greene. Miss Greene was, however, something new to him—a staunch, outspoken abolitionist, a Garrisonian. Phillips spent the next year and a half in serious thought and study about the issue of slavery, trying to sort out his own opinions. With whom could he talk more freely than his friends at Number Four, especially Sumner, who was already knowledgeable about the cause and acquainted with members of Garrison's circle. For years thereafter Sumner would tease Phillips that he had been a reader of the *Liberator* when Phillips "was still indifferent to the cause which has since occupied so much of his time," and Phillips would tease back that he had known Garrison before Sumner had.[78]

Sumner never doubted that emancipation was the proper goal. But how to achieve it? Garrison and his followers used the tactic of "moral suasion" through publications like the *Liberator,* antislavery gift books, conventions, and speeches. Sumner had, in his own private way, used moral suasion on the Harvard students and among his friends. It seemed to him, however, that the best way to combat such a great national and institutional evil was through law. Nothing pained Sumner more than the spirit of lawlessness spreading over the country in the 1830's. From the burning of the Ursuline convent across the river in Charlestown by anti-Catholic rioters to the destruction of "a poor negro [. . .] put to death by the cruel torture of the fagot" in East Saint Louis, Sumner condemned the accumulation of acts "not simply in violation of law, but of the most aggravated and fiendish outrage[. . .]." When the abolitionist editor Elijah Lovejoy, having lost three printing presses to angry rioters, was killed defending his fourth in Alton, Illinois, in 1837, the town's mayor and other officials were among the rioters, and Americans across the country joined in blaming the incendiarism of the abolitionists. To Sumner, Lovejoy was "[a]n American citizen, a husband and father, [who] has been cruelly murdered in the lawful defence of his property from the violence of an armed mob." Sumner often praised "the beautiful remark of the ancient Greek philosopher, that that government was the best, under which an injury to a single citizen was resented as an injury to the state," and deplored the fact that "[t]ried by this test, our government, with all the apparatus of freedom, must fail." The argument of the anti-abolitionists that they were preserving social order by putting down the forces of insubordination was to Sumner perverse. The true basis of social order was law, he believed—law based upon the principles of that Natural Law that was itself suffused with the spirit of a higher moral justice.[79]

Sumner believed that such law had to be at the foundation of real social improvement, and he had faith that this could be accomplished. A series of incidents in the mid-1830's showed that much could be done within Massachusetts to begin a legal campaign to divorce the Bay State from the South's peculiar institution as well as to bring the evils of slavery to general notice. The case of the two fugitive women from Baltimore, whom Samuel Sewall defended in 1836 and for whom Sheriff Sumner had shown such unpopular sympathy, was one such case. In such a situation friends of the accused or antislavery activists wishing to help generally applied for a writ of *habeas corpus,* which forced the pretending master or his agent to sue for the alleged fugitives according to due process. But *habeas corpus* did not require a trial by jury. There had been a stronger statute on the books until just recently. The writ of *de homine replegiando,* later known as personal replevin, went back to the Middle Ages when it had been used principally by landowners to recover serfs from someone who detained them. It allowed for the determination of facts arising out of the case by a jury trial, "a procedural advantage of considerable importance," one scholar has written, "in communities where popular hostility to slave catchers was widespread."[80]

The writ of *de homine replegiando* had been removed from the books in Massachusetts with the general revision of the laws of the Commonwealth in 1835. Southern slaveholders, however—frightened by the 1830 slave uprising led by Nat Turner and incensed by Garrison's *Liberator,* on which they wrongly blamed the rebellion—had become more intransigent in their support of slavery, drifting from the old apologetic acceptance of it as a necessary evil toward the proclamation of it as a "positive good." One part of this reaction was the passage of the congressional gag rule. In turn, many Northerners who had not been sympathetic to the abolitionists were awakened to the danger that slavery represented at least to their own liberties. In 1836 and 1837 therefore the abolitionists had more public support than they could have had before to call for the reinstatement of *de homine replegiando.*[81]

The leader of this fight was the member of the Massachusetts House from Greenfield, the promising young lawyer James C. Alvord, the same young man who had introduced Wendell Phillips to his future wife. Alvord had taught at Harvard Law School for a short time in 1833 while Story was negotiating to have Simon Greenleaf brought on as his colleague. There Alvord and Sumner had become good friends. Alvord had even hoped Sumner might set up in practice with him in Greenfield, a prospect Sumner had declined only because he could not bear trading cultivated Boston for a small town in the western hills of the state. Now the two friends had a warm reunion and quickly got down to the business of restoring *de homine replegiando.* Sumner had already studied aspects of the history of the law when he had written an article on the writ of replevin in 1834, and he spent many hours in Alvord's rooms that winter, undoubtedly discussing the issues with him. Meanwhile Hillard, in full agreement with their efforts, was preparing to speak on behalf of the Massachusetts Anti-Slavery Society before a special committee of the General Court set up against the continued existence of slavery in the District of Columbia and in favor of the right of petition, still under gag rule. Hillard's address came in late February 1837, just about the time Alvord was successful in restoring *de homine replegiando.* The three friends could feel that they had made important contributions to the movement.[82]

Sumner did not speak out himself on any of these issues in public, preferring to be an advisor behind the scenes. He had given public lectures on legal matters, had, of course, spoken before his students at Dane College, and was well-read in the matter of slavery, but his caution about declaring a position without extensive study and his uncertainty of himself caused him to shy away from playing any public role in the movement. Still, on 28 February 1837, he joined with Phillips, now convinced of the justice of abolitionism and on his way to becoming a Garrisonian, and with Hillard in giving a trio of lectures at the Smith Schoolhouse on Belknap, now Joy Street, before the Adelphic Union Society, the lyceum of Boston's black community. Sumner, characteristically, lectured on the Constitution, underlining the "right to petition."[83]

These first steps in the cause of antislavery, however, any more than the intellectual work of editing, writing, and teaching, were not enough to give Sumner the sense of satisfaction he craved. Instead, as the years went by, he grew more discouraged and depressed about his work, his life, and his future prospects. It had started out well enough, and his reputation among jurists, if anything, kept growing. Only a year after he passed the bar Andrew Dunlap, the United States District Attorney for Massachusetts, invited him to become his partner, and, of course, at the same time Story wanted Sumner for the Law School. Given such attentions, it is not surprising that there should have been those who envied the young man's close tie to Story and his rapid rise toward fame. But that first material success had not borne fruit. Clients did not multiply; his cases remained mainly small, as did his fees. Depending entirely upon his income for all his future dreams, Sumner grew frustrated. In 1835 he allowed himself, for the only time in his life, to take part in a land speculation—only to lose a considerable sum, and then have to swallow his pride and borrow a total of $1,100 from his father to make ends meet. Sumner worked extremely hard, sitting at his desk or standing before classes all day long, returning to his rooms late to read long into the night, but a considerable portion of his time was given to editing and teaching and thus took him from his office. As his future friend Edward Pierce noted: "Clients are quick to detect such departures from the professional routine, and prefer some painstaking attorney who is always to be found at his desk."[84]

Most seriously, Sumner was too concerned with the broad principles of jurisprudence and justice to derive satisfaction, moral or intellectual, from the minor disputes that came before him and the mere technicalities of law that might apply to them. He found no greater satisfaction in his editorial and teaching work. They demanded labor and time enough, but being an editor was not the same as being an author, nor was it remunerative. The atmosphere at Dane Law School was refreshingly intellectual, and yet Sumner was secretly troubled by its restrictions as well. On the one hand he had come to think of it as a refuge from the office and to look forward to taking his place there in the future. As he later wrote to Greenleaf: "You know well that my heart yearns fondly to that place, &

that in the calm study of my profession I have ever taken more delight than in the pert debate at the bar." But in a candid moment he also admitted: "My blood demands something more Stirring than the quiet scenes of the Academy."[85]

Sumner did not blame the law for his dissatisfaction. He blamed himself. In his own mind he had never been able to live up to his own high standards of scholarship, and his relative lack of success merely confirmed and deepened his growing lack of self-confidence. He very much wanted the approval of more experienced and learned men than himself, but when he got it he could not think himself deserving. When, while still a law student, he won first prize in the respected Bowdoin essay contest, he considered it mere "*chance*," and confided to Charlemagne Tower about his winning: "I feel a mortification wh perhaps no one may appreciate." Judge Story's friendship, his reliance upon Sumner in the editing and publishing of his voluminous works, and his hopes for Sumner's future—all this Sumner took with embarrassed gratitude and a constant conviction of his own unworthiness. To the Judge in Washington he wrote in a typical letter: "While you are away, remember it will be my highest pleasure to do *every thing* I can for you & yr family. If I can be useful in *any way,* let me know. It is so little that I can do & do really do, in return for all yr kindness to me, that I feel almost ashamed of myself." Even on his solitary vacation in the mid-'thirties Sumner could not escape from such thoughts. As he sat in awe before the rush of Niagara Falls, he thought the cataract sounded "like the voice of God, in my ears." "But," he confided to Greenleaf, "there is something oppressive in hearing & contemplating these things. The mind travails with feelings akin to pain, in the endeavor to embrace them. I do not know that it is so with others; but I cannot disguise from myself the sense of weakness, inferiority, & incompetence which I feel."[86]

Feeling this way, Sumner naturally tended to efface himself before others. Warm and outgoing with people, loving his friends, he spent much more of his time helping others to edit or publish their works than he spent on his own. Joseph Story, for whom Sumner did much work, warned him: "You will have to learn, that those, who are willing to labour for others, will never want ample employment, especially if their services are gratuitous; & you must begin to be chary of your intellectual, as well as physical, strength, or it may be exhausted before you reach the fair maturity of life." But, delighted to help others, Sumner became uncomfortable wherever he was expected to speak in his own voice. He insisted that he was not "a devotee of authorities," and from the start of his legal career he took clear and reasoned sides in the debates at hand, but, whether writing legal articles or arguing before a jury, he used other men's words to supply the authority he could not feel in his own. When this resource was impossible, as in a stagecoach alone with a young lady, he withdrew.[87]

Even on moral issues, where he was already noted for his deep convictions, Sumner preferred to have authoritative company to add the strength to his arguments that he thought wanting in his lone voice. "When he could steady him-self against a statement by an ancient author he felt strong," remembered William Story. "His own moral sense, which was very high, seemed to buttress itself with a passage from Cicero or Epictetus. He seemed to build upon them as upon a rock, and thence defy you to shake him." A phrenologist whom Sumner and Hillard went to visit together in the winter of 1835 proved himself at least a good listener by putting his finger immediately on Sumner's lack of self-esteem as his principal problem. Trying to encourage him to have more confidence in his "fine organization for a literary man," and his ability to "become an interest-ing speaker," the phrenologist urged the young attorney to take heart in his own qualities: "You must rouse up your self respect—take opportunities which do not try your mettle too much, & learn to analyze the talents of others & think it easy to equal others. Read less & think & converse more, review what you have got & reexamine it. Make your reading a mere helper to thought." As though conscious of this fault, Sumner regularly advised friends and young students to cultivate greater self-confidence "without which, if properly tempered by mod-esty, nothing great can be done."[88]

Unable to follow his own advice, however, Sumner grew increasingly de-pressed. The playfulness and eager puns of his college letters and the more seri-ous exuberance of his letters from law school all but completely disappeared. He looked back upon his days at Dane College with melancholy, confiding to Greenleaf that, though he threw himself into his work, "I cannot now achieve that contentment, which once so completely was mine—which made me so deliciously happy in yr society & that of my more than parent Judge Story & in the pines & elms of Cambridge." He feared for a future with neither money nor the more important things it made possible, and he began to speak somberly: "I [. . .] am accustomed to view life & the great change in such colours, as to consider death as very little to be mourned."[89]

Sumner's friends berated him for "croak[ing]" and brooding by himself. To-gether they tried to distract him, and, indeed, nothing could brighten his mood better than finding new friends. Until the mid-'thirties Sumner's society had been mainly confined to his professors and their circle. Then Number Four Court Street became the focus of a new group of friends—Hillard and Phillips most especially, their fellow lawyers Luther Cushing and Rufus Choate, whose offices were upstairs, and another inmate of Number Four, Horace Mann, who gave up his practice just about this time for a full-time career in education re-form. By the latter years of the decade Sumner was making new friends in Cam-bridge. Henry Russell Cleveland was a former English professor who had been forced by precarious health to give up his teaching but not his steady ambition to write something important on the history of English literature. Jolly, round-cheeked Cornelius Conway Felton had started as a tutor at Harvard in 1832 and in 1838 would be named Eliot Professor of Greek. And in 1835 Felton introduced Sumner to another friend of his, Harvard's new Smith Professor of Languages, Henry Wadsworth Longfellow, destined to become Sumner's closest friend of all. Within no time at all Charley Sumner, George Hillard, Hal Cleveland, Corny Felton, and Henry Longfellow had banded together as inseparable friends under the name "The Five of Clubs."[90]

The five shared a common love of literature and history, a common hunger for the riches of Western culture that seemed so sparse in their young country, and a desire to help those riches take root here. Sons of cultivated parents, students of Moral Philosophy, they were bound together in an intellectual and ethical kinship. They were all animated by a conviction in the duty of each individual to develop his faculties to the fullest and to use his abilities to do good unto others, just as they all shared the dream of achieving a well-deserved fame. Among themselves each could admit his deep desire "to do something far higher and better [than] what I now see before me," and urge the others on, as Felton did to Sumner: "Let not one ardent aspiration for honorable renown and the glory of beneficent action be chilled" by any personal consideration or success.[91]

Their conviviality and closeness, the encouragement they gave each other meant everything to the lonely Sumner, but he was also secretly intimidated by his new friends. They were all a bit older than he and more settled in their lives; Cleveland and Longfellow had both been to Europe, Longfellow twice. Once again Sumner felt unsure of himself and his knowledge of the world. His friends reminded him, too, of the domestic happiness he longed for but was too diffident to seek. In October 1837 Wendell Phillips suddenly announced his engagement to the same Ann Greene Sumner had been too shy to escort home to Greenfield two years earlier. "I [. . .] give you joy from my heart," he wrote his friend, but added: "I feel solitary," and if he could he "would *try* to keep you company this very week." The date was approaching, too, of Hal Cleveland's marriage to the lovely and kind heiress Sarah Perkins, who was thus instantly welcomed as a friend by "the Club." Afraid he would see less of Cleveland in the future, Sumner nonetheless warmly congratulated his dear friend and complimented Sarah: "The most priceless possession a man can have is the heart of a pure & intellectual woman, & that I am assured is his." But in a melancholy moment, for which he later apologized, Sumner admitted to Sarah his own sense of hopelessness. Unoffended by his confidence, Sarah replied with the understanding assurances her new friend needed to hear: "You are too much in a hurry." Establish yourself in your profession, see Europe, "then will come this charming lady—you need not doubt it because you do not see when she shall come."[92]

Feeling that his present course had come to a dead end, Sumner became determined to realize a very old dream—one which, he was sure, would complete his formal education, and prepare him for both the social success he craved and the professional success he believed to be the means of accomplishing his true duty in life. Back in 1834, his trip to Washington coming to a close, Sumner had sworn to Judge Story: "My next & sole desire ahead is to visit Europe & my first professional gains shall be devoted to that purpose. This accomplished, I shall be ready for any circumstances of life—even what is called *settlement in life.*" In 1837 Sumner decided that he could wait no longer to see and learn from the Old World.[93]

THE GRAND TOUR

"MY PEN TREMBLES in my hand, as in that of a culprit, who sees before him the awful tree, & counts ye seconds which remain to him." So Sumner wrote his good-byes to his closest friends from a New York hotel room as the hour of his sailing for Europe rapidly approached. He was full of anticipation and excitement. He had placed high hopes on this trip, and its realization was an old dream come true. But a projected absence of a year and a half or more for a young man not yet fully established in his profession was a step not to be taken lightly. Weighing heavily on Sumner's sense of responsibility were the doubts and disapproval of many of his most respected friends and of his family.[1]

Sumner's longing to see Europe, and especially England, was so old he called it an "instinct." European history and literature, much more than the young record of the land of his birth, had formed his education and culture. By the mid-1830's Sumner could withstand the desire no longer: "The thought of Europe fills me with the most tumultuous emotions—there, it seems, my heart is garnered up—I feel when I commune with myself about it, as when dwelling on the countenance & voice of a lovely girl. I am in love with Europa."[2] For months after the new year had started, Sumner would continue to date his letters "1837," so blessed in his mind was the date of the final accomplishment of this dream.

From this trip Sumner anticipated much pleasure, but also study. As a young jurist, interested in comparative and international law, he intended "to observe laws, institutions & the administration of justice," "to go circuits & attend terms and parliaments," and thus better prepare himself for his profession. And yet, as he admitted to his friend Charles Daveis, head of the Portland bar, his purpose in going abroad was not "peculiarly legal." Sumner wanted to study "Europe & its reverend history, [. . .] its governments handed down from old time, its sites memorable in story." He wanted "to see *society* in all its forms which are accessible to me; to see men of all characters," "to see, study, observe & admire."[3] He was also very anxious to learn other languages, to improve his French, and to erase the "mortification" he felt at being unable to read German. To replace the money he would lose by abandoning his practice at such an early stage, Sumner hoped to store up "*intellectual capital*" for the future. "What are the world's goods," he appealed to Lieber, "the dross of gold & silver, compared with the priceless treasures of the mind. One might live content, who could look on all these great minds, even if he lived on humble fare." It was for this "self-improvement" that Sumner longed, and then, he fervently hoped, to "come home and be happy."[4]

It was because Sumner conceived of his trip as a step toward his future usefulness to society, as well as because of his professional promise, that he was able to get the financial support for a stay abroad he could not yet possibly afford himself, despite having put aside all his savings for it. His earnest though diffident request for money was unusual, but not unheard of. The upper class of Boston and Cambridge took seriously its duty to invest in young men of promise. Judge Story had often before invested his influence in up-and-coming jurists and conservative statesmen, including Sumner himself. A number of prominent Bostonians had sponsored the hopeful young sculptor Horatio Greenough's trips to Italy a decade earlier to study art, and Amos and Abbott Lawrence were among those who subsidized the young pastor John Gorham Palfrey's 1825 trip to Europe for his health. Sumner likewise would find help from at least three wealthy leaders of the Boston and Cambridge conservative community who believed enough in him to contribute about $1,000 each toward his goal: Whig congressman and future Supreme Judicial Court judge Richard Fletcher, with whom Sumner had often worked on cases and discussed issues of civic duty arising from their mutual friend Lieber's *Political Ethics;* Samuel Lawrence, the great textile entrepreneur and brother of the future Whig leader Abbott Lawrence; and, of course, Judge Story himself.[5]

Moral approval was harder to get than financial. It was mostly those friends who had themselves been abroad who supported Sumner's trip from the start. Francis Lieber was lavish in his encouragement and advice, and Charles Daveis ever supportive, as were Longfellow and Cleveland, with whom Sumner talked much of his plans. The traditional American uneasiness about the corrupting influence of foreign travel and of loose Continental morals had abated only slightly, however, since Jefferson had warned his young nephew against the dangers to youthful blood of the "glare of pomp and pleasure" of foreign places, and many were Sumner's friends who disapproved of his rashness. William Ellery Channing, though he had once seen Europe himself, gently warned Sumner to be on guard against "the moral perils of travelling. Local prejudices—illiberal notions are worn off—" he admitted, but so may be one's devotion to the "good & true."[6] Josiah Quincy inadvertently wounded Sumner's pride, always sensitive when it came to his own moral strength, by warning him that "you will come home with a cane, mustachios & an additional stock of vanity, that's all." More serious were the doubts of Story and Greenleaf, who privately worried that close exposure to European ideas might weaken Sumner's conservatism, and who frankly expressed their fears that such a trip "would wean him from his profession," despite Sumner's certainty that "I never could be content to mingle in the business of my profession, with that devotion which is necessary to the highest success, until I had visited Europe."[7]

Humbly Sumner offered himself to the scrutiny of his closest friends: "To the candid judgment & criticism of my friends I shall submit myself on my return, & shall esteem it one of ye highest duties of friendship to correct me & to assist in bringing me back to ye path of sense & simplicity, if it shall be found that I have separated from it." Rather than be corrupted by Europe, he fervently hoped that by this trip "I shall return with an increased love for my country, an admiration of its institutions, & added capacity for performing my duty in life."[8]

The approval or disapproval of these men, however important, could not mean so much to Sumner as the reactions of his family. His mother worried about her eldest boy as he prepared to go so far and stay away so long. The trip from her native Hanover to Boston was the longest Relief Sumner had ever made, and her common school education had given her little familiarity with the countries Charles was to visit. His departure was particularly hard as it was not the only one. Her next youngest son, Albert, was off on another of the extended voyages that had kept him from home for most of the last ten years as he worked his way up toward ship's captain, and now her third son, Henry, would leave for Bahia just days after Charles. Only a few months later her next son, George, only just turned twenty-one, would, with characteristic impetuosity, try to outdo his eldest brother by setting sail for exotic Russia. Their mother accepted these separations with pain and patience, but there were no hard feelings between her and her eldest son. Because of her limited education, Sumner would not be able to share with his mother the full significance of his trip, the associations that would be so meaningful to him and for which she was unprepared. He would never write down to her, however, either by simplifying thoughts or by thoughtlessly writing over her head, but did keep his letters to her closely anchored in his concrete experience, never failing to assure her of his health and well-being. Sumner and his mother shared the same deep pride and intense privacy on personal and family matters, and in the compatibility of their natures they understood each other.[9]

Sumner's relationship with his father was not so easy. His admiration for his father had been one of the earliest emotions and motivations of his life, and Charles Pinckney Sumner was equally, though silently, proud of his eldest son's talents and prospects; but their temperaments clashed, and never more so than over Sumner's projected trip to Europe. It had to do with the sense of responsibility on which they both prided themselves so much. Money was one problem. Charles had early come to define his own sense of responsibility according to his father's preoccupation with money, being "anxious—almost morbidly so"—about the cost of college, his year at home, and of law school: "I feel that I ought to be doing something for myself & not to live an expense to my Father, with his large Family looking to him for support & education."[10] But as he began to realize that his father's concerns were exaggerated, that the real poverty of the family's early years had been wiped out by the elder Sumner's appointment as sheriff, Sumner began to feel deceived. His sense of pride and privacy, too, were irritated by his father's continued—increasing—allusions to his own poverty, some made even in public, before audiences of the Massachusetts bar and printed in the *Jurist*. All his adult life, Sumner would hate to speak of money, feeling embarrassed even to ask clients for his modest fees, and preferring to be cheated rather than haggle. What hurt Sumner most of all, perhaps, was that his father continued to make frugality and sacrifice the criteria of responsibility. When his father objected to his 1834 trip to Washington—a trip clearly intended for educational and professional benefit, supported by Judge Story, and considered a standard part of a law student's preparation—Sumner let his annoyance show as he described the arguments of a fellow Bostonian before the Supreme Court: "You, father, may here see ye vanity of my journey in travelling so many hundred miles at such cost & living here at such cost, to confess that ye best treat I have as yet had in ye Sup. Ct.—to attend which was ye main object of my visit—was from a *home* lawyer. You may liken me to those pilgrims, . . ." It is very likely Sumner himself who, when these had later become bad memories, cut out the rest of the sentence.[11]

All these difficulties were made more painful by the elder Sumner's forbidding rigidity and undemonstrativeness and the lack therefore of any real affectionate understanding between father and son. With increasing frequency Sumner spoke privately of this sorrow with close friends, and after that year between college and law school he never again lived with his father, taking his own rooms in town once he returned from Cambridge. Writing to Hillard on the day of his sailing for Europe, Sumner described the warm, truly familial reception he had had from Sarah Perkins and her family in New Jersey as "a delightful *homelike* day (such alas! as *home* has never been to me)[. . .]."[12]

Neither Sumner nor his father left any record of what they said to each other about Sumner's intention to go to Europe in 1837. But it hurt them both deeply. To Sumner's father such a trip at such a time must have seemed the height of irresponsibility. His son had every chance in life to succeed in a profession where he himself had failed, and now he seemed to be throwing it away on a will-o'-the-wisp. Already as a young man, Charles Pinckney Sumner had "declined invitations, the acceptance of which might imply a claim to a social position higher than he held, and even went out of his way by quaint methods to prevent any impression that his household life was more luxurious than it really was." It must have shocked him to think of his son not only abandoning business for a pleasure trip, but doing it on borrowed money. This was made worse by what seemed to him to be Charles' patriotically irresponsible political adherences: "An American travelling in Europe will gain no good name by undermining the reputation of Gen. Jackson or Mr. Van Buren."[13]

For his part, Sumner was fully aware of the dangers he would run. "In going abroad at my present age & situated as I am, I feel that I take a bold, almost a rash, step. One should not easily believe that he can throw off his clients & then whistle them back, 'as a huntsman does his pack.'" He felt in the core of his being that this voyage was necessary to complete his education, to make him a successful and authoritative jurist, and, he thought privately, to give him the experience and the self-confidence necessary to find happiness with friends and family. Nor could he accept his father's definition of patriotism. He knew that his disapproval of the current leadership was due to his love for his country and not contrary to it, and his desire to gain knowledge for the service of his country was an important motive for his journey: "May I return with an undiminished love for my friends and country, with a heart and mind untainted by the immoralities of the Old World, manners untouched by its affectations, & a willingness to resume my hard labors, with an unabated determination to devote myself faithfully to the duties of an American!" But these arguments were not so concrete as his father's. "All this is in the unknown future, which I may not penetrate." How could he convince his father of such things with mere words? How could he be sure his father was not right? His father's old favorite saying kept ringing in his ears: "The duties of life are more than life." The charge of irresponsibility that his father must have flung at him was the most calculated to wound his pride and to touch on his own secret fears.[14]

Nor could such an argument have come at a more emotional time, for it was set against the long-drawn-out and agonizing death from spinal disease of Sumner's oldest living sister Jane. Jane was the one who had shown kindness to Garrison at the time of his mobbing, the one her father admired as "a defender" of the "unjustly accused." She was, indeed, her father's favorite, reminding him perhaps of her mother, for he delighted in her intelligence and discretion, her grace and dutiful resignation, and the natural goodness that "at all times beamed forth from her clear, dark colored benignant eye." With two beloved daughters dead and all his grown sons rushing from home, Sheriff Sumner must have felt he was losing all his family, and the hard words and pain that had passed between him and his eldest son could not be soothed by a shared tragedy. When Sumner left Boston on 25 November he and his father had spoken their last to each other. No letters or greetings would pass between them. Charles Pinckney Sumner recorded his son's departure in his letterbook and then ripped out the page, never to write his name there again.[15]

Father and son could not stop thinking of each other, however. Sheriff Sumner would note his son's movements in his diary, along with any European news that might affect him, especially fires and other calamities that might bode danger. He kept track of the letters received by other members of the family or by friends, and he shared whatever information he had with others. He preserved the letter Felton wrote to thank him for the news that Charles had arrived safely in France, a letter that interceded on behalf of his son: "[I]f ever young man merited such good fortune, by fine talents nobly employed, and generous feelings unceasingly cherished, that man is Charles Sumner." Meanwhile, Sumner's letters to his younger siblings always urged them to love their parents, and to cultivate understanding and sympathy with their father. In response to Mary's complaints that their father did not like Scott's verses, her older brother gently reminded her of their father's deep love for poetry and told her that surely if she were to ask him to read her some of Scott's works aloud he would discover a taste for the Scottish bard—and perhaps father and daughter would be brought closer in the process.[16]

Sumner sailed from New York about noon on 8 December 1837. He had spent his last "hours of *terra firma*" through the night and the next morning feverishly writing letters to his family and friends, assuring his family he would be well, urging his youngest siblings to study hard and look to their self-improvement, admitting to his friends the painful sense of responsibility that hung over him, and assuring them of his love: "And a sad time it was, full of anxious thoughts, & doubts, with mingled gleams of glorious anticipations." After dashing off a few more farewell letters on board ship, Sumner went up on deck as the packet *Albany*, now "bending to the wind," left the spires of New York behind, and there he remained, concentrated on the receding shore as the image of all he left behind until all "that met the most searching gaze was the blue line, which marked the meeting of the waters and the land." When Sumner next saw land, it would be the stone piers of Le Havre, built under the consulship of Napoleon himself. Nineteen days out of New York, after a rough but speedy December crossing, Sumner was poised for his first observations of the Old World.[17]

It was the record of man's accomplishments that first impressed Sumner upon his arrival in Europe. His delight at Europe's age, hardly unusual for someone from a country so conscious of its newness, was intensified by his lifelong love for history. "Houses were older than my country," he wrote excitedly to Henry Cleveland. Every new place he visited was rife with associations: the Channel conjured up the Armada, Le Havre Napoleon, Rouen Rollo and Richard the Lion-Heart. This was more than pleasure for a child of the New World. Now, said Sumner, "I have the image of antiquity in my mind, & the conviction of historical truth derived from actual sight of spots & buildings with which history is connected." "Often, in fancy, have I doubted if such men as history mentions ever lived and did what we are told they did [. . .]. But this fancy, this

Pyrronism of ye imagination, is now exploded." It was this historical significance, which breathed life into the places he was seeing, that was most meaningful to a child of the New World, where everything seemed so precisely without significance: "Cicero could hardly have walked, with a more bounding & yet
placid joy, through the avenues of his Elysium, & conversed with Scipio &
Labius than, I, a distant American, of a country which has no prescription, no
history & no association, walk daily in the places which now surround me."[18]

The bewildering richness of the cultural institutions Europe had built
through that long history made the American blush. He was already delighted
by the art collection at Rouen: "I cannot but record ye admiration, blind & untutored, which was excited by this first view of ye arts in Europe." Paris went beyond his wildest imaginings. The Louvre, "which might have furnished quarters
for the army of Xerxes," was almost incomprehensible in its size and splendor.
This made Boston's little collections seem "shabby" indeed. "You can imagine my
feeli[ngs] in such a scene as I passed through today," Sumner explained to Hillard
of his first visit to the Louvre, "when you think that Mr Sears's house was my type
of a palace, the Athenæum Gallery of a collection of paintings, & the plaister
casts in the Athenæum Reading room & Felton's study, of a collection of an-
tiques."[19]

This was no mere carping on Sumner's part. Boston in the 1830's, despite later
criticisms to the contrary, was an art-conscious city anxious to improve its
knowledge and its collections. Sumner was cordially acquainted with such important patrons as George Ticknor and Edward Everett. His partner Hillard had
written articles of art criticism, and such topics had been a common subject of
conversation in talkative Number Four Court Street. Sumner himself had actively encouraged the artistic interest of Judge Story's son William, the future
sculptor. But Boston's museums and collections, though among the best in the
United States, were as yet embryonic. There was nothing in America to prepare
Sumner for the art galleries and opera houses of the Old World.[20]

Sumner was not alone in these feelings. Thomas Crawford, who would become one of America's greatest sculptors and who had already worked in the
most important studio in New York, was struck dumb by his first entrance into
the Vatican museum: "Only think of it—a green one like me, who had seen but
a half-dozen statues during the whole course of his life—to step then suddenly
into the midst of the greatest collection in the world." When George Hillard first
went to Italy some years later he admitted that "[t]he inward faculty is often paralyzed and discouraged by the too great abundance of external instruments and
faculties." This contrast between the Old and the New World gave Sumner a
sense of "mortification" as to his own country's inferiority. "Never exalt any
building in Boston or its vicinity to the dignity of a *lion,* especially in the pres-

ence of a foreigner," he admonished Hillard, admitting that he was lamenting his own previously prideful conduct more than that of his friend.[21]

At the same time, Sumner conceived an admiration for the public character of France's museums and theaters. Impressed by the Paris Opera, he noted for his own information: "This theater, as many others, is particularly under the patronage of Government, its expenses being included in the *civil list.*" Government support of theaters and art galleries opened them to a larger public in a way that made post-Revolutionary French cultural institutions essentially more democratic than America's private galleries inherited from the aristocratic traditions of England. Most of the Louvre as well as lectures at the Sorbonne and the Collège de France were "open *gratis*" "to all, both citizens and strangers, without question of any kind." "Think of the people of France having free access to these wonderful collections," he declared, and marveled at "the probable influence of this freedom" on the education of the French people and the spread of culture amongst them. Here was a lesson in democracy and public education that France could teach America, and that Sumner would never forget.[22]

Faced with the immensity of Paris and such cultural riches, Sumner felt at first humbled, both as an American and as an individual. Compared to Boston, the whole of which could be traversed by foot in close to half an hour, Paris was "a great world by itself" "where individual man is only a drop in the great Ocean of Mortality. Since I have been here," he confessed to Simon Greenleaf as he had from Niagara Falls, "I have felt my insignificance. It is a good lesson. One may get to believe that he is of some importance, who lives in Boston, or Cambridge, for in both of these respectable places he knows, & is known by, the majority of people that he meets. He bows & is bowed to in return; but here a man may walk the streets 'from morn to dewey eve,' & hardly catch the sight of features, that he has ever seen before."[23]

Lonely, Sumner begged his friends to quench his "parching thirst for letters,"—an impossible task—and he showered them with his own voluminous missives, which they multiplied by sharing them with each other and with his family. But, as he felt so unsure of himself, Sumner's first letters to friends like Henry Cleveland and Longfellow, who had both been abroad, were awkward. "To you I find it difficult to write," he confessed to Cleveland; "for what can I say that you do not know; & what can I describe that you have not seen." Even in the privacy of his own journal Sumner was at first afraid to trust his untrained and inexperienced artistic and musical taste. Over and over he would record his delight at concerts and operas, at music that "entered the chambers of my heart," and then insist "but I am not competent to admire it according to its merits." Moved by the beautiful paintings at the Louvre, he shied away from a judgment: "If I should attempt to describe their effect or appearance, I shld probably make some blunder. They touched my mind, untutored as it is, like a rich strain of music."[24]

Sumner saw and heard all he could, however. The noise and bustle of the metropolis quickly became second nature to the young man who had already been excited by the fast pace of New York and who once complained of a lady that, on rides by the beach, she refused to let her horse break into a gallop. Gradually, too, he came to feel a bit more confident of his artistic taste. He visited the Louvre repeatedly, and did not neglect exhibits of recent works, though he found modern paintings to be "immeasurably below the old masters."[25]

Sumner wanted to do more than just look at pictures; he was determined to enter as fully as possible into French culture and life. How "mortified" he was, therefore, to discover that the French he had known "more or less, almost from childhood" and studied at college, was not up to his principal task of learning about men and institutions. "I could not ask for a dinner in intelligible language," he admitted to his mother. Once settled in Paris, he spent most of the next three months in his rooms on the Left Bank studying grammar books and dictionaries "far into the watches of the night," and practicing conversation with eventually three different teachers. He would "generally, hear two or three lectures of an hour or more each before breakfast," at Paris' various academic institutions, including of course the Ecole de Droit but even the hospitals, in order both to develop a French ear and to learn more about French intellectual and academic life. Meanwhile in the evenings he went frequently to the theater, always with text in hand, enjoying especially the French classics—Molière, Racine, and Corneille.[26]

At his first lecture Sumner was disappointed not to understand a single word, and he complained playfully to his friends about the tortures he was undergoing. "That letter *u;* my lips refuse to utter it. I stumble over it constantly; & despair of being able to compass it." Within days, however, he could follow most of the lectures, and within a month or so he was just beginning to "find myself able to enjoy a conversation; &, I assure you, the sensation is delightful." By the end of April he was even beginning to play with the language, and was justly pleased with himself for a compliment in the best French manner: "It was at dinner at Versailles, & some gentlemen at table said of Madame—*elle est infaillible—elle est le pape.* I mustered all my French, & promptly interposed—'Vous vous trompez—*Madame est la Divinité,* mais le pape est le *representatif* seulement.' Even Frenchmen applauded the sally, & Madame said with a most bewitching smile—*je suis confuse,* at the same time shewing that she was not in the least confused."[27]

Though Sumner still felt diffident about his French, he was by the end of March well on the way to his eventual mastery of the language and was anxious to try it in real conversation. Now he moved from the academic seclusion of the

Left Bank to lodgings in the fashionable place des Italiens next to the Boulevards and for the first time presented his letters of introduction and began his entry into French society. What he found was certainly different from Boston. He could now observe the pleasure-seeking and immorality that he had been warned about from childhood, and even in George Ticknor's college French literature classes. In some ways, Sumner agreed, Paris was "a perfect Sodom," and the more he saw of it the more he appreciated Boston "where elegance & simplicity of manners so distinctly meet, where there is the greatest liberty, & no licence[.]"[28]

What troubled Sumner most was the treatment of women, from peasants to socialites. On his first day at Le Havre he had been dismayed at the heavy work done by women in the markets—the "labor of women" struck him as one of the fundamental differences between the Old World and the New. His first hopes that Parisian society might be different were soon disappointed. Even though ladies and gentlemen did not separate after dinner, as they did in America, Sumner found the ladies nonetheless "more neglected [. . .] than ladies are with us. They sat on the sofas, almost entirely by themselves," the gentlemen apparently not feeling "obliged to entertain" them, not even to the point of escorting them about the room or offering them refreshments.[29] Worst of all, it seemed to Sumner, were the extremes to which female conduct was subjected. He felt sorry for the unmarried girl who was never allowed to be alone, and whose reputation would be ruined by "[a] walk in the street with a gentleman, or even an animated conversation at a ball"—hardly unusual things in Boston. Once she married, however, "[t]he transformation is complete; & from confinement, equal to imprisonment, she passes to actual licence." Under such extremes, friendship between a man and a woman was inconceivable, and Sumner joked to Sarah Cleveland that when he had mentioned to a French lady that he was expecting a letter from her—the "young wife of an intimate friend"—the lady "saw nothing in the distance but jealousy, a quarrel & 'pistols for two & a coffin for one.'" When Sumner discussed these differences with another French lady, she quipped that "a lady should pass her life before marriage in America, & after marriage in France." The saying was "smart" enough, thought Sumner, and as regards "innocent pleasures" he was "no Puritan" who thought that one should do nothing but work, "but what is life? is it for a round of pleasure, of balls, & of rides; & for the equivocal addresses of some adventurer? or, is it not for the enjoyment of the affections, & the doing good."[30]

As he became accustomed to European ways, however, Sumner did appreciate at least the European tendency to live and let live. Ever proud of his own responsibility and dignity, he was much annoyed some time later to learn that back home his name had been connected in gossip with that of a certain young lady—the beloved of his friend Longfellow no less. He bristled at the censoriousness and "narrow impertinence that characterizes our town.(. . .) I cannot but confess, however," he admitted, "that this trait of our character brings with it some attendant good; it preserves society very much from the taint of impurity; but it lowers it by making it a petty prying observer. [. . .] Why can not this intelligence be chastened by charity? and why will not our people confine themselves to regarding the essentials, & cease to watch the unimportant things of life?"[31]

Through his new contacts with French society Sumner began to appreciate the degree to which Americans and Europeans were mutually ignorant of each other in many areas besides morality. Except to those few who took a personal interest in republicanism, the United States remained a small marginal country only fifty years away from its colonial status. Sumner reported to his friends with some amazement that well-educated Europeans inquired of him "if the people of Massachusetts spoke English," and one "very intelligent" gentleman "asked me, with the greatest gravity, if the aristocratic families among us were not descended from Montezuma & the Mexican Emperors!"[32]

Part of the fault for this ignorance lay with Americans themselves, who did not cultivate any interest in questions of larger intellectual or international interest in their public press. In Galignani's Reading Room Sumner immediately saw the general neglect of the American newspapers which "were put away in the dark" while the English and French papers were "in constant demand." "Such is the interest excited by our affairs!" he exclaimed. His disdain for the lack of European curiosity was tempered, however, by the young editor's realization of the inferiority of the American press: "But I must confess, that, as I perused the columns of these papers,—being fresh from the perusal of the elaborate sheets from the English press & the smaller but piquant & vigorous papers of France—I felt strongly the pettiness of the politics of my country, their locality, & their lack of interest for the cosmopolite besides also the ordinary character of their editorial matter. [. . . The French newspapers'] four pages are full of discussion, reports or news, with but a few lines for advertisements; which latter form the bulk of an American newspaper."[33]

The traditional American inability to speak foreign languages very much contributed to this mutual ignorance across the Atlantic. Before leaving the United States, Sumner had assumed Latin to be the language of international culture and had thought French good to learn only because it was fashionable and a mark of cultivation. He had thus advised his sister Jane to learn it "as it were, in *self-defence*." Mingling now in the international society that gathered together in Paris, he understood the fundamental importance of French as an international *lingua franca* for all cultivated, scholarly, and political thought. This had some unfortunate effects on the French character. "The French believe themselves *la grande nation*," and though Sumner was not disposed to disagree, he was struck when "[Victor] Cousin said to me—we do not learn other languages in France *parce que les autres pays nous ont fait le compliment de parler le notre*. They are, therefore, locked up in themselves, & like their own silk-worms, wind them-selves round perpetually in their own glowing thread."[34]

Sumner did not want to see his countrymen fall into the same mistake out of cultural isolation that the French had made out of cultural superiority, especially when it had the effect not only of making them seem arrogant but of cutting them off from other nations, for English did not have the international role that French in fact did. He filled every letter home with injunctions to friends to learn French and to teach it to their children. "I cannot urge you too strongly on this point; it is one on which all Americans fail," he insisted to William Story. "George Cabot is here now; but he cannot speak French, & what does he get from travel but the gratification of his eyes?" Worst of all was the ignorance of American diplomats and ministers, chosen by the internally rather than internationally minded Democratic administrations. Sumner was grateful to Lewis Cass, the American minister to France, for his personal kindness, but he was embarrassed by Cass's failure as a cultural ambassador. Cass had to rely on others, including Sumner, for translations of French letters and documents, and once Sumner winced to hear him say at a diplomatic dinner that his friend "*M. Ticknor savoir parler Français et Allemand* also." Unable to speak French, Cass "therefore, can-not really make acquaintances with Frenchmen, & [. . .] really seems like a fish out of water." It did not help that Cass was also "ignorant of international law." Sumner heard such stories of the absurd ignorance of our other ministers that he could hardly believe the tales, "& yet they are circulated on the best authority." To Judge Story Sumner confided: "Our three ministers at London, Paris, & Madrid are almost the laughing-stocks of Europe." This was a failing that the cultivated and patriotic young Sumner could not take lightly, and one that the future Chairman of the Senate Foreign Relations Committee would actively fight.[35]

Despite their sister revolutions, France and the United States had little in com-mon politically. Like most Americans, Sumner disliked the ubiquitous presence of police and soldiers in the French capital: "They are never out of sight." But he did not believe that France should be forced before her time toward democracy, and he admired Louis-Philippe's masterful statecraft in "rein[ing] in the revolu-tion of July."[36] France and America did, however, to some degree share one im-portant political debate, and here Sumner believed France had the more demo-cratic tendency. Sumner could not help but be constantly reminded of the problem of slavery. He was quizzed about it at every dinner the moment it was known he was an American, for France was herself in the process of debating whether she should emancipate the slaves still held in her own colonies—slaves who had been emancipated by the Revolution and then reënslaved under Napoleon. Sumner discussed the question with most of the men he met, in-cluding Victor Cousin, who disappointed him, despite his great "eloquence" on education reform, by hesitating over the wisdom of emancipation, and the historian Sismondi, who "is a thorough abolitionist," Sumner wrote approvingly to Hillard, "& is astonished that our country will not take a lesson from the ample page of the past & eradicate slavery as the civilized parts of Europe have done."[37]

Such encounters made Sumner profoundly ashamed for his country. Hearing about the latest instance of "the infamous bullying of the South" against their Northern congressional colleagues, Sumner wrote home impetuously: "Dissolve the Union, I say." This disunionism was not deep-seated, but his belief in the equality of all men was, and he was pleased to see evidence to support it in Paris. At the University's law school, where he listened to as many lectures as he could, Sumner observed that the black students "were well received by their fellow-students" for whom "their color seemed to be no objection to them." He admitted candidly that "with American impressions, it seemed very strange," but he "was glad to see this." "It must be, then, that the distance between free blacks & the whites among us is derived from education, & does not exist in the nature of things."[38]

It gave Sumner real pride, however, that there were areas of social and intellectual moment where the United States had been able to make a positive contribution to international discussion. It was the Americans' reputation for having the most advanced prison discipline system that had caused the French government to send Alexis de Tocqueville here to collect information to help in their own efforts to tackle the problem. And Sumner had kept well abreast of the long controversy over prison discipline that Lieber had gotten into with Tocqueville through the publication of his 1835 pamphlet *Education and Crime*. While in Paris, Sumner sought out French authorities on the question of prison discipline including Tocqueville himself and Judge Frédéric Auguste Demetz, founder of the celebrated Reform School of Mettray. Demetz had just returned from his own trip to study prisons in the United States, where he had become, like Lieber and Tocqueville, a supporter of the so-called Pennsylvania or Separate System, for which Sumner himself would later actively campaign. Though Sumner remained scornful of the strong police presence in the capital and of the pride of some French magistrates in "the almost dictatorial power of the *prefect* of police [. . .] over the *intentions,* as well as acts of persons," he reported happily to Longfellow: "The French [. . .] are just waking up on" "the subject of prisons."[39]

The French legal system, too, at first struck Sumner as being less sophisticated and objective than the Anglo-American. His contacts among French jurists quickly became extensive, and through the spring he attended many trials in Paris and Versailles, often invited by the bar and recognized in the newspapers as a distinguished guest.[40] These conversations and observations, however, at first led him to believe that the language barrier and the differences between the two systems were so great that "I do not think it within the power of the French mind to understand our pure municipal law." Indeed, as in other areas, Sumner was dismayed at the mutual ignorance that prevailed between the practitioners of the two systems. Sometimes he was amused by France's adoption of the form of certain English legal practices without any apparent understanding of their spirit. The prisoner's counsel in one criminal trial, the respected lawyer Charles Ledru whose guest Sumner was on the occasion, had newspaper accounts of the trial— "made too by the reporter of this lawyer"—"distribute[d] among the jury" before the next day's session. He merely "laughed at the idea" when Sumner told him that in England or the United States he would be committing the crime of "*Embracery.*" Sumner observed rather scornfully, too, the degree to which emotionalism could dominate in a French courtroom. In one case of a suicide pact gone wrong he recorded: "The defence was theatrical, brilliant, *French.* The counsel grasped the hand of his client, & worked the whole audience into a high pitch of excitement. Women screamed & fainted, & strong men yielded, & tears flowed down even the grim countenances of the half-dozen *police,* or *gens d'armes,* who sat by the side of the prisoner [. . .]." When the jury found the young man "Not Guilty," "[t]he greatest excitement prevailed in the court-room." "Women, & men, too, cried for joy." "So much for a French Criminal trial!" Sumner concluded.[41]

At the same time Sumner was half disappointed and half pleased that the caliber of the French jurists did not reach that of the best Americans. He was particularly proud of Judge Story's solid reputation in France. Jean Jacques Gaspard Fœlix, editor of the *Revue étrangère de législation et d'économie politique* and thus a long-time cordial correspondent of Sumner's, insisted that "there was no lawyer in France equal to him," and that France's principal library "the *Bibliothèque du Roi* did not contain all the books cited in his 'Conflict of Laws,'" Story's latest publication—a testimony to Story's exceptional scholarship and his cosmopolitanism. Sumner lobbied hard to have Story's reputation officially recognized by membership in the French Institute. Though that failed, he was deeply gratified that a fellow American, of a country not so old as a man's lifetime and so generally considered to have no cultural or intellectual merit, had achieved such respect abroad. "Thus has the Judge beaten them on their own ground," Sumner boasted in his journal.[42]

The more time he spent observing French trials, however, and the better acquainted he became with the French *Code,* the more impressed Sumner was. He had already favored the codification of the laws in Massachusetts, and here he found "the simplicity, neatness, & common sense" of the French penal code and especially its *procédure* immensely superior to "the cumbrous antiquated forms & vocabulary" of the common law "which we persist in retaining." He was "glad to find that the *enemies* of codification in England & America have calumniated its plan because they did not understand it." For a time he considered writing "a

Comparative View of the Judicial Institutions of France, England & America," a work he was sure would give him "the clear way of doing good, & gratifying a just desire of reputation," but the work never came to fruition. Sumner was at heart less interested in writing a description, however scholarly, of existing systems than he was in considering how those systems might be improved, and especially what the older established systems of Europe could teach the United States. He showed his characteristic willingness to question tradition by declaring to Hillard: "A *tertium quid* which should be the result of the French and English manner of *procédure* would be as near perfection as I can imagine; but, I am inclined to think—indeed, I am *convinced*—that, if I were compelled to adopt the *whole* of either, without admixture, I should take the *French.*" Meanwhile Joseph Story and Simon Greenleaf watched their protégé's interest in French law with some concern, and Lieber quipped to Sumner that poor Professor Greenleaf "is very much afraid you will become too *principled* and too *unprecedented.*"[43]

Sumner's observations of French life and institutions were constantly made not to exalt European superiority, however, but rather in the desire to learn how best to serve his own country. The ignorance of America that he often met with disappointed not only his national pride, but his belief in the importance of the American democratic experiment for people everywhere. Sumner paid rapt attention to the question then hotly debated in educated European circles "—what is the moral effect of democratic institutions." Tocqueville and Demetz were only two among scores of Europeans who had recently written books on American democracy and society. Sumner's old German acquaintance, Doctor N. H. Julius, was in the midst of his own work, "The Moral State of America," which Sumner understood would be "notoriously strongly *conservative*, [. . .] & more than *tinged* with dissatisfaction at what he saw."[44]

Sumner was "indignant at those men,"—those Americans—"who pervert our institutions, stultify our government, & degrade our just character in the view of Europeans." The existence of slavery in a democracy, the hot-headed belligerent tone being taken by American officials, including the Governor of Maine, in a border dispute with Canada, the outbreaks of mob violence all through the 1830's, all these things tended to weaken the American image abroad and thus the strength of the democratic idea. One French police official contemptuously informed Sumner: "[D]ans votre pays il n'y a pas de justice du tout." No justice in America at all! In exasperation Sumner complained that "some of our country-men are willing to lend the authority of their *assent* to the views of those, who would disparage our form of government," and this just when "our country will need the serried support of its own citizens, to maintain its footing, honorably erect, amidst the family of nations."[45]

The citizens who could contribute the most to undoing these bad impressions were the scholars and literary men who had the most direct access to European opinion, but who also needed to concentrate their energies on informing and elevating American opinion. Thinking of all these things, Sumner queried a friend that autumn whether the congressional elections of 1838 would turn "out Van Buren. My intercourse with men in Europe convinces me of the necessity of doing this, & also of abolishing slavery." In the end, however, Sumner had no doubt that the American democratic experiment would ultimately be successful and influential. And he directly answered those who thought his own patriotic affections would be chilled by the splendors of Europe:

> Who loves & serves antiquity, more than myself? Who is more enthralled by the glories of the Louvre,—by the pavilions of the Thuileries & all these streets about me, so rich with historic associations? Neither am I insensible to the gorgeous spectacle, or to "the sceptered pall of tragedy as it comes sweeping bye" with the verse of Corneille & Racine, or descending lower still in the scale of enjoyment, to the pleasures cheaply bought in the *restaurants* & *cafés* of this wonderful city; & yet, I would not exchange *my country* for all that I can see & enjoy here. And dull must his soul be—unworthy of America—who would barter the priceless intelligence which pervades this whole country, the universality of happiness, the absence of beggary, the *reasonable* equality of all men as regards each other & the law, & the general vigor which fills every member of society, besides the high moral tone, & take the state of things which I find here, where wealth flaunts by the side of the most squalid poverty, where your eyes are constantly annoyed by the most disgusting want & wretchedness, and where American purity is inconceivable.[46]

Sumner left Paris "with the liveliest regret" both for things unseen and things so much enjoyed. He had come to feel more comfortable there than most of the Americans he knew, who shared the traditional disdain for French manners, and he had already stayed two months longer than he had originally intended. Lifelong associations, however, beckoned him with a special urgency to England— "how my soul leaps at the thought! Land of my studies, my thoughts, & my dreams. There indeed I shall 'pluck the life of life.'" Unlike France, so different from the United States in customs, laws, language, England would seem almost like home. "The page of English History is a familiar story, the English law has been my devoted pursuit for years, English politics my pastime, & the English language is my own." Just as the fundamental influence of Ancient Rome led British students to make the Grand Tour, so the closeness of the British heritage to Americans, only half a century removed from being British subjects, cultivated the desire to see the land of their origins. As Sumner put it: "England is the Italy of an American." England, more than any other country, would give Sumner a vantage point from which to scrutinize his homeland.[47]

Despite all his hopes Sumner did not suspect the unprecedented social success he was to know during his eleven months in Great Britain. He presented very few of the many letters of introduction he had brought with him from home, making an ever-increasing circle of acquaintances instead directly from his first entry into London society. Before he returned to the Continent he had met and become familiar with most of the great names of English legal, literary, and political society. As a friend of Joseph Story and the author of two volumes of *Reports* of Story's circuit court decisions, Sumner was welcomed as a brother by the members of the English bench and bar, from the Lords Chief Justice of the Queen's Bench and of the Common Pleas through the Sergeants, or King's lawyers, and the barristers. Indeed, within a month of his arrival in London Sumner could boast, with no little astonishment at himself: "Imagine me in Westminster Hall, in the *Sergeant's Row* in the Common Pleas (as I have declined a seat on the bench!) or in the Queen's Counsel row of the Queen's Bench; there I sit, & hear proceedings, & converse with the very counsel who are engaged in them. I hardly believe my eyes & ears at times; I think it is all a cheat & that I am not in Westminster Hall, at the sacred hearth-stone of the English law." Sumner rode the principal circuits, too, being invited to sit sometimes with the barristers, sometimes with the judges, and wrote to Charles Daveis that "I have made myself master of English practice and of English Circuit Life," an experience that gave him an "admiration of the heartiness & cordiality which pervade all the English bar."[48]

Among literary figures, Sumner strengthened the tie already formed in Boston with Miss Martineau, whom he defended against American strictures as "the uniform and consistent friend of our country." He deepened an acquaintance begun in Paris with Sydney Smith, wit and editor of the *Edinburgh Review,* who had once offended Americans by asking in the *Review* "Who reads an American book?" and by attacking American slavery. Smith delighted many American visitors, however, including Sumner, who thought his "humor makes your sides shake with laughter weeks after you have listened to it."[49]

Sumner was charmed by the gracious and "clever" Mrs. Shelley, and by the "simple, graceful & sincere" William Wordsworth—with whom he discussed the international copyright and slavery,—while he was fascinated by the exotically beautiful Mrs. Caroline Norton. He thought her "a grossly slandered woman" for the freedom of her associations with gentlemen, and "one of the brightest intellects I ever met," author even of a "remarkable" political pamphlet.[50] He found Henry Hallam "a plain frank man," but despite his respect for Thomas Babbington Macaulay's writings he was not entirely pleased by the "instructive but dinning prodigality" of his conversation. Sumner was likewise uncomfortable with Thomas Carlyle, who was "full of genius" but too "unformed" in his style and thinking, a displeasure Carlyle reciprocated, and Sumner could not like the "foppery" of Bulwer-Lytton or forget his snubbing of Longfellow a few years before.[51] Sumner did, however, form a lasting tie with the poet and liberal politician Richard Monckton Milnes and with the Master in Chancery and political economist Nassau Senior, who was also a friend of Tocqueville's.[52]

In the political arena Sumner was "almost sorry" to have seen Lord Brougham, beloved of American Whigs for his great oratory, because of the discrepancy between his public image "as the pure and enlightened orator of Christianity, civilization & humanity," and his private quixotic nature and addiction to oaths.[53] Some of Sumner's deepest and most lasting ties in England were with other statesmen, however, including the liberal M. P. Joseph Parkes, who was fascinated by the beneficial influence the American political system could have on a liberalizing England. It was to Parkes that Sumner was indebted for his introduction to Richard Cobden, who would be a lifelong friend and collaborator in the cause of peace, and most especially George Howard, Lord Morpeth, who became his intimate friend. Through him Sumner became close to the whole Howard family, including Lord Morpeth's mother the Duchess of Sutherland, famous for her outspokenness in favor of the abolition of slavery, and his sister Elizabeth, whose husband the Duke of Argyll would be a member of the British Cabinet during the American Civil War, and a close correspondent of Sumner's.[54]

For the boy who had grown up on the corner of May and Buttolph this was a heady experience. Waiting for a carriage after "the great ball at Lord Fitzwilliam's" Sumner looked around in amazement. "I seemed in a land of imagination, & not of reality [. . .] there was the *elite* of England's nobility, it was all 'lord' or 'lady' [. . .]. I stood there an hour with dowager duchesses pressing about me [. . .]." But mere titles and "high social position"—especially when unaccompanied by intellectual interests—thrilled Sumner infinitely less than the society of cultivated people and of great minds, and when the time came to leave England it was this society that he missed: "I have been familiar with poets & statesmen, with judges & men of fashion, with lawyers & writers; & some of all these I claim as loved friends."[55] Perhaps most exciting of all was that everywhere he was received "not as a young man—but as a person of established position [. . .]." Sumner's old self-doubt was at first great, and he felt "chastened by an ever present sense of my own insignificance. As I recur to the scenes & duties of home I feel my humility to a degree amounting to mortification. I say to myself that I am not what my hosts & English friends suppose me to be. Who am I?— A poor lawyer, hardly recognized at home, or if recognized, only received as a young man; yet here I associate with all as an *equal,* & I fall in with the very leaders & Queen's Counsel, the *elite* of the English bar, as if my place was there."[56]

His friends back home had no such qualms. Felton congratulated Sumner on his social success—"it is as it should be. I rejoice for your sake, for your friends['] sake and for our country, that one like yourself has been thus received."

Governor Edward Everett was no less cordial than Felton: "I consider the country as under obligations to you, for the favorable impression of our means of education & our institutions generally, which must be produced by the specimen of early scholarship and extraordinary attainment you have exhibited." Sumner himself could not remain forever unaware of the fact that he did not disappoint his hosts. His new friends were repeatedly shocked to discover that he was only twenty-eight and not fully ten years older. Sumner began to feel an inspiriting hint of self-confidence. One day he was even emboldened to address Simon Greenleaf in the manner of the English bench and bar not as "Professor" but simply as "My dear Greenleaf." Whether it was Greenleaf's reception of this innovation or his own returning self-consciousness, Sumner never tried it again. With his English friends, however, Sumner tasted for the first time a feeling of equality with men of stature, and even his weariness after a year's round of unending invitations and engagements could not erase that: "And yet the blood does dance to sit at meat with men gifted & good, & more still, with ladies cultivated, refined & beautiful—to see the shifting shadows that cross the countenance, & catch the various conversation, perhaps, to mingle in it & find your voice not unheeded."[57]

Judge Story and Professor Greenleaf must have worried together over the direction in which this new confidence and the whole European experience might take their protégé. Alarmed by Sumner's talk from France of legal reform and fearing the influence of revolutionary French ideas of all sorts on Sumner's already liberal tendencies, they placed their hopes in the corrective of English conservatism. To bring Sumner back to the straight and narrow, Greenleaf sent him apocalyptic visions of the world in the not-so-distant future should the reformers get hold of it—a world in which train wrecks caused by William Lloyd Garrison are excused by the courts on the grounds that he "was bringing to Boston the glorious news that the apprentice system was abolished in S. Carolina, & the blacks were declared free; & that his rate of travel was justifiable, notwithstanding the consequences, as it promoted 'the greatest happiness of the greatest number.'" At the same time, warned Greenleaf, the abolitionist Miss Grimké "practices as chamber counsel in Court Street," and Mrs. Child, also practicing law, is granted a divorce for "*domestic* dissentions" because she and her husband voted for different candidates. Meanwhile punishments in all cases are now being determined "by major vote of the 'circumstantibus.'"[58]

"In sober sadness," concluded Professor Greenleaf, there were many reformers aiming at such a world turned upside down and, though wiser men could not stop the tide of change, they had an obligation to do what they could "to *direct*" its course. Greenleaf reminded Sumner "that *my* duty in the matter is to *educate conservative lawyers* at Dane Hall, & vindicate the honor of the law," seeking no change not strictly necessary. This was certainly Sumner's duty, too, Greenleaf made clear, and expressed his hopeful relief that, for all its dangers, this European trip had "a redeeming consideration in the fact that a wider & deeper view of the elements of society there, has fixed you on the *conservative* side of the great questions which are rending the world asunder."[59]

Story added his own admonitions to Sumner to reassure "your conservative Friends" in England that we Americans "are not all Demagogues, or mad conceited Democrats. [. . .] We dread Radicalism quite as much as they do." Anxious lest this point not be heeded, a few months later Greenleaf urged Sumner anew: "See *quite through* the jacobinism, & radicalism, & atheism of modern Europe; & all its other *isms;* & come home a sound & liberal conservative, as God made you [. . .]." Come home and "occupy an additional professor's chair, with Judge Story & myself, bringing into our Institution all that power, & all the affluence of your mind, to bear upon the great & increasing number of young men who come to us for instruction in constitutional & municipal law," and aid us in the duty of directing our country's future in a sound and responsible direction.[60]

Sumner considered himself entirely responsible in his political opinions, but, from the point of view of his professors, his beliefs justified their worries. Unlike most Americans, who tended to favor England's past over her present, Sumner was well versed in English politics before he set foot on English soil. For years he had been reading two or three British newspapers a day as well as the British literary reviews. He could thus converse knowledgeably with Englishmen of all political sides, and was proud of his own cosmopolitanism in so doing. "It is the privilege of a stranger to be of *no party,*" he later advised his younger brother George; "& it often happened to me to dine on successive evngs with prominent radicals, tories, & whigs, thus crossing from one side to the other." He made friends on all sides, too, and tried to reassure Story and Greenleaf that he appreciated even such staunch Tories as Lord Wharncliffe and Sir Robert Inglis, with both of whom he became very friendly. "Not that I am a Tory; but meeting tories of such a character has made me charitable, & catholic & convinced me that every thing that proceeds from them is from the purest hearts & most cultivated minds." But in his own private views on English policy Sumner harmonized most, not with the Whigs whom American Whigs like Story and Greenleaf most trusted, but with the Radicals. This he candidly admitted to Judge Story, telling him that when his particular friend Lord Morpeth asked him where he should stand were he an Englishman, "I unhesitatingly replied, 'a moderate Radical—much like the *Examiner* newspaper.'"[61]

Sumner was, in fact, convinced that England had a severe ordeal before her. While most American Whigs thought that the Reform Act of 1832 had provided just enough change to make further reform unnecessary, Sumner saw that England had not escaped the democratic yearnings that had caused so many upheavals in France and across the Continent. Having mixed much with the British aristocracy Sumner understood their power and the dangers that menaced it: "[T]hey are not aware of the volcano on which they are sleeping. There is among the middle classes & those lower still a deep & growing discontent; the rumbling begins to be heard, & if, timely changes are not made, there must be an explosion." Sumner did not think the mass of the English people ready in their "present state"—by which he meant primarily in education and in political habits—for democratic government. He was sure, however, that "England needs great reforms," the first of which ought to be the elimination of the so-called rotten boroughs—"a place of 300 votes should not send the same representatives with a place of 5000,"—and the abolition of primogeniture "to break the aristocracy, to reduce estates, & to divide them," as well as to weaken the power of "the established church, the army & navy" which are kept up by the aristocracy as "so many asylums for younger sons." "You will not believe me influenced by any mad democratic tendencies," Sumner tried to reassure Story, "when I say that England has trials of no common character to encounter; that she may go through them in peace I fervently hope."[62]

While England would have to redefine herself to pass peacefully through the great waves of change of the early nineteenth century, the United States was still in the process of defining herself for the first time, of actually forming an identity and giving to it, as to a child, the good habits that would promote her future usefulness and happiness. So believed thoughtful and cosmopolitan Americans, among whom Sumner firmly counted himself. Some Americans still hated England and wanted the United States to be nothing like her; others hoped we would some day take over England's commercial power or rival her imperial status. Sumner believed England and America could help each other through this period of change. Just as England could benefit from America's political experience, America needed to learn from England's cultural and intellectual wealth. "Grateful I am that I am an American; for I would not give up the priceless institutions of my country (abused & perverted as they are); the purity of morals in society, & the universal competence which prevails, in exchange for all that I have [seen] abroad; but still, I see many things in other countries, which I should be glad to see adopted among us. Let us, then, not sigh that we are not Europeans; but cling to our own institutions & model of society & endeavor to engraft upon it, all that is good & fitting in other countries."[63]

European class divisions were one thing the United States did not need to import. As he had been in France, Sumner remained quite sure that "[t]he true boast of our country is in the health, education, happiness, & freedom from poverty of the humbler classes." The dangerous social and political divisions that existed in England were only the most turbulent of the disadvantages of her rigid class system. Sumner was struck by the degree to which England was a closed society. How refreshed he would feel, after his year there, to return to Paris where the great art galleries and cultural institutions were free and open to the public from the wealthiest aristocrat to the humblest working man, and therefore available to the education of the whole population. And, though he delighted in the riches of the upper class into which he had been allowed to enter, Sumner saw how difficult England could be to the one who had no such introduction. "When one is fairly introduced into society, England is the most agreeable country of Europe; but to a stranger, who has not this privilege, it is as cheerless as Nova Zembla."[64]

The English aristocracy still had much to teach us. Sumner was deeply sensible of the general cultivation that reigned in the English upper classes. "Here, civilization has gone further than with us. [. . .] I think that in England one feels the proud prerogative, I will call it, of a liberal education." There were certainly "refined & accomplished persons" in America, but no "society *quâ* society" that proudly maintained and encouraged the broad classical cultivation that was a main badge of the English upper class. A liberal education was thus much valued in England, and "to have had this gives you a rank that at once introduces you to the best society, & distinguishes you from the rest of the world." It meant also that English politics and law were conducted by a well-educated class of men. Sumner had already been disappointed in our ministers abroad. The former Governor of South Carolina, George McDuffie, who was visiting England at the same time, disheartened him even more. Together they attended a proceeding at "the bar of the Common Pleas," with the best of the English legal profession handling the case. Sumner listened scornfully as "McDuffie swore that there were half a dozen judges, & as many lawyers in South Carolina, who would have managed the cause better & with more ability, than did this learned bench & these most distinguished lawyers!! I love my country," Sumner wrote his former master Benjamin Rand, "& profess my American character in all proper ways, but I am disgusted by such ignorant vanity, as prevents its possessor from seeing where we are inferior to England & other countries."[65]

Meanwhile, events back home were no more reassuring. Tensions were mounting between England and the United States over a series of border disputes. Sumner believed the "English were unquestionably justified in the burning of the *Caroline*" in December 1837 for that ship's role in giving private American aid to Canadian rebels. When hostilities broke out along the ill-defined boundary between Canada and Maine, Sumner was ashamed of the ill-considered and even belligerent handling of the dispute by many of his countrymen, and especially of the "ineffable absurdity" of the Governor of Maine, John Fairfield. "As an American I hold down my head while I read his illiterate, undignified & blustering despatches & messages. [. . .] At this distance our politics look petty & dismal."[66]

Such belligerence and unstatesmanlike behavior, combined with the sharp increase in mob violence in the United States during the 1830's, and the reckless impatience of Americans whose trains and steamships were built so carelessly and run so fast that they too often derailed or blew up, all contributed to European skepticism about the viability of democratic government. Once again, as in France, Sumner was constantly confronted by the topic of slavery—a defect all the more humiliating to the democratic United States because the oligarchic England had actually voted the emancipation of her own slaves in 1833. While, following a promise made to "friends," Sumner tried privately to find an English publisher for an American antislavery novel, he made every effort in society to act as cultural ambassador and give a balanced picture of his country. "I never introduce American topics in conversation," insisted Sumner; "but never shun them when introduced by others." Everywhere he tried to maintain that America's republican institutions and egalitarianism were indeed compatible with a strong government and stable institutions. "But, my dear Judge," he confided to Story, "I must confess that the word *Lynch law,* when politely called to my mind, brings up scenes, which I can not apologize for in any way. I always make a clean breast, & confess that the word makes me blush. Do stop these doings."[67]

Sumner did not by any means find that it was always the Americans who came out second in intellectual standing. He saw much to be proud of in his own legal profession. The American bar as a whole, he admitted, was characterized by "shallow learning & pettifogging habits," while he was charmed by "the elevated character of the profession" in England, "& the relation of comity & brotherhood between the bench & the bar. [. . .] Good-will, graciousness, & good manners prevail constantly." But if "the English are better *artists* than we are," Sumner noted that "[t]he state of legal science in England I fear is very low." Indeed, Sumner told Story that however well read and cultivated many of the English lawyers were, few were real scholars. "I know of but one *jurist* in Westminster Hall," he confided to the Judge—"You will understand my meaning." Even before coming to Europe, Sumner had been disappointed by the lacunæ of European law libraries, especially in books relating to American law—a fault that he was anxious to rectify. "I do not despair of seeing American Jurisprudence received with grt distinction in Westminster Hall."[68]

Sumner was likewise proud of America's literary interest and her new productions. He was surprised to discover that "[t]he magazines and reviews are not read here with half the avidity they are in America [. . .]." Just as he hoped to promote American works on jurisprudence in Europe, Sumner devoted much of his time to promoting new American authors. He was proud of his friend William Hickling Prescott's first historical work, newly off the presses, *Ferdinand and Isabella:* "The book reads beautifully, & I am glad that we have produced a work with so much of research, learning, suavity & elegance." He promoted it to all he met, including Spain's "*Procureur Général*" and the deputy of the Cortez, whom Sumner encountered at a dinner party in Paris. "If I could sow the seed with them it might add to the author's just reputation, & to the character of our country. This last consideration is one which I bear not a little in mind in my intercourse with foreigners. Much were my Spanish friends astonished that the great sovereigns of their country should find an historian [on] the other side of the water— *Quod minime veris* &c."[69]

What Sumner did for Prescott in France, he continued to do for him in England, and what he did for Prescott, he did for all his literary friends. He pushed for good English and Spanish reviews of Prescott's work. He tried to interest publishers in an English edition of John Gorham Palfrey's new history of New England, and "on the faith of [his own] testimony," succeeded in getting for Dr. Palfrey an honorary LL.D. from the University of St. Andrews. Likewise he tried to get an English edition of Francis Lieber's *Political Ethics*, superfluously begging his friend to "*rest assured that I will do all that I can.*" Although Longfellow was only just beginning his poetical career, Sumner eagerly worked to distribute his first collection— *Voices of the Night*—as widely as possible, and then solicited good reviews of his next work, *Hyperion*, published just before Sumner left England for the last time. As he explained to Judge Story while urging him to issue an English edition of his works: "A view paramount with me is that the diffusion of the writings of any American calculated to inspire respect, will aid the cause of liberal institutions & tend to remove the ill-founded impressions with regard to their operation."[70]

Sumner's desire that England and the United States should learn greater respect for each other through greater mutual knowledge seemed to find perfect confirmation in the old dispute over the unsettled boundary between Maine and Canada. Simmering for over a decade, the conflict erupted into new violence in the so-called Aroostook War in early 1839, just as Sumner was passing his last weeks in London and returning to Paris. By March 1839, Andrew Stevenson, the American minister to England, told Sumner, "*privately,*" that he was afraid "there is danger of war" between England and the United States. Despite tense moments, Sumner never thought so. There was plenty of hostility—English and American newspaper articles "inciting us to war," the stridency of Governor Fairfield and some congressional speeches, that made Sumner feel "ashamed of my country"—but there was also plenty of good will among well-placed men in England and America alike. Knowledge was the key to disarming the warmongers.[71]

Already before leaving the United States, Sumner had been appalled by the ignorance of the Canadian problem shown by the present and future Secretaries of State, whom he met in Washington. In England, his dear friend Lord Morpeth, "a Cabinet Minister, frankly confessed to me that he had never read a paper on this question." Nor had many other British officials, guilty not of ill will but only "*indifference* to, and *ignorance* of the matters in dispute between us." Sumner thus put his extensive—and well-placed—Anglo-American contacts to work to spread the needed information. His old friend from the Portland bar Charles Stewart Daveis had been the principal American negotiator during an earlier phase of the same dispute. Richard Fletcher, one of the major sponsors of his trip, was just finishing up his term in Congress, while Sumner had a cordial correspondence with Governor Edward Everett of Massachusetts, who had earlier been Minister to the Court of Saint James. Among his British friends, Richard Monckton Milnes and Sir Robert Inglis were both Members of Parliament, while Lord Morpeth was in the Cabinet as Chief Secretary of Ireland.[72]

In response to Sumner's early requests, Daveis began sending Sumner official American reports in January 1839, while Sumner returned the favor with parliamentary papers. In London, Sumner asked Milnes to look into the original maps of the treaty of 1783 that had first created the trouble by laying down an imprecise line. Thus Sumner shared each country's best information with his friends in the other. As he wrote to Governor Everett in mid-March: "I think, then, that it would be desirable to send a large collection of all the reports, articles & documents relating to the Question to London, for distribution. The seed might root in some generous soil, & we should have the benefit of it, if ever a debate arose on the subject." Sumner could not have agreed more with a Philadelphian correspondent who wrote: "Interest is indeed a powerful plea for peace. But it too often fails. A becoming sentiment of mutual respect and regard is a surer guarantee." The way to avert war, Sumner insisted to Congressman Fletcher, was precisely to pour information into the British government: "We should press them to study it and examine it; & I shall not regret all Gov. Fairfield's misguided zeal if it have this effect."[73]

Sumner did more than work behind the scenes. When he reached Paris that April he allowed himself, after some persuasion from the American Minister, General Cass, to make his first published contribution to a question other than such as arose out of his legal career. The article that appeared in *Galignani's Messenger* supported the American claims in the boundary dispute, in agreement with most of his American friends, including Charles Daveis and Simon Greenleaf, as well as a number of prominent British authorities such as the Solicitor-General. But Sumner made it clear in his article and especially in his personal correspondence that the line was not the most important thing.[74] The crucial thing, urged Sumner again and again, was to avoid war. From his Paris hotel on the "*Rue de la Paix*," as he underlined to his correspondents, he urged peace in every way he could. "Peace, and amity, and love, are the proper watchwords of our two great countries," he wrote Lord Morpeth in the sadness of quitting England. His love for England as for his native country made such a war seem "the most fratricidal ever waged." Nor could he accept a war based on "the sordid purpose of securing a few more acres of land." This would be a "crime." Rather than do any such thing, exclaimed Sumner to Richard Fletcher, "I would rather give up the whole state of Maine, & of Massachusetts to boot."[75]

In these sentiments Sumner was unwittingly echoing the conclusions of his father, who was also watching the Maine boundary dispute with a disapproving eye, except that the younger Sumner still had the faith in men's good will and in the future of his country that the elder had long since lost. Sheriff Sumner, disheartened by what he saw as the violent disintegration of the nation in the 1830's, observed: "It is not well for us to buy another foot of land on our frontiers; or to extend our borders in any way untill we have a more consolidated Government." All the more so, it seemed to him, because the faulty geography of the original treaty rendered it useless in settling the question. Though the Sheriff did not believe human nature permitted a hope of the abolition of war, Sumner had surely gotten from his father that sensitivity to peace that was his fundamental concern in this crisis. Even if the two countries involved in this dispute had not been so dear to him as the United States and England, and even if there had been some more substantial cause than a territorial boundary, Sumner could not have imagined a justification for war. To Congressman Fletcher he urged that "*peace* is the duty of nations before all things." For the first time, Sumner put on record the conviction that would play such an important part in his public career: "For myself, I hold all wars as unjust and un-Christian."[76]

Sumner was beginning to feel the press of time. By April 1839 he had been abroad nearly one year and a half—all the time he had originally allotted himself for the whole trip. There were so many things to see and do, so many people to meet that he never could keep to his schedule. His plans merely to stop over in Paris on his way into the Continent were undone by the city's charms and business. Though he had come to love London sincerely, Sumner experienced Paris again with a kind of relief. He reveled in its clean atmosphere compared to London's, and in its museums that were "no fee possession set apart to please the eyes of Royalty." It was not just pleasure, however, as he explained to Hillard, that held him in the French capital, but his quickly spreading reputation for doing anything for a friend, from writing articles on the Northeastern boundary dispute, and letters of introduction, to giving legal advice: "I happen every where upon people, who wish some sort of thing, some information about something which I am supposed to know, who wish introductions to America or England or the like; &, for sooth, I must be submissive & respond to their wishes. I assure you my tour has been full of pleasure, & instruction; but it has not been less full of *work*." Hillard would have occasion more than once to complain of his partner's "facility of temper and disinclination to say No, of which I have so often discoursed to you."[77] By May, however, even Sumner had to tear himself away. In

England he had left behind one land of childhood dreams; now he turned his eyes enthusiastically to another—Italy.

How could Italy fail to beckon to any child of Western civilization and any republican born? And yet by favoring Italy as a destination Sumner was going against the received opinions and recommendations of his friends and community. Italy had become a popular destination for American tourists in the first two decades of the century, and was poised to become as necessary a part of the American Grand Tour as she had been the principal destination of the European Grand Tour for over a century. Among American scholars, however, ever since the German studies of Edward Everett and George Bancroft in the 1810's, the real vogue had been for Germany, where the universities were flourishing in an explosion of serious literary criticism. Italian was considered proper merely "as a recreation," its literature, with the exception of Dante, generally dismissed as unimportant and hardly known. Longfellow, too, chose Heidelberg as his place of study, visiting Italy rather for pleasure. But the classical culture that had meant so much to Sumner from childhood, and Latin, which was his true second language, gave Italy a significance that he could not resist, so casting aside the advice of others and his original plans to favor Germany, he turned his steps southward.[78]

Sumner never regretted the decision. Italy let him relive the first delicious impressions of France. All his life Sumner would fondly remember "Superb Genoa," the home port of Columbus, where, like most travelers, he first landed in Italy. "I doubt if there is any port of Europe so entirely calculated to charm & subdue a voyager fresh from the commercial newness of America." It was not just age, but the ever-present associations of Italy that made it come alive, "dear sunny Italy, where at each step you set your foot on some reverend history [. . .]." Ancient Rome seemed to live again: "What a day I passed at Tivoli!—I was with French companions, one of whom lent me his pocket Horace. The others strolled away to see some ruins, or catch a nearer spray of the falling water. I lay on the grass, with the *præceps Anis* before me in the very Tiburtine grove that Horace had celebrated; & there I read the first book of his odes, & on the spot saw & felt the felicity of his language."[79]

"I go to Italy with letters of all sorts to all sorts of people from the Prince *Borghese* down to *Marquises, Counts,* professors, ambassadors &c in all the towns," Sumner reeled off to Hillard, but in England he had "supped full of society, & am tired of bright lights, & costly curtains & retinues of servants." The republican born wished to return to a simpler existence, and to give himself, as most Americans dreamt of doing, to the visions of the bygone era that was Rome. It was a goal encouraged by Rome herself, the least modernized of all the great western European capitals, her buildings encrusted with age, sheep grazing under the shepherds' gaze in the public squares, her ruins still half-buried in the soil.

In England Sumner had enjoyed a "round of intercourse with *living* minds, in all spheres of thought, study, conduct, & society. Here I have spent my time with the past."[80]

Though Sumner made a tour of the peninsula, visiting the sights of Naples and Pompeii, Florence, Venice, Milan, the core of his visit was a stay of three months in Rome, where he spent a quiet summer enjoying the city of legend and basking in that charm that so appealed to busy, striving Americans driven by a sense of duty—the *dolce far niente*. Sumner joked about the pleasure with which, if only he had "a moderate competence," he would leave the drudgery of the law to others. With what wistful pleasure he reflected on the low cost of living in Italy: "It is a delight to know it; for it gives one a hope that he may—if times should frown & affairs be ungenial at home—after collecting together some of the savings of a few years, come here, & live in the light of all that is fine in art, & under this beautiful sky, & die in peace."[81]

Sumner's own version of the *dolce far niente* was far, however, from the "glorified loafing" Henry James would make fun of. Here Sumner gave himself not only to the study of Italian but to making the unknown Italian literature his own. He centered his Roman routine around these studies, which he undertook with the help of a new friend. George Washington Greene was the American consul in Rome, a grandson of General Nathanael Greene of Revolutionary fame and a bosom friend of Longfellow's whose glowing introduction of Sumner to Greene brought them together: "You will not fail *to make much of him,* as Nature has done before you; for he stands six feet, two, in his stockings. A *colossus* holding his burning heart in his hand, to light up the sea of Life. I am in earnest. He is a very lovely character; as you will find:—full of talent, with a most keen enjoyment of life; simple, energetic, hearty, good with a great deal of poetry and no nonsense in him. You will take infinite delight in his society; and in walking Old Rome with him." The genial young Greene could not fail, indeed, to find much in common with Sumner. Both were of the same age and loved nothing better than to help friends. Though his talents would never be crowned with the success he constantly hoped for, Greene would later occupy a chair in modern languages at Brown and the first in American history at Cornell. Sumner thought that "in accomplishments and attainments our country has not *five* men his peers." The two quickly formed a friendship that would last for life.[82]

With Greene's help Sumner set about his goal of learning Italian. "My habits were simple," Sumner recounted of his Roman summer: "Rose at 6 1/2 o'clk, threw myself on my sofa, with a little round table near well-covered with books,—read undisturbed till about 10, when the servant brought on a tray my breakfast [. . .] the breakfast was concluded without quitting the sofa—rang the bell, & my table was put to rights, & my reading went on—often till 5 & 6 o'clock in the evening, without my once rising from the sofa. Was it not *Gray's* heaven?" In the evenings he would dine in Roman style on fruits and nuts "under a mulberry tree," and then go out to see the sights with Greene. Together "we walked to the Forum, or to San Pietro, or out of one of the gates of Rome; many an hour have we sat upon a broken column or a rich capital in the *via sacra,* or the colosseum, & called to mind what has passed before them, weaving out the web of the story they might tell, & then, leaping countries & seas, we have joined our friends at home & with them shared our pleasures." After some supper or an ice cream the two would part and Sumner would return "to my books again." Such a routine he would remember nostalgically all his life.[83]

Sumner amazed himself with how much he read in those three months at Rome and the next month spent in traveling northward to Milan. Before leaving Italy he had read all or most of the works of Dante—"with great attention, using *four* different editions, & going over a monstrous mass of notes & annotations"—Boccaccio, the plays of Niccolini and Goldoni, the "too elaborate" Tasso, and long-winded but "bright and beautiful" Ariosto, the "delicious" Petrarch, Macchiavelli and Guicciardini—preferring the latter—all the works of Alfieri, and many others, not forgetting the "Diritto Publico" and the "Genesi del Diritto Penale" of Romagnosi, which he considered "the most remarkable work I know on Criminal Law." Nor did Sumner renounce in all of this his addiction to newspapers. "I, habitually, read every American, English, French, Spanish & Italian [journal] I can lay my hands on—I average *ten* a day; but, with my facility in handling these, I despatch the greater part, while taking coffee or ice," he boasted. Thus, for all his desire to devote himself in Italy to the past, his reading spanned all time from the ancients to the latest news, something unprecedented among American travelers. Sumner was struck by how undervalued was Italian literature. This literature that was at home considered to boast of none but Dante and thought unimportant for scholars seemed to him full of treasures, and he became its staunch champion at a time when others all but ignored it. "I know no country that within a few years has produced such great *regenerating writers* as this despised Italy. *Alfieri* is 40,000 strong. I am lost in wonder at his power. What an arch is that of Italian literature spanning from *Dante* to *Alfieri*—two columns fit to sustain the mightiest pressure. I was not aware till I read the latter, that such a mind had shone upon our times; the finding him out seems like getting near Homer or Shakespeare. And *Manzoni* still lives."[84]

Sumner amazed Italians, too, with his unusual interest in their literature. When he and Greene spent a delicious weekend at the Convent of Palazzuola, on the site of Alba Longa within view of Cicero's villa Tusculum, Sumner "amused myself not a little" by going through their library of about one thousand volumes "all in parchment." "The monks have looked with astonishment upon the avidity with which I have examined their books; & I doubt if they have had such an overha[uling] for a century [. . .] a large portion of them I found standing bottom upwards." He soon knew much more about the collection than did the librarian. For another new friend, the Georgian lawyer Richard Henry Wilde, who was then engaged in research on the lives of Dante and Tasso, Sumner looked up manuscripts of the former at Venice and of the latter at Ferrara. And when, at Venice, he sought out the works and manuscripts of Leonardo Bruni known as Aretino "the librarian told me that he had not seen any one so curious & intelligent upon the old Italian writer for a long time [. . .]."[85]

Sumner's studies were not confined to belles lettres, history, and law. Italy was also the land of art. Here he tried to make up for his early want of artistic education. He visited the museums with knowledgeable guides—the Vatican with George Greene and the budding American sculptor Thomas Crawford, the Uffizi with American sculptor Horatio Greenough—and he read the classics of art history and criticism: Vasari, Sir Joshua Reynolds' lectures, lives of the great artists.[86] William Story, who had received art lessons from childhood, gently complained that Sumner had no genuine appreciation of æsthetics, despite his efforts: "The world of art, as art purely, was to him always a half-opened, if not a locked world. He longed to enter into it, and feel it as an artist does; but the keys were never given to him." Sumner was never tempted, however, to follow the ways of such an important Bostonian cultural patron as George Ticknor, whose first reaction to any painting was to record its size and monetary value. Recent art historians have been more impressed by Sumner's "powers of observation" and his "knowledge of and appreciation for" the emerging Neoclassical style. It is not surprising that Sumner's taste in art should have been, in Story's words "historical and literary," rather than "purely" æsthetic. In this Sumner was very much like his countrymen, who were preëminently "a literary people." And the duty that he felt of elevating American culture made him particularly sensitive to the ideas and ideals of Neoclassicism.[87]

American interest in Neoclassicism precisely in the 1830's was indeed much more than just the result of the inevitable time lag in the American adoption of the succeeding artistic trends of Europe. The Græco-Roman inspiration of Neoclassicism appealed strongly to a people who defined themselves as republicans in a monarchical world, and its nostalgia for classical history and literature resonated in American literary taste. Neoclassicism defined itself by its devotion to the idealization of the human spirit as opposed to the mere depiction of reality, and its austere simplicity was meant to dignify and ennoble art after the superficial extravagances of the Baroque and the Rococo. This classical idealism and dignity fitted perfectly not only with the Enlightenment values that still lived in America, but as well with the aspirations of a generation who saw themselves as cultural pioneers for their country, who intended to raise her artistic interest and standards and to ennoble her culture in international eyes. Sumner must have discussed these ideas with friends—especially the art-loving Hillard—before leaving Boston. The two shared an admiration for what Hillard called Neoclassicism's elevation of "the pure and simple over the gaudy and ornate." They agreed also with Neoclassicism, and its great theorist Johann Joachim Winckelmann, in giving the palm to sculpture as the noblest art. For these Americans, Neoclassicism mingled with Moral Philosophy in their belief that painting's greater reliance upon realism, the strength of its merely æsthetic attraction, gave it a less sophisticated appeal, while sculpture's "simplicity and austerity" appealed more to the intellect and the conscience. Likewise, within sculpture, they valued elevated thematic works over portrait busts because "[i]n sculpture we always crave the ideal."[88]

Sumner had been shy of committing his artistic tastes to paper during the 1830's, but he did offer a little patronage—the first of what would become a lifelong career, making him the most important Bostonian art patron of his generation. Judge Story had given his son William art lessons from childhood, but was worried in the mid-'thirties when the temptations of art—and more frivolous things—were tugging his son away from his college duties and bringing down his grades. Sumner was delighted to follow Judge Story's request to tutor William, but perhaps the Judge, who longed to see his son follow in his own legal footsteps, would not have been so pleased had he realized that Sumner was beguiling his son back to his studies not only with his contagious love for classical literature and history, but also with encouragement for the boy's love of art. Before he left for Europe, Sumner rewarded William for his academic progress with a packet of letters of introduction to the major artists of the Boston area, including Washington Allston and Chester Harding, and its major collectors, men like Thomas Appleton and Samuel Cabot. Letters on the great European collections would soon follow from Europe, setting the boy's heart afire. William Story himself considered Sumner one of the most important influences in pushing him in the direction of a career in art and toward a devotion to Neoclassicism.[89]

Now in Italy, Sumner wanted to do all that he could to use his new experiences and contacts to promote art in the United States and American artists. Whereas American authors needed primarily promotion abroad, American artists required promotion at home, where they had as yet only the smallest audience and the most limited patronage. Sumner saw large numbers of American artists in Rome living hand-to-mouth, longing for support from home that rarely came. Of them none impressed him more than the young New Yorker Thomas Crawford. A modern student of William Story's career has praised Sumner for his sometimes "uncanny judgment in ferreting out new artistic talent before the more seasoned connoisseurs had discovered it." This was especially true for Crawford. By the summer of 1839 he was living so close to the edge that he had known hunger and illness and was almost prepared to give up on what he felt to be his calling. George Greene had become a devoted supporter but had not been able to attract any patrons with Crawford's still small output, not even George Ticknor, who had seen his studio only a few months before Sumner arrived. Sumner, however, was delighted by the pieces in Crawford's studio: "They all shew the right direction," he wrote excitedly to Hillard; "they are simple, chaste, firm & expressive, & with much of that air (heaven-descended, I would almost call it) which the antients had [. . .]."[90]

Crawford was pinning all his hopes on a yet unfinished ideal depiction of Orpheus descending into the Underworld, which Sumner thought "without exception the finest study I have seen in Rome," a work that, if properly completed, "will be one of the most remarkable productions that have come from an artist of his years in modern times." Sumner immediately set himself to getting Crawford the much-needed and elusive patronage. He wrote dozens of letters to friends in Boston and beyond, hoping, as Crawford did, that the statue would be bought by an American. Knowing the value of publicity he asked Longfellow to write an article introducing Crawford to the American public, and he even gave in to Crawford's and Greene's incessant importunities that he sit for his own bust. Sumner was doubly embarrassed when Crawford carved the pedestal in the form of a pile of books. The sculptor removed them only after Sumner had repeatedly begged him to: "It will seem to every body a cursed piece of affectation and vanity on my part." For all the discomfort, however, Sumner knew the publicity value of such a bust—not only the most lucrative work for a young artist, portrait busts were also an excellent advertisement of his talents—and he could not resist doing what he could for his friend. "He is poor & I feel anxious to do something for him," Sumner wrote even to young William Story. "If I could convince any body to order this large piece he is now engaged upon, *his fortune would be made. All that he needs is to be known.*"[91]

The sluggishness of the American response was frustrating. "Strange to say, [Crawford's] best orders have come from foreigners; English & Russians. Perhaps, this speaks as strongly in his favor, as it does against his countrymen," Sumner said privately to Hillard. "Americans are sheep & follow the bellwether. Let Crawford once have a good order from some gentleman of an established character; & let the work be exhibited in America & his way will be clear." Sumner scorned this reliance of Americans upon European taste. "Many of our countrymen are so weak, as to make their judgments depend upon Englishmen," he complained to Greene, but he did not hesitate to use that weakness by urging Crawford's talents upon all his English friends in hopes of spurring interest back home. When Sir Charles Vaughn, impressed by Crawford's bust of Sumner, ordered his own, Sumner was delighted: "I know none of his countrymen, whose patronage ought to avail more with Americans."[92]

A buyer for the *Orpheus* would be slow in coming. Sumner did not yet know that he would finally be responsible for its purchase, not by a private patron, but by the Boston Athenæum. For now, however, his experiences made him increasingly certain that the establishment of an artistic tradition in the United States would have to depend upon the creation of a broad foundation of interest through widespread patronage and government support. Sumner had already been impressed by the French government's subsidization of theaters and museums. Now he saw Americans like Crawford, unable to find institutions and encouragement for study at home, flocking to Italy, because of the country's cultural richness, but also because of generous state-sponsored schools and government patronage.

On his way north from Rome, Sumner discussed these issues at length with yet another new friend, the Bostonian sculptor and now Florentine resident, Horatio Greenough. From the first the newly recognized sculptor and essayist impressed Sumner as "a wonderful fellow—an accomplished man & master of his art—I doubt not, the most accomplished artist alive—a thinker of great force—& a scholar, who does not trust to translations, but goes to the great originals." Greenough was then at work on his seated *Washington*. Destined to become his most famous piece, it was highly significant right from the time of its conception, for it was the first work ever to be commissioned by Congress of a native artist, and it was intended for the Rotunda of the Capitol. Sumner shared with Greenough his sense of the opportunity and the responsibility of this trust. The commission had to be handled with such care that it encourage Congress in similar ventures, and that it also accustom the public to the idea of state support of the arts as well as to the æsthetics of great art.[93]

Characteristically, Sumner argued for a cautious, conservative approach to the design of the statue. Much was at stake. He urged that "in a *first great* work, appealing to great national sympathies," Greenough ought "to keep clear, quite clear of debatable ground—so as to carry with [him] all hearts and all consciences as likewise all tastes" as far as possible. Greenough was convinced and agreed to change some of the supporting figures—including the substitution of a Columbus for a black man, thus removing a source of controversy as well as the possible interpretation that slavery was a support of the national idea.[94]

If he thought the statue should be rendered politically noncontroversial, Sumner insisted that it should not skimp on the highest artistic standards. The work was meant in part to educate the public, and it must therefore be in the pure style. Should the standards of that style be strange to the untrained public, the solution was not to diminish the statue, but to train the public taste. Thus from the start, though they both knew it would be controversial, Sumner and Greenough agreed that the statue's Neoclassical undress should be preserved. When this did, indeed, become a subject of "squeamish criticism" as the statue's unveiling approached two years later—ultimately to prove the statue's undoing—Sumner responded once again with the need to educate the public to an appreciation of Neoclassicism. "In Europe an artist is judged at once, in a certain sense, by his peers," Sumner wrote at that time to console Greenough.

> With us all are critics. The rawest Buckeye will not hesitate to judge your work, & will, perhaps complain that Washington is naked; that he has not a cocked hat & a military coat of the Continental cut; that he is not standing etc, etc. The loungers in the Rotunda, not educated in view of works of art, many never before having seen a statue in marble, will want the necessary knowledge to enable them to appreciate your Washington. Should you not prepare them so far as you can? And you can do a great deal. Publish in *Knickerbocker's Magazine,* or such other journal as you may select, some of the papers you read me during my visit to Florence; particularly on the *nude,* [. . .] what you publish with your name (Horatio Greenough, Sculptor) will be extensively read, &, I think, exercise a great influence on the public mind.[95]

Sumner's anxiety for the cultivation of the public's artistic taste, as well as his private delight in art were both souvenirs of his Roman summer that he would keep all his life. That summer would offer another great source of satisfaction, both intellectual and personal. From Rome, Sumner watched his younger brother George blossom. George had always been something of a worry for the family. He was bright and capable, but seemed without direction. Unable to decide what to do in life, tiring of a commercial career almost as soon as he had entered it, he suddenly set sail for Russia at the age of twenty-one with no settled plan for the future. Friends marveled at how like Charles "but yet, oh, how unlike" he was. Both brothers were full of energy and intellectual curiosity, affectionate, devoted to their friends, anxious to do for others. Both brothers had been more deeply impressed than any of their siblings by their father's high standards, and had grown up unsure of themselves, afraid of falling short, sensitive to criticism. But Charles had thus become self-doubting and self-deprecating, cautious and conservative, while George's uncertainties were varnished over with an exaggerated self-confidence, a bold and boasting manner, equally prone to anger as to generosity. And, whereas Charles associated himself with the Whigs and was ready to see his country's faults that he might contribute to undoing them, George became a staunch Democrat and defender of the superiority of his country and of Boston before all other places.[96]

When this forward young man decided to take Europe by storm, his family quailed. "I beg you not to appear knowing," his father wrote him; "Appear *naif;* practise *naiveté;* & do not pass yourself off for any thing more than you are." "In manner always be frank & cordial; but cultivate a *reticence,*" Charles echoed: "'Oh! he has the Yankee *pushing*'! Do not let this be said of you." Undaunted,

George charged across northern Europe, astonishing "the natives" by "making enquiries of *every one*" from the man in the street to exalted generals to get every bit of information he could. In Russia he pushed his way into the circle of the Tsar, and so charmed him that he was invited to accompany him as his personal guest over all his domains, from Saint Petersburg to the Black Sea and into the Caucasus. From there George pushed his way farther south into the Holy Land and on toward Egypt, always boasting about his success, but, too, always questioning, observing, learning, and earning the confidence of heads of state and diplomats wherever he went.[97]

Charles worried constantly about his brother's disconcerting and amazing course, and when George arrived in Rome the year after his eldest brother, Charles asked Greene secretly to keep an eye on him. This resulted in a little conspiracy gently to urge the impetuous young man to acquire greater sophistication and control, but also in a lifelong friendship between George and Greene. For all his worries, however, Charles was being won over by his younger brother's pluck and intelligence. When he read yet another of George's letters describing his travels through Russia and into Palestine, Charles was delighted in spite of himself. "He has seen more of Russia, I doubt not, than any foreigner alive," he boasted to Simon Greenleaf. "He is the most remarkable person of his age I know. Pardon this from a brother." Gradually, Charles stopped writing to George as to a younger brother. He continued to offer guidance and advice, but before he left Europe he had come to see in George an intellectual companion, and upon setting sail for home he wrote to George as to an equal: "It is a glorious privilege that of travel; let us make the most of it. Write me often. Gladden my American exile by flashes from the Old World. I will keep you advised of things at home."[98]

One "shadow" fell across this life of art and literature and the pleasures of study and of friendship. It was in the middle of his summer in Rome that Sumner learned of his father's death. Charles Pinckney Sumner had died on 24 April after a short illness, his post already resigned and his papers meticulously put in order—the event coming as a surprise to everyone but himself. Sumner's friends knew that he could not feel a normal grief for the loss of a man who had never been "like a father" to him. Such grief would have been more consoling. Instead, Sumner could not forget the emotional distance that had denied him his father all his life, nor their last words to each other, spoken in anger. Perhaps, too, he remembered his father's long habit of saying that he should not outlive what the philosopher Thomas Brown called "the grand climacteric of life"—the age of sixty-three, a time that was to fall while his eldest son would be away from home, a prophecy that had now come to pass. The "many painful emotions" Sumner felt were "not the less painful because beyond the reach of ordinary sympathy. To you, who so well understand my situation," he confided to Hillard, "I need say nothing." Nor could he, to his own dying day—at almost exactly his father's age—forget.[99]

Sumner felt responsible for the difficulties between himself and his father, and now instantly felt the duty to look after his fatherless youngest siblings. Mary, Horace, and Julia ranged now from seventeen to twelve years of age, and their eldest brother was anxious about their education. "I wish I were at home to aid them in their studies, to stimulate them, & teach them to be ambitious," he lamented. In their education "I have always interested myself as much as I was allowed to, from the moment in which I had any education myself," and now he took upon himself the whole responsibility of their progress. He was especially concerned that Mary and Julia not be left behind. "I am anxious that my sisters should have the best education the country will afford [. . .]." Their father's estate would provide amply for this, Sumner was sure, but he was all the more sensitive to their deserts that he considered himself so undeserving. Sumner suspected—rightly—that he might not have any share in his father's will, but should he have any, he impressed upon Hillard, "in any division of my father's property *as regards my sisters,* I am to be considered *entirely out of the question.*"[100]

The renewed self-doubt that Sumner felt in the face of this responsibility lent even greater urgency to his anxiety to see American shortcomings corrected. Of his summer in Rome Sumner concluded: "I have studied, making it a rule always to work at least *six hours* a day, which has often been *twelve.* I have found out my ignorance, & my imperfect education." Other American tourists often made him cringe. "You, who travel in yr arm-chair," he informed Hillard, "are not aware of the *stuff* that comes abroad from our country. I think, there have been 375 at Rome this year; of which Greene told me there were not more than *seven* that he regarded as *presentable* persons." The vast majority of them did not even read while traveling.[101]

This was not pure disdain on Sumner's part, but rather a plea to elevate American sights. "We must raise the standard of education at home." Already in England he had witnessed the superior cultivation of the European upper classes. "The difference of education is very much against us," he had written then: "Every body understands French & Latin & Greek [. . .]." It was not enough to be proud that in the United States "the labouring & humbler classes are better educated than in any other I have seen," so long as "the upper classes called by courtesy the *educated class* have less education than the corresponding class of Europe." As he traveled north from Rome, Sumner wrote repeatedly to his friends urging them on in their ambition. When Henry Cleveland admitted that he was preparing yet another lyceum lecture, Sumner protested: "I know your just & honorable ambition; & I am confident that you will not allow the thread of yr life to run out like a skein of Yankee cotton. Circumstances enable you to become, what is so much needed in our country, a *scholar*. You can devote your-self to literature in its highest sense—discarding the vulgar notions of education that abound in America [. . .]."[102]

It was precisely the general notions of education in America that troubled Sumner most, for he believed that they determined the future of American culture. As he looked back on his own schooling at Harvard he felt humbled: "Can we call that smattering of all things, & knowledge of none, which boys have who leave Harvard College, an *education*?" he demanded of Judge Story. "Certainly I left it without knowing any thing, & I do not know a person who at the time he graduated *knew any one thing well*." Harvard gave a veneer of learning, but never instilled a habit or standard of scholarship, Sumner complained. Her teaching methods were out-of-date, and her library, the largest college library in America, was minuscule compared to those of European universities. The school's very prestige thus cheated the country she should be serving. Her graduates "enter upon the duties of life, & pass for educated men, & their example is the pattern of the next generation; & so we are without hope."[103]

Yet Sumner did not really believe there was no hope. "The youth of America do not want ambition; but they cannot be expected to aspire to a scholarship which they do not see about them." Educational standards must be changed, Sumner urged, "& where can it be done better than at Harvard?" When Judge Story brushed aside his recommendation that "the requisites for admission be *doubled*" and that "all candidates for *degrees*" be subjected to "the most rigorous examination," Sumner countered that it was precisely the lack of a general high standard of education that was responsible for the deficiencies of American policy and society apparent under that Democratic rule that they both deplored. If there were greater respect for education "we should cease to applaud the vulgar fustian, that comes for the most part from Congress—& men like Isaac Hill, & Benton, would be lashed back to them who sent them." Despite a few exceptional speakers, the American Congress could not compare with the British Parliament any more than "Joel Barlow's *Columbiad* with the *Paradise Lost*," Sumner insisted, and it was because of the lack of educational standards in the population at large. This went to the heart of the character and viability of popular government, which must not be allowed to fail out of ignorance: "The age, our national character, our future destinies," he urged Story, "demand that there should be some tru[er] standard of taste than is to be found among us—& this will only proceed from a finished education."[104]

Talk of scholarship and the delights of his Roman summer of reading combined with the new urgency of his responsibilities at home to return Sumner's thoughts to his duty. After leaving Italy, he would visit Austria and Germany, converse with statesmen like Prince Metternich, and scholars like the brothers von Humboldt. He would discuss prison reform and jurisprudence with German professors N.H. Julius and Karl Mittermaier, and he would study German. But he would spend only eight months in the German countries, a fraction of what he had originally intended, and his thoughts were now less on his present experiences than on the delights of the recent past and the trials that called him home. It was oh so hard to leave his Italian idyll. As he crossed into Austria, "I rushed back—stood on the border-line—looked in vain for those beautiful fields, which seem Elysian in my memory—said to myself that I should never see them again—took off my hat & made my last salute." Wistfully he dreamt of returning there one day to a life of literature and ease far from the cares of home. "Oh! I love Italy," he would later exclaim when remembering these happy days. "But to other lands, even to England, I can only feel as a friend."[105]

Italy seemed all the more idyllic compared with what awaited him at home. While in England Sumner had still thought of one day returning with equanimity to his law office. What most concerned him then was whether his clients would welcome him back. "Those clients I once had—those duties I once rejoiced in—where are they? shall I find them again?" he asked Greenleaf from London. Occasionally he admitted: "My heart sometimes sinks within me for a moment, when I think of my fate on my return to America [. . .]; when I think of my present days all-jewelled with delights & honorable distinctions, & my lot at home in humble toil & unregarded loneliness."[106]

Sumner never regretted his decision to go to Europe, but Italy made the imminent return to reality seem that much bleaker. His love for the scholarship of the law had now turned to the sad conviction that the law would divide him from the life of scholarship that he loved. At the same time he no longer saw how the law could be the means for his principal duty and ambition, the doing good to his fellow man, and especially for furthering the education and elevation of his countrymen. Urging Cleveland to devote himself to a work of great scholarship such as a history of English literature, Sumner regretted his own lot: "Would that I could do so! My lot is one of stern uninteresting employ, vulgar contracts, dealing with magnified trifles, inhaling bad air, moiling in formal documents, trudging, drudging, where scarce a breath from Heaven can reach me. But how I should rejoice to know that my friends were doing something gracious & good, while I was working in my profession!" He never thought seriously of staying in Europe, however. "I know my duties in life," he assured his friends firmly. "I know my profession better now than when I left Boston, & I can live content at home."[107]

DE PROFUNDIS

THE YOUNG MAN who returned to Boston in May 1840 did not seem to be quite the same person who had left that city two and a half years earlier. Not so long before skin and bones with eyes bloodshot from study, Sumner had filled out and acquired an unwonted glow of health. His complexion was now fair and his thick nut-brown hair fell in a shock over his left temple framing features that, if not perfectly regular, were harmonious, gentle, and expressive and made him seem for the first time strikingly handsome. This, combined with his impressive stature, a dignified, self-assured carriage and a new attention to a European-minded elegance of dress that he brought home with him from his travels, would turn heads wherever he went for the rest of his life.[1]

From over two years' intercourse with the highest European society Sumner had also acquired a sophistication and polish that he had hardly dreamt of before leaving. Often enough at the beginning of his trip he had given his friends leave to laugh at him as he playfully recounted his *faux pas,* his entire innocence of the anatomy of the exotic meats he too generously offered to carve, his unforgivable wearing of boots in a company of shoes. But he quickly learned from his mistakes and from observation, and before he left Europe he knew how to dress himself, address others, and converse even in the most elevated company. Ever after friends seeking advice on matters of etiquette would turn without hesitation to him.[2]

More than this, Sumner brought home a vision of his own future. He would return to his profession. His disappointment in the practice of law could not outweigh his sense of duty. Nor did he ever forget that the material rewards of a successful practice were a necessary foundation for the domestic happiness he dreamt of. But becoming a successful lawyer was not enough. The desire for usefulness and moral satisfaction that since youth had driven Sumner had been intensified by the experiences and connections he had benefited from in Europe. Having mingled and even acted on a larger stage than ever before, he felt the obligation to make a greater contribution to society, and he believed that more was expected of him among his acquaintances in Boston and now in Europe as well. New responsibility intensifying old self-doubt left him daunted. And yet his success in Europe had also given him a fervent hope in the future, an optimism that, if not invulnerable, was stronger and more inspiriting than anything he had felt since law school. He was anxious to prove that he could return to work, be successful in every way, and fulfill his social obligation to do good, just as he was anxious to fulfill his promise to himself to "be happy." Those long years of discouragement and loneliness would now surely have their reward.

Boston seemed very small compared to Paris and London; Sumner missed their activity and excitement. Yet Boston had grown much since his youth. The mercantile town of 30,000 had mushroomed into an industrial capital, its population approaching 100,000. Efforts were intensifying to enlarge the burgeoning little peninsula. Sumner had never known Boston free of construction sites. During the first twenty-five years of his life, the hills of the town's center, including the top of Beacon Hill, with the once-famous Bulfinch column crowning its summit, had been laboriously cut down by as much as sixty feet, the dirt being used to reclaim outlying areas from the old mud flats of the Charles River. By the time Sumner returned from Europe, the poorer waterfront areas of the city were more than ever filled with crowded immigrants hungry for work, while Beacon Hill was all but completely covered with new houses. On the sunny southern slope they were elegant townhouses, inhabited often by families who had made their money in the industrial boom that had started just after the War of 1812 and that had established factories all through the small towns of eastern Massachusetts, especially the great cotton manufactories on the Merrimack River at Lowell and, soon, at Lawrence.[3]

This increasing wealth combined with Boston's traditional desire for culture meant also an increasing familiarity with things European. In this trend Sumner fully participated, for returning to home and work did not mean turning his back on Europe. In many ways his American life now became more European as he combined his interests and friendships from both sides of the Atlantic. The cosmopolitanism he had always felt in spirit he could now live to a greater degree in practice. Sumner continued a close European correspondence over the next years, maintaining personal ties and keeping himself carefully informed on English and Continental politics and reform movements.[4] The Court Street offices themselves rang with talk of Europe and culture. Young William Wetmore Story's own artistic interest was not disappointed when, upon his graduation from Dane College, he took his place in 1840 as assistant in the offices of Hillard and Sumner. He would always fondly remember how the three of them, with whichever of their many friends happened to stop by, "used to talk infinitely, not only of law, but of poetry and general literature and authors, when business would allow—nay, sometimes when it would not allow; but who can resist temptation with such tastes as we all had?" And, of course, everything European became a more important topic of conversation than ever among the Five of Clubs as they entered the closest and liveliest period of their association.

Unhappy to be cut off from the cultural life he had so enjoyed over the past two and a half years, Sumner took the greatest comfort in these good friends and their constant company.[5]

Contemplating his return home from the pleasures of the Old World, which he knew he could not keep forever, Sumner had become keenly aware of the privilege of travel itself. "It is a Free-Masonry," he had written to Longfellow from Paris—feeling from the midst of his European experience a greater sympathy than he had in college with the self-conscious aristocracy of the cosmopolite— "which is only revealed to those who have taken the traveller's staff & scrip." It was a great consolation to him to be able to share those pleasures with others who understood them, and to discover that his European experience had opened up to him a new social circle in Boston. A successful European trip, like a classical education, was prized by Boston society as a kind of pedigree. Henry Adams later recalled that "social success in England and on the Continent [. . .] gave to every Bostonian who enjoyed it a halo never acquired by domestic sanctity." And no Bostonian had ever had such success as Sumner.[6]

An old tie such as the one with Samuel Lawrence broadened to include other members of that prominent industrial family, especially his brother Abbott Lawrence, a leading figure in the Whig party. His marriage in 1839 to Sumner's cousin Harriet added to a common cultivation in bringing Sumner into friendship with cotton manufacturer and avid reader Nathan Appleton. Together they shared their taste for literature and art and their belief in the perfectibility of man, as well as their European correspondence, and Sumner became a regular member of the Appleton household. More than this, the almost familial connection that Sumner had felt with his old professor George Ticknor and his lovely, cultivated wife and daughter in Paris was now resumed in Boston. How Sumner admired Mrs. Ticknor's elegance, goodness, and education. And how he delighted in Mr. Ticknor's books—"the finest private library in our country." This tie was no small matter, for Ticknor had become the veritable arbiter of Boston society. To be welcomed into his elegant Bulfinch mansion at 9 Park Street was to have all Boston's best doors open to one; to be unwelcome there was to be unwelcome everywhere that considered itself anywhere. Charles Daveis teased Sumner from Portland: "Ticknor tells me of your sitting up with him night after night till 12 o'clock. That is tormenting to those who cant have the same privilege."[7]

Europe also brought Sumner into closer contact with John Quincy Adams. Sumner had perhaps first seen the sixth President when he presided over the Latin School awards ceremony in 1826. He had first called on the then Congressman, whom he admired for his outspoken stand against the gag rule, in Washington just before leaving for Europe, but no correspondence had ensued. When Adams heard of George's exploits in Russia, however, his memories of his own trip there as the fourteen-year-old secretary to the American Minister were rekindled. Confusing the two brothers, he eagerly asked Sumner to call on him and tell him of his eastern travels. The initial mistake led to conversation and mutual interest that would ripen into a deeply significant friendship.[8]

Sumner thus became for the first time in Boston and Cambridge, as he had been in London and on the Continent, a social lion. So much kindness was inspiriting. "Consider every opportunity of adding to the pleasure of others as of the highest importance," he had instructed little Julia on the eve of his departure for Europe; "and do not be unwilling to sacrifice some Enjoyment of your own, even some dear plaything, if by doing so, you can promote the happiness of others. If you follow this advice, you will never be selfish or ungenerous and every body will love you." Now his welcome into Boston society confirmed Sumner in this deep faith in human nature. Not that he was unaware of a darker side. "This world is full of harshness," he knew, and knew, too, that "[i]t is easier to censure than to praise," for most people find in the former balm to their "*self-esteem*" and in the latter the threat of "a tacit admission of superiority." Sumner did "not boast myself to be free from blame" in such a tendency to fault-finding—indeed in private he was inclined to reprove himself strongly for it. His own amiability and affectionateness, however, joined with the essentially hopeful view of human nature he had drunk in from the teachings of Moral Philosophy, encouraged him to "cultivate a habit of appreciating others" and of looking for good rather than bad motives to their conduct. "I like to find good in every thing, & in all men of cultivated minds & good hearts," he wrote to George. "Thank God there is a great deal of good to be found."[9]

More even than a strengthened faith in others, these new connections gave Sumner the almost giddying hints of an awakening confidence in himself. It was not the social standing of his hosts—gratifying as that could be—that flattered him, so much as the consciousness of being accepted as an equal by people whom he had always admired for their education and cultivation. To be accepted by them as a friend was the most pleasing of all. Bursting with reminiscences of his trip, lonely at home, eager for the bonds of friendship and the pleasures of society that he had grown accustomed to in Europe, Sumner felt his new ties with the highest Bostonian circles not so much as social privilege but as new springs of the affection and communion that give life its sparkle.[10]

The return to work and clients and to the writing of writs was not so easy after two and a half years of art and literature and high society. "Every morning while I dress I think of Italy, & repeat to myself where I was & what I did a year ago," he confessed to Francis Lieber a few months after his return. And in remembering the scenes of history and the works "of art full of divinity" that he was then contemplating he could "for a moment forget the hard, practical, work-a-day-American present." After a few months of adjustment, however, he was back in his office for regular hours in September 1840. To help him settle in, his friends surrounded him and showered upon him "a perfect Niagara of advice and good counsel," though Hillard jovially remarked that he did not "see that it washes away any of his good-nature." When, shortly after his return, Sumner won a case that "turned on a point that had escaped [his old master Benjamin] Rand & some other lawyers" he could retort with triumph: "So! *allons!* avaunt, ye croakers! who said I could never file my mind to the business of my office. I can always do my duty; & *always will.*"[11]

Raised by the ideals of American Moral Philosophy in post-Revolutionary New England and by a father driven by the dictates of responsibility, Sumner had never questioned that his life should be ordered by the concept of duty, a duty to be determined by reason under the guidance of conscience. That duty, he firmly believed, should consist in being useful to his fellow man, and Sumner had long felt the ambition to do good. Now that he had returned home, he was faced by the practical question of just what that duty entailed. The most obvious and basic answer was, of course, to make a success of his practice. This he desired for the sake of his own personal future. He also believed he owed it to all those who had shown faith in him—men like Judge Story and Simon Greenleaf who had singled him out among their students as their hoped-for successor, men like Judge Story again and Samuel Lawrence and Richard Fletcher who had believed enough in his talent and responsibility to subsidize his trip to Europe. Sumner undoubtedly wanted, too, to show the Josiah Quincys that he was capable of getting more out of Europe than the vanity of a pair of mustachios and a cane. Most importantly, he was anxious to prove that his own father's fears about the irresponsibility of his actions had been unjustified. Though he returned to his practice with this determination, yet Sumner could not face a life of drudgery without purpose, and he sought at the same time, not unlike his father forty years earlier, other endeavors to complement his practice or infuse it with the cultural interest and moral satisfaction he craved.

The first of these endeavors grew naturally out of his duty to his family. As he had promised upon learning of his father's death, Sumner immediately devoted himself to the education of his school-age siblings, not neglecting his sisters. Unlike their brothers, the girls did not need the kind of education that would prepare them for a professional future, but to Sumner's mind that meant that a good general education was, if anything, more important to them. A man of natural talent might become interesting to his fellows and be able to make a contribution to society even without education if he acquired "a large experience of ye world," but this was not the case for a woman. "A female's place is at home—not abroad in ye excited scenes of ye world," Charles had reflected to his sister Jane nearly ten years earlier, perhaps thinking of their mother; "& unless she narrows her mind, so as not to look beyond ye kitchen hearth, she will have many heavy hours if she does not love *books*." More than this, he encouraged her: "Education is ye surest passport to ye best society. Personal appearance invites attention, indeed; & secures, a large circle of admirers, but unless there be also intelligence & information, as its companions, it cannot hold them long. There is nothing more delightful than an accomplished & handsome woman. [. . .] While there is little that is duller than a woman witht education. [. . .] Unless she can charm or interest by her manners or is so educated as to be able at least to *listen intelligently,* she will be able to afford but little pleasure by her company."[12]

Now, in the early 1840's, Sumner had more say in his siblings' education than ever before. In the case of twelve-year-old Julia, Sumner had no trouble persuading his mother, who had always valued education herself, that the baby of the family should have the benefit of an experimental school recently opened in Boston. The girls' high school founded by respected educator George B. Emerson was in fact one of a series of efforts through the 1820's, 'thirties, and 'forties to create a counterpart to the English High School for boys of which Emerson himself had been the first headmaster. His school achieved a fine reputation among educational reformers though it was not destined, any more than the others, to survive the controversies surrounding the whole question of secondary education for girls. The school was thriving when Sumner sent Julia there, however, and she throve at the school, eager to recount to her brother's "kindly, sympathetic ear at dinner the experiences of the morning at school," happy to get his help for her Latin lessons, and so "proud [. . .] of his praise and approval"—with which he was always generous. George Emerson was likewise delighted by Sumner's support for the school and by his deep interest in his sister's education—"a subject," Emerson complained, "which is of such important consequence to me, but which most gentlemen, even well educated and having daughters, look upon with indifference."[13]

Sumner's conception of the appropriate minimum for a girl's education astonished even the progressive Emerson, however. Sumner indeed thought Julia should learn Latin not to become a scholar, but primarily to better understand English grammar and etymology, "& also to enjoy ye numerous allusions to & quotations from the authors of Old Rome, with which elegant composition is so often interspersed." "No lady should be expected to push [the study of Latin] far," answered Emerson: "The only question is how far it should be carried merely as a preparation for other studies. And I confess that your allowance is a very liberal one. In the case of your sister Julia, it lies at a substantial foundation. She has learnt it so exceedingly well, and her recitations in it are so pleasant and satisfactory, that I should like, for my own gratification, to have them continued. But I admit that her thoroughness is a good reason for her stopping where she now is, and devoting herself to what you justly consider essential attainments.

Hereafter I will endeavor to induce her to devote herself with the same resolute fidelity to her French studies as she has always shown in Latin."[14]

The cheerful and bright-eyed Julia would make her brother proud as she grew into an accomplished and cultivated as well as charming young woman. But Sumner's simultaneous efforts to educate his youngest brother Horace would end only in disappointment, a disappointment particularly cruel not only because of Sumner's deep sense of responsibility for his siblings' education, but because he had in some ways seen in his brother a chance to remake his own education. Still pained by what seemed to him the deficiencies of his own formation, Sumner returned to America determined that the fifteen-year-old Horace, at least, should have the benefit of a thorough and polished European education. While still in Europe, Sumner had investigated a number of boarding schools, and finally settled on an excellent one in Geneva—with Bostonian connections to encourage his mother. "I will see him at New York on board a good packet," he desperately tried to reassure her, "& will have the captain put him into a *Diligence* (marked "*this side up with care*") for Paris, where I shall get some of my friends to receive him & forward him to Geneva." Sumner's arguments were to no avail, however, and Horace stayed in Boston.[15]

Perhaps their mother simply did not want her youngest son to follow his elders out of the nest so soon, but perhaps, too, she recognized something that Charles, abroad so long and carried away by enthusiasm, did not yet understand upon his return home. His plans might well have worked for George, who was continually making up for his lack of a classical education by a combination of unquenchable curiosity and charm, and who might have benefited by the academic discipline of a boarding school. It surely would have pleased Albert, who had gone through the Boston Latin School with Charles and who now, despite his years at sea, had grown into a polished and cultivated gentleman with an elegant new wife, together with whom in the early 'forties he moved to Newport to lead a life of refined retirement. Horace shared in the family's kind and affectionate disposition, but not in their active intelligence. He was unscholarly and so unambitious that the family began to worry whether he could ever be even self-sufficient.[16]

This discovery was a blow to Charles, and for a time the two brothers were at odds. Horace must have found his eldest brother even more incomprehensibly demanding than their father. Charles was frustrated at what seemed to him Horace's sluggish incompetence, and for a time thought the boy could do nothing right. If a crate of plaster casts sent from Italy by George arrived "sadly broken," Charles was sure how it had happened: "Perhaps in the passage, though I opine by Horace, who let them fall on the deck of the ship." Horace's horizons were bounded by the beauties of nature and the pleasures of gardening. Pushed by his family to try to find an independent path, he decided on a year at the reform-minded community of Brook Farm and then went on to work on a farm in New Hampshire. As the initial pain of the situation eased, Charles finally became reconciled to Horace's future. "You will see that he is gentle, generous, and inclined to all good things," he told George a few years later, despite his "ignorance of the world, so called, and the absence of those energies which are essential to worldly success." When Horace's New Hampshire experience yielded him "a year or more of happiness," together with a greater measure of self-reliance, Charles wrote to George: "Perhaps you will join with me in thinking that all has been for the best."[17]

Sumner's sad acceptance of his brother's deficiencies was mirrored by his disappointment in the educational reforms going on at the same time at his beloved Harvard. When, filled with his own visions of turning Harvard into a full classical university on a European scale, Sumner returned home to find President Quincy in the midst of strengthening the curriculum and raising the entrance requirements, he at first enthusiastically supported the change. Such reforms seemed all the more crucial to Sumner given the prevailing Jacksonian assault on the whole idea of classical education in favor of schooling oriented toward useful information and practical professional skills. But he was brought up short by some observations by his unhappy college friend Charlemagne Tower. Tower had been forced to give up his study of law to take over the family business when his father fell ill and died. Sumner had encouraged his dreams of someday returning to the law, but they would never be realized. When, after some years of separation, the two met by chance in early 1841 on a train in upstate New York, Tower was working as a schoolteacher in the town of Waterville. Their conversation naturally turned to Harvard and the present reforms, but they found themselves on different sides of the question. While Sumner was still fresh from his European success, Tower was painfully conscious of his own fall from hopeful professional to humble working man, teaching the sons of farmers for his daily bread, and he forced Sumner to reflect on his own perspective when he wistfully defended himself as "one who is on the outposts of society and familiar with the doings of man in common, hard working life, men who [. . .] do not appreciate such loveliness as you do, who dwell in the bright halo of a more ethereal atmosphere."[18]

Both young men wanted American educational standards to be high, but to Sumner's defense of Harvard's present efforts to raise entrance requirements, Tower answered with his fear that such a move—when those requirements were already the highest in the nation—would serve only to cut off more boys from a college education, especially in a country "where prosperity is changeable and acquired more by hard earnings than in any other way," making it difficult for most fathers to afford to prepare their sons thoroughly for college. Against Sumner's defense of a system of higher education geared toward creating an educated class, Tower offered the view that "a college should not be like a European University, venerated and unapproachable,—but, in the spirit of all our political institutions, benevolent and condescending." If Sumner had argued for the raising of academic requirements, however, he had not defended the attendant rise of tuition advocated by Quincy. Perhaps he remembered his own father's arguments in favor of lower school reform back in 1818 to help the children of the poor, and the uncertainty of his own entrance into Harvard due to the already prohibitive tuition in 1826. Sumner was also too fond of his old friend not to be touched by his remarks and by the experience that had prompted them. After his talk with Tower, Sumner never again spoke in defense of Quincy's reforms at Harvard.[19]

One concession of Tower's may have struck Sumner particularly. Tower had ventured that the ideal way to raise standards would be to prepare students more thoroughly for college by giving them better trained teachers in the lower schools. As Sumner thought this over he could not accept Tower's sad objection that these schools "are out of your reach." Instead Sumner turned hopefully to the efforts of his old Number-Four colleague Horace Mann, then becoming outspoken in the cause of education reform. Mann's plea to improve the lower schools with teaching methods and a curriculum inspired by European standards struck Sumner as the perfect solution to Tower's dilemma. When, contrary to tradition, Mann made his reformist proposals the subject of his Fourth of July oration in 1842, Sumner thought his effort "the most noble production ever called forth by that celebration." In 1844 Sumner himself would join with Mann to fight for the improvement of the lower schools and the creation of normal schools for the better training of teachers. He could not shake a sadness, however, at the thought that Harvard, which he wished to be the *alma mater* of the enlightenment of the community, could be blamed for withholding enlightenment from worthy students.[20]

Sumner did not forget his friends any more than his family, and here, too, his services to them combined with his desire to serve the larger community. In Italy Sumner had thrown himself into the work of locating a buyer for his new friend Thomas Crawford's *Orpheus*. By March 1841 Sumner had found the perfect patron. From Rome Sumner had written of his hopes of persuading someone to do for Crawford what James Fenimore Cooper had done for Horatio Greenough. Pleased with one work of the young sculptor, Cooper had ordered another, and then given "Greenough the privilege of exhibiting it in the principal cities. From that moment his success was complete." Such personal patronage could save a young artist from starvation and establish his reputation. Nor had Sumner forgotten his hopes that the government commission for Greenough's seated *Washington* would help to educate the public taste and encourage its support for the arts. Ideal would be a combination of the two types of patronage, and that is essentially what Sumner was able to do by encouraging the Boston Athenæum to buy Crawford's *Orpheus*.[21]

The Athenæum was a private institution and, as a library, remained open only to members, but since the mid-1830's it had been organizing annual public showings of its growing collection of paintings. Under the impetus of the new American interest in Neoclassicism, it had begun, just while Sumner was in Europe, to add to these exhibits such examples of sculpture as it possessed, mainly plaster casts of European works. Sumner's offer of an original American Neoclassical work thus found a willing acceptance from the Athenæum, and he was able to command $2,500 for the *Orpheus*—a handsome sum for a first commission to a young sculptor without previous reputation.[22] During much of 1842 and 1843 Sumner then devoted himself to the work of receiving the statue in Boston, arranging for some repairs, and, in careful coöperation with the artist, organizing the Athenæum's spring show of 1843. Uniting the *Orpheus* with all the available smaller pieces Crawford had so far created in his short career, this became the first show devoted to the works of a single artist ever done in the United States. It launched Crawford's distinguished career.[23] Sumner was thoroughly embarrassed by Crawford's eager thanks for the very successful show and by his thank-you gift, which only the repeated insistence that it was necessary to further Crawford's career could persuade Sumner to include in the Athenæum's show—a marble version of the portrait bust Crawford had modeled of Sumner in Rome.[24]

Sumner's desire to do good and his search for moral satisfaction drew him irresistibly further, into causes less widely promoted by Boston society, but which appealed to his native idealism, and which his European experience—and the larger perspective on his homeland it had given him—now made even more crucial to his eyes.

In May 1840, "the very month" of his return to Boston, Sumner attended a meeting of the American Peace Society—an association he would maintain for some years. On the motion of his family's old friend, the Reverend Ezra Stiles Gannett, he was even placed on the executive committee. Sumner resumed his place as a member of the Boston Prison Discipline Society as well. His dissatisfaction with the conservatism and narrow provincialism of Secretary Louis Dwight had grown even more urgent as he conversed upon the subject in Europe. Now he watched with sympathy the efforts of his new friend Samuel Gridley Howe to dislodge the stubborn secretary, and hoped that Francis Lieber might be persuaded to take his place. Sumner took no action himself, however, beyond frank but private discussions with Dwight.[25]

Through his reform-minded friend Howe, as well as through his own legal work, Sumner also followed with interest the efforts of Dorothea Dix to help the indigent insane—who had been left behind in the recent creation of state asylums and were still most likely to find themselves in prison. Howe got himself elected to the General Court in 1842 to gain state support for Miss Dix's proposals. When he ran into opposition early the next year, Sumner personally inspected the conditions in some of the prisons cited in Miss Dix's report and energetically defended Howe and Miss Dix in an article in the Boston *Courier*. They rejoiced together at the legislature's adoption of the report a few months later.[26]

The fears of Story and Greenleaf seemed to be coming true, even though Sumner's involvement in reform remained private and the few organizations that he belonged to were acceptable to conservative Boston. His professors took hope, however, from the manner in which Sumner defended the social order whenever the question arose of effecting change through violence, as in the so-called Dorr War. When Rhode Island's long-standing dissatisfaction with her constitution and its limited suffrage threatened to explode into open rebellion in the late spring and summer of 1842, Sumner was as horrified as his professors. A rival constitution, written by a "People's Convention," bypassing the General Assembly, had given the state two rival governments and, when the struggling Suffragists under their leader Thomas Dorr tried to strengthen their chances by seizing the Providence arsenal, the established government declared martial law—the first time in American history that any state government had suspended civil law and placed its entire territory under military rule.[27]

"The whole state is in a panic," exclaimed Sumner in June after a business trip to Rhode Island's capital. "Within a few days upwards of three millions of dollars have been sent from Providence to Boston—& women & children also—for safe keeping. The whole state is under arms." Sumner was furious at the failure of President John Tyler to "take the responsibility," as he had been requested by the state of Rhode Island, and send in federal troops. "Is not this clearly a case for the intervention of the Genl Govt. to *protect* the state from *domestic insurrection*?" demanded Sumner. Part of Sumner's anger stemmed from personal circumstances. At that very moment his brother Albert and his wife were in Newport awaiting the birth of their first child, and Sumner's beloved sister Mary was with them. Until order was finally restored at the end of August, he had reason to fear for their safety.[28]

Sumner rejected violence in the cause of social reform as a matter of principle no less than practice. The following year he once again supported the use of force by established authority to put down the threat of violent rebellion. In the case of the *Somers* mutiny, Sumner believed that the young captain, Alexander Slidell Mackenzie, had indeed been faced with an unscrupulous uprising, intended to win gold rather than redress of grievances. In his defense of Mackenzie in the *North American Review*, Sumner offered his greatest sympathy to the "unhappy" officers of any ship overtaken by mutiny, but made it clear that, even where a captain's injustice or the harshness of naval law caused genuine suffering for a ship's crew, they had no right to resort to violent means but must look for succor to the law or, by their testimony, try to have the law changed. Mackenzie he supported on grounds of self-defense—the defense of his own person, of his command, and of all law-abiding persons aboard his ship: "Whatever the commander does [. . .] *in such an emergency, in good faith, and in the conscientious discharge of his duty, believing it to be necessary to the safety of his ship, or of the lives of those on board, receives the protection of the law.*" In the same spirit Sumner had supported the imposition of martial law in Rhode Island.[29]

Sumner was much commended by conservative jurists, foremost by Story himself, for his arguments in Mackenzie's favor—just as he and they had seemed to be in harmony in their judgment about the Dorr Rebellion—and yet below this surface agreement lay philosophical differences that would only gradually become apparent. Story's outrage against the uprising in Rhode Island—which motivated his handling of a circuit court case arising out of the events—came from his fear that the protest and reform movements proliferating at the time constituted an essential threat to republican order. In judging the events in Rhode Island, Story had his eye clearly on Garrisonians in Massachusetts, who now spoke of disunion as a response to the expansion of slavery, and about whom Story was now willing to express his fears openly, not only in correspondence but in his classes as well. If the Dorrites could resort to violence to liberalize the social order—as the Shaysites had done a half century earlier—then could not the abolitionists do the same, as Greenleaf had once prophesied in warning to Sumner? To prevent such a possibility Story was willing to broaden the definition of both martial law and treason, and hoped to see the circuit court case go to the Supreme Court that these changes might be made national. Sumner's refusal to countenance violence on the part of the reformers carried with it no fear of reform in general, as he showed by his increasing ties to reform movements—merely the insistence that change should be pursued through legal means.[30]

Of all the reform movements that Sumner followed, it was antislavery that was beginning to enlist his greatest attention. He could not help but feel that efforts at reform in any domain seemed discredited by America's continued protection of slavery, and her consequent reputation for hypocrisy destroyed any efforts she might make to achieve cultural respect in the international community. Sumner was horrified anew in the early 1840's at the effect of slavery on the South as he relived his own earlier passage there through the travels of friends. He was angered by the brutality and dehumanization of blacks and whites alike that his now very close friend Samuel Gridley Howe described in letters from a trip there in 1842. He was vicariously relieved to read the description that his equally antislavery English friend Lord Morpeth—visiting the United States for the first time—gave of his return from the South into the Northern "soil of freedom, where all labor is honorable, & pursuit is generally philanthropic,"—and where letters were not confiscated by the post office. While most Americans were furious at Charles Dickens for his strictures upon America in the published account of his voyage here in 1842, Sumner and Longfellow, who had become Dickens' good friends and hosts in Boston and Cambridge, were delighted. "He has a grand chapter on Slavery," Longfellow wrote Sumner from Dickens' own study while in England. *"Spitting* and *politics* at Washington are the other topics of censure. Both you and I would censure them with equal severity to say the least."[31]

Still distrusting his own voice, Sumner hesitated to speak out publicly against slavery, though in an 1842 legal article on the slave trade he allowed his feelings to show through for the first time. When antislavery activists, delighted at the possibility of acquiring for the cause such a valuable friend as the well-connected jurist, urged him to do more, he demurred. To the important Garrisonian Maria Weston Chapman's repeated requests that he contribute to the annual antislavery gift-book the *Liberty Bell,* Sumner begged off for himself, sending rather one of Howe's pointed antislavery letters from his recent Southern trip.[32]

Among his friends, however, Sumner was getting a reputation for his attraction to radical causes. Perhaps he even slightly worried his friend Felton, who disliked slavery but also found the abolitionists an unacceptably uncouth lot. One day the quick-witted and sometimes sharp-tongued Greek professor took advantage of one of the habitual ink blots on the busy Sumner's hastily written letters to rally his friend, who submitted with good grace if perhaps just a touch of annoyance. The blot, Felton explained in the margins, was "Charles's seal. You may always verify any document of his by this. He has chosen it as an emblem of his sentiments as un ami des Noirs. You know he subscribes for an abolitionist newspaper, and frequents antislavery FAIRS!!! he differs from Virgil who says *Nimium ne crede COLORI."*[33]

In private correspondence Sumner had become quite outspoken against slavery. Though friends assumed that he voted the Whig ticket in the 1840 presidential election, Sumner told Samuel Sewall how "happy" he was that the Liberty party's candidate—and his future Senate colleague—John Parker Hale was speaking widely, for he was sure it would "do much to promote the establishment of sound principles."[34] Sumner was ever enlarging his circle of antislavery friends, which now included Judge William Jay and his son John Jay of New York, while to old Garrisonian friends like the Reverend Samuel May, Jr., Sumner enthusiastically bestowed his blessings on "every effort for freedom, & especially the self-sacrificing lives of the pioneers in American Anti-Slavery!" In precisely the same terms he praised Garrison as one who "with some faults, has extraordinary virtues & a self-sacrifice heroic." Sumner was "heartily glad" when John Quincy Adams won his long-sought victory in the House of Representatives against the gag rule: "—I am sorry that he had not an opportunity of emptying more from his phials upon the heads of the South!"[35]

Watching these efforts strengthened Sumner's hope in the future. He sent information about American slavery to European lawyers and politicians, encouraging Lord Brougham in 1844 to add his voice to the antislavery debates then going on in Parliament in order to influence American opinion. Sumner's pride in Longfellow's 1842 *Poems on Slavery* was more than just in seeing his friend's name associated with a great humanitarian cause. Sumner was anxious to hear the intellectual and cultural voice of America speak on her moral behalf and touch the public heart. In these poems he rejoiced, "for I detest slavery so thoroughly that I am pleased at every new shaft which it receives. Let the novelist, the statesman, the orator, the poet all in their several ways & moods, utter their testimony against it. Do this, & we will soon surround the Southern States with a *moral blockade*."[36]

Sumner's fundamental antislavery convictions and his attraction to ethics were innate, but in his increasing outspokenness on moral issues, he was aware of the influence of the Reverend William Ellery Channing. Dr. Channing—in all but name the greatest of American moral philosophers—forced Sumner to think carefully about the proper balance between the intellect and the conscience. Antislavery was so natural to the Sumner household as Charles was growing up that it could almost be taken for granted; what Charles had felt he could not take for granted was his own academic achievement and the respect he anxiously desired on that account from his father. Without denying his moral sense, his dream of becoming a scholar and a gentleman like his father caused Sumner in his college years to be particularly impressed by intellectual achievements. It was this feeling that lay behind his indignation when, just in the middle of his college course, the highly respected Reverend Channing published his article attacking Napoleon, the hero of Sumner's youth, on the grounds of the evil done by intellect without virtue.

On that May day in 1830, as he gave his college senior exhibition part, Sumner had been most intent upon defending the Emperor against Channing's denial to him of real intellectual greatness, of that "sublime capacity of thought." Let alone such accomplishments as his legal code, Sumner urged, even his military greatness was proof that Napoleon "was original—he did not choose to trudge on in the same beaten path & trusted tactics, which others had travelled before, he boldly diverged from the common path & trusted the energies of his own mind." But the college senior's argument held more significance than was perhaps apparent at the moment.[37]

Channing had intended his diptych on Milton and Napoleon as a kind of parable on virtue and power, but, as much as he too admired Milton, Sumner bristled at the implication that intellect alone, without the aid of conscience, could accomplish no good. Milton's greatness, Channing had written, came from the exercise of his powers under "self-dominion" or "self-subjection to the principle of duty," whereas Napoleon, possessing perhaps equal intellect and certainly equal dynamic energy, but without the benevolence and responsibility of virtue, had followed the path of evil.[38] But Napoleon had achieved triumphs for the public good through intellect, countered Sumner. His restoration of religion after the Revolution and his healing of "dissention & strife" were great acts of statesmanship, just as was his promulgation of the *Code Napoléon*—"more uniform, complete & effective than any system the world ever saw." If Napoleon was an even greater warrior than statesman, "yet few can be placed before him as such for keenness of observation & depth of research, for quickness to apprehend & readiness to execute." Sadly, this same man had indeed become "the prostrator of the liberties of his country,"—not because he lacked intellectual greatness but because he had succumbed to the tragedy of power. Yet, even then, insisted Sumner, contrary to the "dark, gloomy fanaticism" kindled by the leadership of a Cromwell, Napoleon inspired "an elevated devotion."[39]

Thus intent upon the importance of scholarship and the power of intellect, Sumner had been disappointed by Channing's seeming disregard for intellectuality in the pursuit of conscience. "When I was younger than I am now," Sumner confessed in 1842, "I was presumptuous enough to question his power. I did not find in him the forms of logical discussion, & the close, continuous chain of reasoning—& I complained. I am glad that I am wise enough to see him in a different light."[40]

Sumner began consistently to follow that different light in law school where his imagination was fired precisely by the combination of close logic, of intellect, with a morality that gave it purpose. This was the harbinger of the revulsion he would feel at his first sight of slavery while on his way to Washington, of his resulting interest in Mrs. Child's *Appeal* and in Channing's *Slavery,* and of the close attachment he would form with Channing himself once the two met in 1834. For Channing's characteristic stress upon humanitarian benevolence, the loving nature of God, and the duty of conscience—old ideas in the Sumner household—Sumner's sense of moral awakening gave him a new, exciting appreciation. Under this new sustained desire to follow his conscience, and encouraged by his growing friendship with Channing, Sumner ventured his first involvement in the cause of antislavery in Boston, and then gathered information and made contacts connected with the issue in Europe. With his sense of moral engagement so his admiration for Channing grew, and Sumner felt a compensation for many of America's shortcomings in Channing's European reputation: "One feels proud of being a countryman of Channing. His spirit is worthy of the republic, & does us honour abroad. His is a noble elevation which makes the pulses throb."[41]

During the years of his friendship with Sumner, Channing underwent an awakening of his own, albeit a darker one. His deep faith in man's reason had made his first public pronouncements on slavery moderate and hopeful. He had been sure that a calm and generous voice would have much greater influence in urging Southern slaveholders to emancipation than the abolitionists' stridency. Instead he had found himself as bitterly attacked by Southerners as Garrison had been, while having to suffer the simultaneous coldness and resentment of his Northern neighbors. Instead of giving up, he became bolder. Carefully reëxamining his views, Channing, by 1839, dropped his original faith in the ability of Southerners to find a solution themselves, and came to support a Northern moral movement to pursue the more radical Garrisonian goal of immediate emancipation. Though he never became completely associated with the abolitionists, the mild-mannered Channing came to justify even their belligerent language in terms that he had once used to justify the sometimes harsh invective of Milton:

> The Abolitionists deserve rebuke; but let it be proportioned to the offence. They do wrong in their angry denunciation of slave-holders. But is calling the slave holder hard names a crime of unparalleled aggravation? Is it not, at least, as great a crime to spoil a man of his rights and liberty, to make him a chattel, and trample him in the dust? And why shall the latter offender escape with so much gentler rebuke? I know, as well as the slave-holder, what it is to bear the burden of hard names. The South has not been sparing of its invectives in return for my poor efforts against slavery. I understand the evil of reproach; and I am compelled to pronounce it a very slight one, and not to be named in comparison with bondage; and why is it, that he who inflicts the former should be called to drink the cup of wrath to the very dregs, whilst he who inflicts the latter receives hardly a mild rebuke?[42]

By the early 1840's Channing went further, supporting the political struggle against slavery. He publicly took the side of his abolitionist friend Charles Follen—whose antislavery views had cost him his position as German instructor at Harvard just as his liberalism had once forced him to leave his native Germany—and of John Quincy Adams, who won his fight against the gag rule in the House of Representatives in the last year of Channing's life. For his pains, Channing found his authority in his own parish increasingly questioned and checked, and his person increasingly unwelcome in society until, again in the last year of his life, he was placed under the ban of social ostracism that was the characteristic weapon wielded by George Ticknor in defense of social norms.[43]

Sumner was not discouraged, but struck with admiration. His father had been similarly attacked for his liberal moral principles, but even as a youth Sumner had been unable to accept his father's resulting withdrawal. How great now was his esteem when Channing responded to apathy and disapproval and threats with even greater outspokenness. How deeply was he inspired by Channing's ethical strength and his untiring search for truth. "His moral nature is powerful,

& he writes under the strong instincts which this supplies; & the appeal is felt by the world," Sumner told George. "The elevation & purity of his views always diffuses about him a saint-like character."[44]

Sumner never lost his admiration for intellect and scholarship, but under Channing's influence he was more sensitive now than ever to the appeal and the demands of conscience. The fading of his attraction to Napoleon showed in his loss of faith in Daniel Webster. The Secretary of State was deeply admired in New England as the very model of statesmanship. Webster remained a great intellect, agreed Sumner, and he gave him full credit for his successful negotiation of the Webster-Ashburton treaty with England, which settled most of the long-standing border disputes that had irritated relations between the two nations: "This is owing to his large head!" Sumner exclaimed enthusiastically in the current language of phrenology. "I can see that large head, like an immense battering-ram, behind every sentence he writes." At almost the same moment, however, Webster agreed to serve the Virginian President Tyler's pro-slavery goals, delivering to England in 1842 his so-called *Creole* letter, insisting that England return to the United States a group of slaves who had seized the slave ship transporting them to New Orleans, taking it instead to Nassau and freedom. At this, Sumner could not but compare Webster revealingly to Channing. Webster, like Napoleon, had a great intellect; but without the conscience of a Milton or a Channing, such a force could go horribly wrong. "Who excells, who equals Webster in intellect? I mean in the [mere] dead weight of intellect. With the moral elevation of Channing he would become a prophet. Webster wants sympathy with the mass, with humanity, with truth. If this had been living within him he never could have written his *Creole* letter. Without Webster's massive argumentation Channing sways the world with a stronger influence."[45]

If Channing had encouraged Sumner's appreciation for the need to combine intellectual and moral arguments in the struggle against slavery, Sumner had served Channing in a similar way. When Channing published a collected edition of his works in 1841 he reprinted his thirteen-year-old article on Napoleon without alteration, but with an explanatory footnote that nodded to his young friend. In that "Review, the conqueror of Waterloo is spoken of as having only the merit of a great soldier. No one then believed, that his opponents were soon to acknowledge his eminence in civil as well as military affairs." Likewise, Channing had come to realize that, important as it was, moral suasion could not, without the backing of close legal arguments, carry the struggle against a peculiar institution supported by law.[46]

In 1842 their newly deepened intellectual sympathy was consecrated when Channing chose Sumner as his closest collaborator on his latest and, as it would turn out, his most important antislavery work, a book-length double pamphlet called the *Duty of the Free States* aimed squarely at Webster's offending *Creole* letter. Sumner read through the antislavery and especially the legal literature for Channing, giving his judgment about the sources and about the legal points of all the significant cases. When the book was done, Channing read the whole manuscript to Sumner for his literary opinion, grateful for his suggestions. Sumner and Hillard then saw to the publication of the manuscript while the ailing Channing took some much needed rest. The book would always hold a deep sentimental value for Sumner as the last project that he and Channing would work on together. Within a few months of its completion the always delicate Channing had died. The book was testimony, however, to the decisive influence each had had on the other. Sumner had now helped Channing deepen his appreciation of Natural Law, just as Channing had helped Sumner deepen his appreciation of the meaning of Moral Philosophy. Together they had combined the two great traditions of American philosophical life and of Sumner's own education into the foundation from which Sumner would launch his own campaign against slavery, for the elevation of American culture, and, he hoped, for the infusion of greater ethical significance into his legal practice.[47]

It was thus that Sumner's first public pronouncement against slavery—and his most immediate preparation for the collaboration on the *Duty of the Free States*—came in a pair of legal articles. Within less than a year of his return from Europe, Sumner took one of a series of cases arising out of the question whether England should have the right to search the ships of other nations suspected of violating treaties negotiated in the 1820's and 'thirties to restrict and ultimately end the slave trade. Because the United States, now the world's largest slave trading nation, was not a party to these treaties, illegal slavers of signatory nations sometimes hoisted the American flag to avoid British interference. When England stepped up her own vigilance to catch such renegades, the Royal Navy sometimes mistakenly boarded actual American ships, and it was the owners of one of these ships who asked Sumner to represent them. Characteristically thorough, and also fascinated by the subject, Sumner read through, among other things, "the voluminous correspondence (2 folios) on the subject of the Slave-trade, laid on the table of the British Parlt this last year." Out of this research Sumner published two articles on the right of search in the first two months of 1842.[48]

Sumner supported England's antislavery efforts and showed his friendly faith in her. She had no right knowingly to board and search American ships, of course, but he had none of the fears—shared by many who remembered the War of 1812 and by Democrats generally—of the danger of English impressment of American seamen or other deliberate attacks on American sovereignty. To his Democratic and anglophobic brother George, now living in Paris and friendly with the American minister Lewis Cass—who did fear impressment—Sumner argued England's essential good will. "*Probable cause* is a sufficient defence for any marine tort," he explained. "This has been several times declared by the Supreme Court of the U. States—the highest & most authoritative expounder of the law of nations so far as we are concerned [. . .]." Much of the difference between Sumner and men like Cass or his own brother George was in Sumner's natural inclination to trust British motives. "Should I go out of the way to find dishonorable motives for conduct which is apparently benevolent & philanthropic?" Charles asked his fault-finding brother. Having close ties with English society and established friendships with many influential and antislavery Englishmen, Sumner was offended by Cass's "insinuations about *material interests*" in England's efforts to suppress the slave trade.[49]

Most importantly, Sumner showed his hatred of the slave trade and his belief in the use of international coöperation to improve the standards of international law. England's efforts to choke off the slave trade through international treaties and vigilance—"serving the cause of humanity and civilization, and directing the combined powers of many nations against the infamous traffic in slaves"— was not only permissible, it was morally encouraged by the dictates of Natural Law. In boarding the ships of other nations England was thus acting not so much under the belligerent right of search, but under what Sumner preferred to call the "right of inquiry," her ships becoming essentially "marine constables" set to maintain peaceful order on the seas according to the rule of law.[50]

Speaking against the slave trade was not radical. Even Southern states did it regularly, though more often to protect their internal trade. Congress had labeled it piracy in 1806—without thereby intending to take any strong action against it—and in 1823 Congress called for international coöperation to end the trade, though the resulting treaty was stripped of all its power by the Senate. In the end the United States did not enter into an effective treaty against the trade until 1862, during the Civil War. Even so, as he took the subject more seriously, Sumner's caution and self-doubt made any such first pronouncement formidable for him, and he was encouraged by the round praise he received for his two articles, even by such friends as Judge Story and Chancellor Kent, the pillars of legal conservatism. Kent made Sumner glow with pride when he averred: "I have no hesitation in subscribing to it as entirely sound, logical & conclusive. There is no doubt of it, & the neatness & Elegance with which it is written are delightful." On the second article Story complimented Sumner in the most reassuring terms: "This last article is written with a close logic, & lawyerlike precision, or rather, as I should say, with the comprehensive grasp of a publicist dealing with the general law of nations, & not with the municipal doctrines of a particular country.— I have good reason to believe that Webster entertains the like views; & I rather *guess* that the Atty Genl. does."[51]

In his private correspondence Sumner went further, and here, in discussions about the right of search, the slave trade, and Webster's *Creole* letter, he showed most clearly the ideas he would share with Channing in the preparation of the *Duty of the Free States*. These ideas fell well within the mainstream of the legal thought of the antislavery movement but—something he did not yet entirely appreciate—well to the left of the convictions of his conservative friends. By demanding that England return the fugitive slaves, Webster's *Creole* letter—speaking for the United States Government—urged the universal legal legitimacy of slavery. This, countered Sumner, was in violation of Natural Law. It was England's campaign against the slave trade, rather, that showed the proper effect on international relations of Natural Law and its principle that law should live up to a higher standard of ethics: "She has laid down a rule not to recognize ppty in human beings since the date of her great Emancipation Act. The principle of this is very clear. She will not in any way lend her machinery of justice to execute foreign laws which she has pronounced immoral, unchristian & unjust. She had not so pronounced until her act of Emancipation. It is common learning among jurists that no nation will enforce contracts or obligations of an immoral character, even though not regarded as immoral in the country where they were entered into." And Sumner argued that Webster was fully aware of this. Despite all the characterizations in his *Creole* letter of the black men who took over the ship and ordered her to English territory as "mutineers and murderers" and the "recognized [. . .] property" of American citizens, despite all the Administration's blustering demands for their rendition—despite all this rhetoric, Webster had based his legal call for the rendition of the slaves on "*comity* alone," thus acknowledging England's right to decide. Though Sumner found the *Creole* letter morally repugnant, he thus admitted that legally it was "a most acute & ingenious piece of advocacy."[52]

In his private correspondence, too, Sumner discussed at length the status of the slaves of the *Creole* themselves. His desire for a solution that would be at once morally and legally satisfactory led him back to his belief in Natural Law and to the most prominent legal tradition of the antislavery movement, associated with the seminal case of Somerset *v*. Stewart decided by Lord Mansfield in 1772. Despite his discomfort at having to decide this case of a slave suing for his freedom after his master had brought him from the colonies to England where slavery was not written into law, the Lord Chief Justice had nonetheless expounded the premise that slavery was contrary to Natural Law and could exist only under explicit positive law. Very quickly, with the help of antislavery lawyers and poets alike, the decision was broadened to harken back to the ancient idea that, in the words of Cowper,

> Slaves cannot breathe in England, if their lungs
> Receive our air, that moment they are free
> They touch our country, and their shackles fall.[53]

This principle had been accepted in some American courts as well, prominently in the Massachusetts Supreme Judicial Court starting in 1783. When the father of Charles Pinckney Sumner's future benefactor Levi Lincoln appealed to the Somerset principle in his defense of the freedom of the slave Quock Walker, his argument was accepted and repeated by the Court in a decision that was fundamental to the ending of slavery in Massachusetts. In 1835 the same Court, in the case of Commonwealth *v.* Aves—better known as the case of the Slave Girl Med—decided that even a slave brought by his master from a slave state into Massachusetts had the right to his freedom under Massachusetts and Natural Law.[54] Thinking of the slaves of the *Creole* with this legal tradition in mind, Sumner was "inclined to believe—indeed I entertain scarcely any doubt—that they became *freemen,* when taken, by the voluntary action of their owners, beyond the jurisdiction of the slave-states. Slavery is not a National Institution; nor is it one recognized by the Law of nations. It is peculiar to certain states." A fugitive slave going to another American state would not have the same benefit, conceded Sumner, because of the fugitive slave clause of the Constitution. There was, however, no such clause in the law of nations. Thus Webster had no legal right to demand the recall of the *Creole* slaves. "The courtier of Queen Elizabeth said that the air of England was too pure for a slave to breathe in. I will say, that the air of the ocean is too pure for slavery. There is the principle of manumission in its strong breezes—at least where the slave is carried there by the voluntary act of his owner. If I am correct in this view, these slaves were remitted to their natural rights. They were justified in overthrowing by force, (not *mutinous,* or *murderous,* because justifiable) any power which deprived them of their liberty. In doing what they did, therefore, they have not been guilty of any crime [. . .]."[55]

Sumner did not go so far as the most radical antislavery constitutionalists, who argued that if slavery were contrary to Natural Law then any positive law establishing it was by definition void. To enforce such a principle would have meant violating the so-called federal consensus that Sumner along with most Americans considered a fundamental part of the Union. The several American states could not interfere with each other's municipal laws any more than could separate nations. But, just as Sumner had laid his stress in the *Creole* case on the fact that, though England could not interfere with our laws, she was under no obligation to assist or support foreign laws she considered immoral, so he was anxious to see American laws of slavery remain unassisted and unsupported by the free states, with the hope that ultimately they could not survive in such an atmosphere of "moral blockade."[56]

Sumner felt a deepening commitment to the cause of antislavery, but at the same moment he felt his hopes that such a cause could give his legal practice deeper meaning were crumbling beneath him. He did not, of course, have the luxury of choosing only those cases that he found morally or intellectually stirring, and such cases remained few and far between. As the gap widened between those pursuits that engaged his mind and conscience on the one hand and the day-to-day realities of his practice on the other, Sumner found it harder to concentrate on the details of writs and petty disputes. Even more of his time now than in the 'thirties went into writing articles or teaching at the Law School, or promoting American Neoclassical sculpture, or discussing art and literature and foreign politics, and reminiscing about Europe with friends and colleagues and even surprised clients. Gradually the clients fell away. Then in 1842 the long-struggling *Jurist* published its last issue, its philosophical tone likewise losing readers. Sumner had more than enough other uses for the time this gave him, but he could not afford to lose the income, small as it was. An unpromising-sounding appointment as Standing Commissioner in Bankruptcy did not help. Finally a desperate Sumner was driven to do what he had always sworn he would never do. Heir to his father's pride as well as his disillusioning political experience, Sumner had grown up with a horror of office-seekers. But when in early 1843 his friend Richard Peters was ready to step down as Supreme Court Reporter, Sumner ventured to write to Story:

> If there is a vacancy, I hesitate about making a personal application for the office, much as I value it. I dislike the whole *principle* & *practice* of *office seeking* so thoroughly that I am willing to sacrifice to something of my chances; rather than enroll myself in that "army offensive" which is perpetually saying "Give,["] "give"!
>
> Still I must confess that the office would be a great boon to me. I feel myself competent to its duties, I should be pleased with the labor, with the relation to the bench & bar, & with the opportunities it might open of other professional employment.[57]

The appointment fell prey to politics. The Democratic Taney Court had no intention of replacing one friend of conservative Joseph Story, with his now old-fashioned Natural Law orientation, with another. While Story was sick in bed they chose their own candidate. And so "the demon of party has entered the sacred precincts," Sumner wrote sadly to Richard Peters, "where Marshall once presided with such serenity & justice." Sumner sympathized with Story's discouragement about the future of the Court and his increasingly frequent talk of retirement, while mourning his own personal loss. "The office would have given me $3000 for two months' work, which I should do with pleasure; besides an opportunity of taking business in the highest court of the country." In the end, it was probably Sumner's mother who paid off his remaining European debts out of the family money. Sumner's private hopes for his own future, his dreams of founding his own family, seemed more remote than ever. "Thus, this vision passes away, & I mingle again in the rude realities of life."[58]

If Sumner's hope that he could enrich his practice with cultural and humanitarian pursuits was deceived, so now was his initial faith in the appeal of those pursuits, and especially of antislavery, to the circle of his colleagues and friends. Coming from his father's family, having close ties to antislavery thinkers, surrounded by people who professed their hatred of the South's peculiar institution, Sumner had been able to take a fundamental predisposition in favor of antislavery for granted. What was so natural for him seemed to be echoed in the professions of Boston's reigning Unitarianism, in the city's traditional concern for social improvement, in the universally-mouthed tenets of Moral Philosophy, in the legal profession's traditional belief in the principles of Natural Law. And if the most respectable and influential men of the community expressed such benevolent interest, then it seemed natural that a wiser public policy and better education would soon spread their influence. "The question of slavery is getting to be the absorbing one among us, & growing out of that is that other one of the *Union*," Sumner reported hopefully to his brother George in the spring of 1842. "People now talk about the value of the Union, & the North has begun to return the taunts of the South."[59]

Sumner saw hope in the wide support he received for his articles on the right of search and in the private assurances he received from lawyers of their agreement with him about the effect of the Somerset case on the status of the *Creole* slaves. He saw hope in Channing's increasing outspokenness, despite the obstacles it met with. He saw hope in the increasing strength of the antislavery movement. Why should he not take hope, too, when in January 1842 Joseph Story, speaking for the Supreme Court, gave his decision in the case of Prigg *v.* Pennsylvania. It is true that, in this case of a slave woman who escaped from Maryland into Pennsylvania to save her children from bondage, Story found, following the fugitive slave clause of the Constitution, that the Fugitive Slave Law of 1793 was constitutional and that Pennsylvania's personal liberty laws designed to impede its functioning were not. But he also decided that, though state officials ought to assist in the enforcement of the federal law, the federal government had no right to force them to. He thus gave antislavery activists throughout the North a loophole through which to pass more carefully crafted personal liberty laws.[60]

Some of Sumner's more radical antislavery friends, like Wendell Phillips, were distrustful of Story and thought that, if he had been sincerely opposed to slavery, he would have ruled the Fugitive Slave Law unconstitutional. But Sumner had Story's antislavery interest direct from his own testimony. When Story returned to Boston after the session he told Sumner, "with exulting voice," that this decision was a "triumph of Freedom." This was in part because, as Sumner defended it, "it established by the authority of the Sup. Ct. of the U.S. 'the locality of Slavery,' so that it could not exist any where except where sustained by state laws, & in the case of fugitive slaves." Story added that his decision made clear that "by the law of nations, we cannot require the surrender of *fugitives,* thus throwing the weight of our highest tribunal upon that of the English House of Lords."[61]

Why should Sumner doubt the sincerity of such a close and revered friend, a friend who had emphasized the fundamental role of morality every day in his teaching and his life. He could not know that in the same moment that he handed down the Prigg decision, in correspondence with John Berrien of Georgia, Chairman of the Senate Judiciary Committee, Story was searching for ways to stop the antislavery evasions of the federal Fugitive Slave Law, or that in a private letter Story suggested the appointment of special commissioners with powers to deliver up slaves, as would be legislated in the new Fugitive Slave Law of 1850: "In conversing with several of my Brethren of the Supreme Court, we all thought that it would be a great improvement, & would tend much to facilitate the recapture of Slaves, if Commissioners of the Circuit Court were clothed with like powers. This might be done without creating the slightest sensation in Congress, if the provision were made general."[62] It would be a decade yet before Sumner—then obliged as Senator to speak publicly about the Prigg decision—was forced to accept fully the degree to which Story's personal disapproval of slavery had been overtaken in his mind by his fear of the disorder threatened by abolitionism.[63]

Sumner's ability to take for granted that the leaders of Boston society—men whom he admired and whom he often considered friends—would not only advocate the principles of the Enlightenment and of Moral Philosophy but act in accordance with them, however, received a first and painful shock from a conversation he had one evening in the late autumn of 1843 with his old professor George Ticknor. Neither man recorded what was said. Perhaps Sumner revealed his antislavery sympathies. He was not in the habit of pushing them where they were not solicited, but his feelings on the subject and Ticknor's were so different that an airing could have become a clash. It is more likely that Ticknor said something against another person—very possibly the recently departed Channing, barred not long before his death from Ticknor's home in punishment for his outspokenness on slavery. Sumner's admiration for Channing would have been galled at Ticknor's interference; nor would the loyal Sumner have allowed a harsh word against any friend to pass in silence.[64]

Whatever was said precisely, Sumner for the first time plainly saw that Ticknor's talk of social conscience and of cultivating a moral society boiled down to preserving the status quo, and that vigorously. Sumner's own conviction of the need for reform and his acute sense of social duty, nurtured partly by Ticknor's own college lectures on the decadence of those societies that forgot such duties, were incensed. The young man who had made a philosophy of always seeing the best in people now privately named Ticknor for what he was: "He is the impersonation of *refined selfishness*. [. . .] He sits in his rich library & laps himself in care & indulgence, *doing* nothing himself, treating unkindly the works of those who *do*, looking down upon all, himself having no claim to be regarded, except as a man of *promises*—never, in a life no longer short, redeemed."[65]

It was the first time that Sumner had ever felt real bitterness against an individual. All his life Sumner had learned—in great part from his Harvard professors—that one should not only strive for the improvement of the intellect and the conscience, but use those faculties to do one's duty to the larger society, that good thoughts were not enough but must be followed by deeds. His own sense of guilt at not doing enough was shocked at Ticknor's aggressive idleness. With discouragement and unhappiness overwhelming him from every direction, Sumner now for a time turned away from that society that had once provided him not only amusement but consolation.

Sumner's dream of professional and social satisfaction had abruptly come to an end at the moment when he could perhaps least bear it. It seemed to him that his life was all emptiness and isolation. Hancock Street was no refuge, and Sumner tried to flee it as much as possible. When he had returned to Boston, he had returned to the fatherless house on the northern slope of Beacon Hill. His mother welcomed him fervently and rearranged the house to accommodate her eldest and professional son. To him she ceded the whole second floor for his study, library, and chamber. He did his best to help his mother adjust to running the household and providing for the children's future on her own. His efforts to direct the education of young Horace, however, led only to deep disillusionment. Money was another constant worry as Mrs. Sumner agonized over how best to invest the money her husband had left her that it might support the family, and over the fear of losing it. It hurt Sumner to see his mother in such a state: "She is very anxious, & pains me much by her constant reference to her [investment] troubles." Her eldest sons gave their advice freely, though they did not always agree about money—Charles, uncomfortable with it, always gave conservative advice, while Albert, who had already saved enough from his captainship to retire with his new wife, was inclined to be more adventurous. Mrs. Sumner was well equipped for her new responsibilities. She and her husband had always shared important decisions, and he had confidently left the care of household expenditures to her. Her children respected that authority, and, no matter how old or independent they grew, they none of them ever questioned her right to make all final decisions for the household. But this was one more reason why Sumner never felt truly at home on Hancock Street. The house was too full of gloomy memories, and he felt too much the need for a home and family of his own. As long as he lived at 20 Hancock Street he never failed to refer to it as "my Mother's house."[66]

As he always would, Sumner sought comfort with his friends, the best of whom were like true family to him. Finally reunited, Sumner, Hillard, Felton, Longfellow, and Cleveland spent every free moment together at each other's houses and offices or in the restaurants of Boston, washing down good food and Italian wine or French champagne with bumpers of lively talk about art, literature, history, Europe and America, all liberally spiced with jesting and laughter. Sober Cleveland and Hillard often turned the talk to literary projects and dreams of fame. Soft-spoken Longfellow, looked to by all as a peacemaker, his gentle manner set off by his modish dress and slightly mischievous look, was the pivot around whom the various concerns and personalities of the group turned. Sumner, fresh from Europe, had a million stories with which to fascinate his friends, and Felton a million jokes at which no one laughed more warmly or heartily than Sumner himself.[67]

There were quiet times, too, spent reading or discussing together by the fireside. On a typical Sunday afternoon, Felton and Sumner were sure to be at Longfellow's. Felton would perhaps be reading an article on Greece. Sumner would stretch what Longfellow called "his majestic length" out on the sofa. Delighted at the latest author he was reading, he would break the silence with occasional enthusiastic exclamations—"What a *beautiful* writer Irving is!" Meanwhile Longfellow might catch up on the correspondence he usually disliked, in order to share the scene with a distant friend. Always among the Five of Clubs there was total comfort and confidence. They could handle each other's money or legal affairs, proofread and sharply criticize each other's books, without creating any feeling stronger than gratitude for having such dear and honest friends. They shared tragedy, too, when in 1843 the serious Cleveland, still clinging to his projected history of English literature, succumbed to the ill health that had long stalked him. The Club remained as warmhearted as ever, however, and soon invited Sumner's friend Samuel Gridley Howe to join them and bring their number back up to five. With these friends more than any one else, and especially with Longfellow and Howe, Sumner shared his hopes and dreams and disappointments.[68]

On the surface Sumner and Longfellow seemed an unlikely pair. Sumner was a good head taller than Longfellow, who, as the shortest member of the Club, hated his own name and was sometimes teasingly called "Longo" by his friends. Though Longfellow was four years older than Sumner, the poet's long romantic locks made him seem more modern, almost rakishly so, than the jurist who wore his thick hair conservatively short. From the moment Felton introduced them in 1835, however, they had felt an instant sympathy. It was with Longfellow particularly that Sumner talked over his planned tour of the Old World. The initial awe that Sumner had felt before his new friend, who had then just returned from his second trip to Europe, was by 1840 worn off with his own successful experience abroad, and the two were reunited in an intimacy that, through their whole lives, would never know the slightest cloud.[69]

Warm, affectionate, and loyal, Sumner and Longfellow both preferred to trust their fellow man even at the price of being sometimes cheated or hurt. Longfellow found it no easier to say "no" to his friends or those in need than did Sumner, and both balanced a belief that true friendship demanded frankness with a hatred of quarrels, though both could be downright stubborn when it came to a matter of conviction. Social and convivial, the two friends were also intensely private and let down their guard about the most personal matters only with each other and very few others. Longfellow once admitted that "with me—all deep impressions are silent ones. I like to live on, and enjoy them, without telling those around me that I do enjoy them." Sumner, too, kept family matters and his own personal feelings so well hidden from those who were not his intimates that they were often completely fooled—though unlike Longfellow, he did, privately, desire his friends' understanding of those feelings even when he would not admit to them.[70]

Even in their differences, Sumner and Longfellow complemented each other perfectly. A conscientious worker, Longfellow was nonetheless always conscious of battling an inner streak of lethargy and was amazed at Sumner's unflagging energy and capacity for work: "For my part," he admitted, "I cannot take in so much at once. It fatigues my brain and body." But he found Sumner's energy as inspiriting as Sumner found Longfellow's unhurried conversation and calm study a balm to his own mind after long hours at "the great grind-stone of the law." Like an Atticus to Sumner's Cicero, Longfellow hated public life to the point of refusing to speak at dinners and had no stomach for politics, yet loved to be informed and appreciated Sumner's always ready and accurate knowledge of current events, while Sumner, who craved bustle and activity, found refreshment in Longfellow's life of artistic and literary retirement, just as he had in Rome.[71]

With Longfellow Sumner could share all of his various interests. Longfellow, too, was the son of a Ciceronian lawyer—an acquaintance of Charles Pinckney Sumner's—and had grown up in a cultured if more comfortable and happier home. Sumner could talk freely of literature with Harvard's young Smith Professor of Languages and budding poet, and in after years, when Sumner tired of the unrelieved politicking and backbiting of Washington, he would return to Longfellow's library as to an oasis. From the first Sumner admired Longfellow's literary talent, while Longfellow marveled at his friend's "vast . . . knowledge." Together they discussed art, history, the sights and sounds and society of Europe, the "golden atmosphere" of Italy, in Longfellow's phrase, that "illuminated" both their lives, and especially books—from Dante to Gœthe and Victor Hugo— which they loved with an equal passion, Longfellow's quiet appreciation perfectly complementing Sumner's enthusiastic engagement.[72]

Sumner's deep concern for the rich development of American culture was likewise the intellectual passion of Longfellow's life. As a young professor, hardly in his twenties, at Bowdoin College, Longfellow had devoted himself to urging the creation of a great national literature that, while not ignoring its American origins, would be of that universal spirit "that speaks the same language unto all men [. . .]." The "true glory of a nation," he had written then, "consists not in the extent of its territory, the pomp of its forests, the majesty of its rivers [. . .] but in the extent of its mental power,—the majesty of its intellect,—the height and depth and purity of its moral nature. It consists not in what nature has given to the body, but in what nature and education have given to the mind."[73] Sumner could not have agreed more with the cultural idea or with the principles of Moral Philosophy which lay clearly behind it and which had influenced Longfellow as deeply as himself. Each, too, in his own way felt a similar humanitarian impulse that showed in their shared appreciation of the works of Jean Paul Richter. In this they were inspired by that same Moral Philosophy, and yet were already reaching beyond the Harvard and Bowdoin moralists' desire to promote a rich American literature more for the purpose of steadying a reckless democratic society than for encouraging social change. Longfellow loved Jean Paul for his "boundless love for all that is good in man and all that is beautiful in the world." "I like Jean Paul," agreed Sumner. "He had a soul; big, comprehensive, human as man [. . .]." Sumner could not have sympathized more deeply when Longfellow, struggling with his own desire for fame and his sense of duty in life, came to the conviction that our object should "be, not to build ourselves up, but to build up others, and leave our mark upon the age we live in, each according to the measure of his talent. To oppose error and vice, and make mankind more in love with truth and virtue—this is a far higher motive of action than mere literary ambition." No wonder that each considered the other "more like a brother than a friend."[74]

Sumner and Howe had a more volatile relationship but every bit as warm and loyal. Despite their shared future fame as reformers they were less alike than were Sumner and Longfellow, but Howe, the philanthropic teacher of the blind, spoke directly to Sumner's growing need for moral satisfaction in his life and his increasing engagement in social and humanitarian causes. Though intelligent and well educated, Howe never defined himself as an intellectual. Already at the Boston Latin School young Samuel, the son of a Jeffersonian ropemaker, had taken to defending himself with his fists in the heady days of the War of 1812, and he had not stopped fighting since, at Brown University where he was always in trouble, and then, after getting his degree from Harvard Medical School in 1824, in Greece where he took an active part in the struggle for independence. The closest Sumner had ever come to fighting in school was a lively match of chess, and the only time he had ever carried a gun in seriousness was in 1834 when a mob burned down the Ursuline convent in Charlestown and Sumner spent the night with other graduates patrolling Harvard Yard in case of reprisals. Even then the law student had considerably amused his comrades by speculating on the legality of their defensive action.[75]

Sumner and Howe had the same ability to fight when it came to a cause, however, and the same courage in the face of physical danger. It was, indeed, in the midst of a fight that they met. On 11 June 1837 a company of volunteer firemen—notorious for their hatred of Catholic immigrants and for causing violent disturbances—clashed with the members of an Irish funeral procession. Before the militia finally quelled the riot, groups of concerned citizens had rushed to the scene, including Robert Winthrop, Abbot Lawrence, and Josiah Quincy, Jr., as well as Sumner and Howe. Many commented on how alike were father and son, as Sheriff Sumner coolly read the riot act amid the tumult, while his son waded into the fray and started pulling people apart without thought of himself. When Sumner's uncommon height made him a target for some "heavy missile" it was Dr. Howe who came to his rescue, opening a lifelong friendship.[76]

When it came to internal fears, however, Sumner and Howe were opposites. Howe, standing up for himself from a boy and having acquired the experience of command in Greece at an early age, had grown very self-confident and was sometimes accused of taking himself too seriously, to the annoyance of those who disagreed with him. Even Sumner would chide him for being unable to relax and enjoy a vacation. Sumner, though anxious for a larger role in life, remained deeply unsure of himself, to his friend's great pain. Howe tried always to shore up Sumner's self-confidence—"I love you Sumner, & am only vexed with you because you will not love yourself a little more,"—while Sumner tried to impart a bit of caution to his impetuous friend—"in those words of Spencer—'be bold—be very bold; but be not too bold.'"[77]

They loved each other, however, for how much each loved his fellow man. And all their various interests in humanitarian causes and reform they shared with each other. "[Y]ou, you dog," Howe exclaimed to Sumner, thinking of how close they had become, "are *malgré* moi my *alter ego!*" When Howe on a later day missed Sumner at his office, he wrote: "I know not *where* you may be, or what you may be about, but I know what you are *not* about,—you are *not* seeking your own pleasure, or striving to advance your own interests: you are, I warrant me, on some errand of kindness,—some work for a friend or for the public." "I am very much attached to Howe," Sumner explained to Francis Lieber in the early days of their friendship: "He is the soul of disinterestedness. He has purged his character from all considerations of *self,* so far as mortal may do this; & his sympathies embrace all creatures. To this highest feature of goodness add intelligence & experience of no common order, all elevated & refined by a chivalrous sense of honor, & a mind without fear. I think of the words of the Persian poet, when

I meet Howe—'Oh God! have pity on the wicked. The good need it not; for in making them good, thou hast done enough.'"[78]

Sumner's own restless search for a way to give his life's work ethical meaning and his dissatisfaction with what he had done so far gave a peculiar urgency to his admiration for his friends' accomplishments. Sensitive to the duty of making such a contribution himself, he was temporarily paralyzed by the importance he placed upon it, and by his dread of disappointing the increased expectations that followed his successful trip to Europe. From these fears he shrank more than from any merely physical danger. In the 'thirties he had often lectured in Boston on legal subjects. Now he received frequent invitations to give broader talks before Lyceums, the Society for the Diffusion of Useful Knowledge—where he had often been a listener—and colleges like Bowdoin and Dartmouth desiring him to give their Phi Beta Kappa orations. Sumner refused every one. On one occasion, answering the publicist James T. Fields, he was particularly frank: "I have tried to bring myself to the conclusion, to accept the flattering invitation of the committee of the Mercantile Library Association, to deliver their next Anniversary Address; but, though deeply sensible to the honor which you confer upon me by your invitation, I cannot summon the confidence or courage necessary to the duty."[79]

Sumner's discouragement grew. To his brother George he confessed that his first year back home had been the "[leas]t productive year of my life. I feel that I have done very little—made no advance in any sort of knowledge, nor laid up any materials for happiness." It was entirely without envy, but not without a hint of shame that Sumner admired Howe's career, his humanitarian relief work in Greece, his present teaching of the blind and deaf at the Perkins Institute, his open-minded interest in the latest scientific and social theories, in movements from animal magnetism and phrenology to antislavery. "He is the true Christian hero, never tiring, never shrinking, where any duty is to be done, or any good to be accomplished." Nor did Sumner underestimate Longfellow's more quiet but no less serious contribution to shaping American culture and taste. "I am a lover of books, & of the scholar's life," Sumner wrote in defense of his friend. "To me the learned man, who adds the grace of a blameless life, is more truly respectable than the man of checks & bills of exchange. [. . .] It may be given to him, to strengthen some of his fellow mortals in the love of knowledge, in devotion to truth, perhaps, to revive the sad; & encourage the wavering. Our dear friend Longfellow has done this [. . .]." Sumner was proud of Longfellow's more reform-minded poems—his peace-loving *Armory at Springfield,* which grew out of a trip made with Sumner and which corresponded to Sumner's own efforts on that occasion to persuade the armory's guardian of the evils of war, his *Poems on Slavery* dedicated to Channing but suggested and urged by Sumner. "In truth," he admitted, "I envy Longfellow the good he has done."[80]

Sumner shared with Longfellow and Howe another deeply personal and painful struggle that cemented their friendship in truest sympathy. When Sumner returned from Europe all three were unmarried. Longfellow had lost his too delicate young wife—a tragedy for which he blamed himself—while they were in Europe in 1835. Howe had lamented as far back as 1831 that, since he was still unmarried at thirty, "he would die a bachelor." Long before turning thirty, Sumner had been tormented by the same fear. Even the pleasures of Europe had not been sufficient to quell this suspicion entirely. Pelted with news of betrothals and marriages back home, Sumner sometimes joked about becoming "a curiosity, a very candidate for the New England museum, to be put by the side of stuffed fishes & alligators." But, after attending a wedding in London, he confessed to Sarah Cleveland: "I feel myself hardening into a relentless bachelor, & shall mope about the firesides of my friends, without claiming one of my own." He tried to comfort himself that remaining a bachelor through his twenties unlike Felton, for whom he sometimes said he felt sorry on that account, had made possible his Old World tour and all the future benefits that he hoped it would lead to. As he once advised George: "Keep clear of love & matrimony. You can do better hereafter than [now]." But the greatest benefit he looked for from his European experience was "what is called *settlement in life.*"[81]

When Sumner returned to his friends in Boston, he and Longfellow and Howe were the only specimens left of their species. With each other they shared the pleasures and pains of the bachelor's search for a wife and those times when loneliness becomes a crushing burden. At first, bolstered by the high spirits and taste of self-confidence Europe had given him, Sumner felt greater hope in the future than he ever had before. He submitted with good grace to the inevitable encouragement, advice, and joking from all quarters—even his dearest friends—about his unnatural state. To while away their long bachelor hours, he and Howe would "drive fast & hard, & talk, talk, looking at the blossoms in the fields, or those fairer still in the streets." For the first time, Sumner even permitted himself to take part in that most basic of all social activities in a society that valued love and marriage and family—he flirted.[82]

Sumner's letters were full of the charms of the many "fair ladys" he met and chatted with in Boston, New York, and Philadelphia parlors, of the dreams shared with many bachelors of the beauty of the Misses Appleton, Wadsworth, and Livingston in Boston, and especially of the daughters of the New York banker Samuel Ward, dubbed the "Three Graces of Bond St." by "the lively Cornelius" Felton. To these last, all the members of the Club—including the married ones—swore undying admiration, and Sumner hinted playfully to Lieber that "my visits are so frequent to N. York as justly to awaken suspicion." His friends were never quite sure, however, which of the Ward sisters he liked best. Though he would have indignantly rejected the suggestion, he did not seem truly to warm to the sharp-witted and sometimes sharp-tongued Julia, but he alternately sang the praises of Louisa's "loveliness & natural grace" and rhapsodized about the "gentle, simple, sweet confiding," youngest sister—"Annie is my delight," he once proclaimed.[83]

More serious than his visits to New York, however, were the repeated weekends Sumner spent at Howe's and especially at Longfellow's where "*we* have mused & mourned so often together" as hope faded. "It is a dreary world to travel in alone," he lamented.[84] No personal dream meant more to him than finding the right girl and sharing with her his work and ideas, his love of books and art, and the happiness he longed for. Amidst all the playful flirting of his first years back home he had tried to find her. He was charmed and saddened by every happy couple he knew. He was delighted by what he heard of Mrs. Lieber, whom he had never met, "because she loves her husband so well. Ah! that is the wife's high function—to be his solace & strength & to give him the pride & pleasure of being *her protector.*" He particularly admired Mrs. Greenleaf, who "knows all [her husband's] labors in his profession—& has been over *all his* work *on Evidence*—a heavy 8vo vol. of 650 pages. She thinks his work the *best book ever* written; & my review of it in the Jurist the best review ever written. Give me such a wife; & I'll renounce tomorrow what Cecil calls *single-cursedness.*" When Lieber repeatedly bemoaned his "seclusion" in South Carolina, Sumner reminded him of the difference between a shared seclusion and being alone—"Ah! Lieber, be happy!"[85]

Yet Sumner could not bring himself to take the step from paying court to other men's wives to courting marriageable girls. "It is to those, who belong to others, that I bow," he half joked to Longfellow. He wanted a wife to bring him the supportive affection that his self-doubt craved at the same time that that self-doubt could not bear the danger of revealing itself to another. Nor could he face the responsibility of having to make someone else happy. His friends did not at first fully appreciate his dilemma. In the summer of 1840, in the first enthusiasm of his return, he admitted to his fellow Club members his interest in the beautiful Elizabeth Wadsworth, the daughter of a landowner from Geneseo, New York, who was visiting Boston, only to have them poke merciless fun at him when he let her get away at the end of the summer without ever finding the courage to speak to her. His flirting with the Ward sisters in New York was not so serious. When Felton called Howe "a great blockhead" for declaring his own coolness toward them, Sumner countered: "I am not sure that he is not a very wise man." When the very young Annie Ward, mistaking Sumner's playful attentions, got up her own courage and hopefully sent him a present for his thirty-second birthday, she unwittingly frightened him off altogether, and his once frequent visits to New York ceased.[86]

In his increasing loneliness, Sumner relied more and more heavily on his friends. His tie with Longfellow, most particularly, was forged in their shared unhappiness. Longfellow, too, was suffering the pain of not being able to win the girl of his dreams, except that in his case the girl was very real. He had fallen deeply in love with the beautiful and accomplished Fanny Appleton as far back as 1836, when he had met her in Switzerland. But he had frightened her off with his too precipitate declaration of love, followed by the publication of a thinly veiled account of his feelings in his first novel *Hyperion.* Longfellow remained true to his "dark ladye" through all the years that followed, but often without the hope of ever even speaking with her again. Only his closest friends knew why his health suffered so.[87]

At first Sumner encouraged his friend to give up a hopeless suit. "I cannot bear to see you keep your heart so long in *suspense,*" he had written from Italy; "not to say more than that. I say, then, win her or abandon her." And he added, hinting at the pain his own self-doubt so deeply feared: "I would never be—'*il male amato amante.*'" All the more so because Sumner—not alone in this—was a little afraid of the elegant and dignified Fanny Appleton who, though all "sweetness & sensibility," seemed too full of "that stateliness which bars approach & those gleams, which make you shiver, while you admire their brightness."[88]

On his return, however, Sumner stood solidly by his friend. He had material help to offer in the shape of his cousin Harriet who, as Fanny's new stepmother, could act as go-between, and he offered unlimited sympathy on those constant weekends he spent at Longfellow's rooms in Cambridge, reading, talking, and commiserating—sympathy that was fully and understandingly returned. When Longfellow was particularly depressed, Sumner would take him on a trip. During the Christmas vacation of 1840 Sumner took him to Philadelphia for society and flirting to take both their minds off more serious troubles, and in 1842 the whole Club pitched in to make all the arrangements for a trip to a German spa for Longfellow, whose health had then reached bottom. When Longfellow left, Sumner wrote a parting word from his heart: "We are all sad at yr going; but I am more sad than the rest; for I lose more than they do. I am desolate. It was to me a source of pleasure & strength untold, to see you, &, when I did not see you, to feel that you were near, with yr swift sympathy & kindly words. I must try to go alone; hard necessity in this rude world of ours! For our souls always in this life need support, & gentle beckonings, as the little child when first trying to move away from its mother's knees.— God bless you! my dearest friend, from my heart of hearts! You know not the depth of my gratitude to you. My eyes overflow as I now trace these lines. May you clutch the treasure of health; but, above all, may you be happy!" Later from Marienberg, Longfellow wrote Sumner: "Begging your pardon for the insult, I do not believe anyone *can* be perfectly well, who has a brain and a heart. *You* will not be well long, and I consider Corny an invalid, though he is not aware of it."[89]

Hope died in 1843. That was the year Sumner's last two bachelor friends married. Howe succumbed in February to the talented and intellectual Julia Ward, and in July Longfellow finally won his long-sought Fanny Appleton. Sumner at first feared that he had lost his old intimacy with his dearest friends, and on Longfellow's wedding day he mourned: "I am all *alone—alone.*" That fear was groundless. Instead he gained new friends, especially in Fanny Longfellow, who became a dear friend in her own right as well as a close correspondent about literature and politics. She proved the justness of his original judgment of her "sweetness & sensibility," though not of her daunting "stateliness," when, at the first dinner he took at their house after the wedding, she gave him his "ancient seat" at the head of the table opposite Longfellow while she, the new lady of the house, "sat at the side"—a gesture that deeply touched Sumner.[90]

If he had not lost his friends, however, Sumner had lost whatever illusions he might still have harbored about his own future. He knew in his heart of hearts that he would never marry. His self-doubt hardly gave him a chance to make more than a superficial acquaintance with any marriageable girl. It would be years before Sumner even hinted at another reason, but that same winter of 1843 had also undone his hopes of professional success. His practice was floundering, and the last of his efforts to find other sources of income had just been thwarted by the politics of the Supreme Court. He did not feel he had the right to marry. But the most painful reason to him was that, despite all his social ties and flirting, he had simply never met the right girl. "My solitude & desolation become more pronounced," he confided to Howe in the midst of the weddings of 1843. As for the rumors Howe had heard of his interest in someone: "Never in my life have I been less in love than at this moment. You are much mistaken. *I am not in love.* My heart does not flutter at the mention of a single name. It is *tabula rasa,* on which any name may be scrawled." In a candid moment a year earlier Sumner had written despairingly to Longfellow: "But my dreams are over. No breath stirs in the chambers of my heart. All there is dark & stifled. I live on from day to day. [. . .] Would that Providence wld send me [a loving] wife. Full & overflowing as her woman's love might be, mine should be greater. [. . .] When will these visions, Iris-colored, come to pass, & this weary spirit be at peace?"[91]

There was pain even worse than this. There had been one point of light left to Sumner in the shape of his sister Mary. Hancock Street did not afford much joy; Horace had deeply disappointed him, and bright, cheerful Julia was still too little to be a companion. But there was no one to whom Sumner was closer, nor in whom he took so much pride or felt so much hope as Mary. Mary had blossomed into the most beautiful of the Sumner girls—a softer, feminine version of Charles himself, friends all agreed. Charles described her features as "regular & classical—I have often thought that she resembled the heads of Minerva, but she was truly feminine in her expression & manner." It was her intelligence that most attracted him, however, that had first singled her out in his affections even as a little girl when she would immediately start to cry when any of her unending questions went unanswered. Grown up, she now matched the qualities of her beauty and her mind with an even-tempered sweetness. Charles took no greater pride than in being her constant escort, to balls and concerts, out riding, and in society. The hopes he had had of Horace's being able to enter the best society and be received as an equal were realized in Mary. He introduced her to all his numerous friends, and soon she was a friend in her own right of all the Five of Clubs, of the intellectually demanding Francis Lieber and his charming wife Matilda, of the antislavery lawyer John Jay, of the historian William Hickling Prescott to whom Sumner had now become very close, of Prescott's friend Angel Calderón de la Barca, the former Spanish minister to the United States, and his Bostonian wife Fanny. Always Charles took the pleasure and pride of a brother, of a dear friend, almost of a father in Mary's development and in the rich future he saw ahead for her.[92]

But now, in 1843, Mary, his darling sister Mary, was dying. She had been ill already the year before. Occasionally on a particularly mild winter's day Charles and she would still go riding together, but her doctor denied her further society, directing that she stay "at home *evngs*"—"which I regret very much," Sumner wrote to Lieber. It was during the following winter that it became clear she was suffering from that same consumption that had carried off her eldest sister ten years earlier. "Why this should have fallen upon her is inexplicable," Charles lamented on his own birthday. "She enjoys life; I do not. Why was not I chosen?" As she withdrew from general society, so did her brother, staying at home so often to keep her company and to avoid having to pretend to be cheerful, that friends wondered what had become of him.[93]

For two long years Charles watched her grow slowly paler and thinner and more fragile, unable to deceive himself that there was any hope, in letter after letter helplessly reporting her decline to their friends. "My dear sister Mary is fading," he confided to Howe in the spring of 1844.

> The last two months have made a visible impression on her strength & countenance. A short walk fatigues her, & her cheeks have lost their freshness & fullness. She enjoys life, & I often wish that I could pour into her veins the redundant health which has been wasted on one, who is ungrateful for the blessings he enjoys. She left town yesterday with my mother for Springfield, that she may avoid these unkindly airs, & enjoy the blossoms of spring, which, I fear, she will never see pass into the fruits of autumn. She is gay, & does not know that a stern hand is laid upon her, which neither care, nor affection can

remove. As she talked to me of her plans for the summer, the tears would come to my eyes, &, in the solitude of my chamber, I wept like a child—to think that so much beauty of character & of person, so much truth & goodness, so much grace & culture were to pass away—as a wreath of vapour, rising heavenward dissolves itself into thin air.[94]

He was right. She would pass away with the autumn leaves.

By the start of 1844 every single hope that Sumner had brought home with him from Europe had been crushed. The pleasures of society had been tarnished by unkindness and stifled by unhappiness; his brother had disappointed him; his sister was slipping away; his own dreams of success and happiness had crumbled around him. For a time he was so depressed that he could not even work. Sumner was pursued by the thought that perhaps his father had been right after all, that the trip to Europe had been a mistake and that he had thrown away his own future. Faced with too much pain, he finally threw himself back into his work, desperate not to give in to this possibility, not to give in to these losses and disappointments without one final effort.[95]

In February Little and Brown, then the premier legal publishers, asked Sumner to edit their new edition of the *Equity Reports* of Francis Vesey, Jr. It was not intellectually stimulating work, consisting mainly in explaining references, updating facts, and writing endless biographical sketches of all the legal figures named in a work that would extend to some twenty volumes— and that the publishers expected at the rate of one volume every two weeks. There were two reasons why Sumner could not reject the offer—it was his last hope of proving that he could make an important and remunerative contribution to his field, of proving to himself that he could have a normal and happy life, and the friend who had originally been contracted for the work had fallen ill and asked Sumner's help. Hoping against hope that it would lead to something, but uneasy from the outset, Sumner began work in April "& already [I] begin to tremble under the burthen. There are 57 printers whose *devilish* maws are to be kept filled."[96]

The strain was too much. Feverish work took the place of all society and nearly all sleep. Then everything began to go wrong. A series of letters attacking some of his recent articles for being less than well written or for being too harsh hurt him, and he began uncharacteristically to quarrel with friends. When, in desperation, he asked Little and Brown for a delay in the printing of Vesey, they turned him down in a letter chiding him for his apparent lack of responsibility after they had tried so hard to secure his services. At the same moment as this correspondence, Felton sent Sumner a series of well-meaning but ill-timed and painfully lighthearted letters, urging him to turn his thoughts to matrimony before it was too late and he found himself "a solitary monument, in the deserts of life, like one of those stony Sphinxes, in the wastes of Egypt, buried all but the *head* [. . .] staring out upon the appalling loneliness with deadened eyes [. . .]."⁹⁷

In July Sumner fell ill. For a month he was confined to his bed, prey to a high fever, a raging pulse, and bouts of delirium. His friends cheered him at his bedside while everywhere else it was said that he had succumbed to the same consumption that was carrying away his sister. Longfellow alone did not give up hope. It was not until August that Sumner began slowly to recover. To Howe— then just returning from his honeymoon—Sumner confessed with a particular deliberateness that he could not "find it in my bosom" to feel any "gratitude that my disease was arrested." "If I had been called away it would have been with the regret that I never had enjoyed the choicest experience of life—that no lips responsive to my own had ever said to me—'I love you.' But my life has had too many shadows. My childhood & youth passed in unhappiness, such as I pray may not be the lot of others. From earliest boyhood I have been laborious beyond the example of any I know. You have not seen me in this mood. During our special intimacy I have been blasted by another unhappiness, which unmanned me, & took from me all interest in labor. As this passed away, & the genius of labor again acquired his influence, then comes this illness, which strikes at my life. Why was I spared? For me there is no future, either of usefulness or happiness."⁹⁸

It was this question that Sumner kept asking himself in the long weeks that followed. When, on the first day that he had felt "within me the instincts of recovery" the doctor had decided to tell him that his "case was incurable, &, that, if I should live, I never should be able to do anything," Sumner replied "that I did not shrink from the idea of death; but to pass through life doing nothing— performing no duty—perhaps 'a driveller & a shew'—this was more than I could bear."⁹⁹

There was a deeper dilemma that he confided to no one. During the enforced rest of his recovery—first in his chamber in Boston, and then in the gracious summer home of his dear friends the Appletons, surrounded by the green hills and lush forests of Berkshire County—Sumner carefully pondered the lessons of the last few years. He had been chasing a dream of success and happiness that meant everything to him, but that he had known for some time he was not likely to realize. He had put first his efforts to achieve success in a profession that afforded him neither pleasure nor satisfaction, in the hope of winning the material reward necessary to a life of domestic happiness that continually eluded him, while he had kept in the background the causes that spoke to his conscience and his sense of usefulness in part because he knew that to follow them would mean, by their interference with his professional future, the end of his chances for personal happiness. The moral philosophers had taught that obedience to one's conscience and the performance of one's duty were essentially synonymous, and that they would lead to happiness. To the degree that duty meant the responsible practice of one's profession and ordinary civic obligations, Sumner had found his duty and his conscience to be hopelessly at odds, while he had learned that his higher, conscientious duty would lead only to self-abnegation. Forced to face these facts by his illness, Sumner made a silent but firm decision. As soon as he regained his strength he would all but abandon his law practice, keeping it only to provide his daily bread—and with it, and its potential income, give up not only the hope but the possibility of marriage and a normal life. Instead he would devote himself fully to those causes of social reform that he had long studied and cared about and that spoke to his higher sense of duty. He would give up his own future for the future of others.

PART II

"Be Not Atticus"

V

THE TRUE GRANDEUR OF CIVILIZATION

"TO EACH GENERATION is committed its peculiar task; nor does the heart, which responds to the call of duty, find rest except in the world to come. Be ours, then, the task which, in the order of Providence, has been cast upon us!"[1] Thus Charles Sumner exhorted his fellow citizens on Independence Day in 1845. He spoke as the chosen orator of Boston's city authorities in the traditional celebration inherited from Revolutionary times, but for Sumner the occasion meant also the start of a new career. By both the act of the oration and its content, Sumner proclaimed his answer to the question that had long haunted him of his own personal duty in life. The conflict that he had lived for over a decade between his desire for a successful, happy personal life and his need to satisfy the demands of his conscience, to discover his duty and the means of doing good to others, had led to nothing but the quarrels, depression, and illness that were the outward signs of his turbulence of spirit. In the enforced quiet of his recuperation, he had made the firm and irrevocable decision to give over that law practice which had lost moral significance for him, and instead to dedicate his full energy to those causes of reform that had long claimed his attention. This, he had concluded, was his duty as a citizen and as a human being with a conscience.

The humanitarian and cosmopolitan ideals of the Enlightenment that had shaped his intellectual coming of age gave Sumner a clear vision of the ends at which those reforms should aim, of the kind of civilization for which the United States should and could strive. He knew that not all the particular reforms he would embrace were popular, and that the evangelical religion or the spirit of social radicalism that inspired many outspoken reformers did not recommend their aims to the conservative leaders of educated and propertied society. The vision of a true civilization that animated him, however, and that he had learned from the philosophical principles of the American Revolution and Moral Philosophy was all but universally shared in the intellectual world of New England and in the social circles that had been educated in places like the Boston Latin School and Harvard. Surely, Sumner believed, encouraging the powerful leaders of Boston society to turn their private humanitarian sensibilities into public action was simply a matter of awakening that conscience that they had all been taught to cherish.

Sumner did not yet know how difficult that task would be. Nor was he yet sure in what way he should best work for these ends. He had determined to follow the path of duty without yet seeing where it would lead him, knowing only that he had begun a new life with no possibility of return. When, many years later, he came to collect his own writings as the history of his contribution to the work of building American culture, he ignored everything he had done before that day and began his story with the Fourth of July oration.

The choice of the Fourth of July oration as his starting point was partly symbolic. Sumner did not wait till the summer of 1845 to act on his resolution. In October 1844, filled with the vigor of renewed health and with grief at the loss of his sister Mary, he threw himself as never before into the struggle to build a civilized American society and culture. His interest in education reform was old, impressed upon him by his father and his own experience in youth. Since his return from Europe he had not only helped direct his siblings' education, but had privately encouraged the efforts of his old Number Four colleague Horace Mann—now Secretary of Education for the Commonwealth—to strengthen the public schools. Sumner had enthusiastically cheered Mann's much criticized use of his 1842 Fourth of July oration to urge the issue upon the public mind. By the fall of 1844 Mann and his long-time ally, Samuel Gridley Howe were embroiled in a heated controversy with Boston's pedagogues about his proposed plan. To the degree that Mann's tendency toward stinging attacks had lent bitterness to the debate, Sumner cautioned Howe: "To *you* & to *Mann,* I should say, *moderation.*" Remembering his own comparison of American and European schools, however, Sumner was much impressed by Mann's efforts to improve American education with Prussian teaching and testing techniques.[2]

Before 1844, despite his interest, Sumner had taken no public action himself. But that fall, Mann and Howe needed to win a majority of seats on the Boston School Committee to get Mann's controversial plan implemented. This time Sumner agreed to run with them for the Committee. In the spirit of his own old Anti-Masonic understanding of politics, he even accepted the manœuvering necessary to secure his nomination despite opposition from East Boston, then a part of his ward. It was not so striking a departure as it seemed, however, from his long-declared hatred of office-seeking. The office carried no prestige and therefore no opprobrium, and Sumner's new sense of acting for a cause made it seem to him a duty. This did not save his pride from being wounded when his first bid for election met with failure—especially because the voters of East Boston turned out to be more worried about immigration than education, and rejected Sumner's cosmopolitan support of a European-minded system for his opponent's nativism.[3]

Sumner nevertheless continued his new public work on behalf of school reform. Perhaps remembering his discussion with Charlemagne Tower and their agreement that the best way to increase the number of well-qualified applicants to college was to improve the lower schools, he backed Mann's proposal to establish two model normal schools for the training of professional teachers. Sumner led the efforts to fund the plan, chairing the committee that requested financial backing from the General Court, and directing the drive for subscriptions from municipalities across the state. He put himself personally on the line when, by the spring of 1845, the sluggishness of subscriptions jeopardized the whole project. It was Sumner who, in his own name, advanced the $5,000 necessary to meet the state deadline. His faith in human nature would meet a painful test when, after he had paid the money, fulfillment of the pledges began to dry up out of apathy. Over the next several years he was forced to beg his wealthier colleagues to help him with a debt he could not possibly repay. His offer, however, saved the normal schools. He would never again risk so large a sum, but in these first few months of reform activity Sumner had shown how eager he was to give himself in every way he could to the success of the causes he espoused.[4]

Organizing fund raising with the state legislature and running for office entailed the one activity that Sumner had hitherto most shied away from in the cause of reform—speaking out before civic bodies and the public. His willingness to do so now showed even more clearly in the realm of prison discipline. Here again was an old interest, born of his work in the law and of reminiscences of his father's concerns about the sources of crime and the treatment of criminals. By 1845 Sumner had belonged to the prestigious Boston Prison Discipline Society for a decade. From the start he had been proud of the prominent experiments that had attracted European visitors to the United States, and he had followed with interest the intense debate that had been raging in both America and Europe between partisans of the so-called Auburn System, in which the inmates worked together but under ban of silence, and the Pennsylvania System, where the prisoners worked in their cells completely separated from each other while being permitted to see visitors from the outside.[5]

From the mid-1820's, before the Pennsylvania System had been fairly established, the Boston Prison Discipline Society under its secretary Louis Dwight had championed the Auburn System. Sumner's close discussions of the subject with such as Francis Lieber in this country and N. H. Julius and Tocqueville in Europe had gradually brought him to the conclusion that the European trend in favor of the Pennsylvania System represented the more humane direction. Together with Mann and Howe and Hillard, also involved in the question, he had come to believe that the Boston Prison Discipline Society was lending its prestige to the wrong side of the debate, and felt increasingly dissatisfied with the stubbornness and narrow-mindedness of Louis Dwight's refusal to consider seriously the claims of the Pennsylvania System.[6]

Still, beyond his own correspondence and private conversations with Dwight,

Sumner had taken no active part in the debate—not even when in 1842 Howe had tried officially to challenge Dwight's authority. Then in the late spring of 1845, as he was about to write his Fourth of July oration, Sumner stood up with Howe at the Society's annual meeting in the Park Street Church to give speeches calling for a review of the two rival systems. Challenging the long-accepted authority of the Reverend Louis Dwight, who was himself a respected member of Boston society, as well as of his treasurer, Samuel A. Eliot, former Mayor of Boston and father-in-law of George Ticknor, Sumner asked that the Society's position be referred for serious consideration to a committee, of which Sumner himself and Howe were members. Of this "bomb-shell" Sumner wrote to Lieber: "It is the first interference with [Dwight's] absolute sway that has occurred in the history of the Society." By December, with the proposed construction of a new prison in Boston spurring everyone on, the fight was in full swing. The coming year looked to be tumultuous and, Sumner hoped, more productive than any before. He was not fully prepared for the acrimony of the debate, but having come to a decision as to where his duty lay he was determined to see it through.[7]

If improved methods of education and a more humane treatment of society's wayward were important parts of the building of a higher civilization, so was patronage of the arts. Sumner had not forgotten his friend Thomas Crawford upon his return home from Europe. His success in getting the Boston Athenæum to acquire Crawford's statue *Orpheus,* and his organization of its 1843 showing of Crawford's works launched the sculptor's great career. It did not end Sumner's efforts on Crawford's behalf, however, nor on behalf of the promotion of Neoclassical sculpture to a national audience. Throughout 1845 and 1846 Sumner, with the help of Hillard and Amos A. Lawrence, the nephew of Abbott Lawrence, was writing to Judge Story, their congressman Robert Winthrop, and other prominent Bostonians in the nation's capital to obtain for Crawford a federal commission for an equestrian statue of Washington. Sumner would continue to urge Crawford's merits for bigger and bigger commissions until the sculptor's premature death in 1857.[8]

Sumner's desire to see the arts take root in America was fully shared by his native city. His ability to get for them the *Orpheus,* a fine original Neoclassical work, had caused the Athenæum as much pleasure and pride as Crawford, and when the institution set about designing itself a newer and larger home on Beacon Street, Sumner was named to the committee for determining its plan. Throughout the spring and summer of 1845, while worrying about the normal schools, addressing the Prison Discipline Society, and preparing his Fourth of July oration, Sumner was also going over piles of plans submitted in the contest for the new building. His exalted visions were satisfied with none of them, he wrote to Crawford. "In one I was pleased with the *façade;* in another, with the entrance hall and stairway; and in another with the arrangement of the rooms." His suggestion that "[p]erhaps a new plan might be compassed by adopting features from all," was more than playfulness.[9]

Sumner took the task very seriously, writing regularly to his brother George, who was now in Italy, for information on celebrated buildings there, and especially the measurements of the Bernini staircase at the Vatican. "They were stairs of such exquisite proportions, that you seemed to be borne aloft on wings," he remembered. All his life Sumner felt an especial love for grand stairways, and it was in its stairway that his influence would be most felt at the Athenæum. He pushed a reluctant committee to accept a majestic plan, an elegant foyer and regal stairs that devoted one fourth of the interior space to a celebration of the elevating passion for the acquisition of knowledge and culture. It would be known as the "Sumner staircase." This was a passion he wished the whole community to share in, as he explained to George while the building neared completion a few years later: "My desire is that it shall be made a public library, on condition that the city shall finish the building, & secure to it a permanent income for the purchase of books."[10]

How could a nation successfully build an elevated culture while still harboring evil institutions? Sumner did not want his young country to grow up rich and refined but selfish; he wanted her conscience to be as well developed as her intellect. In Sumner's eyes the events of 1844 thus seemed particularly ominous. The prospect of the annexation of Texas had excited many in the West and especially the South while disturbing Northerners since at least 1836, when Texans had declared their independence from an unwilling Mexico. The fact that most Texans were emigrants from the slaveholding South, who insisted upon maintaining their peculiar institution despite Mexico's attempt to discourage them by abolishing slavery in the 1820's, had done nothing to quiet fears on either side of the border. As Americans poured into the province, Mexicans worried about their expansive northern neighbor, while increasing numbers of Northerners in the United States were sure that a new state of Texas was the project of Southern slaveholders united for the purpose of extending slave territory and their own political power. Texas' ploy to encourage pro-annexation sentiment in the United States by flirting with antislavery England, and the simultaneous difficulties between America and England over control of the Oregon Territory compounded the divisiveness of the Texas issue within the United States as well as in her foreign relations. With Democratic candidate James Polk campaigning for the annexation of both Texas and Oregon, by force if necessary, the presidential election of 1844 made the issue urgent.[11]

Throughout that year the Whig party fought hard to prevent such an outcome. During the spring session conservative Massachusetts political leader Abbott Lawrence organized anti-Texas Whig caucuses. Charles Francis Adams and

Henry Wilson, among the future leaders of the antislavery Whigs, fought successfully in Massachusetts' General Court for the passage of anti-Texas resolutions, while aristocratic Robert C. Winthrop, representative of the conservative manufacturers, tried to do the same in Congress. Sumner, though hopelessly buried in papers for his edition of Vesey, could not help but anxiously watch the efforts of his fellow Whigs and friends. He railed against the "[f]olly, *dementia,* & vulgar weakness [that] now rule the country." Sumner was not opposed to expansion in theory—was more open to it than many Whigs, who insisted that Americans should strengthen their institutions in those areas already settled before acquiring more. He agreed with Whigs, however, that expansion without regard to improvement was a grave mistake. He thought wrongheaded the Democratic tendency—shared by his brother George—to seek territory merely for the "*material* interests of the country. It may be," he answered George, "that these are to be promoted by the accession of Texas; but I know that *right, justice,* & *sound morals* are overthrown by it." Individual motives for desiring Texas might vary, but Sumner was particularly disturbed by the strength of slaveholders' support for annexation. He could only deplore the stubbornness of President Tyler who seemed intent upon using popular "hatred of England" and "love of slavery" to promote his own "chances of a re-election." "If Tyler thinks of anything beyond himself [. . .], it is [. . .] the strengthening of the power of the slaveowners." Sumner saw little hope: "*We are doomed to have Texas,* as I fear."[12]

Sumner's prediction was confirmed in November. In a very close election Polk eked out a victory that he promptly called a mandate. The Whigs were shocked, and blamed the political antislavery movement when the results showed that the gains made by the Liberty party in New York had been enough to switch that state's vote from the Whigs to the Democrats and thereby determine the national outcome. Everyone understood the consequences of the election as to Texas. Pointing to the victorious Democratic banner flying over Washington's slave market, one Vermont Whig declared: "That flag means *Texas,* and *Texas* means *civil war,* before we have done with it."[13]

Popular indignation swept the North, spawning a host of anti-Texas meetings and committees, nowhere more than in Massachusetts. Despite their differences it seemed that the whole spectrum of anti-Texas opinion, from abolitionists to Boston cotton manufacturers, might join forces against the evil. The new year opened with Governor George N. Briggs's antislavery annual message and the passage of yet another set of anti-Texas resolutions in the General Court. Almost simultaneously in Washington, Rufus Choate expressed Massachusetts' disapproval in the Senate, and in the House Robert C. Winthrop gave perhaps a stronger speech than he realized condemning the proposed annexation on both constitutional and antislavery grounds.[14]

Now, in the fall of 1844, Sumner followed developments more closely than ever, and for the first time began personally to attend anti-Texas meetings. Over that Texas winter he also began to form friendships and working ties with the antislavery members of the Whig party who were becoming known as the "Young Whigs." This new generation of the party came from a variety of backgrounds. A number of them, like Stephen C. Phillips of Salem and Richard Henry Dana, Jr.—who would join just a little later,—as well as George Hillard, had been trained as lawyers, though Charles Francis Adams, like his father before him, never practiced his profession with any relish. John Gorham Palfrey, a former protégé of William Ellery Channing, was a Unitarian minister and sometime editor of the prestigious *North American Review* who, with legal help from Sumner and Hillard, had emancipated slaves inherited from his father, while Henry Wilson had come to politics from shoe manufacturing in his adopted town of Natick.[15]

The "Young Whigs" were not all younger in years than the major figures of the party's conservative leadership, but Wilson was the only one in business, and none of them was personally involved in the cotton manufacture that was so important in the lives of the established Whig leaders. Many of these men, like Charles Francis Adams, scion of the Adams dynasty, and Richard Henry Dana, Jr., grandson of the aristocratic Judge and Minister to Russia, seemed destined by their political and social connections to leadership in the Whig party. Others, like the "Natick cobbler" Henry Wilson, whose family was so poor he had had to beg for food on the road as a child, were definitely outsiders. Sumner, of humble background but possessed of a classical education and good connections, fell somewhere in between. What they all shared, however, was a hatred of slavery and a desire that their party be the country's major antislavery voice, a goal that would bind their lives together from now on.[16]

Whig leaders, like the cotton manufacturers Abbott Lawrence and Nathan Appleton and their own hope for the future, Daniel Webster's heir apparent, Robert C. Winthrop—a direct descendant of Massachusetts' famous founder—were by no means comfortable with this more idealistic wing of the party or at finding themselves on the same side as the abolitionists. Though also opposed to Texas they refused party sanction to a large anti-Texas meeting proposed by the Young Whigs. The "popular convention" went forward all the same on 29 and 30 January 1845, and brought together under the roof of Faneuil Hall reformers, radicals, and conservatives to a degree not to be seen again before the Civil War. There were some anxious moments among the conservatives, and even among some of the Young Whigs, when the abolitionists tried to influence the proceedings. William Lloyd Garrison had already, the year before, publicly embraced disunionism and denounced the Constitution as "a covenant with death and an agreement with hell." "[M]ingled hisses and cheers, and one or two solitary cries of 'Treason'" were heard when Garrison offered resolutions calling for the dissolution of the Union should the annexation of Texas be accomplished. Many conservatives stalked out of the hall. In the end, however, the moderates prevailed over both conservatives and Garrisonians; it was by acclamation that the assembly accepted the principal address. Sumner thought it denounced slavery "in terms as strong as any that Channing employed." It proclaimed, in words coauthored by Young Whigs Stephen C. Phillips and Charles Allen in collaboration with conservative icon Daniel Webster himself, that "Massachusetts denounces the iniquitous project in its inception, and in every stage of its progress; in its means and its end, and in all the purposes and pretenses of its authors."[17]

It was already too late. Four days before the Faneuil Hall meeting the House had passed a resolution approving the annexation of Texas—"a most iniquitous vote," wrote Sumner to his old friend Sarah Cleveland. He looked to the other chamber with little optimism: "[I]t is doubtful what will be its fate in the Senate." Whatever hope there might have been quickly evaporated as President-elect Polk worked on the senators' resolve, while President Tyler could not wait to sign the Joint Resolution that would be laid on his desk that first of March, days before he would welcome the Executive Mansion's new occupant.[18]

Massachusetts' most conservative Whig leaders did not wait for the news to reach them. As early as March 1844, when the conservatives began to speak out against annexation, their Young Whig colleagues were aware of an unpromising reticence on their part. When, in that month, Abbott Lawrence held a Whig caucus on the matter at his house, all agreed in opposing annexation, but none wanted to be identified with an anti-Texas committee that might upset Southerners with whom they had political and business ties. At first they passed the chairmanship off on young Charles Francis Adams; then they abandoned the idea altogether. When Robert C. Winthrop stood up in the House to argue against annexation, the new territory it would give to slavery was one of his reasons, but he stressed, as did his conservative associates, the legal and constitutional obstacles to the annexation of a self-proclaimed independent nation, and one whose original parent had not agreed to the arrangement. Though many conservatives attended the Faneuil Hall meeting of January 1845, their leaders Abbott Lawrence, Nathan Appleton, and Winthrop stayed home. Daniel Webster's participation constituted no great exception. More personally troubled by slavery than they, he was also the principal political rival of Abbott Lawrence.[19]

The Whig leaders always put the maintenance of the Union as they knew it above their dislike of slavery. Genuinely opposed to admitting Texas to the Union and believing they had a chance at winning the presidency in 1844, they had coöperated with antislavery elements in their party, and even outside of it, in hopes of capturing power at Washington. The year 1845 found them feeling much weaker. They had lost the presidency. The rivalry in their own party between the Webster and Lawrence factions continued. And now they felt chal-

Boston's Court Street as it appeared when Sumner kept his law office at Number Four, on the corner across Washington Street from the Old State House. Around his second-floor office turned his daily life, professional, social, and political from 1834 until he left for Washington in 1851. *Courtesy, The Bostonian Society / Old State House.*

Sumner's deepening reputation as an art patron gave him a place on the committee to plan the Boston Athenæum's new building in 1848. His principal contribution to the edifice was its noble staircase celebrating the uplifting aspiration for knowledge. From *The Athenæum Centenary*, published by the Boston Athenæum, 1907. *Courtesy, The Bostonian Society / Old State House.*

(left, opposite page) Wendell Phillips, his old classmate from the Law School, became the Garrisonian with whom Sumner most relished the pleasure of intellectual debate. Oil by Charles V. Bond in 1849. *Courtesy, Massachusetts Historical Society.*

(right, opposite page) John Gorham Palfrey in 1848, *Courtesy, U.S. Department of the Interior, National Park Service, Adams National Historical Park.*

(bottom, opposite page) Henry Wilson in 1856. *Brady Collection, U.S. Signal Corps Photo B-4159. Courtesy, National Archives.*

It was Sumner's ability to combine the inspiring moral rectitude for which Palfrey was honored with the political sense Wilson personified that ultimately gave him the leadership of Massachusetts' antislavery Free Soilers.

(above left) The Cotton Lord par excellence, Sumner's friend and kinsman turned political opponent Nathan Appleton standing in front of his calico printing machine in his family's favorite portrait of him. *Courtesy, Pollard Memorial Library, Lowell, Massachusetts.*

(above right) Inspired partly by the contemporaneous revolutions in Europe, Sumner hoped that the American election of 1848 would inaugurate a peaceful social revolution, wresting the United States from pro-slavery control and placing it in the path toward a true popular republicanism based upon broadly shared moral justice and cultural wealth. *Free Soil Songs for the People,* © *Collection of The New-York Historical Society.*

(top, opposite page) Robert C. Winthrop in 1846 by G. P. A. Healy. *Courtesy, Massachusetts Historical Society.*

(bottom, opposite page) Park Street in 1858. *Courtesy, Bostonian Society / Old State House.*

The hub of Boston's social and political universe sat on Park Street across from the State House grounds in George Ticknor's house (foreground) and Whig leader Abbott Lawrence's, just beyond. From these once welcoming houses Sumner would be banned in the tumultuous year 1846 when he first openly criticized Robert C. Winthrop, the groomed Representative of that hub, for the weakness of his stand on slavery and the Mexican War. Both former protégés of Joseph Story, Sumner would finally defeat Winthrop for Massachusetts' Senate seat in 1851 in one of the state's greatest political upheavals.

Sumner thought John Quincy Adams the model of "a Christian statesman," but long feared the mantle Adams was anxious to pass to him, his injunctions to put morality into action through politics, to be Cicero and not Atticus. Daguerreotype of John Quincy Adams in 1843 by Southworth & Hawes. *All Rights Reserved, The Metropolitan Museum of Art. Gift of I. N. Phelps Stokes, Edward S. Hawes, Alice Mary Hawes, Marion Augusta Hawes, 1937. (37.14.34).*

(top and bottom, opposite page) The Boston Courthouse chained in 1851 to prevent the escape of the fugitive slave Thomas Sims; broadside from the same year warning Boston's blacks to be wary in the wake of the passage of the Fugitive Slave Law. *Both Courtesy, Library of Congress.*

The supporters of the Fugitive Slave Law of 1850 said that it would settle the slavery question once and for all; instead it aroused public fear and fury as never before. "Nothing can be settled which is not right," thundered Sumner, and, in an unprecedented upset, he would win Massachusetts' Senate seat in 1851.

Driven into politics by his sense of duty and his own "confidence in Humanity," and despite the pain it had already cost him, Sumner in 1851 looked forward to working for the accomplishment of the peaceful revolution he had long dreamt of. Letter of Sumner to William Wetmore Story, 3 July 1851. *By permission of The Huntington Library, San Marino, California, HM 21972.*

lenged by the rise of the nativist American Republican party. Faced with these dangers, Whig leaders, too closely bound to the cotton manufacturing interest, pulled away from their antislavery associates to strengthen their ties with the South and especially the Southern wing of their own party, which had felt threatened by the choice cast upon them by the Texas question between Whiggery and slavery. Ralph Waldo Emerson gibed: "Cotton thread holds the union together."[20]

The Young Whigs were not always comfortable themselves with the consequences of the association they had begun with the widely hated abolitionists. At the very least there was the fear that such a tie might discredit them before the public. Charles Francis Adams, as leader of the antislavery Whigs, was especially concerned by Garrison's call for disunion at the Faneuil Hall convention and relieved when it was not sustained.[21] Sumner attended the meeting with quite different feelings. This was nearly the first time he had attended any public meeting against slavery—though "in earnest opposition to Slavery, I may almost assume the complacency of a veteran," he thought, as he looked upon the number of new converts that the threat of Texas was bringing to the cause. He was struck by Garrison's eloquence and listened to him "with an interest, hardly ever excited by any other speaker." The abolitionist's words "fell in a fiery rain," he wrote to Judge Story, who must have shaken his head sadly at the growing ideological distance between himself and his former protégé. Sumner was not about to become a Garrisonian, and he voted against Garrison's call for disunion. Unlike so many Whigs, both conservative and antislavery, however, Sumner could say of Garrison's motion that he "was most sincerely glad that he made it, & that he had so good an occasion to explain his views."[22]

In fact, Sumner was anxious to have as wide a spectrum of antislavery defenders as possible. Aware of the reluctance of conservatives and abolitionists to coöperate, he hoped that they might be brought together by shared fundamental principles in the urgency of the final goal, and he believed that they could all contribute to the arousal of that public opinion which was the ultimate weapon against the South's peculiar institution. Sumner was thus delighted to insist that it was to the abolitionists that should go "the honors & consolations springing from" the awakening of the public mind. "Do you not feel animated by the result of the recent Convention?" he exhorted his abolitionist friend Wendell Phillips excitedly. "The people of New England will be lifted up to the new platform of Anti-Slavery, & all must join in the reprobation of Slavery." His optimism was as yet untempered by active participation in the details of politics.[23]

Boston's civic leaders approved of Sumner's final entrance into community affairs. Such activity was, after all, expected of a young gentleman with a classical education—an education itself geared to training him for the role of civic leadership in a republic. During the years that Sumner had been waiting in the wings, many of his friends had already taken their first steps on stage. Hillard had given his Fourth of July oration and been elected to the General Court as early as 1835. Horace Mann and Charles Francis Adams had given their own Fourth of July orations and entered politics in the early 1840's, not to mention Sumner's friend Howe, himself following the path of conscience into public life. There had been efforts to tempt Sumner in the same direction since his return from Europe in 1840. But he had diffidently refused every one, doing no public speaking at all except before the students of Dane College while substituting for Judge Story. But Sumner's involvement in education reform over the winter of 1844–1845, his active contribution to the construction of the new Athenæum, his greater participation—not yet controversial outspokenness—in the Boston Prison Discipline Society, and his attendance at anti-Texas meetings and growing ties to the Whig party—not yet antislavery agitation—all suggested to gratified city leaders that he was at last coming out of his shell. In April 1845 they offered him that honored initiation into republican civic leadership, the principal oration at the city's official celebration of Independence Day.[24]

Suddenly confronted by the task of living up to these expectations, Sumner was struck by his old self-doubt. He refused the invitation of the Mayor and his council. That would not do. He "had kept aloof from public affairs in an unbecoming manner," they informed him; it was his "duty" to accept. This was an appeal he could not escape. Nor could he pretend to himself, as he had before 1844, that he had "no story to tell." For the past two or more years his letters and conversation had been full of the concern, the themes, even the examples, that would make up his Fourth of July oration. Still, it was the middle of June before he could bring himself to start writing. He finished it just under the wire, developing under the strain an uncomfortable case of boils—"one on the shoulder," Felton wrote to Longfellow, with joking reference to the subject of the oration, "just where the epaulette is worn, and another on the side, where the sword hangs."[25]

The Fourth dawned sunny and dry, a perfect day for the planned festivities. The parade started at about 10:30, made up of Bostonian artisans and the membership of charitable organizations escorting the city officials and the chosen orator from City Hall to the Tremont Temple in the heart of the city. There the reading of the Declaration of Independence would be followed by the oration, in a tradition going back to 1774 when John Hancock had spoken on the first anniversary of the Boston Massacre. Some 2,000 people were in the audience on this day, to which was added a more fluid attendance at the back of the hall where the merely curious or impatient young people—among them a sixteen-year-old Edward L. Pierce who was then seeing his future hero and friend for the first time—would come in to catch a glimpse of the speaker and then drift out to enjoy the games and booths of food on the Common.[26]

In the front rows sat the honored guests. There had never before been any significant military presence at the city's celebration of the national birthday. Republican sensibilities had kept the holiday a civic affair. But with the possibility of perhaps two wars in the near future, the city authorities in 1845 decided that the military had been unduly neglected in past years. The visiting ship-of-the-line *Ohio,* bedecked with banners, became the focal decoration in the harbor, and the front rows of the Tremont Temple were filled with "at least one hundred" specially invited army and naval officers from the local forts, all dressed in full uniform.[27]

But when Sumner stepped forward all eyes fixed on him. He was dressed in the traditional blue coat with white waistcoat and trousers, tall and well-built, "dark hair hanging in masses over his left brow," his stateliness softened by his ever genial smile. He struck everyone as "the impersonation of manly beauty and power," and when he began to speak in his resonant, mellow bass voice he seemed the very ideal of the orator. No one seeing him for the first time that day could have guessed how difficult it had been for him to accept this role. As he spoke, Sumner himself discovered, as a kind of revelation, a talent that would become a new career, and a particular form of action that would become for some time his principal means of supporting reform and influencing public opinion. Here he found his public voice.[28]

A Fourth of July oration was expected to be patriotic, and Sumner began by invoking "the Fathers of the Republic" and their "sacrifice." But the pervasive social, cultural, political upheaval of the second quarter of the nineteenth century that was dispersing the population, changing the economy, firing the reform impulse, and slowly dividing the nation had also made the patriotic tradition of the Fourth of July oration a subject of tension. There was increasing dissatisfaction with what had come to seem to many the repetition of celebratory platitudes. Sumner's old professor of rhetoric and oratory, Edward Channing, told his students that the noblest patriotic sentiment would seem "dull, if continued merely out of respect to usage or a town-vote. It gains spirit at once if we can connect with the Declaration and War of our Independence something kindred in the passions, struggles and hopes of our own day."[29]

In recent years the chosen orators had tried to enlarge the scope of the custom and bring it to bear on more immediate concerns. Charles Francis Adams and Peleg Chandler in 1843 and 1844 had spoken to the public's fascination with a history from which they felt increasingly removed, and Horace Mann in 1842 had introduced education reform to the occasion. Even these more experimental efforts avoided great controversy. As his friend Edward Pierce recalled, "Sumner's was the first which attacked a custom and opinions approved by popular judgment and sanctioned by venerable traditions." Sumner did so under the impetus of a definition of patriotism that he would always adhere to, but which itself became a matter of controversy that Independence Day. In the opening of his oration he made the Founding Fathers speak in their own voice to urge their "devotion to duty" directly upon the audience. "Nothing is more shameful for a man," he had them say, "than to found his title to esteem, not on his own merits, but on the fame of his ancestors. The glory of the Fathers is doubtless to their children a most precious treasure; but to enjoy it without transmitting it to the next generation, and without adding to it yourselves, this is the height of imbecility."[30]

Inspired by this sense of duty, mindful of this understanding of patriotism, Sumner had decided in his first public address on the larger social questions of the day to devote himself to the evil of war. It had long seemed to him there were no two greater evils facing the world, no two evils more ripe for eradication, than war and slavery. Sumner's concern about war was older even than his active interest in slavery, dating back by his own reckoning to the age of nine when he had been struck by Josiah Quincy's address on the virtues of peace. Sumner believed further—and the events surrounding the annexation of Texas had done nothing to dissuade him—that war and slavery were intimately linked, the one encouraging and sustaining the other. In the same way that these two institutions harmed humanity and human society, their eradication could promote the highest form of civilization. So it was—to the delight of some, to the shock of most of his audience, and to the especial discomfiture of most of the uniformed officers facing him directly from the first rows—that Sumner began with this proposition: "IN OUR AGE THERE CAN BE NO PEACE THAT IS NOT HONORABLE; THERE CAN BE NO WAR THAT IS NOT DISHONORABLE."[31]

Sumner attacked war not only for its bloody horrors and inherent bestiality, but for the effect of these upon human nature. In this he addressed the intense interest of thoughtful contemporaries—especially those of Whiggish orientation—concerned by questions of rapid change and democratization, in the study of human nature and its effect on improving civilization. Following Moral Philosophy's division of human nature into the three spheres of the animal, the intellectual, and the ethical, Sumner condemned war for reversing their true hierarchy. However masked by talk of honor and by its requirement of technical skill, war enthroned the animal over the higher faculties. Warriors dress like beasts and live by violence, judging themselves by their physical prowess and the harm they commit to others. War "is, in short, a temporary adoption, by men, of the character of wild beasts, emulating their ferocity, rejoicing like them in blood, and seeking, as with a lion's paw, to hold an asserted right."[32]

By glorifying the pursuit of violence, the resort to mere brute force, as well as by staking disputes among nations upon mere chance, "[r]eason, and the divine part of our nature, in which alone we differ from the beasts, in which alone we approach the Divinity, in which alone are the elements of *justice,* the professed object of war, are dethroned." From this intellectual degradation must follow "the moral debasement of man," as the principle of war unleashes all man's "passions,"—a word Sumner nearly always used in the derogatory sense generally given it by the Enlightenment and kept by Moral Philosophy, never with Romantic approval. Man's true duty, Sumner agreed with the moral philosophers, was, by means of reason and conscience, to keep the animal in check within its own sphere, thus freeing himself to develop the higher faculties to their fullest potential. "It is true that in us are impulses unhappily tending to strife," Sumner resumed his thought in a later edition of his oration: "Propensities possessed in common with the beast, if not subordinated to what in man is human, almost divine, will break forth in outrage. This is the predominance of the animal. Hence wars and fightings, with the false glory which crowns such barbarism. But the true civilization of nations, as of individuals, is determined by the extent to which these evil dispositions are restrained."[33]

Sumner did not argue, like more Romantic thinkers, that human nature was all good. In the debate between William Ellery Channing, speaking for the Harvard moral philosophers, and the Transcendentalist minister Theodore Parker, Sumner agreed with Channing that human nature contained both good and evil, and could not accept the hopeful Transcendentalist view that man's conscience was naturally infallible and needed no instruction. Over the next years, Sumner's experience in public life would increasingly tarnish his faith in human nature, and when he revised his Fourth of July oration after the Civil War he could even say that man's warlike tendencies went beyond the example of other animals. "Nay, let me not dishonor the beasts by the comparison," he would add then. "The superior animals, at least, prey not, like men, upon their own species." No such hint of pessimism saddened his delivery of the oration on 4 July 1845, though his philosophy was fundamentally the same. What he stressed to his audience at the Tremont Temple—like Channing—was rather man's natural educability.[34]

As he argued that man is naturally responsive to the treatment he receives from his fellows, and that from them he learns much of his outlook upon life, Sumner showed how all the reforms he espoused were based upon a common understanding of human nature and of the relationship between man and society. As he wrote that winter in an article on prison discipline: "If the society by which he is surrounded is virtuous, his own virtues will be confirmed and expanded. On the other hand, if it be wicked, then will the demon of his nature be aroused in this unholy fellowship." Education laid the foundations of better lives, of better citizenship, and thus of moral progress for the society. Prison discipline should aim to reëducate those who had been led astray, and thus contribute to the same end. It was precisely for the Pennsylvania System's stress on surrounding the prisoner with "good influences" and "virtuous persons," rather than with other criminals, that Sumner preferred it, as well as for its humanity in encouraging self-discipline through the teaching of an independent trade, rather than relying on the discipline of the lash, as was habitually done in the Auburn System. Humane treatment undoubtedly cannot reform all prisoners, but to treat them with the spirit of "*revenge*" is merely to create hardened criminals, Sumner was convinced, and to show the "ignorance" of the society. "In the progress of an enlightened Prison Discipline," he urged, "it may be hoped, that our Penitentiaries will become in reality, if not in name, Houses of Reformation, and that the convicts will be treated with a scrupulous and extreme regard, alike to their physical, moral and intellectual well-being, to the end, that when they are allowed again to mingle with society, they may feel the precious sympathy with virtue and the detestation of vice, and that, though sadder, they may be better men."[35]

Now on the Fourth of July, calling forth the successes of these great experiments then being conducted with human nature, the rehabilitation of criminals as well as the creation of asylums for the insane—traditionally jailed or chained like criminals—Sumner drew the lesson with regard to war: "The warring propensities, which once filled with confusion and strife the hospitals for the insane while they were controlled by force, are a dark but feeble type of the present relations of nations, on whose hands are the heavy chains of military preparations, assimilating the world to one great mad-house; while the peace and good-will which now abound in these retreats, are the happy emblems of what awaits the world when it shall have the wisdom to recognize the supremacy of the higher sentiments of our nature [. . .]." The "universal heart of man," affirmed Sumner, is governed by a "law, according to which the human heart responds to the feelings by which it is addressed, whether of confidence or distrust, of love or hate." If given the choice, however, that heart responds most eagerly not to evil but to good, showing evidence of its divine spark, and illustrating the wisdom of the Christian ideal "that Love is more puissant than Force."[36]

Education could thus work both ways, Sumner conceded. It had traditionally been used to instill an admiration for war and the military. The infant, whose mind is "at that age more impressible than wax," is amused at playtime by the toy soldiers and rocked to sleep by the "images of War" of the nursery rhymes given him by his mother. As he grows older "[h]e draws the nutriment of his soul from a literature, whose beautiful fields have been moistened by human blood," and when he reaches adulthood "his country invites his services in war, and holds before his bewildered imagination the highest prizes of honor." War is further strengthened in the public mind by prejudices repeated from generation to generation—the prejudice of its necessity despite its inability to secure justice, the assumption that what has always been must always be, the militant "infidelity" of the Christian Church, the old-fashioned conception of honor, and the "selfish and exaggerated *love of country,* leading to its physical aggrandizement, and the strengthening of its institutions at the expense of other countries," a sentiment much discussed during the Texas controversy but for which words like chauvinism and jingoism had in 1845 not yet been coined. War, that accepted means of settling disputes among nations, is thus "a practice, or *custom,*" a habit enshrined in law and taught to each succeeding generation.[37]

What can be taught, Sumner urged upon his audience, can be untaught, and different lessons made to take its place. Parents and schools can teach children the virtues of peace, ministers of the Gospel can attend to the true principles of Christianity. Ultimately education is the most important function of society, not that education which merely gives information or repeats old prejudices, but that education which devotes itself to the development of the highest human faculties. From the platform of his Enlightenment faith in mankind, Sumner exhorted his audience to see that the true grandeur of nations lay, not in animalistic and futile military glory, but "in those qualities which constitute the greatness of the individual." The glory and duty of nations as of individuals alike thus became the development of man's highest faculties. "*The true grandeur of humanity,*" he proclaimed, "*is in moral elevation, sustained, enlightened and decorated by the intellect of man.*" This would be the foundation of the truest civilization.[38]

Believing that peace would permit the flourishing of such a civilization, and convinced that war was more likely when its instruments were kept always in readiness, Sumner deplored the money spent by the state on weapons in time of peace. To the objection that Nathan Appleton later made that "occupation is necessary to men" and that the army provided it, Sumner countered—"but let them be occupied *productively,* not uselessly, living actually at the cost of others." His observations in Europe had made Sumner blame taxation for military spending as a primary cause of the Continent's terrible poverty—"poverty & wretchedness are the brood of war. Imagine the wealth, now absorbed in preparation for war, devoted to opening new sources of employment, bringing forward new materials." Sumner exhorted the businessman Appleton, as he had urged his listeners on the Fourth of July, to consider how the lavish sums wasted on the military would, if given to schools, the arts, and productive industry, create a richer and more elevated society than ever known. "Choose ye, my fellow citizens of a Christian State, between the two caskets—that wherein is the loveliness of knowledge and truth, or that which contains the carrion death."[39]

This vision of progress he found beautiful and inspiring, but Sumner wished most particularly to show that it was practicable. The sphere of war had already been restricted. The sword, once the "indispensable companion of the gentleman," would now cause its wearer to "be thought a madman or a bully"; houses, churches, and cities no longer depended upon fortifications. Women and children were now protected as war came under specific rules of international law.

"The principles of free trade, now so generally favored," Sumner argued to his skeptical brother George in the tradition of the Enlightenment, "are antagonistic to war. They teach, and when adopted, cause the mutual dependence of nation upon nation." Reminding his Fourth of July audience of American and European history since the end of the Napoleonic Wars, Sumner saw hope that the principles of arbitration were beginning to take hold among nations: "Since the morning stars first sang together, the world has not witnessed a peace so harmonious and enduring as that which now blesses the Christian nations. Great questions between them, fraught with strife, and in another age, sure heralds of war, are now determined by arbitration or mediation. Great political movements, which only a few short years ago must have led to forcible rebellion, are now conducted by peaceful discussion."[40]

Such progress could continue, Sumner urged. Education, the spread of moral sensibility, and the values of civilization all would contribute to improvement. Sumner thus grounded his oration not on hope and Providence, but in the sense of historical progress that he knew he shared with his audience, and especially in man's ability to shape that progress. For this reason he made his main argument one of law. He began with a legal or, as he put it, a "strictly scientific" definition of war: "*War is a public, armed, contest, between nations, in order to establish* JUSTICE *between them;* as, for instance, to determine a disputed boundary line, or the title to a territory." All recent conflicts or potential conflicts had been of this sort: the War of 1812, the threatenings of war with France in 1834 over spoliation claims owed the United States since the 1790's, and the conflicts at that moment "lowering" with England over Oregon and with Mexico over Texas. In the most important argument of his oration Sumner equated going to war to settle such disputes—dealing as they did with legal, monetary, and territorial claims—with the ancient and mediæval tradition of judicial combat or trial by battle. In both cases, talk of glory and patriotism notwithstanding, armed combat would be resorted to as the institutionally accepted method of determining justice, so that "*all war between civilized Christian nations is a mere* TRIAL OF RIGHT, *or a mode of determining justice between them,* in this respect resembling precisely the *Trial by Battle.*"[41]

The trial by battle, however, could have nothing in common with true justice. "Justice implies the exercise of the judgment in the determination of *right*," and, as Sumner argued, "war not only supersedes the judgment, but delivers over the results to superiority of *force,* or to *chance.*" Who could have predicted Napoleon's victory at the battle of Marengo, "the accident of an accident," asked Sumner; and "[h]ow capriciously the wheel turned when the fortunes of Rome" hung upon the unforeseeable luck of Horatius. Just as men in the nineteenth century had come to "recoil, with horror, from the awful subjection of justice to brute force" in the Middle Ages, and "from the impious profanation of the char-

acter of God in deeming him present in these outrages,"—Sumner urged his listeners—so they could come to behold international war, of identical legal and
logical character, with the same distaste. "As the folly and injustice of [the judicial combat] became apparent," he summarized his argument to George, "men
resorted to Courts and listened to the judgments of Judges. So is the progress of
Nations." In the same way people could avoid international war by establishing
the custom of a resort to: "Negotiation, Arbitration, Mediation, and a Congress
of Nations; all of them practicable and calculated to secure peaceful justice."
When they established these new institutions, and the new modes of thinking
they entailed, then the nations could begin the final and greatest work of disarming, just as individuals had done before them, trusting to their shared belief
in law. Peace rested upon true civilization and allowed true civilization to flourish, while civilization, like true humanity, had "its sources in the loftiest attributes of man, in truth, in justice, in duty." When human society was mature
enough to work for such an ideal, then could it be said that men understood
wherein consisted the "True Grandeur of Nations."[42]

The city authorities were appalled at what their chosen orator had done. They
had intended by their invitation to reward Sumner for his entrance into his civic
duty. As he closed his speech, they thought he had all but entirely abrogated it.
He had forsworn the traditional patriotic oration they had expected, embarrass-
ing them before the community and the special guests they had made such an
unwonted point of welcoming to the ceremony. With them seated beside him on
the stage and the invited military officers stretched out before him in the audience, Sumner had stigmatized the "ear-piercing fife" that had "to-day filled our
streets," "the thump of drum and the sound of martial music" to which Bostonians had been marshaled to the celebration. He had deplored the wasted money
stolen from the country's schools by that engine of war the ship-of-the-line *Ohio*,
lying at anchor in the harbor. And he had arraigned the animalism of soldiers.
Eager for reports of the ceremony he had been unable to attend, Wendell Phillips
imagined the scene: "How did the old 'gray fathers' look at hearing the first time
since *our* fathers['] days a word *up to the times*," he asked with jaunty relish. "—
Startled? I dare say."[43]

The widespread disapproval of Sumner's theme bubbled to the surface at the
ceremonial dinner that closed the festivities. Even friendly Peleg Chandler, sitting in for the ailing Mayor, and John G. Palfrey, Secretary of the Commonwealth and an anti-Texas associate of Sumner's, expressed their disagreement
with Sumner's conclusions, though with every intention of taking the edge off
expected criticism. Others were more blunt. The dozen toasts that followed all
attacked the orator's use of the occasion in one way or another, ranging from
cheerful raillery to angry denunciation. Lawyer and state senator John C. Park's

resentment descended into personal coarseness. General Oliver, one of the invited military guests, was calmer in his disagreement and afterwards praised Sumner for the "exact and refined courtesy" with which he withstood the barrage. Chandler tried to restore good will with a little humor and a toast that all could agree to: "The Orator of the Day! However much we may differ from his sentiments, let us admire the simplicity, manliness, and ability with which he has expressed them." Sumner graciously refused to "follow the apple of discord which he appeared to have thrown out," and, gesturing to the chorus of schoolgirls who had sung during the ceremony, he gave his own toast: "The youthful choristers of the day—May their future lives be filled with happiness, as they have filled our hearts to-day with the delights of their music."[44]

Shocked by Sumner's ideas, the diners had agreed in condemning them as visionary without entirely understanding them. Though Sumner had been at pains to give a different impression, most of his listeners came away thinking that he was an evangelical and a pacifist. One ironically toasted: "The Millennium—[. . .] when the nations shall learn war no more, and when our swords shall be turned into ploughshares and pruning-hooks, the principles of the orator of the day will be susceptible of practical application." Sumner's principal goal, however, had been to show that the establishment of peace was practical. It was on this account that he had rejected religious perfectionism in favor of law and human institutions as the basis of his argument. The peace movement, in which Sumner had taken a quiet part for some years, was strongly influenced by religious thinking. Whether mainstream Protestants or evangelicals, peace activists tended to rely upon Biblical authority to uphold the rightness and godliness of peace, and for this perfectionist stance they were frequently mocked by the public at large. Sumner's close contact over the past decade with reformers, especially with the Reverend Channing, had made him more tolerant of a religious approach to social questions than he had been in law school. In his public addresses from 1845 on he would regularly refer to God and Christianity in defense of the ideals of humanity and civilization. Never did he use such concepts in any strict theological sense, however. The strongly religious character of the peace movement, as well as of the Garrisonian abolitionist movement, was one reason he could never feel entirely at his ease with either.[45]

Sumner took his upbraiding at the Fourth of July dinner placidly, but as letters poured in repeating the same assumption that he was, like most of the peace movement, condemning war on the basis of the Gospel, he began to grow impatient: "[M]y own argt. against war [. . .] is entirely independent of Xstianity," he defended himself. He insisted upon the legal nature of his argument that war in the present age between Christian nations was merely an "*ordeal by battle*" writ large and therefore indefensible. "Now, you will perceive," he repeated to Palfrey, "that this argt. is not touched by any glosses or opinions on the Gospel [. . .]."

Sumner did, however, implicate the Church in his argument. And here he held the ministers of the Gospel to their own higher standard. A militant Church was a moral contradiction, and Sumner attacked the Catholic Church, which "after the first centuries of its existence, failed to discern the peculiar spiritual beauty of the faith which it possessed." Protestant Boston did not find that controversial, but Sumner provoked considerably more heat when he impugned Protestant ministers who, forgetting Christ's injunction to turn the other cheek, continued to deliver sermons "in which we are encouraged to *serve the God of Battles, and as citizen soldiers, to fight for Peace* [. . .]." He thus angered people by appearing at once too religious and too irreligious.[46]

To Sumner's chagrin, his audience misunderstood not only his position on religion, but his stand on self-defense. This was another ground for the public's charge of impracticality against the peace movement—and a cause of dissension within the peace movement itself. With his oration Sumner had hoped to dispel it and perhaps even reunite the advocates of peace. With possibly two wars on the horizon, such a goal seemed especially urgent.

The peace movement had never been without adherents in American history, but it was only in 1828, under the new humanitarian reform impetus, that it finally united into a national organization with the formation of the American Peace Society. This was primarily the work of the tireless publicist and lecturer William Ladd, who envisioned the national organization as a means of uniting radical and moderate peace activists into one stronger movement. It was at about that time that Sumner, just out of college, heard and was inspired by one of Ladd's addresses on peace. The union that Ladd wrought and presided over did not last, however, and in 1838 the Society split into two rival organizations along the same fault line that Ladd had originally been able to bridge. That fault line was the question of self-defense. The American Peace Society accepted it as a right, while the New England Non-Resistance Society, newly created under the leadership of William Lloyd Garrison—himself converted to the cause of peace by Ladd—denied even this recourse to violence.[47]

Sumner was by no means alone in hoping that the threat of war in the mid-1840's might cause a reunion of the peace movement or at least renewed coöperation among its branches, and by 1845 the struggle to broaden the appeal of the American Peace Society was intense. The primary sticking point among the now conservative, moderate, and radical wings of the movement remained the acceptance or rejection of the right of self-defense. At the same time the frequent rejection of self-defense among peace activists tended to cause the public at large to dismiss the whole movement as visionary. It was on this point, therefore, in the spirit of William Ladd, that Sumner tried in his Fourth of July oration to effect a reconciliation in the movement and to reassure the public.[48]

Sumner abhorred physical violence whether on an international or a personal level, but he was not a pacifist. Though he admired the stern logic of the Quakers and conceded that his position was not in accordance with "the requirements of the Gospel," he did believe it to be "ordained by nature," and so he accepted "the right of personal *self-defence;* I believe that human life may be taken to preserve human life." It was a position he had upheld both in private and in public for some years. When the spirited Howe had gotten into a fight and landed in jail on his honeymoon, Sumner had scolded him: "I do not believe in *blows* or force, except in *self-defence.* This is the limit." In 1843 he had published the same opinion in the *North American Review,* when he defended Captain Mackenzie's decision to execute several officers to head off a suspected mutiny aboard the *Somers.* Self-defense is a "right founded in the law of nature," he had written then. "It had its origin in the instincts of humanity, and is ratified by the calm judgments of reason." Such a right must be exercised only "under circumstances of a peculiar character," he insisted. "But the law, while careful to restrain the right within its natural limits, recognizes its force on every just and proper occasion."[49]

Sumner supported the same right of self-defense for the community as a whole through the state's police power. The army and militia he rejected as a waste of money and a temptation to the use of violence, but like his father, who had had occasion to understand the deficiencies of the present system, Sumner did favor the creation of a professional police force—"an active, efficient, ever-wakeful police"—an idea then as yet unimplemented in Boston. In the same way he rejected the navy, but did accept the necessity of a smaller naval establishment to act "as a part of the *police* of the seas, to purge them of pirates, and above all to defeat the hateful traffic in human flesh."[50]

Sumner and two of his legal friends, Wendell Phillips—himself a rare Garrisonian who was not a nonresistant,—and Richard Henry Dana, Jr., whom he had met through the anti-Texas movement, shared with each other the hint of discomfort they felt at this distinction they all made between "the Force of Police, & the Force of Armies," both intended to uphold justice. "I am not entirely satisfied that this distinction accords with the true spirit of the Gospel," Sumner wrote. He defended it nonetheless on the basis of self-defense. "War is a *trial by battle;* it is *monstrous & impious,* as the latter was called, because it is a deliberate appeal to *force* or to *chance* to determine an asserted right. [. . .] But a riot, or other crime puts in jeopardy men, wives, children, society, & awakes the right of *self-defence.*"[51]

What deeply upset Sumner was the misuse of the concept of self-defense to protect what was, in reality, aggression. "It is the phrase '*defensive war*' that vindicates this Texas piracy to the consciences of many," he complained. The United States certainly had the right to defend itself, but "[w]ho would attack [us]?" Sumner playfully reproved his friend and kinsman Nathan Appleton. "England?

or France? Neither of these would think of a *conquest.*" And should a dispute arise between us and such countries about "some asserted right," then "an arbitration would be the proper mode of determining this." Aggression certainly still existed, but Sumner argued that civilization had advanced to the point where there was at least a limited community of nations, the "Christian nations" as he put it, who shared a basic conception of the rule of law and a code of international law, that among these nations the only disputes likely to arise were those based on essentially legal issues, and that among themselves these nations were ready now, "in an age of civilization," to understand that war was neither a just nor a reasonable method of achieving satisfaction. As Sumner put it to his audience on the Fourth of July, "a close consideration of the subject will make it apparent that no war can arise among Christian nations, at the present day, except to determine an asserted right," and such wars, springing "from sentiments of vengeance or honor," are only "falsely called *defensive.*"[52]

Sumner was disappointed at the failure of his arguments to have any influence in reconciling the different wings of the peace movement. His decision to set aside the question of self-defense as no longer applicable in the present state of international affairs merely confirmed the different factions in their disagreement. The American Peace Society, whose positions were closest to Sumner's own, was delighted by the address and circulated it widely, sending in particular one copy to every member of Congress in hopes of influencing them against war with England. Elihu Burritt, the great peace activist in the midst of his campaign to gain control of the American Peace Society for the moderates, told Sumner: "[T]he cause of Peace dates principally from your oration." Nonresistants, however, blamed Sumner for weakening the cause of peace by accepting violence in the guise of self-defense, as well as the police force.[53]

Though Sumner had fully expected the public to be skeptical of his particular arguments—and had thus taken care to underline their practicability—he had felt he had reason to hope they might be receptive to his general intention. After all, public acceptance of the peace movement had become widespread in Massachusetts since the hated War of 1812. In the first year of the war the Unitarian minister Edward Everett—not yet the celebrated orator—condemned in his sermons the exaggerated patriotism that Admiral Stephen Decatur had just proclaimed: "Our country—be she right or wrong." Harvard students at the time, like young John Gorham Palfrey, wrote themes attacking "war as a vestige of barbarism." By the 1830's the American Peace Society had achieved broad support. Its 1833 essay contest attracted so many serious entrants that the final decision had to be postponed seven years, and its judges included the most respected of conservative statesmen—Joseph Story, Chancellor Kent, Daniel Webster. In 1837 the General Court responded to American Peace Society petitions with a resolution urging the creation of a congress of nations and the insertion into every international treaty of a clause calling for arbitration. In 1845 Massachusetts' Whig leaders, accustomed to upholding diplomacy and the rule of law, were speaking against the possibility of war with England and Mexico.[54]

Sumner was taken aback, therefore, by the public's apparent misunderstanding. Confusing his condemnation of the institution of war as a trial by battle with an evangelical denial of the right of self-defense, fearful people showered him with objections: "If a man attacks me," objected Mann, "or threatens to take the life of my wife & family, before my eyes, I can not appeal to the trial by battle; or, even, to the laws of my country." John Quincy Adams, now Sumner's good friend, but who took a more belligerent attitude on American rights in Oregon, also thought Sumner was supporting nonresistance. As he grew frustrated, Sumner's responses shaded from patience into exasperation, and more than once he apologized for the tone of "controversy & dogmatism into which I have plunged."[55]

Sumner's discomfort finally overflowed into a two-year-long quarrel with Francis Bowen. The mild-mannered and bespectacled editor of the *North American Review* was sure he had written a favorable review of the oration, and could not understand why Sumner was so upset over a few criticisms put in just to be fair, while Sumner could not understand how Bowen could have simply disregarded all his main points. Sumner's friends Felton and William Kent, son of the Chancellor, finally convinced him that he had done Bowen "injustice." Sumner immediately wrote to Bowen: "I am unhappy at the thought of this, & feel that I cannot be right, where friends, whom I may claim as much as yourself, think me wrong." Bowen was delighted by the apology, but the two never quite trusted each other again.[56]

Even Edward Everett—despite his denunciation of the War of 1812 and "Decatur patriotism," and though he praised Sumner's "magnificent address" as "an effort certainly of unsurpassed felicity and power"—said that he could not accept its ideas. "I do not see, for instance, that your views of War differ from simple quakerism, & it seems to me demonstrable, that a company of *friends* could not even exist; except in a community which rejects their peculiar views." "I think that my views on war have been misunderstood," Sumner frankly responded to Everett: "I am not a Quaker. I sometimes wish I were." And once again he explained that his opposition to the "*institution* of war" did not prevent his acceptance of the right of self-defense or his rejection of "any principle, which interferes with the stability of government," and compared his opposition to the institution of war, though still accepted by the law of nations, to his opposition to the institution of slavery, still accepted by local American law.[57]

More shocking to Boston's city authorities and social leaders than his idealism was Sumner's seeming failure of patriotic duty. How could he, as J. C. Park an-

grily complained, gratuitously assault the invited military guests as "so many li-
ons, tigers, or other wild beasts,"—and this on the Fourth of July no less, the an
niversary of a national independence won on the battlefield. Sumner had barely
even mentioned the Revolution. His old schoolmate Robert C. Winthrop, now
Boston's representative in Congress and heir to Webster's role as leading statesman of the Whig party, pressed him on this point at the dinner after the oration.
The occasion made Sumner reluctant to give voice to his whole thought, but he
added later that, however much we might have benefited by the winning of independence, it seemed to him a source of sadness rather than of joy that it had
had to be won by violence. National "boasting" under any circumstances he condemned "as indecorous, if not unchristian." There was something else. The
grievance of the two or three million Americans that had led to Revolution "was
the necessity of paying a few pence more or less on certain things, under the direction of a Parliament, in which they were not represented." This they called
"their slavery." "No just or humane person can fail to perceive that all this was as
a feather compared with the rod of oppression, now held by our country over
more than three millions of fellow-men," Sumner wrote Winthrop, and he spelled
out his thought: "If *two millions* were justified in resisting by *force* the assumptions of the British Parliament, as contrary to the law of nature, & the principles
of the common law, & the rights of Freedom; then *a fortiori,* the *three millions* of
blacks, into whose souls we thrust the iron of the deadliest slavery the world has
yet witnessed, would be justified in resisting by *force* the power that holds them
in bondage." Any justification of the American Revolution must lead "with irresistible force" to this conclusion. Sumner put the question to his patriotic friend:
"Can we proclaim such a truth?"[58]

"'Let the Dead Past bury its Dead,'" Sumner quoted to an outraged
Winthrop. We cannot remake history, but we hold responsibility for the shape
of the future. Instead of speaking of the Revolution, Sumner urged his audience
on the Fourth of July to consider the two wars threatening the immediate future,
and to think of what their patriotic duty required of them there. "Who believes
that the *national honor* will be promoted by a war with Mexico or England?" he
asked his listeners. War with England, land of our origins, would be "parricidal,"
he argued now as he had in 1839, and with Mexico, weak from internal divisions,
it "would be mean and cowardly." Here could be "no righteous though mistaken
sentiment, [. . .] no true love of country, [. . .] no generous thirst for fame, that
last infirmity of noble minds," no true grandeur of nations. Sumner arraigned
both potential wars as founded in greed, "springing in both cases from an ignorant and ignoble passion for new territories; strengthened in one case, by an unnatural desire in this land of boasted freedom, to fasten by new links the chains
which promise soon to fall from the limbs of the unhappy slave!"[59]

By linking the traditional patriotic celebration with the ongoing debate over

Texas and the hostilities it might lead to, Sumner made his oration an event in that controversy. This was all the more true as he spoke at the invitation of the conservative Whig leaders of the city who had, after the passage in March of the Joint Resolution in favor of annexation, made it clear they wished an end to all further agitation of the issue—agitation they were afraid might hurt their Southern brethren. How rude and unpatriotic, they cried, that he should thus abuse their trust and attack their invited guests. Sumner may well have thought that it was the city that had been wanting in its duty by so far departing from the civic tradition of the holiday to show such unprecedented attention to the military—especially at such a time. That "selfish and exaggerated *love of country*," that he had arraigned in his oration for its belligerence was, he warned, no more than a "narrow [. . .] heathen patriotism."[60]

It was Robert C. Winthrop who stood up to denounce this view in what became the most significant and celebrated—or notorious—of the toasts at the ceremonial dinner that crowned the Fourth of July festivities. He had been the Massachusetts Whigs' principal national spokesman against annexation until passage of the Joint Resolution, and then, for the good of the party and the Union as he saw it, had ceased all opposition. Now he reminded the dinner guests that annexation was to all intents and purposes accomplished. Texas' required acceptance was a mere formality, word of which was momentarily expected. Giving his listeners the impression that he was, in the name of the Whig party, countering Sumner's plea against the admission of Texas and its consequences, Winthrop gave the toast: "Our Country—Bounded by the St Johns and the Sabine, or however otherwise bounded, or described, and be the measurements more or less,—still *our country*—to be cherished in all our hearts, to be defended by all our hands." To Sumner this was mere "Decatur patriotism." He saw the toast as Winthrop's offering "the hand of fellowship to Texas"—and to the extension of slavery that she represented. Sumner's oration and Winthrop's toast described the rift that Texas had opened up in the Whig party. Together they would add passion to the forces prying open that rift until the party broke in two.[61]

As Sumner succinctly put it, his address was "vehemently praised, & vehemently condemned"—sometimes by the same people. Even conservative dissenters wholeheartedly agreed that its literary elegance and polish, the cultivation that lay behind it, and the courage made it stand out among Fourth of July orations. The judgment of so great an orator as Edward Everett that it was a "magnificent address" must have been gratifying indeed. Nathan Appleton likewise disagreed with the conclusions of the oration, but wrote: "I admire the eloquence, fervor, boldness & truth which it contains. I admire the spirit and grace which run through it [. . .]." The public at large agreed. The beauty and humanity as well as the notoriety of the address made it an unprecedented popular success. No Fourth of July oration had ever sold so well; it quickly went through half a dozen editions, here and abroad. And by autumn Sumner's calendar was full to overflowing with speaking engagements as he found himself an instant celebrity on the lecture circuit—a circuit that would, over the next few years, build for him a base of enthusiastic popular support throughout Massachusetts, New England, and New York.[62]

Sumner's greatest praise came from the reform community, who embraced him with as much fervor as Boston's conservative leaders rejected him. The American Peace Society adopted the oration as its own. Independent-minded John Quincy Adams, whose congressional fight against slavery Sumner had so long admired, was delighted by the "highly wrought, learned, ingenious diatribe," and prophesied in his diary: "Mr. Sumner takes a lofty flight and promises to become a leading politician." Transcendentalist minister and abolitionist Theodore Parker was so moved by it that he initiated a correspondence with Sumner that soon blossomed into a lifelong friendship. William Lloyd Garrison encouraged Sumner that the "denunciations and reproaches" of the lovers of military glory "are your best commendations; but you will also receive the fervent benedictions of all the true friends of the human race." Promptly on the morning after the oration Samuel Gridley Howe sent his own benediction. His efforts in the cause of reform had helped to spur Sumner's crisis of conscience, and no one understood better than Howe the turmoil his friend had gone through to reach this day. To Sumner, no praise meant so much. "I could never love you more than I did yesterday morning," wrote Howe,

> & yet at night, I was far more proud of your friendship than ever before. To say you have done yourself honor is to say but little, but you have done a noble work, even though ridicule and sarcasm should follow you through life. You have struck a blow at the false gods which the people worship; you have proved them to be of wood, hay and stubble; & though their worshippers may rave, their idols will fall.
>
> If I could do as much as you have done on the next 4th, I should be willing to say on the 5th, nunc accipe Diva, and let us retire to private life.[63]

Though hoping to make people think, Sumner had known before he stepped onto the platform of the Tremont Temple that day that his address would be best appreciated by reformers. By it he publicly declared his rejection of the pursuit of ordinary fame and happiness, and his new commitment to reform, to that duty that he had long sought and now understood. Though he never could warm to the drudgery of the lecture circuit, he followed it faithfully, becoming a near stranger to his law office, out of his desire to spread the cause of reform as far as possible. Gratified by the popularity of his address, he encouraged the publication of more and cheaper editions than prestigious Fourth of July orations usually got, to reach as large a public as he could. Contrary to advice, he refused to take out a copyright on the work, "because I was unwilling in any way to restrain its circulation. The sentiments there expressed I believe essential to the welfare of mankind. It will, therefore, be to me a source of unfeigned satisfaction to know that they find favor & circulation in any quarter."[64]

No reaction to the *True Grandeur of Nations* was more symbolic of the distance that Sumner had traveled over the past decade than the letter he received from Joseph Story—the last letter he would ever receive from the man who had been such a deep inspiration and trusted guide, but who had now worn himself out with constant work. Sumner was proud of Story's earnest praise of the oration's "classical" "elegance," and of its sentiments as "such as befit an exalted mind & an enlarged benevolence." "In many parts of your Discourse," wrote Story, "I have been struck with the strong resemblance, which it bears, to the manly moral enthusiasm of Sir James Mackintosh," a jurist about whom Sumner had written with great respect for the *Jurist*. Sumner was probably not surprised when Story felt compelled to add that, though he went "earnestly & heartily along with many of your sentiments & opinions," he believed that "the extent, to which you press your doctrines" was "not in my judgment defensible."[65]

Sumner knew that Story was more conservative about social change than he was himself, and that he had become more conservative with age, but he remembered also that Story had approvingly judged the American Peace Society's 1833 essay contest, and Sumner could write that "I never knew Judge Story more eloquent or earnest than when inveighing against" that sentiment he abhorred himself—"*our country be she right or wrong.*" They did not discuss the question in more detail. Story was ill, disillusioned with the direction of a country "rapidly on the decline" from "corruption & profligacy—demagoguism & recklessness," and, as he put it to Sumner, he felt "too old to desire or even to indulge in controversy." Instead, the Judge gave Sumner his final blessing, assuring him that "no one cherishes with more fond & affectionate pride the continual advancement of your literary & professional fame than myself, & no one has a deeper reverence for your character & virtues." It was, however, in the knowledge that, intellectually and politically, he had lost his star pupil, his hope for the future of the conservative cause and thus of the country, that Judge Story died one month later.[66]

While he deeply mourned the loss of such a dear friend, Sumner knew that his life had taken a very different turn from what they both had once expected. When the possibility finally came up—that possibility that had once meant as much to Sumner as to Story—that Sumner might succeed his master to the headship of the Harvard Law School, he felt within himself that he no longer wanted the post. In such an office "my opinions will be restrained," he confided to George, "& I shall no longer be a free-man."[67]

Sumner did not need to worry. In the end Harvard would never offer him the post for which he had once seemed the natural candidate. It was not unexpected. Harvard had already threatened men—like Henry Ware, Jr.—or even fired them—like Charles Follen—for speaking out against slavery. It was hinted that Webster himself threw his influence against Sumner. As former Mayor Samuel Eliot said just after the Fourth of July oration: "The young man has cut his own throat." Sumner had certainly burned his bridges. Wendell Phillips was struck by the difference between Sumner's former hopes and his present positions in the *True Grandeur of Nations.* "As I closed the last page," he wrote, "I could not help thinking of how far ahead you had strode of the C. S. of '32 & '33—and wondering, at the same time, whether I had been all that while seated still, playing with marbles? I hope not." This touched a reflective vein in Sumner. "I am happy to think, that, in your judgment, I am further on than in those days when I fed so ravenously on the husks of the law," he answered his friend, and confessed: "Life is unsatisfactory & unhappy enough; but one of its chief consolations is the idea of *progress.*"[68]

Sumner's reticence about the American Revolution on the Fourth of July did not imply a lack of respect. His regret that independence had been secured by war and that Americans had so far diverged from the principles on which that independence had been justified was anchored in his own deep admiration for the degree to which the founding of the American nation had been an exercise in idealism. The same spirit of Enlightenment humanism and progress that influenced Sumner's view of war and slavery and their eradication infused his thinking on the whole American republican experiment, its founding documents, and the duties of citizenship. Wendell Phillips had long hoped that Sumner's idea of progress might ultimately lead him to join with the Garrisonians. Instead it drew him closer to the Constitution, the Union, and to an active participation in the political system. It also drew him into a lifelong argument with the Garrisonian Phillips—an argument that, while it mirrored a major split in American antislavery thought, brought the two differently-minded but idealistic friends together in the shared intellectual relish of thoughtful debate.

It was with pride that Sumner asserted that "the Government and Independence of the United States are founded on the adamantine truth of *Equal Rights and the Brotherhood of all Men,* declared on the 4th of July 1776," and that it was for this truth that "the founders toiled and bled, and on account of which we, their children, bless their memory [. . .]." That Americans had not immediately lived up to their own ideals, Sumner did not dispute, but when he looked at the present reform movements and especially at the intensifying struggle against slavery, he believed more firmly that the principles of equality and brotherhood constituted a "truth receiving new and constant recognition in the progress of time [. . .]." And Sumner ardently desired to see the United States respected abroad for its embodiment of that truth which he considered "the great lesson from our country to the world [. . .]."[69]

The Founding Fathers who had written and approved the Declaration of Independence could not have changed their philosophy when, ten years later, they—some the same individuals—sat down to write the Constitution. Both documents, Sumner asserted, were born of the same "divine spirit." The nation took as its "baptismal vows" that "all men are created equal" and then wrote a Constitution under which such a concept of freedom might "be best preserved": "The Constitution was the crowning labor of the authors of the Declaration of Independence. It was established to perpetuate, in the form of an organic law, those rights which the Declaration had promulgated, and which the sword of Washington had secured." A Constitution based upon that foundation, and which declared its own purpose to be the securing of liberty, Sumner believed, was—whatever its practical shortcomings—in its essence antislavery.[70]

To this his friend Phillips cried—hold! Phillips had come to share Sumner's egalitarian principles. On his own first trip to Europe, which overlapped with Sumner's, Phillips had been similarly struck by the mingling of people of different races in schools, churches, society, without antipathy or apparent thought. Like Sumner, he had thought, how different from America, how good. He had as much respect for the ideals of the Declaration of Independence as did Sumner, but he could not accept the Constitution as a part of this tradition. By 1844 and 1845 Phillips had already become Garrison's right-hand man, the intellectual of the abolitionists as well as their most prominent orator. In those years Phillips confirmed this standing in a series of pamphlets directed against the arguments affirming the antislavery nature of the Constitution published by radical antislavery theorists Alvan Stewart, William Goodell, and especially Lysander Spooner. Though within two years these rivals of the Garrisonians would leave the antislavery Liberty party—calling it too narrow and conservative—and establish instead such organizations for political influence as the Liberty League, they remained convinced that the best way to accomplish progress was through politics.[71]

To these men, Phillips argued from James Madison's recently published notes of the Constitutional Convention that the national document had in fact been the result of political compromise, and that protections for slavery had been consciously written into the Supreme Law of the Land. Leading American jurists had confirmed this in their constitutional decisions and writings, Phillips added, and he included Joseph Story among them. Reacting to the recent case of George Latimer, whom Massachusetts Chief Justice Lemuel Shaw ordered returned to slavery despite Latimer's claims that he had already bought his freedom, Phillips insisted bitterly that the federal Fugitive Slave Law of 1793 was in fact binding under a pro-slavery Constitution.[72]

The disagreement between Sumner and Phillips rested in part on their different approaches to law. Though they could remember taking part in moot courts together under Judge Story's direction, they had come away from Dane College with very different understandings of the relationship between Natural Law and the positive law written by man. Phillips' aristocratic self-assuredness, which put him at ease while defying society and allowed him to cultivate a mocking, colloquial speaking style very different from Sumner's classical oratory, may have helped him to take a more radical political stand than the cautious and self-conscious Sumner. In law, however, which the bored Phillips had not read so carefully, it was Sumner who had the ease of an authority.

Phillips' objection to the Declaration of Independence was based upon his belief that as a declaration rather than a piece of legislation it could have no legal bearing upon the interpretation of the Constitution, however much he might prefer its principles to those of the latter document. For Sumner it was the Declaration's status precisely as a statement of principle that made it crucial. They diverged in the same way on Lord Mansfield's 1772 *Somerset* decision, which had long since become legendary in antislavery thought. Phillips did not deny the antislavery potential of a ruling that proclaimed slavery contrary to the Law of Nature, but he rejected it as having no legal jurisdiction beyond the shores of England. It was not just Sumner's antislavery feelings, but his cosmopolitan understanding of Natural Law as well as his acceptance of the deep ties between English and American law that would not permit him to deny its applicability to the United States. Instead, throughout the early and mid-1840's Sumner engaged in a close correspondence with Joshua R. Giddings, antislavery Whig and congressional collaborator of John Quincy Adams, on the precise bearing of *Somerset* not only on the laws of the United States but on the status of slaves on the high seas as well. Phillips respected the ideals of Natural Law but believed that people were bound by the letter of the human laws under the jurisdiction of which they found themselves. For Sumner a decision, like that in *Somerset,* that dealt so explicitly with the universal Natural Law could not be limited to merely local jurisdiction.[73]

Sumner and Phillips looked at the Constitution with the same difference. Sumner consciously followed the Natural Law principle *in favorem libertatis,* while Phillips insisted on interpreting the document according to the practical realities of the present, whatever the ethics. In fact, Sumner used what were the standard traditional rules of interpretation in the legal profession. First categorized by Blackstone, they had been neatly organized and popularized for Americans by none other than Joseph Story—one of his greatest contributions to practicing lawyers across the country. A few years out of law school, Sumner had had occasion to consider these rules even more deeply when he and Hillard and Story himself had helped Francis Lieber prepare his own volume on the subject. It was Sumner who wrote the work's first review—in which he tried to reassure the public that despite its forbidding title, the *Political Hermeneutics* was in fact a valuable manual and discussion of these same rules of interpretation. That laws written by human beings would contain difficult passages, even contradictions, these men all assumed. For their interpretation Story stressed certain basic principles—common sense, he thought—including a recourse to the original intent of the law's framers, a logical understanding of words according to "their ordinary and natural sense," a respect for the spirit of the whole text, and a constant devotion to the public good. These were the rules that Sumner followed in his interpretation of the Constitution.[74]

Phillips had no difficulty countering that slavery was supported by any number of clauses in the Constitution, including the clause for the rendition of fugitives, the clause giving slave states extra representation based on three-fifths of their slave population, and the clause giving Congress power to put down "domestic insurrections." He went into the history of the writing of the Constitution to point out that James Madison's Convention notes revealed the Founding Fathers' consciousness of what they were doing when they placed these safeguards for slavery in the document. Laws based on these clauses, though perhaps completely immoral, were constitutional, and Phillips argued that, under the constitutional system, they must therefore be obeyed or the lawbreaker suffer the consequences.[75]

To Sumner this was missing the forest for the trees. Phillips insisted upon a literal interpretation of the Constitution and biographers have written of his "legal positivism," yet he, too, was interpreting from passages that were inexplicit. As Sumner pointed out, James Madison's notes may have revealed discussion of slavery, but they also contained Madison's own insistence that it was "wrong to admit in the Constitution the idea that there could be property in men." Over the next years Sumner would regularly quote the words and examples of Jefferson, the slaveholder who condemned the evil of slavery and penned the Declaration, of Franklin, who was "President of the earliest Abolition Society in the United States," and of Washington, whose lifelong scruples over slavery caused him to wish the institution might "*be abolished by law*," and who by his last will emancipated his own slaves, thus becoming an "abolitionist." It was "plain" to Sumner that men who showed such personal and public hatred of what was in their time becoming the South's peculiar institution could not have intended the Constitution or the nation it organized to maintain the principle of slavery.[76]

If there were any doubt of the antislavery essence of the founding document, Sumner referred to the Constitution's own preamble—that part of any law meant to express the spirit in which the whole text was intended by its authors to be understood and by which therefore it should be interpreted. To Sumner the preamble's assertion that the Constitution was written "to establish justice, to promote the general welfare, and *secure the blessings of liberty* to ourselves and our posterity" was a restatement of the "unalienable rights" put forth by the Declaration of Independence. The Constitution was written "not to establish *injustice,* not to promote the welfare of a class, or of a few slaveholders, but the *general* welfare; not to foster the curse of slavery, but to secure the blessings of *liberty.*" Following Story's and Lieber's rules of interpreting words in a legal text according to their ordinary dictionary definition, Sumner underlined the fact that the Framers never once "named" the institution of slavery in the Constitution. This meant that, though the authors of the document might have felt unable to abolish slavery at the time, they considered it unacceptable as an integral part of the Union. The Founding Fathers regarded slavery "with aversion" and refused to believe it "*perpetual,*" looking "forward to the day when this evil and shame would be obliterated from the land."[77]

Sumner did not go so far as the "radical constitutionalists" whom Phillips had countered in his recent pamphlets. He agreed with them in upholding the primacy of Natural Law, and used the same rules of interpretation and some of the same examples in showing the Framers' refusal to give slavery ideological sanction in the Constitution that Lysander Spooner had used in his own work, *The Unconstitutionality of Slavery.* Sumner had long been intrigued by the idea Spooner developed that giving primacy to national over state citizenship—contrary to the legal practice of the time—could be a weapon against slavery. Though he considered it desirable, however, Sumner did not feel comfortable that it had clear legal sanction. Likewise, though interested, he was not yet prepared to accept the argument of Alvan Stewart that the Fifth Amendment negated slavery since no one had been made a slave by due process of the law, or that Article IV, section iv of the Constitution—the guarantee clause—did the same because slavery was inherently unrepublican. Sumner was sensitive to Garrison's objection—like Phillips': "Mr. Spooner's reasoning in regard to the language of the Constitution, we admit it to be ingenious—perhaps, as an effort of logic, unanswerable, but *as a matter of fact,* it makes no impression upon us." Unlike Garrison and Phillips, however, Sumner found the legal route by far the better one, and twenty years later would remember and use many of the radicals' arguments in the congressional debates over Reconstruction and the shaping of the Fourteenth Amendment.[78]

What troubled Sumner most about Phillips' position was precisely the danger that it might eliminate law as a solution to the problem. Phillips' insistence upon a pro-slavery interpretation of the Constitution was really meant to defend his primary proposition—the necessity of disunion. By refusing any effort to see hope in the Constitution and the political system it organized, Phillips high-lighted the gravity of the situation and made civil disobedience or outright rev-olution the only possible solution. The only way to abolish slavery, challenged Phillips, was to go "over the Constitution, trampling it under foot," not to use legal hairsplitting "to evade its meaning." That he preferred thereby to arouse public opinion to correct the problem politically before violence broke out was not enough to reassure Sumner of the wisdom of the course. As Sumner hinted to Robert C. Winthrop after the Fourth of July, an acceptance of the American Revolution entailed an acceptance of the right of revolution generally, including by American slaves, but "[c]an we proclaim such a truth?"[79]

Rejecting Phillips' potentially violent solution, without yet following all the arguments of the radical theorists and their limited appeal, Sumner stressed a more cautious but potentially more popular legal route. The Constitution was adaptable. Clauses supporting slavery were not written in stone. The objection of Phillips—as well as of some conservative Whig politicians and Southern pro-slavery theorists—that deference was due to an original compromise between free and slave states in the writing of the Constitution was not valid. "I wish to say, distinctly," Sumner informed his fellow Whigs, "that there is no compromise on the subject of slavery, of a character not to be reached *legally and constitu-tionally,* which is the only way in which I propose to reach it." There could be no compromises "of perpetual character," unless specifically identified as such, in a legal document that expressly sets down "how, at any time, amendments may be made" to it. Thus Sumner argued that the Framers had conferred upon the Con-stitution their own forward-looking spirit, giving the document "a *progressive* character, allowing it to be moulded to suit new exigencies and new conditions of feeling. The wise framers of this instrument did not treat the country as a Chi-nese foot,—never to grow after its infancy,—but provided for the changes inci-dent to its growth."[80]

The Constitution was not an abolitionist document, but it was written ac-cording to the same principles that motivated the abolitionists, Sumner argued, the same principles that made the perpetuation of slavery impossible under hu-man progress. In his *True Grandeur of Nations* he had urged how "shameful" it was for one generation to rest upon the laurels of their fathers, and he insisted now that, though the laws ought not to be expressly broken, he believed "it to be our duty at the North, according to the words of Franklin, to step to the 'very verge of the Constitution in discouraging every species of traffic in our fellow man.'" The antislavery movement was thus not only "the most important since" the Revolutionary period, thought Sumner: "*It is a continuance of the American Revolution.* It is an effort to carry into effect the principles of the Declaration of Independence, and to revive in the administration of our government the spirit of Washington, Franklin, and Jefferson; to bring back the Constitution to the principles and practice of its early founders; to the end that it shall promote Freedom and not Slavery, and shall be administered in harmony with the spirit of Freedom, and not the spirit of Slavery."[81]

Belief in the antislavery potential of the Constitution or in its pro-slavery actuality, appeal to disunion or plea for the Union—these disagreements inevitably pushed Sumner and Phillips to very different conclusions about their duty as citizens. Anxious for his support and agreement, Phillips sent Sumner copies of his pamphlets refuting Spooner and his associates. "Holding that honesty & truth are more important than even freeing slaves," Phillips explained, "—& that duties never can really conflict—" the Garrisonian could not agree to hold office or even to vote under a government and Constitution that sanctioned slavery. Regretting that he had to "differ so decidedly" from his friend, Sumner tactfully passed off his rejection of Garrison's call for disunion in response to the annexation of Texas "to my native hue of *ir*resolution, which leads me to postpone action on important matters." As eager as Phillips for a discussion, however, he went on to explain why he could not accept Phillips' fundamental assumption that participation in government is not a duty. He rejected the possibility of a truly good government—the only kind Phillips' honest citizen could take part in. "I know of no Constitution or form of Government, in the world," he reminded his friend, "from the ancient rule of China to the most newly-fashioned republic of our hemisphere, which does not sanction what I consider injustice & wrong." Sumner believed in no state of nature, no spot however remote that "is not desecrated by the bad passions of men, embodied in the acts & forms of Government." "But because Governments lend their sanction to what I consider unjust, shall I cease to be a citizen?"[82]

Unlike Phillips, Sumner found the Constitution essentially sound,—"with all its imperfections, [it] secures a larger proportion of happiness to a larger proportion of men, than any other Government." His observations of the lot of ordinary citizens in other countries had made him appreciate the relative freedom and enlightenment he found in his own. Thus spurred to greater hopefulness than the Calvinistic Phillips, Sumner urged his friend not to withdraw from government because of its injustices: "Shall I not rather, so far as in me lies, according to the humble measure of my ability, by the various modes in which I may exercise my influence among my fellow-men, by speech, by the pen, by *my vote,* endeavor to procure an alteration in the Constitution, to expurgate the offensive passages? I think that you would *speak* in favor of an alteration of the Constitution, why not *act* in favor of it? Take your place among citizens, & use all the weapons of a citizen in this just warfare."[83]

Where Phillips argued that one had no obligation to support any particular government and that all government was essentially imposed upon the individual by others, Sumner saw government as the natural organizing principle of society, and, as such, he argued that it produced benefits shared by the whole community—a community that included Phillips. Benefits necessarily call forth obligations. "You already support the Constitution of the U.S.," he reminded Phillips, "by continuing to live under its jurisdiction. You receive its protection, & owe it a corresponding allegiance." Merely refusing to vote or hold office is only a "half-way" measure, keeping benefits while giving nothing in return. Reading Phillips' argument, Sumner could not help but remember his own father's abandonment of his right to vote out of disillusionment at his experience in politics, and his continuing injunctions to his sons not to become politically involved. Sumner had been unable by natural inclination to accept such a withdrawal when he was first faced with a burning political issue during the Anti-Masonic campaign of the early 1830's. Now his sense of duty took the place of inclination. He did not put it so categorically to Phillips, but it was not so many years earlier that Sumner had wondered whether the right to vote should not become a legal requirement to do so. He never pursued this idea, but he always felt the duty himself. Even when, as many years later in the presidential election of 1872, he found himself faced with an impossible choice, he never felt he had the right not to vote.[84]

It was a question of more than just voting. Phillips' rejection of participation in the constitutional system included general involvement in politics and the holding of political office. For purely personal reasons Sumner was equally opposed to the idea of holding political office himself, but he would not reject the principle of political involvement. Though the radical constitutionalists' argument with the Garrisonians rested in part on their support of a direct political approach to the problem of slavery, men like Lysander Spooner were no more keen on the established political parties than Phillips. As slavery, through the annexation of Texas and its consequences, threatened more urgently than ever to undo what he saw as the founding principles of the nation, Sumner's sense of duty combined with his predisposition to work through legal and institutional channels quickly pulled him in that one direction that both Phillips and Spooner rejected and that he had himself so long shunned—into the world of party politics. "There are questions of ordinary politics in which men may remain neutral," he told his fellow Bostonians; "but neutrality now is treason to liberty, to humanity, and to the fundamental principles of our free institutions."[85]

This was Sumner's answer to the Whig leadership. They had called for neutrality in the form of acceptance of a *fait accompli* at least since the March passage of the Joint Resolution on Texas annexation. Through Robert C. Winthrop they had repeated that call on the Fourth of July in response to Sumner's oration. And they had made clear their intentions by strengthening their position within the party—tightening economic, political, and personal ties with Southern Whigs, while Nathan Appleton worked to patch up the rivalry between the Daniel Webster and Abbott Lawrence factions. By autumn it looked as though they had secured their desired tariff and parried the outside threat of the rising nativist American Republican party as well as the inside threat of the antislavery Young Whigs.[86]

The Young Whigs, determined to carry on the fight against any effort to admit Texas with a pro-slavery constitution, had now to decide how to proceed and with whom to collaborate. They had organized their January anti-Texas meeting at Faneuil Hall as an event open to all concerned, regardless of party. But with little response from the expansionist Democrats and the increasing cold shoulder from the conservative Whigs, the only significant group that remained willing to coöperate was the Garrisonians. Political and even social outcasts, they did not make very promising colleagues. Cautious Charles Francis Adams, the Young Whigs' leader, though not opposed to coöperation in principle, was personally repelled by Garrisonian disunionism and hesitant about attending abolitionist meetings. It fell to Henry Wilson, who had labored against Texas in the Massachusetts House as Adams had in the Senate, to bridge the gap. Wilson was more politically adventurous than Adams. Like Sumner, he had long read Garrison's *Liberator* and, without agreeing with its disunionism, shared its antislavery passion. Garrison returned the compliment by praising Wilson for "his manly and unfaltering course on the subject of slavery." Adams remained the principal strategist of the Young Whigs, but it was Wilson who accepted the Garrisonians' invitations to abolitionist meetings, and who conceived of the idea of organizing a joint antislavery Whig-abolitionist anti-Texas convention, which itself led that autumn to the formation of a joint effort by abolitionists and Young Whigs, the so-called Massachusetts State Anti-Texas Committee.[87]

Showing his difference not only with Wendell Phillips and Lysander Spooner, but with Charles Francis Adams, it was now that Sumner actively and enthusiastically joined in the work of opposing Texas. No longer just attending meetings, he became an active member of the Massachusetts State Anti-Texas Committee. He helped to edit its short-lived newspaper, the energetically titled *Free State Rally and Texan Chain-Breaker,* and he contributed materially to the organization of the Committee's most important action, its mass meeting at Faneuil Hall on 7 November 1845. Though he did not sign his name to them at the time and let Palfrey read them to the assembly, it was Sumner who wrote the resolutions, the passage of which was the meeting's major accomplishment. In their defense Sumner rose to make the first political speech of his life.[88]

CHAPTER V

As opposition to Texas reached its culminating days, feelings ran high. People on all political sides found the evening's violent electrical storm symbolic "—emblematic of the present moral and political aspects of the country," moralized the *Liberator*. The Democratic *Daily Times* sniped back: "It was proper that such a foul project should have foul weather as an accompaniment." "To oppose the extension of slavery was traitor-like, foul, and dark," echoed Sumner ironically. The mood inside the meeting was anything but dark and violent, however. Instead there reigned a tone of mixed idealistic fervor and political moderation, as the proposed resolutions were considered by various speakers, including Hillard, Phillips, and Garrison. Sumner began the first political resolutions of his career, his first political pronouncement, with the expression of his belief in the Enlightenment ideal of "*Equal Rights and the Brotherhood of all Men*" proclaimed by the Declaration of Independence and thereby made the justification of American nationhood. This, he later resumed, speaking of himself in the third person, was "always, from beginning to end, made the foundation of his arguments, appeals, and aspirations." Condemning the effort to admit Texas as a new slave state, "begun in stealth and fraud, and carried on to confirm Slavery and extend its bounds"—an effort that threatened to enlist the country not only in the extension of slavery but in an "unjust War"—Sumner's resolutions called on the people of Massachusetts, without distinction of party, "to unite in protest" against the extension of an institution so detrimental to the nation's reputation abroad and "in violation of the fundamental principle of our institutions."[89]

Sumner thus laid the ground for his insistence on the conservatism of the political antislavery movement. Understanding of the Garrisonians, very sympathetic to the arguments of such as Lysander Spooner, Sumner still thought the best means of effecting change in a republic was to work directly through the political system, to shape the actions of the major parties and national legislation through the influence of public opinion. In the case of slavery it seemed to him that all that was being asked was to keep the country mindful of its original ideals. The anti-Texas organization thus proposed "no factious or irregular course." "Our movement is conservative," Sumner informed his audience and the Whig leaders beyond. He accepted the common wisdom that the Constitution permitted no interference with local law, including the law of slavery, by other states or by the nation, and insisted that the opponents of Texas had no such designs. It was the pro-slavery forces that proposed change by extending their peculiar institution. More than this, it was the present Massachusetts leadership that proposed a disastrous change in the Commonwealth's stand by acquiescing in the spread of slavery. Her leadership had taken no such course in the past. Sumner appealed to the record of her protest in 1819 against the admission of Missouri as a slave state. He reeled off the names: Josiah Quincy, Daniel Webster, and John Phillips, Boston's first Mayor and father of Wendell Phillips—pillars of the community who had spoken then against the spread of slavery. It was the present Massachusetts leaders who proposed a radical new departure by their acquiescence in the admission of the slave state Texas.[90]

Slavery may or may not be "our original sin," but, Sumner told his audience as he had on the Fourth of July, though we cannot change the past we must take responsibility for the future. "[B]y welcoming Texas as a slave State we do make slavery our own original sin" by "a new and deliberate act," giving our sanction to the spread of slavery and of "*a new slave-trade.*" Instead we must return to the ideals of the Declaration of Independence, to the ideals still followed by the leaders of 1819, Sumner insisted, even should Massachusetts stand alone therefore in "noble solitude." And showing that the power for which his Fourth of July oration had been praised was no accident, he appealed to the idealism and the patriotism of his audience: "God forbid, that the votes and voices of the freemen of the North should help to bind anew the fetter of the slave! God forbid, that the lash of the slavedealer should be nerved by any sanction from New England! God forbid, that the blood which spurts from the lacerated, quivering flesh of the slave, should soil the hem of the white garments of Massachusetts!" "[L]et every man do his duty," Sumner urged, and in so doing, felt that at last he was doing his own.[91]

The resolutions were adopted and the meeting adjourned a success, though the movement as a whole could not hope for the same outcome. The abolitionists denounced the meeting's conservatism. It proved even harder to appease the Whig leadership. A circular letter written by Sumner, Adams, and Palfrey asking for their signatures on a petition to Congress opposing the admission of Texas with a pro-slavery constitution met with cold responses. Abbott Lawrence protested his long-standing opposition to the measure, but condemned further agitation as "useless, as a majority of the people have decided in favor of annexation [. . .]." Nathan Appleton added his conviction of the wisdom of the Constitution as written, and his sentiment that "it is at least questionable whether the Abolition movement is reconcilable with duty under that Constitution." Many Whigs left the now moribund Massachusetts State Anti-Texas Committee. On 29 December 1845 President Polk signed the congressional resolution that made Texas the twenty-eighth state of the Union, and the fifteenth slave state. This did not end but could only intensify the struggle. For now the question was no longer whether a new state would be admitted, but whether that act would lead to war with Mexico.[92]

It had been a sanguine vision—that everyone from conservative Whigs to abolitionists would come together against the annexation of Texas. Political and class prejudices had kept them apart, but the basic tenets of American philosophy and New England tradition—their shared distaste for slavery, their shared belief in the importance of moral leadership working for the public good—

might have united them, thought Sumner. The disappointment of his hopes saddened him. But it had urged only more powerfully to him the necessity of political agitation—not only by politicians, but especially by conscientious private citizens. If the worst came to pass, however, Sumner still hoped that at least all Whigs, conservative and Young alike, could together oppose a war that offended their shared philosophical and moral principles.

"THE VINEGAR OF PARTY"

ON 11 MAY 1846—"a day which will ever be accursed in our history"—the House of Representatives voted to sanction and prosecute a war against Mexico. For Sumner this was more than just the next chapter in the ongoing controversy over slavery. He arraigned a war that, by the baseness of its causes and the inevitable evil of its consequences, degraded the moral character of the United States, threatening the future development of her culture at the same time that it blasted the nation's moral authority in both her domestic and her foreign policy, imperiling the future of republican government and of mankind's eternal struggle for freedom. An Act of Congress, promoting such a crime, "will hardly yield in importance to any measure of our Government since the adoption of the Federal Constitution. It is certainly the most wicked in our history, as it is one of the most wicked in all history. The recording Muse cannot fail to drop a tear over its turpitude and injustice, while she gibbets it for the disgust and reprobation of mankind."[1] Surely, believed Sumner, no conscience touched by such a crime had the right to remain inactive.

Grievances between the United States and Mexico had been accumulating for years. Mexicans had long resented what they saw as the essential takeover of their province of Texas by American immigrants and the aid given them by companies of American citizens during the Texas uprising of 1836. Polk insisted upon claims against Mexico for injuries and losses sustained by Americans during that country's repeated revolutions. He would not be deterred even when the Mexican government went bankrupt in an effort to pay them. The Mexican government grew sure that Polk insisted upon the claims as a way of forcing them to give up even more territory, something they dared not do for fear of retaliation by internal critics. When Polk ignored their agreement to receive a commissioner to settle the claims and in late 1845 sent a minister instead—John Slidell of Louisiana, a man above all hateful to the Mexicans—a furious and frightened Mexico refused to receive him.[2]

When Polk sent the House his war message on 11 May 1846, however, most of the country and even much of Congress was caught off guard. These grievances should not have led to war. The inability of a country to pay claims, even its refusal to receive a minister, had never been considered a legitimate *casus belli*. This was especially true when the United States was itself in default on repayment of substantial British loans. The much more greatly feared war with Great Britain over the Oregon Territory had just been averted by negotiation. Many had awaited the same result with Mexico. Polk, however, had been quietly intent upon disposing peacefully of the Oregon question to free the way for a war with Mexico in order to acquire more southwestern lands. He may well have been most interested in California's Pacific harbors, but his expansionist determination and preference for southern rather than northern lands—both so heartily supported by Southern Democrats and slaveholders—fueled the deep suspicions of Northern Whigs and antislavery men that the annexation of Texas was indeed the design of a Slave Power determined to acquire as much new slave territory as possible.[3]

Behind the scenes Polk had been using aggressive diplomacy—including, in the words of his principal biographer, "bullying and bribery"—to exploit the weaknesses and divisions of the Mexican government. Then, in January 1846, after learning of the Mexican government's refusal to receive the American minister, he openly ordered American troops under General Zachary Taylor to go beyond the Nueces River, the traditional Texas border, into Mexican territory, claiming all the land to the Rio Grande as part of the newly acquired state of Texas—something to which the embattled Mexican Administration could not acquiesce without falling prey to its internal enemies, but which it had little power to stop. When a Mexican contingent finally crossed to the northern bank of the Rio Grande and fired on two of Taylor's companies, the Administration newspaper cried: "*American blood has been shed on American soil!*" Two days later Polk sent his war message to Congress. As "war exists, and, notwithstanding all our efforts to avoid it, exists by the act of Mexico herself," the President called for men and money to repel what he labeled the Mexican invasion and to force Mexico to return to the negotiating table.[4]

Most Americans, especially in the expansionist South and West, were outraged at Mexico and greeted the war with enthusiasm. Even in Massachusetts, some leading Democrats, like the jurist-turned-politician Caleb Cushing and Polk's Secretary of the Navy George Bancroft, supported war. New Englanders generally, however, and Whigs across the North found the Administration's actions unjustifiable. Boston quickly became the center of antiwar protest as both antislavery activists and businessmen worried about the economy spoke out against "Mr. Polk's War." Sumner hoped that a turning point might be at hand within the Whig party.[5]

Feelings between the two factions of the Massachusetts party had been worsening ever since the annexation of Texas. Whig leaders feared that abolitionist talk would divide the party between North and South and began to suspect their juniors of mere political ambition, while Sumner and his antislavery associates deprecated the Northern Whigs' tendency to respond to antislavery agitation by strengthening their ties to Southern slaveholders. When in that winter of 1845 he learned that John C. Calhoun was negotiating a personal loan of $30,000 from none other than Abbott Lawrence, Sumner was appalled. Though he was mistaken in thinking the loan had actually gone through, he would not have been reassured by the cordiality of the correspondence between the South Carolinian Democrat and the Massachusetts Whig. Tariffs and profits seemed more interesting than antislavery to Whig leaders whom Sumner had taken to calling "cottonlords." The phrase early became common currency among antislavery Whigs.[6]

Private doubts quickly spilled into public debate. In January 1846 Governor Briggs set before the General Court a series of resolutions passed by the Georgia legislature attacking Massachusetts for laws protecting her own black citizens while they were in slaveholding states. When an exasperated Whig begged the Court to return to ordinary business and leave off worrying about antislavery petitions, Young Whig Ebenezer Rockwood Hoar—son of the distinguished Judge Samuel Hoar of Concord—answered: "It is as much the duty of Massachusetts to pass resolutions in favor of the rights of man as in the interests of cotton." The conservatives contemptuously labeled Hoar a "Conscience Whig." Hoar proudly declared he would rather be a Conscience Whig than a "Cotton Whig." The names stuck; so did the distrust.[7]

Despite their differences on slavery, however, and on the importance of party unity, Conscience and Cotton Whigs agreed in their desire to see the nation culturally and morally elevated. It was this philosophical agreement which had lent much of the passion to their debate on policy, and which now made Sumner hope that the two groups might be brought together by their shared opposition to the Mexican War. They had all expressed it openly. In 1845 Nathan Appleton had agreed with Sumner on "all you say about the folly and wickedness of going to war for Texas and Oregon," and one year later he agreed that "Mr. Polk [was] unjustifiable in ordering the army into the disputed territory on the Rio Grande [. . .]." The Cotton Whigs' major organ, the *Daily Advertiser,* condemned the President's call for war. Massachusetts' senior Senator, prominent Cotton Whig John Davis, was openly opposed to the war, as was Boston's Representative, the Cotton Whigs' new leader, Robert C. Winthrop.[8]

All through the winter of 1846, Sumner had been anxiously corresponding with Winthrop, hoping to shore up his resolve against both threatened wars. They had never been close, but Sumner had known the long-faced, bespectacled Winthrop since college, and both had been protégés of Judge Story, Sumner in law and Winthrop in politics. They had always shared a friendly regard, and Sumner had always voted for Winthrop, accepting him as "a person of pure life, & good scholarship." He had long been dissatisfied, however, with what seemed to him Winthrop's lack of moral courage and conviction. Boston's Representative did not stand for anything. As early as 1840, Sumner had confided to his brother George that "I think him little more than a *formula* of a man."⁹

It was imperative, however, that war be avoided. Hostilities "for the sordid purpose of securing a few more acres of land" Sumner could not accept now any more than he had in 1839, and a war between England and the United States would be "murder by wholesale." Winthrop's firmness seemed all the more crucial to Sumner because John Quincy Adams, the elder statesman and diplomatist of the House as well as leader of the antislavery Whigs, had in the Oregon debate argued that we should immediately demand an explanation of Great Britain. The wily parliamentarian, as always, had a game. Convinced that Polk had no intention of fighting for Oregon and was using the issue merely as a blind to get support for his real purpose of war with Mexico, Adams pushed the question in order to show the duplicity of the Administration and the true character of the Slave Power lying behind it. Such ploys made Sumner uneasy. "Mr. Adams's course had been expected," he admitted, but its dangers and the belligerence of some of the former President's allusions made Sumner fear that it "will do our national character infinite harm abroad."¹⁰

Sumner thus quickly thanked Winthrop for "the noble resolutions" he had introduced in the Oregon debate "proposing Arbitration instead of War," and encouraged his pride by commenting on the weakness of most "public men & politicians" who are "*behind the moral sense* of the people. [. . .] There were some, undoubtedly, who felt the importance of Peace; but they feared to risk a temporary popularity, not thinking that one vigorous plea for Peace, on this emergency, would confer immortality, besides being the performance of a sacred duty, which would be better far than fame or office." In the very speech calling for arbitration, however, Winthrop had conceded that, should it come to war, "whatever [. . .] previous differences of opinion" there might have been, "the whole country will be *united*." A formal declaration was not enough to make an unjust war just. "I do not believe in *Act of Congress morality*," Sumner rebuked Winthrop. The Representative's position seemed to Sumner merely to echo the "Decatur patriotism" of his toast at the previous Fourth of July dinner. When Polk flung his call for military appropriations at Congress on 11 May 1846, Sumner could hear Winthrop's words still ringing in his ears: "[A]ll wars," Winthrop had admonished him, "involve an element of self-defence, after they have once commenced."¹¹

To Sumner there was no doubt. A war for Oregon would have been folly— the Mexican War was not only indefensible but mean. Texas, whether as a Mexican territory, or an independent state, "had never exercised any jurisdiction beyond the Nueces." To order American troops beyond that river to the Rio Grande was without justification. If a "collision" had resulted it was entirely to be expected. "The Mexicans, in the exercise of the right of self-defence, sought to repel the invaders from their hearths and churches." The fact that the United

States, "a rich, powerful, numerous and united Republic," had avoided war with mighty Great Britain and sought it with a Mexico weak from internal divisions made the war in addition "dishonorable and *cowardly.*" When the Polk Administration then pretended that the war existed "*by the acts of the Republic of Mexico,*" they added falsehood to aggression.[12]

The motivation behind this aggression made it all the worse. Legal and peaceful expansion of the area of free republican government, Sumner would accept. The fact that, as he was sure, this war had "its origin in a series of measures to extend and perpetuate Slavery" made it wicked. Sumner was by no means alone in thinking so. The outspoken support for the war of many slaveholders seemed only to echo the explicit statements of then Secretary of State John C. Calhoun's 1844 Pakenham letter, which sang the praises of slavery to the British minister at Washington and specifically called for the annexation of Texas in order to spread the South's peculiar institution. John Quincy Adams was only the most famous of many antislavery advocates who had collected much circumstantial evidence to implicate slavery as a principal cause of the war.[13]

When it was presented with Polk's call—not for a formal declaration of war, but simply for appropriations to man and fund that war—Congress was confounded. Even in Polk's own party, enthusiasm for a war of expansion coexisted with deep misgivings. Southern Whigs, already nervous about having opposed the acquisition of the new slave state Texas, quailed before a vote on a war to maintain that state. Northern Whigs, sure the war was the result of a conspiracy for more slave territory and sensitive to the difficulties of their Southern brethren, were openly opposed to the war, but at the same time feared being labeled disloyal like the New England Federalists, whose opposition to the War of 1812 had destroyed their party. Polk knew this and had his Democratic forces well marshaled. Debate was limited to two hours. Only at the last minute did Democratic leaders attach to the bill a preamble echoing the President's charge that "by the act of the Republic of Mexico, a state of war exists between that government and the United States." To reject the Administration's explanation of events the House members would have to refuse reinforcements to Taylor's army. The bill passed 174 to 14. The Senate followed suit the next day. John Davis was one of only two senators voting nay, but Winthrop had followed the majority.[14]

The Mexican War was fact. Such a war, begun in unprovoked aggression and for the purpose of spreading an evil institution, Sumner denounced as both illegal and immoral—"wrong by the law of nations, and by the higher law of God." Of the congressional act that sanctioned the war, he declared plainly: "It is a National lie."[15]

The Conscience Whigs had long agreed on the need to act, but while the war had remained only hypothetical they had been unsure how best to proceed. While

Sumner privately encouraged Winthrop's resolve for peace, Henry Wilson, now the leading Conscience Whig in the Massachusetts Senate, was heading the effort there to pass the antislavery resolutions in response to Georgia—a struggle that he would wage to the publication of a minority report. In January John G. Palfrey even suggested that the Conscience men might put up a candidate to run for conservative John Davis' Senate seat, but his friends rejected such a break with the party. For a time, all political discussions stopped among the friends when Charles Francis Adams' five-year-old son fell ill and then died, leaving his father with no heart for political turmoil. Then in May with the suddenly urgent threat of war with Mexico came a perfect opportunity. At a time when newspapers were attached to political leaders or factions, the Whig party's strength in Boston gave it near total control of the local press. How could the Conscience Whigs refuse then, when presented with the chance to buy the faltering *Daily Whig*? Adams, Palfrey, and a more reluctant Stephen C. Phillips would contribute the capital, while Sumner and Wilson, unable to put up any money, would contribute their pens. Adams, recovering from the first shock of grief enough to feel the need for hard work, agreed to be the new paper's editor. By the start of the summer the Conscience Whigs were ready to publish their opposition.[16]

Charles Francis Adams and his colleagues aimed their full fire against the Cotton Whigs. Instead of being opposed to each other, charged the antislavery men, the leaders of the Massachusetts Whig party and of the Democratic party in the South were bound together by the cotton industry, for which the former wove the final product from the latter's raw material. Palfrey spent the summer and fall on a series of articles for the *Whig* on the Slave Power and on the man they believed to be one of its principal Northern allies, cotton manufacturer Nathan Appleton. Adams himself focused on the conservative political influence of manufacturing wealth in the Bay State, and especially on the role of Abbott Lawrence, cotton manufacturer and principal strategist of the Massachusetts Whig party. Sumner took no part in these indictments against dear old friends, but when Adams also condemned what he considered Winthrop's resulting vote, Sumner added his voice to the arraignment in four articles against Boston's Representative.[17]

Whig leaders were nonplussed when the Conscience men chose to protest the war by attacking the heads of their own party. Had an attack like that of the Conscience men "been found in a Democratic paper, although we might have been surprised at it, for its discourtesy," sniffed the *Daily Advertiser*, "it would have been attributed to the zeal of party opposition." Had it come from the abolitionists, added that paper, even its discourtesy "might have passed without remark." After all, objected Nathan Appleton, it was not the Whig but the Democratic party that had started the war and that was "to be called to account for such a wrong." The Whigs, indeed, had been and continued to be outspoken critics of the war, and all sixteen men who had voted against it had been Whigs. Sumner agreed. "I suppose that no person will seriously affirm [the] truth" of the notorious preamble to the appropriations bill, he wrote, "but I have heard Whigs, who have served many winters in the cause, speak of it with shame and regret."[18]

When in a June speech, however, Winthrop defended his own outspokenness against the war by saying that he had "opposed [the Administration's] policy, from beginning to end, to the best of my ability," the Conscience men could only reply with scorn. Winthrop and his fellow Whigs had spoken against the war— but he and the vast majority of his colleagues had voted for it. The Democrats might cultivate party discipline and Romantically set aside reverence for law and community in favor of the modern pursuit of individual and national destiny. The Whigs, urged Sumner, remained attached to their belief that true national glory lay in "a regard for truth, for moral character" that must outweigh mere party considerations. When Winthrop consciously voted for what he believed to be wrong he failed both the Right and the higher standards of his own party. "This has been a suicidal blow to the Whig party," Sumner lamented, for it "has taken from us our moral strength."[19]

Sumner intended no purely political attack against Winthrop. He acted from no political motives, but rather out of a stern sense of conscience and "duty" that did not leave him the choice of silence before such a great moral wrong. His first article against Winthrop's vote was founded in his belief that the Mexican War forced everyone to consider the question of the duty of the individual when faced by wrong sanctioned by his own society or government. This included Sumner's own duty given that the wrong had been sanctioned by the representative for whom he himself had voted. And it required that such a representative be held to account, not as the adherent of a party, but as that moral man and responsible member of the community that Sumner and Winthrop and all their fellow Bostonian Whigs, educated to harken to the duties of conscience under the principles of American Moral Philosophy, had grown up believing they should strive to be.

What Sumner abhorred in the military was precisely its tendency to overthrow individual responsibility and, by its talk of honor and glory, to blind its followers "to a true perception of the moral character of the acts in which they participate." It lowered man to the animal component of his nature and, by denying his intellect and conscience reduced him to "servitude." Not even this could wholly excuse the soldier from his duty as a human being, however. The ordinary soldier might well be "the *least culpable* only," but, as he pondered the matter, Sumner did not "easily see how the soldier can extricate himself from [the] binding force [of the *law of Right*], although his Govt. tells him to fight." Was it not contradictory to expect a Christian to fight "except in defence of life?" As he considered the question, Sumner came to agree with the most liberal clerical opponents of the Mexican War, men like Theodore Parker, that the soldier who does believe a particular cause to be immoral cannot fight for it and then "excuse himself by reason of the orders of his Govt. If in his conscience he believes the war wrong, he cannot serve in it." It was thus to contribute to the elevation of the human spirit by encouraging a devotion to conscience that Sumner would propose an amendment to the ill-fated Massachusetts Constitution of 1853 calling for the legal recognition of conscientious objection.[20]

Could the citizen be less bound by conscience than the soldier? The moralists of the Latin School and of Harvard who had consciously trained Sumner, Winthrop, and all their classmates for their roles as citizens and civic leaders had sometimes fallen into a latent ambiguity on a major philosophical point. They had taught the importance of conscience, of man's moral sense, of thinking about life and society according to the highest ethical standards; but, living in a cultivated and well-ordered place, they had also been attached to the stability of the world they knew. When ethics and stability came into conflict, they, and their students, chose different paths. A milestone of the Reverend Channing's own ethical journey was his realization, growing out of the problem of slavery, "that virtue did not consist in feeling, but in *acting from a sense of duty.*" Another friend of Sumner's, the Reverend Francis Wayland, President of Brown University and author of the most popular American textbook on Moral Philosophy, directly urged his students that each individual must question every act of his government, for he was "morally responsible for all the wrongs committed by that society, unless he has used all the innocent means in his power to prevent them." This was the model that Sumner admired.[21]

If mankind had any dignity, if life had any purpose—as Sumner deeply believed—they derived from that God-given conscience that, properly informed by the intellect, showed every individual the path of right and held him accountable for his choices. It was no good for people to "satisfy their consciences by the utterance of general truth [. . .] without venturing or caring to apply it practically in life." That August, as the principal orator at Harvard's Phi Beta Kappa anniversary, Sumner stood before an audience that included many of his Cotton Whig opponents and celebrated William Ellery Channing precisely for his willingness to accept this responsibility. "He sought to bring his morality to bear distinctly and pointedly upon the world. Nor was he disturbed by another suggestion, which the moralist often encounters, that his views were sound in theory, but not practical. He well knew that what is unsound in theory must be vicious in practice. He did not hesitate, therefore, to fasten upon any wrong he discerned, and attach to it a mark, which, like that of Cain, can never be wiped from its forehead. His Philanthropy was Morality in action."[22] It was this standard that urged Sumner to speak against Winthrop's vote. It was by this same standard that Sumner believed Winthrop had failed in his own duties as a representative.

Sumner had based his first article on the assumption that he and Winthrop, that Conscience and Cotton Whigs alike, agreed on the essential falsehood and injustice of the war against Mexico. All that ought to be required was to remind Winthrop of his duty. It was frustrating therefore to read the angry response of the Cotton Whig press and Winthrop's own self-conscious efforts to defend his vote. In his subsequent articles Sumner felt the need to repeat what had at first seemed too obvious to mention—the details of Polk's aggression against Mexico, the illegality of the war, the sinister role of slavery. Winthrop had not been ignorant of these facts, yet he had voted without regard to them, charged Sumner. In his defense of himself Winthrop had then compounded his error by casting blame on Mexico, among other things for refusing to receive the American minister. Even if the Polk Administration had honored Mexico's request for a semi-official commissioner rather than a full minister, even if that minister had not been an individual hated by Mexico and whose choice was thus doubly a calculated insult by the Polk Administration—even if that minister had been without objection, Sumner reminded Winthrop, under international law the refusal to accept any minister could be "no ground for war." Winthrop's effort to divert blame would not do; nor would his disregard for history and law. As Sumner returned to his desk to make his charges clearer, he attacked more and more directly what he believed to be Winthrop's essential failure, not only of citizenship but of statesmanship.[23]

Just as conscience was at the heart of Sumner's conception of good citizenship, so it formed the core of his definition of statesmanship. True statesmanship must be founded upon the informed conscience striving to elevate mankind and human civilization. It was clear to Sumner that Winthrop had failed to consider the essential consequences of the war against Mexico and therefore of his sanction of the war. First, he had failed to consider the good of the United States. Men and treasure drained from peaceful purposes and poured into aggression would cause twofold harm. "The soul sickens at the contemplation of this incalculable sum, diverted from purposes of usefulness and beneficence, from railroads, colleges, hospitals, schools and churches,—under whose genial influences the country would blossom as a rose,—and prostituted to the wicked purposes of an unjust war." Nor would the end of the war arrest its evil consequences. In 1848 Sumner would lament the indefinite continuation of the war's "most accursed influences"—in terms he would have occasion to employ again nearly two decades later: "There is a squadron of heroes now returning from Mexico to claim honor & office, & to brutalize the public taste."[24]

More than the nation's culture, America's very future would be jeopardized by a war for the expansion of slavery. The consequences of such a "slave-driving war" could be no different from those of other such wars that had been going on for centuries in Africa. Slavery, never satisfied with one territorial gain, would demand ever more, and in its career would not hesitate to engulf the United States in other wars. When, fifteen years later, Sumner's abhorrence for war and for slavery came into conflict with each other, he would in sadness but without hesitation embrace the temporary evil of war to end slavery and what he was convinced was its perpetual threat of violence. In 1846 he was sure that Robert Winthrop had neglected his duty as a public leader to consider these possibilities.[25]

Nor was the future of America alone in the balance, Sumner reminded Winthrop. In a world of monarchies, the United States represented the idea of republican government and the ideal of human equality. During his trip through Europe Sumner had seen all too clearly how the existence of slavery in such a country made all its professions of freedom seem mere hypocrisy. The increasing aggressiveness of the partisans of slavery and the willingness of the government to lie for their benefit could only worsen that reputation, and with it the standing of the ideal of popular government. Under these circumstances it was particularly harmful that the United States should have chosen to declare war "against a sister Republic," a younger and more fragile republic that the United States should instead have tried to support.[26]

To his failure to consider these far-reaching consequences, to his failure to heed his own conscience, which had told him such a war would be wrong, Winthrop had added what seemed to Sumner an insensitivity to such a war's immediate consequences—obvious and terrible—for Mexico herself. As Sumner looked over the horrors of the war just starting—"innocent lives are to be sacrificed; pleasant homes are to be made wretched; [. . .] children are to become fatherless; wives and sisters are to mourn husbands and brothers"—he urged upon Winthrop the seriousness of his action: "All this misery has the sanction of your vote, Mr. Winthrop. Every soldier is nerved partly by you. Away, beyond the current of the Rio Grande, on a foreign soil, your name will be invoked as a supporter of the war. Surely, this is no common act. It cannot be forgotten on earth; it must be remembered in heaven. Blood! blood! is on the hands of the representative from Boston. Not all great Neptune's ocean can wash them clean."[27]

Why would Winthrop do this? Sumner thought that Boston's Representative had been swayed by unstatesmanlike weaknesses. The true statesman should always guard himself against the influence of popular prejudices. Winthrop—who was well known as an "enthusiastic militiaman" and who liked to be called "Colonel"—had been carried away by "the alleged duty of voting succors to General Taylor's troops." As Sumner looked back over Winthrop's Fourth of July toast to "our country, *howsoever bounded*," it seemed to him that Winthrop's vote on 11 May was "the dark *consummate flower*" of that sentiment. Sumner must have shaken his head as Nathan Appleton argued in Winthrop's defense that, however wrong the war might be, "war being actually on foot, it is generally believed that a vigorous prosecution of it is the direct road to peace," and that until the Whigs could win back the White House, "I suppose every good citizen is bound to contribute in defence of his country, in the war in which she is actually engaged. It was the duty of Congress to give support to our citizens composing the army and who were only doing their duty."[28]

What a perversion of duty, thought Sumner. Even if the army had been in danger, and Sumner pointed to evidence that it no longer was by the time Congress considered the matter, Winthrop's vote would still have been unjustifiable—as unjustifiable as his insistence that "all wars involve an element of self-defence, after they have once commenced" was meaningless. "Our troops were in danger," Sumner corrected his Representative, "because they were on a foreign soil, forcibly and piratically displacing the jurisdiction and laws of the rightful government." Such an explanation as Winthrop's "confounds the opposite duties in cases of *defence* and *offence*." The Administration's intentions should have been plain to him on that fateful 11 May, argued Sumner. "[T]he magnitude of the appropriations and the number of Volunteers called for, clearly showed that measures were contemplated *beyond mere self-defence*." It was the Mexicans who were exercising the right of self-defense, Sumner reminded his readers. "We are the aggressors. We are now in the wrong." What should Congress have done when confronted with President Polk's call for men and money? Their statesmanlike duty, said Sumner, was plain: "Clearly to withhold all sanction from the unjust war, from the aggression upon a neighbor Republic, from the spoliation of our fellow-men." General Taylor should have been ordered, "[i]n the words of Col. Washington" when responding to a similar question, to "RETREAT! RETREAT!" To retreat not from an enemy but "from *wrong-doing*," Sumner told Winthrop, "would have been a true victory."[29]

It seemed to Sumner the lamest of excuses when Winthrop's Cotton Whig friends offered in defense of his vote that "his decision is a most difficult one," in "a case in which patriotic and conscientious men might differ and did differ [. . .]." "Surely," answered Sumner, "the case submitted to him had *no* difficulty." Where was the difficulty in a choice between "[*f*]ive-fold *Right*" and "*five*-fold *Wrong*"? The only difficulty, Sumner suspected, had been in the choice between the Right and the majority. Appleton's argument that the President's policy must be followed because "he had been placed in command of the army of the United States by the votes of the people" was repugnant to Sumner. If indeed—and Sumner would not have been satisfied with the definition—"[t]he aim of a deliberative body is to embody in their acts the sentiments of the greatest number, or at least of a majority of the members," as the *Daily Advertiser* contended in Winthrop's defense, that could not remove from each member the responsibility of his individual vote.[30]

Such arguments must have reminded Sumner of the traditional, almost monarchical, view of democracy as the absolute rule of the majority that had poisoned his father's hopes for the future of his country; it was with a different tradition, that of independent republican statesmanship inherited from the Puritans, that Sumner answered the Cotton Whigs. It is indeed "unpleasant" to have to differ with friends and colleagues, Sumner admitted, but "if stern duty summons him" the "man of sensibility and character [. . .] will treat the ties of party as threads of gossamer." It was Charles Francis Adams, in seconding Sumner, who said plainly that "the action of a crowd in itself justifies nothing. For one who aspires to be a leader to be led away to do a thing in itself wrong, by the mere fact that many others do likewise is one of the strongest indications of moral infirmity that he can give." Like their once mutual professor of rhetoric and oratory Edward Channing, the Conscience men warned Winthrop that the legislator "is not to bring his prejudices or his private interests with him, when he professes to act for a whole people. He is not to think of the place, or the honors, or the popularity he may gain or forfeit, by following this or that course of public conduct." And he must always beware any influence that might weaken the "opinions and resolves which he ought never to surrender."[31]

"Believing, as I do, that an *unjust war* is the greatest *crime* a nation can commit," Sumner explained to Appleton, "I think it was the *imperative* duty of every Xtian representative to oppose it, even if he stood *alone*." "In the question of Right or Wrong," Sumner declared to Winthrop, "it can be of little importance, that a few fallible men, constituting what is called a majority, were all of one mind. In all ages supple or insane majorities have been found to sanction injustice. It was a majority which passed the Stamp Act, and Tea Tax, which smiled upon the persecution of Galileo, which stood about the stake of Servetus, which administered the hemlock to Socrates, which called for the crucifixion of our Lord. But these majorities do not cause us to withhold our condemnation from the partakers in these acts. Aloft on the throne of God, and not below in the footprints of a trampling multitude of men, are to be found the sacred rules of Right, which no majorities can displace or overturn."[32]

Sumner willingly accorded Winthrop a faultless personal integrity. "You would not, in your private capacity, countenance wrong, even in your friend or child," Sumner addressed him, but a statesman must show the same integrity in public as in private life. "He will not assert a distinction between the obligations of nations, and of individuals. He will not say that an individual is bound to the strictness of truth, but a nation is not; that *one* man may not tell a lie, but that *many*, in a corporate character, may." Sumner made explicit his appeal to the traditional Puritan ideal of statesmanship by recalling the example of "that true hero, John Milton, that a commonwealth ought to be but as one huge Christian personage, one mighty growth and stature of an honest man, as big and compact in virtue as in body"; such an image as urged the legislator: "[N]ever do for your country what you would not for yourself." There was another ideal of ethical leadership more meaningful yet to the Representative from Boston. Sumner called upon the great founder of the Bay Colony, John Winthrop himself, to speak directly to his descendant. "Our country, right or wrong, or *howsoever bounded,* is a sentiment of heathen vulgarity and impiety. Scorn it; tread it under foot as a serpent beguiling to sin," admonished the ancestor: "For my sake, for the name you bear, that it may always be cherished, for righteousness' sake, do not fear to stand in a small company, or alone, it may be, with truth on your side; scorn the shelter of numbers, howsoever great, when they speak falsehood and injustice."[33]

Winthrop was stunned by the attack. He had never experienced anything like it. As the Conscience Whig articles multiplied, friends wrote to console him, invariably equating invective and reform. "This is Abolitionism," Edward Everett commented sadly. Winthrop's confidant, Massachusetts House member John H. Clifford, tried to reassure his old friend by impugning the motives of his opponents: "When the time comes for *you* to notice [the attack], this whole pack of aspiring, canting, & malignant *Humanitarians* will meet the discomfiture which they are now preparing to make more signal than you could make it for them." Winthrop insisted that he was not upset. "Do not think that I have taken up my pen to scold & fume again about C.F.A. and his compeers," he assured Clifford. "The repetition of the assaults has begun to make me indifferent to them," he added as convincingly as he could, and said of the latest article that he had "accompanied its perusal with reading the 37th psalm, which begins, 'Fret not thyself because of evil doers'[. . .]."[34]

But Winthrop was hurt, deeply hurt by the whole barrage of Conscience articles, and most especially by Sumner's. He was bewildered to find himself so much misunderstood. He disapproved of Polk's actions as much as anyone, and had said so. Such total disagreement seemed to him a "strange hallucination." At the same time, some of Sumner's criticisms were too true. Sumner was right to charge that one motive behind Winthrop's vote was his fear of being associated with the abolitionists. Even before Sumner's article, Winthrop had admitted to Edward Everett that his vote had been partly determined by his desire to avoid having "the whole Mass^ts Delegation [. . .] mixed up with a little Knot of Ultraists against supplies [. . .]." By the following winter Winthrop began to feel that his vote had put him in a box. Angry at Polk's repeated demands for money, Winthrop longed to rein the President in, but could "not see my way quite clear to refusing anything now." In fact, within the year, Winthrop would come closer to the Conscience position than most of his conservative colleagues, refusing a number of Polk's requests for money, especially those intended for the acquisition of territory, but he would never feel free to refuse supplies and demand the return of American troops.[35]

What hurt most was Sumner's arraignment of his statesmanship. Winthrop had always tried precisely to follow the ideal of the statesman, whom he saw as the moderator of overwrought passions. He had been particularly proud of his Fourth of July toast of the previous year, seeing it not as "dishonest patriotism" but as the statesmanlike offer of an olive branch to soothe the emotions elicited on both sides by Sumner's injudicious oration. The youngest of fourteen children, Robert Winthrop early became, through a remarkable series of family tragedies, the only direct descendant to carry his illustrious forebear's name, and he felt the weight of that standard keenly. He sometimes annoyed people by his too easy "habit of blowing a trumpet in honor of his great ancestor." Robert Winthrop often referred to the revered founder of Massachusetts Bay, not only on public occasions but privately, holding up to himself the example of a great man of conviction, who always knew what was right, and who was never troubled by detractors. It was an example that Winthrop secretly felt he himself could not live up to. Despite his efforts to keep his attacks strictly on public matters, Sumner had touched upon what may well have been Winthrop's own greatest source of private dissatisfaction with himself, his own secret cross, and Winthrop could never forget.[36]

The fact that the attacks came from someone Winthrop could only consider a social inferior added insult to injury. Though Clifford had immediately recognized Sumner's style behind the signature "Boston," Winthrop thought it must be Wendell Phillips or even George Hillard, whose backgrounds and literary pretensions seemed to him more in accord with the author's ability and apparent self-assuredness. "The writer is an accomplished person, & does his work with elegance," Winthrop had mused, refusing to consider the sheriff's son.[37]

Because their disagreement was about a matter of public policy—in which Sumner felt implicated because of his own vote for Winthrop—Sumner had published his protest from what he considered an inescapable sense of "duty." The traditional anonymity of political communications might have allowed him to avoid what he expected would be the unpleasantness of Winthrop's reaction, but he could not in his own mind "reconcile" such a silence "with my idea of a proper frankness between us," and so it was Sumner himself who put an end to Winthrop's curiosity. Despite the political matter of their disagreement, Sumner had never thought of his article as the attack of one political opponent against another, but rather as a reminder between two members of the same community of their shared values. As such he had meant it as an act of that true friendship which is always based upon complete honesty. As he explained to their mutual friend Appleton, it was Winthrop's closest friends who ought to have "gently & kindly" set him straight at the start rather than let him "deceive himself into the belief that he had done anything but *wrong*." Appleton, however, made it clear that he thought Winthrop had acted just right and chided Sumner for a want of "Christian charity" toward his Representative. Unwilling to allow his genial relations with Winthrop to be destroyed by politics, Sumner begged him to understand that he had in no way intended to be "disloyal to those pleasant relations, which I have always had the happiness of cherishing with you, & which I trust may always continue."[38]

Winthrop was only infuriated by Sumner's efforts to repeat his points and explain himself. Reading Sumner's articles "afresh," Winthrop swore he could see no arguments in them at all, nothing but "the coarsest personalities," and "the grossest perversions, [. . .] insinuations as to my motives, & imputations on my integrity." Disgusted with what seemed to him Sumner's moral arrogance and vindictiveness, Winthrop sent off a final letter without even making a clean copy. "It is certain, that we do not agree as to what belongs to the intercourse of friends, or even of gentlemen," he wrote, and declared that he must "decline all further communication or conference, while matters stand between us as they now do." Winthrop broke not only with Sumner, but with all the Conscience men. It would be nearly twenty years before he would speak with any of them again. He would never completely forgive Sumner.[39]

The Cotton Whig press was equally blunt. "A True Whig" early tried to berate the Conscience men into silence for subjecting Winthrop to this "public castigation" when "private remonstrance and appeal are open, even without the expense of postage, to any one who feels hurt at the conduct of his Representative." Such a suggestion "trifles with the magnitude of the occasion," answered Sumner. Winthrop had not offended individual feelings, but "the conscience of New-England, and the force of truth." With his eye every bit as much on the public reaction to the issues surrounding the war, Sumner reminded the party leaders how "important" it was that his sentiments against the war and Winthrop's part in promoting it "should be uttered in public, that other pens and tongues may be awakened to call for the arrest of this war, and that Mr. Winthrop may feel the force, not merely of private, but of public disapprobation of his vote, mingled with hope for the future."[40]

To Winthrop's voluble *Atlas* the Conscience men, with Sumner at their head, were guilty of pure "hypocrisy," their articles nothing better than so much "vanity," "arrogance," and "presumption." Winthrop knew that he had gone too far when in his last letter to Sumner he accused him directly of "insolence." He crossed the word out; but believing deep down in its accuracy, he left it clear enough to be read. Sumner and his Conscience friends shared with the Cotton Whigs the traditional conception—most prominent among Whigs and the Federalists before them—of the legislator as a man chosen for his intellectual and moral standing, who should be left to follow his independent judgment and not be imprisoned by the instructions of his constituents. But Sumner rejected any corresponding sense of *noblesse oblige*. The exercise of moral leadership was the statesman's duty, believed Sumner, not his privilege. If Winthrop had failed in that duty, he must be called to account.[41]

Moral leadership was more than a question of class. It had been bound up in Boston's own sense of her ideal self from the Puritan John Winthrop to the Revolutionary James Otis and beyond, so that the debate over far-away Mexico could not help but become a debate over Boston as well. No one felt this ideal more strongly than Sumner himself. Though anxious to see the antislavery movement spread through the whole country, he was eager to have his native city lead the way as she had in all "the generous and magnanimous actions of our history," including the Revolution. The influence that she had often exerted in the country, Sumner exhorted his fellow Bostonians, "is to be referred not to her size, for there are other cities larger far, but to her moral and intellectual character."[42]

Sumner was deeply pained to hear Nathan Appleton say that Boston should be not only understanding, but "proud" of her Representative for making such a difficult decision. In voting for the Mexican War, answered Sumner, Winthrop had "*done the worst act that was ever done by a Boston representative.*" Appleton responded by denying all Sumner's points against the war and rebuking him that "the assumption that our own opinion is the only right one in a complicated case of this kind, implies, it appears to me, a sublimation in our organ of morality incompatible with a perfectly sound judgment." "[E]very Xtian representative," replied Sumner, should stand up against an unjust war. "Above all, it was ye duty of ye representative of Boston, a place of conscience, & morality, to see that the influence of the city of Channing was not thrown on the side of injustice." The disagreement with yet another and much closer friend than Winthrop hurt Sumner. "I *do* wish that I could agree with [Mr. Appleton] more than I can on this great question of slavery & war," Sumner confided to Longfellow. There would be no overt break between Sumner and Appleton, but by the spring of 1847 Sumner sadly told Lieber that he and "*Nathan der Weise*" never saw each other any more. "Politics have parted us."[43]

Sumner's quarrel with Winthrop was representative of the earliest and most advanced American protest against the Mexican War. With the war still in its infancy, the South and West remained overwhelmingly enthusiastic. Since Polk had not yet made his territorial desires overt, only antislavery men and some Northern Whigs were thinking ahead to the danger that war might lead to the acquisition of more slave territory. In New England, however, antislavery men and pacifists were joined by many businessmen, editors, and clergymen in denouncing the war. Maine satirist Seba Smith resumed his anti-expansionist Major Jack Downing letters, while James Russell Lowell began his widely popular

Biglow Papers. No other region sent so small a number of volunteers to the front.[44]

Sumner's opposition to the so-called Decatur patriotism of "my country, be she right or wrong," was fully shared by groups like the American Peace Society, as was his fear that war, with its glorification of the soldier and increased debt, would lead to the moral degradation of the country. In this his friend from the Fourth of July oration, Theodore Parker, fully agreed, and sounded simultaneously from his Unitarian pulpit that war was a violation of the precepts of Christianity, as well as a corrupter of human nature and society by its glorification of the "low, selfish, and animal." John Greenleaf Whittier, Quaker, pacifist, abolitionist, and also a friend of Sumner's, felt no differently. Now—along with Garrisonians and Transcendentalists, many ordinary New Englanders, and antislavery men across the North—they both attacked slavery as the force behind the Mexican War, Sumner in his articles and Whittier in his poems. Sumner's insistence that the only proper solution would be the immediate withdrawal of American troops from Mexico was essentially unheard in the rest of the country, but was the common call of the most outspoken New England critics of the war.[45]

Then, on 8 August, Polk made his territorial plans public, thus unleashing what had been more private misgivings about the war outside New England and even within the Democratic party. On that day Polk set before the House of Representatives a request for two million dollars ostensibly to pay Mexico for the acquisition of Texas, but, Polk hoped and others feared, to take New Mexico and California as well. The expected force of American arms meant that Polk did not need the money to buy the provinces; he wanted it so that the increasingly unstable Mexican government could pay its army and buttress itself against revolution—a revolution that might leave any treaty with the United States in doubt. With the war now overtly for expansion into the southwest, the question of the spread of slavery, which had before been confined to antislavery circles, could no longer be ignored anywhere.[46]

As antiwar sentiment grew, so did the division over slavery within the major parties. Northern Democrats had long been attacked as "doughfaces" or "Northern men with Southern principles" for acquiescing in the pro-slavery policies of their Southern-controlled party. This had become increasingly uncomfortable for Northern Democratic politicians, caught between Southern policy and growing antislavery sentiment among their own constituents. Political resentment among supporters of former President Martin Van Buren, who had been set aside by the Democratic National Convention of 1844 in favor of the dark horse Polk, added to the displeasure of the most antislavery faction of the Democratic party, the New York Barnburners. When the Pennsylvania Van Burenite David Wilmot offered a proviso to Polk's "Two Million Bill" that would exclude slavery from any lands acquired from Mexico, the House thus divided not along party but

along sectional lines, passing both the appropriation and the "Wilmot Proviso"
by a Northern majority. Though a tactical miscalculation by Whig Senator John
Davis, who favored the Proviso, killed the bill in the Senate, and though leaders
of both parties would for some time try to keep the dangerous Proviso quiet, the
national debate over slavery in the territories had begun.[47]

The Conscience Whigs had long hoped for a general awakening across the
North to the evil of slavery. Though the Wilmot Proviso was based on a much
narrower principle than the debate they were engaged in with the Cotton Whigs,
it had potentially a much wider appeal. Just as Southerners, even Southern
Whigs who opposed the Mexican War, could not easily vote for a measure that
sanctioned congressional interference with the spread of slavery into the territories, most Northerners, even those who had never before taken a stand on slavery, would not give their assent to its expansion if they had a choice. Motives
ranged from the hatred of slavery, and the hatred of oligarchy represented by the
Slave Power, to the unwillingness of potential settlers to compete with slave labor or even with blacks, but for the first time a majority of Northerners seemed
ready to support a measure for the restriction of the South's peculiar institution.
Though he had quarreled furiously with the Conscience Whigs all summer,
Robert Winthrop voted aye on the Wilmot Proviso.[48]

The Conscience Whigs knew that their desire to see the Whig party reunited
on an antislavery platform would not be easily accomplished. The quarrel with
Winthrop had engendered bad feelings. So had the simultaneous debate within
the Boston Prison Discipline Society over the relative merits of the Auburn and
Pennsylvania systems, and, equally, about the fitness of the Society's imperious
president Louis Dwight, who rejected any effort to question the Society's cham-
pionship of the Auburn System. In the very month that Congress voted for war,
Sumner begged the Prison Discipline Society not to say: "'Our Society, right or
wrong.'" While Sumner arraigned the Society's intransigeance and privately denounced Dwight as "*lazy*" and insulting, Dwight and his treasurer Samuel Eliot
attacked Sumner as coarse and vindictive. Eliot's honesty and independence, as
well as his "individual sympathies for the slave," Sumner would not deny, but, of
his "obstinate" conservatism, Sumner would one day remark that "[i]n other
days and places he would have been an inquisitor."[49]

Prison discipline and the Mexican War were not unrelated; the leadership of
Boston's politics and of her benevolent organizations overlapped too closely for
that. Dwight was very close to the Cotton Whigs, while Eliot was a leading Cotton Whig himself, former Mayor of Boston and father-in-law of George Ticknor. Howe and Horace Mann as well as Sumner would speak out against the
Mexican War and slavery. Nathan Appleton connected the two struggles when
he quipped of Sumner and Howe: "Their philanthropy continues to be vituperative—and their antimartial zeal highly pugnacious." With American troops

marching through Mexico, however, in a war now plainly intended to gain territory appealing to slaveholders, the Conscience Whigs hoped that the divisions of the summer would give way to a new Northern unity against slavery.[50]

With autumn approaching, the Cotton Whigs were equally concerned about unity—for their party. The coming fall elections made the moment critical, especially with both Robert C. Winthrop's House seat and John Davis' Senate seat in the balance. Long worried about the effect of antislavery agitation on their ties with Southern Whigs, the leaders of the party were afraid now that the Conscience men might throw control of the election results to the Liberty party or to the Democrats. As the Whig State Party Convention approached, the Cotton Whigs thus quieted their tone. The State Committee even offered the Conscience men the carrot of being allowed to make any resolutions they liked, though this was against the better judgment of seasoned leaders like Abbott Lawrence. Winthrop was horrified to learn that Sumner, Adams, and Hillard were all to be delegates and begged his friends to attend in number: "Depend upon it, there is some thing of a crisis in the affairs of the Whig party," he wrote to Clifford. "If the Boston Whig is to be our Organ & Adams & Sumner our fuglemen, I, for one, see nothing further worth fighting for."[51]

Faneuil Hall's long, elegant, white meeting hall, still Boston's usual public gathering place but revered for the Revolutionary oratory that had echoed there, was once again thronged with people the morning of 23 September 1846. Eager, despite their skepticism, to see whether the opportunity could be turned into a real chance to influence the party, the Conscience men arrived armed with resolutions and speeches. The party leaders had pointedly chosen Stephen C. Phillips as one of the Convention's vice presidents, and he used the occasion to offer the Conscience men's resolutions. Though they had greeted the brand-new Wilmot Proviso hopefully, they were not yet ready to limit themselves to its single provision, and instead offered a series of demands long sought by the antislavery movement. The Conscience Whigs wanted the party to put itself on record against the admission of any new slave states. They called for the abolition of slavery in the District of Columbia as well as in the territories, where Congress had direct jurisdiction, and they insisted that no candidates should be accepted who did not support the abolition of slavery "by all constitutional means."[52]

To the Conscience men these all seemed urgent issues. By its constitution Texas could still divide into five separate states. The Mexican War raged on. Polk's desire to take land from Mexico was now on record. The Wilmot Proviso had openly placed before Congress the question of slavery in the territories. Yet when Abbott Lawrence addressed the Whig State Convention and assured the assemblage that there was no dearth of important issues for the Whig party to address, among tariffs and trade issues, he never mentioned slavery.[53]

As the opening business came to a close, a struggle erupted over the next speaker. Shouts arose from all parts of the hall as the newspaper division of the past months was recreated on the convention floor, Cotton men calling for Winthrop to speak, and Conscience men for Sumner. The Conscience men prevailed, and Sumner stepped to the podium. "It will be of Duties that I shall speak," he informed the audience. Tariffs, internal improvements, banks were all potentially worthy issues, but must not be allowed to overwhelm the true spirit of the Whig party, "the party of freedom," and he reproved those in whose minds "[e]ven Right and Liberty are [. . .] of less significance than dividends and dollars." Turning against them the conservatives' choice of Boston as the convention site, rather than the more liberal country, Sumner gestured to the venerable walls of Faneuil Hall, which, "faithful only to freedom," refuse to echo "any but words of morals, of freedom and of humanity."[54]

In choosing a position to urge upon the reluctant Whig party, however, Sumner did not require the pursuit of absolute Right. Instead he took a self-consciously "conservative" and practical approach. First had to be combated the apathy that wondered "[w]hat has the North to do with Slavery? It might almost be answered," countered Sumner, "that, politically, it had little to do with anything else [. . .]." As long as slavery was still sanctioned in lands under federal control, fugitives were pursued into the North, Massachusetts laws and representatives insulted when trying to protect their black citizens in the South, and the Mexican War continued, the North was as deeply implicated in slavery as the South. What was then the duty of the North and of the Whigs in particular? First of all, to recall to mind the principles on which their party and the country had been founded. With Winthrop smoldering, Sumner called upon the Whigs to reject the easy weakness of "Our party howsoever bounded," and, in its place, he introduced to the assemblage his conviction of the antislavery spirit of the federal Constitution and of the Founding Fathers. It was in this sense that the Whig party should consider itself conservative "not of the letter only, but of the living spirit. The Whigs should be conservators of the spirit of our ancestors, conservators of the great animating ideas of our institutions." Upon that basis, Sumner appealed to the Whigs to begin their true work by ending the North's complicity in slavery. Mindful of Daniel Webster's resentment of Abbott Lawrence's control of the party, Sumner offered the great Senator the promise of immortal fame should he lead the antislavery movement. He urged all Whigs to adopt the substance of the Conscience resolutions and thus to devote themselves to the "REPEAL OF SLAVERY UNDER THE CONSTITUTION AND LAWS OF THE UNITED STATES."[55]

As Sumner left the platform, Nathan Appleton, one of the vice presidents of the Convention, leaned over and said to him: "A good speech for Virginia, but out of place here." The remark made clear the Cotton Whig reaction to all the Conscience efforts. As Sumner put it, Appleton "did not recognise, that we were in Virginia, as to the Slave-Power." Influenced perhaps by the enthusiastic reception of Sumner's speech, the resolutions committee added an antislavery resolution to its official list, but of a vagueness that could not satisfy the Conscience men. Any chance of the Conscience men passing their own resolutions was killed that evening when the conservatives pulled off a great show of unity as an answer to Sumner's invitation. Daniel Webster himself arrived at the hall and was escorted to the podium arm-in-arm by Abbott Lawrence.[56]

The Cotton Whigs demonstrated the same unity in the election campaign over the next two months. The press was brought firmly into line. The *Courier* had, alone among the Whig newspapers, maintained the principle—"a strange one," grumbled Winthrop—of keeping its columns open to all opinions. Its editor, Joseph Buckingham, was made to feel the heat for publishing Sumner's article of 13 August decrying the blood on Winthrop's hands. Buckingham defended himself by assuring Winthrop—contrary to what Sumner himself had said—that Sumner had slipped in the most offensive phrases after Buckingham's approval had already been given. But when Sumner offered the *Courier* another article for publication, Buckingham declined. "I am not in *independent circumstances*," the editor explained, "and must submit to influences, from which I should be most heartily glad to be free."[57]

At the same time that they strengthened the Whig press against Conscience invasions, the Cotton Whigs redoubled their efforts to bring the Conscience men back into the fold. Charles Francis Adams, who shared his family's traditional aloofness from Boston's most fashionable circles and who bore the prestige of his own name, weathered the siege better than most, though he did decide to "soften off a little, and not drive them to extremity." Henry Wilson, who had never had any chance of being welcomed into the best homes, was beyond their ability to hurt. It was different for Palfrey. Like Sumner, he had received much help and encouragement from prominent families and had come to rely on their friendship. Appleton sent Palfrey missives "breathing fire and fury" over his accusations in the "Papers on the Slave Power," which had been running in the *Whig,* while, from his own conversations with his cousin Mrs. Appleton, Sumner could testify to what Adams called the "prodigious degree of excitement among the women" the attacks had caused. That intractable Whig leader Samuel Eliot, having warned Sumner back in 1845 that he should expect no applause from respectable quarters for "having chosen the side of the enthusiastic & ardent" who believe reforms "are best promoted by violence," now tried to frighten the shy and meek Palfrey away from a career in politics: "You must either be silent [. . .] or prepared for very rough usage. You will want strong nerves." It was at the cost of much wavering and soul-searching that Palfrey stayed with the Conscience men.[58]

Eliot's son-in-law Andrews Norton, Harvard's most prominent professor of divinity and popularly known as the "Unitarian Pope," aided in Eliot's efforts to subdue Palfrey. Then, just days after the Whig State Convention, he sent a letter of his own to Sumner. Politics was "a dangerous track" for "a poor man," he wrote, singling out Sumner's private concerns as his father-in-law had done with Palfrey, and one in which he "must find it difficult to preserve his moral principles uninjured and his honor unsullied." He warned Sumner that, despite his "fine talents, great goodness of temper, and right principles," his temperament was "particularly unfitted for political life," as proven by his having so quickly offended so many respectable men. Norton aimed at Sumner's pride in his own practicality by illustrating the "mischief" done by the abolitionist faction—with whom Norton associated all who denounced slavery publicly—"by the intemperance of its language, the folly of its measures, and by rejecting all practicable good in aiming at what is impracticable [. . .]." For good measure he tried to add a thrust at Sumner's vanity: "I have a sincere respect for the feelings of many abolitionists," he assured Sumner, "particularly females, and others who may be expected to be governed by their feelings [. . .]." The divine went on to denounce both the conceit of the abolitionists for thinking they had "a monopoly of all the humanity, sympathy for suffering and sense of justice, which exist among us," and, with a perhaps inadvertent reflection upon the leaders of his own party, to impugn the motives of the leaders of the abolitionist party, men like Theodore Parker and Wendell Phillips: "However they may disguise it from themselves, many of its leaders are aiming at political distinction and offices with as great a disregard of principle and of the good of the country, as the leaders of any other party." The success of such men was sure to be productive of nothing but "of a conflict of violent passions, and of all but anarchy."[59]

The tone was sharper and less kindly, but Sumner had gotten such warnings before, including some going back the better part of a decade from old friends like Joseph Story and Simon Greenleaf. It was another once close friend and mentor, however, who now gave the severest blow.

When Appleton's friendly prodding and Norton's stern counsel failed of their intended effect, George Ticknor, Eliot's other son-in-law, decided that stronger action was necessary. Yearning for the genteel, orderly, benevolent Boston of his youth, Ticknor took the duty of civic and moral leadership both seriously and personally. It is imperative, he held, that those who flout the community's moral standards be reprimanded and their influence cut off. What better way, in a place that so valued the bonds of society, than by casting them out. Presiding over the finest cultural gathering place in Boston, his judgment so widely accepted by his peers that he was the effective social arbiter of Boston society, Ticknor controlled by his guest lists the social life of most of the city's first families. To be off his list was to be a virtual pariah. Such a practice was severe, Ticknor coolly admitted, but disruptions to Boston society were worse—"the principles of that society are right, and its severity towards disorganizers, and social democracy in all its forms, is just and wise. It keeps our standard of public morals where it should be, [. . .] and is the circumstance which distinguishes us favorably from New York and the other large cities of the Union, where demagogues are permitted to rule, by the weak tolerance of men who know better, and are stronger than they are. In a society where public opinion governs, unsound opinions must be rebuked, and you can no more do that, while you treat their apostles with favor, than you can discourage bad books at the moment you are buying and circulating them." Thus Ticknor answered Hillard when he tried vainly to intervene on behalf of his partner and dear friend. Ticknor had let fall his ban upon all the Conscience men, and most particularly upon Sumner.[60]

All those families who had first opened their homes to Sumner after his return from Europe, who had flatteringly lionized him as a new light in Boston's cultural constellation, now locked their doors to him. There were indeed a few close personal friends, even in those upper circles, who ignored the ban. William Prescott, a good friend of both Ticknor and Sumner, refused to give up either one, though he could no longer have them at the same table. Those who dared to invite Sumner, however, could expect refusals from other guests because of his presence. Foreign visitors were amazed to discover that the mere mention of his name would cause some to shudder—"*frissoner*"—though they could say nothing against his character but that he was suspected of abolitionism. Former friends would turn away when they saw him on the street. When an uninitiated guest at Ticknor's house once asked whether Sumner would be present, his host informed him: "He is outside the pale of society."[61]

Sumner felt the loss cruelly. "To be admitted to such a house as Mr. Ticknor's was a test of culture and good breeding," explains Edward Pierce; "to be shut out from it was an exclusion from what was most coveted in a social way by scholars and gentlemen who combined the fruits of study and travel." Sumner's entrance into Boston's upper circles had afforded him an oasis of culture away from the drudgery of his law office. It had been his intellectual compensation for the society of Europe that he missed so deeply. More than this, it had offered the delight of sociality to a lonely man. His opposition to Winthrop, Sumner quietly admitted to George, "has cost me friendships which I value much."[62]

Sumner blamed the change squarely on the quarrel with Winthrop, not on the heated debates over prison discipline that George wondered about. "No development, not calculated to bear immediately upon politics, seriously disturbs people," he wrote to George; "but the cotton lords, whose nominee Winthrop was, were vexed with me for that just & righteous opposition."[63] Though Winthrop and Sumner would not speak to each other for years, when Winthrop went abroad the following year Sumner insisted that his brother not "avoid him on my account. [. . .] I have no personal feeling to W. except of kindness." The national crucible of civil war would see the two at least partially reconciled. Ticknor was even more implacable than Winthrop, and never reconciled with Sumner even temporarily. Sumner and Ticknor both thought that a republic required an educated populace and, just as Sumner had hoped the library of the Athenæum might be opened to all, Ticknor devoted his last years to creating such a public institution. As long as he lived, however, Ticknor refused to allow a bust of Sumner, then for many years Massachusetts' senior Senator, to enter the Boston Public Library. When, in 1864, however, Sumner was endeavoring to establish a national academy of arts and letters, modeled on the Académie Française, he included Ticknor's name on the list of American literary men who should be its first members.[64]

The Conscience Whigs did not cave. Rather than give in to the Cotton onslaught, they decided to run one of their own against Winthrop in the fall elections. They had long resisted such a break with the party—as early as January to Palfrey's suggestion that one of them run for John Davis' Senate seat, and as recently as the end of September when Sumner and Adams agreed that Sumner should refuse the congressional nomination just offered him by the Liberty party. Adams told Sumner, however, that he "was inclined to the opinion that he must stand presently as an independent candidate, and that with luck we might effect the defeat of Winthrop." When Winthrop was officially renominated in mid-October it was Sumner himself, with fellow Conscience Whig Francis Bird—a Walpole lawyer who had introduced himself to congratulate Sumner on his speech at the Whig State Convention and who would become a lifelong friend and political associate—who persuaded a skeptical Adams to accept the idea of a splinter campaign. As a first blow in the contest, Sumner then prevailed upon Adams—"[a]fter a proper degree of remonstrance" from the editor—to publish the last of his four articles against Winthrop's vote. The so-called Independent Whigs held their rally at the Tremont Temple on Thursday, 29 October. They did not find the choice of a candidate difficult. It was with "hearty & determined enthusiasm" and "repeated bursts of applause" that the assembly greeted the name of Charles Sumner. "Are you not *the* man, if there is or can be one, for this crisis in our affairs?" the ardent and cherubic John Andrew urged Sumner. "If I know anything, I know that."[65]

Sumner was appalled. He had indeed eagerly supported the independent campaign—but only on the strict understanding that he was by no means to be considered as a candidate. Some fellow Conscience men thought he was just uncomfortable at the likelihood of losing the election. "I would not go to Congress, if I could go by a *unanimous* vote," he swore to them. Thinking all was well, he had thus left for Bangor, Maine, to honor a Lyceum engagement he had made in August, only to return late on the Friday night after the Tremont Temple meeting to the newspaper headlines blaring his nomination. His closest associates knew he would be upset but still hoped he might acquiesce in a *fait accompli.* John Andrew, the antislavery lawyer Ellis Gray Loring and others all had their urgent entreaties ready to greet Sumner that Saturday morning. Adams "reasoned with him rather boldly and perhaps roughly." It was no use. That same morning Sumner fired off a public letter to all the major newspapers refusing the nomination. But he could not shake the feeling of mortification at this use of his name.[66]

Sumner's offensive against Winthrop had given him a new stature in the Conscience Whig movement. Before that summer, though he had been in the inner circle, Sumner had taken no guiding role with his colleagues. His charges against Winthrop, however, were so specific and elaborate, his knowledge of law and of international as well as national affairs so sure, and his language of such evocative imagery and Elizabethan vigor that his articles immediately became the center of attention and forced the Cotton Whigs to respond. They, in turn, attacked and ridiculed none of the Conscience men so thoroughly as they did him. To Winthrop, Sumner became the symbol of enmity, his own *bête noire.* Sumner himself seemed to be growing in assurance. The young man who had held aloof from public office in the 'thirties and who had refused to speak in the early 'forties, had now helped to initiate and organize the Independent Whig movement over Adams' objections, as he had prevailed upon Adams to publish the last of his articles against Winthrop.[67] Adams had deferred, and both the Liberty party and the Conscience Whigs had recognized Sumner's new prominence with their nominations.

With the consequences of this prominence, however, Sumner was not yet comfortable. Though becoming every day more deeply involved in politics, he did not think of himself as a politician. He had not abandoned his lifelong aversion to the idea of holding public office, an aversion rooted not only in the traditional disdain for politicking but in his own father's embittering political experience. Just the previous June, when George had asked his brother to support his request for a secretaryship of legation in Spain, Sumner had agreed despite misgivings—"because I am anxious that yr wishes shld be gratified"—but had added the admonition that as "for myself, I hold in very slight estimation *office & office-holders,* believing that to every honest private man there are better opportunities of influencing the world." Sumner's inside view of politics over the last two years had only lowered his opinion of politicians. Nor did the assurance of his pen and manner mean that his old self-doubt had left him, especially at the thought of officially representing the antislavery movement. The particular circumstances of the election of 1846 added no luster to politics, clouded as it was by the destruction of old and once close friendships. Sumner was only repeating what he had said a hundred times, therefore, when he begged Nathan Hale, editor of the *Daily Advertiser,* "to believe me to speak *ex pectore,* when I say, that I have no desire for public life. If it should be my lot to exert any influence (& I know full well how little it must be) I wish it may be always as a private citizen."[68]

There was yet another reason to refuse the nomination. In the minds of his opponents and of many undecided citizens, the nomination could not but cast a shadow upon Sumner's reputation. It looked as though he had attacked Winthrop only to get his place. It made him look like a liar to Nathan Appleton, to whom he had sworn in August that he knew "of no person who wishes to disturb [Winthrop] in his office [. . .]." Winthrop and his friends were already convinced that office was Sumner's only motive. "[A]ll say," George Ashmun had sneered to Winthrop back in September, "that if Phillips could be made Governor, [Charles] Allen Senator, & Adams Representative from Suffolk, with such small chances for any thing less which might fall to Sumner, the trouble would be at an end."[69]

Immediately upon Sumner's nomination the regular Whig press had a field day impugning the unconscionable motives of the Conscience men. "A Man Killed by his Friends," trumpeted the friendly *Courier,* insisting that it believed in Sumner's integrity but that the *"world"* would say only: "'He wants Mr. Winthrop's place.'" The *Advertiser* accused Sumner of having "sought influence to turn it against those who have fostered him," while the more vituperative *Atlas* declared that the Conscience men had "at last" hoisted their "true colors," and in one short article used the adjective "hypocritical" three times. It pained Sumner deeply that "the disagreeable *tone*" of the *Advertiser's* article was "entirely proper, when I consider the character of political comments, & the circumstances in which I was placed."[70]

One new political associate who had quickly become a personal friend understood. Sumner had first met the bold, eagle-eyed Quaker John Greenleaf Whittier as early as 1829 when the eighteen-year-old Sumner brought copy from his father, or perhaps from himself, to the then editor of the Anti-Masonic newspaper, the *American Manufacturer.* Their correspondence began in 1845 when Whittier wrote to praise Sumner for his "noble address," *The True Grandeur of Nations.* Whittier encouraged Sumner to follow up his Phi Beta Kappa oration with more public action in the political fight against the Mexican War. Yet, though "sorry" to lose Sumner as a candidate that fall, Whittier reassured him that under the circumstances, he was "not surprised," fearing "I might have done the same."[71]

Indeed, everyone who was asked to take Sumner's place agreed. When the nomination was offered to Adams himself—though he thought Sumner's withdrawal "a severe blow to us"—he "peremptorily" refused. In the end only one man was willing to take the plunge. Samuel Gridley Howe, who had preceded Sumner into so many reform movements and so long urged him to join, became involved in politics only at this critical moment, as much to help his friend as out of disapproval of the war and of Cotton Whig policy. Now he was as angry as if he had "swallowed a peppercorn" that no one would step in for Sumner. He was so indignant, in fact, that he finally agreed to run, offering himself, said the old revolutionary, "to stand and be shot at—to fall in a ditch that others may march over it." As Whittier had hoped, Sumner campaigned vigorously "against War & Slavery at this Election" and for his friend Howe, though their efforts were hopeless. In a field of four Winthrop won an absolute majority. There would be one compensation. Across the river in Cambridge, Palfrey, who had managed to get the regular Whig nomination for congressman from Middlesex County, would finally win in a runoff election in December. Even then, the Conscience Whigs as a group seemed to be in their weakest position yet, rejected by Boston society and, in all but name, read out of the party.[72]

Under the strains of the summer and fall of 1846 Sumner began to rely "with fresh tenacity" on the affection of those oldest and dearest friends "who are untouched by the vinegar of party." William Prescott's loyalty, given his closeness to Ticknor, meant a great deal, as did the unshakable kindness of the Josiah Quincy family. Though Josiah Quincy was, in his business dealings and social relations, very much tied to the conservative merchants and lawyers of Boston, the old Federalist never confused his attachment to business with an acceptance of slavery, and he was proud of his son Edmund, who had become a kind of business manager to William Lloyd Garrison and an editor of the *Liberator,* while his daughter Anna and her husband Robert Waterston, an antiwar and antislavery clergyman, kept up a regular correspondence with Sumner.[73]

Even some of the Cotton Whigs kept personal ties separate from politics. Abbott Lawrence himself remained always friendly and sometimes entertained Sumner at his table during the bitterest political days ahead. Though they had never been close, Sumner was gratified that his old tie to Edward Everett also remained untarnished. The benevolence Everett had once felt for the son of his respected Sheriff had now become appreciative admiration for a fellow orator. As for their total political disagreement, the ever "cold & kind" Everett, unlike his more volatile colleagues, was unconcerned: "I do not object to the promulgation of your views. A little ultraism is wanted as well as a little Conservatism. The universe is kept together, by the joint agency of the Centrifugal & Centripetal forces."[74]

Most of all, Sumner found warmth, encouragement, and congeniality with Howe and Longfellow, between whose homes he divided every free moment he had. Especially with the Longfellows, there was no need for invitations. The Craigie House, on Cambridge's elegant eighteenth-century Brattle Street, where Longfellow had roomed in the early 'forties, now belonged entire to him and

Fanny, a wedding present from her father. What belonged to the Longfellows belonged to Sumner. He simply came when he could, regularly on weekends, whenever possible for dinner during the week. His room and his place at table were always waiting for him. When the Longfellows were not there, the servants responded to Sumner as though he were master of the house. Longfellow fully agreed with Sumner's views on the Mexican War. So did Fanny. Nathan Appleton's daughter remained close to her father, but politically she agreed with Sumner. "I am sorry you think Sumner was wrong in condemning Winthrop," she wrote the following spring to her brother Thomas Gold Appleton. "The country is fast agreeing with him, and more than one manly eloquent voice has been raised in Congress for the recall of the army and the cessation of supplies. A Polk cannot make an unjust war righteous and fit to be carried on by a Christian people." When her father or his friends came to dinner, however, she and Longfellow would have to send a quick note to Sumner warning him that it would be best if he did not come over that evening.[75]

If Sumner and Longfellow remained as close as ever, the Five of Clubs were not immune to politics. Of all the members of the Club, it had seemed that Hillard would be the most likely to share Sumner's new course. He had retained his ties to politics ever since he first served in the General Court in 1835, and in 1844 he had joined the anti-Texas fight along with Sumner. They had spoken together from many a podium, and, indeed, Hillard had spoken more often at first. Soon their offices at Number Four Court Street rang with talk not only of art and literature and Europe, but of slavery and politics as well. But over that controversial summer and fall of 1846 Hillard began to step back. His love for orderly and civilized society may well have been upset by the increasingly bitter and unbridled emotions of the battle with Winthrop. He became uneasy about his partner's closeness to abolitionists and reformers who seemed to threaten the social fabric. Plagued by ill health and a resulting "dull drowsy languor which makes all exertion frightful," he had never had Sumner's energy, and deeply attached to cultivated society, he could not bear the pain of being made a social outcast. Whereas Sumner had pulled away from the Ticknors in disgust at their effort to control society and their unkindness to those who disagreed with them, Hillard could not escape their influence. "You do not, cannot, know how sorely I have been tried in all sorts of ways," he later defended himself to Sumner. "You have seen where I have yielded, but not known how much I have resisted." But Sumner could not stop regretting his friend's choice of society. "I wish that Hillard was not blinded to their true character," he confided to George. "He would be a happier & better man. I am not alone in this opinion." In the election of 1846 Hillard supported Winthrop.[76]

Sumner and Hillard never broke their friendship. Their affection for each other remained untouchable. When in January 1847, in the aftermath of Winthrop's election, Hillard gave a series of lectures on Milton, Sumner could not contain his pride in Hillard's accomplishment and success, about which he wrote to all their friends, neglecting the unprecedented success of his own lecture, *White Slavery in the Barbary States*. And when Hillard left for Europe that April, Sumner, who through bad experiences had become very careful about writing letters of introduction, gave Hillard all he could want, while the Sumners welcomed Hillard's wife Susan into their home during part of her year-long widowhood. But on the public stage it was inevitable that hurtful things would be said. The easy intimacy of old was gone.[77]

At the same time Sumner was feeling subtle hints of difficulty with Felton. Sumner and the volatile Schubertian Greek professor—Sumnerius and Feltonius as they often joked—had become especially close in these past few years. Felton's ever gushing sense of humor and keen eye for the ridiculous in life and human nature—including the fun he liked to poke at Sumner's own punctiliousness in "the proprieties of speech" and his patriotic pride in "the purity of our yankee pronunciation" and general education—gave Sumner delightful respite from his own loneliness and dissatisfaction. He would joke to Longfellow about someday editing a collection of Felton's "incomparable little letters."[78]

Sumner in turn had helped Felton through the most painful time in his own life. In 1844 Felton's beloved wife Mary had been gravely ill with cancer. Felton was deeply and repeatedly touched by his friend's kindness, his constant gifts and attentions—at a time when Sumner was battling his own illness. "What a fellow you are, Pinch!" When Mary died the following April, Sumner moved in and kept Felton company. It was to Felton that he practiced his Fourth of July oration and with his help that he revised it for publication. Looking about at all the "Lives of William Penn, Sermons on War, tracts of the American Peace Society" and the like that flooded his little house, Felton joked to Longfellow: "You have no idea what an arsenal of peace arms my house has become." Since then Felton and Sumner had remained much together, sharing their bachelorhood.[79]

They shared their hatred of injustice and especially of slavery, too. If Felton mocked Sumner's fraternization with abolitionists, he also jested about his own ability to uphold the rights of man in discussions at the dinner table and even with willing strangers in the occasional stagecoach. How deeply he shared Sumner's indignation at Webster's 1842 pro-slavery *Creole* letter, and how moved he was with pride by Palfrey's emancipation of his slaves the following year. In 1845 Felton was fulminating against Texas—"Let the sons of iniquity tremble"—and he would support the antislavery Whigs through all their struggles over the next few years.[80]

Antiwar and antislavery Whiggery was one thing, however, while peace activism and abolitionism remained another: Felton could not shake the worry that Sumner was dangerously inclined to forget that. Though he admired Sumner's *True Grandeur of Nations,* he begged him not to write any more against war. "I dont want you to be identified with those Peace men. They are [. . .] weaklings," and "one-idead enthusiasts." Garrison was even worse. Felton could not understand the distinction Sumner made between the *Liberator's* language and the good that Garrison was doing, and he tried over and over to convince Sumner that the *Liberator* had "no trace of Christian spirit" but only "ruthless violence, vulgar and insolent abuse, exaggerations that amount to falsehoods and a spirit that would destroy the happiness of nations if it might possibly effect the carrying out of onesided and stubborn opinions." Garrison's philanthropy, however sincere, was nothing but "the most deadly form of hatred, and it is to be restrained like the frenzy of a madman." Felton did not have a much better impression of the Liberty party, especially after their agitation cost Palfrey victory in the first round of the election of 1846—"the detestable hypocrites."[81]

Felton feared that Sumner was throwing away his professional future by becoming too deeply involved with such agitators and with politics. He still envisioned a rich future for Sumner as a legal scholar and man of letters—the kind of future he dreamt for himself—and he still believed that to be Sumner's own desire. Unlike Howe, Felton was proud of Sumner for turning down the nomination in October 1846. "Forget the intoxicating gas of the last few weeks," he urged his friend, "and come down to cool potations of law and literature." Felton was sure politics was a major reason for Sumner's low spirits: "It is a very bad, not to say virulent complaint, and your constitution not being accustomed to it, it goes hard with you."[82] He thought Sumner needed society and regretted that the Club could not meet so often. "Like you, I am afraid the club is dissolving," he wrote to Sumner, but the fault was clearly with his reforming friend, for "it seems impossible to catch you and Howe. You have gone astray and worship strange gods. Peace and [Pompey?] have usurped the throne of the Club." He could not "quite understand [Howe's] fears of my growing conservative and orthodox." Felton swore that "[t]he only conservation that I can think of is a strong desire to conserve the club," and repeated his strictures upon "you, reformers and philanthropists" for allowing politics to "interfere with its perpetuity."[83]

The members of the Club were solidly joined, however, in worrying about Sumner's unhappiness. Despite all the changes in his life, he had never completely shaken off the depression that had held him since the early 'forties. Felton was the most outspoken, trying to pull him out of it by everything from joking to fighting, tormenting him with a constant stream of reminding letters. "What right have *you* to a heavy heart?" the bereaved Felton wrote after a little quarrel late in 1845. "Of all the men I have ever known, not one ever had less *real* reason for despondency than you." Yet instead of cherishing life "with gratitude," as Felton himself did, Sumner would fall into "expressions of discontent with life," and "the utterance of wishes that it were over."[84]

They all knew what the matter was, but none knew how to help. Sumner was certain that there was no help. When he had given up his future in the law for reform, he had done so knowing that, even if he might work up the courage, the plain loss of income would deny him the right to marry. If he had any feelings beyond friendship for Fanny Longfellow's old neighbor and lifelong confidante, the dignified and constant Emmeline Austin, he never gave any hint. But it was a source of unending pain to him that he could not—and believed he could never—return each day to a home of his own to be cheered by the kind of affection and understanding that she offered him: "Believe me, dear Mr Sumner, in all the circumstances of life a true & faithful friend, who will rejoice ever in your success & happiness, & be ready to offer true sympathy when those trials come which are the lot of all." The following January she resigned herself to a loveless marriage.[85] When Felton chided him for his continuing bachelorhood, Sumner muttered that he was "a poor man." Felton refused to let him get away with that excuse. "[N]o man is poor who has your character, your abilities, your power of gaining both fame and fortune." He begged Sumner not to let any opportunity pass. But Sumner did nothing. He felt himself locked in a hopeless "cage of celibacy" that he could do nothing but bemoan.[86]

At this fatalism his friends rebelled. At first Felton and Howe hatched plans to shake him into action. "Why what an arrant poltroon you are," Howe chided him, "fearless" before the leaders of the army and the city fathers, and "afraid to make an onslaught upon maidens;—get out of that chair of yours go straight up to Beacon Street walk around the Common, seek out the sweetest girl you meet join her at the second round, & offer yourself to her, insist upon her accepting you, and carry off her troth before you are thrice around." Felton agreed and told Sumner that he was a "blockhead" if he refused.[87] It could do no good. Sumner continued to rhapsodize here and there about an "angelic being" he had met or "a fair face" he had seen, which seemed "good, more than fashionable" and "which disturbed my peace of heart." By the summer of 1846, however, Felton was beginning to develop "a fixed disbelief in the probability of your getting married," and only half-jokingly accused Sumner of being "a mere phrase-maker," who did nothing but "talk, talk, talk [. . .]."[88]

Sumner submitted to these assaults in silence. But as politics divided friendships old and new in that autumn of 1846 he felt more isolated and hopeless than ever. Then, during the election campaign that October, Felton took a second wife. Sumner "rejoice[d] in Felton's happiness," as he had for Howe and Longfellow three years earlier, but at the same time he was struck to the heart by this new loss of a cherished intimacy. "I feel—*I do feel*—the desolation of my solitude," he poured out his heart to the more understanding Longfellow. "And Corny has left me. I am again *alone*—more so than ever."[89]

It was then that, for Sumner's attack against Winthrop and the Cotton Whigs and his outspokenness on various reforms, George Ticknor let fall his social ban.

Under the strain of the election of 1846, as had often happened in the past two years, Sumner fell ill. Howe understood, and wrote feelingly:

> I was grieved by learning that you are ill in body, but most grieved by knowing that you are sick at heart. Some would suppose that greater indifference to the opinions of others, contempt for the revilings of the bad, [. . .] would indicate greater independence of spirit, & moral heroism than you exhibit. But those who know you (& all will by & by) know that you are now making greater sacrifices to your principles than you would do by throwing away fortune & station & hopes;—you are sacrificing what is to you dearer than life, or fortune, or fame;—the social regard of those whom you so love as friends. Our fathers pledged their lives fortunes & honors in support of their cause,— you are doing more than they did in the way of sacrifice, & I could not wish you were less affected in spirit because then you would be less warm & true in your affections. I should have thought you a braver man had you stood to the nomination that was forced upon you, but I had not the heart to urge you to do so because I saw you suffering torture. During your whole course in this matter I have watched you closely & have learned to respect & admire you even more than before. It has never been my lot to know a man so perfectly loyal to truth, right & humanity than you have been. Your efforts & sacrifices cannot be lost, for if no other good come out of them this will come that your example will kindle & keep alive high purposes in the souls of hundreds of whom I am one. You are my junior by many years, but to you I owe many of the public aspirations which I feel for progress upward & onward in my spiritual nature.[90]

Friendships were not all that had suffered from the consequences of the quarrel with Winthrop—so had Sumner's once hopeful view of human nature. The ease with which he had always stressed the good in people and brushed aside their faults, his faith in people's ability to be reëducated by the arguments of reason, had all been dealt a severe blow by the venom of the newspapers and more still by the cold looks of former friends. The greatest difficulty was that Sumner could not doubt the honesty of the Cotton Whigs, of men whom in many cases he had known and loved since youth. "I believe you & others with whom you act," he wrote Appleton, "are sincere, & conscientious, as I can claim to be myself, & regret infinitely that we should see such different sides of the shield." And yet these

men of good character and personal integrity could support causes the evil consequences of which they at least partially acknowledged themselves. Regretting
Winthrop's present coldness, Sumner mused to George that Boston's Representative was, "for a *politician,* 'honest'; but he measures his course by the doctrines
of expediency, & by the tactics of party. But I suppose he cannot do otherwise. I
am disposed to believe that there is a *necessity* which controls our course; though
I will not undertake to reconcile this with the seeming freedom of will which we
enjoy. Indeed, this is the speculation where philosophers innumerable have been
'in wandering mazes lost.'"[91]

Sumner had always believed that character and education worked together.
He could not watch the course of the Cotton Whigs without thinking now, however, that the influence of education and professional circumstances was much
harder to escape than he had before believed. Lawyers, he candidly admitted,
"have always been reputed to be under the influence of biases peculiar to their
profession, causing a selfish indifference to the reform of its abuses." Since the
death of Judge Story, Sumner had been made to feel just how unwelcome his interest in reform was to the legal profession. Clergymen were not exempt from the
rule, as Sumner noted to ministers who supported the Mexican War from their
pulpits. He had likewise long assumed the influence of their culture on the slaveholders, based on what he had seen himself in 1834 and had heard from his father
and Howe and Lieber about the backwardness of the Southern economy and culture—an explanation for Southern politics and behavior that he would one day
develop in a speech entitled *The Barbarism of Slavery.* Why should it be different
for merchants? "[T]hough there are brilliant exceptions to the universality of this
law," merchants, too, were generally influenced by "the spirit of trade." Such an
explanation of the actions of the Appletons and Lawrences, as well as of the Ticknors and Winthrops who shared their social circle, accounted for their tendency
to put the maintenance of economic and political ties with the South ahead of
their dislike of slavery, at the same time that it could "be no impeachment of the
motives of a person, and of his *honesty of purpose.*" Sumner did not and never
would deny the importance of the individual character, but he was beginning to
appreciate how strong it must be to withstand such pervasive forces. "It seems to
me that our character & conduct may be referred, in great degree, to the constitution, moral, intellectual and physical,—including, of course, the Will—which
we receive originally from God, *influenced by the circumstances in which we may
be placed.*"[92]

In the midst of the quarrel with Winthrop, Sumner took an opportunity to
explain his own motives in a manner he hoped Boston society might find more
congenial. The controversial May vote had not yet taken place when Sumner was
invited to deliver the prestigious oration at Harvard's annual Phi Beta Kappa celebration. When 27 August arrived, however, he felt a special motivation to speak,

and an audience that included such as Edward Everett and Robert C. Winthrop himself had a special motivation to listen.

Unlike his Fourth of July oration, Sumner's Phi Beta Kappa address conformed to the literary traditions of the occasion. Sumner celebrated the contributions to American culture of four great men associated with Boston and Cambridge and much entwined with his own life—the linguist John Pickering, Joseph Story, the artist Washington Allston, and William Ellery Channing. Harvard Phi Beta Kappa addresses had habitually been used to urge a higher cultural standard for America and to inculcate the duty of conservative moral leadership in future scholars and literary men, but rarely to promote the end of social reform. In painting the accomplishments of his chosen four, however, Sumner quietly evoked the path of his own journey from the love of the intellectual, through the appreciation of beauty, to the understanding of the conscience that had left him no choice but to embrace a career in reform. Whatever the scholarly and artistic achievements of these four representative men, Sumner concluded significantly, what made them all truly great was that "[t]hey are all philanthropists; for the labors of all have promoted the welfare and happiness of mankind." All four had done what Sumner had longed from youth to do himself—to promote the flowering of American culture, to promote justice, to do good. "Their lives, which overflow with instruction, teach one great and commanding lesson, which speaks alike to those of every calling and pursuit,—*not to live for ourselves alone.*"[93]

The difficulties of the past years—from the audience's shocked reaction to his Fourth of July oration to his rejection by Boston society—had also taught Sumner that, if he wished successfully to influence his compatriots, to make them consider and act upon the philosophical values at the heart of their culture, then he must be more patient in advancing his views, take less for granted the shared ideals of the community, and approach his audience more gently. He now personally understood, even if he chafed at the restrictions of the lesson, that slavery was still a "subject [. . .] too delicate to be treated directly." Thus his choice of subject for the Phi Beta Kappa oration, and his decision to devote only small space in it to slavery and war, at the same time that its whole argument was to him a remonstrance against both.[94]

Similarly in his *White Slavery in the Barbary States,* delivered in early 1847, Sumner followed the inspiration of Benjamin Franklin's last published work to lull his audience by apparent acquiescence in common prejudices and then use them to his advantage. He began the address as though it were to be an indictment of the barbarism of the Mahometan people who enslaved white Christians. Having awakened his audience's sympathy for the fate of their fellow Europeans in their degrading captivity, Sumner gradually turned the tables as he painted the indulgent practical character of slavery in the Barbary States and then compared it with the harshness and racial prejudice of slavery in the Southern United States—the "*Barbary States of America.*" When he came to the recent abolition of slavery in the African Barbary States, Sumner could conclude by praising the true christianity of the Mahometans compared to the "selfish and unchristian" prejudices of "exclusive Christendom."[95]

At the same time that Sumner was being ostracized by the Whig party and Boston society, his writings were being crowned with ever increasing success. The Phi Beta Kappa oration confirmed him in everyone's mind as a great orator of the rising generation. Friends had not been sure that the *True Grandeur of Nations* might not be luck, given the strength of his feelings on the subject of war. How would he fare at a grand ceremonial occasion? Sitting in the First Church of Cambridge to hear Sumner's Phi Beta Kappa oration, Howe's wife Julia "did not dare to look at you" for the first fifteen minutes, "dreading some mistake or failure; but when she did look," Howe beamed to his friend, "she lost all fear for you." Sumner's own Julia could only add to the admiration she already felt for her big brother, while his mother, whose quiet pride followed him everywhere, must have wished his father could have been there to see him. Dressed in what became his customary oratorical garb—dark blue dress-coat, buff waistcoat, and white trousers—Sumner spoke from memory in his "singularly musical" voice, "with a clear and distinct elocution" and "great ease and elegance." Though a few gently complained that he should not have mentioned the issues of slavery and war in the oration at all, he captivated ladies and gentlemen alike with his "superb" presence and resonant voice, and impressed forever an audience of Boston's first scholars by his literary and "intellectual powers." Friends and strangers alike were delighted at "how entirely you had commanded and swayed your audience."[96]

As the Phi Beta Kappa oration won Sumner the respect of scholars and literary men, *White Slavery in the Barbary States* quickly became his most widely popular lecture, and would go through many editions over the next fifteen years. Sumner delivered it frequently in lyceums across New England and New York and, as had become his custom, further encouraged its circulation by refusing to take out a copyright on the work. It received praise even from such an unlikely source as George Ticknor. But, though Sumner felt increasing hope that he was contributing to a general change in public opinion on the subject of slavery especially, his experience in the quarrel with Winthrop and the election of 1846 left him with the conviction that it was impossible to change the course of the Whig party. The education of the public would be easier than the reëducation of its leaders.[97]

It was to the students of Amherst College, at the anniversary of their literary societies in 1847, that Sumner delivered what he believed to be the lesson of his struggle with the Cotton Whigs. Without referring specifically to those events, he made clear his refusal to condemn the individual leaders of the party. If an honest man like Winthrop had followed the majority over his own conscience, it could not be out of a disposition to do evil, Sumner was sure, but must be rather from that universal desire for Fame. "This desire is native to the human heart," and is part of the instinctive urge "to provide for our protection." Whether in the child who feels jealous of his parents' attention to other children, or the youth who confuses the desire for "*excellence*" with the desire of "*excelling*," or the adult, driven to conquer new worlds, it adheres to "the desire for the approbation of our fellow-men," that is an essential part of being human.[98]

"'*That last infirmity of noble mind*'" was not a sentiment that a grandson of the American Revolution could completely condemn. "The love of approbation," with whatever of selfishness it might contain, could very well inspire individuals to do good. As Sumner unfolded his observations to the fresh, hopeful, young faces in his audience he urged them not to reject the desire for glory that he knew they all felt. A God-given sentiment was not illegitimate, but all should try to understand and live up to its true function. God instilled in men the desire for fame, but also the "desire of Justice" that urges "the love of duty," and "the desire of Benevolence" that urges "acts of kindness, of disinterestedness, of humanity, of love to our neighbors [. . .]." "[W]hatever may be the temporary applause of men, or the expressions of public opinion" Sumner told the students, "it may be asserted, without fear of contradiction, *that no true and permanent Fame can be founded except in labors which promote the happiness of mankind.*"[99]

How well Sumner knew the price that might have to be paid—"the countenances of companions may be averted; the hearts of friends may grow cold"— but he urged the youths before him to rise above consideration of the merely personal: "the consciousness of duty done will be sweeter than the applause of the world, than the countenance of companion, or the heart of friend." As a youth Sumner had kindled to the vision drawn by Moral Philosophy of devotion to the good of others being rewarded with personal happiness. He now knew that promise to be false. But he clung to the belief that doing good, no matter the punishment, was right, and what was right—said his conscience—was a duty. In private, Sumner was not always sure he could rise above the personal as he had counseled the students at Amherst, but he could accept no other way. It "sounds well" to consider first one's own happiness, "if a person has put behind his back all the duties of life, & has become merely a seeker of pleasure," but Sumner could not do that. "Self-renunciation is sometimes difficult," he admitted to George, "but it is, I believe, a true rule of life—so far as we can follow it. I do not say that I can; but I do strive in what I do to think as little as possible of what others may think of it, & of its influence on my personal affairs. In such a mood criticisms, unfavorable or hostile—neglect & disfavor lose something of their sting. What is it to an earnest laborer, whether one or ten societies recognize him by their parchment fraternization—or whether reviews frown or smile. And yet it cannot be disguised that praise from the worthy is most pleasant & that all tokens of kindly recognition are valuable. But it is not for those that we live & labor."[100]

The events of the year 1846 left Sumner confirmed in hopelessness for his own future, and more confident than ever about the future of the nation. Tried in the kind of crucible that had embittered his father to politics, Sumner felt instead a rekindled desire to fight. When Winthrop left for Washington to resume his seat, it was with Sumner's arguments in hot pursuit. For years Sumner had been enjoying a deepening political friendship and correspondence with the small band of antislavery men in Congress, especially Joshua Reed Giddings. Now, with their help, he would bring the Boston quarrel to the center of the national stage. No one was more eager than he to enter a new phase in the struggle with the Whig party. "The Mexican War & Slavery will derange all party calculations," Sumner predicted to George as the congressional session opened. As "deplorable" as the country's affairs were, it was with real hope that Sumner observed the impact of the opposition: "The Anti-Slavery principle has acquired such force as to be felt by all politicians. In most of the Free States it will hold the balance between the two parties, so that neither can succeed without yielding to it a greater or less degree. The Abolitionists have at last got their lever upon a *fulcrum,* where it can operate. It will detach large sections from each of the parties."[101]

President Polk set the game afoot with his annual message. As they listened to his words, few congressmen felt Sumner's hopefulness. Whigs across the country had been nervously watching the attack of the Conscience Whigs in Massachusetts against men who were leaders of the national party and wondering how the party would pull through. Democrats, too, were increasingly restive under the yoke of a controversial war, some eager to continue in its support while others were lining up behind the Wilmot Proviso and its prohibition of slavery in any new territories acquired from Mexico. The President's message attempted to bring both sides back into line behind his war policy. Instead, he precipitated a fight when he began by directly accusing open opponents of the war, like John Quincy Adams and Joshua Giddings, of giving "aid and comfort" to the enemy. "A more effectual means could not have been devised," he insinuated, "to encourage the enemy and protract the war [. . .]." As he rose to answer, the anger flashing in the eyes of the tall, rather rumpled but powerfully built Giddings must have made him seem even more impressive than usual. Some of his words must also have awakened painful echoes of home in the mind of his sensitive colleague Winthrop, for in defending his refusal to vote supplies for the war effort, Giddings made use of arguments that Sumner, his close correspondent, had just made in Boston.[102]

By supporting the United States' aggression against Mexico, Winthrop had been sadly wanting as both statesman and Whig, Sumner had repeated to crowds of Conscience Whigs in the days before the congressional election. That America should immediately withdraw from the war rather than prosecute it and that the antislavery Whigs were right in their opposition, Sumner defended with an emotional parallel: "I would invoke the example of English Whigs, Chatham, Camden, Burke, Fox, and Sheridan, in opposition to the war of our Revolution,—denouncing it at the outset as unjust, and ever, during its whole progress, declaring their condemnation of it,—voting against supplies for its prosecution, and against thanks for the military services by which it was waged." He followed with dozens of quotations from the great British opposition leaders attacking the war of 1776 in terms that could easily be applied to the war of 1846. Winthrop was furious to hear these same points now being made by Giddings on the floor of the House.[103]

Winthrop had tangled with the Ohioan before, when in January 1845 he had answered a biting anti-Texas speech of Giddings' with apologies to Southerners for his colleague's zealotry. Now Winthrop rose again, in what he considered his most statesmanlike manner, to refute President Polk on the one hand, and, on the other, both Giddings and Sumner. With sarcasm he attacked the President's innuendoes about "aid and comfort" as inimical to the spirit of free speech and democracy. And at almost the same moment, fixing upon Giddings' comparison between the Mexican War and the American Revolution, he hinted that the Ohioan was acting not like Burke but rather like the High Federalist Timothy Pickering, whose opposition to the War of 1812 had tainted him and his party with treason. Like John Jay in his rebuttal to Pickering, Winthrop declared that "'we cannot be too perfectly united in a determination to defend our country [. . .].'" It was the turn of the Conscience Whigs to be furious, and yet another newspaper battle broke out between the *Whig* and the *Atlas*. Sumner turned Winthrop's charge around, believing that it was fear of drawing "upon themselves the odium that covered those who opposed the last war with England" that stopped the Whigs from speaking out against this war. He answered Winthrop both in Congress—by means of notes sent to Giddings and passed on to his antiwar colleague Columbus Delano for another speech—and in Boston, where he once again evoked the image of Mexico as a modern Revolutionary Boston resisting the "iron hand" of an invading army.[104]

It was no longer just the war itself that was fueling the arguments. As Sumner put it that December: "Both parties are now controlled in their conduct, even on the Mexican War, by a reference to the next Presidential election." Leaders of both the Whig and Democratic parties wanted their forces ready for the contest. If the Whigs "shrink from approving [the war], for fear of unpopularity at the South & West," they were also determined to maintain the discipline of their insubordinate antislavery wing, because—with the Democrats dividing over a controversial war of their own making—the ever-disappointed Whigs sensed a real chance of victory.[105]

The Conscience Whigs were no less intent upon 1848. Before the close of 1846 they had put on record their refusal to accept any slaveholder as the Whig presidential candidate. Whom to back was a difficult question. At the Whig State Convention in September, Sumner, trying to take advantage of the split between the Webster and Lawrence forces in the party though without any great hope of success, had symbolically offered the position to Daniel Webster. As he was already known as the "*Defender of the Constitution*" and the "*Defender of Peace*," Sumner flatteringly urged him to become the "*Defender of Humanity*." "The aged shall bear witness to you; the young shall kindle with rapture, as they repeat the name of Webster," Sumner had promised. But he was not surprised when Webster declined, and he could hardly disagree with Whittier's estimate that Webster was "no better on this question than 'a colossal coward.'"[106]

Sumner and his fellow Conscience Whigs looked at a variety of candidates to support. Though his friends were unsure of his stability and integrity on the slavery issue, Sumner nursed a short-lived hope that John McLean might be the one. Joseph Story's sole friend and confidant in his last years among his colleagues on the Supreme Court, McLean had been very kind to Sumner. He had also been much more outspoken against slavery than his judicial brother. But when McLean said "that supplies must be granted," Sumner had to give up on him sadly. In February it was Senator Thomas Corwin of Ohio who "seems to be the man," wrote Sumner, after Corwin gave a stinging speech against the war in Mexico. Stephen C. Phillips was particularly hopeful about Corwin, though Sumner and Adams felt an early disappointment at his failure to follow through on the promise of his speech. By September Sumner had to write him pointedly to ask whether he would be willing to lead the movement. Corwin's evasive answer, as well as his notoriously orthodox Whig "Carthage Speech," made it clear that his real devotion was to the Whig party. Believing deeply himself that "[t]he causes which look to the welfare of man, through justice & benevolence, are kindred," Sumner gave Corwin every benefit of the doubt, but as early as 25 February he had written: "Our first point should be our principles; and if Corwin does not stand firm on those, much as we admire his present position, we could not support him."[107]

Principles were more important than any candidate—or any party. In late 1845 Sumner had felt very optimistic. "The spirit of Anti-Slavery promises soon to absorb all New England." "I doubt if the Whigs of Mass. will ever again vote for a slave-holder as Presdt.," he confidently asserted. The events of 1846 convinced him that, though antislavery was ever-growing, it could win no victories through the Whig party. "It seems to me clear [. . .]," he repeated over and over that following winter, "that we cannot expect candidates from the *United Whig* party on our principles. The party, *as a party,* does not receive them, & would not nominate men who were true & frank in their support."[108] This conviction went hand in hand with an increased disdain for the "*politician*" who, by definition, as he had said of Winthrop, "measures his course by the doctrines of expediency, & by the tactics of party." Jabs at "politicians"—always as opposed to "good men"—began to punctuate his letters.[109]

Sumner's mood, however, was anything but discouraged. Instead, this impasse filled him with excitement. "The signs increase, that the two great parties are breaking up," he predicted to George in January. Northern members of both parties were tiring of "serving their slave-holding allies," and Sumner doubted whether either party could "get through a National Convention [. . .]—that is, the different elements in each party will be so uncompromising, that they cannot unite in support of any one man, or set of men." It was such an uncompromising stand that Sumner urged upon all his colleagues. He was looking far beyond 1848. "The Mexican War has hastened by 20 or 30 years the question of Slavery," he asserted to Lieber. "The issue is now made. It will continue, until Slavery no longer has any recognition under the Constitution of the U.S." Eighteen forty-eight would be the first step in the struggle to create a truly civilized America—one enriched by art and literature, and devoted to equality and justice.[110]

The Conscience men were not fully agreed on the practical question of how best to prepare for the election of 1848. Stephen Phillips was anxious to put up a candidate and continue to try to influence the Whig party from the inside. Giddings was very reluctant to contribute to any break in the party that he had adhered to and taken hope in for so many years. Adams, though willing to consider the possibility, felt more cautious than Sumner. "He always leans to more stringent measures than I," Adams confided to his diary. "Perhaps his course is the wisest one. The point to be aimed at is a union between energy and prudence."[111] With each day, Sumner felt more sure and confident. "We must lay down our principles, & bring all candidates to them as to a touchstone," he tried to persuade Giddings. Such a course, he was well aware, would leave no room for the Conscience men within the Whig party, but would "compel us to a separate organization in conjunction with the scattered fragments of the Democrats." At the end of February, Sumner set down his position to Giddings:

> I am willing to be in a *minority* in the support of our principles. And I am not satisfied, that it would not be preferable to bring forward candidates, who may be beaten in the next contest but who will be carried in 1852. The Anti-Slavery sentiment is not of itself strong enough to place candidates in the chair now. It will be very soon.

Our struggle is not for persons, nor for honors, nor for spoils. It is to advance certain truths, deemed vital to the happiness of the country.[112]

"If the 'Young Whigs' compromise their principles," Sumner urged Giddings, "the Whig party *with their assistance,* may undoubtedly carry the next election." But by standing on principle the Conscience men could make their weight felt and might well throw the election "into the house." "We must stand *firm,*" he repeated over and over again. "*We must stand firm.*"[113]

REVOLUTION

"THE CONTEST is now commencing in earnest," Sumner wrote excitedly to his new antislavery friend Salmon P. Chase on 12 June 1848. Just five days earlier in Philadelphia the Whig National Convention had nominated General Zachary Taylor for president. "The Slave Power has thrown down its gage before the whole country." Sumner assured the Ohioan: "We in Massachusetts shall take it up."[1]

Sumner had been waiting impatiently for this day, but he and antislavery men generally, all across the North, believed that they had given the Whig party—and the Democratic as well—every chance to disclaim complicity in the South's peculiar institution, and that their refusal to do so had made the break inescapable. In the winter of 1847 it had seemed there might be a chance of reconciliation left. As American troops fought their way toward military victory south of the border, the urgent question had become what to do with the land that everyone now knew the Polk Administration wanted to take from Mexico. All Whigs seemed to agree that slavery should not be permitted there. Winthrop himself had declared in Congress that should such land "be conquered and annexed, we shall stand fast and forever to the principle that, so far as we are concerned, these territories shall be the exclusive abode of freemen." Cotton and Conscience seemed poised to agree on the Wilmot Proviso.[2]

In February 1847 the Whig-controlled Massachusetts General Court passed a set of resolves—echoing the 1787 Northwest Ordinance—"solemnly protest[ing] against the acquisition of any additional territory, without the express provision by Congress that there shall be neither slavery nor involuntary servitude in such territory otherwise than for the punishment of crime." A stronger set of resolutions originally confined to a minority report was then reconsidered in April. Presented by Conscience Whig Edward L. Keyes, editor of the Dedham *Gazette*, they had in fact been written by Sumner. They denounced, in terms of both Natural Law and political equity, a war that had been the direct result of the annexation of Texas: "[S]uch a war of conquest, so hateful in its objects, so wanton, so unjust, and unconstitutional in its origin and character, must be regarded as a war against freedom, against humanity, against justice, against the Union, against the Constitution, and against the free states." Whereas the February resolves had supported only the prohibition of slavery in any new territory acquired by the war, Sumner's resolutions, harking back to the Conscience Whigs' efforts at the Whig State Convention of 1846, demanded "all constitutional efforts for the destruction of the unjust system of slavery within the limits of the United States." When, after lively debate, the General Court passed his resolutions, Sumner exulted to Lieber: "Massachusetts is now pledged to uncompromising opposition to the war, & to Slavery. It is not possible, that she can support Genl. Taylor."[3]

Sumner was too sanguine. The Cotton Whigs feared the effect of further antislavery agitation on the already beleaguered Southern wing of the party, especially in light of the coming presidential election, and even the General Court's first set of resolves had made them nervous. As early as February Winthrop had begun subtly to modify his position. From the refusal of slavery in any new territory, Winthrop now began to speak only of his desire to have no land acquired from Mexico at all. By the fall the Whig party had established its official position on the call for "No Territory." To the Conscience men this position was "absurd." President Polk had already requested appropriations to annex new territory, and a large part of the Democratic party was behind him. "It cannot be doubted that territory will be acquired," Sumner wrote plainly, even if Polk did not get all the land he hoped for: "The iron hand which is now upon California will never be removed. Mr. Webster's efforts when Secy of State, to obtain a port there are too well known [. . .]. It is then of vast importance, that we should be prepared for this alternative, & not be cajoled into the simple cry of 'no more territory.'"[4]

At the Whig State Convention in September, the Conscience Whigs made one last effort to strengthen the party's stand. Putting off all questions "of elections or party alliances," they agreed to confine "ourself to the actual issue of this moment—the Wilmot Proviso." For a moment there was even hope that Webster would join them. Seeking their support in his bid for the presidency, he made a strong antislavery speech, which would, however, only cost him Southern support while it could not get him a majority even of the delegates at his own state party convention. Though he did not trust him, Sumner felt for him: "The scene was humiliating." Abbott Lawrence's conservatives remained in firm control. The Wilmot Proviso was rejected. Likewise, Palfrey's proposal that the party pledge itself against any candidate who did not reject slavery expansion "was opposed by Winthrop" and, after "an earnest debate," defeated. Even on the narrowest antislavery ground, Cotton and Conscience proved irreconcilable. Sumner did not confuse the party's conservative Boston leadership with the rank-and-file membership: "I think the heart of the Convention was with us," he wrote to Chase. This was, however, a turning point, Sumner was sure: "I think it doubtful whether we shall ever enter another Convention of the party."[5]

It would take a national event to initiate a break, however, and so the sniping continued through the winter and into the spring of 1848, giving Sumner many discouraging days. "I wish that I could see hope for the country," he lamented to Whittier, "but I cannot. The war & slavery will continue to tear at our vitals." First came the nomination of Robert Winthrop to the speakership of the House. Sumner thought the choice "a subtle & master move on the part of the Whigs to stifle our movements in Massachusetts. State pride, of course, will be stimulated & his influence will be enhanced—against us." Sumner planned closely with Giddings and Palfrey—who now took his seat in Congress—to block his election. It pleased Winthrop that, when his victory did come, he owed it to Southern and not to antislavery votes.[6]

This opposition led only to another quarrel. After Palfrey had spoken openly against slavery on the floor of the House, Sumner rejoiced in the newspapers: "'God be praised; the seal is at last broken!'" he quoted from John Quincy Adams, the vanquisher of the gag rule. The response from the Whig press was a stinging barrage against Sumner's character; he was accused of being "ambitious" and "malignant." "I thought Mr. Palfrey right," he pleaded to Fanny Longfellow. "He was attacked. He was my friend. May this hand lose its cunning, if it ever fails to defend a friend who is right!" Of one "squib" in the *Atlas,* Sumner confided to Palfrey "that I feel the bitter personality of this attack upon myself more than I thought I should ever feel anything a newspaper could say." Sumner had always believed politics to be the best means of accomplishing change in a republic; he had been unprepared for the personal realities of political combat.[7]

One quarrel followed hard upon another when Winthrop charged Giddings with falsely reporting that he had urged members of the Whig caucus to vote for the continuance of the war. Giddings was a man of sterling integrity, but getting supportive testimony, especially against the powerful Speaker, was not easy and took time. Meanwhile, more harsh words flew in the Boston newspapers. How frustrating it was to wait: "I am tired of the anomalous position which is forced upon dissenting Whigs here in Massachusetts," cried Sumner. "Let us have an open field, & direct battle, instead of private assassination & assault, which is our lot here—suspected, slandered, traduced by those who profess & call themselves Whigs."[8]

What Sumner wanted was "a new chrystallization of parties, in which there shall be, one grand Northern party of Freedom." The other Conscience men, including their leader Charles Francis Adams, agreed, but many, like Giddings, continued reluctant to leave a party to which they still felt loyal and in which they continued to hope. If the national party nominated the Louisiana slaveholder and Mexican War hero Zachary Taylor, however, that would change. "In the event of Taylor's nomination," Sumner assured George, "there will be an organized revolt at the North. We in Massachusetts are maturing it in advance; the same is doing in Ohio." It happened in June. The day Taylor was officially nominated Henry Wilson and Charles Allen—the only two dissident Whigs chosen as delegates—stood up and walked out of the convention hall, and with them went the antislavery wing of the party. In August antislavery Whigs and Democrats along with Liberty party men joined forces at Buffalo, New York, to establish the Free Soil party. Eagerly envisioning the moment, Sumner had, a few months earlier, predicted confidently to George that then "there will be a new party, having some *principles,* & looking to the good of Humanity."[9]

Sumner thus remained true to the principle he had defended to Wendell Phillips when he first entered reform, to work for higher ends by political means and by concentrating on the possible. It was thus that he had tried first to reform the Whig party, and then to build a third party, rather than rejecting political compromise. It was thus that he prepared himself for the task of building the Free Soil party in part by steeping himself in the complete works of two authors who were not only among his own most admired but who were among those most admired by New England intellectuals generally—Plato, in Victor Cousin's translation just then coming out, and Burke—alternating between the idealist one night and the statesman the next. "A student of the *ideal,*" wrote Sumner, "I trust never to lose sight of the *practical.*" A later century would tend to see Burke as a pragmatist and positivist. Sumner was, however, in full sympathy with his own time in seeing Burke's importance not in his particular political positions, but rather in his insistence upon responsible reform over reckless change, and upon the need to accomplish that reform according to the dictates of practicality as well as morality, in the tradition of Natural Law. It was thus to work for Platonic ends by Burkean means, to encourage evolution that revolution might not be needed, that Sumner was willing, as a test for the Whig party and a starting point for the Free Soil party, to choose the Wilmot Proviso.[10]

The Proviso was hardly ideal. It had originated in part in Northern Democrats' resentment against Southern control of the patronage, and in their fear of being apologists for the South before their increasingly antislavery constituents. It attracted some who wanted to support the Mexican War, but did not dare so long as it was linked to the expansion of slavery, and others who wanted the territories to be open to free labor or to whites only. But the Proviso also expressed a basic principle that political antislavery men and abolitionists would not reject even if they demanded more. It thus had a very broad appeal and held out the possibility of gaining a majority in Congress. Even though that congressional majority would never quite be realized, it opened the possibility beyond of a national popular majority. Nor did Sumner accept the criticism often used by the Proviso's enemies that it was disunionist. On the contrary, he believed, it would save the Union by breaking the power of the slaveholders. To Sumner such a measure that could be accepted by so many and that could thus practically put the government back on the side of freedom was precisely the right starting point. The new Free Soil party, he insisted, should specifically declare its object as "the prevention of the extension of Slavery" and "the overthrow of the Slave Power, or in other words, the establishment of such a prevailing public opinion, that Slavery shall no longer in any way influence our National Govt. I am thus particular in dwelling on these latter points, because some persons suggest, that, with the settlement of the question of the Wilmot Proviso, our whole platform will disappear. This is not so." He was sure that a movement that started by rejecting slavery in the territories would, by logic, be led to see its evil elsewhere. He hoped that even many Democrats would thus be forced to accept "a broader conclusion" about the evil of the institution their party had so often helped. "They must become Abolitionists."[11]

Sumner never spoke publicly at this time about the actual abolition of slavery. The speculations of radical thinkers on the constitutionality of such a step he found fascinating but impracticable under the present state of opinion. Sumner's father had once lamented that "[i]f we were a consolidated government we might legislate upon slavery, & liberate the slaves; as we are not a consolidated govt. we have nothing to do on the subject in the several states." Sumner—like his father, like most Americans including most antislavery men—accepted the received American understanding of the Constitution, according to which the federal government could not intervene in local laws. To neglect it, he was sure, would jeopardize all that might, with more patience, be solidly accomplished.[12]

The common wisdom among opponents of slavery was that ending its spread would starve the institution economically. The Southern dependence upon single-crop agriculture, nearly everyone agreed, would wear out the soil and thus the need for slavery within a short time if there were no room for expansion. Sumner wanted to go further. Instead of simply trusting to the processes of nature, he wanted to encourage the process of public opinion. He saw the geographical constriction of slavery as one step in a process of moral starvation. It was with satisfaction that Sumner watched the growing antislavery sentiment in Europe. He hoped that not only political speakers and abolitionists but writers as well could contribute to the work of enlightening public opinion in this country. "How much more powerful is a song than a bullet!" he exclaimed in welcome to a new volume of antislavery poems by his friend Whittier. As the literary world, and the whole society in its wake, turned against slavery, Sumner expected to see the peculiar institution "soon in a state of moral blockade. Then it must fall. We will treat it like a besieged city—cut off from all supplies." Sumner believed that human progress itself, hastened by reformers, would awaken moral sensibilities and increasingly direct the world's scorn against the retrograde slave owners. By destroying slavery's political power, such a moral force could destroy the institution—without bloodshed.[13]

What such a siege required was a fundamental reëducation of public opinion.

The history of slavery throughout the United States and its continued existence in the South, Sumner was convinced, influenced not only the present slaveholders, but the thinking and culture of the entire nation. This was clear even in Massachusetts. Sumner's native state had abolished slavery in the 1780's. In the 1840's she was one of only five states that allowed blacks full voting rights, and her citizens were as strongly opposed to slavery as any in the nation. Even most of her conservative political leaders were personally antislavery. And yet, as Sumner pointed out, though every black citizen of the Bay State was "*legally* entitled under our laws to the privileges of the white man," practice did not follow law. "[R]egarded as of a despised caste, [. . .] he is not advanced to office" and "he does not find a seat among the jury." From his father's experience, Sumner had long known the difficulties blacks had in getting proper counsel and protection in the courts and prisons, and he knew himself many whites who condemned slavery but still called for any emancipation to be followed by what Sumner scornfully dubbed "the banishment of free negroes." Sumner urged Americans to see that it was only in the United States that such attitudes and practices were usual. Describing his European experiences to Massachusetts audiences, Sumner reminded them that in the Old World blacks and whites mingled without legal or psychological hindrance. "It is well known that the prejudice of color [. . .] is peculiar to our country." Wrong "in the sight of God and of all just institutions," it was in fact "akin to the stern and selfish spirit that holds a fellow-man in slavery."[14]

Sumner did not make such arguments for national consideration because national public opinion was not yet ready to benefit by them, but he hoped Massachusetts might be more receptive. He applauded the successful efforts of abolitionists to end separation of the races in the railroad cars of the Commonwealth, and the abolition of the ban on interracial marriage—that same ban that his father had deplored—while he himself joined with other speakers like Emerson in declining invitations to lecture in lyceums that separated blacks from the general audience or refused them membership, and was able thus to change policies. Just as his father had once said that he would be pleased to serve on the bench with a black judge, Sumner in 1849 went before the Commonwealth's Supreme Judicial Court with, as his co-counsel, Robert Morris, former law student of the anti-slavery lawyer Ellis Gray Loring and the most promising young attorney of Boston's black community. It was only among the first of Sumner's ties with the black community, ties that would expand greatly after he became Senator.[15]

It was in the case of Sarah C. Roberts *v.* the City of Boston that Sumner appeared with Morris. Ever since the 1790's Bostonians had battled over the question of segregation in the public schools. At first it was blacks themselves, afraid that the stigma of too-recent slavery would put their children at a disadvantage in the classroom, who requested separate schools. By the 1820's, when black parents thought the separation had become a stigma itself and wished to return their children to the regular schools, the Boston School Committee had made the separation mandatory. In the 1830's and 'forties prominent white abolitionists including David Lee and Lydia Maria Child and then Wendell Phillips joined with black activists such as William C. Nell in the struggle to bring Boston's public schools into conformity not only with what they believed to be the Right, but with the practice of the public schools in all other towns of the Bay State. The Boston School Committee, however, refused all change. Thus five-year-old Sarah Roberts was forced to walk every day past better all-white schools to a distant and inferior black school. When her father brought suit in her behalf, he began a case that took forty years of debate to the state's highest court.[16]

The deep importance that Sumner laid on the case showed in his fear of not doing it justice. He was at first very much dissatisfied with his argument, and apologized that he had not been able to give it the attention and labor it deserved—even though he had in fact devoted himself to it fully. In later years, however, he would take great pride in it and in his introduction into American discussions of the phrase "Equality before the law," which he took from the French. During Reconstruction he hoped the argument might be cheaply distributed through the South. At all times, however, its significance seemed to him to go far beyond the individual case, as important as he thought that, and to address the role of education in creating and changing social attitudes.[17]

Sumner based his legal appeal on the Massachusetts Constitution. The School Committee's decision to mandate racial segregation, he argued, was a refusal to conform to the requirements of the Constitution's proclamation that "all men are born free and equal." The Committee's ruling was thus not only contrary to ordinary law, but opposed to the broadest principle of the rights of man. Those rights, he said, had found their most eloquent voice in the constitutions of the French Revolution. They derived, however, according to the conjoined dictates of Natural Law and natural rights, from the highest sentiments of human nature and from the most fundamental law of God.[18]

Sumner did not rest here. In a court room filled with anxious members of the black community, he went on to say that the illegality of racial segregation under the Constitution of the Commonwealth was not its only vice. Founded upon the "heathenish" institution of caste—which, in manner "unreasonable, and therefore illegal," separates races based upon supposed differences in moral and intellectual capacity—the segregation of the schools nursed and perpetuated the public opinion that had allowed racial prejudice to flourish in the United States and that maintained the institution of slavery. The common schools, which Sumner proudly and pointedly called the "*peculiar institution* of New England," taught more than knowledge—they inculcated the values of the society. "The school is the little world in which the child is trained for the larger world of life."

Wherever men were separated, they developed fear of one another. "Prejudice is the child of ignorance. [. . .] Society and intercourse are means established by Providence for human improvement." So should the schools be, urged Sumner, for the good of the children and the adults of both races, and of the state of which they were all citizens. Just as education could be used to instill an admiration for either war or peace, or to encourage vice or virtue, as the society chose, so, by being based upon the principle of equality, it could be the most important instrument in the ongoing work of elevating mankind and creating a true and just civilization.[19]

It would be one hundred and five years before Sumner's argument won in court. Chief Justice Lemuel Shaw said that he agreed with the principle of equality before the law, but decided that such equality existed as long as blacks and whites were equally protected by the laws even if the laws were different for the two races. He thus established for the first time in American law the principle that came to be known as "separate but equal." "[J]udicial trifling," William Jay called it in a letter of consolation to Sumner when the decision was handed down. The New York courts "some time since decided," John Jay's son went on bitterly, "that a black man has no right to ride in an omnibus, & he is not permitted to drive a cart. But the law *protects* him in the right of *walking* & cleaning shoes & *therefore* white & black men are equal before the law!" Lemuel Shaw's principle would be upheld by the Supreme Court of the United States in the 1894 case of Plessy *v.* Ferguson. When that same court struck down its earlier ruling in the Brown *v.* Board of Education case of 1954, however, it sustained an argument anticipated by Sumner in the Roberts case. In 1855, meanwhile, Massachusetts had become the first state in the nation to pass a law mandating the desegregation of the schools, after a reformist coalition, including many Free Soilers, had won the General Court under the leadership of Sumner's colleague and friend Henry Wilson.[20]

Filled with the ideal of an egalitarian society, such as he would urge in the Roberts case, with the vision of a civilization founded on "*moral elevation, sustained, enlightened, and decorated by the intellect of man*" that he had set forth in his first oration and, in one form or another, in every subsequent address, Sumner devoted himself in 1848 to the new Free Soil party as the first stepping-stone to this brighter future. When Union College in Schenectady, New York, invited him to deliver their Phi Beta Kappa oration that 25 July—just over one month, as it turned out, after the antislavery men walked out of the Whig National Convention and two weeks before the first Free Soil National Convention in Buffalo—he had no trouble choosing a subject. His topic would be one that, long dear to him, seemed of especial significance now in the midst of momentous events—the "Law of Human Progress."

Yes, there was a *law* of progress, Sumner urged to the students at Schenectady. Man was not, indeed, capable of absolute perfection, as some modern writers, like Turgot and Condorcet, seemed to suggest. "God only is perfect." Nor did Sumner believe that man's innate potential for improvement grew with time. The limits of that potential, however, were unknown and perhaps unknowable. "Man, as an individual, is capable of indefinite improvement." From the beginning of time he had demonstrated his desire and capacity for improvement in all fields—from the creation and humanization of international law and the enrichment of literature and art, to scientific and material developments like the railroad and the new telegraph, "not forgetting the art of the kitchen." Sumner disdained improvement in no area, and was grateful for any advancement in personal comfort, but just as the intellectual and ethical were above the animal, so was it moral improvement, aiming at the achievement of true civilization, that mattered most. Man was proud of his ability to subdue matter and nature, but Sumner was prouder to think that man himself could be subdued—"subdued to abhorrence of vice, of injustice, of violence,—[. . .] subdued, according to the Law of Human Progress, to the recognition of that Gospel Law [. . .] of Human Brotherhood."[21]

But were some people capable of more progress than others? As he was preparing his oration, Sumner wrote to his old Roman friend who was also much interested in the history of progress, George Greene, to ask his opinion on one of the burning questions of the moment—if there is such a thing as a law of progress, "[w]hy has the Chinese civilization continued immovable?" Greene thought the difficulties of the language and the unprogressive nature of the Chinese religion might be factors, to which "ought to be added those peculiarities or inherent distinctions of race which separate them so widely from the progressive Caucasian [. . .]." Sumner could not accept an explanation of racial predestination. He looked instead to their "habit of unhesitating deference to antiquity, and of 'backward-looking thoughts,'" which isolated them from other nations and discouraged change. For what progress required was "intelligence"—that is, knowledge. "Without knowledge there can be no sure Progress. Vice and barbarism are the inseparable companions of ignorance." By keeping its population in ignorance, want, slavery, a society might temporarily repress its advancement, but never destroy its desire for improvement. Likewise, as Sumner would urge Boston to do through its public schools, a society might promote progress by education and good institutions—"in proportion as knowledge, virtue, and religion prevail in a community, will that sacred atmosphere be diffused, under whose genial influence, the most forlorn may grow into forms of unimagined strength and beauty."[22]

Ultimately, the progress of society depended upon the progress of the individuals of whom it was constituted. Because individuals are capable of improvement, so is society, "for society does not die," but benefits from the work of its individuals in all times. The course of history is thus assured, Sumner pursued, for the "key" to progress is clearly "that the constant desire for improvement, implanted in men, with the constant effort consequent thereon in a life susceptible of indefinite Progress, naturally caused, under the laws of a beneficent God, an indefinite advance; that the evil passions of individuals, or of masses, while unquestionably retarding, could not permanently restrain this divine impulse; and that each generation, by an irresistible necessity, added to the accumulations of the Past, and in this way prepared for a higher Future." Progress, and especially that "[m]oral excellence [that] is the bright, consummate flower of all progress," "is the Destiny of man, of societies, of nations, and of the Human Race." "To labor for this end was man sent forth into the world," pleaded Sumner to the students before him. Surely this was enough to picture "a Future even on earth, an 'All hail hereafter,' to arouse the hopes, the aspirations, and the energies of Man."[23]

Sumner's view of the course of history thus led him to look forward in hope. "The true golden age is before you, not behind you." But the once "amorous votary of antiquity," as his friends had dubbed him in college, had lost none of his belief in the importance of knowing history. As the record of both past successes and failures, history was the stuff from which future progress would be made, without the knowledge of which it could not be made. "History has been sometimes called a gallery, where are preserved, in living forms, the scenes, the incidents, and the characters of the past. It may also be called the world's great charnel-house, where are gathered coffins, dead men's bones, and all the uncleanness of the years that have fled. As we walk among its pictures, radiant with the inspiration of virtue and of freedom, we confess a new impulse to beneficent exertion. As we grope amidst the unsightly shapes that have been left without an epitaph, we may at least derive a fresh aversion to all their living representatives." Though he should never allow himself to be blinded by its drama, the scholar and the statesman had a duty to keep the public well informed about the history that would help build the future. "Let him draw from the Past all that it has to contribute to the great end of life, human progress and happiness; progress, without which happiness is vain."[24]

Sumner would thus never urge upon his audiences the beauties of the future without offering, like most Whig orators, a detailed history of his subject. At Union College he carefully traced the development of the concept of the law of human progress, from Ancient misunderstanding to the first imperfect glimmers of Vico to its full elucidation by Condorcet. Rufus Choate or Webster would have done the same. And they all did so, not to reject change, but in the effort to build that solid foundation they believed to be necessary for responsible change, for true progress. It was this that had drawn Sumner first into the Whig party.[25]

This respect for the necessity of history had likewise helped to keep Sumner from embracing the Democratic party. Despite his conviction in an absolute standard of human equality inspired, originally through his father, by the principle of natural rights, by Thomas Paine and the French Revolution and the writings of Jefferson, Sumner could not—as did his brother George—adhere to a Democratic party that rejected history as the enemy of these same rights. All Americans were struck by the United States' relative lack of history compared to the Old World, but the Democrats were often proud of America's good fortune in having started from a *tabula rasa* that avoided the human oppression and misery of which history seemed to them the record. Sumner, too, could vehemently deplore the hatred and violence of "the Black Forest of the Past," but to forget the past was, he believed with Whigs, the best way to destroy the future. Nor could he accept the Democratic tendency to glory in the present, but always looked to a better future. Sumner knew no sadder example of wasted human endeavor than the life of the political publicist William Cobbett, whose commendable energy was spent upon the "short-lived controversies" of the present with neither historical perspective to give them their true weight nor anticipation of the future to give him "Hope." The present, so it seemed to Sumner, was merely the most recent moment of the past, carrying with it all the faults which a future age would deplore as we deplored those of our past. The great virtue of the present was the opportunity it gave to craft a better future.[26]

But in 1848, what had drawn Whigs together was rending them asunder. In the face of growing individualism and democracy, of increasingly outspoken reform, of defining moral debates about the true direction and scope of progress, Whigs were dividing amongst themselves between those whose attachment to the past outweighed their faith in the future and those whose faith in the future was paramount. Sumner's old Number-Four colleague and once his legal mentor, Rufus Choate, was among those who now publicly denounced him as a "renegade," and thus a false scholar and philosopher. Choate still thought of himself as a progressive, but, like Joseph Story, was appalled at how the actual changes rocking society seemed to abandon the ideals of republican virtue and community he had loved from youth. "History teaches us to appreciate and cherish this good land, these free forms of government, this pure worship of the conscience," he wrote, but the "passionate morality" of the antislavery movement seemed to him rather a denial of civic duty and Puritan ethics. It was evidence only that the Puritan fathers, following Vico, were right in thinking that history turned in cycles, and that America was being forced into a premature senility. How completely he would have understood the despair of Story's final years. "You as a young man should cling to hope," the Judge had written to Sumner in the winter of 1845; "I as an old man, know that it is all in vain."[27]

As Choate and Story and many Cotton Whigs grasped for the past as protection against a future they did not recognize and could not welcome, Sumner had been reaching ever more confidently for that same future. Already in the 'thirties he had been slipping away from Judge Story's insistence that the preservation of civilization required the restraining of reckless reform movements and the creation of increased legal privileges to business, and had instead taken inspiration from Channing's belief "that the grand end of society is, to place within the reach of all its members the means of improvement, of elevation, of the true happiness of man." It was Story's youthful support of the ideals of the French Revolution that Sumner continued to cherish, his discarded belief in the perfectibility of man, his "early confidence in Humanity." "My faith in this is so constant & fixed," Sumner confided to Story's son William, "that I think him more right in those early days than in his later life. Who can doubt, that hereafter, & not before many years are past, we shall all regard distrust in the Future of Man on earth as little better than Heathenism. *The Future is secure;* the Present alone is uncertain."[28]

It was with such hope and determination that Sumner watched over the creation of the new Free Soil party, not to fight against slavery merely, but "to represent Progress, Humanity, Freedom" in all their forms. And no moment seemed more propitious to Sumner than the year 1848 as talk of liberty swept through the whole Western World. At the same time that Americans were beginning to rise up against slavery, Europeans, first in France and then across Germany through Italy to Hungary, were fomenting revolution against the oppressive rule of the aristocracy in what Sumner saw as one great effort for progress. It was at the end of February that the barricades went up in Paris and brought down first the Minister of Foreign Affairs, the historian François Guizot, and then Louis-Philippe himself. It was over almost before people knew what had happened, so quickly did the old régime—born itself of the Revolution of 1830—fall. Within a few days a provisional government had formed under the leadership of the poet Alphonse de Lamartine, and as he declared the establishment of a new republic, Sumner thought "his position is heroic. He speaks not only for France, but for modern civilization."[29]

Sumner's attention to European affairs, newspapers, and literature had never waned, and his European correspondence continued with such as Lord Morpeth, back in the British Cabinet in 1848, Joseph Parkes, in and out of Parliament, and Richard Cobden, whose acquaintance Sumner had recently renewed with a letter of congratulations on his most recent address on international peace. During these years Sumner also paid close attention to French literature, to Victor Hugo, whom he reverenced for both his writings and his political idealism, and Lamartine. Contrary to the general opinion of Boston's upper class that her writings were a bad influence, Sumner was also much impressed by

George Sand, herself deeply involved in the present Revolution, whose *Consuelo* "shews a soul, instinct with humanity, & with virtue." Sumner felt a particular, personal tie to Paris and the events taking place there through his brother George.[30]

From an almost reckless beginning, George had long since lived up to his eldest brother's appraisal of him as "remarkable," and had become an important source of European information for Charles. He had followed his success in Russia and the Middle East by taking the rest of Europe by storm, and soon seemed to have been everywhere. He became fluent in French and Spanish. He researched the history of the Pilgrims at Leyden and of the Spanish monarchy at Malaga; unofficially represented the United States at an international conference on prison discipline at Brussels in 1847; once even acted as a lawyer in the French courts, and won his case; and made uncountable confidential connections with the political, literary, and social leaders of the Continent. When Howe traveled through Europe in the early 'forties he was amazed to hear that everywhere George "is referred to as authority in all matters whatever, from the formation of Cabinets to the tying of shoe strings." The Russian Minister to Prussia remembered him "kindly." The great naturalist and statesman Alexander von Humboldt, while working on his *Cosmos,* "consult[ed] him frequently." George Sand, whom George visited at her country estate at Nohant, thought "qu'il sait l'univers et quelque chose de plus, sur le bout de son doigt." And, in the midst of the events of 1848, Tocqueville was in regular contact with George and recommended him as "a man of superior intelligence, very accomplished, perfectly familiar with all European affairs, and knowing different parties and politics of Europe better than any European."[31]

Success had not cured George of his sensitiveness or his boastfulness, or made him a better correspondent. Charles and the family had to berate him for his "dull & uninteresting" letters—packed full of political and social observations, they said not one word about himself. The family had to learn from the occasional ship's captain that George was in good health, putting on weight, and had grown a beard. But Charles was very "proud" of his younger brother, and never failed to tell him so. Originally hoping that George would put his observations on Russia into a solid and lasting volume, *à la* Tocqueville, he gradually came to agree with George's own desire. "My wish is to see you in diplomacy. I think you are supremely accomplished & fitted for that." For George's sake Charles lamented his now total lack of influence with either the Whig or the Democratic party. To his own and their family's personal desire to see George come home, Charles added the need for George to ingratiate himself with his party if he wished to get a regular post. "[A]ppointments do not turn on fitness for the place," Sumner commented worriedly to Greene, "but on political services [. . .]."[32]

Though he continued to travel, since the early 1840's George had made his home in Paris, where he supported himself by a steady stream of articles on history and politics published there as well as in the United States. But George did more than write. While Charles was speaking and working for the creation of the Free Soil party in the United States, Charles Pinckney Sumner's fourth son was not only observing but actively involved in the creation of the new republic in France. Long before the Revolution broke out in February, George was well acquainted with and trusted by the leading men of the government of Louis-Philippe, including the conservative republican Adolphe Thiers, and by the future leaders of the Revolution, including the socialist Louis Blanc. He had "the ear of Lamartine," and wrote in his defense for the American press. During the events of February he was a member of the National Guard—in effect the military force of the middle class revolutionaries—and "he was very influential in preventing the breaking of the printing presses, which was at one time meditated," while on another occasion he personally arrested a counterrevolutionary in the midst of a demonstration and "harangued a mob with great effect." Charles was delighted—"I admire your readiness and courage, & think they come naturally to you." Just as he shared his knowledge of American political events and personalities with George, he was anxious to hear all George could supply about French leaders, writers, and events. Though the two brothers maintained their different points of view, Charles was immensely pleased to be able to tell George how "much confidence" he had "in yr judgment, & in yr diplomatic tact [. . .]."[33]

Everyone, Sumner wrote to George, was "filled with mingled anxiety, astonishment & hope by the great news from France," and looked to each new "packet with a thrilling interest." He was less sanguine than his brother about how soon the bright republican future they both desired could be achieved, but he saw a great opportunity opening in 1848: "[T]he French Revolution is to render Europe like wax, to receive the impression of new ideas."[34] It was with a "thrilling interest" indeed that Sumner watched as, in the very first days of the February Revolution, a host of reforms were declared: open access to the National Guard, abolition of the death penalty for political offenses, abolition of slavery in the colonies—"It will be a bombshell for our country," Sumner rejoiced,—freedom of assembly and of the press, universal suffrage. Sumner listened, charmed, to Lamartine sing the glories of France's republican future: "Nous allons faire ensemble la plus sublime des poésies." "Can Europe abide King's speeches after these?" demanded Sumner.[35]

Sumner was thinking of more than just Europe. A victory for civilization in one place could not fail to encourage advancement in others. Progress was contagious. Sumner knew, in Burkean manner, that "it is not always safe to argue" for one country from the experience of another. Still, the political and social debate now starting in Europe would provide an unparalleled testing ground for ideas being considered by reformers in the United States, and might help to influence America in turn.

Greater honesty in government was one hoped-for possibility. Sumner had long regretted excessive American electioneering and patronage, and in France it was the charge of government corruption that had triggered the February Revolution. What if the French gave their president a longer term—preferably of seven years, "a Roman lustrum"—but limited him to one term only? "If this were the case," Sumner argued for the future French president as well as the American, "it seems to me that his selfish aspirations would all be quieted, & he would be left to act—not to secure a re-election—but to promote the true welfare of his country." Whatever his term, Sumner believed it was "important that the patronage should be taken from the Executive." In France, where the concentration of power in Paris meant that "a mob may at any time overturn" the government, giving the patronage "directly to the people in their localities" would allow the Republic to be "sustained equally by all France." In the United States, too, the "enormous" executive patronage tended to reward cronies rather than competent public servants, Sumner believed, and he was encouraged by the efforts of New York's new state constitution to strip the governor "of much of his appointing power." Twenty years later Sumner would try to do the same for the national government by urging civil service reform.[36]

Most fundamental was the problem of building intelligent and solid popular support. Sumner feared that here the revolutionary leaders had been rash. "Will it do in the Constitution that shall be established," he questioned George, "to preserve the basis of Universal Suffrage?" Like abolitionism in the United States, republicanism was still controversial in France. A "property qualification" was "obviously impossible," Sumner agreed, since it would restrict the vote to the same monarchists and wealthy bourgeois from whom power had been taken in February. But Sumner's fears of transferring the determining voice to an illiterate and uninformed peasantry—one anxious for the reassurance of a strong man against the new instability—would be confirmed when, within two years, they would give power to Louis-Napoleon Bonaparte. Instead, Sumner hoped in the early months of 1848 that France would institute a literacy requirement, such as Massachusetts herself practiced. True, he granted, there were surely "many persons in France, of no inconsiderable intelligence, who cannot read & write [. . .]; but they must forego the privilege of voting to secure the general good." Not only would the Republic then be supported by an informed public consent, but this would, more effectively than any other method, "secure the cause of education": "In the next generation every body would read & write."[37]

Nearly twenty years later, Senator Sumner would face a similar problem in the American South. When he became, with his colleague Salmon Chase, the earliest congressional champion of universal suffrage for the freed slaves he seemed to be contradicting his stand of 1848. But in 1865 he gave up his initial desire for a literacy requirement not only because such a requirement, he realized, would be used against the freedmen, but also because the blacks, despised as a group, had a stronger sense than the French peasants of 1848 of the civil rights they desired and because they showed such enthusiasm in making up for the education forcibly denied them under slavery.[38]

In 1848, too, what mattered most to Sumner was how the new French government would prepare society not only for popular government but for the better civilization it should lead to. The February Revolution had been launched against the *haute bourgeoisie,* the wealthy industrial and financial class that had dominated the régime of Louis-Philippe. But who should succeed them? The provisional government was divided. The moderate bourgeois under Lamartine—who, as Minister of Foreign Affairs, was essentially prime minister—wanted to establish a republic but not otherwise seriously change the structure of society. Sumner honored Lamartine and thought his history of the Girondins "a marvellous production," but from the start he was most intrigued by the provisional government's gadfly, Louis Blanc. Sumner delighted in his "masterly" history of the French Revolution—a better "analysis of the progress of opinion" had never been written, he asserted. Most striking was his *Histoire de dix ans,* which had criticized the July Monarchy for merely replacing the ruling aristocracy with the ruling industrial class. Sumner was sure this book "must have exerted great influence in undermining the throne of Louis-Philippe," as indeed it had. Louis Blanc—who would become the new government's unofficial minister of labor—did not want a republic to do the same, but rather to spread political power to the still new industrial working class. Sumner begged George for more information about him: "I perceive from that remarkable book, that he aims at a *social* revolution."[39]

Sumner thought that Louis Blanc, more than anyone else, "exert[s] himself in the right direction," and would "cause great good." But he worried, too. "The old is becoming new— very fast. I sometimes fear too fast." It was the idealist and humanitarian in Louis Blanc that Sumner so admired, but he feared the socialist might be lacking the practical sense. "No individual can change an age. It must change itself." To ask a new and nervous bourgeois republic—itself considered radical by many elements of French society—to welcome the working class as brothers was to ignore the present state of public opinion. Such progress "will come with the elevation of the moral & intellectual nature of man—when the social atmosphere is changed to a more genial temperature by gradual but incessant influences." The job of the reformer was to prepare those influences, but he must be patient as well as persevering. "[T]he Future which he seeks cannot be forced. Fraternity cannot be *imposed* upon mankind. [. . .] To expect it now is to expect a full-blown rose in a Northern winter." Full equality and political power for the working class were more than society could yet tolerate, Sumner warned his socialist friends as he warned Louis Blanc through George, because they would require the destruction of the power of the industrial bourgeoisie and strike at the basic support of established power—"*property*"—and that could not be accomplished without a reaction.[40]

One must start with those reforms that are possible. "I may be wrong," Sumner answered Louis Blanc through George, "—perhaps I have my extravagances also; but it seems to me that the *army* question is the question of *our age*. To abolish standing armies is to remove a *cancer*—to *organize labor* is to change the whole constitution of society. The former must be done before the latter." Europe's standing armies had spread nothing but misery, argued Sumner. The great taxation needed to support them was made to fall most heavily on the poorest part of society, especially in a time of drought, famine, financial crisis, and widespread unemployment, such as had, in fact, led to the revolutions of 1848. Sumner was aware, too, as Richard Cobden put it, "that hitherto the governments of Europe have maintained their armies in times of peace almost as much for the purpose of defending themselves against their people as their neighbors." But, this time, the standing army had not helped Louis-Philippe, while the National Guard had actively sided with the revolutionaries. The influence of the peace movement was spreading. Sumner felt it in the continuing popularity of his *True Grandeur of Nations*. Though he knew "that no single nation, in the present state of public sentiment, would undertake to disarm," he was certain that this was "the *age for effort*," and what country could begin the process more effectively than France, renowned for military glory? "A Republic must rest on the voluntary support of the citizens," argued Sumner, while a popular republic could count on her citizens for any legitimate defense. The welfare of the nation and the future of mankind would be secured if France spent the money thus saved on education and the arts—and to "provide for her workmen by appropriating to great industrial enterprises what is now given to soldiers."[41]

Sumner took great inspiration from the opportunity of Europe's fluid state, and from the renewed discussion of international peace. Richard Cobden had promised him that he might have a chance to use the "arguments" of his *True Grandeur of Nations* "in my place in Parliament. If so I shall make free use of your materials without scruple." Sumner urged George to use his "influence" with Lamartine, and reorganized his own thoughts for a new address on the subject.[42] When Sumner delivered the *War System of the Commonwealth of Nations* at a meeting of the American Peace Society in Boston's Park Street Church on 28 May 1849, he was hopeful that public opinion was more open to his ideas than it had been four years earlier and that he did not need to review the horrors of war. Instead he focused directly upon the nature of war as a custom and an institution of the law of nations that, failing utterly of its intended purpose, might well be changed. For centuries men had been joining together in leagues to promote peace, Sumner argued, from the Hanseatic League through the Swiss Confederation to the United States of America. "The next stage must be the peaceful association of the Christian States"—that is, of the nations adhering to international law—ultimately for the creation of "a Congress of Nations, and a High Court of Judicature [. . .]."[43]

To the exception of the right of self-defense from his condemnation of violence, Sumner added this time what he considered a related principle—the "*right of revolt or of revolution.*" Reminding his audience that the acceptance of such a right meant recognizing the right of American slaves to resist "to death the power that holds them," Sumner made it clear that there was nothing romantic about revolution. A right dependent upon means of such "inherent barbarism" and necessarily so "vaguely defined and bounded, must be invoked at any time with reluctance and distrust." Peaceful means should always be sought first. Privately, Sumner took hope that the spread of railroads and especially of the "liberty of the press"—which "alone renders all relapse into barbarism impossible" would soon do away with the need for revolution by violence. "Revolutions, it is said, are not made with rose-water. This will be less true hereafter than now." Yet, the right of revolution could not be dismissed, he told his audience. His dislike of violence had not abated, but Sumner had come to appreciate the danger of vested power much more than he had at the time of the Dorr Rebellion in 1842, or even than when he had discussed the meaning of Independence Day with Robert Winthrop in 1845. His sympathy had grown accordingly for those who felt the need to resort to revolution. "[I]n the present state of the world," even the "lover of Peace" had to admit that "an exigency may unhappily arise for its exercise [. . .]."[44]

Boston did not agree. Sumner thought he knew why. If, in general, "American sympathy is strangely in favor of" the Revolution of 1848, even in the world's foremost republic money felt an international kinship. Louis Blanc may have been too impatient, but Sumner agreed completely that the real danger to the Second Republic and to the entire revolutionary movement came from property. In Boston, as in Paris, "[t]he rich, & the commercial classes feel that property is rendered insecure, & with many of these the pocket is the chief censorium." Sumner thus found himself more alone than ever in his native town. "Mr Cabot told me that I was the first person he had seen, who had hope in the Future of France." George Ticknor, always fascinated by the decay of civilizations, was sure he saw Europe now in its decadence with the United States soon to follow. "John E. Thayer, the rich banker, [. . .] tells me that he regards France as a 'wreck,'" and Sumner heard that "Mr Webster [. . .] condemns this Revolution, saying that it is a movement of *communists & socialists*." No French conservative would have put it differently. Indeed, as Sumner told George, "[t]he people who dominate in Boston are all anti-revolutionists. They have no hope. To them the Future of France is full of guillotines, battles & blood."[45]

Sumner had no illusions that the road ahead for Europe would be smooth. The threat of reaction being ever-present, France had "fearful trials in store [. . .]. She is moving from one house to another. Indeed it is more than this; she is fleeing from a burning house; so doing, she must feel present discomfort; but I do not doubt the Future of that great country." Sumner hoped that counterrevolution would be averted by the curtailment of the patronage and the judicious distribution of power that he had recommended to George, as well as by a firmness of purpose and solidarity on the part of the revolutionary leaders. In mid-April, as the French Republic's first elections approached, Sumner looked forward to a radical victory. He would "not be surprised," he wrote to George, "if the Nat. Assembly should repudiate a portion of the Nat. Debt"—as they had done during the Revolution of 1789—"or should impose taxes upon large properties of such a character as to cause the *rentiers* throughout the world to wince & cry out in sympathy." Though Sumner was personally inclined to be strict about debt—he was insistent that the United States should pay off the debt incurred by the Mexican War as fast as possible that it "not be postponed to the next generation"—a radical economic plan did not disturb him. "The large properties ought unquestionably to pay in a ratio that increases with their ppty."[46]

Sumner was equally concerned about the role of property in American politics. He did not accuse Boston's leading commercial and professional class of hypocrisy any more than he had Robert Winthrop, but he knew that, whatever their personal feelings about slavery, the "spirit of trade" would not allow them to consider action that might disrupt the flow of business or the bonds of party—just as the French aristocracy and bourgeoisie would judge the Second Republic based on its effect on their own power and the continuance of society as they knew it. In 1846 Sumner had watched Boston's leaders respond to anti-slavery agitation by drawing closer to Southern slaveholders with whom they had long-standing ties of business and friendship. Many Southerners chose to vacation in Newport and Saratoga, where they socialized with vacationing Bostonians, just as Bostonian merchants often made extended trips southward, offered help and financial loans to plantation owners, and even discussed plans with them for establishing industry in the South. Within the year President Jared Sparks would begin a concerted and successful effort to entice Southern sons to return to Harvard for their education. All the while the growing and spinning of cotton held their parents in close business partnership, while their efforts to save the national Whig party, and with it the Union as they knew it, held them together politically.[47]

Sumner was not the only one to lose confidence in the will of Boston's leading men to live up to their reputation for benevolence. By 1850 even their friend Hillard felt moved to warn them that the merchant who forgets, in the pursuit of profit, to cultivate his higher faculties will find after a time that "[t]he spring of his mind is broken. He can no longer lift his thoughts from the ground." More than a decade earlier Channing had lamented to Ticknor "the mournful effects of the infinite, intense thirst for gain and accumulation here." This unhealthy state would one day cause the people forcefully to remind their leaders that the end of "republican institutions" is not the accumulation of wealth but "liberty and improvement and the development of human nature [. . .]." At the same time Sheriff Sumner had privately complained that "[i]t does not become the rich to allow the City (in which the[y] made their fortunes) to be in debt" while they wasted their money on "their improvident children. We ought not to have public poverty & private wealth." Early in his own speaking career, when "the Abolitionist was constantly taunted, especially by business men, as 'the man of one idea,'" Charles Sumner replied that it was indeed the "mere man of business" who was the true "'man of one idea,' and his solitary idea has its root in no generous or humane desires, but in selfishness. He lives for himself alone [. . .] nor does his worldly nature, elated by the profits of cent per cent, see with eye of sympathy, in cotton sold or sugar bought, the drops of blood falling from the unhappy slaves out of whose labor they were wrung."[48]

The problem was of national import. Because the Boston merchants were also the leaders of the Whig party of Massachusetts and prominent in the national party, they combined their social outlook with an immense power. The influence of the "cotton-lords" was more than social; they constituted what Sumner and other reformers called the "Money Power," a political group devoted to furthering the interests of business and to blocking attempts at reform, like their French counterparts, and like their counterparts to the South—the more notorious "Slave Power."

Southerners and Northern conservatives alike—as well as many later historians—dismissed the notion of a Slave Power Conspiracy with contempt. Though it became common only in the 1830's, the phrase went back into the eighteenth century along with resentment of the political power of slaveholders. From his earliest years, Sumner had been used to hearing his father complain about the aggressive hypocrisy of united slave owners speaking of liberty or justice, and about their arrogant attempts to control public policy and discussion, as through the gag rule. When Sumner and his fellow Conscience Whigs referred to the Slave Power, their numbers varied somewhat. After the next census Sumner would agree with Charles Francis Adams that it consisted of no more than 350,000 men in fifteen states. Angry at the latest Southern complaints that by Northern efforts to limit slavery "the whole South is insulted & disfranchised," however, Sumner could scoff that if anyone were so treated it was "only the slave-holders. [. . .] How many are they? Less than 100,000." Whatever the precise figures, Sumner and his colleagues knew whom they meant. The Slave Power's implicit assumption that they represented "the whole South," rather than simply their own self-interest, Sumner rejected out of hand. The Slave Power was the South's political leadership. "By the Slave Power," explained Sumner, "I understand that combination of persons, or, perhaps, of politicians, whose animating principle is the perpetuation and extension of Slavery, and the advancement of Slaveholders."[49]

Comparing it to the giant Enceladus, fabled to be trapped beneath Mount Etna and whose every movement threatened to bring "destruction and dismay to all who dwelt upon its fertile slopes," Sumner called the Slave Power "the imprisoned Giant of our Constitution." It was at once "bound" and tolerated by that document, which permitted "the undue proportion of offices [. . .] held by Slaveholders" and thus their disproportionate control of national affairs. The Constitution and the Founding Fathers, however, had only "permitt[ed]" slavery while "regrett[ing]" it. The Slave Power had made a federal government "openly favoring and vindicating it, visiting also with its displeasure all who oppose it." The course of American history told the rest of the story—the Missouri Compromise, the annexation of Texas, "with its fraud and iniquity," the deadly Mexican War. All this was the work of the Slave Power, "a tyranny hardly less hateful than that which sustained the Bastile." To end such a despotism, the friends of freedom had to imitate their "enemies": "[L]et us also be taught by the Slave Power. The two hundred thousand slave holders are always united in purpose. Hence their strength. Like arrows in a quiver, they cannot be broken."[50]

For all the similarities between the opposition of American businessmen and slave-holders on the one hand and of European aristocrats on the other to reform and revolution, Sumner did not think the problems on either side of the Atlantic were identical. Europeans were struggling to establish the very foundations of popular government. Sumner thought these were secure in the United States. By their wealth, by the character of Southern laws giving slave owners near absolute control over their plantations, and, in the older eastern states, by the traditional limitations on the franchise, the slave owners held a commanding position within the South as well as immense power in Washington. But they constituted no *ancien régime*. "We are a republic," Sumner insisted. "[F]or all practical purposes," no American advocated monarchy or hereditary aristocracy. Though, as in other countries, "[t]he passion to *transmit* money" remained strong, the absence of primogeniture kept American estates smaller and more fluid. "Our present struggle is not with a feudal aristocracy, but with a modern substitute [. . .]."[51]

What slaveholders and businessmen and European aristocrats had in common, besides the power they exercised over others, was their belief that they had a right to the power they enjoyed. Just as merchants were generally influenced by the "spirit of trade," just as lawyers generally assumed a bias in favor of their profession and against "the reform of its abuses," just as criminals had generally been raised in vicious rather than virtuous circumstances—and could often, Sumner argued, be reformed by being "withdrawn, so far as is possible by human means, from all bad influences"—so must slaveholders be influenced by the character and values of the society in which they were raised and lived. Human nature combined a native strength—that "disinterestedness which places duty, without hope of reward, without fear or favor, above all human considerations"—and a corresponding weakness—"selfishness." Slavery had made selfishness a basic part of Southern law and culture. Like William Ellery Channing, Sumner argued that it was not out of personal malevolence but under the influence of a culture for two hundred years steeped in the dictates of bondage that slaveholders defended such an evil institution. Sumner thus did "not think it right to abjure slave-holders socially or politically," and "regret[ted]" it when other Free Soilers sometimes did so. The influence of slaveholders on national policy had to be stopped, but they themselves required not chastisement but education.[52]

If Northerners had no right to enter the South and change its society directly, they could deal the Slave Power's hold on national politics a fatal blow by breaking the power of their Northern allies. This would be the first step in reorienting American society toward the principle of freedom. It was with this message that Sumner rallied the cheering crowd at the Free Soil party's first state party convention that summer of 1848. It was none other than the Money Power, the cotton merchants of Boston and their allies, who made the Slave Power's growing victories possible. The Whig party could not have had the slaveholding war hero Zachary Taylor "forced upon" it, Sumner told his audience, had it not been for the help the Slave Power received from Massachusetts' own business leaders: "Yes! It was brought about by an unhallowed union—conspiracy, rather let it be called—between two remote sections of the country—between the politicians of the South-West and the politicians of the North-East; between the cotton planters and flesh-mongers of Louisiana and Mississippi, and the cotton spinners and traffickers of New England; between the lords of the lash and the lords of the loom."[53]

Conspiracy! The Cotton Whigs were furious. After one and a half years of silence Nathan Appleton shot off a series of notes to Sumner, his old playfulness turned to that mocking scorn so infamous among his political enemies. Was this merely a "rhetorical flourish," he jibed, or did it mean "what it says"? Of the charge Appleton declared, mimicking Sumner's own words of defense: "I not only *doubt its accuracy,* but so far as it means what it says pronounce it *utterly untrue,* without the shadow of truth to rest upon. I challenge you to support it."[54]

Sumner defended his accusation by reviewing the history of the Cotton

Whigs' reaction to the antislavery movement since 1845. There was no doubt, he wrote, that "certain prominent gentlemen" of influence in both the cotton manufacture and in politics had "generally discountenanced those measures whose object was to oppose the extension of Slavery & the aggression of the Slave Power." They had "stood aloof from" or discouraged the anti-Texas conventions, accepted the Mexican War, and supported the candidacy of Zachary Taylor, working "*in concert or harmony with*" Southern politicians even in defiance of specific resolutions of their own General Court. "Such a combination, for such a purpose, is odious. It is worse than the combination to carry the Missouri Compromise. It is unholy. It may be justly called a conspiracy." This hardly satisfied Appleton. Conceding that Sumner was "acting under impulses which are a part of your nature rather than from selfish calculation," Appleton dismissed his evidence. Sumner's charge was, after all, he concluded, a mere "rhetorical flourish founded on harmless well known facts.—eked out by suspicious and idle rumours."[55]

Sumner and Appleton were not using the same definition of "conspiracy." Appleton used the word in its narrow legalistic and more modern sense of a cabal for illegal purposes, and declared his conscience clear. This is not what Sumner had in mind. Sumner turned to the example of Abbott Lawrence who had narrowly missed being nominated for the vice presidency at the Whig National Convention and who was deeply implicated in the conspiracy Sumner had outlined—and with whom, despite all their political differences, he maintained a friendly tie. Sumner believed that Lawrence, deep down, knew his alliance with the Taylor men was wrong. "*What can I do about it;*" Lawrence had confided to Sumner one evening after dinner, "*I am in up to the eyes.*" Sumner continued to have the greatest "confidence in the many virtues of his character," he assured Appleton. "I do not believe that he intrigued for the Vice Presidency—nor am I inclined to believe that he desired it. Of course I do not believe that there was a 'bargain' between him and the partizans of Taylor. But I cannot disguise my conviction, that, in an unhappy hour—unhappy for his country & for his own fame—he surrendered to the desire of fraternity with slave-holding politicians, even at the cost of principles, which, as a son of Massachusetts, he should have guarded to the last. I believe that he will yet regret his course."[56]

No one raised under a republican philosophy could consider one's own self-interest a legitimate end of political action, or the self-interest of a group or class the legitimate end of a political party. To do so would be to put "selfishness" above "duty." To Sumner the conspiracy between "the lords of the lash and the lords of the loom" was not—any more than the Slave Power Conspiracy—a felonious bargain in a back room. It was the acquiescence of "worthy but timid men," as Sumner privately called them, in coöperation with those whose values were inimical to their own best ideals, but who shared with them a desire to maintain a comfortable and prosperous status quo. It was a kind of gentleman's agreement to protect property and "'law and order,'" without considering the larger question—the only legitimate question, thought Sumner—of the good of the whole nation, of mankind, of what republicans called the public good. The word "conspiracy," in precisely this meaning, had a long tradition of use in republican thought, just as did the word "faction," which Sumner thought perfectly described both major American political parties. "Whatever may be said of the opinions of individuals belonging to these different" combinations, how better to describe the parties themselves, urged Sumner. "I say factions; for, what are factions but combinations of men whose sole cement is a selfish desire for place and power, in disregard of principles?"[57]

The perversion of the American political system could not be put right without the destruction of the Slave Power. Sumner did not go so far as to advocate the corresponding destruction of the Money Power. Few did. Most antislavery advocates championed free labor in the new system of industrial capitalism. Trade unionism was still a new concept even among industrial workers, while the Workingman's party of the 1830's had never been large and had essentially disappeared with the depression of the early 1840's. Sumner himself, despite disappointment in Boston's financial class, continued to share the traditional eighteenth-century concept of commerce as a civilizing force. Once the Slave Power had been destroyed and the thralldom of the Money Power broken, Sumner imagined that American society as a whole would follow the course already established in the North. "The industrial progress will continue as heretofore," he believed.[58]

Sumner did not, however, want to see the mere replacement of one power by another. Slavery's hold on the federal government could be dismantled only by the active awakening of Northern public opinion in favor of freedom, in favor of America's founding respect for human rights. Once that had been accomplished, America's economic growth might continue as before, "but the Govt. will change from its immoral & pro-slavery course to a moral & anti-slavery course." The nation would begin to promote the public good. "Education, & Peace would then be thoroughly organized; & the enormous means that now go to armaments, & destructive industry will go to beneficence, & productive industry." Sumner hoped that once the influence of the Slave Power had been removed, Northern businessmen would find it easier to follow those principles of the dignity of man and the duty to do good that they, unlike slave owners, had been raised by.[59]

Sumner was aware that this vision was not foolproof. "To all this, the great opposing force, is the selfishness of men, as displayed in business, & in the old combinations of party. I could dwell on this topic at length," Sumner remarked a little bitterly to an English correspondent curious about America's future, but he did not like to. He would rather work toward the vision, trying to be aware of dangers but not giving in to worry. Throughout his life, no matter how deeply disillusioned he might become, Sumner would always say, as he did during the turbulent spring of 1848: "I take counsel of my hopes, rather than my fears." It was with such hope that Sumner looked forward to the establishment of a political organization that might embrace all the North, a party devoted to duty rather than selfishness, devoted to the humanitarian and cosmopolitan ideals of the Enlightenment and to the reforms necessary to make them a reality. "We found now a new party," Sumner would rally his fellow Free Soilers that same spring. "Its corner-stone is Freedom. Its broad, all-sustaining arches are Truth, Justice, and Humanity. Like the ancient Roman capitol, at once a Temple and a Citadel, it shall be the fit shrine of the genius of American institutions."[60]

So many men crowded into Worcester on 28 June 1848 to take part in the Free Soil party's first state convention that the City Hall was not big enough to hold them, and they had to adjourn to the town common. With the Democratic party's choice of a pro-slavery platform and the candidacy of Lewis Cass—whom Sumner remembered as the kindly but bumbling Minister to France during his own stay there and who had supported the annexation of Texas and rejected the Wilmot Proviso—and the Whig party's decision to run Zachary Taylor with no platform at all, rebellious antislavery conventions had quickly been held in Ohio and New York. Massachusetts thus already knew that the foundations of the new party were strongly laid.[61]

As one fervent speaker followed another that day in Worcester, Sumner told Palfrey that the "enthusiasm [. . .] rose to fever heat." Both Judge Samuel Hoar and his son E. Rockwood Hoar spoke, as well as Henry Wilson, Joshua R. Giddings and a dozen others. It was near the end of the meeting that Charles Francis Adams captured the imagination of the crowd by declaring his allegiance to the new movement in the words his grandfather had used as he signed the Declaration of Independence: "'Sink or Swim, Live or Die, Survive or Perish, to go with the liberties of my country, is my fixed determination.'" Sumner followed immediately after, and took up Adams' theme by reminding his audience of the moment when a courtier informed Louis XVI of the taking of the Bastille. Louis responded: "'It is an *insurrection*.' 'No, Sire,' was the reply of the honest courtier, 'it is a *revolution*.' And such is our Movement to-day," Sumner proclaimed. "It is a REVOLUTION." Working his audience into a crescendo of excitement, Sumner urged Massachusetts to take up the banner and go on to Buffalo, and linked the Revolutionary heritage of their fathers with the present stirrings in Europe: "Let Massachusetts—nurse of the men and principles which made our earliest revolution—vow herself anew to her early faith. Let her elevate once more the torch, which she first held aloft. Let us, if need be, pluck some fresh coals from the living altars of France. Let us, too, proclaim 'Liberty, Equality, Fraternity,'—Liberty to the captive—Equality between the master and his slave—Fraternity with all men, the whole comprehended in that sublime revelation of Christianity, the Brotherhood of Mankind."[62]

The zeal with which the Free Soilers convened in Buffalo on 9 August 1848 for their first ever national convention was enough to justify the party organizers' most sanguine hopes. Even the normally guarded Charles Francis Adams was moved to look forward to victory that fall, while Sumner excitedly measured "[t]he development of public opinion. [. . .] Even in Boston, the stronghold of the commercial spirit, we find most unexpected sympathy." "The whole country seems to be arousing at last," he gloried "—God be praised!"[63]

Perhaps twenty thousand delegates came to Buffalo. Massachusetts, Ohio, and New York led the way, but eighteen states in all—including Delaware, Maryland, and Virginia—sent delegates from all political backgrounds. Former Whigs, Democrats, and Liberty men showed their eagerness to make a distinct party by the willingness with which they compromised on economic and land issues to write the party's platform. The platform's major issue—slavery—found them already united. For men who came from three previously rival parties, settling on a presidential candidate was touchier. Still, present good will and hope in the future united them with remarkable swiftness on the favorite of New York Democrats— former President Martin Van Buren. The vice presidential candidate was an easier choice. Though he had not sought it, Charles Francis Adams was gratified for the memory of "my fathers" to be nominated by acclamation. "We shall have candidates of our own every where," Sumner exulted to Giddings. "*We are a new party*—entirely."[64]

The old parties felt threatened—and skeptical at the Free Soilers' pretensions to idealism. How sincere could they really be, asked Whigs and Democrats, as well as many subsequent historians, when they, former Whigs and Liberty party men, professing their hatred of the moral evil of slavery, picked for their standard-bearer Martin Van Buren? The "Old Fox of Kinderhook" had long since become famous as a political machinator and as the original "Northern man with Southern principles." As President he had opposed the abolition of slavery in the District of Columbia—now called for in the Free Soil party's platform—and had upheld the gag rule and the censorship of abolitionist publications from the mails. What kind of antislavery leader was that? Democrats were as angry at Van Buren's apostasy, as Whigs were incredulous that Conscience men could abandon their party out of indignation at its choice of a slaveholding candidate and then fly to the South's most famous Northern friend. The Free Soilers' apparent self-confidence in the face of their former colleagues' taunts was itself a goad. It was more in teasing than in malice that Abbott Lawrence and a friend joked to Sumner in June that his decision to reject Taylor forced him to follow Van

Buren. Lawrence was puzzled all the same that Sumner could announce with such firmness: "*I am ready.*"[65]

The choice of Van Buren, of course, had not been easy. The formation of a new party necessitated coöperation among old political enemies. Van Buren's past record on slavery made the choice particularly unpleasant. The Liberty men had at first hoped the Free Soil party would choose their favored candidate, John P. Hale. The Liberty party's presidential candidate in 1840 and 1844, he was now the only antislavery man in the United States Senate. But Liberty men knew that Hale was too closely associated in the popular mind with abolitionism to be viable, and it was no surprise when he voluntarily withdrew his name. It was the association with abolitionism that had doomed the whole Liberty party to obscurity and that had, by 1848, caused its adherents to divide amongst themselves in the search for more practical political avenues to fight slavery. The Conscience Whigs for a time supported Judge John McLean. As a Supreme Court justice he was a prominent Whig, and was personally opposed to slavery. He had already disappointed them, however, by his failure to speak out against voting supplies for the Mexican War, and was now worried that attaching his name to the Free Soil movement might hurt his standing as a Whig. McLean's own Ohio delegation would withdraw his name as well, leaving Van Buren the only practicable candidate.[66]

The Free Soilers faced a dilemma. They were a new party, founded upon an idea, which they wished to see prevail in the nation at large. To do this they needed leaders who had both, as Sumner put it, "devotion to the cause," and the "ability to maintain it to a successful result [. . .]." As both major parties had tried for years, however, to keep the issue of slavery out of national politics, the men most famous for their devotion to the cause had been branded dangerous fanatics in the public eye, while the nation's respected statesmen had all survived politically by compromising with slavery. Van Buren had the advantage of being the favorite of the largest and least certain contingent of the Free Soil coalition. Still, the wary Conscience men remained frustrated by Van Buren's politicianly refusal to commit himself against a veto of abolition in the District of Columbia. Afraid Van Buren might maintain his former presidential position, Sumner considered adding a plank to the Free Soil platform calling for the removal of the government from Washington should slavery not be abolished there. As the Buffalo Convention approached, they all watched the "Red Fox" carefully.[67]

Van Buren, like most of the political men of his generation—sons of the Revolution, anxious to preserve their fathers' legacy—put the maintenance of the Union and of his party above ideology. His belief in the importance of party unity to the maintenance of the Union could be called his ideology. Yet he was not insensible to the problem of slavery. Even as President he had opposed the annexation of Texas, and he now supported the Wilmot Proviso. He had long been deeply concerned about the danger to Northern Democrats of their sub-servient role to the slaveholding leaders of the party. It was said that resentment of those leaders for slighting him and his wing of the New York Democrats in 1844 pushed him to join the Free Soil movement. Certainly he felt deep loyalty to his New York followers, the antislavery Barnburners, and to their leader, his flamboyant and quixotic son John. More important was his sense that Southern leaders had not reciprocated fairly for the compromises of their Northern col-leagues. The lack of such comity threatened the Union, he believed, and his sense of civic duty demanded that he rebuke Southern recklessness in an effort to re-store the balance of the Democratic party and of the country.[68]

Sumner knew that such a man, however honest, put political above moral questions, and he carefully debated with himself about the prospect of giving the former President his support. So often accused of being a visionary idealist, Sum-ner remained proud of his own sense of practicality. He had chosen the political rather than the Garrisonian path of reform, not because he thought it purer but because he thought it more effective. Having chosen that path, he was willing to accept help from anyone, whatever his history or private interests. As Sumner had told the students at Amherst College the year before, "[i]t were churlish, in-deed, not to offer our homage to those acts by which happiness has been pro-moted, even though inspired by a sentiment of personal ambition, or by consid-erations of policy." Sumner could have said of Van Buren what he would later say of his son John: "Van Buren is a politician, not a philanthropist or moralist, but a politician, like Clay, Winthrop, Abbott Lawrence, & has this advantage that he has dedicated his rare powers to the cause of Human Freedom. In this I would welcome any person from any quarter."[69]

And Sumner became convinced that Van Buren could do the cause important service, if only by fixing the voters' attention on the newborn party. "The more I hear of Van Buren," he wrote to Adams on the eve of the Convention, "the more I become reconciled to him as our candidate. His name gives our movement a national character." The other former Conscience Whigs agreed—Charles Francis Adams accepted the nomination as Van Buren's running mate, and Stephen C. Phillips, whose reputation for principle was respected by Free Soilers and Garrisonians alike, gave Van Buren the first Conscience Whig vote of the Convention, thus rallying his colleagues to the standard of coöperation.[70]

It was in this spirit of using the practical to advance the ideal that Sumner accepted the whole Free Soil movement. Not all its adherents were equally advanced on the subject of slavery. Most New York Barnburners disliked aboli-tionism and blacks; a few of the delegates at Buffalo were disappointed support-ers of Clay, there to spite the Whigs; while some Liberty men had long pro-nounced slavery void under the Constitution, and Sumner himself would soon make his Roberts case appeal for complete civil equality regardless of color. Some historians have argued that for abolitionists to join with supporters of the Wilmot Proviso, or to accept the leadership of Van Buren, for egalitarians to join with those who had accepted the racial discrimination that was standard at the time, was an abnegation of principle, or evidence even that they had never had strong principles to start with. With such a conclusion, Sumner emphatically disagreed.[71]

For all their differences, it was concern about slavery and its national implications that had brought the Free Soilers together. At Buffalo they all agreed "with great enthusiasm" to a platform that went beyond the Wilmot Proviso to call for what was known as "divorce" of the federal government from slavery, that is, that slavery no longer find protection in but rather banishment from all territories and jurisdictions controlled by the federal government, including—hinted the platform on this controversial subject—the District of Columbia. In the campaign ahead, Free Soilers would stand by their platform, turning the canvass into the ideological debate that the major parties had tried to avoid. Many Free Soilers would act upon their principles by working to end discriminatory state laws denying blacks equal civil and political rights. Van Buren would reciprocate the good will of his new supporters by expressly accepting the entire Free Soil platform, and adding his pledge not to veto any bill to abolish slavery in the District of Columbia. Of those who had thought the Buffalo platform "should leave the moral question of Slavery untouched & should allude only to the inequality under the Constitution for its expansion," Sumner had answered plainly: "This will not do." The fact that the Free Soilers, whatever their backgrounds, readily agreed on a platform that condemned slavery and looked to its extinction was to Sumner evidence of progress indeed.[72]

Still, Sumner's hopefulness expected a little more than all his Free Soil colleagues were yet ready to give. His deep disillusionment at the tergiversation of his former Whig friends found balm in the crusading spirit of his new Buffalo colleagues. He was entirely willing to forgive Van Buren his past and to forgive the Barnburners their hesitancy about abolition in part because he believed that, once their sensibilities had been awakened to the evil of slavery, their own vision would be enlarged and their principles strengthened. This was the same process of education he expected the Free Soil movement to effect in public opinion throughout the North. Sumner's faith in the Barnburners would indeed be sorely tested over the coming years, especially in those much hoped-for elections of 1852—by which time the intervention of the Compromise of 1850 had caused many former Democrats, including the Van Burens, father and son, to return to the successful Democratic party. Still, Sumner would maintain his conviction in the ultimate victory of that progress of public opinion that the Barnburners had already by their actions in 1848 materially advanced.[73]

Van Buren was not the only former president whose influence was felt at the

Buffalo Convention. The delegates had certainly thought about the need to balance the ticket when they chose Charles Francis Adams as Van Buren's running mate. They were also remembering his father. Just the previous February "Old Man Eloquent" had died. John Quincy Adams had been struck by his final illness in the Hall of the House of Representatives where he had served the last seventeen years of a lifetime devoted to public service, and where the vigor, parliamentary skill, and *panache* he had brought to the fight for freedom of speech had so dramatized the universal urgency of the struggle against slavery and brought it a wider public sympathy. Impelled by the respect they felt for him, the delegates now "crowded about the son, shook his hands, spoke of their admiration for the 'old man', & seemed by a natural process of the mind to show him the respect they could not show to the father."[74]

"It is a source of lasting satisfaction to me," Sumner had written that spring to Charles Francis Adams, "that I had the privilege of seeing so much of [your father] at such an interesting moment of his life." A difference of forty-four years between their ages and John Quincy Adams' long record of public service, including one term as president, as well as his illustrious parentage, had all imparted a natural formality to their relations that could not, however, obscure a warm feeling of friendship and close philosophical kinship. Sumner had lost an important friend in John Quincy Adams, a man he esteemed too deeply to trust himself to write the eulogy that friends expected of him. As a memento, Charles Francis gave Sumner the silver writing-ring which his father had worn in later years to steady his hand, and which had his initials engraved upon it. Sumner would wear it upon his watch-chain for the rest of his life.[75]

Sumner and the elder Adams had been shaped by the same traditions of the Enlightenment and American Moral Philosophy. They shared the same ideal of human nature, of the faculties held in balance and developed by the guidance of the informed conscience. Within the republican balance between the rights of the individual and his duty to society, Sumner and Adams, both trained in the traditions of Natural Law, stressed the natural rights of all men, which they equated with the Christian ideal of the Brotherhood of Man. It was an emphasis that had led them, like William Ellery Channing, to the antislavery struggle, and, despite an early and strongly felt conservative loyalty, in a political direction steadily more liberal.[76] No human right was to them more precious than that of self-improvement, and what was true for the individual, they believed was true for the nation. They both aimed at that true national self-improvement which was the progress of civilization, the moral and cultural development of the whole people. "The Constitution itself," Adams had said in 1833, "is but one great organized engine of improvement—physical, moral, political." Both strong nationalists, they loved the Union most as the means to a higher end. Nor should the international community uphold a different standard. Both cosmopolites, Sumner and Adams shared a commitment to a family of nations with communal responsibilities under the governance of international law.[77]

The former President was not without his human failings. Sumner regretted that, though "[h]is cause was grand," Adams could be downright "violent, uncandid, & wrong-headed" as he debated slaveholders in the House. In Adams' willingness to indulge in personalities, to make on-the-record references to "'the puny mind' of the gentleman from Kentucky," or "to his intemperance," Sumner was sorry to see Adams "governed by the lower part of his nature," and feared that he sometimes set an unparliamentary example in a capital city where "fear of bullies or interruptions" might begin to threaten the necessary "freedom of speech." Later, when Sumner had personally to face the taunts of Southern opponents on the floor of the Senate, he would learn how difficult it could be to keep one's temper, but, though his political rhetoric could be sharp, he would never indulge in the game of personalities that seemed rather to amuse Adams.[78] But, if Adams was guilty of "errors, & eccentricities," Sumner never doubted his "unquestioned purity of character"—he was "of honesty 'all compact.'" And it was precisely the purity and strength of his character that Sumner "prize[d] more than genius." In a society captivated by the untutored common man and mass democracy, Adams was an all too rare contemporary example of the kind of statesman, like Roscoe's Lorenzo and Charles Fox, who easily mingled statecraft and scholarship. "[P]articularly in our country," such an example was crucial, and Sumner was grateful that Adams had been so long "spared to guide & enlighten the land."[79]

What Sumner honored most in John Quincy Adams was that he brought his philosophy, his idealism, and his vast intellectual culture directly to bear upon the political arena. After a lifetime of public service, at a time when he could have retired, instead—his mind full of his favorite Cicero, whom Adams called "the moral philosopher of Rome"—the ex-President had returned to Congress, there to do his greatest service of all, defending the people's right to speak and petition against the slave owners' efforts to silence them, fighting for the Right when most were too afraid to speak. It was for "his high *morale*, & his comprehensive attainments" that Sumner had long "reverence[d]" Adams. He was a true model of "a Christian statesman," whose life showed "the important truth, that *politics & morals* are one & inseparable."[80]

But who would carry on a tradition that seemed to be considered more and more old-fashioned, worried Adams. In his search for a successor, he naturally looked first to Joshua Giddings. Their collaboration in the House against the gag rule, the Mexican War, and the Slave Power stretched back nearly ten years, and the mutual confidence that had grown between them had soon become a deep friendship, almost like that between father and son. It was Giddings who, in February 1848, sat by Adams in his last day to wipe his brow and hold his hands. Shortly before, Adams had passed the mantle to Giddings: "I have more hope from you than from any other man." When, fifteen years later, Giddings felt his own time approaching, he would do as Adams had done and confer the same blessing in the same words upon his own best hope—Charles Sumner. In so doing he followed the original hope of John Quincy Adams himself.[81]

Adams had eyed appreciatively in Sumner many of the same qualities that Sumner admired in Adams—his constitutional impulse to industry, his high intellectual and cultural ideals and corresponding humility, his devotion to the principle of moral statesmanship, his commitment of conscience, and his unrelenting sense of duty. It disturbed Adams that these qualities should be combined with such self-doubt and such aversion to public office, for to Adams, civic duty almost inevitably meant the holding of public office. In truth, Adams liked politics and relished a good political fight and even the personal quarrels that could go with it. What Sumner suffered as a personal sacrifice, Adams admitted he could not live without. But Adams had been pushed into the public arena no more by his taste than by his experience and philosophy. From a youth filled with vivid memories of the Revolution, from a personal experience dating back to the age of fourteen when he had served as secretary to the American Minister to Russia, and from the example and lessons of his parents, who had very consciously sacrificed their personal comfort and even safety to serve the young Republic, Adams had learned to identify service to the common good with the holding of public office. To be fitted for it and refuse to serve seemed to him an abdication of responsibility. At least as early as 1845 Adams had seen in Sumner the makings of a statesman. His hopes had been confirmed by Sumner's Phi Beta Kappa oration the following year. Eagerly he had written then: "Casting my eyes backward no farther than the 4th of July of the last year, when you set all the vipers of Alecto a lisping, by proclaiming the Christian Law of universal Peace and Love, and then casting them forward perhaps not much farther, but beyond my own allotted time, I see you have a mission to perform—I look from Pisgah to the promised Land. You must enter upon it [. . .]."[82]

From then on Adams had regularly urged Sumner to reconsider his refusal to enter politics, undeterred by Sumner's repeated insistence that he preferred to serve as a private citizen. One day, after he had suffered a stroke in the winter of 1847, Adams harangued the younger man with particular intensity. Public service was not something Sumner could choose or reject according to his fancy, Adams pressed him; it was a solemn obligation. Sumner repeated that he "was unwilling to renounce literature." Cicero himself, Sumner liked to point out, wrote of how "he preferred to sit in the library of Atticus, beneath the bust of Aristotle, to any curule *sella*," and, "except that I would rather place myself beneath the bust of Plato," this was his own dream as well. But that would not do,

Adams enjoined. Public service had not forced Adams to "renounce" literature, and whatever Cicero's preferences, he had done his service in the Senate. As Sumner took his leave and turned to part, the old warrior called out to him once more: "Be not Atticus."[83]

Sumner had reached a crossroads in his life. He knew it, and dreaded to make the final decision. Politics had, in fact, become his primary occupation. Friends who regretted this complained repeatedly that they could never find him in his law office. Felton was relieved on one occasion to learn that his absence had been due to his actually having been in court. Usually Sumner was out researching a new speech, traveling to deliver a lecture, or meeting with political associates. When he was in his office, it was more often to talk politics than law. Hillard was dismayed to return from Europe in October 1848 only to discover that Number Four Court Street—which Rufus Choate's office had once made a famous center of Whig policy-making—had become a headquarters for planning Free Soil campaign strategy and "such a place of rendez-vous for abolitionists, free soilists and all other *ists,* that it was quite impossible to think of doing any business there."[84] If Hillard had been there in June and July, he would have seen Sumner all day at his desk "moiling at the law,"—but only to catch up on the pressing cases and bills left over from his utter neglect of his practice that spring. How Sumner's priorities had changed since, as a young law student, he had believed that the animal temptation of politics threatened to lure him away from his true intellectual and conscientious duty in the law. Since then the law had disappointed both his mind and his desire for moral satisfaction, while reform and the politics it led to had awakened his conscience. That July, when Palfrey wondered what had become of him, Sumner apologized for being "so much occupied" that he had to give up politics a month longer: "After that I will endeavor to do my duty." Law had become the distraction and politics the duty.[85]

That fall—the fall of the presidential election and of the Free Soil party's first elections—Sumner gave himself to his new duty more completely than ever before. Though anxious for rest, he spent part of his short August vacation observing the Buffalo Convention. By the twenty-second he was back in Boston to preside over a Free Soil rally at Faneuil Hall. Two weeks later it was the party's state convention, of which Sumner had been one of the principal organizers. There his work was recognized when he was made Chairman of the State Committee to manage the fall campaign. After that, when he was not holding the meetings that made their law offices so uncongenial to his Whiggish partner, Sumner was out on the campaign trail, speaking, to his own amazement, "in N. Hampshire, Maine, & from one end of Massachusetts to the other—in all the large towns— from Nantucket to Berkshire," and too busy to accept invitations to speak in the rest of New England, New York, and Ohio.[86]

Nor did Sumner neglect the constant stream of letters that he had been writing for some time now to encourage his fellow antislavery men in their own duty. Already that spring, when Horace Mann had been asked to take John Quincy Adams' seat in Congress, Sumner had written to inspirit him. "You can shew, as no other man can," he told the anxious antislavery Whig, "how supreme is duty—above all the suggestions of '*expediency*' or the urgency of party dictation." And when, over the summer, Mann failed to speak out on the issues surrounding the territory taken from Mexico because he feared it would force him "to bear about, this autumn, wherever I may go, on educational errands"—for Mann remained Secretary of Education for the Commonwealth—"a political badge," Sumner again reminded him of his duty. Hoping that Mann would keep both offices, Sumner nonetheless told him that he could retain the secretaryship "only so far as is consistent with the complete & earnest discharge of all the duties of Representative." If that was impossible, he must resign the one or the other. With apologies for his frankness, Sumner told him flatly: "I should not delay 24 hours." Mann scolded Sumner for being "rather the hardest task-master since Pharaoh [. . .]."[87]

Sumner's energetic guidance, however, contributed to an enthusiastic fall campaign. Whigs and Democrats, worried by the Free Soilers' ideological upper hand and by their excitement, lustily hurled billingsgate at them. Adams was "a political huckster," characterized by "egoism" and "selfishness," Palfrey was labeled "Judas," while Sumner was dismissed as a "transcendental lawyer." Across the country Free Soilers were called "sectional," "disunion[ist]," and more than that, "infidels," "political vipers," "lousy curs." The Free Soilers responded with more condemnation of the spread of slavery into the territories, and put the major parties on the defensive. Even the Whig party acknowledged Sumner as "the Demosthenes" of the Free Soil party, and his speech was hailed everywhere with "thunderous applause." When he occasionally ran into "shouts and hisses and [. . .] vulgar interruptions," as he did among the Whiggish and Southern Harvard students at Cambridge—Longfellow thought his speech there "was like one of Beethoven's symphonies played in a saw-mill!"—Sumner showed himself master of the situation by silencing his pro-Taylor hecklers. "The young man who hisses will regret it ere his hair turns gray," he declared, as all eyes turned to the source of the disturbance. "He can be no son of New England; her soil would spurn him."[88]

The campaign left Sumner hopeful for the party and personally dispirited. Longfellow worried as his friend became "somewhat worn." By election day Sumner had "spoken almost every night for the last two months," and he complained that "[m]y voice is hoarse & shattered, & I am weary." Never "in my wildest visions" had Sumner "expected" such an experience, and never did he want such again. He would always marvel at how William Seward seemed actually "to like" the work of campaigning. More than the sheer labor was "the mendacity of the public press" and the "violence" of the Whigs, which seemed to Sumner "most unprecedented," even after 1846. For his public role, Sumner had "been attacked bitterly." He tried to console himself "by what J. Q. Adams said to me during the last year of his life—'No man is abused whose influence is not felt.'" The vituperation, however, and the continued erosion of old friendships hurt. Longfellow regretted how their conversations had changed. "Nothing but politics now. Oh, where are those genial days when literature was the theme of our conversation?" Under the effect of constant labor and hostility, Sumner felt empty. "I am alive; that is, continue to draw breath, & stride through the streets," he wrote to Howe. "But what is this? I am becoming every day duller & duller; I have nothing to say to any body. I am like an extinct volcano." It was the direction his future was taking that most disturbed Sumner, and the danger that he might become permanently enmeshed in politics.[89]

Sumner imagined a completely different future for himself. Rather than of drudging at the law or of being a slave to demanding constituencies, he had long dreamt of the artistic and intellectual independence of the writer's life. Never trusting his own ability, he had for years encouraged his friends to write the book that he secretly wished he might write himself. Thus he had told Hal Cleveland not to waste time on articles and lyceum talks but to write that history of English literature, and thus he had encouraged Hillard's writings and Longfellow's first mature literary steps. Thus he had urged George in 1840 to write his book about Russia, and thus now, after some years of silence, he revived the subject: "I wish you would write a book—a solid volume—into which you would pour the conclusions & experience of the last ten years. Think of this." Though he was too unsure of himself to admit his thoughts openly to anyone but Longfellow, his own success as orator and political activist was beginning, little by little, to make Sumner feel that perhaps he, too, could achieve such a dream. In 1848 he began to hint of a change. With his *Law of Human Progress,* he said cryptically, "I think [. . .] I shall close my labors of this class." By 1849 he was refusing all new lyceum engagements, and he told George that his *War System of the Commonwealth of Nations* was not only his "best," but "the last address I shall ever give." By the middle of 1849 Sumner had made arrangements to publish an edition between hard covers of his collected orations and speeches, to put an elegant close to his political career. Then, he promised himself, he would start his own book.[90]

Sumner never intended thereby to abandon the cause of social improvement to which he had devoted himself over the past five years. He shared his countrymen's belief in the power of words. Since law school at least, he had emphasized the ability of writers and scholars to influence the development of society—and to him such an ability was synonymous with duty. As he watched European events in the spring of 1848 he found his subject, one that he hoped would be a serious, scholarly contribution to the human struggle for progress in his time. It was to be a history of the Mexican War, as Longfellow described it, "after the fashion of Louis Blanc's '*Dix Ans.*'" Sumner hoped it would have something of the same influence as the Frenchman's work. Because he proposed to fight slavery slowly, constitutionally, through public opinion and education, Sumner believed he would avoid the descent into violence caused by France's precipitousness. In his own way, however, he aimed at the same result Louis Blanc had envisioned—the remaking of American society. In the process he hoped to remake his own life to find a way to balance his need to work for the benefit of society with his desire for an existence of scholarly fulfillment and intellectual freedom.[91]

It was in mid-October 1848—as he was preparing himself to make this dream a reality—that the Free Soil party of the Boston district nominated Sumner for Congress. "Sumner stands now, as he himself feels," Longfellow noted in his journal, "at just the most critical point of his life. Shall he plunge irrevocably into politics, or not?" Urging George yet again earlier that spring to come home and help in the struggle against slavery, Sumner had reminded him of their father's constant saying "that the duties of life were more than life." The words echoed in Sumner's mind. Following that sense of duty he had already lost many of "the pleasures of friendship," without which "I have small satisfaction left except in the performance of my duty." It had subjected him to hounding by the newspapers, where he was accused of hypocrisy, mendacity, ambition, vindictiveness. "I have sought little for myself," he replied, "—not office or wealth—or worldly favor. No small chance for all of these I have dismissed." In the midst of the controversy the winter before over Winthrop and Palfrey and Giddings, Sumner had poured out his heart to Fanny Longfellow: "I dislike controversy. It is alien to my nature; but I do love what seems to me true & right; nor do I speculate much with regard to personal consequences in their maintenance. Believe me now, dear Fanny, as I look back upon all that has passed during the last year—groping among the wrecks of friendships that might have been argosies—I feel that I have done nothing but a duty, poorly, inadequately, but a duty which my soul told me to perform."[92]

Yet, faced with a life of such duty, with such consequences, as Longfellow observed, "he shrinks a little from the career just opening before him." More than ever Sumner felt the true starkness of his father's creed. Had every pleasure of life to be sacrificed to duty? Might one reserve nothing for oneself? He had already surrendered the dream of wife and family, had lost friendships, been forced to give up his easy confidence in the generosity of others, and been compelled to suffer the constant torment of his own unrelenting self-doubt faced with the growing expectations of his colleagues and the public. Now it seemed that duty asked him to lay down also his prized independence and the hope for a peaceful literary future that was his last personal dream.[93]

What made the choice the more difficult was that the dilemma was, to a greater degree than Sumner realized, within himself. It was not just a choice between duty on the one hand and dreams on the other, but between conflicting requirements of his own nature. Though he rejected its legitimacy throughout, his attraction to politics had been real and steady. He had never ceased from college on to follow both national and international affairs, reading all the available newspapers, corresponding with political friends, reading congressional and parliamentary documents and reports. Trying to keep himself informed, he had been giving himself a political education. His craving to help friends had pulled him in the same direction. They had only to ask. "Will you do me a favor?" ran a typical letter. "I see your ready response & the charming smile indicating assent." Whether it was making sure that one of their books got proper attention from the publisher, or that a pamphlet got to the right hands in Washington, or that a brother or son found consideration for a patronage job or diplomatic post, Sumner was always ready and knew what to do and whom to see. Even that love of excitement, of the whirl of public affairs and bustle of big cities pulled him away from the retired life.[94]

None of this could have tempted him to enter politics, however, had it not been for the cause. Starting with the Anti-Masonic movement, Sumner had been unable to resist a struggle that called to his conscience. As much as he genuinely loved the intellectual luxury of the library, he could not give himself to the satisfaction even of the highest private senses, when he felt called into the world by duty. "He is a man of moral enthusiasm," Hillard observed; "made to identify himself with some great Cause and accept and surrender himself to it unconditionally." Such a cause seemed all the more impelling to Sumner given the loneliness and dissatisfaction he felt in his own life. That had never seemed worth fighting for. Hillard thought that "[h]is mind and character require the stimulus of something outward and exoteric, some strong pressure, to take him out of himself and prevent him from a morbid habit of inactive brooding." More than a simple distraction, the antislavery struggle and the quest for a higher civilization of which it was a part were ideals that Sumner had imbibed from earliest youth and cherished all his life. They had been from the start his true faith, and now they had become his duty. The Free Soil party "aimed at the highest interests of mankind," Sumner told Horace Mann: "Nothing but my deep conviction of the importance of sustaining these principles would have impelled [me] into the strife of affairs."[95]

Close friends had none of Sumner's doubts. Would he accept the nomination tendered him that October, would he enter politics once and for all? The question "is already answered," Longfellow noted in his journal the day Sumner learned of the nomination. "He inevitably will do so, and after many defeats will be very distinguished as a leader." He imagined Sumner as "Member of Congress, perhaps; Minister to England, certainly." As Sumner agonized over his decision, Longfellow wrote: "When he has once burned his ships there will be no retreat. He already holds in his hand the lighted torch."[96]

On 26 October Sumner gave his answer. "Earnestly urging others to active support of the cause," he later recalled, "he could not refuse the post assigned to himself." To the committee which had informed him of his nomination he repeated his desire to remain a private citizen, but this time, in the name of duty, accepted their call. "In my view a crisis has arrived, which requires the best efforts of every citizen; nor should he hesitate with regard to his peculiar post. Happy to serve in the cause, he should shrink from no labor, and no exposure."[97]

It was not a final decision, however. Sumner reconciled himself to the nomination in part because he knew, as did everyone, that in the Boston district, the Whig stronghold, running against Robert C. Winthrop, no Free Soil candidate had the slightest chance of winning. On election day Sumner won fewer than one third the votes cast for Winthrop. He accepted defeat as a reprieve. With a lighter spirit he looked forward to the future. The Free Soil party had done superbly well for a new party in 1848, especially in Whig Massachusetts, which Sumner thought "the best-fought field." There they won a higher percentage of votes than in any other state besides Vermont, and won more than the Democrats: "It is no longer the 3d party," exulted Sumner. Though the Whigs kept control of the General Court, the Free Soilers elected members there and to Congress and were able to deny Taylor a majority. Sumner's hopefulness was widely shared: "As I view it, the Democratic party is not merely *defeated*, it is entirely broken in pieces. It cannot organize anew except on the Free Soil platform. Our friends feel happy in the result. We shall form the opposition to Taylor's administration—& secure, as we believe, the triumph of our principles in 52. You know that there will be a new census in 50, & a new apportionment of representatives & electors, securing to the North a large preponderance of power. This will count for us."[98]

There was still work to be done. Sumner agreed to become the Free Soilers' first State Party Chairman for 1849. But the Free Soil party would soon be victorious—perhaps indeed by 1852. Then, Sumner told himself, he could lay down his burden and devote himself to writing that book.

VIII

"*DIES IRÆ*"

"[*D*]*IES IRÆ dies illa.*" So Sumner would characterize 7 March 1850, the day
Daniel Webster stood up in the United States Senate to support what would become known as the Compromise of 1850 with its infamous Fugitive Slave Law.
Outraged as he was, Sumner was not entirely surprised. The events of 1848 had
been to him the rising up of the Enlightenment spirit of moral and humanitarian progress. From the first days of the revolutions of 1848, however, he had eyed
the danger of reaction—from the monarchists and the *haute bourgeoisie* in Europe, in the United States from the Slave Power and its ally the Money Power,
everywhere from those forces that put the maintenance of property and power
above the improvement of man. Now, he believed, it had come. The future of
the country, of freedom, of civilization was at stake. He had not anticipated the
effect it would have on his own future.[1]

Sumner was deeply disappointed to see how quickly the reaction began in
France, and the degree to which his worries about Louis Blanc had been right.
The socialists had been kept in check from the start of the February Revolution.
Louis Blanc's desire to give political power to the working class and the demands
of armed workers for "*le droit au travail*" had been whittled down by the suspicious bourgeois leaders of the provisional government to a system of National
Workshops designed simply to hand out public works jobs and the dole in a time
of fifty percent unemployment. But Sumner, "solicitous for his success," was
"troubled not a little by the *cochonnerie* of Louis Blanc," when, after the elections
of April 1848 yielded a moderate rather than a radical victory, the disappointed
socialists tried to establish a rival government with Louis Blanc at its head. It was
the beginning of the end. When the dole dried up and the National Workshops
were closed in June, the hungry workers took to the barricades once again, only
this time it was the revolutionary government that called out the army and the
National Guard to put them down. Over one thousand people were killed. "Alas!
France! poor France!" Sumner lamented to Whittier. "I sigh over her great Republican lie!" The republican experiment Sumner had hoped to see strengthened
by a cautious and practical approach was now endangered by the government's
mistrust and instability.[2]

When George first mentioned Prince Louis-Napoleon Bonaparte in June it was with an uncharacteristic note of dismay. "When you despair, or seem to lose hope," Sumner replied, "what must be the condition of things?" Sumner had met the nephew of the great Napoleon "once or twice" in London in 1839. "He seemed to me an ordinary character," he enquired anxiously. "Surely he cannot overturn France." But in December it was this prince, with his glorious name and his promises of restoring stability, who was elected, by a landslide, the Second Republic's first president. Sumner was "shocked by the press-gag, & the retrenchment of the suffrage" that the Prince President and his rightist Assembly soon instituted. George crisscrossed France trying to shore up support for the republic, and assured his brother that "every honest man is _for_" it. Sumner agreed that "the Future is secure," but knew that, for the present, the reaction had won. By 1850 the Second Republic was no republic "except in name." "It is a kingless monarchy," Sumner wrote scornfully, "a despotism in the disguise of a republic." The coup-d'état of 2 December 1851 and the Second Empire were only a step away.[3]

Sumner watched sadly as roughly the same pattern repeated itself across Europe, and revolutionaries, inspired by the French example, tried to jump from absolutism to constitutional democracy in one step. In each case fledgling liberal governments were weakened by internal class or national divisions, which paved the way for an often bloody reassertion of power by the old authoritarian régime. The nostalgic affection Sumner had felt for Italy since his sojourn there gave him a particular desire to see that land freed from her various foreign overlords and united for the first time since the Roman Empire. And so he was particularly disappointed to see Austria reassert her control over Milan and northern Italy, as he was in 1849 to see Mazzini's Roman Republic crushed—by French troops under orders from President Louis-Napoleon. "What a sacrilegious piece of piracy this French expedition against Rome is!" Sumner complained to Lieber. Perhaps no country seemed to have a better chance of success in 1848 than distant Hungary. "The feeling for Hungary throughout the U.S. is very strong," Sumner was pleased to say. Longfellow for one would host many Hungarian patriots over the next few years, and Tokay would long remain the wine of choice at his table. Sumner "share[d this sympathy] entirely," pleased by the combination of lawyerly practicality and idealistic enthusiasm of Hungary's revolutionary leader Louis Kossuth, and encouraged in the summer of 1849 by Hungary's ability to drive the Austrian army completely off her territory. But by that fall, with the help of Russian troops, the Austrian army reasserted control over a Hungary increasingly divided among her own nationalities, as was Austria herself.[4]

Over the next twenty-five years Sumner would continue to follow the progress of liberalism and self-determination in Europe, ever hopeful in their ultimate success despite the difficulties that stood in the way. He wished that the United

States could help—but he would countenance no action that violated the law of nations. Moral encouragement and friendly legislation were legitimate, direct intervention was not. Back in 1842 when England had been at war against China to maintain the lucrative trade in opium, Sumner had disagreed with both Lieber and John Quincy Adams. That English representatives and subjects had been maltreated was a legitimate justification for war, he conceded, but "[t]he Chinese were justified in demanding the opium & burning it [. . .]," and he declared himself "at a loss to see how Mr Adams can invoke Xtnty as a cloak for" the principle of intervention. Such a war was neither ethical nor legal: "Much as policy & the feelings of our social nature may dictate to nations commercial intercourse, I cannot find in the law of nations, as expressed in the writings of publicists & reduced from the practice of the world, any rule, which would authorize the *scourging* a state into the circle of nations. If it chooses to be a hermit, & live on its own springs & the fruits of its own soil, we cannot interfere. It is churlish & barbarian; but we cannot impose our Christian yoke upon them."[5]

The same principle obtained when it was a question of intervening to help a new nation establish itself. In the summer of 1849, when Hungary had chased the Austrian army off her land, Sumner was anxious for the United States to recognize the new nation. Hungary had, like the United States in her own war for independence, "sustained herself against" the empire to which she had belonged, and this should define her as an independent nation. "Surely it is not necessary that she should sustain herself against the combined world—nor against any combination of nations; but simply against the single unaided nation which claims to rule it." Austria had been unable to maintain control. "The Russian soldiers, as they descended the Carpathians, at the summons of Austria, virtually proclaimed the Independence of Hungary." But the moment passed quickly, and when Austria had, before winter, reëstablished control and chased the "*de facto*" Hungarian government into exile, Sumner would not consider any intervention. When Senator Cass offered a resolution to suspend diplomatic relations with Austria in protest against her treatment of Hungary, Sumner thought it "a dangerous precedent. Where could we stop our system;—not with Austria, or Russia. We must give up our relations with England on account of Ireland."[6]

In April 1848, George asked Sumner if another form of help might not be possible. Would the United States consider helping the new French Republic by lowering its tariffs against her? Sumner liked the idea and wrote immediately to Vice President George Dallas. Sumner was not very much interested in or attuned to financial questions, but accepting economics as a branch of Moral Philosophy, he did believe that it should be exercised for ethical and humanitarian advancement. He was thus sorry to have to warn George that, despite the Vice President's sympathetic response, no action should be expected.[7]

The Mexican War had just ended and had left the United States with a great debt. "People begin to clamor for a higher Tariff," not a lower one, Sumner told George. He was thinking more of opinion in Massachusetts than in the nation at large. After forty years of contention over rising tariffs—especially unpopular in a South both agricultural and fearful of the effect of positive government on slavery—most Americans had greeted the moderate lowering of duties in 1846 with pleasure. Disappointment reigned only in the industrial regions of Pennsylvania and Massachusetts. Among Whig leaders in Boston, however, desire for higher tariffs coexisted with skepticism about the European revolutions, and Sumner could only express his scorn for those "who do not feel that a generous idea is worth more than a Tariff."[8] Meanwhile, though the Senate passed resolutions congratulating France on its new republican government, national Democratic leaders would do more to acquire new southwestern lands and even Cuba, than they would to give material help to republicanism in Europe. Once again it seemed to Sumner that the Slave Power and the Money Power agreed in putting self-interest above the good of others.[9]

Sumner could only regret that the mere existence of slavery made any effective American action impossible. It was this that defeated the Cass resolution. Sumner was so aggrieved by Austria's repression of Hungary that he admitted privately that he would be "willing to see" such a departure from "international usage." Shortly after Senator Cass made his resolution against Austria, however, American filibusters tried to take over Cuba to add more slave territory to the United States—an action, Sumner lamented, that "has dishonored us before the world." For decades European authors and statesmen like Harriet Martineau and Alexis de Tocqueville, and Tocqueville's partner on his American expedition Gustave de Beaumont, had denounced American prejudice and hypocrisy on the subject of slavery, so that American talk of liberty was often greeted in Europe with snickers and sneers. "[A]las! while we have Slavery our voice is powerless," Sumner sighed to his brother. "Every word for Freedom exposes the horrid inconsistency of our position."[10]

The power of America's own reactionary forces had undermined her moral authority to help those who yearned for her republican ideal. The defenders of property, whether in man or textile mills, had worked to stem the tide of humanitarian progress. Now, in 1850, Sumner saw those forces regrouping, as their counterparts in Europe had already done, to quash what he had proudly thought of as the American revolution of 1848. Just "as 'law and order' are the words by which reaction has rallied in Europe," Sumner told George, "so these very words, or perhaps the 'Constitution and Union,' are the cry here."[11]

It had been no surprise to Sumner, or to any of his fellow Conscience Whigs and Free Soilers, that the occasion for the next great clash over slavery and the reassertion of control by the Slave Power would come over the settlement of the lands to be acquired from Mexico. Sumner had no more objection in principle to the acquisition of new land now than at the time of the annexation of Texas. Indeed, he believed that "Canada is destined to be swept into the orbit of her neighbor," and he looked forward to her "annexation to the United States," which he thought "inevitable." "But," he cautioned, "Canada must make the advance." The acquisition of land by war, and for the purpose of spreading slavery he condemned. Ralph Waldo Emerson had predicted pungently: "The United States will conquer Mexico, but it will be as the man swallows the arsenic, which brings him down in turn. Mexico will poison us." Sumner fully shared his disapproval, but, readying himself to take part in the coming struggle, he took greater hope in its outcome.[12]

It was on the very day that John Quincy Adams died that the United States Senate received the treaty of Guadalupe Hidalgo, with the new territory which Adams had warned that Polk and the Slave Power would take. The divisions in the Senate followed a well-established pattern. Most Whigs wanted no territory, but would not consent to oppose the treaty and thus prolong the war. A number of Democrats, including Stephen A. Douglas of Illinois but mostly from slave-holding states, supported an amendment proposed by Senator Jefferson Davis of Mississippi to take even more land, something President Polk himself wanted. Some slaveowners wanted all of Mexico. Though the opposition was in the majority, it could not unite. The treaty thus passed quickly, and ratifications were exchanged with Mexico on 30 May 1848. By this treaty the United States took what had been more than one third of Mexico's original territory and made it one fifth of her own—stretching from Texas to the sea, including the widely coveted California. The two million dollars Polk had asked for in 1846 to keep Mexico stable enough to make any treaty last were now increased to fifteen million, and the United States assumed the damage claims that had been pending against Mexico. By force of arms and bribery the United States had acquired a vast new territory—and a dilemma about whether it would be free or slave.[13]

It was to President Zachary Taylor's first Congress that all eyes turned for a resolution of this dilemma. Tensions had only mounted since the signing of the treaty. The discovery of gold in California had caused that territory's population to mushroom to a size and lawlessness begging statehood. Texas and New Mexico seemed on the verge of war over boundary disputes. Southern leaders were openly disunionist, and Southern states had already elected delegates to a planned bipartisan convention to be held in Nashville the following June to discuss whether Northern hostility and threats of enacting the Wilmot Proviso should be met with secession.[14]

The strength of the antislavery vote of 1848 made Sumner hopeful, however, not least because it had elected the largest organized antislavery delegation Washington had ever seen. With these associates Sumner eagerly began to plan strategy for the coming session of Congress. "It seems to me," he told Giddings, that "there must be a *break-up* of parties on the choice of Speaker at the next session." It was not a visionary prospect. The Congress that convened on 3 December 1849 was so divided over slavery that the Free Soilers had reasonable hopes of holding the balance of power. Indeed, the first action of the House was to deadlock over the speakership.[15]

The Whigs, intent themselves on party unity, could not believe that the Free Soilers would completely abandon their old party ties. When faced with a decision, surely the Free Soil members, who were mostly former Whigs, would prefer a Whig to a Democrat for Speaker. Reasoning thus, the Whigs put up Robert C. Winthrop for the third time. It was a miscalculation. The Free Soilers stood firm, and supported David Wilmot. Indeed, as days passed by and the debates grew rancorous, even some Whigs began to break away and vote for antislavery members of their party such as Horace Mann or Thaddeus Stevens of Pennsylvania. In the end it was impossible to elect a Speaker according to the traditional majority rule. The election was resolved only when the House agreed, for the first time, to accept a plurality vote—in favor of Georgia Democrat Howell Cobb. The Whigs were livid. The Free Soilers were delighted at their show of strength and solidarity. Cobb was certainly no abolitionist, but the Free Soilers' determination had given promise of the future. "The Slave Power has rec[d] its first serious check," Sumner boasted to George, "& all parties see that the Slavery Question is soon to be paramount to all others. The Northern man who sets his face against the Anti-Slavery sentiment will surely be crushed."[16]

Free Soilers were not yet strong enough to set the course of the coming debate, however. That fell to the new President, and to congressional leaders, of whom none was more closely watched than Henry Clay. Nearly everyone had assumed that the all but unknown Zachary Taylor, a Louisiana slaveholder, would follow the interests of his section and class. It was to a rush of general surprise therefore that he angrily rejected all Southern talk of secession: "Whatever dangers may threaten [the Union], I shall stand by it and maintain it in its integrity." Forty years' service in the United States Army had made a staunch unionist of the Southern President, and the father-in-law of Jefferson Davis chose as his closest personal advisor the nationalistic and antislavery New York Senator, William Henry Seward. For the lands ceded by Mexico, Taylor proposed a compromise that would admit California with her antislavery constitution, and leave the status of slavery in New Mexico to be determined by the vote of the local territorial government that he insisted should be speedily organized.[17]

Southerners felt as betrayed by the President's effort at evenhandedness as Free Soilers were pleased. Sumner left no record of his own thoughts. He could not approve the President's plan, which accepted the possibility that New Mexico might become a slave state, but he was very likely impressed by the President's independence and determination. Sumner always admired "backbone" wherever he found it. Where he found it most prominently in the months to come was in the congressional leader Henry Clay. The "Great Pacificator," who had pushed through the Missouri Compromise thirty years earlier, had returned to the Senate to offer a new compromise to restore calm to a violently unsettled Congress and, as he said, to settle the slavery question once and for all. Compromise, Sumner was convinced, could never settle such an issue, but as the struggle went on he envied Clay's resoluteness. "Clay is determined, & portential, & he is daily shewing what a strong _WILL_ can do," Sumner wrote to Howe. "Such a person with such a _WILL_, & such capacity as a _leader_, would have carried Freedom long ago."[18]

Sumner could not accept Clay's proposed plan, however. Clay offered a package designed to give something to each section of the country. For the North he would accept California with her antislavery constitution, but he included no specific rejection—as the Wilmot Proviso would have—of slavery in the other new territories, New Mexico and Utah. He would also ban the slave trade, though not slavery itself, in the District of Columbia—a provision that, sounding good, would in reality affect very few people. To placate the South, Clay proposed that Congress declare its lack of authority to interfere with the interstate slave trade—an interference slave owners had often denounced and abolitionists had often called for. Most importantly for the South, Clay called for a new and more stringent fugitive slave law.[19]

Slave owners had been furious ever since a wave of personal liberty laws had swept the North in the 1840's. Taking their cue from loopholes in the Supreme Court's 1842 Prigg _v._ Pennsylvania decision, these laws had been passed to limit the states' ability to enforce the federal Fugitive Slave Law of 1793, and to provide the accused runaway with legal protections. Slave owners now complained that they had eviscerated the old law and had encouraged thousands of slaves to run away. As the issue became increasingly contentious throughout the spring months, Clay would offer a fugitive slave bill that provided for trial by jury for the fugitive in the state from which he had run away—meaningless compromise, thought abolitionists, for they could not forget that when Clay first outlined his plan in January and February he said that he would follow "the furthest Senator from the South to impose the heaviest sanctions on the recovery of fugitive slaves." That seemed to nod to the bill already being debated on the Senate floor. In the first days of the new year, Senator James Mason of Virginia had offered a bill that required the fugitive to be delivered up to the slave owner, or his agent, upon his presenting evidence of his title to the runaway. It denied the fugitive any right to testify, gave marshals pursuing him the power to force any citizen in a free state to join their posse, imposed a one-thousand-dollar fine on anyone who tried to rescue or otherwise help the runaway, and gave special commissioners the power to try the cases—for a fee of five dollars should they free the accused and for what abolitionists lost no time in dubbing a "bribe" of ten dollars should they find for the slave owner.[20]

The Thirty-First Congress would remain forever celebrated for its oratory. Here, for the last time, the "Great Triumvirate" of Henry Clay, John C. Calhoun, and Daniel Webster would meet and do battle over the future of the Union, and, though no one could match their reputation and eloquence, they would be seconded by a host of younger members, each anxious to speak on this momentous and controversial proposal. Henry Clay led off, defending his compromise on 5 and 6 February, feeling old and ill, but his famous voice still silvery and resonant. John C. Calhoun was already too wasted by consumption to deliver his own speech; it would be read for him by James Mason. No one was surprised, however, to hear his words as firm and unforgiving as ever as they opposed Clay's plan as unacceptable for a South that demanded concessions or else threatened to leave the Union. Among the antislavery voices, none got more attention than that of Whig William Seward who opposed the compromise, especially the Fugitive Slave Bill, as unacceptable not only to Northerners but, in a phrase that would ring in all ears, as contrary to "a higher law than the Constitution," that is, to God's own Natural Law.[21]

Everyone waited in anticipation for the third member of the Great Triumvirate to speak. Until Massachusetts Senator Daniel Webster stood up on 7 March 1850, no one knew what stand he would take. Privately he had promised Clay to support him, but to Southern colleagues he had called himself uncommitted. Robert Winthrop had told him that Boston expected him to support the President's plan and not even mention the divisive Wilmot Proviso. As he listened to the debates, however, Webster had been struck by the sincerity of the Southerners' disunionism and by the gravity of the crisis that menaced his beloved Union. Intending to blame both sections for damaging the bonds that held them together, he made every effort to conciliate the South, promising not to vote for any exclusion of slavery in the West, nor for the Wilmot Proviso, nor even to receive antislavery petitions. He pleaded with Southerners to see that there could be no such thing as "peaceable secession." He told Northerners that, however bad slavery might be, they had been wrong to evade their constitutional obligation to render up fugitives. Law must come before sentiment. Daniel Webster— "the Godlike," New England's already mythic statesman, the nation's towering orator—thus threw his full support behind Clay's resolutions, and Mason's Fugitive Slave Bill.[22]

It was "a heartless apostasy," mourned Sumner. Webster "is another Strafford or archangel ruined. In some moods, I might call him Judas Iscariot or Benedict Arnold." "With all his majestic powers," Sumner shook his head, "he is a traitor to a holy cause." Antislavery men across the North were indignant at Webster's rejection of human rights. Sumner's friend the Ohioan Salmon Chase, serving his first session in the Senate, was shocked, and more determined than ever to respond, when he overheard Webster, at the conclusion of his address, lean over to Stephen Douglas and whisper: "You don't want anything more than that, do you?" Theodore Parker was not alone in thinking his action could be explained only "as a bid for the Presidency." Emerson scorned Webster's prostitution of the word "liberty," while Whittier lamented Webster's "fall" from grace in immortal lines:

> Of all we loved and honored, naught
> Save power remains;
> A fallen angel's pride of thought,
> Still strong in chains.
>
> All else is gone; from those great eyes
> The soul has fled:
> When faith is lost, when honor dies,
> The man is dead![23]

The sense of betrayal felt by antislavery men saw its reverse in the delight of the Southern press and the Democrats generally. The major Washington papers, too—which were read across the country by those who followed politics—and even the leading Whig paper of Boston, the *Advertiser,* praised Webster's performance. As the debate continued, Sumner complained about the influence of the established parties on the national voice: "The saying of Fisher Ames is now verified. 'A lie will travel from Maine to Georgia while truth is putting on her boots.' [. . .] Oh! when, oh! when shall this dynasty of Slavery be overthrown, & the press at Washington be *openly, actively & perpetually on the side of Freedom.* Never until both these old parties are overthrown." In this case, however, the national press could not control the popular reaction. In Massachusetts especially, many ordinary citizens were shocked by Webster's stand. It seemed to many grimly appropriate that just two days after Webster's speech a Harvard professor by the same name should go on trial for a grisly crime. The public had been appalled less by the fact that Dr. John Webster, deeply in debt, had murdered his colleague and creditor Dr. George Parkman, than by the manner in which the professor of chemistry had tried to dispose of the body. If it had not been for the gruesome discovery of the remaining parts of Dr. Parkman in the laboratory, the public might have accepted Dr. Webster's story that the murder had been an unpremeditated accident. As it was, Dr. Webster would soon meet the ultimate penalty at Boston's Leverett Street jail. Thus were two Websters at the same time "set to the bar of public opinion," Sumner explained to George. Despite horror at the murder, however, "many feel against [the Senator] a warmer indignation than against Prof. Webster."[24]

It was Webster's party that suffered most from his speech. "The merchants of Boston"—and throughout the Northeast—"subscribe to" Webster's speech, Sumner granted; "it is their wont to do such things." They had been as frightened as Webster by Southern threats of secession—for the future of the country, but especially, as they repeated in their letters, for the financial disaster they were sure would follow. They would rally behind anything, however distasteful, that might avert such a calamity. They were joined by the most conservative of their non-merchant associates. The Boston *Courier* swallowed its discomfort and continued to support Webster. When a runaway slave was hunted down the following year in Boston, Rufus Choate would defend the law as a patriotic duty, and Sumner thought Ticknor was "vindictive for Webster."[25]

Even Ticknor, however, expressed private reservations about the Fugitive Slave Law's effect on public opinion. For most Whigs the Seventh of March speech, as it came to be known, brought consternation. Robert Winthrop was shocked by how "tremendously Southern" the speech was. Edward Everett went so far as to say of the proposed fugitive slave law that he could not himself "perform the duty which it devolves 'on all good citizens.'" He admitted privately "the theoretical right of the South to an efficient extradition law; but it is a right *that cannot be enforced.*" A few individuals protested by breaking with the party, including the leading merchant John Murray Forbes, while the *Atlas,* which had been the most vituperative of the Whig papers against antislavery men, now initiated a long barrage against Webster's speech and his defenders. Hillard described the general misery as he recounted to Winthrop "how our little state has been reeling and staggering under the blow dealt by Webster's speech [. . .]. You can hardly imagine the embarrassment and perplexity into which those members of the Whig party in the legislature were thrown who, without approving of the doctrines of Webster's speech, at least not all of them, were anxious that nothing should be said or done inconsistent with the gratitude, admiration and respect which we feel for his commanding powers and eminent public services."[26]

Sumner was more blunt. He had heard "from various Whig quarters the strongest condemnation of [Webster's] speech," he admitted, but he did "not expect from Whigs any open protest" against the party or its leaders, however much they might have pained "the moral sense of the people." "The shibboleth of party is too potent," he explained to Salmon Chase. "The independent Whigs or *protestants,* have already left the party. All the rest are in servile bonds."[27]

Webster had realized from the start the political danger he was putting himself in—especially since he would come up for reëlection the following January. He immediately tried to soften the pro-Southern aspects of his speech before publishing it in Boston: "Altered for the Mass. market," observed Sumner.

Popular indignation was so strong, however, that Sumner was sure that 7 March had ended Webster's elective career. To George he remarked that "I should not be astonished if he were Sec. of State within a short time." "He can hardly dare to confront the people of Mass. at the next election," Sumner explained, "as he must do, if he is a candidate for re-election. The disaffection towards him among leading Whigs of the North" was too "strong" to allow him to keep his Senate seat. It was not strong enough, however, to permit those leading Whigs to refuse when the great man asked them to sign a public letter supporting him and his speech. Webster's old rival Abbott Lawrence probably would not have signed even if he had not been in England as Minister to the Court of St. James, and Nathan Appleton left his name off the list, but in all eight hundred "gentlemen of property & standing," as William Jay scornfully called them, swallowed their concerns and signed. "Eight hundred gentlemen in Boston avowedly ready to catch slaves!!" Jay sighed to Sumner. "How the trade of politics paralyzes the moral sense & ossifies the heart!" Sumner was hardly surprised to see names like Choate and Ticknor and Samuel Eliot there, but there were others that hurt more—his once close friend Samuel Lawrence, his still—and always—dear friend William H. Prescott, and, dearer than all, Cornelius Conway Felton.[28]

Sumner could not allow New England's leading statesman and her most famous and influential citizens to take such a stand unanswered. He could not allow Webster to speak unchallenged in support of the spread of slavery into the territories, nor allow such a measure as the Fugitive Slave Bill to go uncombated. Throughout that spring and summer of 1850, as Congress furiously debated the elements that made up the proposed compromise, and as his friends in Congress—especially Giddings, Chase, and Mann—prepared their replies, Sumner sent them never-ending encouragement to speak tellingly. "You have a grand opportunity," Sumner exhorted Chase. "I hope yr speech will be thorough, & *high-toned*. The people will bear a strong tone; & what is more, the occasion requires it, even if they would not bear it." Along with his encouragement, Sumner sent reams of letters amounting to a detailed response of his own to Webster's speech.[29]

Sumner agreed with Webster that if the slavery question were not settled, Americans could expect increasing violence in their public life and even, perhaps, civil war. He thought that the slave owners were not only "bent on securing the new territories for slavery," but that "they see, in perspective, an immense slave-nation, embracing the gulf of Mexico, & all its islands, & stretching from Maryland to Panama. For this they are now struggling; determined while in the union to govern it, & direct its energies; or, if obliged to quit, to build up a new nation, slave-holding throughout."[30]

Their method would always include the threat of violence. "It is true, most true," Sumner had long argued, "that slavery stands on force and not on right," and thus violence had become a foundation of Southern culture, whether in whipping slaves, dueling with other slave owners, or threatening duels against Northerners. Compromises had not stopped and would not stop this. Instead, with each compromise Southerners became bolder. The debates over the proposed compromise of 1850 would spur more than one duel, including one occasion in the Senate chamber when Senator Henry S. Foote of Mississippi rushed at Senator Thomas Hart Benton of Missouri with a cocked gun. Sumner thought Webster's assumption that concessions would restore calm and end the danger of violence was illogical as well as unjust. "Let him preach Peace to the South," Sumner retorted. It was the slaveholder who "vex[ed] the land by his profane demands." Sumner was convinced that to "sacrifice" freedom for peace was to lose both. A society that tried to maintain calm by forcing the acceptance of injustice merely turned itself into a volcano. "*Atque, ubi solitudinem faciunt, Pacem appellant,* are the words of Tacitus; & Webster, true to their spirit, seems to call that only *Peace* which is obtained by trampling on the North, & Human Rights. [. . .] Let him, in the spirit of his earlier efforts, raise his voice for Freedom; & Peace will soon ensue. I want no Peace, except with Freedom; nor is Peace *possible*, except with Freedom."[31]

All his life, Sumner had striven after that ideal of civilization that he had inherited through his parents and through the professors and leaders of the New England community from the Enlightenment and from its understanding of the ancient tradition of Natural Law. It was an ideal founded upon a belief in man's human rights and civic duties, in his fundamental dignity, an ideal that sought the fullest development of the human intellect and conscience, and that imagined the rich and ethical society that his best efforts could build. It was the ideal upon which the United States had proclaimed its independence, and according to which Sumner hoped that his young homeland would encourage its developing culture that it might become an envy and an example to the rest of the world.

Sumner found many things to quarrel with in Webster's speech—his misjudgment that compromise with slavery would settle the country's divisions and bring peace, his false statement that the annexation of Texas was "constitutional originally," his absurd argument that the climate of New Mexico would make slavery impossible and thus render the Wilmot Proviso unnecessary— in New Mexico "there will be houses," Sumner countered, and slaves could always be used in "household[s]," and "mines," and wherever labor was needed. But Sumner's profound quarrel with Webster lay elsewhere. Fearful for the stability of society, the Senator had preferred to sacrifice individual rights. Sumner believed that ultimately—just like peace—social stability, the common good, progress itself were impossible if individual rights were not respected. "Ferdinand of Spain, the Catholic, said he would rather lose an army," Sumner recalled to Mann, "than have the curses of a single poor widow. It is this regard for the *individual,* which is the triumph of Xtianity & civilization." Sumner's quarrel with Webster was not that the Senator had made errors of fact or of judgment, but rather that he, who had once championed it, now actively struck at the heart of that ideal of civilization that was the foundation of American philosophy and culture, and the hope of human progress.[32]

Sumner saw that, while Webster had accepted the compromise out of fear of disunion, he had felt obliged to defend it to his Northern constituents in terms of its constitutionality. Sumner was outraged to observe that, in so doing, Webster had eviscerated the Constitution itself and the common law upon which it was founded. This from Webster who was not only a statesman but a lawyer, and who continued to argue cases before the Supreme Court. Sumner the lawyer marveled at Webster's argument that "'the reclaiming of a fugitive slave is not a *suit at the common law.'* What is a suit at common law?" Sumner exclaimed, incredulous. Where is a "question of *human liberty*" to be determined—"not in equity, or admiralty; but at *common law.*" Webster had had to remove the question of reclaiming fugitives from the jurisdiction of the ordinary body of Anglo-American law, with its traditional protections for the accused, in order to justify the Fugitive Slave Bill's denial to the accused fugitive of the right of trial by jury.[33]

A fugitive slave law was not different in principle, argued Sumner, from the mediæval writ of *de homine replegiando,* still a part of the common law, and the reinstatement of which into the Massachusetts statutes Sumner had so closely observed in the 'thirties. But this writ, like all writs at common law, entailed a trial by jury to determine its applicability to the case at hand. The Constitution, thus like the common law, provided for laws governing the reclaiming of fugitives. Distasteful as he found this, Sumner did not deny it as a matter of law. He had always believed that everything should be done "for the *abolition of Slavery,* by moral means—I would add by & *through, & under* the constitution, & not *over* it." But the Constitution also, like the common law upon which it was founded, guaranteed certain protections in the enactment of its requirements. Nor could any one clause of the Constitution, or of any law, as America's foremost constitutional scholar Joseph Story had taught, be favored to the exclusion of others. If the Constitution's fugitive slave clause was to be activated, pursued Sumner, so must all others.[34]

Even before the Constitution, the founders of the American nation had reaffirmed the right of trial by jury throughout their legal documents, from "[t]he very first law 'for the general good of the colony of New Plymouth'" to the Declaration of Independence. As Sumner pointed out in a barrage of letters to Mann in Washington, in following this tradition the Constitution amply, even redundantly, protected the right of everyone to trial by jury in any case in which the cause of the dispute exceeded twenty dollars. It did so explicitly, as well as in clauses guaranteeing "due process of law,"—which, as Sumner quoted Story, "in effect affirms the right of trial according to the process & proceedings of the common law"—and by the wording of the fugitive slave clause itself, which referred to "persons from whom service or labor *MAY BE DUE*"—thus requiring that it be "determined to whom is service *DUE*."[35]

Sumner acknowledged that the related right against self-incrimination— "[*n*]*emo tenetur accusare seipsum*"—had usually "been restrained to criminal matters." Its purpose was essentially the same, however, for Sumner reminded Webster through Mann that it "was originally established as a security of the subject against oppression & power—in short, against men acting like slave-masters." Why should not a fugitive, like any accused, wondered Sumner, be allowed to deny the truth of the charge "& compel the dealer in human flesh to prove every part of his case." For himself, Sumner saw no reason why a fugitive slave should not be treated rather as a political refugee. "Webster assimilates the case of a fugitive slave to a *fugitive from justice*," Sumner noted to Mann. "Capital mistake. Fugitive from *injustice*." Criminals were subject to their fate, but in treaties, such as Webster's own 1842 treaty with Lord Ashburton, "[*p*]*olitical offenders* are not delivered up."[36]

Webster had disregarded not only the letter of the Constitution and of the common law, but, more importantly, Sumner continued, its very spirit, that spirit without respect for which all interpretation was violation. Freedom was a cherished principle of the common law—as Sumner reminded Webster, marshaling the great names of Anglo-American jurisprudence, including the commentator and chancellor of Henry VI, Sir John Fortescue, who had written that "Slavery is introduced through human wickedness; but God advocates liberty by the nature which he has given to man. Wherefore, liberty torn from man, always seeks to return to him [. . .]. *On this account it is that* the man who does not favor liberty, must be *regarded as impious & cruel;* & hence the English law always favors liberty." The American Constitution was a part of this same tradition, and "as all laws are to be construed *in favorem libertatis* the constitution of [the] U.S. must be so construed, & every privilege of liberty thrown about the fugitive." This was not something that could be abandoned lightly for convenience' sake, or to placate an angry class of men—"this is a question of freedom," urged Sumner; "& it is an insult to the constitution, a mockery of all principles of freedom, an apostacy to Magna Carta, to suppose that this can be done without the highest & most solemn proceedings known to our law." Webster could not deny such precedents without showing up his "law & constitutional learning" as "trivial," Sumner counseled Mann. "Ask if this be the *Defender of the Constitution?* Charge home upon him."[37]

Webster had done worse than this. Already in his Seventh of March speech and even more pointedly in the many speeches he gave immediately afterwards to defend it, he turned his most cutting sarcasm upon the abolitionists' insistence on the dictates of a law higher than the Constitution. "His ridicule of a law above the Constitution may be turned against him sharply," Sumner told Mann, for it showed the famous defender of the Constitution and of America's founding traditions turning his back upon precisely the most important tradition of all—the spirit of that Natural Law and of the Enlightenment from which the nation had sprung. "'The law of nature,'" Sumner quoted from Blackstone, "'being co-eval with mankind, & dictated by God himself, is, of course, superior in obligation to any other. It is binding over all the globe; in all countries at all times. No human laws have any validity, if contrary to this; & such of them as are valid, derive all their force & all their authority, mediately or immediately from the original.'"[38]

This was the tradition, going back to Aristotle and beyond, in which all Western jurisprudence had developed, and in which both Sumner and Webster had been trained. The Webster of 1820, who at Plymouth Rock had denounced the slave trade as "contrary to the principles of justice and humanity within the reach of our laws," had spoken, Sumner pointed out to Mann, in the true Western legal and philosophical tradition. The votes that he now gave in the Senate in accord with his Seventh of March speech "expose him to the rebuke of his former self." The betrayal of this tradition threatened infinite harm. The purpose of Natural Law, as both Sumner and Webster had been taught and had once believed together, was to balance rights and duties as a check against arbitrary power, to remind men of the very concept of right and wrong, to uphold an eternal moral standard against which to measure human law. Without it, Sumner still believed, there was nothing to prevent the rule of law being sacrificed to the rule of men.[39]

What "deep regret" Sumner's old conservative friends felt, to see "the pupil of Story, [. . .] the ardent apprentice to the law,—the admirer of English jurisprudence,—the friend of Morpeth," go off on what they thought "the high road to ultra democracy." "You are a *liberal*," Chancellor Kent's son William scolded Sumner playfully yet not so playfully, "in feeling, mind, & ex necessitate [. . .]." But to Sumner Natural Law, its principle of human rights, and the ideal of civilization were rather a true conservatism that, neither reactionary nor reckless, "reconcile[d] order with change, stability with Progress." He believed the true ideal was to be "[a] conservative of all that is good—a reformer of all that is evil; a conservative of knowledge—a reformer of ignorance; a conservative of truths and principles, whose seat is the bosom of God—a reformer of laws and institutions which are but the wicked or imperfect work of man; a conservative of that divine order which is found only in movement—a reformer of those earthly wrongs and abuses, which spring from a violation of the great Law of Human Progress."[40]

To Sumner it was the Webster Whigs and their kin who had succumbed to the temptation of reaction, of that false conservatism which was, in truth, "bigotry." Fearful of change, of the threat to traditional privilege embodied in the ideals of their own cherished culture, in the principles of Natural Law and of Moral Philosophy, they preferred to abandon the culture altogether and follow the newer, morally less demanding and less elevating paths of legal positivism and political expediency. Like Milton's Satan they, "knowing well the sins and offences of mortals, would keep them ever in their present condition; holding them fast in their degradation; binding them in perpetual slavery [. . .]." As a new lawyer, just leaving Dane College for the practice of his profession, Sumner had been much disillusioned by the tendency among so many young lawyers—especially rural, western, Jacksonian—to abandon the ancient concept of Natural Law. He had not then dreamt that one day it would be the stalwarts of the legal profession itself, the men who had once taught the principle of Natural Law and embodied the Ciceronian ideal, and its requirement upon society's intellectual leaders to be its moral leaders,—he had not dreamt that one day it would be the jurists and statesmen and orators themselves who would deal the moral foundations of the American experiment their deadliest blow. This, he believed, was what Webster had done on 7 March 1850.[41]

Webster's speech rent asunder the final threads holding Boston society together. They had been fraying since 1846, each new dispute in the slavery controversy pulling the pieces farther apart, until, by 1850, they were too weak to resist. It was no longer just Sumner and Wendell Phillips and the inner circle of Conscience Whigs who were ostracized, but all their friends and families, so that Boston society was split down the center. When a young Harvard instructor was befriended by George Ticknor, he was informed that their connection would open his way "to the homes of the Lawrences, to those of Mr. George Hillard and Judge Parker and Professor Parsons of Cambridge, but that I should not enter those of the Lowells or the Quincys or that of Mr. Longfellow." Some young patricians began to revolt. Henry Bowditch, son of a Harvard scholar, abandoned the Ticknor circle: "I was unwilling to be treated as Charles Sumner told me he was treated by Mr. Ticknor, before whom all had to deferentially bow on this subject of slavery in the South." "There was a time when I was welcome at almost every house within two miles of us," Sumner would say one day to Richard Henry Dana, Jr., as they drove together down Beacon Street, "but now hardly any are open to me."[42]

Already pained by the loss of that general convivial society that had been his greatest pleasure, Sumner now worried that he might lose those dearest friends, even members of the Five of Clubs, who had been the heart of his life. They had always been frank with each other. Sharing an ever-flowing affection, complete confidence and trust in each other, they had believed deeply in that duty of frankness among friends. There were no better acts of friendship, they agreed, than defending a friend when he was wronged and correcting him when he wronged others. But now their wrongs were becoming too sensitive. Sumner appeared to some of his friends to have become reckless in the pursuit of change, while he saw them shrinking from their highest moral ideals and most humane impulses out of fear of change. They tried to save their friendship and each other, but by 1850 politics were corroding their old faith in one another, and, with it, Sumner's own faith in friendship.

Perhaps Hillard understood best, for he, too, was active in politics, speaking and campaigning for Webster and the Whigs. Longfellow described the two partners as "working in separate shafts of the dark, dirty political coal-mine!" Their old intimacy had been strained by public political divisions, but not their affection—"I have never loved you the less," wrote Hillard. Sumner would try to revive his friend's reformist feelings, but when he objected to Hillard's opposition to antislavery resolutions presented to the General Court in 1850 to counter Senator Clay's proposed compromise, Hillard replied simply that "true friendship rests upon mutual respect for the moral and intellectual rights of others."[43]

Into 1850 they continued to work together, sometimes even using their political differences to help each other. When in 1849 it looked, for a moment, as though the United States might have occasion to appoint a minister to a newly independent Hungary, Sumner immediately thought George "ought to be the man." Then he "felt keenly the constraint of my position," for as a Free Soiler he had no influence to use in his brother's behalf. "Of course I cannot speak directly to the other side," he explained to George. But Hillard could and, "with entire concurrence," agreed "to see Abbott Lawrence" to plead George's case. It was in early 1850 that Thomas Crawford got the chance to compete for a prestigious commission offered by the city of Richmond, Virginia, for an equestrian statue of George Washington. He was anxious to receive it; together Sumner and Hillard worked to get it for him. Sumner wrote to important legal acquaintances in Richmond as well as sending letters of recommendation to all the judges, while "Hillard, who prefers the winning side, [made] up for my deficiencies," by sending his own more proper Whig letters to the judges. The Hungarian post never materialized for George, but Crawford got his commission—which would lead directly to the most important commissions of his life, granted by the United States Congress.[44]

The Seventh of March dealt a blow to such efforts at coöperation, however. Now Hillard spoke out for Webster more vigorously than ever. As one of its editors, he gave the *Courier* a new decisively pro-Compromise stance, accepting many an article defending the Fugitive Slave Bill, and taking a sharp and bitter tone against the opposition at the same time that Sumner became so deeply involved in attacking Webster and his work. Hard as they both tried, the two old friends and partners were driven yet further apart.[45]

Sumner's efforts to be frank with Francis Lieber failed. When Sumner felt his demanding but intellectually stimulating friend growing reticent about the evils of slavery, Sumner worriedly pressed him about it. Still trying hard to find Lieber a teaching position in the North, he began to fear—rightly—that Lieber was giving up on this hope and reconciling himself to a future in the South. A candidate for the presidency of South Carolina College had to accept slavery, own slaves himself, and be careful what he said—even on trips northward—and now Sumner's questions only made Lieber angry. When, one evening at Longfellow's in 1849, Lieber staunchly defended the humanity with which slaves were treated in the South, Sumner mustered every bit of evidence he could think of to correct the German liberal, but a "vigorous discussion" only turned sour. Afraid to reopen a fight but anxious to reopen his eyes, Sumner began to send Lieber abolitionist documents and newspaper clippings, but in 1850 a Lieber desperately defending the Union to his secessionist and very skeptical neighbors resented these subversive missives. Soon Lieber stopped writing altogether; it took Sumner a few years to resign himself to do the same.[46]

Felton never had been able to understand why his "beloved Charley," the fine jurist and high-minded orator, should allow himself to mix with Garrison and the sort who wrote for the *Liberator,* why he would abandon the law for politics and reform that seemed to promote nothing but social disintegration. His marriage in 1846 into the prominent Cotton Whig Cary family only confirmed this tendency. "You are like the Englishman who was forced to dig up the pavements in Paris, in the Revolution of July," he had chided Sumner, "and seems so delighted with it, that he has been digging pavements ever since, wherever Revolutions turn up." But when the revolution hit home in 1848, Felton lost his sense of humor. Sumner's address at the Free Soil convention in Worcester with its revolutionary imagery and attacks against the "lords of the loom," was, despite its elegant garb, "nothing more nor less than old fashioned Jacobinism," Felton remonstrated, appalled at the specter of violent and seemingly uncontrollable change. That speech, he told Sumner, "contained a violent assault upon Massachusetts Institutions, Massachusetts policy, and Massachusetts men; it embodied what I thought was an insidious appeal to class prejudices—an attempt to rouse the hatred of the poor against the rich, and to organise vulgar passions of envy and jealousy into political action."[47]

Sumner was worried by Felton's fear as well as by his increasingly violent attacks against the antislavery movement. Political discussions became quarrelsome. After an emotional "passage" early in 1850, Sumner began to avoid the subject of politics altogether, only sending to Felton, as he did to Lieber, occasional abolitionist newspaper clippings in hopes of quietly reawakening his antislavery sensibility. Even when on 3 April Sumner opened the newspapers and discovered, with a pang, Felton's name among the eight hundred signatures subscribed to the letter supporting Webster, his Seventh of March speech, and the Fugitive Slave Bill, Sumner did not dare say anything directly to Felton. But what could he do, he asked himself, when Felton began to attack dear friends of Sumner's, charging Theodore Parker, for example—who had attacked the eight hundred—with an "*atrocious disregard for truth.*" Sumner had first met Parker in Felton's own house. "He seems to me to be 'clean daft,'" Sumner exclaimed to Longfellow. "—Oh! I wish these things were not so." Longfellow urged Sumner to "[l]et the matter drop," because Felton was too "sensitive about it." But as Sumner wrote to Felton: "Justice to the absent friend is a sacred duty, &, as I have, of late had occasion to say something in extenuation of yr public course in politics when impugned, I must now say something for others, who are impeached by you."[48]

Sumner hoped that a frank talk, such as they used to have, would shake Felton out of his fear and back to a realization of what he had been defending. He had contradicted himself like a "passionate man," Sumner told him, condemning "'a purpose at which humanity shudders,'" and yet, by signature, "you stand pledged to sustain before the world a system of slave-catching, more cruel & vindictive than any the world has yet seen." This was all the worse as Felton was "[*a*]*lone of all the professors of Harvard*" to sign the infamous letter. His attacks against the motives and veracity of others, Sumner went on, had been entirely unjust. Felton had taken to condemning the *Liberator* for its tone. Sumner did not defend it. "It has seemed to me often vindictive, bitter & unchristian. But let me say frankly," he went on, "I have never seen any thing in that paper at any time so vindictive, bitter & unchristian as yr note. You beat Garrison." "I deny you no rights," Sumner replied to Felton's angry rebuttal, "[I] simply vindicate the rights of others, to which you have become insensible." Desperately, he countered Felton's charges: "I break off no friendship. In anguish I mourn yr altered regard for me; but more than my own personal loss, I mourn the present unhappy condition of yr mind & character."[49]

Felton was furious. To Lieber he exclaimed that Sumner and Wendell Phillips and the rest of "this philanthropic concern" should be "shut up" in a "great insane hospital" along with the most extreme Southerners. He thought Sumner's newspaper clippings "scurrilous" and "lying," and felt that he had been "abused, [. . .] accused of 'malignity'—'venom[,]' insulted [. . .]." "I have been written to about my 'vindictiveness'," he complained to their mutual friend Palfrey, "and the 'enormity of my conduct' by one whom I once regarded as my friend,—whose friend I have certainly proved myself to be in every conceivable method for twenty years past [. . .]—and all this because I judged for myself, instead of walking by the light of other men's eyes."[50]

A newspaper quarrel that summer, perhaps all the more bitter because it substituted the unimportant question of Webster's misuse of a Latin phrase for the grievous issues of the Compromise, dealt the final blow. Felton threw himself into the controversy with all the anger he had been nursing against the antislavery movement for years. Sumner agonized over the fact that to defend his friend Horace Mann, who had initiated the quarrel, he would have to attack Felton for his "castigatory" articles against Mann. In the end neither wrote directly against the other, but each came to feel a kind of mission to correct the other's errors. Yet all the while, Sumner kept writing to Howe, begging him to return an old letter of Felton's in which "he poured out his soul to me with friendship, gratitude & admiration. He then exaggerated me—very, very much. But do find the letter for me."[51]

Felton and a grateful Sumner would be reconciled six years later. But, looking now upon what he called "the wreck of my past life, with friends leaving me," Sumner could no longer trust even his closest friendships the way he once had. He had been aware since youth of his own tendency in quarrels to press "his view aggressively," as his friend Pierce later put it. Confident in his beliefs but not in himself, he sometimes allowed intensity to supply the want of authority he felt in his own voice. "I know that I need charity & candour," he confided to Howe; "God grant that I may always shew them to others." But at least among friends, he had believed, frankness and even honest emotion should be understood. Instead now, "I have learned," he sadly told Mann, "that, in controversy, caution & skill are required, in order not to say things, which, though true, may yet jeopard the main cause." Over the coming years, when political disagreements arose even with such close friends as Howe, Sumner would "shrink" from discussions for fear that they might become quarrels. "[P]eople, who differ in politics," he had learned, "give no quarter."[52]

Only with Longfellow, of all his friends, could Sumner continue to feel the easy, familial comfort of old. Longfellow agreed with him on slavery as well as on Latin phrases, disagreed with him on how to handle Felton, regretted his involvement in politics—but understood it—and remained ever constant. Though he disliked politics, Longfellow felt none of the fear that troubled Hillard and Felton. He was as comfortable in his beliefs as in his home and friends. Once the heat of the 1848 campaign was over, Sumner and Longfellow returned to their favorite conversations. How Longfellow and Fanny both loved "Sumner's Sunday visits, with their free, fresh variety of topics and nice literary talks which he best loves." Sumner and Fanny had become the best of friends, too, and he discussed literature and even politics as freely with her as with her husband. In 1849 they read together through some of the works of Lamartine. Though she expressed some dissatisfaction with their sentimentality, he admitted that, for all their faults, they contained some most charming parts: "I confess it—I cannot help it. All that sensibility & love move me much." She, like her husband, deeply admired Sumner's own writings, and told him "what a sisterly pride I take in the author of words so strong in truth & wisdom."[53]

Sumner's own family, too, was proud of him—especially his mother. The second floor of their house, which she had abandoned to him, was now filled with *objets d'art*—souvenirs of Europe—and especially bookshelves, even under the windows and into the hallway. As she watched him there at the mahogany writing table, in the upstairs front room that was his study, composing his articles and orations, she must have felt that her husband's highest idealism and deepest conscientiousness were still alive in their eldest son. As in the old days, when she and her husband had hosted such as Garrison, she was pleased to welcome her son's political and abolitionist associates to the house. Sometimes, when Sumner was absent, she helped by carrying messages or by searching out for him or for a friend a book or pamphlet on one of those overflowing shelves.[54]

Albert helped by giving his hard-working eldest brother a yearly vacation spot at the Newport home where he, his wife, and daughter were still living their life of genteel retirement. They came to Boston every winter for an extended stay, and then welcomed any of the family who could come in the summer. Charles readily took the habit of going when his yearly work was done, usually in September.[55] Indeed, Albert played host to a good part of Boston, all of Charles' friends being his friends as well. Everyone delighted in his gentlemanly taste, "cordial kindness," ever-ready "chat & good humor," and never-ending "obliging courtesies." Though he never played any public role, Albert shared his brother's political opinions, resenting the degree to which Southern influence swayed Newport, and he took a "warm interest" in Charles' speeches and anti-slavery work.[56]

But the house on Hancock Street still had its troubles. Charles had tried to reconcile himself to his little brother Horace's lack of ambition and simple horizons, but by 1848 Horace was twenty-four and, though he was a loving son and a sweet brother to his sister Julia, he was still unsettled in life and, more than this, he seemed to be slowly but irrevocably declining in health. Charles worried about his self-reliance and his future. Though it was now too late to think of schooling, he had never given up his hope that Horace might benefit from a trip to Europe. Gradually Horace had come to share the idea, and by October 1849 he had been to Malta and was on his way slowly northward to Paris, enjoying his own grand tour. The family were eagerly anticipating his meeting in the French capital with George. But their mother was "anxious about him." Charles had to reassure her constantly. "I tell her it will do him good to see the world, & to be thrown upon himself," he wrote to George. She was counting the days till Horace's return that

December and was "very much disturbed" when he changed his plans and decided, for his health, to spend the winter in Florence.[57]

Charles was "pleased with the tone of Horace's letters from Florence." He was making friends among the American community there, becoming "much attached" in particular to Margaret Fuller and her new husband, the Marchese Ossoli. With their infant son, they had been forced to flee the Marchese's native Rome when Mazzini's 1848 Revolution, in which they had been much involved, was put down by Louis-Napoleon's troops. Horace promised his family that he would return home in the summer with his new friends, but Charles still had to calm their mother's continuing fears, assuring her that the extra winter in Florence "would do him good. Any thing that teaches self-dependence, & practical ideas will do him good."[58]

On Monday, 22 July 1850, the family were "anxiously expecting" Horace's imminent arrival. Instead, they received a telegram. His ship, the *Elizabeth,* had been wrecked in a storm in sight but just out of reach of land. Charles rushed instantly to New York to join other friends and relatives combing the beaches of Fire Island for survivors. Horace and the Ossolis were not to be among them. Charles tried to console himself that Horace had been "an invalid, & would probably have never been able to enter upon any active usefulness. He has been released from trial & disappointment."[59]

But the anguish of his mother and sister tore at Charles. Why had he not been more content with Horace as he was, why had he disregarded his mother's all too prescient fears? His mother had already lost her husband and three daughters, while three of her sons had left home, Henry in anger when his family disapproved of his intended, causing the lady to withdraw, and George seemingly forever. Charles was always busy, either at law or politics. He kept turning over in his mind his youngest brother's perfect goodness. He was "gentle, loving," "pure in heart, & without guile or selfishness." Remembering Horace's letters from Italy, Charles repeated again and again, as if in reproach to himself, that he was "particularly struck by his unselfish life." Horace had been the great comfort of his mother, and his sister's closest "companion [. . .], particularly at concerts, & on horse-back," he lamented, "& enjoyed more than I can her musical zeal." Charles was afraid she would "miss his brotherly attentions very much. I feel painfully," he admitted to George, begging him to come home, "my own inability to supply them."[60]

Julia disagreed. She adored her eldest brother. Nothing could bring a smile to her lips like the name "Charles," and, out of his own gloom, he looked upon her ever "bright face" as an object of wonder and delight. She was now twenty-three, and her brother had introduced her to all his friends, as he had once done for Mary. She loved to talk with his political associates, too, just to hear about his work and enjoy their praise of him. Solicitous for her happiness, he guided her love of literature, and got her access to all the best private art collections to gratify her desire to learn and to copy. As concerned about him as he was about her in their depression at the loss of Horace, she was all the more anxious to do what she could to return his kindness and draw him closer.[61]

She had long wanted to awaken his interest in music. Though secretly he had always enjoyed it, Charles was too keenly aware of his lack of musical training to trust his own feelings, and her love for music was so great that he hesitated even to accompany her to a concert—he had always sent Horace with her. That May she had finally "persuaded Charles to go" to see the highly acclaimed Havana Opera Company, then on tour in Boston, and to her joy he was "charmed" and agreed to accompany her to more of their performances. Now, to lift both their spirits, she continued his musical education, taking him to concerts, talking about music with him, bringing musical journals to his attention. When Jenny Lind came to Boston that October he was still diffident about giving his opinion, but he eagerly took Julia to several of her recitals. By the following spring he felt sure enough to praise the Swedish Nightingale and soon, though sometimes he marveled to hear himself doing it, he not only attended all the concerts and operas he could but took pleasure in discussing music with friends and even critics. It seemed to him that he had "acquired a new sense," one that he would always associate with Julia.[62]

Sumner continued to be plagued by a painfully conscious self-doubt—especially acute after the death of Horace. Yet, just as Julia's lessons would gradually give him confidence in his musical taste, so five years of oratorical and political experience were beginning to awaken a still unconscious but inspiriting assurance. Gone were the days when Sumner had refused invitations to speak because he could not muster the courage. Now he could nonchalantly tell George that, though it was hard work full-time, "[l]ecturing is not unpleasant as a pastime [. . .]." Wherever he went to speak he made a point of asking for a stage. "*I will not speak from a pulpit,*" he told a fellow-lecturer. "It is a devilish place. I do not wonder that people in it are dull." Sumner's memory never needed notes, and he had come to enjoy the *rapport* between speaker and audience. When he went to lecture in Newport, William Kent waggishly assured him that "[t]he whole of your person—every wish of the orator—will be seen by the bright eyes, that will be beaming around you."[63]

Bright eyes beamed at him, indeed, in great numbers. But it was widely remarked that Sumner evoked admiration in both intellectually inclined ladies and young men. As his biographer noted, "for that period, with its great causes, there was no voice so potent as Sumner's in inspiring and guiding the hopes and aims of American youth." The combination of his vigorous and evocative style with his forthright defense of principle and his reputation for the purest integrity made him an object of intense interest and trust among young people, clergymen, and ordinary families throughout New England and New York. Through his published addresses, Sumner was becoming known even in the West. Indiana Free Soiler George Julian thought that his *White Slavery in the Barbary States* had "exerted a powerful influence," and "surprised" Sumner by telling him "how many admirers he had in Indiana."[64] A farming couple from the tiny western Massachusetts hill town of Colrain wrote in 1850 to tell him that they had just named their first-born son for him. In March he had his first meeting with a young college student named Edward Pierce, who had begged the interview of his hero in his painstakingly best hand. Working-class newspapermen who looked down their noses at his "lamp-smelling periods" and thought them "rather deep for common folks" were forced to admit that Sumner raised the enthusiasm of his audiences "up to fever-heat." Sumner's popular prominence was even acknowledged by his first hate mail—purporting to be from an old Harvard classmate who hailed from the South.[65]

At the same time that Sumner heard the plaudits of popular audiences, he received sincere praise from experienced and respected writers. Richard Henry Dana, Jr., already the author of *Two Years before the Mast,* was "struck" not only by the "humanness of feeling" of Sumner's Fourth of July oration, but by its "picturesque, & dramatic effect [. . .]. I left it with distinct pictures of images of scenes, persons & places in my mind, & felt as though I had seen & acted in some great & terrible crisis. How rare this power is, in a writer!" In 1850 Edward Everett, one of the deans of American oratory, thought Sumner's works "are among the most finished productions of their class in our language,—in any language. I am sure they will be read & admired as long as any thing English or American is remembered."[66]

The repetition of high praise from strangers and established writers was like a balm to Sumner's self-doubt. It was indeed hard for him to believe it was more than flattery, and after hearing Emerson lecture one night he felt "almost a nausea at all that I can do—at my scarlet, green-baize, holyoke-flower stuff." Yet, this praise combined with his own growing experience and facility as a writer and speaker slowly fostered that sense of assurance that he had so long craved. With a mixture of disbelieving delight and doubting belief he took to sharing his good reviews with his friends, as when he returned from Amherst in 1847. He had left lonely and "sad" to deliver his *Fame and Glory,* but returned warmed by his reception. "The papers have been loud in praise," he gushed to Longfellow. "Somebody says, I set the river on fire." For this habit Sumner would later be accused of vanity, but it had been prompted by too little rather than too much self-esteem, and never contained in it anything of envy.[67]

Sumner's growing assurance had been evident in the profusion of his advice to congressional friends for the preparation of their responses to Webster's Seventh of March speech. "Let yr points be clear; & the arrangement careful—divided & subdivided," he authoritatively urged Mann, known as a loose writer. "These resting-places help the understanding of a long document," added Sumner, always mindful of the audience. His letters to Chase and Mann had been more than just helpful hints. He sent them excited promptings, exuberant details, hosts of legal references, literary quotations, suggested turns of phrase, even outlines. In his anxiety to see Webster properly answered, Sumner had sent them what amounted to the rough draft of a complete oration.[68]

This was the oration that Sumner would have given had he been in Congress. Yet at the same time that he was secretly disappointed by the final efforts of Chase and Mann, he refused suggestions to publish his own answer to Webster in a pamphlet. He felt similarly daunted by the publication of his collected speeches. The two volumes had been planned since 1848, agreed to by the publishers by August 1849, and advertised for that winter. By the spring of 1850, however, friends were delicately inquiring where the volumes were. So were the publishers. "The public begin to feel that we are deluding by advertisement," James Fields reproved Sumner in March. Unlike a pamphlet, a complete collection between hard covers was intended for posterity, and Sumner spent months tightening and dramatizing his prose, clarifying his thoughts where there had been controversy. He could not bring himself to put down his revising pen and declare the volumes ready. Even when proofs were given to him later that spring, Sumner returned them with so many corrections that the publishers berated him for the extra cost it would take to redo the entire edition. Finally, he gave in and let them go forward with the printing of what he deprecatingly called "my *Plays*— in contradistinction to *Works* [. . .]." "My *ideal* is so much above any thing *actual* in my poor life," he apologized to Whittier after sending him the two volumes that fall, "that I have little satisfaction in any thing I am able to do."[69]

Through practice, Sumner now felt comfortable with his pen and with an audience. When the cause he had at heart was threatened, he felt sure of what action was necessary and urged others to fight. Despite the approval of his peers and a large popular following, however, he still feared he could not rise to the expectations of others, and that on momentous occasions his voice would fail. Torn between ripeness to take on a larger role and a continuing sense of unworthiness, Sumner felt depressed. "When I think of you, & your labors," he wrote sadly to Howe, who was researching prison discipline and the education of the blind in Europe, "I feel my own littleness, & the little that I do—'muddling away my life' in writing letters, & in doing infinitesimal things of little avail."[70]

It was with such conflicting feelings in mind, only days after the death of Horace, that Sumner received a nomination for Congress from the Free Soil party of the Boston district. As Sumner had predicted, by the end of July Webster was Secretary of State. The Free Soilers were deeply disappointed when the supposedly antislavery Governor Briggs bowed to Webster's pressure and chose Winthrop as his Senate successor, instead of Samuel Hoar or Horace Mann. "Such are the performances of a Governor pledged to the Wilmot proviso!" noted Adams scornfully in his journal. Sumner walked right up to Briggs and "took the liberty of telling him [. . .], that he had missed an opportunity of doing an act of justice." "Briggs always *talks* anti-slavery," Sumner wrote to Howe, but "when the *tight punch* comes, where is he?"[71]

Now the question was whether an antislavery man could be elected to Winthrop's vacant House seat. Timing made the election crucial. Whoever was chosen would cast his votes on what was likely to be the final version of the proposed compromise over slavery in the new territories. On 9 July its great foe in Washington, President Taylor, had suddenly died. When Clay's unwieldy Omnibus Bill failed on 31 July, canny young Stephen Douglas of Illinois thought he could muster discrete majorities to pass all the provisions of the Compromise separately. If he could, the new President, pro-Compromise New Yorker Millard Fillmore, would sign it. Friends feared that Sumner might refuse to run. Salmon Chase, who had just lost a baby daughter and whose wife was dangerously ill, begged him not to allow either his mourning or his dislike of office to keep him from accepting the proffered nomination. "It is a time of trial for the friends of Freedom," he urged from Washington. "You are looked to as a leader. You know it though your modesty would fain disclaim the title and shun the position. [. . .] [I]f Boston is to be yoked in with Slavehunters and their apologists, let no part of the sin lie at your door."[72]

Sumner had already accepted the nomination. In this decision his new assurance and his old self doubt could agree. The situation was critical, and he had decided in 1848 that he would offer his name whenever required. "[N]otwithstanding the hatred of enemies, or the coldness of friends," Sumner told the nominating committee in words reminiscent of his *Fame and Glory,* the "laborer" in such a cause would have at least "the happy consciousness of duty done." The pending Compromise represented a danger beyond ordinary legislation. Now that "the cause of Human Liberty," attacked in Europe, "has been betrayed where it should have been defended," Sumner wrote, "I confess a new motive to exertion." Still, when he told the committee that he wished "[f]rom the bottom of my heart" that another had been chosen, he was sincere. If he had accepted the nomination with equanimity it was in great part because he knew, as he had in 1848, that he would lose. "I am in politics accidentally," he answered Chase, "certainly without design & unconsciously. Personally I resign all their fruits"; and he added, perhaps remembering his father's words but following a different conclusion, "their thorns and bitterness I will share."[73]

Sumner lost the election by a wide margin. While antislavery men and politicians awaited the passage of the Compromise, the general public knew only that the Omnibus Bill had failed, and, afraid that, with no compromise at all, the country was headed for a crisis, the electorate looked anxiously to Congress for a solution. Antislavery agitation lost favor. Victory went to the candidate whose friends had represented him as the friend of compromise—caustic Cotton Whig Samuel Eliot. Webster was elated—the results showed that "I was not a dead man." Sorry for the cause, Sumner was relieved for himself. To Mann, who had thought the whole effort a lost cause, Sumner insisted that "yielding my name" for such a loss was not "profitless. It was a new sally, & a new token of my willingness to be sacrificed, if need be, for the principles I have at heart." Still, his self-doubt was not unscathed. Though he denied it, he gave his friend Chase the impression that his pride had been wounded by the "humiliation of a small vote."[74]

Within the month the Free Soilers' fears came to pass. Already by the end of August, Stephen Douglas had guided nearly all the Compromise measures successfully through the Senate. It took only another two weeks for all the bills to pass the House—Samuel Eliot giving the Massachusetts delegation's only yea vote for the Fugitive Slave Bill. By 20 September President Fillmore had signed them all into law. Most Americans breathed a sigh of relief. Washingtonians fired canons, organized bonfires, and serenaded Webster from the streets. The disunionist Nashville Convention was defused, while newspapers across the South hailed the Compromise. Politicians North and South, starting with Henry Clay and Stephen Douglas themselves and followed by President Fillmore, proclaimed the Compromise of 1850 a "permanent" settlement of the nation's divisions.[75]

Then, for the first time only one week after its passage, the new Fugitive Slave Law began to be enforced. Fugitives in New York and Pennsylvania were apprehended—"kidnapped," said abolitionists—and sent back into slavery. Significant numbers across the North, not only abolitionists, but Whigs and Democrats groaned in outrage. Actual fugitives, free blacks, whites, men, women, and children alike, felt threatened by a law that stripped the accused of the right of self-defense, forced the bystander to join a posse to catch a suspected fugitive, and punished anyone for giving food or shelter—Christian charity, many pointed out—to a runaway. The new law threatened even the formerly apathetic. People of all parties joined in public protest meetings across the North to call for its repeal. Henry Wilson spoke his indignation at a protest meeting in Lowell, Massachusetts, at the beginning of October, while a meeting in Faneuil Hall on the fourteenth was presided over by Charles Francis Adams, addressed by Wendell Phillips, Theodore Parker, and black abolitionist Frederick Douglass. It adopted resolutions written by Richard Henry Dana, Jr., and Sumner took his place on one of the meeting's committees to give legal protection to fugitives.[76]

Soon there would be more than talk in Boston. In late October three slave catchers arrived in the city looking for William and Ellen Craft, who had escaped their North Carolinian master two years earlier. George Hillard's wife Susan—with or without her husband's knowledge—warned the Crafts, as she would do for many fugitives, of the arrival of the slave hunters. A newly formed committee of vigilance including Samuel Gridley Howe among its large membership and under the leadership of Theodore Parker—who began to keep a loaded and cocked gun within reach at all times—devoted its attention to the slave catchers. Under the new law, the three Southerners had expected to enlist citizens to help in the capture. Instead they became the hunted. "[T]hey were followed about in the streets," remembered Wilson, "pointed out as slave-hunters, waited upon at their hotel, and advised to leave while they were unmolested." The jeering crowds and veiled threats were too much for the bewildered men; they finally fled the city. Daniel Webster, anxious to see the new law enforced, intervened with national and state leaders, but by then the Crafts were on their way to England. "The consummation of the iniquities of this most disgraceful session of Congress is now reached," Charles Francis Adams had written to the antislavery Indianan George Julian shortly after the passage of the new law " —I know not how much the people will bear."[77]

On 10 August 1850 Sumner hosted a meeting of the Free Soil leaders in his office. Henry Wilson, as State Committee Chairman, had called the meeting to put forth a proposal. Like all his colleagues, Wilson hated the impending compromise, but he did not think it enough merely to speak against it and trust to the slow strengthening of the Free Soil party. He reminded them that the problem was a political one. The people of Massachusetts were strongly and increasingly antislavery, but their state's districts were divided in such a way that her political machinery remained in the hands of those who controlled the major eastern industrial towns, especially Boston. The rest of the state might be Free Soil, but if Boston remained Whig, so would her General Court and her congressional delegation. Wilson thus laid before his colleagues a frankly political solution.[78]

Over the past few years, Free Soilers from Maine to Iowa, unable to win majorities by themselves, had been trying political coalitions with other minority parties—either Whigs or Democrats according to local conditions. Already in 1847, antislavery Whigs and antislavery Democrats in New Hampshire, anticipating the fusion that led to the Free Soil party, had elected John P. Hale to the Senate, and in 1849 Ohio Free Soilers and Democrats sent Salmon P. Chase to join him. Massachusetts Free Soilers and Democrats had made the same experiment at the local level in 1849, but remained the only ones not to have tried it at the state level. Wilson wanted them now to do just that. For the November elections he proposed a coalition with the state's Democratic party, a coalition between the state's two parties of opposition in order to wrest control of the General Court from the Whigs. The Free Soilers would then concede the state offices to the Democrats, who were most interested in local reforms, while the Democrats would help elect a Free Soiler to take Daniel Webster's seat in the United States Senate.[79]

None of the Free Soilers was immune to the poetic justice of replacing Ichabod with an antislavery voice, but they were divided about the means. Everyone knew that Wilson and Adams, the traditional leader of the group, had been at odds about the matter for some time. Now Adams, feeling that "[i]f I can defeat this scheme, I shall feel that I have done great good," voiced his "uncompromising opposition to the whole thing," and was seconded by Palfrey and Dana. Sumner and Whittier were sympathetic to the plan, but neither wanted to cause a rupture in the group. To preserve the peace, Whittier offered a motion to lay the proposal on the table, and all agreed.[80]

The Conscience Whigs had accepted fusion with antislavery Democrats to create a new antislavery party in 1848. Adams had agreed to be Van Buren's running mate. But fusion and coalition were not the same. Coalition would mean coöperation with the regular Democratic party. The hope might exist of further fusion to come, but for the time being Free Soilers and Democrats would retain their separate organizations. The consequences of this difference divided the Free Soil leaders. Adams, Palfrey, and Dana did not trust the Democrats. During the 1849 experiment in local coalitions, Adams was deserted by the Democrats of his county in his bid for a seat in the General Court. He swore that he had accepted the coalitions then particularly "for the sake of Mr Palfrey," who was trying for reëlection to Congress from Middlesex County, and "in whose cause I feel the deepest interest." When, after painful months of runoffs, Palfrey lost, too, they both blamed the Democrats—Dana was sure that Palfrey had not gotten a single Democratic vote.[81]

Neither Adams nor Palfrey had "that confidence that the 'instincts of the Democracy' are on our side wh. Sumner has," commented Dana. For Palfrey's loss Sumner blamed rather—probably more accurately—the complacency of the Free Soilers and especially the power of the Whigs. The "manufacturing power" had greater patronage "in Massachusetts, even than that of the General Court," he had complained in 1848. When he thought that Whigs like Edmund Dwight could give "$2000 to influence a single election," Sumner sympathized with John Van Buren's saying "that we have more to fear from the corruption of wealth than from mobs." "It is *money, money, money,*" Sumner exclaimed in 1850, "that keeps Palfrey from being elected." When Governor Briggs appointed Winthrop, rather than Hoar or Mann, to succeed Webster in the Senate, Sumner lost his last hope in the Whigs. "Put not your faith in *politicians*," he told a sympathetic Howe. "They may talk fairly, but they will ACT *always as politicians*. At last I understand them."[82]

By contrast, Sumner was inclined to trust the Democrats. He had closer personal ties with members of the other party than did Adams, Palfrey, or Dana. Sumner had been corresponding for some years with Barnburners like John Van Buren, Theodore Sedgwick, Henry B. Stanton, and now especially John Bigelow, the editor of the New York *Evening Post*, which Sumner called "the most scholarly paper in the country [. . .]." Sumner was a close friend of Massachusetts Democrat George Bancroft, and had long admired many of the reformist stands of Robert Rantoul, Jr. Despite the return of the Barnburners to the Democratic fold in 1849, Sumner still hoped, and would continue to hope, for "the entire absorption of the Dem. party by our force [. . .]."[83]

This continued hope sprang partly from Sumner's own nature. Whig politicians had sadly disillusioned him, yet his faith in men was too deep to be destroyed all at once. If Whigs had been corrupted by power, he still hoped that the liberal idealism at the root of the Democratic party would hold sway over mere politics. Even as his hopes were gradually deceived by the events of 1849, 1851, and 1852, however, Sumner did not give up on the coalition as Adams and Palfrey would. If it was impossible to fuse with the Democrats, Sumner admitted in 1851, "yet I am willing to *use them*, and also for other matters to co-operate with them, on the best terms, we can get." The important point to him was that "Websterized Whiggery must be defeated." If idealism could not muster enough numbers to fight for the destruction of selfish power, then politics must be made to do the work.[84]

It was more than just Democratic politicians who excited the antipathy of the conservative Free Soilers. They also rejected Democratic principles. In the old republican debate over the relative importance of the community and of the individual, the Whigs tended strongly to stress the citizen's duty to the community and the public good, while the Democrats, especially their most liberal wing called the "loco-focos," favored the rights of the individual. Old Whigs like Adams, Palfrey, and Dana found irresponsible the Democratic rejection of all regulation upon the individual, of state support to economic growth, and of government-sponsored internal improvements. To Adams especially, who rather disdained Sumner's idealism, talk of human perfectibility and of a law of human progress, as well as such reforms as socialism and Transcendentalism and the peace movement were at best hopeless and at worst dangerous to social stability. Dana agreed with his friends "that our cause addresses itself to a sense of justice & national honor, rather than to the instincts of *personal freedom* wh. wd. insure the support of the *loco-foco* part of the Democratic party."[85]

Their disapproval of Democratic policies was reinforced by the conservative Free Soilers' discomfort with the kind of men who advocated them. New England tradition made politics the civic duty of those gentlemen whose education and connections stamped them as society's moral leaders. By definition, such a civic duty could not be a profession in itself, should never be confused with self-interest or personal desire, but must remain disinterested and separate from one's personal business. Yet many Democrats and now many Free Soilers—especially but not exclusively former Democrats—constituted a new generation of young men of modest background who tended to see politics not as a privilege reserved to society's upper class, but simply as the business of getting things done in a democracy, and as a profession. Such a man was Henry Wilson, and Adams and Palfrey mistrusted him instinctively.[86]

Wilson openly loved politics. Handsome, affable, tireless, he was in his element shaking hands, making friends, making deals. It was he, not any of the other Free Soil leaders, who crisscrossed the state, meeting with local political workers, creating alliances, building grassroots loyalties. Wilson eagerly replaced Adams as chief Free Soil editor in 1848, and, despite the controversy over coalition, frankly used his position to push the coalition in the Free Soil newspaper, the old *Daily Whig,* which was renamed the *Republican* and then the *Emancipator and Republican.* He would help set up a special campaign newspaper, the *Free-Soiler,* to do the same during the fall elections. Nor did Wilson disdain to seek office. Even his best friends admitted that he was "intensely ambitious," and, since he had abandoned his shoe manufactory for good in the excitement of the political summer of 1848, political office was his only source of income.[87]

Wilson likewise approved of Democratic reforms. Born in a hut, indentured to a farmer, apprenticed to a shoemaker, the young Jeremiah Colbath, desperate to escape his origins, had cast off the name his drunkard father had given him, educated himself, and pulled himself up through business and now through politics. Unlike his well-connected, classically educated associates, Wilson had known want and had always been a working man. By his history and his embracement of politics as a profession he represented much of the rank and file of the Free Soil party, and, most specifically, those who favored coalition with the Democrats—men like hard-working newspaperman William Robinson, "the workers' editor" James Stone, political worker John Alley, the self-educated blacksmith and reformer Amasa Walker, and self-made businessman and working-class advocate Francis Bird. This was not company that Adams and Palfrey understood.[88]

Sumner found himself increasingly at the center of the controversy. He had never tried to take a leading role within the inner circle of Conscience Whigs turned Free Soilers, and had never been considered more than a valuable member of the close-knit group. Stephen C. Phillips stood out as the group's founder, Adams as its voice of authority. Yet the question of coalition was turning Sumner into the pivotal figure. Though he was of more modest origins, Sumner shared the classical education and upper-class connections of Adams, Palfrey, and Dana. He shared, too, their concern about culture and civilization, about the public good. But his conviction that the public good and social stability were impossible without respect for individual rights brought him closer than they to a Democratic sensibility. He was the one member of the aristocratic Free Soil leaders who might coöperate with the plebeian coalitionists.[89]

Sumner was not an economic revolutionary. Still, as early as his disagreement with Judge Story over his 1837 decision in the Charles River Bridge case, Sumner had shared a Democratic mistrust of monopoly and consolidated wealth that did not allow him to be hostile to working-class reforms. His attacks on the Money Power were more pointed than those of Adams and Palfrey, whose shafts were always aimed at money's effect on slavery alone. To other Democratic reforms and reformers, Sumner was very sympathetic. Since the 'thirties he had been developing a deep respect for Robert Rantoul, Jr., who championed the codification of the laws, the abolition of the death penalty, and many other reforms as well as the abolition of slavery. The ban—which Sumner's father had condemned—against interracial marriage had been abolished by a Democratic General Court and governor, Marcus Morton, who had also passed the Commonwealth's first personal liberty law in 1843. The same Ohio Democrats who had delighted Sumner by their election of Chase to the Senate had then repealed the black laws that had until then denied blacks most civil and political liberties in that state. With former Democrat, now Free Soiler, Amasa Walker, Sumner had had a long correspondence on cheap ocean postage, the elimination of "taxes on knowledge," that is, on books—common Democratic demands—and international peace. It was Walker, with the great peace activist Elihu Burritt, who had anxiously pushed Sumner to represent the United States at the 1849 Paris Peace Conference. Sumner had had neither the money nor the confidence to go, but he did agree to their desire that he serve as chairman of the committee to organize American participation in the 1850 conference.[90]

As his social principles inclined Sumner more toward the Democracy, so his frank acceptance of political means brought him closer than his upper-class colleagues to Wilson and the rank-and-file Free Soilers. From the days when he had first rejected his father's abdication of his political voice and embraced the partisan agitation of the Anti-Masons, to his defense of political involvement to Wendell Phillips and beyond, Sumner had always accepted the legitimacy of political means in a republic, and association with anyone who shared the same goals. Their disagreement over Wilson was not the first such difference between Sumner and Adams. They had already taken opposite views of the trustworthiness of Ohio's new senator, Salmon Chase.

Chase's rise to prominence had also divided the Ohio Free Soil party, as sincere and self-sacrificing Joshua Giddings and his supporters had been repelled by the openly political and ambitious Chase. Giddings had been propelled into antislavery politics by a religious conversion, while Chase, not unlike Sumner, had grown up craving education and striving after the Ciceronian ideal. He had become interested in antislavery through his legal practice, and for years specialized in the defense of fugitive slaves. Despite the eye he kept on his own prospects, Chase's hatred of slavery was genuine, as was his devotion to the principles of the Declaration of Independence and of the Northwest Ordinance, on which he based his legal arguments. "I find no man so congenial to me as yourself," Chase told Sumner, though, not feeling Sumner's faith in human nature, he admitted that "I do not pretend to be *up* to your theories in all respects." Admiring Sumner's learning, he would have been deeply flattered to hear Sumner praise him as "a learned & well-trained lawyer," and "a man of decided ability."[91]

Giddings and Adams mistrusted Chase's unhidden ambition and his frank desire for the Senate seat he would win in 1849, while Sumner judged him only on the genuineness of his antislavery sentiment, and was thus puzzled by their antipathy. The division Chase spawned in Ohio politics "increases the perplexity with regard to yr local politics," Sumner told him. "We have [Giddings] already," he added wonderingly, "& now we have you." As he had once written of John Van Buren, who had turned out to be less sincere than Chase, "I would welcome any person from any quarter" who was willing to devote his "powers to the cause of Human Freedom." With equal equanimity Sumner accepted Henry Wilson's ambition; with equal delight he welcomed Wilson's ability. As for the Natick Cobbler's social background, Sumner never once mentioned it. Nor did he treat Wilson with condescension, but rather with genuine respect. Sumner judged Wilson and the other new Free Soilers solely on their character, talent, and devotion to the cause, and he never found them wanting.[92]

While Adams and Palfrey held aloof, Sumner had been for several years cultivating closer ties with the men who, in 1850, would advocate coalition. Since 1848 Sumner, Wilson, Edward Keyes, James Stone, and others had been meeting for dinner and political talk every Saturday at Young's Hotel at the invitation of Francis Bird. By 1850 their association was well known as the "Bird Club." Sumner had acted confidentially with all these men. His first active political participation in the anti-Texas struggle had been as a member of Wilson's Massachusetts State Anti-Texas Committee—established against Adams' judgment. When Robert Winthrop had been renominated for Congress in the fall of 1846 after his vote to supply the Mexican War effort, it was Sumner and Francis Bird who persuaded a reluctant Adams to run a splinter campaign against him. In early 1847 Sumner wrote the resolutions denouncing the Mexican War that Edward Keyes would introduce in the General Court. In August 1850 it was James Stone of the Boston District committee, among others, who helped nominate Sumner for Congress.[93]

Meanwhile, Sumner, as State Party Chairman in 1849, had actively helped Wilson prepare the way for coalition. Wilson was already in close contact with Democratic leaders by that fall, and Benjamin Hallett, erstwhile Anti-Masonic editor, consulted with him before offering the pointedly antislavery resolutions that his Democratic State Convention would adopt. At the Free Soil State Convention, while Wilson worked the floor, Sumner offered corresponding resolutions that incorporated a number of traditional Democratic positions, including calls for cheaper postage, free land grants to western settlers, reduction of the patronage, and an expression of disapproval at the consolidation of industrial wealth.[94]

Disappointed at the results of the 10 August meeting held in Sumner's office, the impatient Wilson tried to bypass Adams' traditional authority in the group by not inviting him to the State Committee meeting at the end of the month. Fearing to act against Adams' wishes, however, the assembly refused to support the coalition plan in his absence. Wilson's tactlessness touched Adams' most sensitive spot—that sense at once of duty to lead and prerogative inherited with his name. "This is the way I am to be treated by these traders of principle for place!" Adams fumed in his journal. "I see the game and will defeat it if I can. If not, I will clear my skirts." The coalition was turning associates into enemies.[95]

These developments made Wilson all the more anxious to have Sumner's support. And, privately, Sumner remained interested in the plan. "When I think of the insignificance of the state offices," he confided to Howe, "& the importance of Senator, to our cause I confess the strength of the temptation." But he would not act to divide the group. Wilson hoped Sumner would back him at another meeting he had called for 10 September to try to make amends. But Sumner remained in Newport with his brother. Nor would he write the kind of letter Wilson had hoped to be able to read at the meeting. He did not object to the idea of coalition, Sumner assured Wilson, but "[f]or myself I should incline against any departure from our customary course which did not enlist the sympathies of all who have thus far acted together in our movement."[96]

Then the Compromise of 1850 with its Fugitive Slave Bill became law. Sumner had to reconsider Free Soil strategy. A great deal was at stake in the rapidly approaching November elections. If the Whigs chose the new senator, Massachusetts' voice would be used to condone the Compromise. Samuel Eliot, running now for the regular House seat, defended the Fugitive Slave Law in the papers as "necessary for the preservation" of the original compromise of the Founding Fathers "in *statu quo*." But the Fugitive Slave Law "has shocked the people of New England," and Sumner thought it the paramount Free Soil duty to fight for its repeal and against the power of those who had championed it.[97]

To Sumner's mind coalition with the Democrats, before only a temptation, became now a necessity. He begged dissenting Free Soilers to accept Wilson's proposal. "[N]othing seems clearer to me than our duty," he urged Palfrey in October, "in utter disregard of all state issues, & placing our Anti-Slavery above all other things—to try to obtain the *balance of power* in the Legislature, at least in the Senate, so that we may influence *potentially* the choice of a senator in Congress." The "only" way to do this was by coöperating with the Democrats, he pleaded. That some Free Soilers considered acting with the Whigs in order to win local races appalled him. The election of a Whig majority would "render us powerless; so that the nominee of the Whig caucus would walk over the course next winter." "Oh! *back-bone—back-bone—back-bone!*" he cried. "This is what is needed [. . .]."[98]

Palfrey was shocked. Only the year before, while he was in the midst of his endless runoffs, Sumner had promised him: "Do not fear any coalitions which can impeach yr Anti-Slavery position." To Palfrey the qualification was redundant, and he was puzzled by Sumner's apparent change of mind. Palfrey shared Adams' dislike of Democrats and discomfort with the new lower-class Free Soilers, but to these feelings he added a traditional moral repugnance to party politics. It was aristocratic disdain that prevailed in Adams' mind when he rejected any deal with Democrats "merely for the sake of the bait of a Senator's place," and spurned Wilson's plan with the reply that the Democrats should be made to know that "we had higher purposes in view than the mere bargaining for offices." Though Adams spoke scornfully of mere politics, William Robinson swore that "I have heard him suggest expedients by the hour together." A former Unitarian minister and editor, Palfrey had become involved in politics only out of his moral concern about slavery. As a minister, Palfrey had been deeply imbued by American Moral Philosophy, which—though it accepted the practical necessity of politics—continued to share the eighteenth century's distrust of political parties. Political principles and political economy were important, but politicking and deal-making were morally tainted. In Palfrey's mind there was no such thing as a good coalition.[99]

Palfrey's shock was reinforced when, on the very day that Sumner wrote his letter, Wilson came to call at his Cambridge home. Misjudging Palfrey as badly as he had Adams, Wilson tried to win him over to the coalition by promising him the presidency of the state senate if he would abandon his newest bid for reëlection and be the coalition's candidate for Webster's seat. Palfrey thought he was hearing an offer from the devil. Wilson, whom he had once thought "a man of great courage," now became the very model of an unprincipled "jobber and intriguer." Palfrey would never forget or forgive. He was sure that Sumner's motives were more honest, but had to question his judgment. Palfrey and Sumner would never quite be able to trust each other again when it came to the fine line between politics and morality.[100]

Even Howe agreed with the anticoalitionists. As little experienced in politics as Palfrey, Howe told Sumner that he had felt "always inclined to defer to your judgment" in political matters. But now he drew the line. In making such a bargain with the Democrats, countered Howe, the party "had failed to act up to the highest dictates of morality." The end of electing a Free Soil senator was certainly desirable, Howe agreed, but he could not accept "the political morality of the means [. . .]." "Argue it as we may," he scolded Sumner, "—blind our eyes & our consciences as we may, this is doing wrong that right may come out of it."[101]

Sumner could not understand such moral objections to the coalition. They were not trading principle for office, because they were not seeking office for its own sake, but precisely to pursue their antislavery principles. Sumner had long avoided political office for himself, but he had never shared the traditional assumption that political means were essentially tainted. To set aside principles for popularity or power, to vote for the continuance of the Mexican War, to urge passage of a fugitive slave bill—that was immoral. But to Sumner it was clear that to use political means to send antislavery voices to Washington was to fight for morality.

His conviction in the necessity of the coalition, however, put Sumner in a dilemma. Adams would go no further than to agree to another experiment in local coalitions and to leave the state coalition up to each man's conscience. Throughout October in vain, Sumner entreated the conservative Free Soilers to accept what the majority of the party already supported. But, despite constant urging from the coalition's friends, Sumner would not speak out and support it publicly. Sumner's and Wilson's overtures to Palfrey showed that few of them thought they could actually win the Senate seat that was the dream of the coalition. They hoped to win enough seats in the General Court "at least [to] dictate to the Whigs whom they shall send"—perhaps an antislavery Whig like Mann. Nonetheless they had discussed who might be their candidate—Stephen Phillips, Adams, Palfrey. But in addition to their dislike of the plan, these traditional leaders of the group lacked enough sympathy with the Democrats to appeal to the other half of the coalition. Nor did they have the kind of popular following to raise the excitement of the electorate. The one man among the Free Soilers who had these qualities and whose name had been considered with more enthusiasm than any other was Sumner himself.[102]

Soon Sumner was receiving letters from all quarters entreating him to take a public stand on the issue of coalition. Whig friends told him to return to the fold, where "you will do more in a year to put a stop to the encroachments of slavery than by a lifetime of free soilism!" while Free Soilers begged him to speak, as he had begged others to do. On 29 October he read Samuel Eliot's defense of the Fugitive Slave Law in the newspaper, and, perhaps on the same day received yet another anxious Free Soil letter. "No man has so great an influence with the masses" as yourself, wrote Albert Browne, a party activist in Salem. "The enquiry is, what says Sumner?" he urged. "Does he approve of this arrangement? What does your silence imply—I tell you frankly what they think, that you do not approve of it. [. . .] If we lose this election, we lose it by our own folly, by the indifference, the want of exertion, on the part of our leaders." The result would be a certain Whig victory and the return of Winthrop, Webster's successor, to the Senate in vindication of the Compromise. "*It depends upon you,*" Browne implored. "I say it deliberately, & with a full conception of what I say. *It depends upon you* whether the coalition ticket succeeds."[103]

On 6 November, just under a week before election day, Sumner stood up on the dais of Faneuil Hall before a meeting of expectant Free Soilers, and spoke. "[I]t is because I place Freedom above all other questions," he began, "that I cordially concur in the recent unions or combinations, made in different parts of the Commonwealth [. . .]." By this means "our cause will be much advanced; since, by these combinations, the friends of Freedom have a well-grounded hope *to secure a controlling influence* over the Legislature [. . .]." This, he declared to a burst of cheers, would allow Free Soilers to "contribute more powerfully than they otherwise could to the cause which has drawn us together."[104]

The coalitionists were jubilant, and encouraged Sumner with repeated and enthusiastic applause as he entered into the matter at the heart of his speech and of the canvass. Whatever "small" measures of good might be contained in the Compromise, such as its admission of a free-soil California or its abolition of the slave trade in the District of Columbia, nothing the recent Congress had done could mitigate its blessing upon the spread of slavery into the new territories or its passage of the "Fugitive Slave Bill"—as Sumner would always call it—"a most cruel, unchristian, devilish law," which threatened fugitive slaves, free blacks, and white men and women alike, anyone who might be charged by the slave catcher and thus lose his right to defend himself. Such a law "sets at naught the best principles of the Constitution, and the very laws of God!"

In terms that he had already outlined to Horace Mann that spring, Sumner condemned the law as unconstitutional—a violation of the guarantee against "*unreasonable seizures,*" a violation of the right of trial by jury explicitly and repeatedly guaranteed by the Constitution, a violation of the guarantee of an impartial judiciary in its allowing fugitive slave cases to be decided by commissioners whose posts and fees depended upon the decisions they gave. Many other acts of shame had been perpetrated "[i]n the dreary annals of the Past," Sumner conceded, but the United States claimed to be a free country and the nineteenth century prided itself upon its advanced civilization. "[W]*hen we consider the country and the age,* I ask fearlessly, What act of shame, what ordinance of monarch, what law can compare in atrocity, with this enactment of an American Congress?" And yet Americans were told that by this Compromise "the Slavery

Question is settled." He looked out over the assembly and presiding officers. "Yes: settled—settled—that is the word." To the thrilling of his audience, he replied with a phrase that he would come to think of as his motto: "*Nothing, Sir, can be settled which is not right.* Nothing can be settled, which is adverse to Freedom. Nothing can be settled, which is contrary to the precepts of Christianity. God, nature, and all the holy sentiments of the heart, repudiate any such false seeming settlement."

Faced with such an enormity, voted by the people's representatives, asked Sumner, what are the citizen's duties? Until now, he had felt very uncomfortable at the idea of breaking even an unjust law. Two years earlier he had admitted that he could not help but "regard [. . .] with honor" men who helped slaves to escape their masters, but "as at present advised I would not myself be a party" to such an effort.[105] The passage of the new Fugitive Slave Law had changed his mind. To his present audience Sumner explicitly refused to condemn even those who would "protect [the fugitive's] liberty by force. But let me be understood, I counsel no violence." Recalling Revolutionary Boston's resistance to hated British laws, and remembering also perhaps the more recent treatment of abolitionists, Sumner called for the complete isolation of the slave hunter. "The contempt, the indignation, the abhorrence of the community shall be our weapons of offence," he cried out to the cheering crowd. "Wherever he moves, he shall find no house to receive him—no table spread to nourish him— no welcome to cheer him. [. . .] The villages, towns and cities shall refuse the monster; they shall vomit him forth, never again to disturb the repose of our community." "The Stamp Act could not be executed here," he appealed to his fellow Bostonians. "Can the Fugitive Slave Bill?"

Sumner promised to do as he counseled. He told his audience that, years earlier, Judge Story had made him a commissioner, such as now, under the new law, was vested with the power to decide the fate of fugitives brought before him. To his audience he vowed: "I cannot forget that I am a *man,* although I am a *Commissioner.*" What "office," "salary," or "consideration" could be worth "enslaving my brother-man," asked Sumner to the "[r]apturous applause" of the assembly: "Where for me would be comfort and solace, after such a work! In dreams and in waking hours, in solitude and in the street, in the meditations of the closet, and in the affairs of men, wherever I turned, there my victim would stare me in the face; from the distant rice-fields and sugar plantations of the South, his cries beneath the vindictive lash, his moans at the thought of Liberty once his, now alas! ravished from him, would pursue me, telling the tale of his fearful doom, and sounding in my ears, 'Thou art the man!'"

To resist such a law was not enough, Sumner pursued. Every citizen who understood the evil of the Compromise must act in every way that he could to repeal it, and more than this, to "overthrow the Slave Power" that had forced it upon the nation. Such a cause was "not sectional," Sumner replied to its critics, "for it simply aims to establish under the Federal Government the great principles of Justice and Humanity, which are as broad and universal as man." Nor was this cause "aggressive," or "contrary to the Constitution," or "hostile to the quiet of the country," for it proposed not to harm these things but to preserve them all. Having "correct opinions," he said in the spirit of Channing, was not enough; one must act upon them. "Living in a community where political power is lodged with the people, and where each citizen is an elector, the vote is an important expression of our opinions. The vote is the cutting edge." And that vote must be given not to purveyors of "lip-service" but carefully to men of "backbone."

At such a time of crisis, Sumner cautioned in conclusion, no one retained the right to abdicate his responsibility and remain silent. Recounting the transformation in his own life over the past five years, he admitted that "the strife of politics had seemed ignoble to me," but that now "my own course is determined." He was defending his involvement in politics against Cotton Whig charges that he was motivated by mere political ambition. It was not desire, but principle and duty that had forced him into politics. He intended no more. Earlier in his speech, however, while urging the people before him to exercise their duties as citizens, he had voiced a principle that would ultimately force him to do more. The overthrow of a system of slavery "sustained by law" was necessary to the survival and flourishing of civilization in the United States and thus to the spread of free government throughout the world. "I am sorry to confess that this can be done only through the machinery of politics. The politician, then, must be summoned. The moralist, the philanthropist, must become for this purpose a politician; not forgetting his morals or his philanthropy, but seeking to apply them practically in the laws of the land."[106]

Sumner spoke, to the joyous relief of the coalitionists and to the excitement of the electorate, on the Wednesday before election day. Two days later, as Whigs set upon Sumner's "inflammatory" "Marc Antony speech," a desperate Chairman of the Massachusetts Whig State Committee issued a circular imploring every merchant "to use all the influence he can over those in his employ, or in any way under his control" to block the victory of Free Soilers and Democrats. It was too late. "I called to tell you *such* good news," a Free Soil newspaperman dashed off to Sumner as the results came in. "We have carried everything in the State. Senate sure, house nearly certain, Governor, *Senator* & all—You are bound for Washington this winter."[107]

"'Into what pit thou seest, from what height fallen,'" Winthrop quoted disconsolately to his friend Clifford. "Our predictions are verified.—A noble party has been crushed, by what agencies or influences history will pronounce." Whigs and their newspapers traded recriminations over "our defeat." Some blamed the Fugitive Slave Law as the Free Soilers had, while others angrily countered that it was the fault of the personal liberty laws of the past decade for having made the Fugitive Slave Law necessary. Reading their mutual denunciations, Sumner wondered whether the Whig party was "not beyond any resurrection." He added only that, when the party leaders would finally be discredited, "I hope Hillard may be saved." He looked forward to a permanent victory for the coalition, and, he hoped, to the creation of that larger party of civilization that he had long called for—that "*true* Democratic party [. . .] which pledges itself to Humanity & to the Future."[108]

In the meantime, Whigs groaned as the actual Democratic and Free Soil parties took over the General Court that they themselves had so long controlled. "Wilson & Banks presiding Officers of the Massachusetts Legislature!" cried Winthrop after the General Court convened on 1 January 1851. "My fate—let me rather call it my fortune—can not be far off." Wilson, the former cobbler, and his coalition partner Democrat Nathaniel Banks, who had started out as a bobbin boy in the cotton mills of Lowell, presided over strong majorities for the coalitionists in both houses, and oversaw the peopling of state offices with so many former clerks, shopkeepers, blacksmiths, and cobblers, that former-Whig-turned-Democrat Caleb Cushing, a learned and aristocratic jurist, wondered indignantly whether "the state is to be shoemakerized or not."[109]

But the matter to which everyone looked anxiously was the choice of a successor to Daniel Webster. Now that the coalition had swept the elections, the Free Soilers had a real chance of electing one of their own. They were ready to back his candidacy, too, with a new newspaper. The *Republican* had been faltering for months, if not years, and had for some time existed only as a weekly. By pooling resources and buying up several papers in late 1850, however, the Free Soilers managed to bring out a new paper exactly on 1 January 1851. They called it the *Commonwealth*—"a name proud in English liberty," said Howe. The first issue declared that "THE POLE STAR toward which it will ever point will be THE RIGHT; but the right of All." Their prospects were more hopeful than ever before.[110]

But would they have a candidate, they wondered? Sumner's dislike of office was so well known that fellow Free Soilers were afraid he might even now refuse to run. Chase hastened to exhort him: "[Y]ou have no right to *take yourself* out of the list from which a selection shall be made. [. . .] You *cannot* withdraw to more quiet pursuits whether elected to the Senate or not. Freedom has need of all and more than all her able champions." A Vermont Free Soiler agreed: "Your name is known across the water, but not so is that of Phillips, or any of the rest of them. They never wrote 'the True Grandeur of Nations' [. . .]." "You cannot escape from your position." The final decisions about the senatorial race were made in party caucuses during the first days of January. The Whigs offered their leading candidate, Robert Winthrop. After several days of delicate negotiations and conferences guided by Wilson, the Free Soilers and Democrats agreed, with near unanimity, on Sumner.[111]

The nomination was too important to be refused, but Sumner acquiesced with deeply mixed feelings. His taste and his unyielding solitude craved the bustle and excitement and sense of purpose of public affairs at the same time that the personal consequences repelled him, and so it would always be. The very thought of living in Washington was distasteful. His most recent trip there in 1846 had reminded him of the realities of that half-finished and hardly civilized city—all "annoying dust" and "tobacco juice on costly carpets" so that no one in "pure sweet Boston" could imagine it. His new assurance as a writer made him cling more hopefully to those old "dreams & visions" of a literary life, and to his more recent desire to write an historical work that might be of permanent usefulness and also assure his lasting reputation. More than this, politics had already brought Sumner greater pain than he had ever anticipated. In abandoning the law for reform he had known that he was giving up the hope of professional success and the dream of marriage. He had not realized that he must also see existing social ties and even close friendships broken by political passions. To leave behind family and those friends who remained and were his sole consolation, made him "shrink unfeignedly from the work." As much as he had struggled over his initial decision to devote himself to reform, he told Theodore Parker that he would "now find it more difficult to make a personal sacrifice for the True or Right than in 1845."[112]

But Sumner cared too much about the great issues he had become involved in to abandon them. The cosmopolitan and humanitarian ideals of the Enlightenment had determined all his personal and professional choices from boyhood. From the desire to educate himself and to be good, he had moved to the work of building the nation's culture and moral character. From youth his ambition had been to follow that principle urged by Moral Philosophy—to do good. He felt driven to it by his own craving for moral satisfaction and by his relentless sense of duty—both inherited from his father and encouraged by the culture of post-Revolutionary New England. Political means appealed to Sumner's sense of practicality, and held out the hope of escaping from the sense of futility that had poisoned his father's quest. No matter how much use Sumner made of political means, however, as he told Parker, he always considered himself to be "in *Morals* not in *Politics*."[113]

For these reasons Sumner felt the importance of electing a Free Soil senator. The "defeat" of "Websterized Whiggery" and of the Slave Power required that Free Soilers become the majority party. Nor could he be indifferent to his own nomination. As his assurance increased Sumner had felt frustrated at the limitations upon his actions as a private citizen—especially in the critical days of the passage of the Fugitive Slave Law—and the Senate would be an excellent platform from which to influence public opinion. As an orator he was well prepared to take advantage of this, and there was no better position for one who had so long sought to devote his life to doing good and who longed for moral satisfaction.[114] Election to the Senate would also be a flattering token of recognition for someone whose desire to make a noble contribution to his country had struggled so long against the fear of unworthiness. Sumner conscientiously rejected all such considerations as motives for action, but, experience having given him greater ease in politics, he did not deny that such feelings had run through his mind. Though "I have never been accustomed to think highly of political distinction," he confided to Adams, "I am not entirely insensible to the honor that post would confer [. . .]. I feel that it would, to a certain extent, be a vindication of me against the attacks, to which, in common with you & others of our friends, I have been exposed. And I am especially touched by the idea of the sphere of usefulness in which it would place me."[115]

Yet to everyone, stranger and closest friend alike, Sumner repeated over and over again, with increasingly anguished tone that "I have not been able, at any time, in my inmost heart, to bring myself to desire the post, or even to be willing to take it." Though he condemned Webster's "devilish" "course on the Fugitive Slave Bill," Sumner told George: "I have searched my heart, & have its response. I do not desire to be Senator." Thanking Dana for a welcome expression of sympathy for the difficulty of his situation, Sumner added: "I have implicit faith in the propriety of the Coalition, but I regret that it pivots on me."[116]

Of course Sumner would not, nor would any polite Bostonian, have admitted publicly to such a desire even if he had felt it deeply. Especially in New England the tradition of moral leadership required that public service be taken with disinterested concern for the public good, and the trumpeting of a personal desire for office would have been regarded not only as immodest but as a sign of dishonesty. Raised on Ciceronian ideals and his father's disillusionment, Sumner did more than conform to this custom—he had cherished it from boyhood. "My ambition is to live without office," he had always said. If he should take the Senate seat, Sumner told all according to the principle he had held since youth, "the office must seek me, not I the office." Such an ideal spoke strongly to Sumner's appreciation for the concept of moral leadership and to his deep sense of personal dignity. These principles, however, had not stopped him in the past from admitting his desire for other posts to close friends; nor would they stop him from doing so in the future. In 1843 he had swallowed his dislike of office-seeking to ask Judge Story and his colleague John McLean for the post of Supreme Court Reporter. In 1856, when his Senate seat came up for reëlection, Sumner would tell Longfellow and Howe frankly that he wished very much to keep it, and ask them therefore to look after the proper publication and advertisement of his latest volume of speeches. In 1851, however, Sumner's protestations were sincere. He did not want to be elected to the Senate.[117]

Why, it might be asked? For Sumner seemed to have every reason to desire it. But beyond the pain of lost friends and personal sacrifice, the very importance that he attached to the election daunted him. There was nothing in the world that Sumner took more seriously than responsibility and duty, and nothing that more painfully intensified his self-doubt. Through experience over the past years he had gradually felt a new assurance in public speaking and political debate. Yet, faced with a momentous occasion such as Webster's Seventh of March speech, Sumner still feared to publish his own answer. His future success as Senator would reconcile him to a post that did give the sense of usefulness and moral satisfaction he had long sought. But in 1851, Sumner had never yet held any political office, and the one he had been nominated for was attracting more public attention and popular hope than any in memory. He could not look forward with an easy mind to taking on such a heavy responsibility and to meeting—he feared disappointing—such high expectations. The anxiety he had already felt at the contemplation of a possible candidacy in December grew only worse as the candidacy became real and the election in the General Court approached. "It almost preys upon me," he cried later, as the reality of his situation sank in.[118]

Deeply worried himself about it, Sumner did not at first realize that his nomination had also perturbed some of his fellow Free Soilers. The general body of the party and their leader Wilson supported him wholeheartedly. So did Palfrey, Dana, and Howe, though they continued to disapprove of the coalition. Indeed, Palfrey circulated an open letter in the General Court opposing the coalition, which cost him his two-day-old editorship of the *Commonwealth*. But Robert Winthrop was mistaken when he sourly remarked that even Palfrey found "Sumner's pretensions to principle & disinterestedness [. . .] wanting." Palfrey, Dana, and Howe easily made a distinction between the propriety of the coalition, which they rejected, and the ability and integrity of its candidate, which they never questioned. "No one, acquainted with your course in this matter," Palfrey told Sumner, "can ever say that it has not been most high & honorable."[119]

The difficulty came rather with the traditional leaders of the Conscience Whigs turned Free Soilers. The same kinds of sensibilities over seniority and class that had contributed to the difference of opinion over coalition with the Democrats, now irritated Stephen Phillips and Adams against Sumner. Because of his popular standing and ties with the Democrats, Sumner had been elevated without regard to his traditional standing in the movement. Phillips, whom his colleagues credited with being the founder of the Conscience Whigs, had disapproved of the coalition from the start. When his friends nominated him anyway for the governorship on the coalition ticket, he hoped for the Senate nomination, not for his own benefit, but, as Adams put it, "as a manifestation of confidence." Instead, once the coalition won and his actual gubernatorial nomination—following the agreement for all state offices—was cast aside in favor of a Democrat, the Senate nomination went to Sumner. "[M]ortified and disgusted" at such a slap in the face and at what he perceived as the end of his whole political career, Phillips berated a surprised and deeply pained Sumner for not having saved him from "*such a ceremony of desertion.*" Phillips never forgave the coalition, but he did apologize to Sumner once his anger had cooled, absolving him "of all unfriendly intentions or acts" and urging him to stay in the race.[120]

Adams' authority rested on his political experience, and especially his political heritage and name. This deference he both expected and craved. The devotion of much of his time over recent years to editing his grandfather's and now his father's diaries for publication had only increased his native anxiety "to stand upon something like a level with my family." He had felt keenly the decline of his own popularity within the party while Sumner's rose. At the party's state convention in October he had attributed to his disapproval of the coalition "a diminution of the warmth of manner with which I have always heretofore been received [. . .]." It was with a touch of resentment that Adams noted that the coalitionists' belief that Sumner "sympathise[d] with them," made Sumner "therefore much more vehemently applauded."[121]

Unsure of himself, Sumner naturally turned to Adams, as both a friend and an experienced politician, for advice on how best to proceed. He had no idea that in so doing he gave offense. Irritated, Adams jumped eagerly at a rumor, heard just after the November election, that Sumner had in fact "wanted the place" and manoeuvered for the Senate nomination. Palfrey quickly disabused him, and Adams himself had to admit that Sumner was simply "incapable" of "so great a share of duplicity." But, pained at seeing himself displaced and politically "isolated," Adams continued to vent his resentment in his diary, a document private at the time but intended for posterity.[122]

In that diary, Adams criticized Sumner for sacrificing the independence and future of the Free Soil party to what Adams came to think was his unconscious desire for the post. It was "clear," Adams commented, that Sumner could have "shown a particle of energy in directing off from him the tide which he must have seen setting towards him [. . .]." Adams reassured himself "that my sense of right and wrong leads me with less and less of uncertainty to my conclusions" while Sumner was guilty of "weakness of moral purpose [. . .]." It was not merely political displacement that caused Adams to make such a cynical error, but the humiliation of seeing his authority taken by men—whether by Sumner or Wilson—of lower social standing. "To him who is rising in the world a little abrasion of this sort will do no harm," Adams tried to dismiss the affair, "whilst to me who am constantly contrasted with my predecessors, it would be discreditable." But however keen the resentment felt by Adams the scion of a great political dynasty, Adams the antislavery man, like Phillips, believed throughout that it was only in "his mode of operation" that his colleague had erred and that "Sumner will make an efficient and true Senator in the cause." For this, despite his personal feelings, Adams genuinely looked forward to Sumner's election.[123]

Whatever their opinion of the coalition, or their feelings about how it had treated them, all the Free Soilers thus stood behind Sumner's candidacy. The remaining question was, what would the Democrats do? Wilson, the coalition's chief architect, watched nervously as the day of balloting approached. Despite the agreement of the Free Soil and Democratic caucuses, grumblings had been heard from some Democrats. Then, after the state offices were filled with Democrats, the senatorial election in the House was several times delayed—from Friday 10 January to Saturday and finally to Tuesday the fourteenth. On that day the galleries were thronged with spectators "on the tiptoe of expectation," each "man's politics" written in varying smiles or disappointment upon "his countenance." But when the votes were counted, Sumner came out five short of the needed majority. A core of conservative Democrats under Caleb Cushing—calling Sumner an agitator and disunionist—had reneged. On 22 January the Senate approved Sumner. But as January yielded to February, and then to March and April, the twenty-some Democratic "Indomitables" remained inflexible. The House remained deadlocked, and the Commonwealth in suspense.[124]

The Whig leaders rushed into action to defeat Sumner. The State Central Committee levied contributions from industry, while Amos A. Lawrence, nephew of Abbott Lawrence, led private subscription drives to compensate Whig legislators for time lost from work that they might stay in their seats as long as it would take. With some rank-and-file Whigs almost as angry at Webster and the Compromise as were the Free Soilers, and some even ready to vote for Sumner, Whig leaders did everything they could to keep the party in line. The "dishonorable" coalitionists had to be stopped from pursuing their "corrupt bargain,"—a phrase infamous in American ears ever since the 1824 House election of John Quincy Adams to the presidency. They had to be stopped from putting the Senate seat up "for sale" to such a man as Sumner, "an Abolitionist—an agitator, a promoter of party strife, and an instigator of sectional animosities."[125]

Former friends like Nathan Appleton, once "disturbed [. . .] by the apprehension at one time pretty violent that he would be chosen," hoped now that "the future is secure." But Robert Winthrop was not so sure. Webster's successor had himself been shocked by Webster's speech and had voted against the Fugitive Slave Bill—and now felt himself caught in the middle. "Personally, I am glad at getting out of Congress," he insisted over and over, but "I wish [. . .] it could be any body else but Sumner." Any Democrat would do. "Even Phillips or Mann

would not nauseate me. But I should find my stomach revolting from Sumner."
To Winthrop, Sumner was nothing but an "unscrupulous" hypocrite. "And what
became of Mr. Sumner's vainglorious pretensions to disinterestedness, & his
clamorous abnegations of all ambitious aspirations & selfish objects, in view of
so infamous a compact!" Winthrop knew, however, that he was "taking the fall"
for Webster, and believed "that Sumner will be chosen in the end."[126]

From the start, from before the balloting began, Sumner consciously adhered
to the strict statesmanlike independence he had admired since youth. He saw
Wilson nearly every day, but took no part in his own election, leaving all the details to his capable colleague. "I have kept myself entirely aloof from all the
arrangements at the State House," he could say, "making no suggestion on any
points, or persons." For fear that any public action at all on his part might back-
fire from the appearance of a selfish motivation, Sumner carried this traditional
delicacy to unusual lengths. Though Palfrey was in another tight race for reëlection, Sumner refused to heed the calls to speak on his behalf. With Dana he tried
quietly to get a writ of *habeas corpus* to free fugitive slave Thomas Sims, and together they presented a new set of personal liberty laws to the General Court. But
publicly he said nothing—not even when Sims was led back into slavery.[127]

Pledges, of course, were out of the question, though the Democratic Indomitables tried. Sumner reported to Adams one "ludicrous" exchange, in which
several Democrats, worried about Sumner's outspokenness against slavery,
"wished me to say that in the Senate I should devote myself to *Foreign* politics!!"
To all such offers Sumner answered, "1st, that I did not in any way, directly or
indirectly seek the office, 2ndly, if it came to me, it must find me *an absolutely
independent man.*" Adams for one, was "exceedingly relieved." "His position
was now much stronger than it had been," he thought, and Sumner's high-
mindedness "removed all barriers between us."[128]

The public, and many colleagues, were mystified at Sumner's apparent equanimity during the interminable struggle, through ballot after ballot that left him
dangling within a few votes of election but without foreseeable resolution.
"Amidst all the pell-mell about me I am undisturbed," Sumner told Longfellow,
and he took to referring to himself in the third person as "the present Free Soil
candidate." It was not indifference so much as resignation. Torn between the desire to see the coalition win and the fear of being Senator, Sumner could neither
rejoice nor lament at any vote no matter which way it went. Dismayed at the
strong feelings in Boston and at the "prodigious" "pressure from Washington,"
from both Webster and Lewis Cass, Sumner nonetheless felt a kind of relief after mid-January in the thought that his chances of election were "lost *beyond* recovery."[129]

The election was a trial for Sumner all the same. There were times, especially
as the pattern became established in late January and early February, when he

found the process humiliating. The disagreeable smallness of his August vote paled in comparison to being the object of the most difficult senatorial election in Massachusetts history. Adams thought it was "with a little bitterness" that Sumner said that "he was no longer in the way of the political prospects of any body." Even more painful to his pride and his craving to be trusted, was the knowledge that "I shall not generally be believed if I say, *I do not desire*" the office. When even some correspondents wondered, Sumner became increasingly impatient. "I do regret *ex meo pectore* that circumstances have pressed me into my present position," he wrote over and over, only to have to explain that he had written "that you might understand my position, not in any way to promote my election." And again, after Mann offered consolation for another failed attempt at election: "I pray you to believe that I have no personal disappointments. I do not desire to be Senator. [. . .] The world will not do me the justice to believe this. But you & the friends who know me will."[130]

Conflicting advice poured in from all sides as friends and foes alike hung on each new development in the canvass. Sumner's old college friend Charlemagne Tower was "so much enlisted" that he had to write to tell Sumner "that I hope you will not, for any consideration whatever, suffer your name to be withdrawn." John Greenleaf Whittier, the first to push Sumner to accept the candidacy but now disconcerted by Democratic faithlessness, told Sumner to "*decline at once.*" By March, however, confessing himself completely baffled, Whittier "fear[ed] there would be no prospect of electing any true man if thou shouldst withdraw." Mann urged pertinently from Washington: "If you don't prevail now, Massachusetts goes over to Hunkerdom. This may the gods avert." "[T]he conviction is pretty general that I am the only person who can be elected," Sumner wrote Giddings. For this reason Sumner would not withdraw from the race "absolutely." Instead he decided to leave the election entirely to Wilson's discretion. On 22 February he wrote Wilson a letter to use as he saw fit. "I have no political prospects which I desire to nurse," he repeated, and authorized Wilson: "Abandon me, then, whenever you think best, without notice or apology. The cause is every thing; I am nothing."[131]

With all sides manœuvering to break the deadlock, there were many opportunities for Wilson to use Sumner's letter. More than once Caleb Cushing and his Indomitables—many of them anxious now for a way out of what had become an unpopular position—suggested that the Free Soilers put up a different candidate. Playing on his well-known ambition, Cushing even offered the Senate seat to Wilson himself. The "active and restless" Wilson worked unflaggingly throughout the canvass, energizing Free Soilers, buttonholing Democrats, shaming renegades, negotiating with Indomitables—but unswervingly for Sumner, while the February letter remained undisturbed in his desk. During the long election months a deep esteem had developed between the two men. Sumner ad-

mired Wilson's great industry and ability, and his devotion to the cause, while he
felt grateful for Wilson's unwavering confidence in him. Wilson admired Sumner's intellectual and literary brilliance and his self-sacrificing devotion to principle, while he felt a deep personal gratitude for Sumner's refusal to speak down
to him despite the difference in their education and social background. Before it
was all over they had cemented the foundations of a partnership that would last
the rest of their lives.[132]

Meanwhile January snows had given way to March wind and April blossoms
with still no choice in the senatorial election. At the beginning of April, Wilson
and the coalitionists agreed on a three-week hiatus in the balloting to regroup,
while Wilson redoubled his efforts to bring everyone into line. Public interest,
keen from the start, became even keener with the events of April.

The Crafts had escaped Boston unharmed in October. In February the Fugitive Slave Law was again flouted in Boston. The young man who called himself
Shadrach was brought before a commissioner. When his battery of antislavery
lawyers, including Samuel Sewall, got an adjournment, however—as had happened in 1836—an armed mob spirited him away from the courthouse to freedom. When Thomas Sims, a fugitive from Georgia, was arrested on 3 April, the
authorities were determined not to be made fools of again. Coming to save Sims,
the Vigilance Committee found the courthouse encircled by a heavy chain. After the judge denied a writ of replevin, Sumner and Dana tried twice to get a writ
of *hubeas corpus*. Even once it was granted, however, Judge Levi Woodbury, after
declaring the necessity of the Fugitive Slave Law, refused to discharge the accused. To the disgust of abolitionists and many ordinary citizens alike, Thomas
Sims was adjudged a slave and, on 13 April, escorted by armed guards from the
courthouse down to Long Wharf—over the very ground of the Boston Massacre, cried abolitionists—to the ship that would return him to slavery.[133]

Deeply "stirred" by Parker's sermon denouncing the outrage, Sumner could
not be surprised at the outcome. "I have had no confidence from the beginning [. . .] in our courts," he told Parker. "I was persuaded that with solemn
form they would sanction the great enormity. Therefore I am not disappointed."
With law held hostage by the "Slave Power," there was no remedy except through
"Public Opinion." By strengthening this force, Sumner hoped not only to render the Fugitive Slave Law "a dead letter," but to destroy slavery's hold on the national government and its laws. The Fugitive Slave Law had this of good in it,
Sumner was sure—it was "so offensive" that it "cannot for any length of time be
tenable" and would in the process arouse unprecedented "discussion" in the free
states.[134]

Ten days later the balloting for senator began again. Shortly after noon on the
twenty-third there was a momentary burst of excitement at the State House as

the rumor spread through the galleries and into the city that Sumner had been elected. The Adams family, thrilled, sent young Charles Francis, Jr. to Sumner's office to invite him to dinner. The breathless sixteen-year-old was perhaps disappointed by the reaction when he told Sumner the news—"He took the matter very quietly indeed." The boy's father, usually scornful of Sumner's emotional and demonstrative nature, marveled now at what he thought his "self-command"—he "did not to appearance change a muscle nor a tone." But presently they were all quieted as the rumor turned out to be false. Two more ballots had been cast than the number of members present. If they could not elect Sumner now, even after three weeks of special preparation and the return of Sims to slavery, the prospects seemed slim, indeed. "What a disappointment!" wrote Adams in his diary.[135]

On 24 April they tried again. Sumner and Adams had met in the street that morning and so Sumner came to dine with the family again—as he generally did at least once a week. This delighted young Henry who, like his older brother, idolized Sumner as "heroic," and hoped that this time he might get the scoop. As the adults sat down to eat a little before three in the afternoon, Henry, with all the enthusiasm of his fourteen years, ran the two blocks from their 57 Mount Vernon Street home to the State House. He returned not long after, with slow step and downcast eye. Struggling to sound grave, he answered the family's questions: Sumner had received 193 votes, the exact number necessary for election. The family was elated. It had happened on the twenty-sixth trial, explained Henry proudly, after a controversial decision to cast the votes by secret ballot. Charles Francis, Jr., turned to Sumner immediately: "'Mr. Sumner, I want to shake hands with you first;' upon which he very kindly gave me his hand, and accepted my congratulations." But there was no joy in Sumner's eyes. Young Charles Francis was once again struck by his demeanor: "He received the news [. . .] with as perfect calmness and absence of any appearance of excitement as was possible."[136]

It was never known for certain which was the deciding vote. But Whigs and conservative Democrats both contributed to the final decision. The secret ballot—moved by a Whig in hopes of defeating Sumner—allegedly allowed at least one Indomitable quietly to change his vote. But many Whigs had grown restless, too. Under Free Soil pressure, many town meetings had been instructing them to vote for Sumner—instructions a number of them, never happy about the Fugitive Slave Law, became more inclined to follow the more Webster pushed them to vindicate the Compromise. Webster even wanted Winthrop—who had voted nay to the Fugitive Slave Bill—to be replaced with a candidate less soft on antislavery.[137]

Everyone knew what the election meant: 24 April 1851 was Massachusetts' answer to 7 March 1850. The day was "important," noted Adams, "as dating the downfall of Mr. Webster." "Sumner is now fairly installed as a leader of the party," wrote Adams, "and upon him must rest all the responsibility of its course hereafter. I think he will do himself and the country credit." Unlike Webster, added Wilson, Sumner would represent "the whole country, [. . .] not merely [. . .] the few rich planters of the South and the still fewer rich merchants and manufacturers of the North." Among all the duties and possibilities that his new position gave him, Sumner would never forget that "I was chosen to the Senate for the first time immediately after the passage of the infamous [Fugitive Slave] Act of 1850. If at that election I received from the people of Massachusetts any special charge, it was to use my best endeavors to secure the repeal of this atrocity."138

All over town, festivities were quickly mounted. That evening, from the rooftop of the *Commonwealth* building, at the corner of Washington and State Streets, a fireworks display lit up the sky, while perhaps 10,000 spectators came to hear Free Soil speakers, starting with Henry Wilson himself, as they addressed the crowd from the balcony of the Old State House across the street. "Massachusetts is for freedom to-day [. . .] to-morrow and forever," Wilson told the cheering crowd. The next day the paper boys were all crying "Sumner, Sumner!" and Longfellow in Cambridge could hear the one-hundred-gun salute fired from Boston's Public Garden—in answer to the hundred canon shots fired in celebration of the passage of the Compromise.139

Whigs appeared in the streets wearing black crepe armbands. The *Courier* denounced the "craven-skulking" of the secret ballot—proposed by a Whig member—while a rumor circulated "that real-estate had gone down twenty-five percent!" The *Commonwealth* bemusedly reported that a "barber in this city, last evening, charged a Whig double price for shaving him, on account of his having such an extraordinarily long face." The Whigs did more than mourn. Articles in the newspapers called on merchants to withdraw their business from Sumner and other antislavery lawyers, like Dana and even Mann. One public letter signed by Whig members of the General Court called the coalition "an indictable offence." The letter's author, leading Cotton Whig Benjamin R. Curtis, was the commissioner who had returned Thomas Sims to slavery. The Whigs began to plan, too, for the annual fall elections—which would determine the membership of the entire state government—hoping at least to undermine Sumner's position with a big Whig victory before he could even take his seat. But the fall elections would confirm the coalition's majority—all the Democrats who voted against Sumner failing of reëlection.140

Soon Sumner began receiving a flood of letters. Some were sad, reflecting the wounds felt by all sides from the struggle. Hillard wrote that he could not congratulate Sumner, because "with my political connections, that would be insincere." But, looking ahead to Sumner's "noble career," he wished his old friend:

"May you walk in it with a statesman's steps, and more than gratify the good wishes of your friends, and more than disappoint the ill wishes of your enemies." Free Soilers, coalitionist and anticoalitionist alike, were jubilant. "Laus Deo," wrote both Mann and Chase. "Good; better, best, better yet," added Mann: "By the necessity of the case, you are now to be a politician,—an honest one." Fanny Longfellow agreed. Lamenting that Sumner was "far too good and pure and noble for a politician," she reluctantly admitted that "he has an energy and eloquence which, as well as the times, seem to claim him for such work [. . .]."[141]

Alone amid all the excitement, Sumner was quiet and somber. On the evening of the twenty-fourth, bands of Free Soilers crisscrossed Beacon Hill looking for him, first at his mother's house, then at the Adamses', then at the Dana house, giving cheers all along the way—but they never found the object of their search. As soon as he had been able that afternoon, Sumner had slipped away to the "retreat" of Longfellow's Cambridge home. He wrote the next day to Mrs. Adams to apologize for the upheaval he had caused at her house when dozens of supporters from the State House had come to congratulate him, and to tell her how "touched" he was by her and her family's warm "interest" in his situation. That day he also wrote to Wilson. In saying that he would "follow the line of reserve" he had kept from the start and not appear for the celebrations, he knew that "[y]ou, who have seen me familiarly & daily from the beginning to the end will understand me." Sumner gave Wilson all the credit for the outcome:

> To yr ability, energy, determination, & fidelity our cause owes its present success. For weal or woe, you must take the responsibility of having placed me in the Senate of the U.S.
>
> I am prompted also to add, that, while you have done all this, I have never heard from you a single suggestion of a selfish character, looking in any way to any good to yourself. Yr labors have been as disinterested, as they have been effective. This consideration increases my personal esteem & gratitude.[142]

As he took stock, in Longfellow's secluded home, Sumner was not immune to what he had once called the "vindication" of such a victory. When Richard Henry Dana, Sr. told him what "gall and bitterness" the election was to some, Sumner admitted that he had thought of that, "but I at once suppressed all feeling of triumph." He felt no temptation of triumph, however, when he thought of what the election meant to him personally. Fanny Longfellow assured her father that Sumner "has no political ambition whatever, and was more depressed at the moment of his success than during the long and doubtful contest." Sumner was, in fact, awed by the duty that lay before him. "I am humbled by the importance attached to the election," he wrote to George. As he thought of the "bon-fires, firings of canon, ringing of bells, public meetings, & all forms of joy to celebrate the event," he confided to his brother: "I feel my inability to meet the expectations aroused." Nor could the thought have failed to pass through his mind—even if he never gave it voice—that the date of his election fell on the twelfth anniversary of his father's death.[143]

During the quarrels of the previous years, Sumner had sharply criticized others for not living up to the dictates of true statesmanship. Now he had to live up to them himself, and his conscience would allow him no slack. He was painfully aware of the peculiarly deep but skeptical hope of his demanding constituents. Antislavery citizens, Free Soilers, even abolitionists, Garrisonians like his friend Wendell Phillips, looked now to Sumner as the representative not of their interests but of the cause of Right—and required that he prove himself faithful.

Theodore Parker, for one, had been troubled by Sumner's unwillingness to take on the task. Fearing that the new Senator might be lulled into the ways of Washington and forget his duty, Parker sent him a "sermon" to warn him of the "peril" of his new elevation. For all their "understanding and practical sagacity," wrote Parker, "all our Politicians" are, "in moral power, in desire of the True & the Right, [. . .] behind the carpenters & blacksmiths." Even John Quincy Adams, he said plainly, "never *led* in any moral movement." Not yet appreciating that the cause of Sumner's fear was precisely his own relentless sense of duty, Parker borrowed his words to say that Sumner must now be "still in Morals *although* in Politics." He told Sumner that he must be "bound more & more to forget yourself for the sake of the State—; to deny yourself for the sake of the State," and put aside personal "Reputation [. . .] for the eternal Right." "Now I look to you to be a leader in this matter," Parker tried to inspirit the new Senator, "to represent justice, *quae semper et ubique eadem est*. If you do not do this you will woefully disappoint the expectations of the people in the Country." Parker expected nothing less, he told Sumner, than "heroism—of the most heroic kind."[144]

In his upbraiding, Parker expressed nothing less than Sumner's own daunting but unyielding determination: "I hope you will be *the Senator with a Conscience*."[145]

"BOUND FOR WASHINGTON"

TO BE IN HIS SEAT on the first day of the congressional session, Sumner left Boston on 25 November. "Three times yesterday I wept, like a child," he wrote to Howe the next day from New York. "I could not help it. First, in parting with Longfellow, next in parting with you, & lastly, as I left my mother & sister." His "soul [was] wrung" at the "sacrifice" of their constant and warming presence, at a future that was uncertain except for its difference from the past. "Be happy, & think kindly of me," he begged each of them. He brooded over his mother's quiet pride and the exuberant enthusiasm of Julia in whose eyes he could do no wrong—and over the awesome responsibility of remaining worthy of them. He must have thought, too, of his father, who, though he rarely spoke of him, was never far from his mind. He could never forget how he had once disappointed his father's expectations. Now he had taken the habit of saying, like his father, that the duties of life were more than life. It was a standard that he would never cease to hold up to himself.[1]

The long months of waiting from April until the start of the session on the first Monday of December were among the most painful Sumner had ever passed. "From the bottom of my heart I say that I do not wish to be Senator," he repeated to one and all, telling proud young Edward Pierce, now a student at Harvard Law School, that perhaps it would "be the best thing for me" if death intervened before he could take his seat. Deeply depressed, he asked all his friends for "sympathy & friendly succor." The advantages that he had been able to see in the post of senator when it was still only a theoretical possibility were now forgotten. Even the demanding Parker came to realize that he had been overly nervous about Sumner's conscientiousness, and tried to reassure his friend that his congratulations were not "invidious," and that his election truly was "both an *Honor* & a *Reward*"—a mark of esteem of the people of Massachusetts for "your actual deservings," and the opportunity for "a higher & wider field for the same activity you have previously displayed."[2]

His fears did not stand in the way of Sumner's preparation for Washington, however. Democrats and Whigs alike had misrepresented him as a mere agitator. For both himself and the cause, Sumner was anxious to undo this image, and to show himself a statesman. He began by offering the General Court a highly unusual formal letter of acceptance. This allowed him to repeat that he was and always had been a constitutionalist and a unionist. Thus, "by simply stating my position, I have spiked [my opponents'] guns,—at least for the present." He warned himself that, once he arrived in Washington, he should not speak too quickly, but make it his "first duty to endeavor to understand the body in which I have a seat, before rushing into its contests." The more his colleagues could accept him as a statesman, the more effectively he could press his cause.[3]

Nor did Sumner forget that, though opposition to slavery had become the most urgent question before the nation, the establishment of true freedom and civilization depended on a wide range of issues, starting with peaceable and lawful relations with other countries. Young Pierce eagerly hoped that Sumner's "first speech in the Senate would be on foreign affairs." In August, while on vacation in Newport with Albert, Sumner gave Democratic leaders, including Stephen Douglas, "warning" about the "danger" they were flirting with by seeking the "annexation of Cuba," an island long sought by expansionist slave owners. "I see in it the chances of foreign war," he instructed them, "—the disturbance of all our domestic repose & a hideous servile war in Cuba, xtending sympathetically to our own country." In the midst of his depression, unconsciously, Sumner was already finding his senatorial voice and exercising the authority that would finally overcome his self-doubt.[4]

Perhaps, as he set out for Washington, Sumner's thoughts returned to his first trip there, seventeen years earlier. How much material progress there had been since then. The difficult two-week journey by stagecoach and ferry and train had become a rapid and comfortable two-day ride entirely by rail. But the moral evil that had first shocked him then seemed in the interval only to have grown more powerful. How far away, too, those days when he had given himself so ardently to the law, the reminder of which now struck him like the sight of a ghost.[5] Even as he continued in the pursuit of his ideal of Natural Law, he knew how different that had become from the vision taught at Dane College, once so dear to him. The young man groomed to become Story's successor as leader of a resurgent conservative movement had become instead a leader of what Story saw as the advocates of reckless change. Nor could Sumner then have guessed that, as he would abandon the law, those politics that he had once despised would replace it as his career and duty.

As he thought of the changes in his own life, perhaps Sumner thought, too, of how the people and society around him seemed to have changed. His love for the Ciceronian ideal had once been dismayed by the positivism and materialism of the new Jacksonians. Likewise the antislavery visions of the Founding Fathers, men of the Age of Light, seemed to have been repudiated by their descendants in the South, while the once-cherished ideals of the Law of Nature seemed to have been equally repudiated by their Northern counterparts, men educated by the Enlightenment but now devoted to property and stability.

Whatever unforeseen turns his own life had taken, however, Sumner had always followed the ideals he had cherished from youth. Born in a Boston that hailed Adams and Washington and tried to imitate Roscoe and Lorenzo, raised in the spirit of the Enlightenment, by a father who loved Cowper and Paine, educated by American moral philosophers who admired Stewart and Reid, Sumner could not remember when his soul had not kindled to the ideal of the dignity of man and the progress of civilization, nor felt the stern dictates of duty. They had driven him in his studies, drawn him to the ethical ideal of Natural Law, awakened him to the richness of man's artistic and literary achievements. They had first drawn him to Story, then awakened his admiration of Channing, and made him cherish the example of John Quincy Adams. And, from an early age, they had made him dream of devoting his life to doing good to his fellow man.

As a youth Sumner had hoped that this work would lead to happiness and fame, but even when it led instead to loneliness and vituperation he followed it, putting his belief in the Right above personal considerations. As America became rapidly more industrial, more materialistic, more cynical, talk of stern duty and high ideals would come to sound strange or amusing, if not suspect, to most Americans. Young politicians of the age of Grant would look upon Sumner as an oddity from another time and place, later historians would assume that he must have been hiding more selfish if not more sinister motives. But Sumner's idealism was as deeply rooted in his own nature as it was in the Enlightenment from which both he and his country had sprung. Even as he came to fear that America was turning away from those ideals, he would always insist upon the principle of hope in man's future—hope without which, he believed, man had no future.

As he looked to Washington, Sumner thus hoped to do on a larger stage what he had tried to do from the start. He longed to foster the nation's intellect—its artistic and cultural enrichment—and its conscience—its devotion to humanity and justice. He wanted the country he loved to become a beacon to the world of the humanitarian ideals of the Enlightenment, a model of true civilization. He wanted that country, and the world beyond it, to say, like himself: "Nothing can be settled which is not right."

NOTES

Abbreviations Used in the Notes

CCF   Cornelius Conway Felton
CFA   Charles Francis Adams
CPS   Charles Pinckney Sumner
CS   Charles Sumner
FL   Francis Lieber
GS   George Sumner
GSH   George Stillman Hillard
HL   Harvard Law School Library
HUA   Harvard University Archives
HW   Widener Library Manuscripts, Harvard University
HWL   Henry Wadsworth Longfellow
JS   Joseph Story
MHS   Massachusetts Historical Society
NA   Nathan Appleton
PCS   [Charles Sumner]. *The Papers of Charles Sumner.* Edited by Beverly Wilson Palmer. Alexandria, Va./Cambridge, Eng.: Chadwyck-Healey, 1988. Microfilm. 85 Reels.
RCW   Robert Charles Winthrop
SGH   Samuel Gridley Howe

Introduction

1. Joseph Parkes to CS, Westminster, 12 Apr. 1850, PCS reel 7, frame 0177 (hereafter cited thus: PCS 7/ 177).

2. For an excellent overview of this question see Louis Ruchames, "Charles Sumner and American Historiography," *Journal of Negro History,* xxxviii (1953): 139–160.

3. J. G. Randall, "The Blundering Generation," *Mississippi Valley Historical Review,* xxvii (1940): 3–28.

4. Paul Goodman, "David Donald's *Charles Sumner* Reconsidered," *The New England Quarterly,* xxxvii(iii) (Sept. 1964), esp. pp. 373–374, 376, 379, 386–387; David Herbert Donald, "Toward a Reconsideration of Abolitionists," in *Lincoln Reconsidered: Essays on the Civil War Era,* 2d. ed. (1961), esp. pp. 27, 31, 33–36; David Herbert Donald, "An Excess of Democracy: The American Civil War and the Social Process," in *Lincoln Reconsidered,* esp. pp. 224–235.

5. David Herbert Donald, *Lincoln's Herndon,* new ed. [c. 1988]), p. viii.

I. Father and Son

1. John Adams to Abigail Adams, 12 May 1780, in *Adams Family Correspondence* (Series II of *The Adams Family Papers*), L. H. Butterfield, Editor-in-Chief, III (1973): 342.

2. Edward L. Pierce, *Memoir and Letters of Charles Sumner*, I (1877): 1–3. See also William Sumner Appleton, *Record of the Descendants of William Sumner* (1879).

3. Jedediah Dwelley and John F. Simmons, *History of the Town of Hanover Massachusetts* (1910), *Genealogical Work* p. 239; Pierce 1: 3, 20.

4. Robert A. McCaughey, *Josiah Quincy, 1772–1864* (1974), p. 118; Elias Nason, *The Life and Times of Charles Sumner* (1874), p. 311; Pierce 1: 20.

5. Pierce 1: 4–7.

6. David Donald, *Charles Sumner and the Coming of the Civil War*, rev. ed. (1989), p. 5 (hereafter cited as Donald 1); CS to GS, (6, 8 &) 15 July 1842, PCS 62/ 550.

7. Pierce 1: 7–9; "An Elderly Man," [CPS], to "Messrs. Ballard & Wright," *Boston Patriot and Mercantile Advertiser*, 4 Mar. 1828.

8. Job Sumner to Ebenezer Pemberton, 9 Oct. 1788, in Pierce 1: 13; Job Sumner to "his agent in Boston," 14 Dec. 1788, in Pierce 1: 13–14; Pierce 1: 11.

9. Samuel Eliot Morison, *Three Centuries of Harvard, 1636–1936* (1936), pp. 185–186; Daniel Walker Howe, *The Unitarian Conscience* (1988), p. 84.

10. CPS, Valedictory Poem "for the Speaking Club," 8 July 1795, CPS Papers [box 1, folder "Addresses"], MHS.

11. CPS, *The Compass* ([1795]), p. 12; Pierce 1: 15 n2; Charles Pinckney Sumner's Notebook for 1796–1797 shows the great interest he was then (and very likely was earlier) taking in the antislavery writings of Thomas Paine and William Cowper; CPS Papers [box 1, folder 2], MHS.

12. Rayford W. Logan, *The Diplomatic Relations of the United States with Haiti, 1776–1891* (1941, 1969), ch. 11.

13. See especially Alfred N. Hunt, *Haiti's Influence on Antebellum America* (1988), pp. 42, 108–132, 150–155. See also Herbert Aptheker, *American Negro Slave Revolts* (1963), pp. 209–234; Philip S. Foner, *History of Black Americans* (1975), pp. 443–460, 472–474; Winthrop D. Jordan, *White over Black* (1969), pp. 378–388; and David Brion Davis, *Revolutions: Reflections on American Equality and Foreign Liberations* (1990), pp. 50–54.

14. James Spear Loring, *The Hundred Boston Orators Appointed by the Municipal Authorities and Other Public Bodies from 1770 to 1852*[. . .] (1852), p. 328.

15. CPS, Notes 1811–1813, CPS to Rev. [John Sylvester John] Gardiner, 1823 or 1824 in Letterbook I (1825–1829), CPS to the *Standard* (printed 28 Oct. 1835) in Letterbook III (1832–1837), p. 116, note of payment to Charlestown convent in CPS, Notes 1834–1837 [all in box 2], CPS, Miscellany Notebook, p. 56 [box 1], all in CPS Papers, MHS; Pierce 1: 27–28.

16. CPS, Miscellany Notebook, p. 152 (27 Dec. 1835), CPS Papers [box 1], MHS; CS to his Parents, Washington, 24 Feb. [1834], PCS 62/ 037; Pierce 1: 24.

17. CPS, Miscellany Notebook, pp. 66, 78 (Aug. 1835) [box 1], and Notes 1836, pp. 91, 180 [box 3], all in CPS Papers, MHS; Pierce 1: 24; CS, Autobiographical Notes, [1851], [bMS Am 1704.15 (74)], by permission of the Houghton Library, Harvard University, (hereafter cited as Autobiographical Notes).

18. CPS, "Addresses," including the college theme on the line of Virgil: "Non omnia possumus omnes," CPS Papers [box 1], MHS; Leonard Woods to CS: Theological Seminary, Andover, 17 June 1846, PCS 5/ 108–109, and 26 Mar. 1852, PCS 8/ 703–704, and 29 Dec. 1851, PCS 8/ 383–384, and 26 Oct. 1852, PCS 9/ 463–464; Pierce 1: 14–16; CS, *The Scholar, the Jurist, the Artist, the Philanthropist* (1846). See also his "Hon. John Pickering," in *Orations and Speeches* (1850), II: 441–468; CPS to JS, [Hingham? 1796–1797], CPS Papers [box 1, folder 2], MHS.

19. William Wetmore Story, *Life and Letters of Joseph Story* (1851), 1: 71; CPS to JS, [Hingham? 1796–1797], and CPS Notebook 1796–1797, pp. 7, 15, 8, both in CPS Papers [box 1, folder 2], MHS; William Charvat, *Literary Publishing in America* (1993), pp. 64–66. For a superb discussion of the relationship between law and literature see Robert A. Ferguson, *Law and Letters in American Culture* (1984), for example pp. 92–94.

20. JS to CPS, 8 Sept. 1798, in W. W. Story, *Joseph Story,* 1: 71–72; CPS to JS, Boston, Judge Minot's Office, 29 Sept. 1798, CPS Papers [box 1, folder 3], MHS.

21. Pierce 1: 16.

22. Paul Goodman, *Towards a Christian Republic* (1988), pp. 11–16; CPS, *A Letter on Speculative Masonry* (1829), pp. 6–7, 15.

23. Pierce 1: 27; Loring, *Boston Orators,* p. 328; CPS to Rev. John Sylvester John Gardiner, 1823 or 1824, Letterbook 1 (1825–1829), CPS Papers [box 2], MHS.

24. D. W. Howe, *Unitarian Conscience,* p. 314; CS to John Gorham Palfrey, Court Street, [3?] Oct. 1845, PCS 67/ 345.

25. Arthur Brown, *Always Young for Liberty* (1956), pp. 158–159, 163–164; CS to Ezra Stiles Gannett: 11 Oct. 1844, PCS 67/ 208, and 13 Oct. 1844, PCS 67/ 210, and [Nov. 1844], PCS 67/ 219; CPS, Miscellany Notebook, p. 79, CPS Papers [box 1], MHS.

26. CPS, Address at Milton, 5 Mar. 1804, CPS Papers [box 1, folder 4], MHS; CPS, *Eulogy on the Illustrious George Washington* (1800), pp. 17, 19–21, 23–24; Pierce 1: 18.

27. CPS, to "Messrs. Russell and Cutler," *Boston Gazette,* 29 Aug. 1811.

28. Paul Goodman, *The Democratic-Republicans of Massachusetts* (1964, 1986), pp. 128–130; R. Kent Newmyer, *Supreme Court Justice Joseph Story* (1985), pp. 45–48; Donald 1: 6; CPS, Address at Milton, 5 Mar. 1804, CPS Papers [box 1, folder 4], MHS.

29. CPS to Thomas Jefferson, Boston, 11 Jan. 1804, Coolidge Collection of Thomas Jefferson Papers [reel 7], MHS; CPS, Address at the Third Baptist Meeting House, Boston, 4 July 1808, CPS Papers [box 1, folder 5], MHS.

30. CPS, note in Letterbook 1 (1825–1829), pp. 116–117, CPS Papers [box 2], MHS.

31. "Communications," *Boston Gazette,* 19 Aug. 1811.

32. CPS, to "Messrs. Russell and Cutler," *Boston Gazette,* 29 Aug. 1811.

33. Newmyer, *Joseph Story,* pp. 45–48, 189–190, 60–63, 38–39, 66, 59.

34. Pierce 1: 35; CPS to Thomas Kittera, 12 Aug. 1811, in Donald 1: 6; CPS, Notes 1811–1813, CPS Papers [box 2], MHS.

35. Donald 1: 6–7; Pierce 1: 20–21; Gerard W. Gawalt, *The Promise of Power* (1979), pp. 111–115. Donald guesses that Charles Pinckney Sumner's salary was "about $1,000 a year." But even after his change of profession in 1819 Sumner was making "less than a thousand dollars a year," and he very likely had been making less than that as a lawyer. See CPS to Josiah Quincy, 13 May 1823, in Letterbook 1 (1825–1829), pp. 15–16, CPS Papers [box 2], MHS.

36. Pierce 1: 30, reference to C. P. Sumner's letter to Josiah Quincy on p. 21; Donald 1: 7, 10; CPS to JS, 27 June 1815, in "Selections from the Story Papers," in MHS *Proceedings,* xxxv (2d ser., xv) (1901–1902): 203–204; JS to CPS, 30 June 1815, in W. W. Story, *Joseph Story,* 1: 273–274; see also JS to William F. Channing, Cambridge, 23 Sept. 1843, in W. W. Story, *Joseph Story,* 1: 49.

37. Quote—"an emaciated, attenuated figure"—from Loring, *Boston Orators,* p. 330; Pierce 1: 30–31, 11: 96; Donald 1: 6; Nason, p. 311; CS to Jane Sumner, Washington, 4 Mar. 1834, PCS 62/ 043–042; CS to Charles Vaughn, Boston, 1 Sept. 1840, PCS 66/ 066. There is little surviving direct evidence of the character and personality of Mrs. Sumner. What there is suggests a proud and private woman, more dignified than demonstrative. But I find no reason to suppose, as David Donald says, that "[s]he did not know how to express affection." Donald supports this view by selectively quoting from the description in Elias Nason's biography of her son (p. 311) those phrases that refer to her stateliness and leaving out those that refer to her warmth. Her children did not fail to recognize her affection for them, however, and remained close to her all their lives even when they had difficulties with their father. See, e.g., GS to Henry Sumner, Paris, 1 Nov. 1844, R. C. Waterston Autograph Collection, MHS.

38. Donald 1: 8–9; Nason, p. 19; CS, Autobiographical Notes; Pierce 1: 39.

39. [CPS], articles on the Town Schools, Boston *Yankee,* 15 May–31 July 1818, esp. 15 May, 11 June, 9 & 13 July.

40. Richard Henry Dana, Jr., Journal, Sept. 1854, in [Richard Henry Dana, Jr.], *The Journal of Richard Henry Dana, Jr.,* ed. Robert F. Lucid (1968), II: 661–662; CS, Autobiographical Notes.

41. Frank Preston Stearns, *Cambridge Sketches* (1905), p. 181; Pierce I: 39–41, 37; Irving H. Bartlett, *Wendell Phillips* (1961), p. 11; Donald I: 7.

42. Pierce II: 38–39; D. W. Howe, *Unitarian Conscience,* pp. 139–140; Frank Otto Gatell, *John Gorham Palfrey and the New England Conscience* (1963), pp. 20, 40–41; Henry F. Jenks, *Catalogue of the Boston Public Latin School* (1886), pp. 50–51, 60–64; James Brewer Stewart, *Wendell Phillips* (1986), p. 11.

43. Pierce I: 38–39; Mary S. Withington, "The Home of Charles Sumner," *Boston Beacon and Dorchester News-Gatherer,* 26 Jan. 1878; Donald I: 10.

44. CPS, Notes 1836, p. 103 [box 3], and CPS to Josiah Quincy, 13 May 1823, in Letterbook I (1825–1829), pp. 15–16 [box 2], both in CPS Papers, MHS. See also Charles Pinckney Sumner's tribute, "Reminiscences of the Old College Company, or Marti-Mercurian Band," in which his father had surely served at Harvard, in Boston *Columbian Centinel,* 2 Apr. 1828; and Loring, *Boston Orators,* p. 329.

45. Pierce I: 20–21, 42–44; Donald I: 11; CPS, Miscellany Notebook, pp. 86, 90, and passim [box 1], CPS to Levi Lincoln: 27 Sept. 1837, in Letterbook IV (1837–1839), p. 20 [box 3], and 21 Jan. 1834, in Letterbook III (1832–1837), p. 78 [box 2], CPS Papers, MHS. It was not unusual for lawyers in the late eighteenth and early nineteenth centuries to have to take such posts as deputy sheriff and sheriff to make ends meet. See Gawalt, *Promise of Power,* pp. 28, 110–111. David Donald (I: 11) differs from Pierce (I: 21) in giving 1826 rather than 1825 as the date of Charles Pinckney Sumner's appointment as sheriff, but there is ample evidence that the earlier date is correct. Sheriff Sumner himself, in the letter quoted above, gave his age at the time of the appointment as "forty nine," and his letterbooks contain letters from the year between September 1825 and September 1826 showing him to be already Sheriff. See, e.g., CPS, "To the Honorable Mayor & Aldermen of the City of Boston," Boston, 17 July 1826, in Letterbook I (1825–1829), pp. 29–32, and CPS to the "Hon. City Council of the City of Boston," Boston, 11 Feb. 1826, in Letterbook I (1825–1829), pp. 35–39, both in CPS Papers [box 2], MHS.

46. See Ronald Story, *The Forging of an Aristocracy* (1980). In his *Towards a Christian Republic,* Paul Goodman—who is inclined to moderate Story's argument—points out that the great push to make Harvard more exclusive came after the period of Sumner's studies, pp. 45, and 257 n42; Morison, *Three Centuries of Harvard,* chs. IX and X; Gawalt, *Promise of Power,* pp. 148–150.

47. Morison, *Three Centuries of Harvard,* chs. IX and X; Stewart, *Wendell Phillips,* pp. 19–20; David Tyack, *George Ticknor and the Boston Brahmins* (1967), pp. 100, 112–123; CPS to CS, [1826], PCS 65/ 001–002.

48. Pierce I: 47–48; Donald I: 13–14. Because of Sumner's excellent performance in literary subjects at college and because of his early prominence in his chosen profession, however, he would be inducted into Phi Beta Kappa in 1837.

49. Tyack, *George Ticknor,* pp. 90–92; George Ticknor to CPS, 7 July 1828, in Pierce I: 47; Richard Henry Dana, Jr.'s introduction to Edward Tyrell Channing, *Lectures Read to the Seniors in Harvard College* (1856), pp. xi–xiii; Pierce I: 47, 53; Rev. Samuel Emery—Sumner's speaking noted for its "great degree of earnestness . . ."—quoted in Pierce I: 58–59.

50. Pierce I: 48–49; Nason, p. 32; Donald I: 15–16; John White Browne to Jonathan French Stearns, 6 May 1832, in Pierce I: 99; John W. Browne to CS, Salem, 6 Mar. 1831, PCS 1/ 006; see also CS to Charlemagne Tower, Boston, 1 Mar. 1831, PCS 65/ 013–014.

51. Pierce I: 11–13, 45–46.

52. Donald I: 17; Pierce I: 51; CS to Jonathan F. Stearns, 12 Dec. 1829, PCS 62/ 002–001; "Amicus" [CS], "The English Universities," *Boston Patriot and Mercantile Advertiser,* 27 and 30 Oct. 1829.

53. CPS to CS, [1826], PCS 65/ 002; Donald I: 12, 16–17; Pierce I: 50–51, 60–70.

54. Rev. Samuel Emery, quoted in Pierce I: 59; CS to Jonathan F. Stearns, 13 Feb. 1831, PCS 62/ 012.

55. Tyack, *George Ticknor,* pp. 97–98; Nason, pp. 27–29; Pierce I: 52–53; Donald I: 15.

56. Sumner never left a written explanation of his motives in the affair of the buff-colored waistcoat, and previous biographers have recorded the story with possible explanations either of youthful rebellion, early reformist activity, or youthful joking. David Donald even tosses in the idea that it was "stubborn unwillingness to admit that he could be wrong" (I: 15). But the interpretation given here fits well with a pattern of behavior by which Sumner shows his pride in his character and desire to be trusted. He reacted similarly in 1840 when the famous ballerina Fanny Elssler visited Boston. As he had met her in London, Sumner was expected by mutual friends in Europe to escort her about Boston. He knew that in that "puritan place[. . .] [t]'were social death to be seen in public with her" because of her loose reputation as a dancer, but he did his duty and was then deeply annoyed that people who should know his integrity spoke of him in scandalous terms. See CS to FL, Boston, 1 Sept. 1840, PCS 62/ 461, and CS to Henry Cleveland, 4 Court Street, 23 Sept. 1840, PCS 66/ 063. Likewise in 1852, in his first session in the Senate, Sumner would be pained by the lack of trust of fellow antislavery men who would not let him choose his own time to give his first antislavery address but quickly lost faith in his intention to do so at all. See letters by Sumner, spring and summer 1852, PCS reels 63 and 70.

57. Henry F. May, *The Enlightenment in America* (1976), part IV; D. W. Howe, *Unitarian Conscience,* pp. 4–7, 36–38, 67–68; Donald H. Meyer, *The Instructed Conscience* (1972), pp. 9, 13, 41–42, 72, 77, 84.

58. Daniel Walker Howe, *The Political Culture of the American Whigs* (1979), pp. 158–160; Howe, *Unitarian Conscience,* pp. 36–41, 50–51, 57–59, 116.

59. Edgeley Woodman Todd, "Philosophical Ideas at Harvard College, 1817–1837," *The New England Quarterly,* XVI(i) (Mar. 1943): 69–71, 73–74, 76–79, 88; D. W. Howe, *Unitarian Conscience,* ch. IV. Sumner himself referred to Thomas Brown throughout his life, but rarely to William Paley, who, he found, did not touch the "higher chords" of other philosophers. See CS, *Prophetic Voices Concerning America* (1874), p. 145.

60. CS to Jonathan F. Stearns, Cambridge: 10 Feb. 1830, PCS 62/ 005–006, and 24 Nov. 1830, PCS 62/ 009.

61. CS, "The Character of Bonaparte," Senior Exhibition Part, delivered 4 May 1830, in *Exhibition and Commencement Parts, 1829–1830,* by courtesy of the Harvard University Archives (hereafter cited as *Commencement Parts*).

62. CS, article in the *Boston Patriot and Mercantile Advertiser,* 20 Nov. and 3 Dec. 1829; CS "The Religious Notions of the North American Indians," 25 Aug. 1830, in *Commencement Parts,* and "Tom Paine's Creed," in CS, Commonplace Book, p. 1, by courtesy of the Harvard University Archives (hereafter cited as Commonplace Book). Sumner inadvertently wrote "citizen's" instead of citizens.

63. CPS to CS, 16 May 1830, quoted in Pierce I: 54.

64. CS to Charlemagne Tower, Boston, 8 Dec. 1830, in Pierce I: 84; CS to Jonathan F. Stearns: 28 Sept. 1830, PCS 62/ 007–008, and Boston, 24 Nov. 1830, in Pierce I: 83; CS to Charlemagne Tower, 29 Aug. 1831, PCS 65/ 023–024; Pierce I: 71–72.

65. Pierce I: 74–75; CS, notes on the lectures of the Society for the Diffusion of Useful Knowledge, CPS Papers [box 1, folder 8], MHS; CS to Jonathan F. Stearns, Boston, 28 Sept. 1830, PCS 62/ 008.

66. CS to Charlemagne Tower, Boston, 27 Sept. 1830, in Pierce I: 80–82; Pierce I: 77.

67. Pierce I: 71; CS to Charlemagne Tower, Boston, 8 Dec. 1830, in Pierce I: 84. The word "boxes" in the quote appears in Pierce as "bores"—probably a simple misreading or a typographical error.

68. CS to Rev. George Putnam, —— Apr. 1848, PCS 63/ 244. For early examples of Sumner's

sympathy for peace, see CS, journal of a walking tour of New England, 23 July 1829, in *Boston Patriot and Mercantile Advertiser,* 3 Dec. 1829; CS to Charlemagne Tower, Boston: 11 May 1832, PCS 65/ 033, and 29 July 1832, PCS 65/ 037.

69. CPS to CS, 10 Aug. 1828, in Letterbook 1 (1825–1829), CPS Papers [box 2], MHS.

70. William Preston Vaughn, *The Antimasonic Party in the United States* (1983), gives a good overview of the Anti-Masonic movement and political organization, while Goodman, in his *Towards a Christian Republic,* intelligently explores the cultural background and implications of the movement; D. W. Howe, *American Whigs,* pp. 54–56; Leonard L. Richards, *The Life and Times of Congressman John Quincy Adams* (1986), pp. 42–43; Steven C. Bullock, *Revolutionary Brotherhood* (1996), pp. 277–279.

71. D. W. Howe, *American Whigs,* pp. 56–57; Richards, *Congressman John Quincy Adams,* pp. 45–46, 50–53; Vaughn, *The Antimasonic Party,* pp. 9, 12, 21, 53, 55ff., 120–123.

72. Vaughn, *The Antimasonic Party,* pp. 9, 12; CPS, *A Letter on Speculative Masonry,* pp. 6–7, 10, 15–16, quote from p. 9.

73. Boston *Masonic Mirror,* 31 Oct., 7 Nov. 1829, 19 Dec. 1829–27 Feb. 1830; see esp. 7 Nov. 1829, 2, 9, 30 Jan. 1830, 13, 20 Feb. 1830; CPS, Notes 1834–1837, pp. 36, 12, 13, 17, 22, and passim, CPS Papers [box 3], MHS.

74. Pierce 1: 76; CS to Jonathan F. Stearns, 25 Sept. [1831], PCS 62/ 018. Paul Goodman treats the motivation of Sumner and of his father in the Anti-Masonic movement, though briefly, better than anyone else in his *Towards a Christian Republic,* pp. 160–161.

75. Goodman, *Towards a Christian Republic,* pp. 105–108. Scholars disagree on just when parties became acceptable in the American mind, as, of course, did Americans throughout the early nineteenth century. Perhaps the best discussion of the philosophical debate behind antipartyism and the idea of a legitimate opposition is to be found in Richard Hofstadter's *The Idea of a Party System* (1969). Ronald Formisano gives a less philosophical discussion of the same question with specific reference to Massachusetts in *The Transformation of Political Culture* (1983), esp. ch. IV.

76. CS to Jonathan F. Stearns, 25 Sept. [1831], PCS 62/ 018.

77. Ibid.; Pierce 1: 76; John W. Browne to CS, Salem, 6 Mar. 1831, PCS 1/ 006.

78. Pierce 1: 76; CS to Charlemagne Tower, Cambridge, 29 Sept. 1831, PCS 65/ 028.

79. CPS to CS, 10 Aug. 1828, in Letterbook 1 (1825–1829), pp. 106–107, 109 [box 2], and Miscellany Notebook, pp. 105, 106, 14, 78, and passim [box 1]; see also his Notes 1834–1837 passim, esp. pp. 19, 36, 41, 57, 63 [box 2], all in CPS Papers, MHS.

80. CS, "The Character of Bonaparte," Senior Exhibition Part, 4 May 1830, p. 5, in *Commencement Parts,* and Commonplace Book, 29 Oct. 1830, p. 62.

81. CS to Charlemagne Tower, Boston, 10 June 1831, PCS 65/ 018–019.

82. More has been written about the ideal of fame in the Revolutionary period than later. Though the concept was beginning to break down in the Jacksonian period, it remained strong with those educated in traditional eastern classical schools, or who looked up to traditional ideals. See, for example, John Schutz and Douglass Adair, eds., *The Spur of Fame* (1966), introduction, and James M. Farrell, "John Adams's Autobiography: The Ciceronian Paradigm and the Quest for Fame," *The New England Quarterly,* LXII(iv), (Dec. 1989): 505–528. References to fame recur throughout the correspondence of Sumner and his friends for this period. See, e.g., Barzillai Frost to CS, Framingham, 25 Sept. 1830, PCS 1/ 005; CS to John Bosman Kerr, 14 Aug. 1833, typescript, PCS 62/ 028; John W. Browne to Jonathan F. Stearns, 5 Apr. 1831, in Pierce 1: 74.

83. CS to Charlemagne Tower, Boston, 8 Dec. 1830, in Pierce 1: 84; CPS, notes in Letterbook 1 (1825–1829), p. 67, CPS Papers [box 2], MHS; Pierce 1: 22, 75; CS to Charlemagne Tower, Boston, 10 June 1831, PCS 65/ 018–019; CS, Commonplace Book.

84. CS to Charlemagne Tower, Boston, 8 Dec. 1830, in Pierce 1: 84; CS to Jonathan F. Stearns: 13 Feb. 1831, PCS 62/ 012, and [20] Mar. [1831], PCS 62/ 014.

85. CS to Jonathan F. Stearns: 13 Feb. 1831, PCS 62/ 012, and [20] Mar. [1831], PCS 62/ 014; CS

to Charlemagne Tower, Boston, 21 July 1831, PCS 65/ 020; Pierce I: 78; Thomas Hopkinson to CS, Summer 1831, in Pierce I: 79.

86. CS to Jonathan F. Stearns, 7 Aug. 1831, PCS 62/ 016.

87. CS to Charlemagne Tower, Boston, 29 Aug. 1831, PCS 65/ 023–024.

II. The Jurist

1. CS to Charlemagne Tower, Law School, Div[inity] Hall No. 10, 29 Sept. 1831, PCS 65/ 027.

2. Ferguson, *Law and Letters,* pp. 27–28, 74–76, 126, 199–200; Gawalt, *Promise of Power,* pp. 6–8, 18–19, 140–145, 163; Samuel Haber, *The Quest for Authority and Honor in the American Professions* (1991), pp. xii–xiv, 4–14; Perry Miller, *The Life of the Mind in America* (1965), pp. 109–113; Daniel H. Calhoun, *Professional Lives in America* (1965), pp. 178–179.

3. CS to Charlemagne Tower, Boston, 27 May [1831], PCS 65/ 015. David Donald (I: 18–19) gives the unfortunate impression that Sumner's rejection of the "mere lawyer" is a reflection upon his own father: "Remembering his father's uninteresting and unsuccessful legal career, Sumner judged that 'a *mere* lawyer' must be 'one of the veriest wretches in the world.'" Charles Pinckney Sumner's career had certainly been financially and even intellectually unrewarding for him, but when his son rejected the "mere lawyer" he was declaring his desire to follow in the same intellectual tradition that had shaped his father's life. From childhood Sumner had admired his father precisely for his cultivation.

4. Gawalt, *Promise of Power,* pp. 130, 136, 148–150.

5. CPS to JS, Boston, 27 June 1815, in "Selections from the Story Papers," pp. 202–203; CPS, "Addresses," p. 73, CPS Papers [box 1], MHS.

6. CS, *The Scholar, the Jurist, the Artist, the Philanthropist,* p. 24; Morison, *Three Centuries of Harvard,* p. 239; CS, "A Tribute of Friendship: The Late Joseph Story," in *Orations and Speeches,* II: 427, and Review of Joseph Story's "Commentaries on the Law of Bills of Exchange[. . .]," *The Law Reporter,* v(xi) (Mar. 1843): 519; W. W. Story, *Joseph Story,* II: 38–39; Pierce I: 112; CS to Charlemagne Tower, 31 Jan. 1832, PCS 65/ 029.

7. CS, "Sketch of the Law School at Cambridge," *The American Jurist and Law Magazine,* XIII(xxv) (Jan. 1835): 114, 107, and *The Scholar, the Jurist, the Artist, the Philanthropist,* p. 25.

8. Newmyer, *Joseph Story,* pp. 112–113, 210–211, 246, 285; Miller, *Life of the Mind,* pp. 159–164; JS, "Value and Importance of Legal Studies," in *The Miscellaneous Writings of Joseph Story,* ed. W. W. Story (1852), pp. 527–528.

9. Newmyer, *Joseph Story,* pp. 287–290, 83, 92–93; Simon Greenleaf's 1832 inaugural address at Harvard Law School, quoted in CS, "Sketch of the Law School at Cambridge," *Jurist,* XIII(xxv) (Jan. 1835): 116–117; JS quoted in James McClellan, *Joseph Story and the American Constitution* (1971), pp. 182–183.

10. Miller, *Life of the Mind,* pp. 164–170; JS, "A Discourse on the Past History, Present State, and Future Prospects of the Law," quoted in McClellan, *Joseph Story,* p. 345.

11. JS, "Natural Law," *Encyclopædia Americana* (1836 edition, IX: 150–158), quoted in McClellan, *Joseph Story,* p. 313; JS, "The Value and Importance of Legal Studies," in *Miscellaneous Writings,* pp. 533–534; William Blackstone paraphrased in Miller, *Life of the Mind,* p. 164.

12. McClellan, *Joseph Story,* pp. 70–71, 74–76, 83–84.

13. JS, "Natural Law," in McClellan, *Joseph Story,* pp. 313–315.

14. CS to Charlemagne Tower, Cambridge, 17 Dec. 1832, in Pierce I: 116–117; CS to Jonathan F. Stearns, Cambridge, 25 Sept. 1831, PCS 62/ 017, 019; CS to Charlemagne Tower, Law School—Divinity Hall No. 10—29 Sept. 1831, PCS 65/ 027. See also Miller, *Life of the Mind,* pp. 139–140; selections from the diary of Rutherford B. Hayes in Arthur E. Sutherland, *The Law at Harvard* (1967), pp. 131–133.

15. Rev. Dr. Osgood quoted in Pierce I: 101; CS to Jonathan F. Stearns: 7 Aug. 1831, PCS 62/ 015,

and Boston, 28 Sept. 1830, PCS 62/ 007, and Cambridge, 12 Jan. 1833, PCS 62/ 025–026; Asaph Churchill to CS, Milton, 3 Jan. 1852, PCS 8/ 433–434

16. CS to Jonathan Cogswell Perkins, Boston, 10 July 1835, PCS 62/ 065; CS to Jonathan F. Stearns, Cambridge, 25 Sept. 1831, PCS 62/ 017; Pierce I: 93–94, 96–97; CS, Autobiographical Notes; CS to William Frederick Frick, New York, 7 Dec. 1837, PCS 62/ 141–143; John W. Browne to Jonathan F. Stearns, 6 May 1832, in Pierce I: 98–99; Thomas Hopkinson to CS, 17 July 1832, in Pierce I: 99; Story quoted by Mrs. Robert Waterston *née* Anna Quincy in Pierce I: 103.

17. Nason, p. 39; CS quoted by the Rev. Dr. Samuel Emery in Pierce I: 104; Sutherland, *The Law at Harvard,* pp. 102, 118, 121; W. W. Story quoted in Pierce I: 106; Miss Peters quoted in Pierce I: 127.

18. Pierce I: 92–93; John W. Browne to Jonathan F. Stearns, 6 May 1832, in Pierce I: 98–99; CS to Jonathan F. Stearns, 34 Div[inity] Hall, [May? 1832], PCS 62/ 022–021; CPS to CS, 4 Apr. 1832, in Pierce I: 98; CS to Charlemagne Tower, Boston, 10 June 1831, PCS 65/ 018.

19. CPS, Letterbook III (1832–1837), p. 6 [box 2], and Notes 1836, p. 129 [box 3], CPS Papers, MHS; Pierce I: 33; CS to his Parents, Washington, 24 Feb. [1834], PCS 62/ 036, and to Jane Sumner, Washington, 4 Mar. 1834, PCS 62/ 043–042; CS to Charlemagne Tower, 11 May 1832, PCS 65/ 032–033. David Donald (I: 7) uses this last letter, about the death of Sumner's sister Matilda, to show his supposed coldness. A reading of the whole letter, however, shows clearly Sumner's sensitivity in not trying to compete in his grief with the fresh wound of his friend, who had just lost his father and felt guilty about whether he had done his full duty toward his parent.

20. CS, Autobiographical Notes; Nason, pp. 39–40; Pierce I: 90–91, 102, Story quoted on p. 96; CS to JS, 27 Jan. [1834], PCS 65/ 069; W. W. Story quoted in Pierce I: 105; W. W. Story, *Joseph Story,* II: 38–39; Pierce II: 3; CS, "Duty of the Colored Lawyer," 3 Feb. 1871, *The Works of Charles Sumner* XIV (1883): 146 (hereafter cited as *Works*).

21. CS to his Parents, Washington, 24 Feb. [1834], PCS 62/ 036; CS to JS, Boston, 21 Mar. [1834], PCS 65/ 89A.

22. CS to his Parents, Washington, 24 Feb. [1834], PCS 62/ 037; CS to JS, Boston, 12 Feb. 1834, PCS 65/ 074; CS to Simon Greenleaf, Washington, 3 Mar. [1834], PCS 65/ 080. On Whig respect for the Senate see, e.g., Thomas Brown, *Politics and Statesmanship* (1985), p. 11.

23. CS to CPS, Washington, 19 (& 20) Mar. [1834], PCS 62/ 047; CS to Simon Greenleaf, Washington, 18 Mar. [1834], Simon Greenleaf Papers [box 2, folder 12], HL; CS to JS, Washington, 20 Mar. [1834], PCS 65/ 086; CS to CPS, Washington, 21 Mar. [1834], PCS 62/ 049.

24. CS to Charlemagne Tower: Boston, 10 June 1831, PCS 65/ 018–019, and 17 Dec. 1832, in Pierce I: 117. David Donald follows his general interpretation of the relationship between Sumner and Story by saying: "Under the tutelage of Story, who had conveniently forgotten his own earlier career as a Jeffersonian partisan and had now become John Marshall's chief support in the Supreme Court, Sumner developed, during his Washington trip, a decided aversion to politicians and to 'the unweeded garden in which they are laboring'" (I: 30). Sumner had already explained his intellectual and moral aversion to politics during the period of his interest in Anti-Masonry, before his trip to Washington, or even his meeting Story.

25. Pierce I: 96, 123–125; CS, Autobiographical Notes; JS to CS, Washington, 10 July 1836, PCS I/ 0215.

26. CS to his Parents, Washington, 3 Mar. 1834, PCS 62/ 039; CS to JS, Washington, 20 Mar. [1834], PCS 65/ 086; Pierce I: 98, 123–124; John W. Browne to CS, 2 May [1834], in Pierce I: 128. For a full discussion of the effect of the loss of the Ciceronian tradition on the generation of 1830 see Ferguson, *Law and Letters,* e.g., pp. 199–206.

27. Pierce I: 127, 129, 147; Boston *Atlas,* 14 Oct. 1834, in Pierce I: 146; W. W. Story, *Joseph Story,* II: 38–39.

28. JS to CS: 30 Jan. 1836, PCS I/ 212, and 10 Feb. 1836, PCS I/ 215–216; Francis J. Humphrey, a classmate of Sumner's in Rand's office, quoted in Nason, p. 44.

29. CS to his Parents, Philadelphia, 21 Feb. [1834], PCS 62/ 035; Simon Greenleaf to CS, Washington, 11 Jan. 1837, PCS 1/ 302; Donald 1: 28; Pierce 1: 136, 140; Chancellor James Kent to JS, 23 June 1837, in W. W. Story, *Joseph Story,* II: 270–271.

30. Frank Freidel, *Francis Lieber* (1947, 1968), pp. 109–110; Pierce 1: 74, 125–126.

31. Freidel, *Francis Lieber,* pp. 1–2, 15–16, 52, 63–81, 122–124, 141–142, 144–153; McClellan, *Joseph Story,* pp. 283–284; [CS], Review of Francis Lieber's *Legal and Political Hermeneutics, North American Review,* XLVI(xcviii) (Jan. 1838): 300.

32. McClellan, *Joseph Story,* pp. 283–285; CS to Charlemagne Tower, Boston, 27 May [1831], PCS 65/ 015; Pierce 1: 74, 159–160; JS to CS, 2 Dec. 1837, PCS 1/ 372; FL to Mrs. Francis Lieber *née* Matilda Oppenheimer, 12 Aug. 1837, quoted in Freidel, *Francis Lieber,* pp. 201–202. David Donald belittles the relationship between Sumner and Lieber by suggesting that it was merely an instance of Sumner trying to copy Judge Story: "Identifying himself completely and enthusiastically with the judge, Sumner ran into the danger, common to all students of great teachers, of becoming a caricature of his professor. [. . .] If Story was impressed by the earnest, learned German expatriate, Francis Lieber, to whom he introduced Sumner, his student promptly annexed Lieber as an admired friend, whose works he humbly praised and whose career he sought to forward [. . .]" (1: 24). This underestimates a relationship that Lieber valued as much as Sumner, and that would endure most of their lives, providing each with great intellectual stimulation.

33. CS, Autobiographical Notes.

34. CS, "Are Challenges to Jurors in Massachusetts Determinable by Triors?" *Jurist,* XII(xxiv) (Oct. 1834): 332–333; Pierce 1: 147–149; Donald 1: 31–32.

35. CS to JS, on board the Steamer *Robert Morris,* 3 Dec. 1837, PCS 65/ 340.

36. CS to William F. Frick, New York, 7 Dec. 1837, PCS 62/ 142–143; CS to Arthur James Johnes, Boston, 12 Aug. 1836, PCS 65/ 187.

37. CS, "American Law Journals," in *The Law Reporter,* VII(ii) (June 1844): 66, 73–74; *Jurist,* XVI(xxxi and xxxii) (Oct. 1836–Jan. 1837), cover. See, e.g., *Jurist,* I(i) (Jan. 1829): i–ii, 1–2, 141, and II(iv) (Oct. 1829): 267–270, 272. See also Ferguson, *Law and Letters,* p. 36.

38. CS to William F. Frick, New York, 7 Dec. 1837, PCS 62/ 141–142; CS, "The Juridical Writings of Sir James Mackintosh," *Jurist,* XIV(xxvii) (July 1835): 100–134, quote on p. 101, and "Sketch of the Law School at Cambridge," *Jurist,* XIII(xxv) (Jan. 1835): 107–130.

39. CS, "Mr. Sumner's Catalogue of the Law Library of Harvard University," *Jurist,* XI(xxi) (Jan. 1834): 263–268, and "The Advocates Library in Edinburgh," *Jurist,* XIII(xxv) (Jan. 1835): 387–388; quote from "The Library of the Inner Temple," *Jurist,* XIV(xxviii) (Oct. 1835): 311; GSH, "On the English Inns of Court," *Jurist,* XIII(xxvi) (Apr. 1835): 310–332.

40. CS to GS, on board Packet *Albany,* 8 Dec. [1837], PCS 62/ 152–153.

41. CS, Autobiographical Notes; Pierce 1: 150, 187–188; Sutherland, *The Law at Harvard,* pp. 124–125; W. W. Story, *Joseph Story,* II: 430; JS to CS, Washington, 9 Feb. 1835, PCS 1/ 110.

42. Pierce 1: 98; Newmyer, *Joseph Story,* pp. 37–39; Miller, *Life of the Mind,* pp. 136, 142, 182–183.

43. JS to W. W. Story, 23 Jan. 1831, in Newmyer, *Joseph Story,* p. 37; Henry Adams quoted in Tyack, *George Ticknor,* p. 183; JS, "Statesmen: Their Rareness and Importance," *The New-England Magazine,* VII (Aug. 1834): 90. See also Thomas Brown, *Politics and Statesmanship,* pp. 8–12.

44. Newmyer, *Joseph Story,* pp. xvi, 38–39, 44, quote on p. 38.

45. My understanding of Story's political mission is indebted to the writings of R. Kent Newmyer. See especially his "Harvard Law School, New England Legal Culture, and the Antebellum Origins of American Jurisprudence," *The Journal of American History,* LXXIV(iii) (Dec. 1987): 814–835, and his *Joseph Story,* pp. 155–156, 161–163, 172–177, 247–248. JS, "The Value and Importance of Legal Studies," *Miscellaneous Writings,* pp. 513–514. My interpretation of the relationship between Sumner and Story differs substantially from that of David Donald (see generally Donald 1, ch. 11). That Sumner was much influenced by Story there is no doubt, but Donald's portrait is rather a caricature. He says essentially that Sumner, lacking approval from his own father, found

in Story a father figure and tried obediently to copy everything Story did and said (1: 24–25). Thus ignoring the Ciceronian tradition, the history of the legal profession, the influence of Sumner's father, and Sumner's own long-standing inclination, Donald writes: "When Story announced that a good lawyer must also be broadly versed in literature, Sumner promptly agreed" (1: 25), and that "As Story thought lawyers should be acquainted not merely with cases, but with the broad literature of the law, Sumner tried to learn" all the works and authors in the field (1: 25). Likewise Donald attributes Sumner's decision to submit articles to legal journals to Story's "suggestions"—hardly indication of an unusual relationship between a professor and an advanced student (1: 29). Donald again mistakenly says: "As Story and Greenleaf thought that a young attorney should, after his theoretical training, get practical experience in the office of some established lawyer, Sumner went, with Story's strong letter of recommendation, to study with Benjamin Rand [. . .]," ignoring the fact that Sumner was required by Massachusetts law to undergo a year's apprenticeship (1: 28). Donald's only concession to Story's admiration for his favorite student is based on Sumner's eagerness to please and his industry (1: 27)—thin support for Story's hopes that the young man would succeed him at Harvard Law School. Donald concludes by saying that "Sumner, as a worshipful student, treasured every word the judge had ever written and adopted every opinion he had ever expressed—including some that Story had himself discarded." This last concession is highly significant given Story's own discarding of his earlier liberal idealism in favor of a conservative outlook, which, however, was not done "conveniently" as Donald says (1: 41, 30).

46. CS to Simon Greenleaf, Boston, 25 Jan. 1837, PCS 62/ 112. For the increasingly close relationship between law and corporate capitalism, and the transformation of the legal profession to suit that relationship, see Charles Sellers, *The Market Revolution* (1991), pp. 47–55ff. Sellers stresses the social affinity between lawyers and merchants and argues that "lawyers became the main purveyors of capitalist ideology." In the context of his argument, he thus sees them as crucial in the breakdown of American democracy. He does not discuss, however, the degree to which the democratic ideology itself could be seen as a breakdown of the older republican ideology, which many of the best-educated lawyers still professed adherence to. Nor does he make a clear distinction between the intentions of lawyers in the Jacksonian period, the type of capitalism and society they wished to build, and the type of capitalism and society that had by the end of the century actually resulted from the forces at work at its start. Compare Sellers' view of the legal profession as a whole with the discussion of Story's own view of commerce and republicanism in the context of Enlightenment thinking, in Newmyer's *Joseph Story,* pp. 66–68, 118–120, 133–135, 282, 305–306, 333, 342, quote from Story on p. 118. See also Newmyer, "Harvard Law School."

47. CS, Review of "*The Americans, in Their Moral, Social, and Political Relations [. . .],*" *North American Review,* XLVI(xcviii) (Jan. 1838): 115–116.

48. CS to JS, 4 Court Street, 25 Mar. 1837, in "Selections from the Story Papers," pp. 210–211; McClellan, *Joseph Story,* p. 225; Newmyer, *Joseph Story,* pp. 224–234.

49. CS to Charlemagne Tower, Cambridge, 17 Dec. 1832, in Pierce 1: 116–117. Thomas Brown, *Politics and Statesmanship,* pp. 18, 24–25.

50. Newmyer, *Joseph Story,* pp. 211–217; D. W. Howe, *American Whigs,* pp. 188–190, 210–211.

51. Simon Greenleaf to CS, Cambridge, 3–4 May 1838 (intentionally misdated 10 Dec. 1845), PCS 1/ 399.

52. CS, "Are the most important Changes in Society effected Gradually or in Violent Revolutions?" Bowdoin Prize Essay, 1832, in *Bowdoin Prize Essays,* V (1832–1834), by courtesy of the Harvard University Archives; Pierce 1: 163; CS to FL, 26 Oct. 1837, PCS 65/ 290–291; Newmyer, *Joseph Story,* pp. 240–241.

53. Quote from Howard Mumford Jones, *O Strange New World* (1964), p. 441; Newmyer, *Joseph Story,* p. 208; *Prize Essays on a Congress of Nations* (1840).

54. Newmyer, *Joseph Story,* pp. 277–278; CS to Theophilus Parsons, Tuesday Evening [1836], PCS 65/ 214–215; Theophilus Parsons to CS, [Boston, Apr. 1836], PCS 1/ 233–234.

55. Robert Rantoul, Jr., *Memoirs Speeches and Writings of Robert Rantoul, Jr.* ed. Luther Hamilton (1854), p. 279. Many histories of the law in America give good discussions of the codification debate. See especially: McClellan, *Joseph Story,* pp. 87–91; Newmyer, *Joseph Story,* pp. 272–275; Miller, *Life of the Mind,* p. 109; Maxwell H. Bloomfield, *American Lawyers in a Changing Society* (1976), pp. 69, 73–77, 80; Gawalt, *Promise of Power,* pp. 179–183; Charles M. Cook, *The American Codification Movement* (1981).

56. CS to Karl Joseph Mittermaier, Boston, 27 Mar. 1837, PCS 62/ 123; Newmyer, *Joseph Story,* pp. 271–272, 276–278; JS to CS, Washington, 25 Jan. 1837, PCS 1/ 307; JS to George Ticknor, 16 Dec. 1836, quoted in Newmyer, *Joseph Story,* p. 278.

57. CS to Theophilus Parsons, Tuesday Evening [1836], PCS 65/ 214–215; Newmyer, *Joseph Story,* pp. 280–281; CS to FL, 17 Nov. 1836, PCS 62/ 110.

58. CS, "Tribute to Robert Rantoul, Jr.: Speech in the Senate, on the Death of Hon. Robert Rantoul, Jr., August 9, 1852," in *Works,* III (1875): 79; Pierce IV: 293. For a discussion of Robert Rantoul, Jr., that suggests the influence upon him of Moral Philosophy as well as republicanism, see Marvin Meyers, *The Jacksonian Persuasion* (1960), pp. 206–233.

59. Negley K. Teeters and John D. Shearer, *The Prison at Philadelphia, Cherry Hill* (1957), pp. 205–206; Pierce I: 160; Freidel, *Francis Lieber,* pp. 96–98, 103, 185–186. See, e.g., Nicolaus H. Julius to CS: Hamburg, 7 Feb. 1840, PCS 2/ 423, and Berlin, 22 Oct. 1846, PCS 5/ 323–324.

60. Pierce I: 189; [Anon.], editorial notice of "Reports on the abolition of Capital Punishment [. . .]," *Jurist,* XVII(xxxiii) (Apr. 1837): 236–238. The editors of the *Jurist* never signed their editorials and affected a common style as well as agreeing on this subject, but it is likely that this notice was written by Sumner, given the closeness with which he watched the debate and was questioned about it by others, as well as the similarity of the arguments with his later positions. See also miscellaneous correspondence with Sumner on this question, PCS reel 12 passim.

61. CS, "The Juridical Writings of Sir James Mackintosh," p. 115; CS to FL: Boston, 7 Apr. 1835, PCS 62/ 055, and 25 Aug. 1835, PCS 62/ 071.

62. Pierce I: 154–155, 164; CS to FL, 19 Nov. 1837, PCS 62/ 138.

63. CS to Wendell Phillips, "Private," Washington, Sunday [30 Jan. 1853], PCS 70/ 680; CS to SGH, Washington, 3 Aug. 1871, PCS 64/ 706; CS to Edward Coles, 23 Aug. 1852, in *Works,* III: 85.

64. CS to his Parents, Washington, 24 Feb. [1834], PCS 62/ 037.

65. Leonard L. Richards, *"Gentlemen of Property and Standing"* (1970), gives a comprehensive discussion of the wave of mob violence against the abolitionists in the mid-1830's and of its causes; see especially pp. 71–73, 131–133, 155, 165–170. JS to Rev. R. R. Gurley, Salem, 17 Aug. 1822, JS Papers [box 2, folder 2], HL; Newmyer, *Joseph Story,* pp. 166–167, 208, 345–350, 354–358. See also, for example, Rutherford B. Hayes, Diary, 21 Dec. 1843, quoted in Sutherland, *The Law at Harvard,* pp. 132–133.

66. Lydia Maria Child, *An Appeal in Favor of that Class of Americans Called Africans,* ed. Carolyn L. Karcher (1996), pp. xliv–xlv; Lydia Maria Child (Mrs. David Lee Child) to CS, Wayland, 7 July 1856, PCS 14/ 232.

67. Arthur Brown, *Always Young for Liberty,* pp. 225–226; William Ellery Channing, *Slavery,* in *The Works of William E. Channing, D.D.* (1847), II: 46–48, 51–52, 74–76, 32–35, 38. The friendship of Sumner and William Ellery Channing may date from December 1834 when Sumner served as watcher at Channing's house for his friend and Channing's nephew George Gibbs during the latter's illness. See William Ellery Channing to CS, Wednesday Evening [Dec. 1834], PCS 1/ 102; CS to William Ellery Channing, Paris, 21 May 1838, in Pierce I: 295–296.

68. CS to CCF, 9 Apr. 1850, PCS 63/ 340–341.

69. Richards, *"Gentlemen of Property and Standing,"* pp. 15–19; Wendell Phillips Garrison and Francis Jackson Garrison, *William Lloyd Garrison, 1805–1879* (1885), II: 2, 8, 20–32 (quotes on pp. 21 and 24).

70. W. P. Garrison and F. J. Garrison, *William Lloyd Garrison,* II: 29; CPS to Joseph Bartram, 24 Aug. 1834, in Letterbook III (1832–1837), pp. 92–93 [box 2], and CPS, Notes 1836, p. 129 [box 3], CPS Papers, MHS; William Lloyd Garrison to Mrs. William Lloyd Garrison *née* Helen Benson, Boston, 14 Nov. 1835, in *The Letters of William Lloyd Garrison,* ed. Walter E. Merrill and Louis Ruchames, I (1971): 556.

71. Samuel E. Sewall to Comfort H. Winslow in Nina Moore Tiffany, *Samuel E. Sewall* (1898), pp. 62–64.

72. "Supreme Judicial Court" in the Boston *Morning Post,* 2 Aug. 1836; the *Morning Post,* 3 Aug. 1836; CPS in the Boston *Evening Transcript,* 3 Aug. 1836, in which the lawyer's name is spelled "Sewell" and the word "freeman" mistakenly printed in the plural; CPS, Notes 1836, p. 9, CPS Papers [box 3], MHS.

73. Charles Stewart Daveis to CS, 6 Aug. 1836, PCS 1/ 268; CS to Charles S. Daveis, Boston, 8 Aug. 1836, PCS 65/ 181.

74. Charles P. James and Rufus King quoted in Pierce 1: 165–166.

75. CS to FL: Boston, 9 Jan. 1836, PCS 62/ 089–090, and (17 &) 19 June 1837, PCS 62/ 125.

76. CS to Rev. Samuel May, Jr., Boston, 18 Feb. 1836, PCS 65/ 146; Pierce 1: 156, 160; JS to CS, Washington, 10 July 1836, PCS 1/ 215; CS to FL, Boston, (17 &) 19 June 1837, PCS 62/ 125.

77. Stewart, *Wendell Phillips,* pp. 40–46, 55; Bartlett, *Wendell Phillips,* pp. 32–37.

78. CS to Rev. George Putnam, Boston, —— Apr. 1848, PCS 63/ 245; Wendell Phillips, "Philosophy of the Abolition Movement," *Speeches, Lectures, and Letters* (1864), p. 135.

79. CS, Review of "*The Americans, in their Moral, Social, and Political Relations,*" pp. 120–121.

80. William M. Wiecek, Jr., *The Sources of Antislavery Constitutionalism in America* (1977), pp. 157, 197, 189.

81. Ibid., pp. 178–191. An excellent general discussion of the effect of slavery and pro-slavery outspokenness on Northern public opinion is Russel B. Nye, *Fettered Freedom* (1963).

82. CS, Autobiographical Notes; Pierce 1: 163; James C. Alvord to CS: 9 Sept. 1833, PCS 1/ 051, and 3 May 1836, PCS 1/ 237–238; CS, "Replevin of Goods Taken in Execution [. . .]," *Jurist,* XII(xxiii) (July 1834): 104–117.

83. Pierce 1: 153–154; CS, Notes for a Lecture on the Constitution delivered before the Adelphi Society, 1837, in Misc. Papers of CS [MS Amer 1.60], by permission of the Houghton Library, Harvard University.

84. Theophilus Parsons to CS, [Boston, Apr. 1836], PCS 1/ 233; Pierce 1: 147–149; Donald 1: 31–32.

85. T. Jones to CS, 12 Nov. 1835, PCS 1/ 195; CS to Simon Greenleaf: Holkham House, 2 Nov. 1838, PCS 62/ 277, and 4 Court Street, 9 Jan. 1837, PCS 65/ 216.

86. CS to Charlemagne Tower, Boston, 29 July 1832, PCS 65/ 037; CS to JS, Saturday Morning [June 1835?], PCS 65/ 121; see also CS to Charles Folsom [c. 14 Sept. 1835], PCS 65/ 129; CS to Simon Greenleaf, Niagara Falls, 30 Aug. 1836, PCS 65/ 194.

87. CS to JS, 20 Jan. 1834, PCS 65/ 066–067; CS to Simon Greenleaf, [15 Feb. 1834], PCS 65/ 075; JS to CS: 4 Feb. 1834, PCS 1/ 061, and 10 Feb. 1836, PCS 1/ 215–216. See also CS to William F. Frick, New York, 7 Dec. 1837, PCS 62/ 143; CS to J. C. Perkins, Boston, 28 July 1835, PCS 62/ 068.

88. W. W. Story quoted in Pierce 1: 106; T. Jones to CS, 12 Nov. 1835, PCS 1/ 196. See also CS to FL, 11 Sept. 1837, PCS 62/ 132.

89. CS to Simon Greenleaf, 4 Court Street, 9 Jan. 1837, PCS 65/ 216; CS to GSH, Montreal, 12 Sept. 1836, PCS 62/ 106.

90. Mrs. George Hillard *née* Susan Tracy Howe to CS, 11 May 1835, PCS 1/ 154; Pierce 1: 161–163; Donald 1: 39–40.

91. Henry Russell Cleveland to CS, Pine Bank, 3 June 1838, PCS 1/ 416; CCF to CS, Cambridge, 9 Dec. 1838, PCS 2/ 006.

92. CS to Wendell Phillips [Boston, Oct. 1837], PCS 65/ 296; CS to Miss Sarah Perkins: 4 Court

Street, 9 June 1837, PCS 65/ 249–251, and Albion, 24 Nov. 1837, PCS 65/ 323–324; Mrs. Henry R. Cleveland *née* Sarah Perkins to CS, Pine Bank, 15 July 1838, PCS 65/ 464.
93. CS to JS, Washington, 20 Mar. [1834], PCS 65/ 086.

III. The Grand Tour

1. CS to Simon Greenleaf, Astor House, 7 Dec. 1837, PCS 65/ 343; CS to Mrs. Joseph Story *née* Sarah Wetmore, 25 Nov. 1837, PCS 65/ 329.
2. CS to JS, 13 July 1837, PCS 65/ 256–257; CS, Travel Journal, 25 Dec. 1837, in Misc. Papers of CS [MS Amer 1.60], by permission of the Houghton Library, Harvard University (hereafter cited as Travel Journal); Pierce 1: 196; Donald 1: 10; CS to Charles S. Daveis, Boston, 28 Oct. 1837, PCS 65/ 289; N. F. Bryant to Edward L. Pierce, 2 Apr. 1878, quoted in Donald 1: 43 n7; CS to FL, Boston, 17 June 1837, PCS 62/ 124–125. There is ample evidence, including the circumstances of his education and upbringing, as well as his own repeated testimony, that Sumner's desire to visit Europe was an old dream, and that it was not, as Donald states, "Story who originally caused him to fall 'in love with Europa.'" Donald himself quotes Sumner's letter to Story of 13 July 1837 [PCS 65/ 256], which says the desire "dates back to my earliest memory." His interpretation allows Donald to suggest that Story's original belief "that the well-rounded lawyer should travel abroad" had changed since Story himself never went abroad and opposed Sumner's trip, while Donald labels Sumner "inflexibly stubborn" for never changing his ideas—though Donald does not explain why it should be a virtue to reject foreign travel (1: 43–44). Donald's interpretation of this point follows his interpretation of the whole relationship between Sumner and Story, for which see the footnotes to chapter II above.
3. CS to Jared Sparks, 4 Court Street, 28 Oct. 1837, PCS 65/ 292; CS to Charles S. Daveis, Boston, 4 Aug. 1837, PCS 65/ 262; CS, Travel Journal, 25 Dec. 1837.
4. CS to GSH, Montreal, 12 Sept. 1836, PCS 62/ 107; CS to FL, Boston, 21 Oct. 1837, PCS 62/ 135–136; CS to Simon Greenleaf, Astor House, 7 Dec. 1837, PCS 65/ 342; CS to JS, 4 Court Street, 13 July 1837, PCS 65/ 256–257; Allison Lockwood, *Passionate Pilgrims* (1981), pp. 15–16.
5. CS to Jared Sparks, Boston, 28 Oct. 1837, PCS 65/ 292; CS, Travel Journal, 25 Dec. 1837; Pierce 1: 199, 162; CS to JS, 4 Court Street, 13 July 1837, PCS 65/ 256; David Bernard Dearinger, "American Neoclassical Sculptors and Their Private Patrons in Boston" (Diss., City University of New York, 1993), p. 42; Gatell, *John Gorham Palfrey,* p. 56; Donald 1: 44; CS to FL, Boston, 19 Nov. 1837, PCS 62/ 138.
6. Thomas Jefferson to Peter Carr, Paris, 10 Aug. 1787, in *The Portable Thomas Jefferson,* ed. Merrill D. Peterson (1975), pp. 427–428; William Ellery Channing to CS, [15 Nov. 1837], PCS 1/ 370; CS to Henry R. Cleveland, Athenæum Club, 1 Jan. 1839, PCS 65/ 559.
7. Pierce 1: 198–199; CS to Joseph Story, Heidelberg, 10 Feb. 1840, PCS 62/ 436; Simon Greenleaf to CS, Dane Hall, 18 Jan. 1839, PCS 2/ 134–133; CS, Travel Journal, 25 Dec. 1837.
8. CS to Simon Greenleaf, Astor House, 7 Dec. 1837, PCS 65/ 342–343.
9. CS to his Mother, Paris, 8 Mar. 1838 [misdated 1837], PCS 62/ 115–116; CPS, Letterbook II (1829–1832), pp. 86, 91–92 [box 2], Letterbook III (1832–1837), pp. 30–31 [box 2], and Letterbook IV (1837–1839), pp. 40, 42 [box 3], CPS Papers, MHS; CPS, Diary and Memoranda, 29 Nov. 1837, and 18 Mar. 1838, in the *Boston Almanac,* HW.
10. Pierce 1: 71; CS to Charlemagne Tower, Cambridge, 11 May 1832, PCS 65/ 032.
11. CPS, "A Discourse on Some Points of Difference between the Sheriff's Office in Massachusetts and in England [. . .]," *Jurist,* II(i) (July 1829): 18; CS to FL, Boston, 10 Dec. 1841, PCS 62/ 512; CFA to CS, 5 July [1850], PCS 7/ 273; CS to GS: Boston, 6 Aug. 1850, PCS 63/ 388, and Boston, 10 Sept. 1851, PCS 63/ 447–448; CS to his Parents, Washington, 3 Mar. 1834, PCS 62/ 038–039.
12. Pierce 1: 29–30; CS to GSH, Rome, 13 July 1839, PCS 62/ 401; CS to Simon Greenleaf, Convent of Palazzuola, 27 July 1839, PCS 65/ 669; CS to GSH, Astor House, 8 Dec. 1837, PCS 62/ 148.

13. Pierce 1: 29; CPS, Notes 1836, p. 51 (3 Apr. 1837), p. 106 (9 Nov. 1837), CPS Papers [box 3], MHS.

14. CS, Travel Journal, 25 Dec. 1837; CS to Simon Greenleaf, Astor House, 7 Dec. 1837, PCS 65/ 342; CS to Sarah Perkins, Albion, 24 Nov. 1837, PCS 65/ 324.

15. Pierce 1: 33; CPS, Letterbook IV (1837–1839), pp. 22ff., 40, Notes 1836, p. 129, CPS Papers [box 3], MHS. Inevitably, the reconstruction given here of the argument between Sumner and his father is largely speculation based on the little evidence that remains. There is no direct description of such a quarrel in any surviving papers, and most of the references to Sheriff Sumner in his son's letters were carefully cut out. In the same way most of the purely family correspondence had already disappeared by the time Edward Pierce, who was one of Sumner's three executors, saw the papers. Given Sumner's very strong sense of privacy about family matters, it is likely that he destroyed the papers himself. In Sheriff Sumner's Letterbook IV there are careful notations of the departures of his sons Albert and Henry, who both left Boston about the time Charles did, and, in the chronological place corresponding to the date of Charles' departure there is a paragraph beginning "Charles S" with all the rest of the page torn out. There are no more references to Charles in his father's letterbooks or notebooks where the travels of Charles' brothers are carefully recorded, but in his pocket diaries there are a few notations of Charles' arrivals in various places and of the receipt by his mother, siblings, or friends, of letters from Charles while in Europe. CPS, Diary and Memoranda, in *Boston Almanac*, 1839, passim, HW.

16. CPS, Diary and Memoranda, in *Boston Almanac*, e.g., Jan. and Oct. 1838, HW; CCF to CPS, Cambridge, 1 Feb. 1838 [bMS Am 1.10 (7)], by permission of the Houghton Library, Harvard University; CS to Julia Sumner, Astor House, 7 Dec. 1837, copy, PCS 65/ 344–345; CS to Horace Sumner, Paris, 21 Apr. 1838, PCS 62/ 172; CS to Mary Sumner, Dublin, 14 Oct. 1838, PCS 62/ 262.

17. CS, Travel Journal, 25 Dec. 1837; CS to Simon Greenleaf, Astor House, 7 Dec. 1837, PCS 65/ 342.

18. CS, Travel Journal, 25 and 28 Dec. 1837; CS to Henry R. Cleveland, Paris, 6 Jan. 1838 [misdated 1837], PCS 65/ 358, 360; CS, Travel Journal, 30 Dec. 1837; CS to FL, Paris, 9 Mar. 1838 [misdated 1837], PCS 62/ 117.

19. CS, Travel Journal, 30 Dec. 1838; CS to GSH, Paris, 13 Jan. 1838, PCS 62/ 160–161; CS to Sarah Perkins Cleveland, Paris, 5 Mar. 1838 [misdated 1837], PCS 65/ 390. David Sears was most famous for his imposing stone house on Beacon Street, now the home of the Somerset Club, but he was also an important art patron, supporting the work of Washington Allston, Thomas Cole, Horatio Greenough, and others, as well as institutions such as the Athenæum, Harvard, and the Massachusetts Historical Society. See Dearinger, "American Neoclassical Sculptors," pp. 599–600. In Paris, Sumner first stopped at the Hôtel Montmorency at 10–12, boulevard Montmartre. After a week his friend the law review editor Jean Jacques Gaspard Fœlix got him a room in a *pension* at 3, rue Saint-Dominique, the site of which is today near the intersection of the boulevard Saint-Germain and the rue des Saints-Pères. Soon thereafter he moved to lodgings of his own at 25, rue de l'Odéon.

20. On Boston's interest in art in the 1830's see, for example, Jan M. Seidler, "A Critical Reappraisal of the Career of William Wetmore Story" (Diss., Boston University, 1985), pp. 88–104, and Dearinger, "American Neoclassical Sculptors," which includes sketches of the artistic enterprise of Everett, Ticknor, and Hillard, as well as Sumner. See Dearinger for a discussion of Boston's peculiar role in American art history, pp. 26–29, 493, 658–669. See also Paul Goodman, "Ethics and Enterprise [. . .]," *American Quarterly*, XVIII(iii) (Fall 1966): 437–451, and Ronald Story, "Class and Culture in Boston [. . .]," *American Quarterly*, XXVIII(ii) (May 1975): 178–199.

21. Thomas Crawford to Robert Launitz, Rome, 27 June 1837, in Robert Launitz, "Reminiscences of Thomas Crawford," *The Crayon*, VI(i) (1859): 28, quoted in Jan M. Seidler, "William Wetmore Story," p. 162; GSH, *Six Months in Rome*, quoted in Jan M. Seidler, "William Wetmore Story," p. 163; CS to GSH, Paris, 13 Jan. 1838, PCS 62/ 160. David Donald (1: 48–49) suggests that

Sumner's overestimation of Boston's artistic offerings was the result of local prejudice: "Like most Bostonians, he had been provincially conceited when he sailed for Europe." In fact, Sumner had some reason to think highly of Boston's interest in the arts, for Boston was artistically active in the 1830's and already well on its way to becoming the most important center of artistic patronage in the United States. Other cities had patrons, too, of course, but none developed a more sustained and broad-based support of the arts. Sumner was amazed at Europe's artistic offerings, not because he had overestimated Boston's offerings compared to those of other American cities, but because no American city, even Boston, could come close to the richness of Europe's well-established collections. Compare the discussion in Dearinger, "American Neoclassical Sculptors," pp. 493, 645–669.

22. CS, Travel Journal, 5 Feb. 1838, and 11 Jan. 1838; CS to GSH, Paris, 13 Jan. 1838, PCS 62/ 160–161.

23. CS to JS, Paris, 30 Mar. 1838, typescript, PCS 65/ 399; CS to Simon Greenleaf, Paris, 6 Jan. 1838 [misdated 1837], PCS 65/ 362.

24. CS to Henry R. Cleveland: Paris, 30 Jan. 1838 [misdated 1837], PCS 65/ 373, and Paris, 21 Mar. 1838, PCS 65/ 393; see also CS to Henry R. Cleveland, Paris, 30 Jan. 1838 [misdated 1837], PCS 65/ 370; CS, Travel Journal, 29 Mar. 1838, 14 and 19 Jan. 1838.

25. CS, Travel Journal, 13 Feb. and 14 Mar. 1838; CS to GSH, Paris, 21 Mar. 1838, PCS 62/ 169; Pierce I: 155–156; CS to GSH, Newport, 1 Oct. 1844, PCS 63/ 059–060. See also Dearinger, "American Neoclassical Sculptors," p. 371.

26. CS to his Mother, Paris, 8 Mar. 1838 [misdated 1837], PCS 62/ 115–116; CS, Travel Journal, 29 Dec. 1837; CS to W. W. Story, Paris, 14 Apr. 1838, PCS 65/ 414–415; Pierce I: 228; CS, Travel Journal, 8–10, 12, 15, 24, 28, and 31 Jan. 1838, and 10 and 15 Feb. 1838; CS to JS, 14 Feb. 1838 [misdated 1837], typescript, PCS 65/ 377.

27. CS to JS: Paris, 30 Mar. 1838, PCS 65/ 399, and Paris, 14 Feb. 1838 [misdated 1837], PCS 65/ 377; CS to Henry R. Cleveland, Paris, 30 Jan. 1838 [misdated 1837], PCS 65/ 371; CS to JS, Paris: 14 Feb. 1838 [misdated 1837], typescript, PCS 65/ 377, and 21 Apr. 1838, PCS 65/ 417.

28. CS, Travel Journal, 6 Mar. 1838, and 31 Dec. 1837; CS to GSH, Paris, 8 Mar. 1838, PCS 62/ 164; CS to Sarah Perkins Cleveland, Paris, 22 May 1838, PCS 65/ 450–452. Sumner lodged at 5, place des Italiens, today place Boïeldieu.

29. CS, Travel Journal, 28 Dec. 1837, 15 and 19 Feb. 1838, 5 Mar. 1838.

30. CS to Sarah Perkins Cleveland, Paris, 22 May 1838, PCS 65/ 450–452; CS to GS, on board packet *Albany,* 8 Dec. [1837], PCS 62/ 153. See also Paul Baker, *The Fortunate Pilgrims* (1964), p. 100, for similar impressions by other Americans of the treatment of women in Italy.

31. CS to HWL, Athenæum Club, 24 Jan. 1839, PCS 65/ 570–571.

32. CS to Henry R. Cleveland, Paris, 21 Mar. 1838, PCS 65/ 394.

33. CS, Travel Journal, 13 Jan. 1838.

34. CS to Jane Sumner, Washington, 4 Mar. 1834, PCS 62/ 043–042; CS, Travel Journal, 20 Mar. 1838; CS to JS, Paris, 10 May 1838, PCS 65/ 428.

35. CS to W. W. Story, Paris, 14 Apr. 1838, PCS 65/ 415; CS to JS, Paris, 14 Feb. 1838 [misdated 1837], typescript, PCS 65/ 377; CS to Sarah Perkins Cleveland, Paris, 22 May 1838, PCS 65/ 445–447; CS to JS, Paris, 14 May 1838, PCS 65/ 439.

36. Bloomfield, *American Lawyers,* p. 196; CS, Travel Journal, 14–15 Jan. 1838.

37. Pierce I: 251; CS, Travel Journal, 28 Jan. 1838, 20 Feb. 1838, and 9 Mar. 1838; CS to GSH, Paris, 11 May 1838, PCS 62/ 181; CS to William Ellery Channing, Paris, 21 May 1838, in Pierce I: 296.

38. CS to GSH, Paris, 30 Jan. 1838, PCS 62/ 162; CS, Travel Journal, 20 Jan. 1838. Of Sumner's observation of black students at the Ecole de Droit, Donald (1: 49) concludes that, though Sumner found it strange, "he promptly decided that French tolerance was superior to American racial proscription." Donald does not discuss Sumner's private but extensive interest in antislavery

throughout the 1830's, but if one keeps this in mind, there is nothing at all "prompt" about Sumner's feelings in Paris, nor is Sumner's interest in antislavery limited to this one episode. Beverly Wilson Palmer insists that through the 1830's at home and abroad Sumner showed "only a passing interest in politics and none in the antislavery cause." In *The Selected Letters of Charles Sumner,* ed. Beverly Wilson Palmer (1990), (1: 4). This might be compared with Elias Nason's statement (pp. 53–54), referring to Sumner's stay in Paris in the spring of 1839: "While in France, his thoughts were turned especially to the leading social questions of the day; and, from his intercourse with the liberal philosophers of that period, his views of prison-discipline, of universal peace and brotherhood, which came so grandly forth in his first remarkable orations, received fresh coloring and confirmation. Through Mr. Sumner many of the advanced ideas of France in respect to legal and social science were introduced into America." Mrs. Palmer would undoubtedly object to Nason's celebratory tone. The fact remains that he is closer to the truth as revealed in Sumner's correspondence than is she. Sumner, in fact—as should be clear here as well as from the first two chapters of this biography—showed a sustained interest in politics, despite his own disapproval of them, as well as a sustained interest in antislavery and other reforms, such as prison discipline. What he had not yet decided upon was a *public career* in reform.

39. Freidel, *Francis Lieber,* pp. 96–103; CS, Travel Journal, 31 Mar. 1838; CS to HWL, Paris, 27 Feb. 1838, PCS 65/ 388.

40. CS, Travel Journal, 16 Mar. and 2 Apr. 1838; Pierce 1: 273.

41. CS to JS, Paris, 14 May 1838, PCS 65/ 438; CS, Travel Journal, 17 Mar. 1838.

42. CS, Travel Journal, 14 Feb. 1838.

43. CS to Simon Greenleaf, Paris, 13 Apr. 1838, Simon Greenleaf Papers [box 2, folder 12], HL; CS to JS: Paris, 30 Mar. 1838, PCS 65/ 399, and Paris, 21 Apr. 1838, typescript, PCS 65/ 417–418; CS to GSH, Paris, 10 Apr. 1838, PCS 62/ 170; FL to CS, 9 Oct. 1838, in Pierce II (1877): 7.

44. CS to JS, Paris, 21 Apr. 1838, typescript, PCS 65/ 416.

45. CS, Travel Journal, 15 Apr. 1838; CS to JS, Paris, 21 Apr. 1838, PCS 65/ 416.

46. CS to John O. Sargent, London, 20 Nov. 1838, PCS 65/ 542; CS to JS, Paris, 21 Apr. 1838, PCS 65/ 416. Mrs. Palmer does a disservice, as she admits to a degree, to both Sumner and Emerson by using them as representative types of American travelers in Europe. She portrays Emerson essentially as the proud American who refuses to be influenced by Europe—neglecting both his intellectual curiosity and the self-doubt in his attitude—and Sumner as the naïve American, impressed indiscriminately by everything—a view that I hope in this chapter to counter. See Beverly Wilson Palmer, "The American Identity and Europe: View of Emerson and Sumner," *Harvard Library Bulletin,* xxx(i) (1982): 74–86.

47. CS to JS, Paris, 14 (& 21) May 1838, PCS 65/ 437; Lockwood, *Passionate Pilgrims,* pp. 18–19, 89, 174–175; CS to GSH, (16 Feb. etc. &) 13 Mar. 1839, PCS 62/ 355.

48. CS to JS, Travellers' Club, 12 (& 15) July 1838, PCS 62/ 204–217; CS to Simon Greenleaf, Travellers' Club, 1 July 1838, PCS 65/ 462; CS to Henry R. Cleveland, London, c. July 1838, PCS 65/ 473–474; CS to GSH, Athenæum Club, 4 Dec. 1838, PCS 62/ 290–289; CS to JS, Travellers' Club, 9 Mar. 1839, PCS 62/ 363–372; CS to Charles S. Daveis, 2 Sept. 1838, PCS 65/ 496–497. See also CS to GSH: Oakland, 2 Sept. 1838, PCS 62/ 232, and Liverpool, 12 Aug. 1838, PCS 62/ 221. In London, Sumner lodged at 2 Vigo Street.

49. CS to GSH: Travellers' Club, 16 Feb. 1839, PCS 62/ 352; Sydney Smith to CS, Combe Florey, Taunton, 16 Aug. 1838, PCS 1/ 549; CS to GSH, Athenæum Club, 4 Dec. 1838, PCS 62/ 289; Lockwood, *Passionate Pilgrims,* pp. 198, 186.

50. CS to GSH: Athenæum Club, 4 Dec. 1838, PCS 62/ 291, and Stratford-on-Avon, 6 (& 23) Jan. 1839, PCS 62/ 321, and Keswick, 8 Sept. 1838, PCS 62/ 243, and London, 16 Feb. 1839, PCS 62/ 344.

51. CS to GSH: Athenæum Club, 4 Dec. 1838, PCS 62/ 289, and Travellers' Club, 16 Feb. 1839, PCS 62/ 345; CS to Mrs. Judge (Sarah L.) Howe, Athenæum Club, 22 Nov. 1838, in Pierce II: 18.

52. Pierce I: 329, II: 22.

53. CS to GSH, Brougham Hall, 6 Sept. 1838, PCS 62/ 239.

54. See, e.g., CS to JS: London, 23 July 1838, PCS 62/ 218, and 9 Mar. 1839, PCS 62/ 373; CS to George Washington Greene, London, 30 Mar. 1840, PCS 66/ 028; CS to Richard Cobden, Boston, 12 Feb. 1848, PCS 68/ 155; CS to GSH, 9 Mar. 1839, in Pierce II: 78.

55. CS to JS, Alfred Club, 27 June 1838, PCS 62/ 198; CS to GSH, Travellers' Club, 16 Feb. (& 13 Mar.) 1839, PCS 62/ 353, 355.

56. CS to GSH, 4 (& 5) Dec. 1838, PCS 62/ 293; CS to GSH, Liverpool, 12 Aug. 1838, PCS 62/ 221; CS to John Gorham Palfrey, Liverpool, 12 Aug. 1838, PCS 65/ 484.

57. CCF to CS, Cambridge, 5 Nov. 1838, PCS 1/ 630; Edward Everett to CS, Boston, 20 May 1838, PCS 2/ 345; CS to Simon Greenleaf, Holkham House, 2 Nov. 1838, PCS 62/ 275; CS to GSH, Oxford and London, 11 (& 14) Dec. 1838, PCS 62/ 304.

58. Simon Greenleaf to CS, Cambridge, 3 (& 4) May 1838 [intentionally misdated 1845], PCS 1/ 399–400.

59. Ibid.

60. JS to CS, Cambridge, 11 Aug. 1838, PCS 1/ 546; Simon Greenleaf to CS, Cambridge, 7 Sept. 1838, PCS 1/ 564–565.

61. CS to GS, Boston, 14 Apr. 1842, PCS 62/ 538; CS to JS, London, 12 (& 15) July 1838, PCS 62/ 213, and (9 &) 18 Mar. 1839, PCS 62/ 376. A preoccupation with English history, according to William Brock, caused the majority of American visitors to miss current events, including the development of a school of philosophical radicalism; see William Brock, "The Image of England and American Nationalism," *Journal of American Studies*, v(iii) (Dec. 1971): 225–245. CS to Arthur James Johnes, Boston, 12 Aug. 1836, PCS 65/ 186–187.

62. CS to JS, London, 9 (& 18) Mar. 1839, PCS 62/ 375–377; D. W. Howe, *American Whigs*, p. 77.

63. See Brock, "The Image of England [. . .]," pp. 225–245; Lockwood, *Passionate Pilgrims*, pp. 15–16, 27; CS to Simon Greenleaf, Travellers' Club, 1 July 1838, PCS 65/ 462–463.

64. CS to Benjamin Rand, Athenæum Club, 20 Feb. 1839, PCS 65/ 580; CS to GS, Boston, 30 Apr. 1842, PCS 62/ 540.

65. CS to Benjamin Rand, Athenæum Club, 20 Feb. 1839, PCS 65/ 580–581.

66. CS to GSH, London, 16 Feb. (& 13 Mar.) 1839, PCS 62/ 354; CS to FL, Boston, 23 Mar. 1841, PCS 62/ 479; CS to John O. Sargent, Travellers' Club, 15 Mar. 1839, PCS 65/ 600–601.

67. Richards, "*Gentlemen of Property and Standing*," pp. 8–9, 13; CS to GSH, Travellers' Club, 16 Feb. 1839, PCS 62/ 343; CS to Richard Bentley, Athenæum Club, 3 Dec. 1838, PCS 65/ 546–547; CS to JS, Lanfire House, 28 Sept. 1838, PCS 62/ 254–253. Consider Dickens' popular description of the talk in a New York boardinghouse in *Martin Chuzzlewit*: "Thus, Martin learned in the five minutes' straggling talk about the stove, that to carry pistols into legislative assemblies, and swords in sticks, and other such peaceful toys; to seize opponents by the throat, as dogs or rats might do; to bluster, bully, and overbear by personal assailment, were glowing deeds—not thrusts and stabs at Freedom, striking far deeper into her House of Life than any sultan's scimitar could reach, but rare incense on her altars, having a grateful scent in patriotic nostrils, and curling upward to the seventh heaven of Fame": *The Life and Adventures of Martin Chuzzlewit* (1906), p. 298.

68. CS to Mrs. Judge Howe, Athenæum Club, 22 Nov. 1838, in Pierce II: 18; CS to William F. Frick, Rome, 4 Aug. 1839, PCS 62/ 405–406; CS to Simon Greenleaf, Travellers' Club, 1 July 1838, PCS 65/ 462; CS to JS: London, 9 (& 18) Mar. 1839, PCS 62/ 368, and London, 12 (& 17) July 1838, PCS 62/ 215, and London, 23 Jan. 1839, in Pierce II: 54; CS to GSH, 21 Mar. [1839], PCS 62/ 387–388.

69. CS to Mrs. Judge Howe, Athenæum Club, 22 Nov. 1838, in Pierce II: 18; CS to GSH: Paris, 8 Mar. 1838, PCS 62/ 164, and Paris, 11 May 1838, PCS 62/ 181.

70. CS to GSH, London, 16 Feb. (&c) 1838, PCS 62/ 343, 345–346; William Hickling Prescott

to CS, Boston, 18 Apr. 1839, PCS 2/ 330–331; David Brewster to CS, St. Leonards St. Andrews, 8 Dec. 1838, PCS 65/ 553–554; CS to FL, Oakland, 3 Sept. 1838, PCS 62/ 234; CS to HWL, Vienna, 10 Nov. 1839, PCS 66/ 008; CS to GSH: London, 18 Mar. 1840, PCS 62/ 443–442, and 21 Mar. [1839], PCS 62/ 387–388; CS to JS, Lanfire House, 28 Sept. 1838, PCS 62/ 253.

71. CS to JS, London, 9 (& 18) Mar. 1839, PCS 62/ 369; CS to Richard Fletcher, Travellers' Club, 20 Mar. 1839, PCS 65/ 613–614.

72. CS to JS: on board Steamer *Robert Morris,* Sunday, 3 Dec. 1837, PCS 65/ 339–340, and London (9 &) 18 Mar. 1839, PCS 62/ 378; CS to Richard Fletcher, Travellers' Club, 20 Mar. 1839, PCS 65/ 613–614.

73. I. R. Ingersoll to CS, Philadelphia, 22 Apr. 1839, PCS 2/ 333; Charles S. Daveis to CS, Portland, 18 Jan. 1839, PCS 2/ 132–131; CS to GSH, 21 Mar. [1839], PCS 62/ 385–386; CS to Richard Monckton Milnes, Paris, 10 Apr. 1839, PCS 65/ 629–630; CS to Edward Everett, Travellers' Club, 18 Mar. 1839, PCS 65/ 607; CS to Richard Fletcher, Travellers' Club, 20 Mar. 1839, PCS 65/ 613–614.

74. See, e.g., CS to Edward Everett: Travellers' Club, 18 Mar. 1839, PCS 65/ 607, and Paris, 6 Apr. 1839, PCS 65/ 623; CS to GSH: Paris, 15 Apr. 1839, PCS 62/ 393, and Rome, 13 July 1839, PCS 62/ 402.

75. See, e.g., CS to Edward Everett, Paris, 6 Apr. 1839, PCS 65/ 623; CS to George William Frederick Howard, Viscount Morpeth: 2 Vigo Street, 5 Mar. 1839, in Pierce II: 71–72, and Ship Hotel, Dover, 22 Mar. 1839, in Pierce II: 81–82; CS to Richard Fletcher, Travellers' Club, 20 Mar. 1839, PCS 65/ 614.

76. CPS, Miscellany Notebook, pp. 40, 52, CPS Papers [box I], MHS.

77. CS to GSH, Paris: 15 Apr. 1839, PCS 62/ 393–394, and 20 Apr. 1839, PCS 62/ 397; GSH to CS, quoted in Pierce II: 150.

78. Baker, *Fortunate Pilgrims,* pp. 1–2, 7, 11; Orie W. Long, *Literary Pioneers* (1935, 1963), pp. 94–95, 160–163; Pierce II: 83, 115–116. See also, e.g., HWL to Stephen Longfellow, Paris, 19 Oct. 1826, in *The Letters of Henry Wadsworth Longfellow,* ed. Andrew Hilen, I(1966): 187–188.

79. CS to W. W. Story, 14 Jan. 1848, PCS 68/ 115; Baker, *Fortunate Pilgrims,* pp. 27–30, 49; CS to Sarah Perkins Cleveland, Boston, 31 Jan. 1845, PCS 67/ 248; CS to GSH, Rome, 13 July 1839, PCS 62/ 401.

80. CS to GSH, Paris, 15 Apr. 1839, PCS 62/ 393; Otto J. Wittman, "The Italian Experience," *American Quarterly,* IV(i) (Spring 1952): 13; CS to GSH, Venice, 29 Sept. 1839, PCS 62/ 422.

81. Pierce II: 91; Jones, *Strange New World,* pp. 220–221; CS to George W. Greene, Munich, 18 Oct. 1839 [misdated Sept.], PCS 66/ 006; CS to GSH, Venice, 29 Sept. 1839, PCS 62/ 424.

82. Henry James, *Roderick Hudson,* quoted in Seidler, "William Wetmore Story," p. 154; HWL to George W. Greene, Portland, 6 Aug. 1838, in *Letters of Longfellow,* II (1966): 93–94; Hilen, ed. *Letters of Longfellow,* I: 9–10; Pierce II: 93–94; CS to GSH, Palazzo Giustiniani, Venice, 29 Sept. 1839, PCS 62/ 423.

83. CS to GSH, Palazzo Giustiniani, Venice, 29 Sept. 1839, PCS 62/ 423. It may be remembered that, in daily life, Thomas Gray was Professor of Modern History at Cambridge and delighted in nothing so much as passing his days, as Sumner did in Rome, reading voluminously on every subject, taking, as he put it, "verse and prose together with bread and cheese." Quoted in John Bradshaw's biographical introduction to *The Poetical Works of Thomas Gray,* p. 30.

84. CS to GSH, Palazzo Giustiniani, Venice, 29 Sept. 1839, PCS 62/ 422–423.

85. CS to Simon Greenleaf, Convent of Palazzuola, 27 July 1839, PCS 65/ 669; CS to GSH, Convent of Palazzuola, 26 July 1839, PCS 62/ 403; Pierce II: 97; CS to Richard Henry Wilde, Venice, 28 Sept. 1839, PCS 65/ 689; Edward L. Tucker, "Charles Sumner and Richard Henry Wilde," *Georgia Historical Quarterly,* XLIX(iii) (Sept. 1965): 320–323; CS to GSH, Palazzo Giustiniani, Venice, 29 Sept. 1839, PCS 62/ 423–422.

86. CS to GS: Berlin, 8 Jan. 1840, PCS 62/ 432, and Florence, 6 Sept. 1839, PCS 62/ 414.

87. W. W. Story quoted in Pierce II: 95; Dearinger, "American Neoclassical Sculptors," pp. 370, 405; Tyack, *George Ticknor,* pp. 71–72, 88; Baker, *Fortunate Pilgrims,* pp. 27–30, 143, 149–150; Lauretta Dimmick, "A Catalogue of the Portrait Busts and Ideal Works of Thomas Crawford [. . .]" (Diss., University of Pittsburgh, 1986), pp. 4–5, 19; Seidler, "William Wetmore Story," p. 83.

88. GSH, articles on art from the 1830's, quoted in Dearinger, "American Neoclassical Sculptors," pp. 542–547; Dimmick, "Thomas Crawford," pp. 4–5, 19.

89. W. W. Story quoted in Pierce I: 105; Dearinger, "American Neoclassical Sculptors," p. 403; Seidler, "William Wetmore Story," pp. 17, 21–22, 46–47, 78–79, 83; CS to Thomas G. Appleton, Boston, 20 Nov. 1837, PCS 65/ 310–311; CS to Chester Harding, Boston, 20 Nov. 1837, PCS 65/ 314–315; CS to W. W. Story, Boston, 20 Nov. 1837, PCS 65/ 316–318, and others.

90. Seidler, "William Wetmore Story," pp. 82–83; Dimmick, "Thomas Crawford," pp. 20–23, 28, 137, 547, 551–555; CS to GSH, Palazzuola, 26 July 1839, PCS 62/ 404; Baker, *Fortunate Pilgrims,* pp. 125–127.

91. CS to GSH, Palazzuola, 26 July 1839, PCS 62/ 404; CS to HWL, Convent of Palazzuola, 26 July 1839, PCS 65/ 667; William F. Frick to CS, Baltimore, 16 July 1840, PCS 2/ 537; CS to George W. Greene: Florence, 11 Sept. 1839, in Pierce II: 110, and Berlin, 30 Dec. 1839, PCS 66/ 017; CS to W. W. Story, Rome, 6 July 1839, PCS 65/ 661.

92. CS to GSH, Palazzuola, 26 July 1839, PCS 62/ 404; CS to George W. Greene: 30 Dec. 1839, PCS 66/ 017, and London, 30 Mar. 1840, PCS 66/ 027–028.

93. CS to GSH, Venice, 29 Sept. 1839, PCS 62/ 424; Horatio Greenough to CS, Florence, 16 Nov. 1839, PCS 2/ 378–379.

94. Horatio Greenough to CS, Florence, 16 Nov. 1839, PCS 2/ 378–379 (repeating Sumner's advice to himself).

95. Ibid.; CS to Horatio Greenough, Boston, 28 Feb. 1841, copy, PCS 62/ 476–477.

96. SGH to CS, Paris, 12 (& 17) June 1844, typescript, PCS 67/ 177; CPS to T. B. Curtis, 20 Sept. 1832, in Letterbook III (1832–1837), p. 30, in CPS Papers [box 2], MHS; CS to GS, on board packet *Albany,* 8 Dec. [1837], PCS 62/ 152–153; CS to his Mother, Paris, 8 Mar. 1838 [misdated 1837], PCS 62/ 116; GS to Henry Sumner, Washington, 25 Sept. 1837, Miscellaneous Bound Manuscripts, MHS.

97. CPS to GS, in Letterbook IV (1837–1839), p. 70, CPS Papers [box 3], MHS; CS to GS, Florence, 6 Sept. 1839, PCS 62/ 414; GS to Mary Sumner, Copenhagen, 1 May 1838, Miscellaneous Manuscripts, MHS; Loring, *Boston Orators,* pp. 331–332.

98. George W. Greene to CS, Rome, 19 Nov. 1840, PCS 2/ 623–624; CS to Simon Greenleaf, Convent of Palazzuola, 27 July 1839, PCS 65/ 668; CS to GS, Berlin, 8 Jan. 1840, PCS 62/ 433; Theodore S. Fay to CS, Berlin, 31 Oct. 1840, PCS 2/ 598–599.

99. CS to Simon Greenleaf, Palazzuola, 27 July 1839, PCS 65/ 669; Edward Everett to CS, Boston, 20 May 1839, PCS 2/ 345–344; CCF to CS, Cambridge, 29 Apr. 1839, PCS 2/ 337; Henry R. Cleveland to CS, Burlington, 2 May 1839, typescript, PCS 65/ 645; CS to GSH, Rome, 13 July 1839, PCS 62/ 401. As Pierce points out (I: 29): "In length of life, [Sheriff Sumner] and his son Charles differed less than one month." Needless to say, I disagree with David Donald's suggestion (I: 72) that Sumner reacted "coolly" to his father's death. Sumner and his father did not have a happy relationship, but it was, if anything, too heavily weighted with unhappy emotions rather than cool. Donald's suggestion here is in keeping with his opinion (I: 7) that Sumner reacted "coolly" to the deaths of other family members as well, especially that of his sister Matilda. The letter on which Donald bases this interpretation, however, clearly shows Sumner's sensitivity and consideration for another's grief. See the discussion in chapter II: note 19 above.

100. CS to Simon Greenleaf, Palazzuola, 27 July 1839, PCS 65/ 669; CS to GSH, Rome, 13 July 1839, PCS 62/ 401.

101. CS to JS, Venice, 24 Sept. 1839, PCS 62/ 420–421; CS to GSH, Venice, 29 Sept. 1839, PCS 62/ 422.

102. CS to GSH, London, 16 (&c) Feb. 1839, PCS 62/ 353; CS to JS, Venice, 24 Sept. 1839, PCS 62/ 420–421; CS to Henry R. Cleveland, Florence, 27 Aug. 1839, PCS 65/ 674.

103. CS to JS: Venice, 24 Sept. 1839, PCS 62/ 420–421, and Heidelberg, 10 Feb. 1840, PCS 62/ 436–437; D. W. Howe, *Unitarian Conscience,* p. 263.

104. CS to JS: Venice, 24 Sept. 1839, PCS 62/ 420–421, and Heidelberg, 10 Feb. 1840, PCS 62/ 436–437.

105. CS to George W. Greene, Munich, 18 Oct. 1839 [misdated Sept.], PCS 66/ 006; CS to Mrs. Sarah Cleveland, Boston, 31 Jan. 1845, PCS 67/ 248.

106. CS to Simon Greenleaf, London, 21 Jan. 1839, PCS 62/ 329; CS to Henry R. Cleveland, Athenæum Club, 1 Jan. 1839, PCS 65/ 559–560; CS to HWL, Vienna, 10 Nov. 1839, PCS 66/ 009.

107. CS to Henry R. Cleveland: Florence, 27 Aug. 1839, PCS 65/ 674–675, and Athenæum Club, 1 Jan. 1839, PCS 65/ 560; CS to George W. Greene, Munich, 18 Sept. 1839, PCS 66/ 006; CS to HWL, Vienna, 10 Nov. 1839, PCS 66/ 009.

IV. De Profundis

1. Pierce II: 147.

2. CS to JS, Paris, 7 Feb. 1838, typescript, PCS 65/ 375; CS to GS, Florence, 6 Sept. 1839, PCS 62/ 413.

3. Walter Muir Whitehill, *Boston: A Topographical History,* 2d ed. (1968), pp. 73–94, 105–112; Allen Chamberlain, *Beacon Hill* (1925), chs. I–III, passim.

4. Pierce II: 159–160. See, for example, Theodore S. Fay to CS, Berlin, 23 Sept. 1840, PCS 2/ 572; Joseph Parkes to CS: Reform Club, 30 June 1840, PCS 2/ 528–529, and Cologne, 1 Sept. 1840, PCS 2/ 561; Charles R. Vaughn to CS, Oxford, 2 Nov. 1840, PCS 2/ 604–605; J. Randolph Clay to CS, Heitzing near Vienna, 22 Aug. 1840, PCS 2/ 549–550.

5. W. W. Story quoted in Seidler, "William Wetmore Story," p. 84; Pierce II: 148.

6. CS to HWL, London, Alfred Club, 15 June 1838, PCS 65/ 460; Tyack, *George Ticknor,* pp. 164, 180; Henry Adams, *The Education of Henry Adams* (1918), p. 30.

7. Frances W. Gregory, *Nathan Appleton* (1975), pp. 303–304; CS to NA: 4 Court Street, Monday [July? 1841], PCS 66/ 167, and 4 Aug. [1841], PCS 66/ 169; Tyack, *George Ticknor,* pp. 157, 183–185; CS to GS, Cambridge, 18 Apr. 1841, PCS 62/ 480–481; Charles S. Daveis to CS, 21 May 1840, PCS 2/ 508.

8. CS to JS, on board the Steamer *Robert Morris,* Sunday, 3 Dec. 1837, PCS 65/ 339–340; CS to FL, Boston, 11 Sept. 1837, PCS 62/ 131; CS to John Quincy Adams, Boston, 4 Court Street, 16 Oct. 1840, PCS 66/ 081–082.

9. HWL to George W. Greene, Cambridge, (2 &) 5 Jan. 1840, in *Letters of Longfellow,* II: 203; CS to Julia Sumner, Astor House, 7 Dec. 1837, copy, PCS 65/ 344–345; CS to GS, Boston, 6 & 8 July 1842, PCS 62/ 545–547. See also CS to Horace Sumner, Paris, 21 Apr. 1838, PCS 62/ 172, and CS to SGH, Athenæum, Monday, [c. 1842], PCS 62/ 084–085. The microfilm dates the letter to Howe as "c. 1835." Sumner and Howe did not meet, however, until 1837, and their intimate friendship did not begin until after Sumner had returned from Europe. The tone of this letter is much more in keeping with Sumner's letters from the period of 1842 and 1843, and closely parallels his letter to George of 6 & 8 July 1842.

10. Charlemagne Tower to CS, Waterville, New York, 23 Feb. 1841, PCS 2/ 685–686; CS to GS, Boston, 6 & 8 July 1842, PCS 62/545–547; Pierce I: 153–154.

11. CS to FL, Boston, 6 July 1840, PCS 62/ 453; P.S. by GSH in CS to Sarah Perkins Cleveland, Boston, 4 Court Street, 23 Sept. 1840, PCS 66/ 075; CS to Henry R. Cleveland, 4 Court Street, 23 Sept. 1840, PCS 66/ 062.

12. CS to Jane Sumner, Washington, 4 Mar. 1834, PCS 62/ 043–042. David Donald (1: 38) gives a severely distorted view of Sumner's letter to his sister Jane, and thus of Sumner's views on female education and on the ideal relationship between a husband and wife. Speaking of marriage Donald says that Sumner "thought a woman should know her role. 'A female's place is at home,' he somewhat heavily instructed his young sister Jane when she was but fourteen years old, 'not abroad in the excited scenes of the world,' and her principal charm should be the ability 'to listen intelligently.'" This reading contradicts the words of the original letter.

13. George B. Emerson to CS, Pemberton Square, 28 Jan. 1844, PCS 3/ 645; Mrs. John Hastings *née* Julia Sumner [Oct. 1874], in Pierce II: 157–158.

14. George B. Emerson to CS, Pemberton Square, 28 Jan. 1844, PCS 3/ 645–646.

15. CS to his Mother, Vienna, 31 Oct. 1839, PCS 62/ 427.

16. GS to Henry Sumner, 16 rue de la Paix, Paris, 1 Nov. 1844, R. C. Waterston Autograph Collection, MHS.

17. CS to GS: Cambridge, 18 (& 29) Apr. 1841, PCS 62/ 481, and (in Mary's hand), Boston, 15 July 1844, PCS 63/ 025–026, and Boston, 15 May 1844, PCS 63/ 012–013.

18. Charlemagne Tower to CS, Waterville, New York, 23 Feb. 1841, PCS 2/ 684–686.

19. Ibid.

20. Ibid.; CS to GS, (14 Sept. &) 16 Oct. 1842, PCS 62/ 567. In many ways, the discussion between Sumner and Tower parallels the thesis argued by Ronald Story in his study of Harvard at this time, except that they never suggest that President Quincy's reforms were made for the purpose of turning Harvard into a class-oriented institution. Sumner himself, though he favored educational reforms and the creation of an educated class, would have rejected the idea of limiting Harvard in any way to the service of any particular social class. See Ronald Story, *The Forging of an Aristocracy.*

21. CS to GSII, Convent of Palazzuola, 26 July 1839, PCS 62/ 404.

22. Ibid.; George W. Greene to CS, Rome, 31 Mar. 1841, PCS 66/ 147; Dearinger, "American Neoclassical Sculptors," p. 437; Dimmick, "Thomas Crawford," p. 563.

23. Dimmick, "Thomas Crawford," pp. 576–577, 662–663; Thomas Crawford to CS, 16 Mar. 1843, PCS 3/ 230.

24. Thomas Crawford to CS, Rome, 3 Nov. 1842, PCS 3/ 393; CS to Thomas Crawford, Boston, 1 Aug. 1843, in Pierce II: 265.

25. CS to Rev. George Putnam, Boston, —— Apr. 1848, PCS 63/ 245; Charles K. Whipple to CS, Boston, 7 July 1845, PCS 4/ 349–350; CS to FL, 5 Sept. 1842, PCS 62/ 563; CS to Francis Wayland, Boston, 30 May 1845, PCS 67/ 289–290.

26. CS, article in the Boston *Courier,* 25 Feb. 1843; Harold Schwartz, *Samuel Gridley Howe* (1956), pp. 98–100; David Gollaher, *Voice for the Mad* (1995), pp. 137–139, 160–162.

27. George M. Dennison, *The Dorr War* (1976), chs. III and IV.

28. CS to FL, Boston, 27 June 1842, PCS 62/ 543; CS to GS, Boston, 13 June 1842, PCS 62/ 541.

29. CS, "The Mutiny of the Somers," *North American Review,* LVII(cxx) (July 1843): 206–211, 231–236, quote from pp. 236–237.

30. Newmyer, *Joseph Story,* pp. 361–365. The case of Luther *v.* Borden was decided by the Supreme Court in 1849, four years after Story's death. The Court did not, however, probe into the issues of republican order as Story had wished, but rather let his own incomplete circuit court decision stand. See Dennison, *The Dorr War,* pp. 118, 149–154.

31. SGII to CS, Richmond, [6?] Dec. 1841, PCS 66/ 203–204; Schwartz, *Samuel Gridley Howe,* pp. 152–154; Lord Morpeth to CS: Louisville, 2 May 1842, PCS 3/ 258–259, and Cincinnati, 6 June 1841, PCS 3/ 297, and St. Louis, 12 June 1841, PCS 3/ 302; HWL to CS, 16 Oct. 1842, PCS 66/ 369. In his letter from St. Louis, Lord Morpeth expressed relief at the receipt of a letter from Dr. Channing, "unconfiscated by the P.O."

32. Theodore Sedgwick to CS, New York, 11 Oct. 1842, PCS 3/ 382; Maria Weston Chapman

NOTES TO CHAPTER IV

(Mrs. Henry Grafton Chapman) to CS, 39 Summer Street, 24 Sept. [1842], PCS 3/ 375–376; CS to Maria Weston Chapman, 4 Court Street, 30 Nov. [1842], PCS 66/ 387–388; Maria Weston Chapman to CS, [Oct.–Nov. 1843], PCS 3/ 583–582.

33. Note by CCF in CS to Samuel Ward, Boston, 4 Aug. 1842, PCS 66/ 332.

34. Pierce II: 158; CS to Samuel E. Sewall, Court Street, 16 Oct. 1840, PCS 66/ 083–084.

35. CS to John Jay, Boston, 5 June 1844, PCS 67/ 168–169; CS to Rev. Samuel May, Jr., Court Street, Tuesday [July 1840], PCS 66/ 043; CS to HWL, Court Street, Tuesday Morning [Mar. 1844], PCS 67/ 133; CS to GS, Boston, 29 Mar. 1842, PCS 62/ 534; CS to JS, 10 (& 12) Feb. 1842, PCS 66/ 244.

36. Thomas Denman to CS, Middleton, 29 Sept. 1840, PCS 66/ 067–068; CS to Lord Brougham, Boston, 15 May 1844, PCS 67/ 163–164; CS to Henry R. Cleveland, Court Street, 28 Nov. 1842, PCS 66/ 379–380.

37. William Ellery Channing, "Remarks on the Life and Character of Napoleon Bonaparte,"in his *Works,* I: 119; CS, "The Character of Napoleon Bonaparte," Senior Exhibition Part, 4 May 1830, pp. 2–5, *Commencement Parts.*

38. William Ellery Channing, "Remarks on [. . .] Napoleon Bonaparte," in his *Works,* I: 71, 73–76, 91–97, 118–120, 146–149, quotes from p. 149; Andrew Delbanco, *William Ellery Channing* (1981), pp. 41–42.

39. CS, "The Character of Napoleon Bonaparte," pp. 2–5, *Commencement Parts.*

40. CS to GS, 14 Sept. 1842, PCS 62/ 567.

41. CS to GS, Boston, 29 Mar. 1842, PCS 62/ 534. David Donald slights the relationship between Sumner and Channing by saying vaguely that "it is difficult to explain the enormous influence" of Channing on the young people of Sumner's generation, and then discussing his "frail" constitution and unprepossessing appearance, and likewise by saying, erroneously, that Sumner discovered a liking for Channing only after learning that the minister had a good reputation in Europe. See Donald I: 99–100.

42. William Ellery Channing, "Remarks on the Slavery Question in a Letter to Jonathan Phillips, Esq.," in his *Works,* V: 60, 96–97, and "Remarks on the Character and Writings of John Milton," *Works,* I: 23–25. For a detailed and compelling discussion of Channing's increasing disillusionment and his reconsideration of his views in the light of the response to his antislavery attitudes, see Delbanco, *William Ellery Channing,* pp. 131–150.

43. William Ellery Channing, "Remarks on the Slavery Question [. . .]," in his *Works,* V: 81, 97–99, 105, and "A Discourse Occasioned by the Death of the Rev. Dr. Follen," *Works,* V: 231–260.

44. CS to GS, Boston, 14 Sept. 1842, PCS 62/ 567.

45. Ibid.; CS to FL, Boston, 5 Sept. 1842, PCS 62/ 562.

46. William Ellery Channing, "Introduction," in his *Works,* I: xxx.

47. See William Ellery Channing to CS: Duncan's Island, Pennsylvania, 23 May 1842, PCS 3/ 278–279, and Wilkesbarre, 4 June 1842, PCS 3/ 294; and CS to William Ellery Channing, Boston, 31 May 1842, PCS 66/ 299. Once again, as he did for the relationship of Sumner to Joseph Story, David Donald (I: 100, 103–104) suggests that the relationship between Sumner and Channing was one in which Sumner merely copied his mentor. "Where Channing led, Sumner followed." Whereas the evidence shows that, despite the difference in age, both men helped and influenced each other.

48. Wiecek, *Antislavery Constitutionalism,* pp. 92–93, 97; David Eltis, *Economic Growth and the Ending of the Transatlantic Slave Trade* (1987), pp. 86–87; CS to GSH, New York, 24 Jan. 1841, PCS 62/ 471.

49. CS to GS: Boston, 29 Mar. 1842, PCS 62/ 533–534, and Boston, 6 July 1842, PCS 62/ 546–545.

50. CS, "Right of Search on the Coast of Africa," (second article), Boston *Daily Advertiser,* 10 Feb. 1842, p. 1, columns 2 and 3.

51. Richards, *Congressman John Quincy Adams,* pp. 100–101; Chancellor James Kent to CS, New York, 7 Jan. 1842, PCS 3/ 171; CS to JS, Boston, 31 Jan. 1842, PCS 66/ 233; CS to GS, Boston, 29 Mar. 1842, PCS 62/ 534; JS to CS, Washington, 20 July 1842, PCS 3/ 215.

52. Daniel Webster to Edward Everett, Minister to the Court of St. James, Department of State, Washington, 29 Jan. 1842 (the *Creole* letter), in [Daniel Webster], *Diplomatic Papers,* ed. Kenneth Shewmaker et al., (Series III of *The Papers of Daniel Webster,* ed. Charles M. Wiltse), 1 (1983): 179; CS to Jacob Harvey, 17 Mar. 1842, PCS 62/ 531; CS to Jacob Harvey, Boston, 14 Jan. 1842, PCS 62/ 521–522.

53. Wiecek, *Antislavery Constitutionalism,* pp. 31–39, quote of Cowper, from "The Task," on p. 34.

54. Wiecek, *Antislavery Constitutionalism,* pp. 40, 45–46, 195–196.

55. CS to Jacob Harvey, Boston, 14 Jan. 1842, PCS 62/ 521–522.

56. Wiecek, *Antislavery Constitutionalism,* pp. 38–39, 15–17.

57. Pierce II: 150–151; CS to HWL, Sunday Night [16 Aug. 1840?], PCS 66/ 053; CS to JS, Court Street, 31 Jan. 1843, PCS 66/ 408–409.

58. CS to John McLean, Boston, 2 Feb. 1843, PCS 66/ 411–412; CS to Richard Peters, Boston, 2 Feb. 1843, PCS 66/ 413; CS to John McLean, Boston, 7 Feb. 1843, PCS 66/ 415; CS to Henry R. Cleveland, Boston, 15 (& 17, 27) Feb. 1843, PCS 66/ 438.

59. CS to GS, Boston, 29 Mar. 1842, PCS 62/ 534.

60. McClellan, *Joseph Story,* p. 261; Wiecek, *Antislavery Constitutionalism,* pp. 99–100.

61. McClellan, *Joseph Story,* p. 261; Newmyer, *Joseph Story,* pp. 370–378; Wiecek, *Antislavery Constitutionalism,* pp. 99–100; Wendell Phillips to CS, 29 July 1851, PCS 8/ 140–143; CS to John Jay, Boston, 23 Nov. 1852, PCS 70/ 571; CS to Jacob Harvey, Boston, 17 Mar. 1842, PCS 62/ 532.

62. Joseph Story to John McPherson Berrien, 29 Apr. 1842, quoted in McClellan, *Joseph Story,* pp. 262–263.

63. For Sumner's pronouncements and conclusions about the Prigg case in the early 1850's see his "Freedom National, Slavery Sectional," in *Recent Speeches and Addresses* (1856), p. 124, his "The Powers of a State over the Militia," in *Recent Speeches,* pp. 193–194, 200–201, and his "The Duties of Massachusetts at the Present Crisis," in *Recent Speeches,* p. 405.

64. Pierce III (1893): 10; Donald I: 93–94; Tyack, *George Ticknor,* pp. 185–186. In private, Sumner invariably referred over the years to Ticknor as "vindictive, venomous & wicked" toward others, and as failing to do productive work. When, in 1864, it came to drawing up lists for a proposed National Academy of Literature, however, Sumner included Ticknor's name among possible members in recognition for his work on Spanish literature and in the establishment of the Boston Public Library. See, e.g., CS to George Bancroft, Boston, 3 July 1849, PCS 68/ 614–613; CS to Horace Mann, Boston, 5 Aug. 1850, PCS 69/ 305; CS to Mrs. Charles Francis Adams *née* Abigail Brooks, Stuttgart, 7 Nov. 1858, PCS 73/ 281–282; CS to FL, Senate Chamber, 3 Feb. 1864, PCS 64/ 299. Liberal-minded friends shared Sumner's estimate of Ticknor's character. HWL to CS, 17 Dec. 1858, PCS 73/ 305; SGH to CS, Newport, 20 Aug. 1859, PCS 73/ 473.

65. CS to FL, Boston, 29 Jan. 1844, PCS 62/ 618. David Donald (I: 93–94) leaves an unclear impression of the difference between Sumner and Ticknor, admitting "the essential justice of Sumner's characterization" of Ticknor, yet trying to portray the break as Sumner's fault. "Lonely and discouraged, Sumner grew increasingly sensitive." Donald argues: "Soon Sumner convinced himself that he was surrounded by dangerous enemies in Boston society. Though he had been an intimate of the Ticknors since his return from Europe, he came to think, for reasons that are not at all clear, that Ticknor had 'a peculiar prejudice and ill will' toward him. Once Sumner suspected a slight, he magnified every occurrence, real or fancied, into an insult. The turn of a phrase in conversation, the casual laughter that might drift out as he entered one of Ticknor's soirees would be enough to persuade him that there was a conspiracy against him." Ticknor's character and use of social ostracism as a weapon of social conformity were well known at the time, however, and even

Ticknor's recent biographer, David Tyack, has no trouble understanding the cause of their es-
trangement, justifying Sumner's remarks against Ticknor in terms of Ticknor's high-handedness
and "reproachful[ness]." See Tyack, *George Ticknor*, pp. 185–186.

66. CS to Horace Sumner, Boston, 14 Apr. 1842, PCS 62/ 535–536; Nason, p. 58. See, e.g., CS
to Edward Lillie Pierce, Senate Chamber, 28 Dec. 1852, PCS 63/ 591; CS to William Henry Seward,
Boston, 15 Aug. 1860, PCS 74/ 213.

67. Pierce II: 156; Edward Wagenknecht, *Longfellow: A Full-Length Portrait* (1955), p. 144, 82–
83; Edward Wagenknecht, *Henry Wadsworth Longfellow: Portrait of an American Humanist* (1966),
p. 13.

68. Wagenknecht, *Longfellow Humanist*, pp. 52–53, 144; Rufus Griswold to CS, Philadelphia,
28 July 1842, PCS 3/ 332; HWL to Samuel Ward, Cambridge, 11 Oct. 1840, in *Letters of Longfellow*,
II: 256, and to Stephen Longfellow, Cambridge, 21 Mar. 1841, in *Letters of Longfellow*, II: 291; CS to
GS, Cambridge, 18 Apr. 1841, PCS 62/ 480; Pierce II: 247, 156; Donald I: 86.

69. Stearns, *Cambridge Sketches*, pp. 63–64; Pierce I: 161.

70. Wagenknecht, *Longfellow Humanist*, pp. 15, 33–35; Lawrence Roger Thompson, *Young
Longfellow* (1938), p. 231; HWL to his sisters, L'Ariccia, 1 Sept. 1828, in *Letters of Longfellow*, I: 279.

71. Wagenknecht, *Longfellow Humanist*, pp. 21–22, 25–27, 40–41, 54; HWL to George W.
Greene in 1877, quoted in Wagenknecht, *Longfellow Humanist*, p. 22; Hilen, ed., *Letters of Longfellow*, I: 10–11; HWL to Stephen Longfellow: Bowdoin, 11 Dec. 1823, in *Letters of Longfellow*, I: 63,
and Cambridge, 22 June 1840, in *Letters of Longfellow*, II: 236; CS to George W. Greene, Munich,
18 Sept. 1839, PCS 66/ 006.

72. HWL to George W. Greene in 1877, quoted in Wagenknecht, *Longfellow Humanist*, p. 22;
HWL to CS, Portland, 25 Nov. 1840, in *Letters of Longfellow*, II: 266–267.

73. HWL, *Kavanagh* (1849), ch. XX, quote on p. 115, and "Defence of Poetry," quoted in
Thompson, *Young Longfellow*, p. 173.

74. D. W. Howe, *Unitarian Conscience*, pp. 193, 195, 202–203; HWL, Journal, 9 Feb. 1846, in
Long, *Literary Pioneers*, p. 194; HWL quoted in Wagenknecht, *Longfellow Humanist*, pp. 85–86;
CS to SGH, Athenæum, Monday [c. 1842], PCS 62/ 085; HWL to Stephen Longfellow, Göttingen, 10 Mar. 1836, in *Letters of Longfellow*, I: 300–301; HWL to the Duchess of Argyll, Cambridge,
5 Apr. 1874, in *Letters of Longfellow*, V (1982): 734; Pierce II: 154.

75. Schwartz, *Samuel Gridley Howe*, pp. 1–6; Pierce I: 128–129. Howe's father owned a ropewalk
near the present Public Garden.

76. Oscar Handlin, *Boston's Immigrants* (1979), p. 187; Pierce I: 23, 162; Nason, p. 47.

77. CS to SGH, Boston, 30 July 1850, PCS 63/ 383; Schwartz, *Samuel Gridley Howe*, pp. 39, 107;
SGH to CS, Monday Evening, 9 o'clock [Apr. 1845], PCS 67/ 272; CS to SGH, Court Street, Monday [1840's], PCS 66/ 112; CS to HWL, Court Street, Monday [Mar. 1844], PCS 67/ 131–130.

78. SGH to CS: Frankfort, Ky., 1 Feb. 1842, PCS 66/ 235, and Monday Evening [Apr. 1845],
PCS 67/ 271; CS to FL, Boston, 3 June 1841, PCS 62/ 486; Pierce II: 156.

79. CS to James T. Fields, 4 Court Street, 26 Aug. 1841, PCS 66/ 174–175. For other examples
of Sumner's refusing invitations to lecture, see Charles S. Daveis to CS: Portland, 17 June 1840,
PCS 2/ 520, and 29 June 1840, PCS 2/ 524; N. L. Frothingham (for the Society for the Diffusion
of Useful Knowledge) to CS, 28 Apr. 1841, PCS 2/ 714; CS to HWL, Boston (6 &) 7 June 1842,
PCS 66/ 300.

80. CS to GS, Cambridge, 18 (& 29) Apr. 1841, PCS 62/ 480; CS to Samuel Ward: Boston,
21 Feb. 1843, PCS 66/ 426–427, and Hudson on the North River, Tuesday Evening [Oct. 1841],
PCS 66/ 189–190; CS to FL, Boston, 6 Jan. 1843, PCS 62/ 580–581.

81. Schwartz, *Samuel Gridley Howe*, pp. 103–104; CS to Henry R. Cleveland, Paris, 22 May 1838,
PCS 65/ 443–444; CS to Sarah Perkins Cleveland, Travellers' Club, 10 Mar. 1839, PCS 65/ 597; CS
to GS, Boston, 30 Nov. 1840, PCS 62/ 467.

82. CS to FL, Boston, 3 June 1841, PCS 62/ 486.

83. CS to FL: Boston, 10 Dec. 1842, PCS 62/ 468, and Boston, 8 Dec. 1842, PCS 62/ 572–573; CS to Samuel Ward, Boston, Monday [Sept. 1842], PCS 66/ 357; CS to FL, Boston: 5 Sept. 1842, PCS 62/ 563–562, and 18 July 1842, PCS 66/ 318.

84. CS to HWL: Friday [6 Aug. 1847] (& Sunday [8 Aug.]), PCS 68/ 015–017, and Boston, 15 Oct. 1842, PCS 66/ 366; CS to FL, Boston, 27 June 1842, PCS 62/ 544.

85. CS to FL, Boston: 5 Sept. 1842, PCS 62/ 563–562, and 8 Dec. 1842, PCS 62/ 575, and 13 July 1842, PCS 62/ 553.

86. HWL and CCF to CS, 29 Aug. 1840, PCS 66/ 056; CS to FL, Boston: 5 Sept. 1842, PCS 62/ 563–562, and 8 Dec. 1842, PCS 62/ 575; CS to Mrs. Henry W. Longfellow *née* Frances Elizabeth Appleton, Court Street, Friday Noon, 20 Oct. 1843, PCS 67/ 026; Miss Annie Ward to CS, 25 Jan. 1843, PCS 3/ 428.

87. Thompson, *Young Longfellow,* pp. 257–259; Wagenknecht, *Longfellow Humanist,* pp. 12–13, 163, 167–168.

88. Thompson, *Young Longfellow,* pp. 315, 320–321, 323–328; Wagenknecht, *Longfellow Full-Length,* p. 224; CS to HWL, Convent of Palazzuola, 26 July 1839, PCS 65/ 666–667; CS to FL, Boston, 8 Dec. 1842, PCS 62/ 573.

89. Rufus Griswold to CS, [Philadelphia, 28 July 1842], PCS 3/ 332; CS to HWL, Court Street, 23 Apr. [1842], PCS 66/ 277; HWL to CS, 1842, quoted in Wagenknecht, *Longfellow Humanist,* pp. 16–17.

90. CS to FL, Boston, 11 (& 12 & 13) July 1843, PCS 62/ 586–587; CS to Samuel Ward, Court Street, 20 July 1843, PCS 66/ 532.

91. CS to SGH, 31 Aug. 1843, PCS 62/ 593; CS to HWL, Boston, 10 (& 14) July 1842, PCS 66/ 316.

92. Pierce I: 33; II: 157; CS to GS, Boston, 15 Oct. 1844, PCS 63/ 062–061; Fanny Longfellow to CS, Astor House, 13 Oct. 1843, PCS 67/ 015; CS to John Jay, Boston, 6 Apr. 1844, PCS 67/ 135; Mrs. Angel (Frances) Calderón de la Barca to CS, Chestnut Street, 13 Feb. 1843, PCS 3/ 438–439.

93. CS to FL: Boston, 20 Jan. 1842, PCS 62/ 525, and Boston, 6 Jan. 1843, PCS 62/ 580; CS to Henry R. Cleveland, Boston, 15 Feb. 1843, PCS 66/ 435; William H. Prescott to CS, Wednesday Morning [1 Mar. 1843], PCS 3/ 447.

94. CS to FL, Boston, 12 Sept. 1843, PCS 62/ 599, and Boston, 6 Oct. 1843, PCS 62/ 603; CS to GS, Boston, 1 June 1844, PCS 63/ 018; CS to SGH, Boston, 30 Apr. 1844, PCS 67/ 144–145.

95. I base the idea that Sumner kept recurring to what his father must have said to him before his trip to Europe upon the frequent repetition in Sumner's writings after that date of references to Thomas Brown's theory that the life of man is naturally divided into seven-year periods, of which "the grand climacteric" falls at the age of sixty-three. This was the age Sumner's father had long assigned as the time of his death, and he himself had based this idea upon Thomas Brown. The first time Sumner referred to this idea was precisely in his article on the number seven, published in April 1844, the unusual nature of which puzzled contemporaries and later writers alike. CS, "The Number 'Seven'," *The Law Reporter,* VI(xii) (Apr. 1844): 529–541.

96. CS to Jonathan C. Perkins: Boston, 7 Feb. 1844, PCS 63/ 001–002, and Boston, 9 Apr. 1844, PCS 63/ 009. Little and Brown offered $2,000 for the editing of Vesey. See Pierce II: 282.

97. Peleg W. Chandler to CS [Mar. 1844], PCS 3/ 685–686; George Gibbs to CS, New York, 21 Mar. 1844, PCS 3/ 679; Little and Brown to CS, 112 Washington Street, 2 Apr. 1844, PCS 3/ 693; CCF to CS: Cambridge, 2 Apr. 1844, PCS 3/ 691, and 10 Apr. 1844, PCS 3/ 694–695.

98. CS to SGH, Boston, 16 Aug. 1844, PCS 67/ 190–191.

99. Ibid.

V. *The True Grandeur of Civilization*

1. CS, *The True Grandeur of Nations,* from the 2d Boston ed. (1846), p. 6. Citations are from this edition except as noted otherwise.

2. CS to SGH, Pittsfield, 11 Sept. 1844, PCS 63/ 046; Stanley K. Schultz, *The Culture Factory* (1973), pp. 126–128, 132–133. For Sumner's earlier private support of Horace Mann's educational activities see, for example, CS to Horace Mann, London, 13 Mar. 1839, PCS 65/ 598–599, and CS to GS, Boston, 14 (& 16) Sept. 1842, PCS 62/ 567.

3. Schultz, *Culture Factory,* p. 139; Michael B. Katz, *The Irony of Early School Reform* (1970), p. 152; Pierce II: 324–325; Donald I: 101–103. Once again, David Donald reduces his explanation of Sumner's motivation to the mere copying of a friend. In the case of education reform that friend is Samuel Gridley Howe, as in law it is Joseph Story, and in ethics William Ellery Channing. This leaves the question of Sumner's real motivation untouched, and his frequent allusions, especially in the early 1840's, to his struggle with the question of duty untapped.

4. Pierce II: 326–328; Donald I: 102–103.

5. Teeters and Shearer, *The Prison at Philadelphia,* pp. ix, 200, 205.

6. Ibid., pp. vii, ix, 203, 205–209; W. David Lewis, *From Newgate to Dannemora* (1965), pp. 107–110, 178, 220, 227–228.

7. CS to FL, Boston, 8 Dec. 1842, PCS 62/ 572–574; CS to Francis Wayland, Boston, 30 May 1845, PCS 67/ 289–290; CS to FL, Boston, 3 June 1845, PCS 63/ 082; Pierce III: 80; Teeters and Shearer, *The Prison at Philadelphia,* pp. 208–209; Lewis, *From Newgate to Dannemora,* pp. 227–228.

8. CS to JS, Boston, 5 Feb. 1845, PCS 63/ 072; CS to RCW, Boston, 15 Mar. 1846, PCS 67/ 426–427; Dimmick, "Thomas Crawford," pp. 111–112. Amos A. Lawrence had met Crawford in his Roman studio in the spring of 1840, shortly after Sumner's visit there, and had been likewise impressed by the sculptor's ability. Amos A. Lawrence to Amos Lawrence, Rome, 16 Apr. 1840, in William Lawrence, *Life of Amos A. Lawrence* (1888), pp. 37–38.

9. CS to Thomas Crawford, 17 Apr. 1845, in Pierce II: 332.

10. CS to GS, Boston, 1 June 1845, PCS 63/ 080; Dearinger, "American Neoclassical Sculptors," pp. 386–387; CS to GS, Boston, 18 Feb. 1850, PCS 63/ 334–335. The Athenæum is still located in the Beacon Street building erected in the 1840's. To its later regret, however, the institution commissioned Edward Clarke Cabot in 1889 to redesign the foyer and remove the grand staircase in order to make room for more stacks.

11. Charles Sellers, *James K. Polk: Continentalist* (1966), pp. 48–55, 67–76, 99–100, 110–112, 128, 170–172; Kinley J. Brauer, *Cotton versus Conscience* (1967), ch. III. In a recent book, Michael Morrison argues that fear of a Slave Power Conspiracy did not become important until the 1850's, and that the debate over the annexation of Texas focused instead on the issue of westward expansion and its expected consequences for the ideals of freedom and equality inherited from the American Revolution. Morrison does not discuss the fact that slavery as well as expansion raised serious questions for anyone concerned about the ideals of the Revolution, however, nor does he make clear that the annexation of Texas and the Mexican War turned many Northerners toward antislavery or free soil before the 1850's. In suggesting that North and South shared precisely the same culture and ideals and that the institution of slavery was the only difference between them Morrison, I believe, overlooks the seminal influence of slavery upon Southern culture as well as the depth of philosophical opposition to slavery in New England. See Michael A. Morrison, *Slavery and the American West* (1997), for example pp. 1–12, 14, 16–22, 25, 31–34, 44, 81, 98.

12. Brauer, *Cotton versus Conscience,* pp. 62–63, 65–66, 68–80; Sellers, *James K. Polk,* pp. 133–136; CS to GS, Boston, 30 Sept. 1845, PCS 63/ 095; CS to Richard Monckton Milnes, Boston, 1 May 1844, PCS 67/ 151.

13. Sellers, *James K. Polk,* pp. 108, 145–161, 168, quote on p. 159.

14. Brauer, *Cotton versus Conscience,* pp. 105–112; Thomas H. O'Connor, *Lords of the Loom* (1968), pp. 63–64; RCW, "The Annexation of Texas" (6 Jan. 1845), in RCW, *Addresses and Speeches on Various Occasions* (1852), pp. 438–459, esp. pp. 441–442, 459.

15. Martin Duberman, *Charles Francis Adams* (1960), p. 29; Gatell, *John Gorham Palfrey,* pp. 12–13, 18–19, 30, 79ff., 121–126; Schwartz, *Samuel Gridley Howe,* pp. 155, 170–171.

16. Richard H. Abbott, *Cobbler in Congress* (1972), pp. 3–4, 24–25.

17. Brauer, *Cotton versus Conscience,* pp. 115–124; Donald I: 136; Pierce III: 101–102; *Daily Advertiser,* 30 Jan. 1845; CS to Sarah Cleveland, Boston, 31 Jan. 1845, PCS 67/ 251.

18. CS to Sarah Cleveland, Boston, 31 Jan. 1845, PCS 67/249; Sellers, *James K. Polk,* 205–208.

19. Brauer, *Cotton versus Conscience,* pp. 103–104, 64, 68–72; O'Connor, *Lords of the Loom,* pp. 63–64; Sellers, *James K. Polk,* pp. 172–173, 206–208; RCW, "The Annexation of Texas," *Addresses and Speeches,* pp. 441–442, 446–459.

20. O'Connor, *Lords of the Loom,* pp. 64–71, quoting Ralph Waldo Emerson, p. 67; Sellers, *James K. Polk,* p. 172.

21. Brauer, *Cotton versus Conscience,* pp. 122–123; Duberman, *Charles Francis Adams,* pp. 104–105.

22. CS to JS, 5 Feb. 1845, PCS 63/ 072; CS to Sarah Cleveland, Boston, 31 Jan. 1845, PCS 67/ 251; CS to Wendell Phillips, Court Street, 4 Feb. 1845, PCS 67/ 256–257.

23. CS to Wendell Phillips, Court Street, 4 Feb. 1845, PCS 67/ 254–256.

24. Pierce II: 338–340.

25. CS to Rev. George Putnam, Boston, —— Apr. 1848, PCS 63/ 244–245; CS to James T. Fields, 4 Court Street, 26 Aug. 1841, PCS 66/ 174–175; CCF to HWL, Cambridge, Saturday, 9 Aug. 1845, [bMS Am 1340.2 (1941)], by permission of the Houghton Library, Harvard University (hereafter cited as CCF-HWL Letters); Donald I: 106–108. "Inexplicably," says Donald, Sumner refused the Mayor's first invitation to speak, but Sumner had made clear, in numerous refusals to speak all through the early 1840's, his fear of not being up to the task of an important address. See chapter IV above.

26. Pierce II: 340–341; Donald I: 108; On Fourth of July orations generally see, for example, Jean Matthews, *Rufus Choate* (1980), pp. 42–50; D. W. Howe, *American Whigs,* pp. 25–28; and Ferguson, *Law and Letters,* pp. 78–81. City Hall was at the time in the old Court House on the same site as the present Old City Hall.

27. Pierce II: 341–342.

28. Ibid., p. 342.

29. [CCF], "Sumner's Oration," *Christian Examiner and Religious Miscellany,* XXXIX (Fourth Series, IV[iii]) (Nov. 1845): 409–410; E. T. Channing, *Lectures,* p. 69.

30. Pierce II: 340; CS, *The True Grandeur of Nations,* pp. 5–6.

31. CS to the Rev. George Putnam, —— Apr. 1848, in another's hand, PCS 63/ 244–245; CS, *The True Grandeur of Nations,* p. 8.

32. D. W. Howe, *Unitarian Conscience,* pp. 57–59, 116; D. W. Howe, *American Whigs,* pp. 158–160; CS, *The True Grandeur of Nations,* pp. 12–13.

33. CS, *The True Grandeur of Nations* (1846), pp. 12–13, and in *Works,* I(1875): 13.

34. Arthur Brown, *Always Young for Liberty,* pp. 215–216; CS, *The True Grandeur of Nations, Works,* I: 115. Compare the 1846 ed., p. 70.

35. CS, "Prisons and Prison Discipline," *Christian Examiner and Religious Miscellany,* XL (Fourth Series, V[i]) (Jan. 1846): 130–131, 137, and Notice of *On Punishments and Prisons* (. . .), *The Law Reporter,* VIII(x) (Feb. 1846): 477; Teeters and Shearer, *The Prison at Philadelphia,* pp. 114, 202, 205–206, 210–211, 216–218; Lewis, *From Newgate to Dannemora,* pp. 227–228, 276.

36. CS, *The True Grandeur of Nations,* pp. 65–66. Sumner never became deeply involved in the efforts to improve the lot of the insane in Massachusetts, but he followed the debate with interest. In the early 1840's the question was being much discussed in both reforming and legal circles.

Dorothea Dix was then beginning her campaign to end the placement of the indigent insane in prisons, and Sumner was simultaneously aware of the issue through his legal work. Dr. Isaac Ray of Maine, a leading medical superintendent, wrote a number of works arguing that the insane should not be treated as criminals by the law. Sumner published several of his articles in the *Jurist* as well as giving him friendly reviews in *The Law Reporter.* Schwartz, *Samuel Gridley Howe*, pp. 98–102; Gollaher, *Voice for the Mad,* pp. 134–139, 141–142, 154–158, 161; Sumner's notice of a report on the insane by Dr. Ray, *The Law Reporter,* VI (Mar. 1844): 521.

37. CS, *The True Grandeur of Nations,* pp. 28–43, quotes from pp. 9, 40, 74.

38. Ibid., pp. 74–76.

39. NA to CS, Pittsfield, 11 Aug. 1845, PCS 4/ 382–383; CS to NA, Boston, 18 Aug. 1845, PCS 67/ 317–318; CS, *The True Grandeur of Nations,* pp. 46–54, quote from p. 51.

40. *The True Grandeur of Nations,* pp. 68–70; CS to GS, Boston, 26 Aug. 1844, PCS 63/ 033.

41. CS, *The True Grandeur of Nations,* pp. 10–11, 23–28, 82.

42. Ibid., pp. 22–23, 25, 28–29, 85–88, 40, and in *Works,* I: 16, 67; CS to GS, Boston, 26 & 27 Aug. 1844, in Julia's hand, PCS 63/ 031–034, quote from frame 032.

43. CS, *The True Grandeur of Nations,* pp. 10, 12–13, 33, 51–52; Wendell Phillips to CS, [5? July 1845], PCS 4/ 375.

44. Pierce II: 355–358; Donald I: 110–111; "Celebration of the Fourth by the City Authorities," Boston *Morning Post,* 7 July 1845.

45. "Celebration of the Fourth," *Morning Post,* 7 July 1845; Pierce II: 356. For an excellent overview of the American peace movement and its religious orientation, see Valarie H. Ziegler, *The Advocates of Peace in Antebellum America* (1992), e.g., pp. 3, 12–16, 27–30, 32–37, and passim.

46. CS, *The True Grandeur of Nations,* pp. 31–35, 88–92; CS to John G. Palfrey, Thursday Evening [11? Sept. 1845], PCS 67/ 334–339, quotes from frame 335; CS to RCW, Sunday, 6 July 1845, PCS 67/ 308; CS to Wendell Phillips, Court Street, 19 Aug. 1845, PCS 67/ 319–320.

47. Ziegler, *Advocates of Peace,* pp. 26–27, 40–41, 43, 49; CS to the Rev. George Putnam, Boston, —— Apr. 1848, PCS 63/ 244–245.

48. Ziegler, *Advocates of Peace,* pp. 91, 96. Sumner did not make explicit a strategy to unite the peace movement in 1845, though he did in 1849 when he gave his address *The Commonwealth of Nations.* He felt no need to do so in 1845 because he did not anticipate the kind of misunderstanding that would greet his oration. His interest in William Ladd, however, his insistence upon themes held in common among the peace activists, and the downplaying of divisive issues all lead to the conclusion that reconciliation was a part of his intention. See CS to Amasa Walker, Boston, 11 June 1849, PCS 68/ 583–584.

49. CS to Edward Everett, Boston, 7 Sept. 1846, PCS 67/ 544; CS to SGH, Boston, 30 Apr. 1844, PCS 67/ 144 (in response to SGH to CS, Rome, 6 Mar. 1844, PCS 67/ 113–114); CS to RCW, Sunday, 6 July 1845, PCS 67/ 307–308; CS to John G. Palfrey, Thursday Evening [11? Sept. 1845], PCS 67/ 334–339, quote from frames 335–336; CS, "The Mutiny of the Somers," pp. 231–232.

50. CS, *The True Grandeur of Nations,* pp. 58–59, 56.

51. Wendell Phillips to CS, Natick, 17 Aug. 1845, PCS 4/ 409–410; CS to Wendell Phillips, Boston, 19 Aug. 1845, PCS 67/ 319; CS to Richard Henry Dana, Jr., [after 22 Aug. 1845], PCS 67/ 321–323.

52. CS to John G. Palfrey, Thursday Evening [11? Sept. 1845], PCS 67/ 334–339; CS to NA, Boston, 18 Aug. 1845, PCS 67/ 317–318; CS, *The True Grandeur of Nations,* pp. 10–11. David Donald (I: 119) implies that Sumner's ideas on nonresistance and the right of self-defense were confused and that "he was repeatedly obliged to modify his positions" in response to criticism. In fact, his positions throughout this period are perfectly consistent. He had put his opinion about self-defense on the record long before 4 July 1845. He always explicitly said that his respect for the Quakers' position was not agreement with it. His belief in the unlikelihood of the need for self-

defense among nations was based upon the present state of international relations among Western countries, not upon a rejection of the principle of self-defense.

53. Valerie Ziegler, *Advocates of Peace*, pp. 31–32, 89–105; Elihu Burritt to CS, 19 Nov. 1845, PCS 4/ 572.

54. Ziegler, *Advocates of Peace*, pp. 50–53; Stuart Joel Horn, "Edward Everett and American Nationalism" (Diss., City University of New York, 1973), pp. 44–46, 48; Gatell, *John Gorham Palfrey*, p. 26.

55. CS, *The True Grandeur of Nations*, p. 8; Horace Mann to CS, Concord, 8 Sept. 1845, PCS 4/ 466–467; John Quincy Adams to CS, Quincy, 29 Aug. 1846 [misdated 1829], PCS 5/ 226; CS to John Quincy Adams, Boston, 4 Sept. 1846, PCS 67/ 541–542; CS to John G. Palfrey, Thursday Evening [11? Sept. 1845], PCS 67/ 334–339.

56. Francis Bowen to CS, Saturday, 4 July 1846, PCS 5/ 143; [Francis Bowen,] "Critical Notices: The True Grandeur of Nations [. . .]," *North American Review*, LXI(cxxix) (Oct. 1845): 519, 521, 522–523; CS to Francis Bowen, 4 Court Street, 10 Aug. 1847, PCS 68/ 018; Francis Bowen to CS, Cambridge, 11 Aug. 1847, PCS 5/ 597; Francis Bowen to RCW, Cambridge, 10 June 1852, Winthrop Family Papers [reel 27], MHS.

57. Edward Everett to CS, Cambridge, 5 Sept. 1846, PCS 5/ 242–243; CS to Edward Everett, Boston, 7 Sept. 1846, PCS 67/ 544–545. See also James Russell Lowell to CS, Elmwood, 16 Aug. 1845, PCS 4/ 404.

58. Donald 1: 111; CS to RCW, 6 July 1845, PCS 67/ 305–307.

59. CS to RCW, 6 July 1845, PCS 67/ 305; CS, *The True Grandeur of Nations*, pp. 7–8.

60. CS, *The True Grandeur of Nations*, pp. 40–41.

61. Pierce 11: 355–356; Donald 1: 111; "Celebration of the Fourth," *Morning Post*, 7 July 1845; CS "To the Hon. Robert C. Winthrop [. . .]," *Daily Whig*, 27 Oct. 1846. This toast became very controversial, and many versions of it circulated, to Winthrop's great dismay. According to the Conscience Whigs, this version, originally published in the *Morning Post* and quoted in the article listed above, is the one Winthrop pointed to as the correct one, he himself having given the copy of it directly to the editor of the *Post*. Winthrop complained that the *Post* had put mistakes into his speech, but did not mention the toast itself. This is also the version used by Pierce, though not by Donald. Robert Winthrop's son uses this version also, though with different punctuation. See Boston *Daily Whig*, 2 Nov. 1846; RCW to John H. Clifford, Saratoga Springs, 11 July 1845, Winthrop Family Papers [reel 24], MHS; RCW, Jr., *A Memoir of Robert C. Winthrop* (1897), p. 45.

62. CS to GS, 30 Sept. 1845, PCS 63/ 095; Edward Everett to CS, Cambridge, 5 Sept. 1846, PCS 5/ 243–242; NA to CS, Pittsfield, 11 Aug. 1845, PCS 4/ 382; CS to "My dear Sir" [E. W. Bard], Boston, 5 Dec. 1845, PCS 67/ 370; CS to John C. Randall, Boston, 4 Feb. 1846, PCS 67/ 412.

63. John Quincy Adams, Diary, 13 Aug. 1845, Adams Family Papers [reel 48], MHS; Theodore Parker to CS, West Roxbury, 17 Aug. 1845, PCS 4/ 407–408; William L. Garrison to CS, Boston, 23 Aug. 1845, PCS 67/ 326; SGH to CS, 5 July 1845, PCS 67/ 304.

64. CS to James Miller McKim, Boston, 17 Nov. 1845, PCS 67/ 360.

65. JS to CS, Cambridge, 11 Aug. 1845, PCS 4/ 386–387.

66. CS to RCW, Boston, 9 Jan. 1846, PCS 67/ 396–397; JS to CS, Washington, 4 Jan. 1845, PCS 4/ 198; JS to Simon Greenleaf, Washington, 4 Jan. 1845, Simon Greenleaf Papers [box 2, folder 10], HL; Donald 1: 113.

67. CS to GS, Boston, 30 Sept. 1845, PCS 63/ 095.

68. Donald 1: 129; D. W. Howe, *Unitarian Conscience*, p. 282; Wendell Phillips to CS, Natick, 17 Aug. 1845, PCS 4/ 409; CS to Wendell Phillips, Court Street, 19 Aug. 1845, PCS 67/ 319.

69. CS, Resolutions of 4 Nov. 1845, in "The Wrong of Slavery," *Works*, 1: 150, and ["Antislavery Duties of the Whig Party,"] Boston *Courier*, 24 Sept. 1846.

70. CS, "Speech for Union Among Men of All Parties Against the Slave Power and the Extension of Slavery," *Orations and Speeches*, 11: 253–254.

71. Wiecek, *Antislavery Constitutionalism,* pp. 250–252.

72. Gilbert Osofsky, "Wendell Phillips and the Quest for a New American National Identity," *Canadian Review of Studies in Nationalism,* I (Fall 1973): 33, 35–36; Stewart, *Wendell Phillips,* pp. 120–121, 123–124.

73. Wiecek, *Antislavery Constitutionalism,* pp. 214–215, 240–241, 244–246; Stewart, *Wendell Phillips,* pp. 123–124. See also, e.g., CS to Joshua R. Giddings, 21 Dec. 1846, PCS 67/ 600–601; Joshua R. Giddings to CS, Washington City, 25 Dec. 1846, PCS 5/ 391–392; CS to Joshua R. Giddings, Boston, 30 Dec. 1846, PCS 67/ 612.

74. Stewart, *Wendell Phillips,* p. 123; [CS], Review of the *"Political Hermeneutics* [. . .]," *North American Review,* XLVI (Jan. 1838): 300–301; JS, "Law," in McClellan, *Joseph Story,* pp. 360–361. Story's article originally appeared in Lieber's *Encyclopædia Americana* in 1831.

75. Stewart, *Wendell Phillips,* pp. 123–124.

76. Ibid., p. 123; CS, "The Free-Soil Party Explained and Vindicated. Address to the People of Massachusetts, Reported to and Adopted by the Free-Soil State Convention at Worcester, September 12, 1849," in *Works,* II (1875): 293–295.

77. CS, ["Antislavery Duties of the Whig Party,"] *Courier,* 24 Sept. 1846; "Speech for Union," *Orations and Speeches,* II: 253–255.

78. Wiecek, *Antislavery Constitutionalism,* pp. 259–273; CS, "Are We a Nation?" *Works,* XII (1877): 195–197; Lysander Spooner, *The Collected Works of Lysander Spooner,* ed. Charles Shively (1971), I: 35, 39, IV: 7–12. At this time it was the states that had explicit rules governing citizenship (sometimes excluding even certain native-born groups such as blacks or women), while national citizenship, lacking any specific legal definition, was generally assumed to belong to all who had state citizenship. In Dred Scott *v.* Sanford (1857) Chief Justice Taney would deny even this, saying that blacks could not be national citizens under any circumstances, even if considered citizens of their state. This situation would be rectified by the Fourteenth Amendment. See Sumner's discussion of this problem in a letter to RCW of 9 Feb. 1843, PCS 66/ 419–420.

79. Wendell Phillips quoted in Stewart, *Wendell Phillips,* p. 124; Osofsky, "Wendell Phillips and the Quest for a New American Identity," p. 33.

80. Stewart, *Wendell Phillips,* pp. 123–124; CS, "Speech for Union," *Orations and Speeches,* II: 253–254, and ["Antislavery Duties of the Whig Party,"] *Courier,* 24 Sept. 1846.

81. CS, "Speech for Union," *Orations and Speeches,* II: 261, and *The True Grandeur of Nations,* pp. 5, 78–79; CS to Rev. George Putnam, —— Apr. 1848, PCS 63/ 245–246; CS, ["Antislavery Duties of the Whig Party,"] *Courier,* 24 Sept. 1846.

82. Wendell Phillips to CS, Sunday, 17 Feb. 1845, PCS 4/ 227; CS to Wendell Phillips, Court Street, 4 Feb. 1845, PCS 67/ 254–256.

83. CS to Wendell Phillips, Court Street, 4 Feb. 1845, PCS 67/ 254–256.

84. Ibid.; Wendell Phillips to CS, Sunday, 17 Feb. 1845, PCS 4/ 227–229. See also CS to FL, 19 Nov. 1837, PCS 62/ 138, in which Sumner not only muses on the possibility of making a legal obligation of the right to vote, but rebukes certain wealthy citizens for not exercising that right: "Their immense property was protected by the law, & yet they would not interfere or assist in the choice of the law-maker."

85. CS, "Speech against the Admission of Texas as a Slave State, Made at a Public Meeting at Faneuil Hall, Boston, Nov. 4, 1845," *Orations and Speeches,* II: 115.

86. Brauer, *Cotton versus Conscience,* pp. 125–126, 128–130; O'Connor, *Lords of the Loom,* pp. 66–71.

87. Brauer, *Cotton versus Conscience,* pp. 135–140; Gatell, *John Gorham Palfrey,* pp. 123–126; Duberman, *Charles Francis Adams,* pp. 104–105; Abbott, *Cobbler in Congress,* pp. 24–25.

88. *Daily Advertiser,* 7 Nov. 1845; CS, "The Wrong of Slavery," (4 Nov. 1845), *Works,* I: 149; Brauer, *Cotton versus Conscience,* pp. 143–149; Pierce III: 103; Donald I: 139.

89. CS, Resolutions, in "The Wrong of Slavery," *Works*, I: 149–150; *Daily Advertiser*, 7 Nov. 1845; Henry Wilson, *History of the Rise and Fall of the Slave Power in America*, I (1872): 645–646.

90. CS, "Speech against the Admission of Texas as a Slave State," *Orations and Speeches*, II: 108–109, 112–114.

91. Ibid., pp. 111–114.

92. Abbott Lawrence to CFA, Boston, 7 Nov. 1845, and NA to CFA, John G. Palfrey, and CS, Boston, 10 Nov. 1845, *Daily Advertiser*, 27 Nov. 1845; Brauer, *Cotton versus Conscience*, pp. 155–156; Henry Wilson, *Slave Power*, I: 646–647.

VI. *"The Vinegar of Party"*

1. CS, "To the Hon. Robert C. Winthrop," *Daily Whig*, 27 Oct. 1846.

2. Frederick Merk, *History of the Westward Movement* (1978), pp. 359–362; Sellers, *Market Revolution*, pp. 420–421; Justin H. Smith, *The War with Mexico* (1919), I, chs. III & IV.

3. Richards, *Congressman John Quincy Adams*, pp. 182–183, 186–187; Sellers, *James K. Polk*, pp. 406–409; John H. Schroeder, *Mr. Polk's War* (1973), pp. 4, 10; Merk, *Westward Movement*, p. 360.

4. Sellers, *James K. Polk*, pp. 400–409, 422, the Washington *Union* quoted on p. 408, and the war message on p. 409; Richards, *Congressman John Quincy Adams*, pp. 187–188; Schroeder, *Mr. Polk's War*, pp. 9, 11–12.

5. For public reaction to the war see Schroeder, *Mr. Polk's War*, esp. pp. 24, 33–36, 41, 90, 92.

6. O'Connor, *Lords of the Loom*, pp. 66–67; Brauer, *Cotton versus Conscience*, p. 163; CS to GS, Boston, 30 Nov. 1845, PCS 63/ 102.

7. Henry Wilson, *Slave Power*, II (1874): 115–118; Moorfield Storey and Edward W. Emerson, *Ebenezer Rockwood Hoar* (1911), pp. 43–44; Brauer, *Cotton versus Conscience*, pp. 159–163.

8. NA to CS, Pittsfield, 11 Aug. 1845, PCS 4/ 382, and 20 Aug. 1846, PCS 5/ 215–216; O'Connor, *Lords of the Loom*, pp. 73–76.

9. "Boston" [CS], *Daily Whig*, 22 July 1846; RCW, Jr., *Robert C. Winthrop*, p. 52; Newmyer, *Joseph Story*, p. 177; CS to NA, Boston, 11 Aug. 1846, PCS 67/ 515–516; CS to GS, Boston, 30 Oct. 1840, PCS 62/ 465.

10. Richards, *Congressman John Quincy Adams*, pp. 182–183; CS to RCW, Boston, 9 Jan. 1846, PCS 67/ 396–397; RCW to CS, Washington, 4 Jan. 1845, PCS 4/ 635–636; CS to GS, Boston, 30 Nov. 1845, PCS 63/ 103–102.

11. CS to RCW, Boston: 22 Dec. 1845, PCS 67/ 379–380, and 9 Jan. 1846, PCS 67/ 396–397 (including the paraphrase of Winthrop's speech of 3 January 1846); RCW to CS, Washington, 2 Feb. 1846, PCS 4/ 671.

12. CS, "To the Hon. Robert C. Winthrop," *Daily Whig*, 27 Oct. 1846, and "Mr. Winthrop's Vote on the War Bill," *Courier*, 13 Aug. 1846.

13. CS, "To the Hon. Robert C. Winthrop," *Daily Whig*, 27 Oct. 1846; Richards, *Congressman John Quincy Adams*, ch. VI, esp. pp. 153–154, 157–160, 165–168.

14. O'Connor, *Lords of the Loom*, pp. 72–73; Sellers, *James K. Polk*, pp. 416–417; Richards, *Congressman John Quincy Adams*, pp. 189–190; Schroeder, *Mr. Polk's War*, pp. 14–16, 29, 72–73.

15. CS, "Mr. Winthrop's Vote," *Courier*, 13 Aug. 1846, and "To the Hon. Robert C. Winthrop," *Daily Whig*, 27 Oct. 1846.

16. Henry Wilson, *Slave Power*, II: 115–118; Brauer, *Cotton versus Conscience*, pp. 159–165; Duberman, *Charles Francis Adams*, pp. 110–111; CFA, Diary, 19, 24, 27, 28 Jan., 4–9 Feb, 23, 28 May 1846, Adams Family Papers [reel 68], MHS.

17. Brauer, *Cotton versus Conscience*, pp. 167–169; Duberman, *Charles Francis Adams*, p. 112. Charles Francis Adams' "Sagitta Letters" against Abbott Lawrence and John Gorham Palfrey's "Papers on the Slave Power" appeared in the *Whig* from mid-June through September 1846.

18. "Mr. Winthrop and the Whig Members of Congress," *Daily Advertiser*, 27 July 1846; NA to CS, Pittsfield, 20 Aug. 1846, PCS 5/ 215–216; [CFA, CS, and Stephen C. Phillips], "Mr. Winthrop and the Daily Advertiser," *Daily Whig*, 29 July 1846; "Boston" [CS], *Daily Whig*, 22 July 1846.

19. RCW, "The Wants of the Government and the Wages of Labor" (25 June 1846), in RCW, *Addresses and Speeches*, p. 526; "Boston" [CS], *Daily Whig*, 22 July 1846.

20. CS to George Ellis, Court Street, 2 June 1846, PCS 67/ 464–465; CS to Edward L. Pierce, Senate Chamber, 30 Dec. 1852, PCS 63/ 592–593; CS, "The Powers of a State over the Militia [. . .]" *Recent Speeches*, pp. 194–195.

21. D. W. Howe, *Unitarian Conscience*, pp. 270–271, Channing quoted on p. 279; Francis Wayland, *Sermons Delivered in the Chapel of Brown University*, 3d ed. (1854), quoted in Schroeder, *Mr. Polk's War*, p. 111.

22. CS, *The Scholar, the Jurist, the Artist, the Philanthropist*, p. 54.

23. CS, "To the Hon. Robert C. Winthrop," *Daily Whig*, 27 Oct. 1846.

24. CS, "Speech of Charles Sumner, Esq. at Faneuil Hall, February 4th, on the Withdrawal of the American Troops from Mexico," *Courier*, 6 Feb. 1847; CS to GS, Boston, 14 Jan. 1848, PCS 63/ 211; Thomas Brown, *Politics and Statesmanship*, pp. 8–9. These sentiments that Sumner expressed during the Mexican War he had already made public in his *True Grandeur of Nations*, and had been expressing privately for some years before that. See, for example, CS to GS, Boston, 26 & 27 Aug. 1844, in Julia's hand, PCS 63/ 032–033.

25. CS, "Withdrawal of the American Troops," *Courier*, 6 Feb. 1847, and "Mr. Winthrop's Vote," *Courier*, 13 Aug. 1846. See also Sumner's correspondence from early 1861 (PCS reel 74), e.g., CS to Nathaniel Hawthorne, Washington, 16 Apr. 1861, PCS 74/ 652, and CS to HWL, Washington, 17 Apr. 1861, PCS 74/ 662–663.

26. CS, "Mr. Winthrop's Vote," *Courier*, 13 Aug. 1846, and "To the Hon. Robert C. Winthrop," *Daily Whig*, 27 Oct. 1846.

27. CS, "Mr. Winthrop's Vote," *Courier*, 13 Aug. 1846.

28. RCW, Jr., *Robert C. Winthrop*, pp. 7, 9–10, 52; NA to CS, Pittsfield, 20 Aug. 1846, PCS 5/ 215–216; CS to NA, Boston, 22 Aug. 1846, PCS 67/ 527–528.

29. CS, "To the Hon. Robert C. Winthrop," *Daily Whig*, 27 Oct. 1846, and "Withdrawal of the American Troops," *Courier*, 6 Feb. 1847.

30. NA to CS, Pittsfield, 20 Aug. 1846, PCS 5/ 215–216; CS, "Mr. Winthrop and the Whig Members of Congress," *Daily Advertiser*, 27 July 1846, and "To the Hon. Robert C. Winthrop," *Daily Whig*, 27 Oct. 1846, and "Mr. Winthrop's Vote," *Courier*, 13 Aug. 1846.

31. "Boston" [CS], *Daily Whig*, 22 July 1846; CS to NA, Boston, 11 Aug. 1846, PCS 67/ 515–516; [CFA], "The Daily Advertiser and Mr. Winthrop," *Daily Whig*, 6 Aug. 1846; E. T. Channing, *Lectures*, pp. 77–78; Thomas Brown, *Politics and Statesmanship*, pp. 8–12.

32. CS to NA, Boston, 22 Aug. 1846, PCS 67/ 526–527; CS, "To the Hon. Robert C. Winthrop," *Daily Whig*, 27 Oct. 1846.

33. CS, "To the Hon. Robert C. Winthrop," *Daily Whig*, 27 Oct. 1846; "Boston" [CS], *Daily Whig*, 22 July 1846; [CS], "Mr. Winthrop's Vote," *Courier*, 31 July 1846.

34. Edward Everett to RCW, Cambridge, 1 Aug. 1846; John H. Clifford to RCW, 31 July 1846; RCW to John H. Clifford, Washington, 2 Aug. 1846, all in Winthrop Family Papers [reel 25], MHS.

35. RCW to CS, Washington, 17 Aug. 1846, PCS 5/ 211; "Boston" [CS], *Daily Whig*, 22 July 1846; RCW to Edward Everett, Washington, Sunday Evening, 7 June 1846, Edward Everett Papers [reel 12A, frame 0150], MHS; RCW to "My Dear Sir," Christmas Eve, 1846, Winthrop Family Papers [reel 25], MHS.

36. RCW to CS, Washington, 17 Aug. 1846, PCS 5/ 211; RCW, Jr., *Robert C. Winthrop*, pp. 2, 4–5, 44–46, 53, 55, 65, 84, 104–105, 144, 231–232; RCW to John H. Clifford, Washington,

Sunday, 2 Aug. 1846, in Winthrop Family Papers [reel 25], MHS; D. W. Howe, *American Whigs,* p. 31.

37. John H. Clifford to RCW, 31 July 1846, and RCW to John H. Clifford, Washington, 2 Aug. 1846, both in Winthrop Family Papers [reel 25], MHS. Winthrop's willingness to accuse Sumner of "insolence," as will appear later in the text, and the emphasis he placed upon his recollection, thirty years later, of John C. Park's insulting toast at the Fourth of July dinner in 1845, which ridiculed Sumner "as the son of a Sheriff," are among the details that lead me to conclude that Winthrop was irked by the fact that the attacks against his unworthiness as a statesman and a scion of the Winthrop name came from a social inferior. See RCW, "The Mexican War Bill, & the personal controversy to which it gave occasion" (1872), pp. 81–82, Winthrop Family Papers [reel 39], MHS. His son speaks of his "native *hauteur.*" RCW, Jr., *Robert C. Winthrop,* p. 126. Compare Donald (1: 144), who suggests that Winthrop was surprised only because he had thought Sumner more friendly—but this could be said of Hillard as well, whom Winthrop at first suspected.

38. CS to RCW, Boston, 5 Aug. 1846, PCS 67/ 509–510, and 10 Aug. 1846, PCS 67/ 511–512; CS to HWL, Court St., Wednesday [12 Aug. 1846], PCS 67/ 520; CS to NA, Boston, 11 Aug. 1846, PCS 67/ 517; NA to CS, Pittsfield, 20 Aug. 1846, PCS 5/ 216.

39. RCW to CS, Washington, 7 Aug. 1846, PCS 5/ 197. Compare the original unsent draft of Sumner's letter of 10 August 1846 (PCS 63/ 137–136), in which he included a more pointed conclusion that he cut from the final version (cited above, PCS 67/ 511–512). RCW to CS, Boston, 17 Aug. 1846, PCS 5/ 211–214.

40. "A True Whig," *Courier,* 1 Aug. 1846; [CS], "Mr. Winthrop's Vote," *Courier,* 13 Aug. 1846.

41. *Atlas,* 28 Oct. 1846; "The 'Conscience' Candidate," *Atlas,* 31 Oct. 1846; RCW to CS, Boston, 17 Aug. 1846, PCS 5/ 212.

42. CS, "Withdrawal of the American Troops," *Courier,* 6 Feb. 1847.

43. NA to CS, Pittsfield, 10 Aug. 1846, PCS 5/ 198; CS to NA, Boston, 11 Aug. 1846, PCS 67/ 515–516; NA to CS, Pittsfield, 20 Aug. 1846, PCS 5/ 215–216; CS to NA, Boston, 22 Aug. 1846, PCS 67/ 527–528; CS to HWL, Court Street, Wednesday, 12 Aug. 1846, PCS 67/ 520; CS to FL, Boston, 22 Mar. 1847, PCS 63/ 162.

44. Schroeder, *Mr. Polk's War,* p. 35.

45. See ibid., pp. 90, 94–95, Theodore Parker quoted on p. 114; Charles J. Beirne, S.J., "The Theology of Theodore Parker and the War with Mexico," *Essex Institute Historical Collections,* CIV(ii) (Apr. 1968): 133–137; J. Welfred Holmes, "Whittier and Sumner [. . .]," *The New England Quarterly,* XXX(i) (Mar. 1957): 58–59.

46. Chaplain W. Morrison, *Democratic Politics and Sectionalism* (1967), especially pp. 3–4, 16. In August Polk was confidently anticipating American victories. General Zachary Taylor would begin the major offensive against the Mexican provinces of New Mexico and California in September, taking Monterey on 25 September. See Smith, *War with Mexico,* I, chs. XI–XII.

47. C. W. Morrison, *Democratic Politics,* pp. 6–7, 10–20, 25–26; Schroeder, *Mr. Polk's War,* pp. 46–49.

48. C. W. Morrison, *Democratic Politics,* ch. IV; Eric Foner, "The Wilmot Proviso Revisited," *The Journal of American History,* LVI(ii) (Sept. 1969): 265–266, 270–271, 276–279. Southern proslavery activists, like John C. Calhoun, saw the Wilmot Proviso both as part of a Northern threat to Southern institutions and rights and as a potential tool to build Southern unity in defense of these issues. This position would be at the base of William Lowndes Yancey's "Alabama Platform" accepted by the Alabama Democratic State Party Convention in March 1847. Pro-slavery activists quickly tried to use it as a test of party loyalty in the South, but were not yet able to succeed. See Morrison, *Democratic Politics,* pp. 112–120.

49. CS to Francis Wayland, Boston, 8 June 1846, PCS 67/ 470–473; CS to Horace Mann, Boston, 28 July 1846, PCS 67/ 502; CS to John Bigelow, 2 Sept. 1850, in Pierce III: 217.

50. Pierce III: 5–6, 84–85; NA to RCW, Boston, 15 June 1847, Winthrop Family Papers [reel 25], MHS.

51. Brauer, *Cotton versus Conscience,* pp. 184–186; RCW to John H. Clifford, Boston, 9 Sept. 1846, Winthrop Family Papers [reel 25], MHS.

52. Wiecek, *Antislavery Constitutionalism,* p. 224.

53. Brauer, *Cotton versus Conscience,* pp. 189–190; Wiecek, *Antislavery Constitutionalism,* p. 224; Gatell, *John Gorham Palfrey,* pp. 130–131.

54. CS, ["Antislavery Duties of the Whig Party,"] *Courier,* 24 Sept. 1846.

55. Ibid.

56. CS, "Antislavery Duties of the Whig Party," *Works,* 1: 303, 316; CS to Salmon Portland Chase, Boston, 12 Dec. 1846, PCS 67/ 595; Brauer, *Cotton versus Conscience,* pp. 193–194; Duberman, *Charles Francis Adams,* pp. 114–118.

57. RCW to John H. Clifford, Washington, Sunday, 2 Aug. 1846, and George Ashmun to RCW, Tremont House, Thursday P.M. [Oct. 1846], and Joseph T. Buckingham to RCW, 12 Oct. and 13 Oct. 1846, all in Winthrop Family Papers [reel 25], MHS; Joseph T. Buckingham to CS, Courier Office, 30 Sept. 1846, PCS 5/ 284. Sumner's article, declined by the *Courier,* would be printed in the *Whig,* 10 October 1846.

58. Pierce III: 120–121; Duberman, *Charles Francis Adams,* p. 119; Brauer, *Cotton versus Conscience,* pp. 196–197; CFA, Diary, 3, 17 Oct. 1846, Adams Family Papers [reel 68], MHS; Samuel A. Eliot to CS, 19 Aug. 1845, PCS 4/ 417; Gatell, *John Gorham Palfrey,* pp. 132–134.

59. Andrews Norton to CS, Monday, 29 Sept. [1846], PCS 5/ 278–279.

60. Tyack, *George Ticknor,* pp. 16–17, 23, 185–186; George Ticknor to GSH, 17 July 1848, in GSH, Mrs. George and Miss Anna Ticknor, *Life, Letters and Journals of George Ticknor* (1877), II: 235.

61. Pierce III: 7–10, 119–120.

62. Ibid., pp. 10, 121; CS to GS, Boston, 31 July 1847, PCS 63/ 186.

63. Pierce III: 10, 121; CS to GS, Boston, 31 July 1847, PCS 63/ 185–186. George Sumner was not entirely wrong in blaming the prison discipline debates. They had indeed caused strong feelings and violent rhetoric in the newspapers. Ticknor's defense to Hillard of his practice of social ostracism was immediately in reference to the prison discipline debates rather than the quarrel with Winthrop. The two were closely connected, however. Many of the same men were players in both—including Sumner, Howe, and Mann on the one side, and Samuel Eliot and his family on the other. In Ticknor's mind, furthermore, the actions of the reformer in both struggles were very much of a piece. He was as deeply and as publicly opposed to abolitionism and antislavery politics as he was to challenges to the Boston Prison Discipline Society. See also Tyack, *George Ticknor,* pp. 228–231.

64. CS to GS, Boston, 15 July 1847, PCS 63/ 180; Pierce III: 121; RCW, Jr., *Robert C. Winthrop,* p. 220; John Sibley, Manuscript Private Journal, 1: 669 (HUA), quoted in Tyack, *George Ticknor,* p. 186; CS to FL, Senate Chamber, 3 Feb. 1864, PCS 64/ 298–299. Winthrop was very much upset at Sumner's election to the Senate in 1851. When Winthrop published the first volume of his speeches the following year, he included a note—the entire text of his final letter of 17 August 1846 to Sumner breaking off relations, including the passages he had stricken out in the original. See RCW, *Addresses and Speeches,* pp. 770–773. When the first volume of Sumner's *Works* came out, Winthrop prepared his own impassioned recollections of the whole quarrel for publication, though they never actually appeared. In spite of this, the intermittent social relations between him and Sumner were not entirely ended. See, e.g., RCW to HWL, Brookline, Wednesday, 10 Sept. 1873, [bMS Am 1340.2 (6128)], by permission of the Houghton Library, Harvard University.

65. Pierce III: 128; Brauer, *Cotton versus Conscience,* pp. 200–202; Duberman, *Charles Francis Adams,* pp. 119–120; CFA, Diary, 29 Sept. and 19, 26 Oct. 1846, Adams Family Papers [reel 68], MHS; John Albion Andrew to CS, Boston, Friday 9 a.m., 30 Oct. 1846, PCS 5/ 329–330.

66. Pierce III: 135–136; Brauer, *Cotton versus Conscience*, pp. 202–203; Ellis Gray Loring to CS, 31 Oct. 1846, PCS 5/ 332–333; John A. Andrew to CS, Friday 9 A.M., 30 Oct. 1846, PCS 5/ 329–330; CFA, Diary, 29, 31, Oct. 1846, Adams Family Papers [reel 68], MHS; CS, "To the Public," in CS to Nathan Hale (editor of the *Daily Advertiser*), Hancock Street, Saturday Evening [31 Oct. 1846], PCS 67/ 579–581. Sumner's letter of refusal appeared also in the *Whig* and the *Courier* on Monday, 2 November 1846. See also [William S. Robinson], *"Warrington" Pen-Portraits* (1877), pp. 30–31. Donald (1: 148–149) implies that Sumner really desired the nomination when he says that Sumner was "[d]iscreetly out of town when the nomination was made," but all the evidence supports Sumner's assertion that he knew nothing of the decision to nominate him and that he did not want it. Charles Francis Adams in his diary says of the event: "Sumner is absent and this is a surprise upon him." CFA, Diary, 29 Oct. 1846, Adams Family Papers [reel 68], MHS.

67. CFA, Diary, 22 Oct. 1846, Adams Family Papers [reel 68], MHS.

68. CS to GS, Boston, 24 June 1846, PCS 63/ 130; CS to Nathan Hale, Hancock Street, Saturday Evening [31 Oct. 1846], PCS 67/ 579–580.

69. CS to NA, Boston, 11 Aug. 1846, PCS 67/ 515–516; George Ashmun to RCW, Springfield, 27 Sept. 1846, Winthrop Family Papers [reel 25], MHS. See also Levi Lincoln to RCW, Monday Evening, 9 Nov. 1846, Winthrop Family Papers [reel 25], MHS. J. P. Kennedy thought that "Charles Adams, Sumner and Howe, if left to their own way, would [?] annex every Mexican Province from the Isthmus up to the Bravo," and thus accused them of rank "hypocrisy." J. P. Kennedy to RCW, 15 Nov. 1846, Winthrop Family Papers [reel 25], MHS.

70. "A Man Killed by His Friends," *Courier*, 2 Nov. 1846; "The Nomination of Mr. Charles Sumner," *Daily Advertiser*, 30 Oct. 1846; "The 'Conscience' Candidate," *Atlas*, 31 Oct. 1846; CS to Nathan Hale, Hancock Street, Saturday Evening [31 Oct. 1846], PCS 67/ 579–580.

71. Samuel T. Pickard, *Life and Letters of John Greenleaf Whittier* (1894), 1: 77, Whittier quoted on p. 308; Holmes, "Whittier and Sumner," pp. 58–59; John Greenleaf Whittier to CS, Amesbury, 3 Nov. 1846, PCS 5/ 343–345.

72. CFA, Diary, 31 Oct. and 2 Nov. 1846, Adams Family Papers [reel 68], MHS; Schwartz, *Samuel Gridley Howe*, pp. 159, 161; SGH to CS, [Nov. 1846], PCS 67/ 591; SGH to the Nominating Committee, *Daily Whig*, 4 Nov. 1846.

73. CS to Mrs. George Bancroft *née* Elizabeth Davis, Thursday [20 Sept. 1849], PCS 69/ 017; McCaughey, *Josiah Quincy*, pp. 204ff.

74. CS to GS, Boston, 28 Aug. 1849, PCS 63/ 313–314; CS to FL, Boston, 19 Nov. 1845, PCS 63/ 100; CS to NA, Boston, 31 Aug. 1848, PCS 68/ 408–409; Edward Everett to CS, Cambridge, 17 Dec. 1847, PCS 5/ 690.

75. Fanny Longfellow to Thomas Gold Appleton, 28 Feb. 1847, in [Frances Appleton Longfellow], *Mrs. Longfellow: Selected Letters and Journals*, ed. Edward Wagenknecht (1956), p. 126; Wagenknecht, *Longfellow Humanist*, p. 52; CS to HWL, Friday [6 Aug. 1847] & Sunday, PCS 68/ 015 017; HWL to CS, [19 June 1849], PCS 68/ 589–590, and in Hilen, ed., *Letters of Longfellow*, III (1972): 204.

76. GSH to FL, quoted in Freidel, *Francis Lieber*, p. 142; Pierce III: 121; Stearns, *Cambridge Sketches*, p. 191; Donald 1: 171; GSH to CS, [1847], quoted in Pierce III: 51; CS to GS, Boston, 14 Apr. 1848, PCS 63/ 235.

77. CS to GS, Boston, 28 Feb. 1847, PCS 63/ 159; CS to FL, Boston, 22 Mar. 1847, PCS 63/ 160, 162; CS to GS: Boston, 30 Apr. 1847, PCS 63/ 169, and Boston, 14 Jan. 1848, PCS 63/ 211.

78. CCF to CS: Bond Street, 13 Feb. 1842, PCS 3/ 203, and Worcester, 8 Feb. 1842, PCS 3/ 200; CS to HWL, New York, 15 Apr. 1846, PCS 67/ 438, 440.

79. CCF to CS [May? 1844], PCS 4/ 052–053; CCF to HWL, Cambridge, Saturday, 9 Aug. 1845, [bMS Am 1340.2 (1941)], by permission of the Houghton Library, Harvard University (hereafter cited as CCF-HWL Letters); CS to Sarah Cleveland, Cambridge, 15 Aug. 1845, PCS 67/ 313.

80. CCF to CS: Bond Street, 13 Feb. 1842, PCS 3/ 204, and Sunday Evening, 6 Mar. 1842, PCS

3/ 221; CCF to John G. Palfrey, Thursday, 11 Sept. [1845], [bMS Am 1704 (314)], by permission of the Houghton Library, Harvard University (hereafter cited as CCF-Palfrey letters); CCF to CS, Thursday Morning [Sept.–Oct.?] 1845, PCS 4/ 524–525.

81. CCF to HWL, Cambridge, [1 Aug. 1845], CCF-HWL Letters; CCF to CS: Sunday Evening [Oct. 1845], PCS 4/ 549, and [Nov. 1845?], PCS 4/ 593–594, and 11 Nov. [1846], PCS 5/ 355.

82. CCF to CS, Saturday [Oct.–Nov. 1846], PCS 5/ 335–336. The microfilm edition of Sumner's papers suggests the date of October 1846 for this letter; however, given the fact that Sumner returned to Boston only late on 30 October and declined the nomination on 31 October, it seems unlikely that Felton squeezed in his letter before November. CCF to CS, 11 Nov. [1846], PCS 5/ 355.

83. CCF to CS: [27 Jan. 1846], PCS 4/ 658, and Tuesday Morning [Mar. 1846], PCS 5/ 025–026.

84. CCF to CS, [Nov. 1845?], PCS 4/ 593–594.

85. [Fanny Longfellow], *Mrs. Longfellow,* p. 11; Miss Emmeline Austin to CS, Brookline, Thursday, 15 July [1845], PCS 4/ 360. See also Emmeline Austin to CS, Monday, 7 Apr. [1845], PCS 4/ 259–260; Fanny Longfellow to Mrs. Robert Mackintosh *née* Mary Appleton, Cambridge, 31 Dec. 1845, in [Fanny Longfellow], *Mrs. Longfellow,* p. 120.

86. CS to John G. Palfrey, Court Street, Friday, [3?] Oct. 1845, PCS 67/ 345; CCF to CS, [27 Jan. 1846], PCS 4/ 658.

87. "Chev" [SGH] to CS, No. 8 Bond Street, 28 Oct. 1845, PCS 67/ 354–353; CCF to CS, Thursday [30 Oct. 1845], PCS 4/ 544.

88. CCF to CS, [27 Jan. 1846], PCS 4/ 658; CS to HWL, New York, 15 Apr. [1846], PCS 67/ 440; CCF to CS: Tuesday Morning [Mar. 1846], PCS 5/ 025–026, and Saturday Morning [July–Aug. 1846], PCS 5/ 185–184.

89. CS to HWL, New York, 15 Apr. 1846, PCS 67/ 440. This letter, written at the time of Felton's engagement, expressed feelings that did not change.

90. SGH to CS, New York, 7 Nov. 1846, PCS 67/ 586–587. David Donald (1: 176) says that Sumner, contrary to what he said, loved being persecuted—"this holy, blissful martyr thrived upon his torments." Donald argues that Sumner fell ill only when he was away from politics, but that as soon as he returned to them and to the hatred of conservative Boston "his health was amazingly restored." Despite the popularity of such concepts in mid-twentieth century historiography, however, there is no psychological mystery about Sumner's illnesses, and Donald's argument jibes with neither the correspondence of Sumner and his acquaintances nor the dates of his illnesses. All of Sumner's major illnesses, from the fever of 1844, to the boils of July 1845, and beyond to his illness during his first term in the Senate, came at times when the responsibilities of civic duty and of politics put him under great stress—precisely when it is most likely for a person (especially one who takes such responsibility seriously) to become ill.

91. CS to NA, Court Street, 1 Oct. [1846], PCS 67/ 563; CS to GS, Boston, 1 June 1847, PCS 63/ 175.

92. CS to Rev. George Putnam, Boston, —— Apr. 1848, PCS 63/ 240–242. See also, for example, SGH to CS, Richmond, Sunday Evening, [6?] Dec. 1841, PCS 66/ 203–204; CS to CCF, Wednesday Afternoon [10? Apr. 1850], PCS 63/ 343–342.

93. D. W. Howe, *Unitarian Conscience,* pp. 179–181; CS, *The Scholar, the Jurist, the Artist, the Philanthropist,* pp. 68–69.

94. CS, introductory note to *White Slavery in the Barbary States. A Lecture before the Boston Mercantile Library Association, February 17, 1847, Works,* 1: 384.

95. CS, *White Slavery in the Barbary States* (1847, 1969), pp. 6, 59. Citations are from this edition except as noted otherwise. Sumner was familiar with Benjamin Franklin's story from its appearance in Jared Sparks's edition of Franklin's works. Sumner had looked out for letters of Franklin during his travels in Europe and had sent copies to Sparks. Historicus [Benjamin Franklin], "To the Editor of the Federal Gazette," 23 Mar. 1790, in *The Works of Benjamin Franklin,*

ed. Jared Sparks, II (1836): 517–521; CS to Jared Sparks, Vienna, 26 Nov. 1839, PCS 66/ 014. Sumner also refers to Franklin's story in later works of his own. See "Freedom National," *Recent Speeches,* pp. 101, 132, and "The Barbarism of Slavery," *Works,* V (1874): 91 & n3.

96. SGH to CS, [after 27 Aug. 1846], PCS 67/ 531–532; Pierce III: 16–18; George Washington Julian, *Political Recollections* (1884), p. 100; Edward Everett Hale to CS, Worcester, Friday Morning, 4 Sept. 1846, PCS 5/ 239.

97. CS to John G. Palfrey, Boston, 14 Feb. 1848, PCS 68/ 159–160; George Ticknor to CS, 17 May 1847, PCS 5/ 521.

98. CS, "Fame and Glory [. . .]," *Orations and Speeches,* I: 324–325.

99. Ibid., pp. 324, 326–328, 331–332.

100. Ibid., p. 330; CS to GS, Boston, Friday Evening [10 Mar. 1848], PCS 63/ 227.

101. CS to GS, Boston, 31 Dec. 1846, PCS 63/ 143.

102. President Polk's message in the *Congressional Globe,* 29th Cong., 2d sess., p. 4; James Brewer Stewart, *Joshua R. Giddings and the Tactics of Radical Politics* (1970), pp. 123–124.

103. CS, "Slavery and the Mexican War. Speech at a Public Meeting in the Tremont Temple, Boston, November 5, 1846," *Works,* I: 340–351; Joshua Giddings' speech in the *Congressional Globe,* 29th Cong., 2d sess., appendix, p. 51.

104. Stewart, *Joshua R. Giddings,* pp. 107, 125–126; Winthrop's speech in the *Congressional Globe,* 29th Cong., 2d sess., p. 143; CS to GS, Boston, 30 Jan. 1847, PCS 63/ 145; CS, "Withdrawal of the American Troops," *Courier,* 6 Feb. 1847.

105. CS to GS, Boston, 31 Dec. 1846, PCS 63/ 143.

106. CS, ["Antislavery Duties of the Whig Party,"] *Courier,* 24 Sept. 1846; Daniel Webster to CS, Marshfield, 5 Oct. 1846, *Works,* I: 316; John G. Whittier to CS, Amesbury, 26 Sept. 1846, PCS 5/ 268.

107. CS to Joshua R. Giddings, Boston, 6 Jan. 1847 [misdated 1846], PCS 67/ 623; CS to FL, Boston, 22 Mar. 1847, PCS 63/ 161–160; CS to Salmon P. Chase, Boston, 1 Oct. 1847, PCS 68/ 032–033; Duberman, *Charles Francis Adams,* pp. 124–125; Brauer, *Cotton versus Conscience,* pp. 214–215; CS to Thomas Corwin, Boston, 7 Sept. 1847, PCS 63/ 187–188; Thomas Corwin to CS, Lebanon, 25 Oct. 1847, PCS 5/ 641; CS to Joshua R. Giddings, Boston, 25 Feb. 1847, in Pierce III: 141.

108. CS to GS, Boston, 30 Nov. 1845, PCS 63/ 102; CS to FL, Boston, 19 Nov. 1845, PCS 63/ 101; CS to Joshua R. Giddings, Boston, 25 Feb. 1847, PCS 63/ 157.

109. CS to GS, Boston, 1 June 1847, PCS 63/ 175; CS to Joshua R. Giddings, Boston, 1 Feb. 1847, PCS 63/ 147.

110. CS to GS, Boston, 30 Jan. 1847, PCS 63/ 145; CS to FL, Boston, 22 Mar. 1847, PCS 63/ 161–160.

111. CS to Joshua R. Giddings, Boston, 19 Feb. 1847, PCS 63/ 155; Stewart, *Joshua R. Giddings,* pp. 126, 134–135; CFA, Diary, 14 Aug. 1847, Adams Family Papers [reel 69], MHS; CFA to Joshua R. Giddings, Quincy, 19 Oct. 1847, in CFA, Letterbook, Adams Family Papers [reel 159], MHS.

112. CS to Joshua R. Giddings: Boston, 6 Feb. 1847, PCS 63/ 153, and Boston, 25 Feb. 1847, PCS 63/ 157–156.

113. CS to Joshua R. Giddings: Boston, 1 Feb. 1847, PCS 63/ 146–147, and 19 Feb. 1847, PCS 63/ 155, and Boston, 6 Feb. 1847, PCS 63/ 149, and 25 Feb. 1847, PCS 63/ 157–156.

VII. Revolution

1. CS to Salmon P. Chase, Boston, 12 June 1848, PCS 68/ 298.

2. RCW, "The War with Mexico. A Speech Delivered in the House of Representatives of the United States, in Committee of the Whole on the State of the Union, January 8, 1847," *Addresses and Speeches,* p. 585; Brauer, *Cotton versus Conscience,* pp. 208, 210–211.

3. Pierce III: 140–141; Brauer, *Cotton versus Conscience,* pp. 211–212, quoting *Massachusetts Acts*

and Resolves, 1847, pp. 506–507, 541–542; CS to FL, Boston, (3, 12 &) 13 May 1847, PCS 63/ 171–170.

4. RCW, Provisos to the Army Bill, in "The Conquest of Mexican Territory. A Speech Delivered in the House of Representatives of the United States, in Committee of the Whole on the State of the Union, February 22, 1847," *Addresses and Speeches,* pp. 593, 598–599; "absurd" in CFA to Joshua R. Giddings, 19 Oct. 1847, in CFA, Letterbook, Adams Family Papers [reel 159], MHS; CS to Thomas Corwin, Boston, 7 Sept. 1847, draft, PCS 63/ 188; Pierce III: 159–160.

5. CS to John G. Palfrey, Boston, Friday [Sept.? 1847], PCS 68/ 030–031; CS to Joshua R. Giddings, Boston, 1 Oct. 1847, PCS 68/ 035; CS to Salmon P. Chase, Boston, 1 Oct. 1847, PCS 68/ 033 (typescript 68/ 034); Pierce III: 144–145; Brauer, *Cotton versus Conscience,* pp. 216–218.

6. CS to John G. Whittier, Boston, 5 Jan. 1848 [misdated 1847], PCS 68/ 102–103; CS to Joshua R. Giddings: [10 Dec. 1847], PCS 68/ 068, and Boston, 1 Dec. 1847, PCS 68/ 066; CS to John G. Palfrey, Circuit Court, [10 Dec. 1847], PCS 68/ 069–070; Stewart, *Joshua R. Giddings,* pp. 135–136; Gatell, *John Gorham Palfrey,* pp. 143–145, 147; CS to GS, Boston, 14 Jan. 1848, PCS 63/ 211; Pierce III: 146–152.

7. CS, "Honor to John Gorham Palfrey," *Courier,* 23 Dec. 1847, and "Mr. Palfrey's Speech," *Courier,* 1 Feb. 1848; CS to Fanny Longfellow, Court Street, Friday Afternoon [Feb. 1848], PCS 68/ 178–181; John G. Palfrey to CS, 30 Jan. [1848], PCS 68/ 125; CS to John G. Palfrey, Boston, 27 Jan. 1848, PCS 68/ 123–124.

8. CS to Salmon P. Chase, Boston, 7 Feb. 1848, PCS 68/ 141; Pierce III: 152–153; Donald I: 161–162; Stewart, *Joshua R. Giddings,* pp. 142–151. David Donald's picture of this episode—that the quarrel was initiated by Sumner, who naïvely trusted Giddings' promise to provide evidence, and was then disappointed by the flimsiness of the evidence finally given, thinking himself caught in a lie—is effectively refuted by Stewart. Giddings had published his charges in Ohio for some time before the Boston newspapers repeated them. Donald dismisses Giddings' evidence as "a weak collection of statements from congressmen who disagreed as to whether a caucus had been held, whether Winthrop had been present, and whether he had spoken in favor of the war bill." Giddings had hoped for stronger evidence yet, but he was able to publish several letters showing that Winthrop, whether in the caucus room or on the floor of the House, had, as Giddings had charged and Winthrop had explicitly denied, "urged the necessity of voting for the bill (authorizing the Mexican War)." Sumner did not think himself misled by such evidence. See Stewart, *Joshua R. Giddings,* pp. 161–162 n11, 164 n40; [CS], "Mr. Giddings and Mr. Winthrop," *Daily Whig,* 18 Mar. 1848; CS to Joshua R. Giddings: Boston, 8 Feb. 1848, PCS 68/ 148, and 15 Feb. 1848, PCS 68/ 161, and 20 Feb. 1848, PCS 68/ 165–166. Compare Donald I: 162.

9. CS to Salmon P. Chase, 12 Dec. 1846, PCS 67/ 595–596; Stewart, *Joshua R. Giddings,* pp. 151–155; CS to GS, Boston, 30 (& 31) May 1848, PCS 63/ 251–252; Pierce III: 165; Gatell, *John Gorham Palfrey,* pp. 160–161. See also CS to GS: Boston, 30 Apr. 1847, PCS 63/ 168–169, and 16 May 1848, PCS 63/ 249, and 13 June 1848, PCS 63/ 256; and CS to Joshua R. Giddings, Boston, 1 Dec. 1847, PCS 68/ 065.

10. CS to Salmon P. Chase, Boston, 18 Sept. 1849, PCS 69/ 010; CS to HWL, [1847], PCS 68/ 094. Plato was, naturally enough, the favorite philosopher of the American moral philosophers. Burke was equally admired by American statesmen and political thinkers who considered themselves both progressive and responsible, including Joseph Story and the conservative Whigs generally, but also such serious liberal minds as Wendell Phillips. Both philosophers were much read at Harvard. D. W. Howe, *Unitarian Conscience,* pp. 102–103, 123, 273–274; Francis P. Canavan, S.J., *The Political Reason of Edmund Burke* (1960), pp. vii, ix–x, 3, 5–6, 168–169, 194; Raymond Williams, *Culture and Society* (1983), pp. 5–7; D. W. Howe, *American Whigs,* pp. 230–236; Newmyer, *Joseph Story,* p. 186; Stewart, *Wendell Phillips,* pp. 28, 30, 60.

11. Eric Foner, "The Wilmot Proviso Revisited," esp. pp. 265–266, 270–271, 276–279; Richard H. Sewell, *Ballots for Freedom* (1976), pp. 171–175; Wiecek, *Antislavery Constitutionalism,* pp. 221–

226, Sumner quoted on p. 221; CS to Joshua R. Giddings, Boston, 1 Nov. 1847, PCS 68/ 052; CS to Salmon P. Chase, Boston, 16 Nov. 1848, PCS 68/ 444–445.

12. CPS, Notes 1836, p. 37, CPS Papers [box 3], MHS.

13. Sewell, *Ballots for Freedom,* pp. 190–191; CS to John G. Whittier, Boston, 6 Dec. 1848, PCS 68/ 453–454.

14. CS to RCW, Boston, 9 Feb. 1843, PCS 66/ 419–422; CS to Salmon P. Chase, Boston, 22 Mar. 1850, PCS 69/ 116; CS, "Equal Rights in the Lecture-Room. Letter to the Committee of the New Bedford Lyceum, November 29, 1845," *Works,* I: 161–162. The other four states to allow full voting rights to blacks were all in New England—Maine, Vermont, New Hampshire, and Rhode Island. The only other state to allow even partial voting rights was New York, which, in its new constitution of 1821, imposed a heavy property qualification on blacks that was not imposed on whites.

15. CS, "Argument against the Constitutionality of Separate Colored Schools, before the Supreme Court of Massachusetts, in the Case of Sarah C. Roberts *vs.* The City of Boston, Dec. 4, 1849," *Orations and Speeches,* II: 375, and "Equal Rights in the Lecture-Room," *Works,* I: 160; Schultz, *Culture Factory,* pp. 186–187; James Oliver Horton and Lois E. Horton, *Black Bostonians* (1979), pp. 9, 55–56.

16. Schultz, *Culture Factory,* pp. 157, 180–183, 195–198; Horton and Horton, *Black Bostonians,* pp. 70–72; Bartlett, *Wendell Phillips,* pp. 87–91; Louis Ruchames, "Race and Education in Massachusetts," *Negro History Bulletin,* XIII(iii) (Dec. 1949): 53–54.

17. CS to GS, Boston, 10 Dec. 1849, PCS 7/ 039 (also 63/ 321); CS, introductory note to "Equality before the Law: Unconstitutionality of Separate Colored Schools in Massachusetts. Argument before the Supreme Court of Massachusetts, in the Case of Sarah C. Roberts *v.* The City of Boston, December 4, 1849," *Works,* II: 326; CS to Edward L. Pierce, Boston, 11 Sept. 1868, PCS 64/ 586–587.

18. CS, "Argument against the Constitutionality of Separate Colored Schools," *Orations and Speeches,* II: 334–348.

19. Ibid., pp. 352, 358, 362–363, 333, 371–377, quotes from pp. 333, 352, 363, 373, 374.

20. William Jay to CS, New York, 17 Apr. 1850, PCS 7/ 184; Leonard W. Levy and Harlan B. Phillips, "The Roberts Case [. . .]," *American Historical Review,* LVI(iii) (Apr. 1951): 510–518; Horton and Horton, *Black Bostonians,* pp. 73–75; Ruchames, "Race and Education in Massachusetts," pp. 56–58, 71; Pierce III: 40–41. As he does also for Sumner's interest in the European revolutions of 1848 (see note 41 below), David Donald (I: 180–181) subordinates Sumner's involvement in the Roberts case to his interest in a political coalition between Massachusetts Free Soilers and Democrats in 1849 and 1850—after having implied that Sumner's desire for the coalition was dictated by his desire to gain office. Of the Roberts case, Donald writes that Sumner "borrow[ed] from the Jacksonian Democrats the idea of equal opportunity," and that he was now in a "new, equalitarian mood [. . .]." Sumner had upheld the essential principles that formed the basis of his argument in the Roberts case since the 1830's and even in college. It was because of his early belief in human equality and dignity—ideas he was exposed to within his own family before the Jacksonian Democrats were even established as a party—that Sumner was outraged by slavery in the 1830's and that, in 1849, he took on the Roberts case. He did not uphold equality and take the Roberts case because he wished for political office, but rather he took the Roberts case, supported the possibility of coalition, and would eventually take public office, because he believed deeply in human equality and in the necessity of abolishing slavery. As Donald points out, Sumner took no fee for his appearance in this case. Stanley Schultz, following his thesis that reforms in the public schools at this time were efforts at "social control," suggests (*Culture Factory,* pp. 203–206) that Sumner based his case upon a paternalistic appeal to superior whites to be generous to inferior blacks. Sumner does add to his argument a final paragraph, of a different character from the rest of his appeal, asking for generosity from the court, showing his fear that the arguments that seemed undeniable to him would nonetheless be rejected by the court. He makes clear in his argument, however, that

he does not believe in moral or intellectual differences grounded in race, that such distinctions are purely the product of prejudice and are unconstitutional. His argument is based upon the principle of equality before the law, not on charity—and is thus based upon a desire to eliminate unfair social control, not to establish it.

21. CS, "The Law of Human Progress. An Oration before the Phi Beta Kappa Society of Union College, Schenectady, July 25, 1848," in *Orations and Speeches,* I: 385, 370–372, 395, and *Works,* II: 108; CS to Jane Sumner, Washington, 4 Mar. 1834, PCS 62/ 043.

22. CS to George W. Greene, Boston, 10 May 1848, PCS 68/ 273–274; George W. Greene to CS, Providence, 15 June 1848, PCS 6/ 189; CS, "The Law of Human Progress," *Orations and Speeches,* I: 388–389, 387, 392–393.

23. CS, "Fame and Glory," *Orations and Speeches,* I: 329, and "The Law of Human Progress," *Orations and Speeches,* II: 372, 385, 395.

24. CS, *The True Grandeur of Nations,* p. 78, and *White Slavery in the Barbary States,* (1847), p. 3, and *The Scholar, the Jurist, the Artist, the Philanthropist,* p. 15.

25. Major L. Wilson, *Space, Time, and Freedom* (1974), pp. 63–67; D. W. Howe, *American Whigs,* pp. 69–75, 107–109; Miller, *Life of the Mind,* p. 225; CS, "The Law of Human Progress," *Orations and Speeches,* I: 365–385.

26. Major Wilson, *Space, Time, and Freedom,* pp. 63–67; CS, "The Employment of Time," *Works,* I: 199.

27. Matthews, *Rufus Choate,* pp. 172, 92, 197–198; D. W. Howe, *American Whigs,* pp. 69–74; JS to CS, Washington, 4 Jan. 1845, PCS 4/ 198.

28. McClellan, *Joseph Story,* pp. 47–48; Newmyer, *Joseph Story,* pp. 66–68, 118–120, 333, 342; Delbanco, *William Ellery Channing,* pp. 177–179; William Ellery Channing, "The Duty of the Free States. Part II," in *Works,* VI: 331; CS to W. W. Story, On board the steamer for Newport, Thursday Evening [3 July 1851], PCS 69/ 647.

29. CS to GS, Boston, 16 May 1848, PCS 63/ 250–249; Pierce III: 36.

30. William Staughton Chase to CS, 7 1/2 Tremont Row, Rooms of the American Academy, 29 June 1848, PCS 6/ 217; CS to Fanny Longfellow, Boston, Monday [July 1849], PCS 68/ 649–650; CS to GS: Boston, 14 Apr. 1848, PCS 63/ 235–236, and 4 Apr. 1848, PCS 63/ 233, and 16 May 1848, PCS 63/ 249–250, and 30 Nov. [1845], PCS 63/ 103; D. W. Howe, *Unitarian Conscience,* p. 192.

31. GS to CS, Malaga, 19 Nov. 1843, PCS 67/ 040–041; "Penitentiary Congress at Brussels" (Speech by GS with leader by CS), *Daily Advertiser,* 22 Oct. 1847; SGH to CS, Boppard, 26 Sept. 1850, PCS 69/ 395–394; Theodore S. Fay to CS, Berlin, 31 Oct. 1840, PCS 2/ 598–599; SGH to CS, Vienna, 6 Oct. 1843, PCS 67/ 006; George W. Greene to CS, Rome, 27 Mar. 1845, PCS 4/ 251; George Sand to René Vallet de Villeneuve, Nohant, 18 oct. 1845, in [George Sand], *Correspondance,* VII (1970): 136; Alexis de Tocqueville to General Cavaignac, quoted in Loring, *Boston Orators,* pp. 331–332.

32. CS to GS, Boston, 16 Sept. 1847, PCS 63/ 194–193, and 29 Aug. 1848, PCS 63/ 270; CS to George W. Greene, Boston, 27 Feb. 1849, PCS 68/ 508–507.

33. CS to GS: Boston, 4 Apr. 1848, PCS 63/ 232, and Boston, 13 June 1848, PCS 63/ 255, and Boston, 1 Nov. 1845, PCS 63/ 099, and Boston, 2 Sept. 1850, PCS 63/ 392, and Boston, 30 Apr. 1847, PCS 63/ 169, and Boston, 13 June 1851, PCS 63/ 256, and 18 July 1851, PCS 63/ 442. After staying for a while on the rue de la Paix, George took lodgings at 4 bis, rue des Beaux-Arts. Before Christmas 1849 he moved into a more fashionable apartment at 84, rue Neuve des Mathurins, today rue des Mathurins.

34. CS to GS: Boston, 4 Apr. 1848, PCS 63/ 231, and 18 Apr. 1848, PCS 63/ 237; CS to Richard Cobden, Boston, 1 Apr. 1848, PCS 68/ 217.

35. Pierre Miquel, *Histoire de la France* (1976), II: 39–40, Lamartine quoted on p. 39; CS to John G. Palfrey, Boston, 24 May 1848, PCS 68/ 288; CS to GS, Boston, 30 May 1848, PCS 63/ 251.

36. CS to GS: Boston, 4 Apr. 1848, PCS 63/ 232–231, and 14 Apr. 1848, PCS 63/ 235–236. See,

e.g., CS, "A Single Term for the President, and Choice by Direct Vote of the People," *Works,* XI (1875): 98–101; Pierce III: 149, and IV (1893): 190–192.

37. CS to GS, Boston, 4 Apr. 1848, PCS 63/ 232–231.

38. Pierce IV: 252–253. See, e.g., CS to FL, Boston, 14 Aug. 1865, PCS 64/ 427–428.

39. Miquel, *Histoire de la France,* II: 39–41; CS to GS: Boston, 14 Apr. 1848, PCS 63/ 235–236, and 16 May 1848, PCS 63/ 249–250, and 4 Apr. 1848, PCS 63/ 233.

40. CS to GS, Boston, 16 May 1848, PCS 63/ 249–250; CS to George Perkins Marsh, Boston, 6 Apr. 1848, PCS 68/ 224.

41. CS to GS, Boston, 16 May 1848, PCS 63/ 250; Richard Cobden to CS, London, 9 Mar. 1848, PCS 6/ 055–058; CS to GS: Boston, 31 July 1847, PCS 63/ 186, and 4 Apr. 1848, PCS 63/ 232. As he says of Sumner's involvement in the Roberts case (see note 20 above), David Donald likewise subordinates Sumner's interest in the European revolutions to his interest in the possibility of a coalition between the Free Soil party and the Democrats in order, as he ambiguously puts it, "to win offices [. . .]." Donald writes (I: 180): "Shortly after the election of 1848 Sumner began making statements he once would have condemned as Jacksonian demagoguery. [. . .] He grew enthusiastic about the European revolutions of 1848, of which he regarded the Free Soil movement as an American counterpart, and hoped that they would destroy the outrageous social and economic injustices that had, to tell the truth, seemed anything but outrageous to him only a few years earlier when he visited England." It will be immediately apparent that Donald's comments ignore the calendar. Sumner's interest in the European revolutions, which broke out in February (Sumner's most detailed letters on the subject date from April), predated the elections of 1848, held in November. In April, the Free Soil party, and therefore the possibility of a coalition between Free Soilers and Democrats, did not yet exist. Donald confuses the question of fusion between antislavery Whigs and Democrats to form the Free Soil party—which was happening in 1848—with the question of coalition between the already formed Free Soil party and Democrats in Massachusetts in the elections of 1849 and 1850. More important is Donald's suggestion that Sumner's interest in the European revolutions was somehow gotten up to please the Democrats in order to further their coöperation. Sumner's interest in Europe and its politics was by 1848 of too long standing for such a suggestion to be taken seriously. It is not true that he had been unaware of or undisturbed by the social and economic injustices in England and throughout Europe while he was there, as is discussed in chapter III above. He had, indeed, become increasingly outspoken about such injustices as, through his involvement in reform in the 1840's, he had become even more keenly aware of how inequalities of wealth and power were used to put down dissent. On the purposes of the coalition, see chapter VIII.

42. CS to GS, Boston, 31 July 1848, PCS 63/ 186; Richard Cobden to CS, London, 9 Mar. 1848, PCS 6/ 055–056; William H. Prescott to CS, Beacon Street, Saturday Morning [Apr. 1848], PCS 6/ 113–114; CS to GS: 4 Apr. 1848, PCS 63/ 231–232, and 14 Apr. 1848, PCS 63/ 235–236.

43. CS, "The War System of the Commonwealth of Nations. An Address before the American Peace Society, at Its Anniversary in Boston, May 28, 1849," *Orations and Speeches,* II: 50–91, quotes pp. 59, 89.

44. Ibid., 11–13, and "The Law of Human Progress," *Orations and Speeches,* I: 388; CS to GS, Boston, 31 July 1849, PCS 63/ 311–312.

45. CS to GS: Boston, 4 Apr. 1848, PCS 63/ 231–233, and 14 Apr. 1848, PCS 63/ 235–236, and 18 Apr. 1848, PCS 63/ 237; Pierce III: 36; Tyack, *George Ticknor,* pp. 195–196ff.; Henry Blumenthal, *France and the United States* (1970), pp. 57–61.

46. CS to GS: Boston, 14 Apr. 1848, PCS 63/ 235–236, and 18 Apr. 1848, PCS 63/ 237; CS, "Speech for Union," *Orations and Speeches,* II: 260; [Robinson], *"Warrington" Pen Portraits,* p. 522.

47. CS to Rev. George Putnam, Boston, —— Apr. 1848, PCS 63/ 240–242; Goodman, "Ethics and Enterprise," pp. 437–440; O'Connor, *Lords of the Loom,* pp. 44–55, 66–71; Duberman, *Charles Francis Adams,* pp. 139–140; William Lawrence, *Amos A. Lawrence,* pp. 73–74. For much of the

antebellum period Southern students had kept away from Harvard because of her "reputation for religious heterodoxy." D. W. Howe, *Unitarian Conscience,* p. 377 n1.

48. GSH, "The Dangers and Duties of the Mercantile Profession," and William Ellery Channing to George Ticknor, 22 Apr. 1837, both quoted in Tyack, *George Ticknor,* p. 176; CPS, Notes 1836, p. 1, CPS Papers [box 3], MHS; CS, "The Employment of Time," *Works,* 1: 208–209.

49. See, e.g., CPS, "Inconsistencies," in Notes 1811–1813 [box 2], and Miscellany Notebook, p. 152 [box 1], CPS Papers, MHS; Pierce 1: 24; Richards, *Congressman John Quincy Adams,* p. 154; CS, "Freedom National; Slavery Sectional," *Recent Speeches,* pp. 108–109; CS to Salmon P. Chase, Boston, 7 Mar. 1850, PCS 69/ 101; CS, "Speech for Union," *Orations and Speeches,* II: 252. Historians have long debated the legitimacy of the claim that there was a Slave Power. Some recent historians have looked more favorably upon the charge than previous ones. See, e.g., D. W. Howe, *American Whigs,* pp. 286–288, and Eric Foner, *Politics and Ideology in the Age of the Civil War* (1980), pp. 39–43; Richards, *Congressman John Quincy Adams,* pp. 9–10, 153–154ff.

50. CS, "Speech for Union," *Orations and Speeches,* II: 252–255, 262; CS, "Speech for Political Action against the Slave Power," *Orations and Speeches,* II: 246–247.

51. CS, "Speech for Union," *Orations and Speeches,* II: 250–252; CS to John Pringle Nichol, Boston, 17 Sept. 1849, PCS 69/ 008–009.

52. CS to Salmon P. Chase, Boston, 18 Sept. 1849, PCS 69/ 010–011; CS to Rev. George Putnam, Boston, —— Apr. 1848, PCS 63/ 240–242; CS, "Prisons and Prison Discipline," p. 130, and "Fame and Glory," *Orations and Speeches,* I: 322, and *The Scholar, the Jurist, the Artist, the Philanthropist,* pp. 58–59; Pierce III: 157. Selfishness was a common charge made by abolitionists against the slave system. See the discussion in Daniel J. McInerney, "'A State of Commerce' [. . .]," *Civil War History,* XXXVII(ii) (June 1991): 101–119, which relates the concept of selfishness to republicanism.

53. CS, "Speech for Union," *Orations and Speeches,* II: 256–257.

54. NA to CS: [4 July 1848], PCS 6/ 229, and Pittsfield, 31 July 1848, PCS 6/ 277–278 (referring to Sumner's letter of 8 July), and 17 Aug. 1848, PCS 6/ 291 (referring to Sumner's letter of 12 Aug.), and 31 Aug. 1848, PCS 6/ 291–292. The letter of 4 July 1848 is tentatively dated on the microfilm as of 6 July 1848, but Appleton himself refers back to it as of 4 July. See NA to CS, Pittsfield, 4 Sept. 1848, PCS 6/ 331.

55. CS to NA, Boston, 31 Aug. 1848, PCS 68/ 405–409; NA to CS, Pittsfield, 4 Sept. 1848, PCS 6/ 332–333.

56. CS to NA, Boston, 31 Aug. 1848, PCS 68/ 405–409.

57. CS to Karl Mittermaier, 8 July 1851, in Pierce III: 253; CS, "Speech for the Buffalo Platform and Candidates; on Taking the Chair as Presiding Officer of a Public Meeting to Ratify the Nominations of the Buffalo Convention, at Faneuil Hall, Aug. 22, 1848," *Orations and Speeches,* II: 266–267; Pierce III: 179–180. For a discussion of the republican understanding of conspiracy see D. W. Howe, *American Whigs,* pp. 53, 63, 80–82, 171, 263, 302. In the same way that many recent historians have criticized the Wilmot Proviso as appealing to selfishness rather than altruism, so have they criticized the concepts of the Slave Power and the Slave Power Conspiracy. See Larry Gara, "Slavery and the Slave Power," *Civil War History,* XV(iii) (Mar. 1969): 5–18, e.g., p. 14. It is argued that attacks against the Slave Power were characteristic of political antislavery men and their adherents, rather than of the abolitionists, and that the appeal of the target was the threat it represented to Northern white civil rights and political power, not concern for the civil rights of slaves or of free blacks. The more slavery threatened Northern rights, the larger the number of people who became involved in antislavery, it is true. It is also true that people who opposed slavery on moral grounds naturally opposed the political power—disproportionately large—of the slaveholding interest. Like the Wilmot Proviso, the idea of the Slave Power had the advantage as a rallying cry of appealing to a wide variety of people. In the same way that Sumner hoped antislavery sentiments awakened by the narrow grounds of the Wilmot Proviso would grow with increased knowledge,

so he hoped that people initially interested by attacks against their own rights would by the experience learn sensitivity to the rights of others. As Sumner's ideas on slavery and race—as expressed, for example, in his argument in the Roberts case—show, his attacks on the Slave Power were not an indication of lack of concern for the rights of slaves and free blacks. He deprecated the slaveholding oligarchy for its contempt for the rights of all, everywhere, and most especially for its foundation—material, cultural, and philosophical—in that slavery that he considered an immoral attack against the dignity of man. As he put it later in a favorite autograph: "Ours is a noble cause; nobler than that of our Fathers, inasmuch as it is more exalted to struggle for the Freedom of *others* than for our *own*" (CS to unknown, autograph, Boston, 19 May 1853, PCS 71/ 079, also 6 Aug. 1853, PCS 71/ 106). It is thus misleading to quote Sumner's strictures against the Slave Power as evidence of the selfishness of the appeal of the Slave Power concept. Unfortunately it appeared too late to be used for this volume, but an excellent and much needed new study of the Slave Power thesis has now been published. Leonard L. Richards, *The Slave Power: The Free North and Southern Domination, 1780–1860* (2000).

58. CS to John Pringle Nichol, Boston, 17 Sept. 1849, PCS 69/ 008–009. On the history of the workingman's movement in this period see Formisano, *The Transformation of Political Culture,* and Sean Wilentz, *Chants Democratic* (1984). On the concept of free labor specifically in the ideology of the Republican party, successor to the Free Soil party, see Eric Foner, *Free Soil, Free Labor, Free Men* (1970).

59. CS to John Pringle Nichol, Boston, 17 Sept. 1849, PCS 69/ 008–009.

60. Ibid.; CS to George Perkins Marsh, Boston, 6 Apr. 1848, PCS 68/ 224; CS, "Speech for the Buffalo Platform," *Orations and Speeches,* II: 272.

61. Pierce III: 161–163, 165–166.

62. Ibid., pp. 166–167; Gatell, *John Gorham Palfrey,* pp. 164–165; CS to John G. Palfrey, Boston, 4 July 1848, PCS 68/ 355; Duberman, *Charles Francis Adams,* pp. 142–143; [Robinson], *"Warrington" Pen-Portraits,* pp. 184–185; CS, "Speech for Union," *Orations and Speeches,* II: 251–252, 262–263.

63. Duberman, *Charles Francis Adams,* p. 144; CS to Salmon P. Chase, Boston, 7 July 1848, PCS 68/ 363.

64. Duberman, *Charles Francis Adams,* pp. 144, 147, CFA quoted on p. 151; Brauer, *Cotton versus Conscience,* pp. 239–240; CS, "Speech for the Buffalo Platform," *Orations and Speeches,* II: 267; CS to Joshua R. Giddings, Boston, 3 Sept. 1848, PCS 68/ 412. Detailed accounts of the Buffalo Convention are given by Joseph G. Rayback, *Free Soil* (1970), pp. 218–230, and by Frederick J. Blue, *The Free Soilers* (1973), pp. 70–80.

65. Pierce III: 169 170; Sewell, *Ballots for Freedom,* pp. 152–153; Julian, *Political Recollections,* p. 59; CS to Joshua R. Giddings, Boston, 23 June 1848, PCS 68/ 317.

66. Pierce III: 169–170; Sewell, *Ballots for Freedom,* p. 159; Rayback, *Free Soil,* pp. 1–3, 99–106, 213, 217–218; Duberman, *Charles Francis Adams,* pp. 144–146.

67. CS, "Speech for the Buffalo Platform," *Orations and Speeches,* II: 270; Duberman, *Charles Francis Adams,* pp. 144–146.

68. John Niven, *Martin Van Buren* (1983), pp. viii, 567, 579–580, 585–586; Donald B. Cole, *Martin Van Buren and the American Political System* (1984), pp. 4–5, 411–412, 419; Rayback, *Free Soil,* pp. 176, 215–216, 299.

69. Pierce III: 170; CS, "Fame and Glory," *Orations and Speeches,* I: 327; CS to HWL, Court Street, 24 Jan. 1850, PCS 69/ 069–068.

70. CS to CFA, Saratoga Springs, Sunday [30 July 1848], PCS 68/ 383; Richard Henry Dana, Jr., Journal, 10 Aug. 1848, in *Journal of Dana,* I: 351. George W. Julian of Indiana recounts similar reasons for his decision to give up old Whig sentiments and to support Van Buren. At first skeptical of Van Buren's past record, Julian decided that he had shown a principled attachment to the Wilmot Proviso even to the detriment of his career, and that, as the nominee of an antislavery party, he could not go back on the platform to which he was pledged and the new associations he had

made. In addition, Van Buren's political experience and the support of his Barnburners would be a boon to the Free Soil movement. Julian, *Political Recollections,* pp. 58–60.

71. Rayback, *Free Soil,* pp. 218–222; Sewell, *Ballots for Freedom,* pp. 158–159; Julian, *Political Recollections,* pp. 57–58. For a criticism of the Free Soilers' political opportunism and racism, see Blue, *The Free Soilers,* pp. x, 81–103, 118–119, 126. Blue (p. 125) incorrectly uses Sumner's "lords of the lash and lords of the loom" speech from the Worcester Convention as the example of a Free Soiler concerned that the Democrats and Whigs might win more votes than Free Soilers on the issue of the Wilmot Proviso. For a discussion of the skepticism of many historians toward the Free Soilers, and a refutation of their arguments, see Sewell, *Ballots for Freedom,* pp. 158–165, 170–201. David Donald (1: 166) describes the Free Soil party as "a mongrel assortment of disgruntled Conscience Whigs, a few Webster followers, furious that their chief had been spurned at Philadelphia, some patronage-hungry Democrats, assorted Liberty men, and other disaffected persons." Having disparaged the party, Donald (1: 167) mocks Sumner: "None of these discords and inconsistencies troubled Sumner; he was marching to Zion." This is an editorial comment, not a probing into character. On Donald's slighting of Sumner, see Louis Ruchames, "The Pulitzer Prize Treatment of Charles Sumner," *The Massachusetts Review,* II (Summer 1961): 763–764.

72. Dana, Journal, 10 Aug. 1848, in *Journal of Dana,* I: 350; CS to CFA, Saratoga Springs, Sunday [30 July 1848], PCS 68/ 383; Sewell, *Ballots for Freedom,* pp. 159–160, 174–175ff., 189–191, 224–226; Rayback, *Free Soil,* pp. 224–230, 249; Blue, *The Free Soilers,* pp. 104–105, 121–122.

73. CS to Salmon P. Chase, New York, 25 Sept. 1849, PCS 69/ 022; Pierce III: 312–313.

74. Brauer, *Cotton versus Conscience,* p. 243; Dana, Journal, 10 Aug. 1848, in *Journal of Dana,* I: 352–353; Duberman, *Charles Francis Adams,* p. 151.

75. CS to CFA, Boston, 26 Apr. 1848, PCS 68/ 245; Pierce III: 47. In answer to his request Sumner read over William Seward's eulogy and returned it covered with pencil corrections and suggestions. But when asked to give his own eulogy, Sumner declined, saying too many good ones had already been written. See William H. Seward to CS, Auburn, 18 May 1848, PCS 6/ 138–139; CS to Timothy Walker, Boston, 22 Apr. 1848, PCS 68/ 241–242.

76. D. W. Howe, *American Whigs,* p. 173; Richards, *Congressman John Quincy Adams,* p. 98; George A. Lipsky, *John Quincy Adams* (1950), pp. 56, 66–69, 75–78, 82, 124–131.

77. D. W. Howe, *American Whigs,* pp. 44–45, 51–52, 59–60, 67; Lipsky, *John Quincy Adams,* pp. 55–56, 70, 140–143, 212–216, 98–100; Major Wilson, *Space, Time, and Freedom,* pp. 53, 63–67, Adams quoted on p. 102; Thomas Brown, *Politics and Statesmanship,* pp. 15–17.

78. CS to FL: Boston, 5 Sept. 1842, PCS 62/ 562, and Boston, 21 Feb. 1842, PCS 62/ 530; Lipsky, *John Quincy Adams,* pp. 21–22, 52–56; D. W. Howe, *American Whigs,* pp. 61, 65. In the very heated debate following his speech on the "Crime against Kansas" in May 1856 Sumner did once allow his long pent-up disgust at the intemperate language and what he considered the criminal behavior of the leaders of the efforts to permit slavery in the Kansas territory to express itself in personal remarks. Condemning Senator Stephen Douglas' mischaracterizations of himself, and Douglas' well-known habit of indulging in coarse language and "offensive personality," Sumner concluded that "[t]he noisome, squat, and nameless animal to which I now refer is not the proper model for an American Senator." His political opponents made much of it, but the remark was notable for its unusualness in Sumner's speech. CS, "The Crime against Kansas: The Apologies for the Crime; the True Remedy," *Works,* IV (1875): 254–255. On Douglas' coarseness see Stephen B. Oates, *The Approaching Fury* (1997), p. xv.

79. CS to Timothy Walker, Boston, 22 Apr. 1848, PCS 68/ 241–242; CS to SGH, Boston, 31 Dec. 1843, PCS 62/ 614.

80. "John Quincy Adams on Cicero," *National Intelligencer,* 3 Dec. 1839, quoted in D. W. Howe, *American Whigs,* p. 44; CS to SGH, Boston, 31 Aug. 1843, PCS 62/ 593; CS to Timothy Walker, Boston, 22 Apr. 1848, PCS 68/ 241–242; CFA to CS, Quincy [22? Apr. 1848], PCS 68/ 240; CS to CFA, Boston, 26 Apr. 1848, PCS 68/ 245.

81. Stewart, *Joshua R. Giddings*, pp. 38–40, 150; D. W. Howe, *American Whigs*, pp. 173, 176–177, 179; Richards, *Congressman John Quincy Adams*, p. 190.

82. Richards, *Congressman John Quincy Adams*, pp. 4–9, 55–57, 125, 128ff.; D. W. Howe, *American Whigs*, pp. 46–47; Lipsky, *John Quincy Adams*, pp. 61–63; John Quincy Adams to CS, Quincy, 29 Aug. 1846 [misdated 1849], PCS 5/ 226.

83. CS, Autobiographical Notes; Loring, *Boston Orators*, p. 630. There is no record that Sumner made a specific reference to Cicero during this interview with Adams, but he was as fond of the comparison as Adams was fond of the Roman orator. The quote about Cicero given here comes from CS to William H. Seward, Boston, 22 Oct. 1851, PCS 70/ 037–038; see also CS to Edward Everett, Philadelphia, at Mr. Furness's, 16 Oct. 1856, PCS 72/ 353. Sumner says only that the interview took place "during [Adams'] illness," which would seem to refer most obviously to the winter of 1847, after Adams' stroke. The two men did see each other often at the time, and Adams was then especially concerned about making all necessary provisions for the future. See CS to Joshua R. Giddings, Boston, 6 Feb. 1847, PCS 63/ 153–152. David Donald (1: 153) characterizes the relationship between Sumner and Adams in exactly the same terms he used to describe Sumner's relationship with Joseph Story and then with William Ellery Channing. According to Donald, Adams became to Sumner "a new, fatherly advisor." Disparaging Adams as well as Sumner, Donald attributes Adams' respect for Sumner to his seeing in the younger man the equivalent of his own "bad temper and stubborn disposition," while of Sumner, Donald writes: "Always responsive to praise, Sumner became Adams's adoring admirer. [. . .] Whenever the old President was in Quincy, Sumner came out to sit at his feet, and he undiscriminatingly adopted all of Adams's opinions, from his enthusiastic nationalism to his injunction that a statesman should '*Never accept a present.*'" Donald offers no attempt to understand the philosophical bonds that drew them together—a philosophical worldview that Sumner had been developing long before he came to know Adams personally. That he then learned from Adams' lifelong experience in public service and later used some of his constitutional ideas is what one would expect from a serious open mind. Donald's denial of any disagreement between Sumner and Adams is contradicted by Sumner's own words over the years. Sumner regretted Adams' belligerence in the House, as discussed above, as well as Adams' support for war with England over Oregon in 1846, which Sumner strongly denounced. See ch. VI above, and CS to RCW, Boston, 9 Jan. 1846, PCS 67/ 396–397. Sumner likewise disagreed with Adams' support of the Opium War. See ch. VIII below, and CS to FL, Court Street, 5 Jan. 1842, PCS 62/ 516–515. For a similar criticism of Donald's handling of Sumner's friendship with Adams, see Ruchames, "The Pulitzer Prize Treatment of Charles Sumner," pp. 761–763.

84. CS to Joshua R. Giddings, Boston, 3 Feb. 1848, PCS 68/ 134; Matthews, *Rufus Choate*, p. 39; GSH to FL, 5 Dec. 1848, in Freidel, *Francis Lieber*, p. 249.

85. CS to CFA: Saratoga Springs, Sunday [30 July 1848], PCS 68/ 383, and Saratoga Springs, 31 July 1848, PCS 68/ 385; CS to SGH, Court Street, Friday [15 Nov. 1850], PCS 63/ 401–400; CS to John G. Palfrey, Boston, 4 July 1848, PCS 68/ 355–356. See also CS to John G. Whittier, Boston, 12 July 1848, PCS 68/ 367–368.

86. Pierce III: 170–172; CS to Rev. Samuel J. May, Boston, 15 July 1848, PCS 68/ 370; CS to Joshua R. Giddings, Boston, 10 Nov. 1848, PCS 68/ 441; CS to Timothy Walker, Boston, 18 Oct. 1848, PCS 68/ 429.

87. CS to Horace Mann: Sunday [20 Mar. 1848], PCS 68/ 208, and Boston, 2 July 1848, PCS 68/ 346–347; Horace Mann to CS: Washington, 28 June 1848, PCS 68/ 333, and 24 June 1848, PCS 68/ 321; Gatell, *John Gorham Palfrey*, pp. 168–169, 315 n22.

88. Pierce III: 172–174, 177–178; Rayback, *Free Soil*, pp. 244–245; Blue, *The Free Soilers*, p. 131; Julian, *Political Recollections*, pp. 62, 64–66; HWL, Journal, 26 Oct. 1848, in Samuel Longfellow, *Life of Henry Wadsworth Longfellow* (1886), II: 127.

89. CS to Joshua R. Giddings, Boston, 10 Nov. 1848, PCS 68/ 441–442; CS to John G. Palfrey, Boston, 7 Nov. 1848, PCS 68/ 437; CS to Mrs. William H. Seward *née* Frances Elizabeth Miller,

Boston, 18 Sept. 1860, PCS 74/ 244–245; CS to John Jay, Boston, 5 Dec. 1848, PCS 68/ 449–448; CS to GS, Boston, 15 Nov. 1848, PCS 63/ 285; HWL, Journal, 17 Sept. 1848, in Samuel Longfellow, *Life of Longfellow,* II: 123–124; CS to SGH, Boston, Sunday [26 July 1848], PCS 63/ 265.

90. CS to GS: Boston, 13 June 1848, PCS 63/ 256, and 18 July 1848, PCS 63/ 261; CS to Gilbert Lewis Streeter, Boston, 5 June 1849, PCS 68/ 575; CS to GS: 5 June 1849, PCS 63/ 304–303, and 28 Aug. 1849, PCS 63/ 314; HWL to GSH, Cambridge, 4 Apr. 1848, in *Letters of Longfellow,* III: 168. Felton had once jokingly encouraged Sumner to "put up a set of your 'opera omnia.'" CCF to CS, Friday Morning [1846–1847?], PCS 5/ 398.

91. HWL to GSH, Cambridge, 4 Apr. 1848, in *Letters of Longfellow,* III: 168.

92. Pierce III: 175; HWL, Journal, 22 Oct. 1848, in Samuel Longfellow, *Life of Longfellow,* II: 126; CS to GS, Boston, 12 Feb. 1848, PCS 63/ 225; CS to Fanny Longfellow, Court Street, Friday Afternoon [Feb. 1848], PCS 68/ 177–180.

93. HWL, Journal, 3 Sept. 1848, in Samuel Longfellow, *Life of Longfellow,* II: 122.

94. William Kent to CS, 2 Apr. 1849, PCS 6/ 466.

95. GSH to FL, 28 Mar. 1849, in Lieber Papers, Huntington Library, quoted in Donald I: 176; CS to Horace Mann, Boston, 19 Oct. 1849, PCS 68/ 036–038. David Donald (I: 168) writes: "This time feelings of duty, ambition, and revenge obliged [Sumner] to accept the nomination in a platitudinous letter declaring: 'Morals is the soul of all true politics.'" To dismiss the ideas of this letter as "platitudinous" is to belittle fundamentally important currents in the history of Western thought and political philosophy, as well as to ignore that Sumner was living at a moment when the relationship of morals to politics was being violently contested. Donald's insinuation about Sumner's motives likewise belittles what was an agonizing decision for him. Sumner may have been ready for a sphere of greater usefulness, but he was not actuated by a desire for personal preferment. The desire for "revenge" was completely foreign to Sumner's nature.

96. HWL, Journal, 22 Oct. 1848, in Samuel Longfellow, *Life of Longfellow,* II: 126.

97. CS, "Letter on Parties, and the Importance of a Free Soil Organization; Addressed to a Committee of the Free Soil Party in Boston, Oct. 26, 1848," *Orations and Speeches,* II: 275–276, and *Works,* II: 148.

98. Duberman, *Charles Francis Adams,* pp. 156–157; Pierce III: 175; Rayback, *Free Soil,* pp. 303–306, 309; Blue, *The Free Soilers,* pp. 143–146; CS to GS, Boston, 1 Nov. 1848, PCS 63/ 284–285.

VIII. "Dies Iræ"

1. CS to SGH, Washington, 7 Mar. [1856?], PCS 63/ 677.

2. Miquel, *Histoire de la France,* II: 41–46; CS to GS, Boston, 13 June 1848, PCS 63/ 255–256; CS to John G. Whittier [June 1848], PCS 68/ 339–340.

3. Miquel, *Histoire de la France,* II: 49–56; CS to GS: Boston, 4 July 1848, PCS 63/ 257–258, and 6 Aug. 1850, PCS 63/ 388, and 2 Sept. 1850, PCS 63/ 392; GS to CS, quoted in CS to FL, Boston, 3 Aug. 1850, PCS 63/ 386; CS to Fanny Longfellow, Boston, 26 July 1849, PCS 68/ 635.

4. Priscilla Robertson, *Revolutions of 1848* (1952), esp. pp. 339–346, 352–355, 371–377, 266–267, 274–278, 290–304; CS to FL, Boston, 17 July 1849, PCS 63/ 305; Stearns, *Cambridge Sketches,* p. 68; CS to GS: Boston, 31 July 1849, PCS 63/ 311–312, and 28 Aug. 1849, PCS 63/ 313–314.

5. CS to FL, Court Street, 5 Jan. 1842, PCS 62/ 516–515.

6. CS to GS: Boston, 28 Aug. 1849, PCS 63/ 313–314, and 8 Jan. 1850, PCS 63/ 328–329.

7. CS to GS, 14 Apr. 1848, PCS 63/ 235.

8. Ibid., and 18 Apr. 1848, PCS 63/ 237. Nathan Appleton and Abbott Lawrence were among the strongest critics of the lower duties of the so-called Walker Tariff of 1846 and among the strongest proponents of higher tariffs to promote industry. See Abbott Lawrence's letters on the tariff to Hon. William C. Rives of Virginia, in Hamilton Andrews Hill, *Memoir of Abbott Lawrence* (1883), esp. pp. 142–146; Frank William Taussig, *The Tariff History of the United States* (1964),

pp. 126–145; Glyndon Van Deusen, *The Jacksonian Era* (1959), pp. 201–204; and Sellers, *Market Revolution,* pp. 74–75, 192, 277–278, 289–290, 315, 424–425.

9. Donald S. Spencer, *Louis Kossuth and Young America* (1977), pp. 15–18; Blumenthal, *France and the United States,* pp. 57–61.

10. CS to GS: Boston, 25 June 1850, PCS 63/ 376, and 8 Jan. 1850, PCS 63/ 328–329. See Lorman Ratner, *Powder Keg* (1968), ch. 11, esp. pp. 29–33.

11. CS to GS, 26 Nov. 1850, in Pierce III: 230.

12. CS to Richard Cobden, Boston, 2 May 1849, PCS 68/ 549–550; [Ralph Waldo Emerson], *The Journals and Miscellaneous Notebooks,* ed. William H. Gilman et al., IX (1971): 430–431.

13. David M. Potter, *The Impending Crisis* (1976), pp. 5–7; Merk, *Westward Movement,* pp. 371–373.

14. Holman Hamilton, *Prologue to Conflict* (1964), pp. 15–16, 69; Potter, *Impending Crisis,* pp. 88, 94–95.

15. Stewart, *Joshua R. Giddings,* p. 180; CS to Joshua R. Giddings, Boston, 3 July 1849, PCS 68/ 618.

16. Hamilton, *Prologue to Conflict,* pp. 41–42; Stewart, *Joshua R. Giddings,* pp. 180–182; CS to GS, Boston, 8 Jan. 1850, PCS 63/ 328.

17. Zachary Taylor, annual message, *Congressional Globe,* 31 Cong., 1 sess., p. 72; Hamilton, *Prologue to Conflict,* pp. 10–12, 14–16, 30; Potter, *Impending Crisis,* pp. 86–88.

18. Hamilton, *Prologue to Conflict,* pp. 25–26; CS to SGH, Boston, 25 June 1850, PCS 69/ 257–258.

19. Merrill D. Peterson, *The Great Triumvirate* (1987), pp. 455–456; Hamilton, *Prologue to Conflict,* pp. 53–59; Potter, *Impending Crisis,* p. 99.

20. Peterson, *The Great Triumvirate,* pp. 455–458, 470; Hamilton, *Prologue to Conflict,* pp. 59, 96; Robert V. Remini, *Henry Clay* (1991), pp. 732–733; Stanley W. Campbell, *The Slave Catchers* (1970), ch. 1.

21. Hamilton, *Prologue to Conflict,* pp. 71–74, 84–86; William H. Seward's speech in the *Congressional Globe,* 31 Cong. 1 sess., appendix, pp. 264–265, quote on p. 265; Robert V. Remini, *Daniel Webster* (1997), p. 667.

22. Daniel Webster's speech in the *Congressional Globe,* 31 Cong., 1 sess., pp. 476–484; Remini, *Daniel Webster,* pp. 664–666, 668–672.

23. CS to GS: Boston, 18 Mar. 1850, PCS 63/ 337, and 16 Apr. 1850, PCS 63/ 344–345; Theodore Parker and Ralph Waldo Emerson quoted in Remini, *Daniel Webster,* pp. 676–677; John Niven, *Salmon P. Chase* (1995), p. 135; John G. Whittier, "Ichabod," in *The Complete Poetical Works of John Greenleaf Whittier* (1894), pp. 186–187.

24. Remini, *Daniel Webster,* pp. 673–675; CS to Horace Mann, Boston, 26 June 1850, PCS 69/ 261–262; CS to GS, Boston, 18 Mar. 1850, PCS 63/ 337; Morison, *Three Centuries of Harvard,* pp. 282–286.

25. CS to GS, Boston, 18 Mar. 1850, PCS 63/ 337; Pierce III: 205; O'Connor, *Lords of the Loom,* pp. 83–85; Matthews, *Rufus Choate,* pp. 194, 202; CS to John Bigelow, Boston, 6 June 1851, PCS 69/ 630; CS to Horace Mann, Boston, 5 Aug. 1850, PCS 69/ 305. For Whig reactions to Webster's speech see, e.g., the *Courier,* 11 Mar. 1850 and 3 Apr. 1850.

26. Edward Everett to RCW, 21 Mar. 1850, Winthrop Family Papers [reel 26], MHS; O'Connor, *Lords of the Loom,* p. 83–85; GSH to RCW, Boston, 14 May 1850, Winthrop Family Papers [reel 26], MHS. See, for examples of newspaper reaction, the *Atlas,* 13 Mar. 1850 and 17 June 1850; the *Daily Advertiser,* 3 Apr. 1850.

27. CS to GS, Boston, 18 Mar. 1850, PCS 63/ 337; CS to Salmon P. Chase, Boston, 9 Mar. 1850, PCS 69/ 105.

28. CS to GS: Boston, 18 Mar. 1850, PCS 63/ 337, and 16 Apr. 1850, PCS 63/ 344–345; CS to Horace Mann, Boston, 1 June 1850 (no. 1), PCS 69/ 192–194; "Address to Mr. Webster," *Courier,* 3

April 1850. The letter was also printed in the *Advertiser* of the same date; Gregory, *Nathan Apple-ton,* pp. 302–303; William Jay to CS, New York, 17 Apr. 1850, PCS 7/ 184–185.

29. CS to Salmon P. Chase: Boston, 9 Mar. 1850, PCS 69/ 105, and 22 Mar. 1850, PCS 69/ 117.

30. CS to Richard Cobden, Boston, 9 July 1850, PCS 69/ 278.

31. CS, *White Slavery in the Barbary States,* p. 9; Hamilton, *Prologue to Conflict,* pp. 92–94; CS to Horace Mann, Boston, 1 June 1850 (no. 1), PCS 69/ 193–194.

32. CS to Salmon P. Chase, Boston, 22 Mar. 1850, PCS 69/ 114–117 (typescript 69/ 118); CS to Horace Mann: Boston, 23 June 1850, PCS 69/ 248, and 21 June 1850, PCS 69/ 243–245, and 1 June 1850 (no. 1), PCS 69/ 192–193.

33. CS to Horace Mann, Boston, 1 June 1850 (no. 3), PCS 69/ 198–200, and 3 June 1850, PCS 69/ 202.

34. CS to Horace Mann: Boston, 1 June 1850 (no. 2), PCS 69/ 195–196, and 1 June 1850 (no. 3), PCS 69/ 198–200; CS to William I. Bowditch, Court Street, Monday [1840's], PCS 66/ 100.

35. CS to Horace Mann: Boston, 30 May 1850 (no. 2), PCS 69/ 184–183, and 1 June 1850 (no. 2), PCS 69/ 195–196, and 1 June 1850 (no. 3), PCS 69/ 198–200, and 24 June 1850, PCS 69/ 255–256.

36. CS to Horace Mann: Boston, 3 June 1850, PCS 69/ 201–202, and 26 June 1850, PCS 69/ 261–262, and 30 May 1850 (no. 1), PCS 69/ 182.

37. CS to Horace Mann, Boston, 1 June 1850 (no. 3), PCS 69/ 197–198 (quoting from Sir John Fortescue's *De Laudibus Legum Angliæ,* cap. 42), and Boston, 30 May 1850 (no. 1), PCS 69/ 182, and 30 May 1850 (no. 2), PCS 69/ 184–183; CS to William Jay, 1 June 1850, in Pierce III: 216; CS to Horace Mann, Boston, 1 June 1850 (no. 2), PCS 69/ 195–196.

38. CS to Horace Mann, Boston, 1 June 1850 (no. 3), PCS 69/ 197, quoting from Blackstone's *Commentaries.*

39. Daniel Webster quoted in Ferguson, *Law and Letters,* pp. 233–234; CS to John Bigelow, Boston, 8 June 1850, PCS 69/ 213.

40. William Kent to CS: Newport, 24 Nov. 1848, PCS 6/ 386–387, and 19 Jan. 1849, PCS 6/ 425, and [Sept. 1849], PCS 6/ 700; CS, "The Law of Human Progress," *Orations and Speeches,* I: 409.

41. CS, "The Law of Human Progress," *Orations and Speeches,* I: 403–404. This discussion is indebted to the excellent analysis of Webster and the significance of his speech in Ferguson, *Law and Letters,* pp. 199–206, and esp. pp. 232–234.

42. Tyack, *George Ticknor,* pp. 228–229; Sumner quoted in Pierce III: 120.

43. HWL to FL, Cambridge, 18 Nov. 1849, in *Letters of Longfellow,* III: 226; GSH to CS: [1847], and [early 1850], quoted in Pierce III: 51.

44. CS to GS, Boston, 17 July 1849, PCS 63/ 307; CS to Thomas Crawford, 18 Jan. 1850, PCS 63/ 332; Dearinger, "American Neoclassical Sculptors," pp. 445–447; Dimmick, "Thomas Crawford," pp. 266–267.

45. Pierce III: 49–51, 206–207.

46. Freidel, *Francis Lieber,* pp. 122–127, 135–136, 234–242, 249–254, quoting HWL, Journal, 14 Sept. 1849, on p. 250; CS to FL, Boston, 17 July 1849, PCS 63/ 305.

47. Pierce III: 219–220; CCF to CS, [Mar.–Apr. 1846?], PCS 5/ 027–028; CCF to John G. Palfrey, Cambridge, 13 Sept. 1850, CCF-Palfrey Letters.

48. *Courier* and *Daily Advertiser,* 3 Apr. 1850; Pierce III: 45; HWL to CS, Cambridge, 8 Apr. 1850, PCS 69/ 130; CS to HWL, Court Street, Tuesday [9 Apr. 1850], PCS 69/ 134; HWL to CS, Cambridge, 11 Apr. 1850, PCS 69/ 139; CS to CCF, Court Street, 9 Apr. 1850, PCS 63/ 340.

49. CS to CCF: Court Street, 9 Apr. 1850, PCS 63/ 340–341, and Wednesday Afternoon [10 Apr. 1850], PCS 63/ 343–342. The Harvard faculty was divided as was the rest of Boston and Cambridge, some professors, like Longfellow, being staunchly anti-Compromise, others supporting the Compromise. Even though Felton was the only one to sign the letter, however, the majority of the faculty stood behind Webster. In this they followed the lead of the Harvard Corporation—the prominent Boston businessmen and lawyers who controlled the College—which included such signers

of the letter as Charles G. Loring, Benjamin R. Curtis, and Samuel A. Eliot. Young Edward L. Pierce, already an enthusiastic Free Soiler and friend of Sumner's, remembered sitting "restlessly" through lectures at the Law School where the Fugitive Slave Law was defended. Pierce III: 207; Duberman, *Charles Francis Adams,* p. 167; Morison, *Three Centuries of Harvard,* p. 286.

50. CCF to FL, 6 May 1850, quoted in Freidel, *Francis Lieber,* p. 251; CCF to John G. Palfrey, Cambridge, 13 Sept. 1850, CCF-Palfrey Letters; John G. Palfrey to CCF, Cambridge, 15 Sept. 1850, [bMS Am 1704.1 (109)], by permission of the Houghton Library, Harvard University.

51. Pierce III: 210–211; CS to Horace Mann: Boston, 27 Aug. 1850, PCS 69/ 339, and 3 Sept. 1850, PCS 69/ 368, and 27 Sept. 1850, PCS 69/ 397–398; CS to SGH, Boston, 30 July 1850, PCS 63/ 383. Quotes from CS to SGH: Boston, 27 Aug. 1850, PCS 63/ 390–389, and Court Street, Wednesday [Nov. 1850], PCS 63/ 403–404. On the Latin quarrel see, e.g., "Boston Latin School" [CS], *Daily Evening Transcript,* 29 July and 2 Aug. 1850; "Codex Alexandrinus" [CCF], *Daily Advertiser,* 3 and 4 Oct. 1850.

52. Pierce III: 220; CS to SGH, Boston, [c. 1842], PCS 62/ 084–085; CS to Horace Mann, Boston, 5 Aug. 1850, PCS 69/ 306, and 3 Sept. 1850, PCS 69/ 367–368; CS to SGH, Court Street, Friday [15 Nov. 1850], PCS 63/ 401–400. See CS to SGH: [Washington, 2–5? Jan. 1852], PCS 63/ 482–483, and Senate Chamber, 9 Jan. 1852, PCS 63/ 484–485, and Washington, 3 Aug. 1871, PCS 64/ 705–708; CS to Edward L. Pierce, Washington, 3 May 1871, *"Private,"* PCS 64/ 709–710.

53. Fanny Longfellow to Emmeline Austin Wadsworth, 16 Apr. 1852, in [Fanny Longfellow], *Mrs. Longfellow,* pp. 186–187; CS to Fanny Longfellow, Boston, Monday [July 1849], PCS 68/ 649–650, and Fanny Longfellow to CS, Portland, 19 July 1849, PCS 68/ 631.

54. Nason, pp. 58, 16–17; CS to HWL, 7 Jan. 1861, PCS 74/ 363.

55. CS to GS, Boston, 16 Dec. 1845, PCS 63/ 107; HWL to CS, Cambridge, 14 Jan. 1856, PCS 72/ 012; Albert Sumner to HWL: Newport, 17 May 1849, and Newport, 22 July 1849, [bMS Am 1340.2 (5391)], by permission of the Houghton Library, Harvard University (hereafter cited as Albert Sumner-HWL Letters); CS to SGH, Boston, 27 Aug. 1844, PCS 63/ 036; CS to GS, 2 Sept. 1850, PCS 63/ 391; Pierce II: 290.

56. SGH to CS: Newport, 25 Aug. [1852], PCS 70/ 502, and Boston, 15 Jan. 1856, PCS 72/ 017; John Jay to CS, New York, 13 Dec. 1856, PCS 15/ 049; Albert Sumner to HWL, Newport, 23 July 1856, Albert Sumner-HWL Letters.

57. CS to GS: Boston, 16 Sept. 1847, PCS 63/ 193, and 1 Oct. 1847, PCS 63/ 195, and 23 Oct. 1849, PCS 63/ 320, and 10 Dec. 1849, PCS 7/ 039, and 8 Mar. 1849, PCS 63/ 336.

58. CS to GS: 29 July 1850, PCS 63/ 380–381, and 18 Mar. 1850, PCS 63/ 336; CS to SGH, Boston, 30 July 1850, PCS 63/ 384.

59. CS to SGH, Boston, 30 July 1850, PCS 63/ 383–384; CS to HWL, Court Street, 31 July 1850, PCS 69/ 294.

60. CS to GS, Boston, 29 July 1850, PCS 63/ 380–381; CS to SGH, Boston, 30 July 1850, PCS 63/ 383–384; CS to HWL, Court Street, 31 July 1850, PCS 69/ 294.

61. James W. Stone to CS, Boston, 5 Apr. 1852, PCS 9/ 001–002; SGH to CS, Boston, 6 Dec. 1851, PCS 70/ 071; CS to HWL, [1847], PCS 68/ 093–094; CS to GS, Boston, 2 Sept. 1850, PCS 63/ 392.

62. James W. Stone to CS, Boston, 5 Apr. 1852, PCS 9/ 001–002; CS and Julia Sumner Hastings quoted in Pierce III: 52; Katherine K. Preston, *Opera on the Road* (1993), 153–154. See, for examples of Sumner's interest in music, CS to Horatio Woodman, Hancock Street, Monday Morning [25 Sept. 1854], PCS 71/ 440–441; CS to the Duchess of Argyll, Brougham Hall, 26 Oct. 1857, PCS 72/ 615; CS to HWL, Nuremberg, 31 Oct. 1858, PCS 73/ 274–275.

63. CS to GS, 5 Aug. 1851, PCS 63/ 444; CS to George Perkins Marsh, Boston, 4 Sept. 1847, PCS 68/ 026; William Kent to CS, Newport, 8 Sept. 1847, PCS 5/ 613. See also CS to George W. Greene, Boston, 27 Feb. 1849, PCS 68/ 507; George Perkins Marsh to CS, North Burlington, 6 Sept. 1847, PCS 5/ 509–510.

64. Pierce III: 13, 32; Edwin Percy Whipple, *Recollections of Eminent Men* (1887), pp. 216–219; Julian, *Political Recollections,* pp. 100, 102.

65. C. H. Cape to CS, Glenquiet, Colrain, 12 Dec. 1850, PCS 7/ 467–468; Edward L. Pierce to CS: Milton, 14 Dec. 1849, PCS 7/ 043, and Brown University, 4 Mar. 1850, PCS 7/ 140; Warrington, "The Worcester Convention," [28 June 1848], in [Robinson], *"Warrington" Pen-Portraits,* pp. 184–185; "A former Classmate & a Southerner" to CS, New York, 28 Feb. 1850, PCS 7/ 131–132.

66. Richard Henry Dana, Jr. to CS, 22 Aug. 1845, PCS 4/ 420; Edward Everett to CS, Cambridge, 6 Dec. 1850, PCS 7/ 451–452.

67. CS to HWL: Court Street, Tuesday [5 Dec. 1848], PCS 68/ 450–451, and Friday [6 Aug. 1847], PCS 68/ 016, and Boston, Wednesday [18 Aug. 1847], PCS 68/ 022–023; HWL to CS, Portland, 14 Aug. 1847, PCS 68/ 019–020; Pierce III: 70–73; Stearns, *Cambridge Sketches,* pp. 198–199. See also John Greenleaf Whittier, "Sumner," in *Complete Poetical Works of Whittier,* p. 209; Ralph Waldo Emerson, Journals, [1870], in *Journals of Emerson,* XVI (1982): 189–190. Describing Sumner's oratory, David Donald writes (1: 216): "Though long, Sumner's sentences were considerably shorter than those of the orotund Rufus Choate and Daniel Webster. The thundering clauses, the intricately balanced phrases, and the poetic effusions of these orators Sumner belittled as 'scarlet, green-baize, holyoke flower stuff,' and he tried to follow Channing's advice and keep his metaphors to a minimum." As will be seen by the longer citation in my paragraph, Sumner was indeed belittling an orator when he spoke of "holyoke-flower stuff"—but that orator was not Choate or Webster, but rather himself.

68. CS to Horace Mann, Boston, 23 June 1850, PCS 69/ 250.

69. CS to GS, Boston, 28 Aug. 1849, PCS 63/ 314; Salmon P. Chase to CS, Washington, 13 Apr. 1850, PCS 7/ 179; James T. Fields to CS, 7 Mar. [1850], PCS 7/ 142; Ticknor and Company to CS, Wednesday Morning, 29 May [1850], PCS 7/ 229–230; CS to Horace Mann, Boston, 5 Aug. 1850, PCS 69/ 305; CS to John G. Whittier, Boston, 3 Dec. 1850, PCS 69/ 433–434.

70. CS to SGH, Boston, 25 June 1850, PCS 69/ 257.

71. Remini, *Daniel Webster,* pp. 683–684, 686; CFA, Diary, 28 July 1850, Adams Family Papers [reel 71], MHS; CS to SGH, Boston, 30 July 1850, PCS 63/ 383.

72. Hamilton, *Prologue to Conflict,* pp. 102–117; Niven, *Salmon P. Chase,* p. 139; Salmon P. Chase to CS, Washington, 13 Aug. 1850, PCS 7/ 323–324.

73. CS to William Bates and James W. Stone, committee, 12 Aug. 1850, Boston *Emancipator and Republican,* 15 Aug. 1850 and PCS 69/ 315–326; CS to Salmon P. Chase, Boston, 29 Aug. 1850, PCS 69/ 343.

74. Pierce III: 207–208; Hamilton, *Prologue to Conflict,* pp. 102–117; Remini, *Daniel Webster,* p. 686, including quote of Webster; CS to Horace Mann, Boston, 29 Aug. 1850, PCS 69/ 349; CS to Salmon P. Chase, Boston, 29 Aug. 1850, PCS 69/ 343; Salmon P. Chase to CS, Washington, 8 Sept. 1850, PCS 7/ 343; CS to SGH, 27 Aug. 1850, PCS 63/ 390; Donald 1: 185–186.

75. Pierce III: 208; Hamilton, *Prologue to Conflict,* pp. 133–150, 160–161, 166–167, 191–200; Remini, *Daniel Webster,* p. 693; Potter, *Impending Crisis,* pp. 104–105, 121; Henry Clay, in *Congressional Globe,* 31 Cong., 1 sess., p. 1858. The Nashville Convention had adjourned in June to await the outcome of the compromise debates, with the promise of reuniting later if Southern demands were not answered.

76. Hamilton, *Prologue to Conflict,* p. 167; Henry Wilson, *Slave Power,* II: 304–307; Pierce III: 192; Harold Schwartz, "Fugitive Slave Days in Boston," *The New England Quarterly,* XXVII(ii) (June 1954): 192. For a detailed discussion of the effect of pro-slavery legislation on Northern public opinion, see Nye, *Fettered Freedom.*

77. Henry Wilson, *Slave Power,* II: 307–308, 325–326; Hamilton, *Prologue to Conflict,* p. 169; Schwartz, "Fugitive Slave Days in Boston," pp. 192–193; Pierce III: 192–193; Remini, *Daniel Webster,* pp. 695–696; Richard Henry Dana, Jr., Journal, 13 Feb. 1853, in *Journal of Dana,* II: 531–532;

CFA to George W. Julian, Quincy, 14 Sept. 1850, in CFA, Letterbooks, Adams Family Papers [reel 160], MHS.

78. Pierce III: 187, 223. It is not recorded whether Wilson attended the meeting and put forth the proposal in person. He was recognized from the start, however, as the leader of the coalitionists. Free Soilers had long complained about this inequity in the state's electoral distribution, which was heightened by the fact that, Boston being the capital, the conservative Boston delegates could more regularly attend the General Court, whereas members from other parts of the state often had to absent themselves to take care of business at home. The Free Soil State Convention of September 1849 had adopted an address written by Sumner, as State Party Chairman, making precisely these points. This would become a motivating issue behind the constitutional convention held in Massachusetts in 1853. This problem has, indeed, been a point of contention throughout Massachusetts history, most notably during the Shays Rebellion of 1786. See CS, "Address to the People of Massachusetts, Explaining and Vindicating the Free Soil Movement; Reported to the Free Soil State Convention, and Adopted by that Convention, at Worcester, Sept. 12, 1849," *Orations and Speeches*, II: 329.

79. Henry Wilson, *Slave Power*, II: 341–342; Pierce III: 184; Duberman, *Charles Francis Adams*, pp. 160–162, 170–171; Ernest A. McKay, *Henry Wilson* (1971), p. 63.

80. CFA, Diary, 15 Oct. 1849, and 10 Aug. 1850, Adams Family Papers [reel 71], MHS; Duberman, *Charles Francis Adams*, pp. 170–171; McKay, *Henry Wilson*, p. 63–64; Ernest A. McKay, "Henry Wilson and the Coalition of 1851," *The New England Quarterly*, XXXVI(iii) (Sept. 1963): 339–340.

81. CFA, Diary, 17 Oct. 1849, and 15 May 1850, Adams Family Papers [reel 71], MHS; Duberman, *Charles Francis Adams*, pp. 161–162, 167–168; McKay, *Henry Wilson*, pp. 60–61; Abbott, *Cobbler in Congress*, p. 39.

82. Richard Henry Dana, Jr., Journal, 8 [Sept. 1849], in *Journal of Dana*, I: 389; Duberman, *Charles Francis Adams*, pp. 162, 453 n7; CS to Joshua R. Giddings, Boston, 10 Nov. 1848, PCS 68/441; CS to HWL, Court Street, Thursday [24 Jan. 1850], PCS 69/ 069–068; CS to SGH, Boston, 30 July 1850, PCS 63/ 383.

83. CS to Horace Mann, Boston, 27 Sept. 1850, PCS 69/ 397; CS to John G. Whittier, Boston, 11 Sept. 1851, PCS 70/ 011; Pierce III: 170. See also CS to Salmon P. Chase, New York, 25 Sept. 1849, PCS 69/ 022.

84. CS to John G. Whittier, Boston, 11 Sept. 1851, PCS 70/ 011; Pierce III: 170.

85. Duberman, *Charles Francis Adams*, pp. 68–69; McKay, "Henry Wilson and the Coalition of 1851," p. 340; Richard Henry Dana, Jr., Journal, 8 [Sept. 1849], in *Journal of Dana*, I: 389.

86. D. W. Howe, *Unitarian Conscience*, pp. 133–134; Meyer, *Instructed Conscience*, p. 63.

87. Abbott, *Cobbler in Congress*, pp. 35–36; Pierce III: 221, 227; CS to Joshua R. Giddings: Boston, 14 Apr. 1848, PCS 68/ 226, and 19 Oct. 1849, PCS 69/ 034–035.

88. Gatell, *John Gorham Palfrey*, p. 192; Abbott, *Cobbler in Congress*, p. 39; McKay, "Henry Wilson and the Coalition of 1851," pp. 342–343.

89. Gatell, *John Gorham Palfrey*, p. 171.

90. CS to JS, 4 Court Street, 25 Mar. 1837, in "Selections from the Story Papers," pp. 210–211; McKay, *Henry Wilson*, pp. 60–61; Pierce III: 39; Stewart, *Joshua R. Giddings*, p. 175; Amasa Walker to CS, North Brookfield, 8 May 1849, PCS 6/ 486; Elihu Burritt to CS, London, 18 May 1849, PCS 6/ 497–498; CS to GS, 5 June 1849, PCS 63/ 304–305. David Donald (I: 179–180) writes that Sumner was equally tempted by maintaining the Free Soil party aloof, returning to the Whigs, or making a coalition with the Democrats, and that what tipped the balance was his desire for office. "With his growing ambition," writes Donald, "Sumner must have realized that an independent antislavery party had no chance to win offices, that he could look to the Whig hierarchy for no future favors, and that fusion with the Democrats could be politically profitable" as it had proved to

be in other states. Donald never makes it clear that Sumner desired the Free Soilers to win office because that was the way to get the necessary strength in Congress ultimately to abolish slavery. There is no evidence for Donald's statement that Sumner "secretly hankered for a restoration of his ties with Boston Whiggery." On the contrary, Sumner had been among the first of the Conscience Whigs ardently to desire a break with the Whig party, and, once the break had been accomplished, Sumner repeatedly looked forward to the creation of an even larger antislavery party, toward which he believed the coalitions of 1849 and 1850 with the Democrats were a first step. Donald's footnote to the paragraph that contains this assertion refers exclusively to a letter to Judge Story dated 25 March 1837, cited to back Donald's mention of Sumner's disagreement with the Judge at the time over the Charles River Bridge case. See, e.g., CS to Salmon P. Chase, Boston, 9 May 1849, PCS 68/ 555–554, and CS to John Bigelow, 2 May 1851, in Pierce III: 247–248.

91. Salmon P. Chase to CS, New Haven, 15 Sept. 1849, PCS 6/ 673; CS to GS, Boston, 8 Jan. 1850, PCS 63/ 329; Stewart, *Joshua R. Giddings*, pp. 23–26, 32–34, 176, 202–203, 215; Niven, *Salmon P. Chase*, ch. 11, passim, and pp. 30–33, 37–38, 41 on Chase's attachment to education and the Ciceronian ideal, pp. 50–56, 62–65, 76–79, 84 on Chase's defense of fugitive slaves, pp. 57–59, 60–62, 65–70 on Chase's involvement in political antislavery, pp. vii, 45–46, 54–57, 60, 79, 83, and passim on his combination of antislavery sincerity and ambition. See also, e.g., Salmon P. Chase to CS: Cincinnati, 27 Nov. 1848, PCS 6/ 388, and Portland, 2 Sept. 1849, PCS 6/ 658.

92. Abbott, *Cobbler in Congress*, pp. 35–36; Niven, *Salmon P. Chase*, pp. 114–115, 120; CS to Salmon P. Chase, Boston, 27 Feb. 1850, PCS 68/ 504–505; CS to HWL, Court Street, Thursday [24 Jan. 1850], PCS 69/ 069–068.

93. Dale Baum, *The Civil War Party System* (1984), pp. 3–5; Stearns, *Cambridge Sketches*, pp. 162–165, 168, 172–173, 174.

94. Henry Wilson, *Slave Power*, II: 339; Pierce III: 188; McKay, *Henry Wilson*, p. 60; Abbott, *Cobbler in Congress*, pp. 37–38; Donald I: 182.

95. Pierce III: 221–222; Henry Wilson, *Slave Power*, II: 342–343; McKay, "Henry Wilson and the Coalition of 1851," pp. 344–345; CFA, Diary, 27 Aug., 16 Nov., 16 Dec. 1850, Adams Family Papers [reel 72], MHS.

96. CS to SGH, Boston, 27 Aug. 1850, PCS 63/ 389; CS to Henry Wilson, Newport, 9 Sept. 1850, in Pierce III: 222–223; CFA, Diary, 10 Sept. 1850, Adams Family Papers [reel 72], MHS.

97. "Letter from the Hon. Samuel A. Eliot," *Daily Advertiser*, 29 Oct. 1850; CS to GS, Boston, 22 Oct. 1850, PCS 63/ 399.

98. CS to John G. Palfrey, Boston, 15 Oct. 1850, PCS 69/ 411–412.

99. CS to John G. Palfrey, 13 Sept. 1849, PCS 69/ 007; Gatell, *John Gorham Palfrey*, p. 192; CFA, Diary, 15 May 1850, Adams Family Papers [reel 71], MHS; [Robinson], *"Warrington" Pen-Portraits*, p. 418; Meyer, *Instructed Conscience*, pp. 114–116; D. W. Howe, *American Whigs*, pp. 176, 198.

100. Gatell, *John Gorham Palfrey*, p. 192; Palfrey quoted in Abbott, *Cobbler in Congress*, p. 39.

101. SGH to CS, Boston, [1850], PCS 69/ 462–463.

102. Pierce III: 13, 32, 222; CS to Charles Allen, 15 Oct. 1850, in Pierce III: 218–219. David Donald (I: 186–187) portrays Sumner as, at the same time, secretly paving the way for coalition behind his friends' backs—"A far better politician than even his friends believed, he knew the advantages of rowing toward his objective with muffled oars"—and vacillating between his friends' opinions—"Uncertain in his own mind about the propriety of a coalition, he found it easy to agree both with Adams's theory and with Wilson's practice." In fact,—as Sumner's colleagues well knew—Sumner had long favored coalition in theory and recommended it to his friends, but made it clear that he would not insist upon it at the state level—where there was the most objection to it—against their wishes. By working for local coalitions in 1849, Sumner was not acting behind the backs of Adams and Palfrey; they, too, accepted such coalitions then, which were necessary to Palfrey's effort to win reëlection in Middlesex County. (See CFA, Diary, 13 Oct. 1849, [reel 71]). Donald writes that "even while making public disclaimers, Sumner was quietly co-operating with Wil-

son's plans" for coalition. In evidence, Donald writes of Sumner's letter to Wilson of 9 September. Donald says that the letter "was deliberately not read" at the meeting. If Sumner, in collusion with Wilson, had intended to keep the letter secret from the start, meaning it only for Wilson but not for the general meeting, why then had it been announced ahead of time that the letter was to be read aloud at the meeting? Later, while nurturing momentary suspicions about Sumner's purposes, Charles Francis Adams brought up the unfulfilled promise to read the letter as one reason for thinking Sumner had been manœuvering for the Senate nomination. (See Adams' Diary, 16 Nov. 1850, [reel 72], and my own discussion of Adams' feelings about Sumner's position later in this chapter.) As evidence that Sumner's personal ambition was behind his October support for the coalition, Donald quotes him describing the Senate seat as "a mighty pulpit from which the truth can be preached"—well might Sumner say so in a letter looking forward to speeches by Senators Hale and Chase against Clay's proposed compromise (CS to William Jay, 19 Feb. 1850, in Pierce III: 212). Sumner ardently desired—as did his colleagues—to see a Massachusetts Free Soiler in Daniel Webster's seat. He desired it for the furtherance of the cause of antislavery, not for himself. It was because of the possibility of his own candidacy that Sumner so long refused to support the coalition publicly, despite his belief in its necessity. Donald apparently did not consider the passage of the Compromise and of the Fugitive Slave Law sufficient reason for Sumner to change his mind and urge the coalition.

103. Benjamin Douglas Siliman to CS, 6 Nov. [1850], PCS 7/ 400; Pierce III: 225; Albert G. Browne to CS, Salem, Monday Evening, 28 Oct. 1850, PCS 7/ 384–385.

104. Pierce III: 227–228; "Mr. Sumner's speech at Faneuil Hall, Nov. 6, 1850," *Emancipator and Republican*, 14 Nov. 1850. All quotes from this speech in the following paragraphs refer to this edition. See also CS to Edward L. Pierce, [Washington, 21 Dec. 1869], PCS 64/ 643.

105. CS to Joshua R. Giddings, Boston, 6 May 1848, PCS 68/ 266–267.

106. Sumner gave evidence of his conviction that the political destruction of the Compromise was paramount in the publication of his *Orations and Speeches*. After having spent months laboring to present a polished work to posterity, he now rushed to include the unpolished original version of his 6 November speech—which had not made reference to the coalition—given by him at a Free Soil meeting on 3 October, and he had the volumes appear just in time for the election. David Donald (I: 186–187) concludes that the publication of the two volumes "at this strategic time" was evidence of Sumner's apparent desire for the Senate seat. But, of course, it was clearly evidence of his desire to see a Free Soil—that is, anti-Compromise—victory, no matter who the senatorial candidate might be. See Sumner's *Orations and Speeches*, II: 415, 420. Larry Gara ("Slavery and the Slave Power," pp. 14–16) argues—as he does for the concept of the Slave Power—that Northern objections to the Fugitive Slave Law were founded in concern not for the victims of slavery, but for the civil rights of Northerners, and rarely even for the rights of Northern blacks. As a generality this is undoubtedly true, as is the fact that many Northerners were first awakened to the issue of slavery by their outrage at the Fugitive Slave Law. The law did, of course, genuinely threaten the rights of all Americans, including Northern whites. It is clear from the whole of Sumner's career, however, that his denunciation of the threat to Northern rights was not evidence of a narrow view on his part. Concerned as he was with the concepts of Natural Law and natural rights, he was disturbed by the threat to the rights of all men. Aware that many people had been first outraged by the threat to their own rights, he hoped that an appeal that linked their rights with those of others would gradually teach them to take a larger view. It should also be remembered that, though he did not speak publicly about the abolition of slavery at a time when he did not think it was constitutional for the federal government to abolish it directly, Sumner always aimed at the destruction of slavery by "moral blockade" aided by positive government influence.

107. Pierce III: 228, 231–233; George Morey, Chairman, for the Massachusetts Whig State Committee, Circular, 8 Nov. 1850, quoted in O'Connor, *Lords of the Loom*, pp. 87–88; Seth Webb, Jr. to CS, [Nov. 1850], PCS 7/ 447.

108. RCW to John H. Clifford, Boston, 12 Nov. 1850, "*Private,*" Winthrop Family Papers [reel 26], MHS; Pierce III: 231; CS to GS, Boston, [26 Nov. 1850], in Pierce III: 230; CS to FL, 25 June 1851, PCS 63/ 439; CS quoted in Pierce III: 253; CS to Salmon P. Chase, Boston, 9 May 1849, PCS 68/ 555–554. For examples of Whig reactions to the election results, see the *Atlas,* 14, 15 Nov. 1850; *Courier,* 15 Nov., 16 Dec. 1850; *Daily Advertiser,* 18, 21, 22 Nov. 1850.

109. RCW to John H. Clifford, Washington, Sunday Night, 5 Jan. 1851, Winthrop Family Papers [reel 26], MHS; Pierce III: 230; Duberman, *Charles Francis Adams,* p. 172; McKay, *Henry Wilson,* p. 67; Abbott, *Cobbler in Congress,* pp. 41–42; McKay, "Henry Wilson and the Coalition of 1851," p. 354.

110. SGH quoted in Schwartz, *Samuel Gridley Howe,* pp. 178–179; Boston *Commonwealth,* 1 Jan. 1851.

111. Salmon P. Chase to CS, Washington, 14 Dec. 1850, PCS 7/ 469; E. A. Stansbury to CS, 31 Dec. 1850, PCS 7/ 489; Henry Wilson, "History of the Legislative Coalition," *Commonwealth,* 30 Jan. and 18 Feb. 1851.

112. CS to Mrs. William H. Prescott *née* Susan Amory, Baltimore, Tuesday Morning [7 Apr. 1846], PCS 67/ 432–433; CS to CFA, Boston, 16 Dec. 1850, PCS 69/ 441–442; Sumner quoted in Theodore Parker to CS, Boston, 26 Apr. 1851, PCS 7/ 686–687.

113. Sumner quoted in Theodore Parker to CS, Boston, 26 Apr. 1851, PCS 7/ 686.

114. CS to CFA, Court Street, Thursday Afternoon [2 Jan. 1851], PCS 69/ 475–476.

115. Thomas Brown, *Politics and Statesmanship,* p. 11; CS to Thomas Brown, Boston, 24 June 1851, PCS 63/ 436–435; CS to CFA, Boston, 16 Dec. 1850, PCS 69/ 441.

116. CS to CFA, Boston, 16 Dec. 1850, PCS 69/ 441; CS to GS, Boston, 23 Feb. 1851, PCS 63/ 413–414; CS to Richard Henry Dana, Jr., Court Street, Monday [Jan. 1851], PCS 69/ 510.

117. CS to GS, Boston, 23 Feb. 1851, PCS 63/ 413–414; CS to John Bigelow, Boston, 11 Jan. 1851, PCS 69/ 483; CS to HWL: Washington, 9 Jan. 1856, PCS 72/ 007–008, and Senate Chamber, 10 Mar. 1856, PCS 72/ 110.

118. CS to John G. Palfrey, Monday Morning [c. June 1851], PCS 69/ 645. See also notes 127 and 140 below.

119. Gatell, *John Gorham Palfrey,* pp. 194–198, 201–202; John G. Palfrey to CS, 25 Feb. 1851, PCS 69/ 527.

120. CFA, Diary, 21 Dec. 1850, Adams Family Papers [reel 72], MHS; Stephen C. Phillips to CS, 9 Jan. 1851, PCS 7/ 509–510; Jason W. Thompson to CS, Salem, 10 Jan. 1851, PCS 7/ 516; Stephen C. Phillips to CS: 15 Jan. 1851, PCS 7/ 520, and Salem, 26 Feb. 1851, PCS 7/ 589–590; Pierce III: 240.

121. CFA, Diary, 21 Dec., 3 Oct. 1850, Adams Family Papers [reel 72], MHS.

122. Ibid., 16 and 19 Nov. 1850, 12 Jan., 21 Mar. 1851 [reel 72].

123. Ibid., 12 Dec. 1850, 12 Jan., 21 Mar., 7 Feb. 1851 [reel 72], and 10 Aug. 1850, [reel 71]; "Letter from the Hon. Charles Francis Adams," *Commonwealth,* 9 Jan. 1851.

124. Henry Wilson, "History of the Legislative Coalition," *Commonwealth,* 30 Jan. and 18 Feb. 1851; Pierce III: 236–238; CFA, Diary, 14 Nov. 1850, Adams Family Papers [reel 72], MHS; Henry Wilson, *Slave Power,* II: 348–349; McKay, *Henry Wilson,* pp. 68–71; "The Beginning of the End," *Courier,* 15 Jan. 1851.

125. O'Connor, *Lords of the Loom,* pp. 88–89; "The Beginning of the End," *Courier,* 15 Jan. 1851; RCW to NA, Washington, 17 Jan. 1851, and RCW to George Morey, Washington, Friday, 17 Jan. 1851, Winthrop Family Papers [reel 26], MHS; Pierce III: 242; Donald I: 191–192.

126. NA to RCW, Boston, 21 Jan. 1851; RCW to John H. Clifford, Washington, Sunday Night, 5 Jan. 1851; RCW to George Morey, Washington, 9 Jan. 1851; RCW to Mrs. Gardner, Washington, 23 Jan. 1851; RCW to George Morey, Washington, 25 Jan. 1851, "*Private,*" all in Winthrop Family Papers [reel 26], MHS.

127. CS to Horace Mann, 11 Jan. 1851, 11 o'clock, PCS 69/ 487–486; Richard Henry Dana, Jr., Journal, 23 Mar. 1851, in *Journal of Dana*, 11: 416. After his election, however, Sumner's first use of his senatorial frank was to promote Palfrey's election. See Pierce 111: 246 n1.

128. CS to CFA, Court Street, Tuesday [7 Jan. 1851], PCS 69/ 479–480; CS to John Bigelow: Boston, 21 Jan. 1851, "*Private*," in *Selected Letters*, 1: 320, and Boston, 11 Jan. 1851, PCS 69/ 483; CFA, Diary, 5 Jan. 1851, Adams Family Papers [reel 72], MHS.

129. CS to HWL, Court Street, Saturday, 11 Jan. 1851, PCS 69/ 484–485; CS to Horace Mann, Boston, 10 Feb. 1851, PCS 63/ 412–411; CS to John Bigelow, Boston, 21 Jan. 1851, "*Private*," in *Selected Letters*, 1: 320.

130. Pierce 111: 233–234; CS to John Bigelow: Boston, 11 Jan. 1851, PCS 69/ 483, and 21 Jan. 1851, in *Selected Letters*, 1: 319–320; CS to Horace Mann: Boston, 11 Jan. 1851, 11 o'clock, PCS 69/ 487–486, and 22 Jan. 1851, PCS 69/ 493; CFA, Diary, 13 Feb. 1851, Adams Family Papers [reel 72], MHS.

131. Charlemagne Tower to CS, Orwigsburg, Schuylkill County, Pennsylvania, 18 Jan. 1851, PCS 7/ 540; John G. Whittier to CS: Amesbury, 16 Jan. 1851, PCS 7/ 530, and 28 Mar. 1851, PCS 7/ 617; Horace Mann to CS, Washington, 14 Feb. 1851, PCS 69/ 517; CS to Joshua R. Giddings, Boston, 3 Apr. 1851, PCS 69/ 551; CFA, Diary, 13 Feb. 1851, Adams Family Papers [reel 72], MHS; CS to Henry Wilson, Boston, 22 Feb. 1851, *Commonwealth*, 26 Apr. 1851. See also Sumner's *Works*, 111: 153–154. David Donald (1: 199–200) defends the coalition against the Whig charge that it was corrupt, and then reverses himself: "If the Whig charge that the coalition was 'unprincipled' was not tenable, the Free Soil counterclaim that some weighty principle of antislavery was involved in Sumner's election was equally dubious. Whatever idealism the Free Soilers may have had in the beginning had disappeared by the time two dozen ballots were taken, each followed by higgling for office and spoils." Donald illustrates his contention with a pungent quotation from Cotton Whig George Hillard to the effect that the Free Soilers were prostituting themselves. The distribution of offices, however, was agreed to in the first days of January, before the senatorial balloting began. Thereafter Wilson remained adamant in his support of Sumner. Earlier, Donald (p. 188) had similarly questioned Sumner's own motivation by writing that, in his speech before the Free Soil State Convention on 3 October, he "attempted simultaneously and somewhat contradictorily to prove that he was willing to co-operate with the Democrats and that his antislavery principles were simon-pure." Sumner supported the coalition, however, in order to further the antislavery cause. Since the Democrats were most interested in state reforms and therefore in state offices, while the Free Soilers were most interested in the national issue of slavery and therefore in national office, Sumner, for one, did not see how the coalition sacrificed any real principle, except the principle—which he scorned—of loyalty to party. Massachusetts Democrats, in addition, whatever the position of the national party, were—like most of the state's citizens—overwhelmingly antislavery in sentiment. Donald's dismissal of this coalition is particularly strange, when one remembers that it was a major step on the road towards the creation of the Republican party, and that many of the Democrats who took part in it would later become Republicans along with the Free Soilers. After decades of struggle by various groups, it was that Republican party that finally abolished slavery in 1865. For similar imputations see, for example, Donald 1: 197, 200. Sumner's letters do not support these charges. Compare, for example, CS to Salmon P. Chase, Boston, 9 May 1849, PCS 68/ 555–554, and CS to John Bigelow, 2 May 1851, in *Selected Letters*, 1: 330–331.

132. CS to Joshua R. Giddings, Boston, 3 Apr. 1851, PCS 69/ 551; Pierce 111: 242, 248; McKay, *Henry Wilson*, pp. 71–73; McKay, "Henry Wilson and the Coalition of 1851," pp. 354–355; Stearns, *Cambridge Sketches*, p. 177.

133. Schwartz, "Fugitive Slave Days in Boston," pp. 195–201; Pierce 111: 193–194.

134. CS to Theodore Parker, 19 Apr. 1851, PCS 69/ 555.

135. CFA, Jr., quoted in Pierce 111: 244; CFA, Diary, 23 Apr. 1851, Adams Family Papers [reel 72], MHS; Pierce 111: 242; McKay, *Henry Wilson*, p. 72.

136. CFA, Diary, 24 Apr. 1851, Adams Family Papers [reel 72], MHS; CFA, Jr., quoted in Pierce III: 245; Henry Adams, *The Education of Henry Adams,* p. 31; CFA, Jr., *Charles Francis Adams, 1835–1915* (1916), pp. 32, 37; Pierce III: 242–243; McKay, *Henry Wilson,* p. 72; Donald I: 173.

137. Pierce III: 242–243; Donald I: 200–202; McKay, "Henry Wilson and the Coalition of 1851," p. 356.

138. Pierce III: 202, 249–250; Donald I: 200–202; CFA, Diary, 25 and 24 Apr. 1851, Adams Family Papers [reel 72], MHS; *Commonwealth,* 25 Apr. 1851; CS, "Final Repeal of All Fugitive Slave Acts," in *Works,* VIII (1874): 412.

139. The *Commonwealth,* 25 Apr. 1851; HWL, Journal, 25 Apr. 1851, quoted in Pierce III: 245–246; Pierce III: 205, 243.

140. "The End of the Senatorial Struggle," *Courier,* 25 Apr. 1851; Donald I: 202–203; CS to John Bigelow, 2 May 1851, in Pierce III: 248; O'Connor, *Lords of the Loom,* p. 89; Pierce III: 210, 238, 252; "Address to the People of Massachusetts," *Daily Advertiser,* 28 May 1851; Schwartz, "Fugitive Slave Days in Boston," p. 199; CS to GS, Washington, 15 Dec. 1851, PCS 63/ 464. Again in the fall canvass of 1851, Sumner refused to take any part, unwilling to appear to be campaigning for himself, and also because "I do not wish to seem to pursue Winthrop." CS to GS, Boston, 30 Sept. 1851, PCS 63/ 450. See also CS to John G. Whittier, Boston, 11 Sept. 1851, PCS 70/ 011.

141. GSH to CS, 25 April 1851, in Pierce III: 250; Salmon P. Chase to CS, Columbus, 28 Apr. 1851, PCS 7/ 693; Horace Mann to CS, [24+ Apr. 1851], PCS 69/ 561; Fanny Longfellow to Mrs. James Greenleaf *née* Mary Longfellow, 27 Jan. 1851, in [Fanny Longfellow], *Mrs. Longfellow,* p. 175.

142. CS to Abigail Brooks Adams, Craigie House, 25 Apr. 1851, PCS 69/ 562; CS to Henry Wilson, Craigie House, Cambridge, 25 Apr. 1851, PCS 69/ 565–566.

143. Pierce III: 244n; Fanny Longfellow to NA, 4 May 1851, in [Fanny Longfellow], *Mrs. Longfellow,* p. 179; CS to GS, Boston, 29 Apr. 1851, PCS 63/ 419–420.

144. Theodore Parker to CS, Boston, 26 Apr. 1851, PCS 7/ 686–687.

145. Ibid.

Afterword— "Bound for Washington"

1. CS to SGH, New York, Delmonico's, 26 Nov. [1851], PCS 63/ 453–454; CS to HWL, New York, Delmonico's, Thanksgiving Day, 26 Nov. [1851], PCS 70/ 057–058; CS to Julia Sumner, New York, Delmonico's, 26 Nov. 1851, in Pierce III: 259.

2. CS to GS, Boston, 29 Apr. 1851, PCS 63/ 419–420; CS to Thomas Brown, Boston, 24 June 1851, PCS 63/ 436–435; Pierce III: 246 n2; Theodore Parker to CS, Brookline, 11 July 1851, PCS 8/ 119.

3. CS, "Acceptance of the Office of Senator of the United States," 14 May 1851, in *Works,* II: 437–440; CS to GS, Boston, (17 &) 24 June 1851, PCS 63/ 427; CS to John Jay, 23 May 1851, PCS 69/ 601.

4. Pierce III: 246 n2; CS to GS, Boston, 10 Sept. 1851, PCS 63/ 448–447.

5. CS to Richard Henry Dana, Jr., 1 Nov. 1851, in Pierce III: 75–76.

BIBLIOGRAPHY

Charles Sumner—Collected Works

Orations and Speeches. Boston: Ticknor, Reed, and Fields, 1850. 2 volumes.

The Papers of Charles Sumner. Edited by Beverly Wilson Palmer. Alexandria, Va., and Cambridge, Eng.: Chadwyck-Healey, 1988. Microfilm. 85 reels.

Recent Speeches and Addresses. Boston: Higgins and Bradley, 1856.

The Selected Letters of Charles Sumner. Edited by Beverly Wilson Palmer. Boston: Northeastern University Press, 1990. 2 volumes.

The Works of Charles Sumner. Boston: Lee and Shepard, 1875–1888. 15 volumes.

Charles Sumner—Selected Articles, Speeches, and Monographs in Chronological Order

["Amicus," pseudonym.] "The English Universities." *Boston Patriot and Mercantile Advertiser.* 27 and 30 October 1829.

[On Bennington and the Erie Canal]. In the *Boston Patriot and Mercantile Advertiser.* 20 November and 3 December 1829.

"Short Review" of "*What are Courts of Equity?* A Lecture Delivered at King's College, London, April 6, 1832, by J. J. Park, Esq., the Professor of English Law and Jurisprudence. London. 1832." *The American Jurist and Law Magazine.* x(xix) (July 1833): 227–237.

Review of "*Report of the Trial of James H. Peck, Judge of the United States District Court for the District of Missouri, before the Senate of the United States, on an Impeachment Preferred by the House of Representatives against Him for High Misdemeanors in Office.* By Arthur J. Stansbury. Boston: Hilliard, Gray & Co., 1833." *American Monthly Review.* iii(iv) (April 1833): 315–327.

Review of "*Commentaries on the Laws of England.* By Sir William Blackstone; in Two Volumes, from the Eighteenth London Edition; with a Life of the Author and Notes, by Christian, Chitty, Lee, Hovenden and Ryland; and also References to American Cases, by a Member of the New York Bar. New York: 1832." *American Monthly Review.* iii(v) (May 1833): 430–433.

"Lex Loci. Can the Assignee of a Scotch Bond Maintain an Action in His Own Name in the Courts of this Country?" *The American Jurist and Law Magazine.* xi(xxi) (January 1834): 101–115.

"Mr. Sumner's Catalogue of the Law Library of Harvard University." *The American Jurist and Law Magazine.* xi(xxi) (January 1834): 263–268.

Review of "*Chitty's Pleadings. A Treatise on the Parties to Actions . . .* By Joseph Chitty, Esq. of the Middle Temple, Barrister at Law; Sixth American from the Fifth London Edition, Corrected and Enlarged; with Notes and Additions, by John A. Dunlap, Esq. and Additional Notes and References to Later Decisions, by E. D. Ingraham, Esq. 3 vols. Springfield. 1833." *The American Jurist and Law Magazine.* xi(xxii) (April 1834): 320–338.

"Character of Law Books and Judges." *The American Jurist and Law Magazine.* xii (xxiii) (July 1834): 5–66.

"Replevin of Goods Taken in Execution.—Error in the Books." *The American Jurist and Law Magazine.* xii(xxiii) (July 1834): 104–117.

Notice of "*The Law Glossary . . .* By Thomas Tayler, Late of Clement's Inn, London, Solicitor in His Majesty's High Court of Chancery. Albany. Published by W. & A. Gould, and by Gould, Banks & Co. New York. 1833. 8vo. pp. 501." *The American Jurist and Law Magazine.* xii(xxiii) (July 1834): 248–270.

"Are Challenges to Jurors in Massachusetts Determinable by Triors?" *The American Jurist and Law Magazine.* xii(xxiv) (October 1834): 330–340.

Review of "*The Practice in Civil Actions and Proceedings at Law, in Massachusetts.* By Samuel Howe, Late Judge of the Court of Common Pleas. Edited by Richard S. Fay and Jonathan Chapman, Counsellors at Law. Boston. Hilliard, Gray, and Company. 1834. 8vo. pp. 599." *The American Jurist and Law Magazine.* xii(xxiv) (October 1834): 554–567.

"Right to Sue the United States." *The American Jurist and Law Magazine.* xiii(xxv) (January 1835): 34–39.

"Sketch of the Law School at Cambridge." *The American Jurist and Law Magazine.* xiii(xxv) (January 1835): 107–130.

"The Advocates Library in Edinburgh." *The American Jurist and Law Magazine.* xiii(xxv) (January 1835): 382–389.

Notice of "*Suggestions for a Reform of the Court of Chancery, by a Union of the Jurisdiction of Equity and Law; with a Plan of a New Tribunal for Cases of Lunacy.* By Arthur James Johnes, Esq. of Lincoln's Inn. London. 1834. 8vo. pp. 134." *The American Jurist and Law Magazine.* xiii(xxvi) (April 1835): 459–465. ("Probably" by Sumner, according to Pierce 1: 160 n5.)

"The Juridical Writings of Sir James Mackintosh." *The American Jurist and Law Magazine.* xiv(xxvii) (July 1835): 100–134.

"The Library of the Inner Temple." *The American Jurist and Law Magazine.* xiv(xxviii) (October 1835): 310–316.

Review of Lieber's "Reminiscences" in the Boston Daily *Atlas.* 6 January 1836.

"Barbour's Equity Digest." *The American Jurist and Law Magazine.* xvii(xxxiv) (July 1837): 366–372.

"Phillips on the Law of Patents." *The American Jurist and Law Magazine.* xviii(xxxv) (October 1837): 101–119.

"Law and Literature." Review of "*Miscellaneous Thoughts on Men, Manners and Things.* By Anthony Grumbler, of Grumbleton Hall, Esquire. Baltimore; Published by Coale & Co, 1837. pp. 374." *The American Jurist and Law Magazine.* xviii(xxxv) (October 1837): 119–120.

Review of "*Miscellaneous Thoughts on Men, Manners, and Things.* By Anthony Grumbler, of Grumbleton Hall, Esquire. Baltimore. Published by Coale & Co. 1837. 12 mo. pp. 374." *North American Review.* xlv(xcvii) (October 1837): 482–484.

Review of "*The Shipmaster's Assistant, and Commercial Digest; Containing Information Useful to Merchants, Owners, and Masters of Ships.* By Joseph Blunt, Counsellor at Law. New York. Published by E. & S. W. Blunt. 1837. 8vo. pp. 683." *North American Review.* xlv(xcvii) (October 1837): 502–504.

"The Judgments of Sir Edward Sugden." A Review of "*Reports of Cases argued and Determined in the High Court of Chancery in Ireland, during the Time of Lord Chancellor Sugden, from the Commencement of Hilary Term, 1835, to the Commencement of Easter Term, 1835.* By Bartholomew Clifford Lloyd and Francis Gould, Esquires, Barristers at Law. London. 1836." *The American Jurist and Law Magazine.* xviii(xxxvi) (January 1838): 328–334.

Review of "*The Americans, in Their Moral, Social, and Political Relations.* By Francis J. Grund. From the London Edition of Longman, Rees, Orme, Brown, Green, & Longman. Two Volumes in One. Boston. Marsh, Capen, & Lyon. 1837. 12 mo. pp. 423." *North American Review.* xlvi(xcviii) (January 1838): 106–126.

Review of "*Political Hermeneutics, or an Essay on Political Interpretation and Construction, and also on Precedents.* By Francis Lieber, Professor of History in South Carolina College. Boston. Charles C. Little & James Brown. 1837. 8vo." *North American Review.* XLVI(xcviii) (January 1838): 300–301.

"Crawford, the American Sculptor." Boston *Daily Evening Transcript.* 31 December 1840.

"Right of Search on the Coast of Africa." Boston *Daily Advertiser.* 4 January and 10 February 1842.

Review of "*Commentaries on the Law of Bills of Exchange, Foreign and Inland, as Administered in England and America; with Occasional Illustrations from the Commercial Law of the Nations of Continental Europe.* By Joseph Story, LL.D., One of the Justices of the Supreme Court of the United States, and Dane Professor of Law in Harvard University. Boston: 1843." *The Law Reporter.* v(xi) (March 1843): 519–522.

Review of "*De Vera Judicii Juratorum Origine, Natura et Indole.* Dissertatio inauguralis quam illustri jurisconsultorum ordini in alma literarum Universitate Ruperto-Carola Heidelbergensi ad Gradum Doctoris summos in Jure Civili et Canonico honores rite obtinendos submisit Auctor Thomas Caute Reynolds, Carolina-Americanus. Heidelbergæ: 1842. pp. 90." *The Law Reporter.* VI (May 1843): 43–44.

"Crawford's *Orpheus.*" *The United States Magazine and Democratic Review.* XII (May 1843): 451–455.

"The Mutiny of the Somers." *North American Review.* LVII (cxx) (July 1843): 195–241.

"The Eightieth Birthday of Chancellor Kent." *The Law Reporter.* VI(vii) (November 1843): 289–296.

Notice of "*The Relation of the Poet to His Age. A Discourse Delivered before the Phi Beta Kappa Society of Harvard University, on Thursday, Aug. 26th, 1843.* By George S. Hillard. Second Edition. Boston. Charles C. Little and James Brown. 1843. pp. 53." *The Law Reporter.* VI(vii) (November 1843): 330–331.

Notice of "*Proceedings and Debates in the House of Representatives of the Commonwealth of Massachusetts, during the Four Days Previous to the Election of a Speaker, in January, 1843; Compiled from the Several Reports of the Same, Revised, Corrected and Enlarged, and Preceded by an Introduction.* By Luther S. Cushing, Clerk of the House of Representatives. Boston: Dutton and Wentworth. 1843. pp. 84." *The Law Reporter.* VI(viii) (December 1843): 377–378.

"University of Heidelberg." *The Law Reporter.* VI(viii) (December 1843): 381.

Notice of "*The Reporters Chronologically Arranged, with Occasional Remarks upon Their Respective Merits.* By John William Wallace. Philadelphia: L. R. Baily, Printer. 1844. pp. 77." *The Law Reporter.* VI(ix) (January 1844): 425–426.

Notice of "*Reports of Cases in the Supreme Judicial Court of the State of Maine.* By John Shepley, Counsellor at Law. Vol. VIII. (Maine Reports, Volume XXI.) Hallowell: Glazier, Masters, and Smith. 1843." *The Law Reporter.* VI (March 1844): 519–520.

Notice of "*Report of the Trustees of the Maine Insane Hospital, Embracing the Fourth Annual Report of the Superintendent of the Hospital, November 30, 1843.* (Document of the Legislature of Maine—24th Legislature—No. 1—House.) pp. 38." *The Law Reporter.* VI(xi) (March 1844): 520–521.

"The Number 'Seven'." *The Law Reporter.* VI(xii) (April 1844): 529–541.

Notice of "*Reports of Cases Argued and Determined in the Supreme Court of Judicature of New Hampshire.* Volume X. Concord. Published by Asa McFarland, 1843." *The Law Reporter.* VII(i) (May 1844): 48–51.

Notice of "*Reports of Cases in Chancery, from 1778 to 1794.* By William Brown, Esq.; with the Annotations of Mr. Belt and Mr. Eden. Edited by J. C. Perkins, Esq. Vol. I. Boston: Little and Brown, 1844." *The Law Reporter.* VII(i) (May 1844): 51–52.

"American Law Journals." *The Law Reporter.* VII(ii) (June 1844): 65–77.

"Diversions in Philology." *The Law Reporter.* VII(iii) (July 1844): 155–157.

Notice of "*The Constitution and Revised Statutes of the United States, and Additional Laws to 1844, Reduced to Questions and Answers; for the Use of Schools and Families.* By William B. Wedg-

wood, A. M., Member of the New York Bar. Philadelphia: published by Thomas, Cow-
perthwait & Co. 1844." *The Law Reporter.* VIII(i) (June 1845): 88.

*The True Grandeur of Nations: An Oration Delivered before the Authorities of the City of Boston, July
4, 1845.* From the Second Boston Edition. Philadelphia: Henry Longstreth, 1846.

"Tribute of Friendship: The Late Joseph Story." Boston *Daily Advertiser.* 16 September 1845.

Notice of "*Compendium of Modern Civil Law. By Ferdinand Mackeldey, Professor of Law in the University of Bonn.* Edited by Philip Ignatius Kauffman, Ph.D. of the University of Freiburg.
From the Twelfth German Edition. In Two Volumes. Vol. 1. New York: Published by the Editor. 1845." *The Law Reporter.* VIII(ix) (January 1846): 427–428.

"Prisons and Prison Discipline." *Christian Examiner and Religious Miscellany.* XL [Fourth Series
V(i)] (January 1846): 122–138.

Notice of "*On Punishments and Prisons; Written by His Majesty the King of Sweden and Norway.*
Translated from the Second Swedish Edition, by A. May. London: D. Nutt, 158 Fleet Street.
1844. 8vo. pp. 162." *The Law Reporter.* VIII(x) (February 1846): 477–479.

"O'Brien on Military Law." *The Law Reporter.* VIII(xii) (April 1846): 529–532.

"Boston" [pseudonym]. Article against Robert C. Winthrop's vote of 11 May 1846. Boston *Daily
Whig.* 22 July 1846.

"Mr. Winthrop's Vote on the War Bill." Boston *Courier.* 31 July 1846.

"Mr. Winthrop's Vote on the War Bill." Boston *Courier.* 13 August 1846.

*The Scholar, the Jurist, the Artist, the Philanthropist. An Address before the Phi Beta Kappa Society of
Harvard University, at Their Anniversary, August 27, 1846.* Second Edition. Boston: William
D. Ticknor and Company. 1846.

["Antislavery Duties of the Whig Party."] In "Whig State Convention." Boston *Courier.* 24 September 1846.

"To the Hon. Robert C. Winthrop, Representative in Congress from Boston." Boston *Daily Whig.*
27 October 1846.

"Speech of Charles Sumner, Esq., at Faneuil Hall, February 4th, on the Withdrawal of the American Troops from Mexico." Boston *Courier.* 6 February 1847.

*White Slavery in the Barbary States. A Lecture before the Boston Mercantile Library Association, Feb-
ruary 17, 1847.* Boston: William D. Ticknor, 1847. Reprint Miami: Mnemosyne, 1969.

"Honor to John Gorham Palfrey." Boston *Courier.* 23 December 1847.

"Mr. Palfrey's Speech." Boston *Courier.* 1 February 1848.

"Mr. Giddings and Mr. Winthrop." Boston *Daily Whig.* 18 March 1845.

"Boston Latin School." [pseudonym]. Boston *Daily Evening Transcript.* 29 July and 2 August 1850.

"Mr. Sumner's speech at Faneuil Hall, Nov. 6, 1850." *Emancipator and Republican.* 14 November
1850.

Prophetic Voices Concerning America: A Monograph. Boston: Lee and Shepard/New York: Lee,
Shepard, and Dillingham, 1874.

Manuscripts

Charles Francis Adams Papers [microfilm]. Massachusetts Historical Society.

John Quincy Adams Papers [microfilm]. Massachusetts Historical Society.

Nathan Dane Papers. Harvard Law School Library.

Edward Everett Papers [microfilm]. Massachusetts Historical Society.

Simon Greenleaf Papers. Harvard Law School Library.

Henry Wadsworth Longfellow Papers. Houghton Library, Harvard University.

John Gorham Palfrey Papers. Houghton Library, Harvard University.

Joseph Story Papers. Harvard Law School Library.

Charles Pinckney Sumner Papers. Massachusetts Historical Society.

Charles Sumner Papers. Harvard Law School Library.
Charles Sumner Papers. Harvard University Archives.
Charles Sumner Papers. Houghton Library, Harvard University.
Charles Sumner Papers. Massachusetts Historical Society.
Robert C. Winthrop Papers [microfilm]. Massachusetts Historical Society.

Newspapers and Journals

The American Jurist and Law Magazine (Boston).
The Daily Atlas (Boston).
The Boston Gazette
The Boston Yankee
The Morning Commonwealth (Boston).
The Congressional Globe (Washington).
The Daily Courier (Boston).
The Daily Advertiser (Boston).
The Masonic Mirror (Boston).
The Law Reporter (Boston).
The Morning Post (Boston).
The Daily Whig (Boston, 1846–1848). Then the Republican (1848–1849), later the Emancipator and Republican (1849–1850).

Published Sources

Abbott, Richard II. Cobbler in Congress: The Life of Henry Wilson, 1812–1875. Lexington: The University Press of Kentucky, 1972.
Adams, Charles Francis, Jr. Charles Francis Adams, 1835–1915: An Autobiography. Boston: Houghton Mifflin, 1916.
———. Richard Henry Dana: A Biography. Boston: Houghton, Mifflin, 1890. 2 volumes.
Adams, Henry. The Education of Henry Adams: An Autobiography. Boston: Houghton Mifflin, 1918.
[Adams, John, et al.]. Adams Family Correspondence. (Series II of The Adams Family Papers). L. H. Butterfield, Editor-in-Chief. Cambridge: The Belknap Press of Harvard University Press, 1973. 4 volumes.
[Anonymous.] Editorial notice of "Reports on the abolition of Capital Punishment; reprinted by order of the House of Representatives, from the Legislative documents of 1835 and 1836. Boston, Dutton & Wentworth, State Printers, 1837, pp. 136." The American Jurist and Law Magazine. XVII(xxxiii) (April 1837): 236–238.
Appleton, William Sumner. Record of the Descendants of William Sumner of Dorchester, Mass. 1636. Boston: David Clapp & Son, 1879.
Aptheker, Herbert. American Negro Slave Revolts. New York: International Publishers, 1963.
Aumann, Francis R. The Changing American Legal System: Some Selected Phases. New York: Da Capo, 1969.
Baker, Paul. The Fortunate Pilgrims: Americans in Italy, 1800–1860. Cambridge: Harvard University Press, 1964.
Bartlett, Irving H. Wendell Phillips: Brahmin Radical. Boston: Beacon Press, 1961.
Baum, Dale. The Civil War Party System: The Case of Massachusetts, 1848–1876. Chapel Hill: The University of North Carolina Press, 1984.
Beard, Charles A., and Mary R. Beard. The American Spirit: A Study of the Idea of Civilization in the United States. (Volume IV of The Rise of American Civilization). New York: Macmillan, 1942.

Beirne, Charles J., S.J. "The Theology of Theodore Parker and the War with Mexico." *Essex Institute Historical Collections.* CIV(ii) (April 1968): 130–137.

Bloomfield, Maxwell H. *American Lawyers in a Changing Society, 1776–1876.* Cambridge: Harvard University Press, 1976.

———. "Law vs. Politics: The Self-Image of the American Bar (1830–1860)." *American Journal of Legal History.* XII (October 1968): 306–323.

Blue, Frederick J. *Charles Sumner and the Conscience of the North.* (American Biographical Series). Arlington Heights, Ill.: Harlan-Davidson, 1994.

———. *The Free Soilers: Third Party Politics, 1848–54.* Urbana: University of Illinois Press, 1973.

Blumenthal, Henry. *France and the United States: Their Diplomatic Relations, 1789–1914.* Chapel Hill: The University of North Carolina Press, 1970.

Botein, Stephen. "Cicero as Role Model for Early American Lawyers: A Case Study in Classical 'Influence'." *Classical Journal.* LXXIII (Spring 1978): 313–321.

[Bowen, Francis.] "*Critical Notices: The True Grandeur of Nations: an Oration delivered before the Authorities of the City of Boston, July 4, 1845.* By Charles Sumner. Second Edition. Boston: Published by the American Peace Society. 1845. 8vo. pp. 96." *North American Review.* LXI(cxxix) (October 1845): 518–523.

Brauer, Kinley J. *Cotton versus Conscience: Massachusetts Whig Politics and Southwestern Expansion, 1843–1848.* Lexington: The University of Kentucky Press, 1967.

Brock, William. "The Image of England and American Nationalism." *Journal of American Studies.* V(iii) (December 1971): 225–245.

Brown, Arthur. *Always Young for Liberty: A Biography of William Ellery Channing.* Syracuse: Syracuse University Press, 1956.

Brown, Thomas. *Politics and Statesmanship: Essays on the American Whig Party.* New York: Columbia University Press, 1985.

Bullock, Steven C. *Revolutionary Brotherhood: Freemasonry and the Transformation of the American Social Order, 1730–1840.* Chapel Hill: The University of North Carolina Press, for the Institute of Early American History and Culture, Williamsburg, Va., 1996.

Cady, Edwin H. *The Gentleman in America: A Literary Study in American Culture.* Syracuse: Syracuse University Press, 1949.

Calhoun, Daniel H. *Professional Lives in America: Structure and Aspiration, 1750–1850.* Cambridge: Harvard University Press, 1965.

Campbell, Stanley W. *The Slave Catchers: Enforcement of the Fugitive Slave Law, 1850–1860.* Chapel Hill: The University of North Carolina Press, 1970.

Canavan, Francis P., S.J. *The Political Reason of Edmund Burke.* Durham: Duke University Press, 1960.

Cayton, Mary Kupiec. *Emerson's Emergence: Self and Society in the Transformation of New England, 1800–1845.* Chapel Hill: The University of North Carolina Press, 1989.

Chamberlain, Allen. *Beacon Hill: Its Ancient Pastures and Early Mansions.* Boston: Houghton Mifflin, 1925.

Channing, Edward Tyrell. *Lectures Read to the Seniors in Harvard College.* Boston: Ticknor and Fields, 1856.

Channing, William Ellery. *The Works of William E. Channing, D.D.* Seventh edition. Boston: James Munroe, 1847. 6 volumes.

Chaplin, Jeremiah, and J. D. Chaplin. *Life of Charles Sumner.* With an Introduction by Hon. William Claflin. Boston: D. Lothrop/Dover, N.H.: G. T. Day, 1874.

Charvat, William. *Literary Publishing in America, 1790–1850.* Amherst: University of Massachusetts Press, 1993.

Child, Lydia Maria. *An Appeal in Favor of that Class of Americans Called Africans.* Edited by Carolyn L. Karcher. Amherst: University of Massachusetts Press, 1996.

Cole, Donald B. *Martin Van Buren and the American Political System.* Princeton: Princeton University Press, 1984.

Cook, Charles M. *The American Codification Movement: A Study of Antebellum Legal Reform.* Westport, Conn.: Greenwood Press, 1981.

Corwin, Edward S. *The "Higher Law" Background of American Constitutional Law.* Ithaca: Cornell University Press, 1955.

[Dana, Richard Henry, Jr.] *The Journal of Richard Henry Dana, Jr.* Edited by Robert F. Lucid. Cambridge: The Belknap Press of Harvard University Press, 1968. 3 volumes.

Darling, Arthur Burr. *Political Changes in Massachusetts, 1824–1848: A Study of Liberal Movements in Politics.* Cos Cob, Conn.: John E. Edwards, 1968 (reprint of 1925 edition).

Davis, David Brion. *Revolutions: Reflections on American Equality and Foreign Liberations.* Cambridge: Harvard University Press, 1990.

———. "Some Themes of Counter-Subversion: An Analysis of Anti-Masonic, Anti-Catholic, and Anti-Mormon Literature." *Mississippi Valley Historical Review.* XLVII(ii) (September 1960): 205–224.

Dawes, Anna Laurens. *Charles Sumner.* New York: Dodd, Mead, 1892.

Dearinger, David Bernard. "American Neoclassical Sculptors and Their Private Patrons in Boston." Ph.D. dissertation in Art History. City University of New York, 1993.

Delbanco, Andrew. *William Ellery Channing: An Essay on the Liberal Spirit in America.* Cambridge: Harvard University Press, 1981.

Dennison, George M. *The Dorr War: Republicanism on Trial, 1831–1861.* Lexington: The University Press of Kentucky, 1976.

Dickens, Charles. *The Life and Adventures of Martin Chuzzlewit.* London: Thomas Nelson and Sons, 1906.

Dimmick, Lauretta. "A Catalogue of the Portrait Busts and Ideal Works of Thomas Crawford (1813?–1857), American Sculptor in Rome." Ph.D. dissertation in Art History. University of Pittsburgh, 1986.

Donald, David Herbert. *Charles Sumner.* Revised edition in one volume. New York: Da Capo Press, 1996.

———. *Charles Sumner and the Coming of the Civil War.* Revised edition. New York: Fawcett-Columbine, 1989.

———. *Charles Sumner and the Rights of Man.* New York: Alfred A. Knopf, 1970.

———. *Lincoln Reconsidered: Essays on the Civil War Era.* Second edition, enlarged. New York: Vintage Books, 1961.

———. *Lincoln's Herndon.* New edition. New York: Da Capo [c. 1988].

Duberman, Martin. *Charles Francis Adams, 1807–1886.* Stanford: Stanford University Press, 1960.

Dwelley, Jedediah, and John F. Simmons. *History of the Town of Hanover Massachusetts with Family Genealogies.* Hanover: Town of Hanover, 1910.

Ellis, David. *Economic Growth and the Ending of the Transatlantic Slave Trade.* New York: Oxford University Press, 1987.

[Emerson, Ralph Waldo]. *The Journals and Miscellaneous Notebooks of Ralph Waldo Emerson.* Edited by William Gilman et al. Cambridge: The Belknap Press of Harvard University Press, 1960–1982. 16 volumes.

Farrell, James M. "John Adams's Autobiography: The Ciceronian Paradigm and the Quest for Fame." *The New England Quarterly.* LXII(iv). (December 1989): 505–528.

Felton, Cornelius Conway. "Professor Channing and His Lectures." *North American Review.* LXXXIV(clxxiv) (January 1857): 34–48.

[————.] "Sumner's Oration." *Christian Examiner and Religious Miscellany.* xxxix [4th Series IV(iii)] (November 1845): 407–417.

Ferguson, Robert A. *Law and Letters in American Culture.* Cambridge: Harvard University Press, 1984.

Foner, Eric. *Free Soil, Free Labor, Free Men: The Ideology of the Republican Party before the Civil War.* New York: Oxford University Press, 1970.

————. *Politics and Ideology in the Age of the Civil War.* New York: Oxford University Press, 1980.

————. "The Wilmot Proviso Revisited." *The Journal of American History.* LVI(ii) (September 1969): 262–279.

Foner, Philip S. *History of Black Americans: From Africa to the Emergence of the Cotton Kingdom.* Westport, Conn.: Greenwood Press, 1975.

Formisano, Ronald. *The Transformation of Political Culture: Massachusetts Parties, 1790's–1840's.* New York: Oxford University Press, 1983.

[Franklin, Benjamin.] *The Works of Benjamin Franklin. Containing Several Political and Historical Tracts Not Included in any Former Edition and Many Letters Official and Private Not Hitherto Published with Notes and A Life of the Author.* Edited by Jared Sparks. Boston: Hilliard, Gray and Company. 1836–1839. 9 volumes.

Freidel, Frank. *Francis Lieber: Nineteenth-Century Liberal.* Baton Rouge: Louisiana State University Press, 1947. Reprint Gloucester, Mass.: Peter Smith, 1968.

Gara, Larry. "Slavery and the Slave Power: A Crucial Distinction." *Civil War History.* xv(iii) (March 1969): 5–18.

Garrison, Wendell Phillips, and Francis Jackson Garrison. *William Lloyd Garrison, 1805–1879: The Story of His Life, Told by His Children.* New York: The Century Company, 1885. 4 volumes.

[Garrison, William Lloyd]. *The Letters of William Lloyd Garrison.* Edited by Walter E. Merrill and Louis Ruchames. Cambridge: The Belknap Press of Harvard University Press, 1971–1979. 6 volumes.

Gatell, Frank Otto. *John Gorham Palfrey and the New England Conscience.* Cambridge: Harvard University Press, 1963.

Gawalt, Gerard W. *The Promise of Power: The Emergence of the Legal Profession in Massachusetts, 1760–1840.* Westport, Conn.: Greenwood Press, 1979.

Gollaher, David. *Voice for the Mad: The Life of Dorothea Dix.* New York: The Free Press, 1995.

Goodman, Paul. "David Donald's *Charles Sumner* Reconsidered." *The New England Quarterly.* xxxvii(iii) (September 1964): 373–387.

————. *The Democratic-Republicans of Massachusetts: Politics in a Young Republic.* Cambridge: Harvard University Press, 1964. Reprint Westport, Conn.: Greenwood Press, 1986.

————. "Ethics and Enterprise: The Values of the Boston Elite, 1800–1860." *American Quarterly.* xviii(iii) (Fall 1966): 437–451.

————. *Towards a Christian Republic: Antimasonry and the Great Transition in New England, 1826–1836.* New York: Oxford University Press, 1988.

Gray, Thomas. *The Poetical Works of Thomas Gray: English and Latin.* Edited with an Introduction, Life, and Notes by John Bradshaw. New York: A. L. Burt, n.d.

Gregory, Frances W. *Nathan Appleton: Merchant and Entrepreneur, 1779–1861.* Charlottesville: University Press of Virginia, 1975.

Grimké, Archibald H. *Charles Sumner: The Scholar in Politics.* (American Reformers Series). New York: Funk and Wagnalls, 1892.

Haber, Samuel. *The Quest for Authority and Honor in the American Professions, 1750–1900.* Chicago: University of Chicago Press, 1991.

Hamilton, Holman. *Prologue to Conflict: The Crisis and Compromise of 1850.* New York: W. W. Norton, 1966.

Handlin, Oscar. *Boston's Immigrants: A Study in Acculturation.* Cambridge: Harvard University Press, 1979.

Haynes, George H. *Charles Sumner.* (American Crisis Biographies). Philadelphia: George W. Jacobs, 1909.

Hill, Hamilton Andrews. *Memoir of Abbott Lawrence.* Boston: Printed by the University Press, Cambridge, for private distribution, 1883.

Hillard, George Stillman. "Farewell to Number Four." *The Law Reporter.* xvIII (March 1856): 653.

————. "On the English Inns of Court." *The American Jurist and Law Magazine.* xIII(xxvi) (April 1835): 310–332.

————. "Remarks" on Cornelius Conway Felton. Massachusetts Historical Society *Proceedings.* v (March 1862): 446–457.

Hillard, George Stillman, and Mrs. George and Miss Anna Ticknor. *Life, Letters and Journals of George Ticknor.* Boston: James R. Osgood, 1877. 2 volumes.

Hofstadter, Richard. *The Idea of a Party System: The Rise of Legitimate Opposition in the United States, 1780–1840.* Berkeley: University of California Press, 1969.

Holmes, J. Welfred. "Whittier and Sumner: A Political Friendship." *The New England Quarterly.* xxx(i) (March 1957): 58–72.

Horn, Stuart Joel. "Edward Everett and American Nationalism." Ph.D. dissertation in History. City University of New York, 1973.

Horton, James Oliver, and Lois E. Horton. *Black Bostonians: Family Life and Community Struggle in the Antebellum North.* New York: Holmes & Meier, 1979.

Horwitz, Morton. *The Transformation of American Law, 1780–1860.* Cambridge: Harvard University Press, 1977.

Howe, Daniel Walker. *The Political Culture of the American Whigs.* Chicago: University of Chicago Press, 1979.

————. *The Unitarian Conscience: Harvard Moral Philosophy, 1805–1861.* Middletown, Conn.: Wesleyan University Press, 1988.

Howe, Julia Ward. *Reminiscences, 1819–1899.* Boston: Houghton Mifflin, 1899.

Hunt, Alfred N. *Haiti's Influence on Antebellum America: Slumbering Volcano in the Caribbean.* Baton Rouge: Louisiana State University Press, 1988.

James, Henry. *William Wetmore Story and His Friends, from Letters, Diaries, and Recollections.* Boston: Houghton Mifflin, 1903. Reprint New York: Kennedy Galleries/Da Capo Press, 1969. Two volumes in one.

[Jefferson, Thomas]. *The Portable Thomas Jefferson.* Edited by Merrill D. Peterson. New York: Viking Penguin, 1975.

Jenks, Henry F. *Catalogue of the Boston Public Latin School, Established in 1635: With an Historical Sketch.* Boston: Boston Latin School Association, 1886.

Jones, Howard Mumford. *O Strange New World. American Culture: The Formative Years.* New York: Viking Press, 1964.

Jordan, Winthrop D. *White over Black: American Attitudes toward the Negro, 1550–1812.* Baltimore: Penguin Books, 1969.

Julian, George Washington. *Political Recollections, 1840 to 1872.* Chicago: Jansen, McClurg, 1884.

Katz, Michael B. *The Irony of Early School Reform: Educational Innovation in Mid-Nineteenth Century Massachusetts.* Boston: Beacon Press, 1970.

Lane, Roger. *Policing the City: Boston, 1822–1885.* Cambridge: Harvard University Press, 1967.

Lawrence, William. *Life of Amos A. Lawrence, with Extracts from His Diary and Correspondence.* Boston: Houghton, Mifflin, 1888.

Ledbetter, Bill. "Charles Sumner: Political Activist for the New England Transcendentalists." *The Historian.* xLIV(iii) (May 1982): 347–363.

Lester, C. Edwards. *Life and Public Services of Charles Sumner.* New York: United States Publishing Company, 1874.

Levy, Leonard W., and Harlan B. Phillips. "The Roberts Case: Source of the 'Separate but Equal' Doctrine." *The American Historical Review.* LVI(iii) (April 1951): 510–518.

Lewis, W. David. *From Newgate to Dannemora: The Rise of the Penitentiary in New York, 1796–1848.* Ithaca: Cornell University Press, 1965.

Lieber, Francis. "On Political Hermeneutics, or, on Political Interpretation and Construction, and also on Precedents." *The American Jurist and Law Magazine.* XVIII(xxxv) (October 1837): 37–101, and XVIII(xxxvi) (January 1838): 281–294.

Lipsky, George A. *John Quincy Adams: His Theory and Ideas.* New York: Thomas Y. Crowell, 1950.

Lockwood, Allison. *Passionate Pilgrims: The American Traveler in Great Britain, 1800–1914.* New York: Cornwall Books/Rutherford, N.J.: Fairleigh Dickinson University Press, 1981.

Logan, Rayford W. *The Diplomatic Relations of the United States with Haiti, 1776–1891.* Chapel Hill: The University of North Carolina Press, 1941. Reprint New York: Kraus Reprint, 1969.

Long, Orie W. *Literary Pioneers: Early American Explorers of European Culture.* Cambridge: Harvard University Press, 1935. Reprint New York: Russell and Russell, 1963.

Longfellow, Ernest Wadsworth. *Random Memories.* Boston: Houghton Mifflin, 1922.

[Longfellow, Frances Elizabeth Appleton.] *Mrs. Longfellow: Selected Letters and Journals of Fanny Appleton Longfellow (1817–1861).* Edited by Edward Wagenknecht. New York: Longmans, Green, 1956.

Longfellow, Henry Wadsworth. *Kavanagh, a Tale.* Boston: Ticknor, Reed, and Fields, 1849.

[———]. *The Letters of Henry Wadsworth Longfellow.* Edited by Andrew Hilen. Cambridge: The Belknap Press of Harvard University Press, 1966–1982. 6 volumes.

Longfellow, Samuel. *Life of Henry Wadsworth Longfellow.* Boston: Ticknor and Company, 1886. 2 volumes.

Loring, James Spear. *The Hundred Boston Orators Appointed by the Municipal Authorities and Other Public Bodies from 1770 to 1852; Comprising Historical Gleanings, Illustrating the Principles and Progress of Our Republican Institutions.* Boston: J. P. Jewett and Company/Cleveland: Jewett, Proctor and Worthington, 1852.

Matthews, Jean. *Rufus Choate: The Law and Civic Virtue.* Philadelphia: Temple University Press, 1980.

May, Henry F. *The Enlightenment in America.* New York: Oxford University Press, 1976.

McCaughey, Robert A. *Josiah Quincy, 1772–1864: The Last Federalist.* Cambridge: Harvard University Press, 1974.

McClellan, James. *Joseph Story and the American Constitution: A Study in Political and Legal Thought with Selected Writings.* Norman: University of Oklahoma Press, 1971.

McInerney, Daniel J. "'A State of Commerce': Market Power and Slave Power in Abolitionist Political Economy." *Civil War History.* XXXVII(ii) (June 1991): 101–119.

McKay, Ernest A. "Henry Wilson and the Coalition of 1851." *The New England Quarterly.* XXXVI(iii) (September 1963): 338–357.

———. *Henry Wilson: Practical Radical. A Portrait of a Politician.* Port Washington, N.Y.: Kennikat Press for National University Publications, 1971.

Merk, Frederick. *History of the Westward Movement.* New York: Alfred A. Knopf, 1978.

Meyer, Donald Harvey. *The Instructed Conscience: The Shaping of the American National Ethic.* Philadelphia: University of Pennsylvania Press, 1972.

Meyers, Marvin. *The Jacksonian Persuasion: Politics and Belief.* New York: Vintage, 1960.

Miller, Perry. *The Life of the Mind in America from the Revolution to the Civil War.* New York: Harcourt, Brace and World, 1965.

Miquel, Pierre. *Histoire de la France.* Paris: Librairie Arthème Fayard, 1976. 2 volumes.

Morison, Samuel Eliot. *Three Centuries of Harvard, 1636–1936*. Cambridge: Harvard University Press, 1936.

Morrison, Chaplain W. *Democratic Politics and Sectionalism: The Wilmot Proviso Controversy*. Chapel Hill: The University of North Carolina Press, 1967.

Morrison, Michael A. *Slavery and the American West: The Eclipse of Manifest Destiny and the Coming of the Civil War*. Chapel Hill: The University of North Carolina Press, 1997.

Nason, Elias. *The Life and Times of Charles Sumner: His Boyhood, Education, and Public Career*. Boston: B. B. Russell, 1874.

Newmyer, R. Kent. "Harvard Law School, New England Legal Culture, and the Antebellum Origins of American Jurisprudence." *The Journal of American History*. LXXIV(iii) (December 1987): 814–835.

———. *Supreme Court Justice Joseph Story: Statesman of the Old Republic*. Chapel Hill: The University of North Carolina Press, 1985.

Niven, John. *Martin Van Buren: The Romantic Age of American Politics*. New York: Oxford University Press, 1983.

———. *Salmon P. Chase: A Biography*. New York: Oxford University Press, 1995.

Nye, Russel B. *Fettered Freedom: Civil Liberties and the Slavery Controversy*. Revised edition. East Lansing: Michigan State University Press, 1963.

Oates, Stephen B. *The Approaching Fury: Voices of the Storm, 1820–1861*. New York: Harper Collins, 1997.

O'Connor, Thomas. *Lords of the Loom: The Cotton Whigs and the Coming of the Civil War*. New York: Charles Scribner's Sons, 1968.

Osofsky, Gilbert. "Cardboard Yankee: How Not to Study the Mind of Charles Sumner." *Reviews in American History*. I(iv) (December 1973): 595–606.

———. "Wendell Phillips and the Quest for a New American Nationality." *Canadian Review of Studies in Nationalism*. I (Fall 1973): 15–46.

Palmer, Beverly Wilson. "The American Identity and Europe: View of Emerson and Sumner." *Harvard Library Bulletin*. XXX(i) (1982): 74–86.

———. "Towards a National Antislavery Party: The Giddings-Sumner Alliance." *Ohio History*. XCIX (1990): 51–71.

Peterson, Merrill D. *The Great Triumvirate: Webster, Clay, and Calhoun*. New York: Oxford University Press, 1987.

Phillips, Wendell. *Speeches, Lectures, and Letters*. Boston: Walker, Wise, 1864.

Pickard, Samuel T. *Life and Letters of John Greenleaf Whittier*. Boston: Houghton, Mifflin, 1894. 2 volumes.

Pierce, Edward Lillic. *Memoir and Letters of Charles Sumner*. Boston: Roberts Brothers, 1877, 1893. 4 volumes.

Potter, David M. *The Impending Crisis, 1848–1861*. New York: Harper and Row, 1976.

Preston, Katharine K. *Opera on the Road: Traveling Opera Troupes in the United States, 1825–60*. Urbana: University of Illinois Press, 1993.

Prize Essays on a Congress of Nations, for the Adjustment of International Disputes and for the Promotion of Universal Peace without Resort to Arms. Boston: Whipple & Damrell for the American Peace Society, 1840.

Randall, James G. "The Blundering Generation." *Mississippi Valley Historical Review*. XXVII (1940): 3–28.

Rantoul, Robert, Jr. *Memoirs Speeches and Writings of Robert Rantoul, Jr.* Edited by Luther Hamilton. Boston: John P. Jewett and Company/Cleveland: Jewett, Proctor, and Worthington/London: Low and Company, 1854.

Ratner, Lorman. *Powder Keg: Northern Opposition to the Antislavery Movement, 1831–1840*. New York: Basic Books, 1968.

Rayback, Joseph G. *Free Soil: The Election of 1848.* Lexington: The University Press of Kentucky, 1970.

Remini, Robert V. *Daniel Webster: The Man and His Time.* New York: W. W. Norton, 1997.

———. *Henry Clay: Statesman for the Union.* New York: W. W. Norton, 1991.

Rhodes, James Ford. "Memoir of Edward L. Pierce." Massachusetts Historical Society *Proceedings.* Second Series. XVIII (9 June 1904): 363–369.

Richards, Leonard L. *"Gentlemen of Property and Standing": Anti-Abolition Mobs in Jacksonian America.* New York: Oxford University Press, 1970.

———. *The Life and Times of Congressman John Quincy Adams.* New York: Oxford University Press, 1986.

———. *The Slave Power: The Free North and Southern Domination, 1780–1860.* Baton Rouge: Louisiana State University Press, 2000.

Robertson, Priscilla. *Revolutions of 1848: A Social History.* Princeton: Princeton University Press, 1952.

Robinson, William S. *"Warrington" Pen-Portraits: A Collection of Personal and Political Reminiscences from 1848 to 1876, from the Writings of William S. Robinson.* Edited with an Introduction by Mrs. William S. Robinson. Boston: Edited and Published by Mrs. W. S. Robinson, 1877.

Rolle, Andrew F. "A Friendship across the Atlantic: Charles Sumner and William Story." *American Quarterly.* XI (Spring 1959): 40–57.

Ruchames, Louis. "Charles Sumner and American Historiography." *Journal of Negro History.* XXXVIII (1953): 139–160.

———. "The Pulitzer Prize Treatment of Charles Sumner." *The Massachusetts Review.* II (Summer 1961): 749–769.

———. "Race and Education in Massachusetts." *Negro History Bulletin.* XIII(iii) (December 1949): 53–59, 71.

[Sand, George]. *Correspondance.* Paris: Garnier Frères, 1964–1991. 25 volumes.

Schroeder, John H. *Mr. Polk's War: American Opposition and Dissent, 1846–1848.* Madison: University of Wisconsin Press, 1973.

Schultz, Stanley K. *The Culture Factory: Boston Public Schools, 1789–1860.* New York: Oxford University Press, 1973.

Schurz, Carl. *Charles Sumner: An Essay by Carl Schurz.* Edited by Arthur Reed Hogue. Urbana: University of Illinois Press, 1951.

Schutz, John and Douglass Adair, editors. *The Spur of Fame: Dialogues of John Adams and Benjamin Rush, 1805–1813.* San Marino, Calif.: The Huntington Library, 1966.

Schwartz, Harold. "Fugitive Slave Days in Boston." *The New England Quarterly.* XXVII(ii) (June 1954): 191–212.

———. *Samuel Gridley Howe: Social Reformer, 1801–1876.* Cambridge: Harvard University Press, 1956.

Seidler, Jan M. "A Critical Reappraisal of the Career of William Wetmore Story (1819–1895)." Ph.D. dissertation in Art History. Boston University, 1985.

"Selections from the Story Papers." Massachusetts Historical Society *Proceedings.* XXXV (Second Series XV) (1901–1902): 201–224.

Sellers, Charles. *James K. Polk: Continentalist, 1843–1846.* Princeton: Princeton University Press, 1966.

———. *The Market Revolution: Jacksonian America, 1815–1846.* New York: Oxford University Press, 1991.

Sewell, Richard H. *Ballots for Freedom: Antislavery Politics in the United States, 1837–1860.* New York: Oxford University Press, 1976.

Smith, Justin. *The War with Mexico.* New York: Macmillan, 1919. 2 volumes.

Spencer, Benjamin T. *The Quest for Nationality: An American Literary Campaign.* Syracuse: Syracuse University Press, 1957.

Spencer, Donald S. *Louis Kossuth and Young America: A Study in Sectionalism and Foreign Policy, 1848–1852.* Columbia: University of Missouri Press, 1977.

Spooner, Lysander. *The Collected Works of Lysander Spooner.* Biography and Introductions by Charles Shively. Weston, Mass.: M & S Press, 1971. 6 volumes.

Stearns, Frank Preston. *Cambridge Sketches.* Philadelphia: J. B. Lippincott, 1905.

Stewart, James Brewer. *Joshua R. Giddings and the Tactics of Radical Politics.* Cleveland: The Press of Case Western Reserve University, 1970.

———. *Wendell Phillips: Liberty's Hero.* Baton Rouge: Louisiana State University Press, 1986.

Storey, Moorfield. *Charles Sumner.* (American Statesmen Series). Boston: Houghton Mifflin, 1900.

Storey, Moorfield, and Edward W. Emerson. *Ebenezer Rockwood Hoar: A Memoir.* Boston: Houghton Mifflin, 1911.

Story, Joseph. *The Miscellaneous Writings of Joseph Story.* Edited by William Wetmore Story. Boston: C. C. Little and J. Brown, 1852.

———. "Statesmen: Their Rareness and Importance." *The New-England Magazine.* VII (August 1834): 89–104.

Story, Ronald. "Class and Culture in Boston: The Athenæum, 1807–1860." *American Quarterly.* XXVIII(ii) (May 1975): 178–199.

———. *The Forging of an Aristocracy: Harvard & the Boston Upper Class, 1800–1870.* Middletown, Conn.: Wesleyan University Press, 1980.

Story, William Wetmore. *Life and Letters of Joseph Story, Associate Justice of the Supreme Court of the United States and Dane Professor of Law at Harvard University.* Boston: C. C. Little and J. Brown, 1851. 2 volumes.

———. [A verse account of Number 4 Court Street]. Massachusetts Historical Society *Proceedings.* XIX (June 1882): 346–348.

Sumner, Charles Pinckney. *The Compass: A Poetical Performance at the Literary Exhibition in September, m, dcc, xcv, at Harvard University.* Boston: Printed by William Spotswood for the Subscribers, [1795].

———. "A Discourse on Some Points of Difference between the Sheriff's Office in Massachusetts and in England: Read in the Hearing of a number of the Gentlemen of the Bar." *The American Jurist and Law Magazine.* II(i) (July 1829): 1–24.

———. *Eulogy on the Illustrious George Washington, Pronounced at Milton, Twenty-Second February, 1800.* Dedham, Mass.: H. Mann, 1800.

———. *A Letter on Speculative Masonry: By Charles Pinckney Sumner, Sheriff of Suffolk County. Being an Answer to a Letter Addressed to Him on that Subject by the Suffolk Committee.* Boston: John Marsh, 1829.

———. To "Messrs. Russell and Cutler." *Boston Gazette.* 29 August 1811.

———. "Ode. Written by Charles P. Sumner, Esq. For the Seventh Anniversary Celebration [of the Massachusetts Charitable Fire Society]. May 31—1801." In *An Address Delivered Before the Members of the Massachusetts Charitable Fire Society, at Their Anniversary Meeting, June 1, 1804.* By Edward Gray, Esq. Boston: Russell and Cutler, 1804. p. 25.

———. "Reminiscences of the Old College Company, or Marti-Mercurian Band." Boston *Columbian Centinel.* 2 April 1828.

———. "To His Excellency Governor Gerry." *Boston Gazette.* 29 August 1811.

———. ["An Elderly Man," pseudonym.] To "Messrs. Ballard & Wright." *Boston Patriot and Mercantile Advertiser.* 4 March 1828.

Sutherland, Arthur E. *The Law at Harvard: A History of Ideas and Men, 1817–1967.* Cambridge: Harvard University Press, 1967.

Taussig, Frank William. *The Tariff History of the United States.* New York: Capricorn Books, 1964.

Teele, A. K., editor. *The History of Milton, Mass., 1640 to 1887*. Boston: Press of Rockwell and Churchill, [1887].

Teeters, Negley K. and John D. Shearer. *The Prison at Philadelphia, Cherry Hill: The Separate System of Penal Discipline, 1829–1913*. New York: Columbia University Press for Temple University Press, 1957.

Thompson, Lawrence Roger. *Young Longfellow, 1807–1843*. New York: Macmillan, 1938.

Tiffany, Nina Moore. *Samuel E. Sewall: A Memoir*. Boston: Houghton Mifflin, 1898.

Todd, Edgeley Woodman. "Philosophical Ideas at Harvard College, 1817–1837." *The New England Quarterly*. xvi(i) (March 1943): 63–90.

Tucker, Edward L. "Charles Sumner and Richard Henry Wilde." *Georgia Historical Quarterly*. xlix(iii) (September 1965): 320–323.

Tyack, David. *George Ticknor and the Boston Brahmins*. Cambridge: Harvard University Press, 1967.

Van Deusen, Glyndon. *The Jacksonian Era, 1828–1848*. New York: Harper Brothers, 1959.

Vaughn, William Preston. *The Antimasonic Party in the United States, 1826–1843*. Lexington: The University Press of Kentucky, 1983.

Wagenknecht, Edward. *Henry Wadsworth Longfellow: Portrait of an American Humanist*. New York: Oxford University Press, 1966.

———. *Longfellow: A Full-Length Portrait*. New York: Longmans, Green, 1955.

[Daniel Webster]. *Diplomatic Papers*. Kenneth E. Shewmaker, Editor. Kenneth R. Stevens and Anita McGurn, Assistant Editors. (Series III of *The Papers of Daniel Webster*. Charles M. Wiltse, Editor-in-Chief). Hanover, N.H.: University Press of New England for Dartmouth College, 1983–1987. 2 volumes.

Whipple, Edwin Percy. *Recollections of Eminent Men with Other Papers*. Boston: Ticknor, 1887.

Whitehill, Walter Muir. *Boston: A Topographical History*. Second edition. Cambridge: The Belknap Press of Harvard University Press, 1968.

Whittier, John Greenleaf. *The Complete Poetical Works of John Greenleaf Whittier*. Boston: The Riverside Press, Houghton, Mifflin, 1894.

Wiecek, William M., Jr. *The Sources of Antislavery Constitutionalism in America, 1760–1848*. Ithaca: Cornell University Press, 1977.

Wilentz, Sean. *Chants Democratic: New York City & the Rise of the American Working Class, 1788–1850*. New York: Oxford University Press, 1984.

Williams, Raymond. *Culture and Society: 1780–1950*. New York: Columbia University Press, 1983.

Wilson, Henry. "History of the Legislative Coalition." *Commonwealth*. 30 January and 18 February 1851.

———. *History of the Rise and Fall of the Slave Power in America*. Boston: Houghton, Mifflin, 1872–1877. 3 volumes.

Wilson, Major L. *Space, Time, and Freedom: The Quest for Nationality and the Irrepressible Conflict, 1815–1861*. Westport, Conn.: Greenwood Press, 1974.

Winthrop, Robert C. *Addresses and Speeches on Various Occasions*. Boston: Little, Brown, 1852.

Winthrop, Robert C., Jr. *A Memoir of Robert C. Winthrop, Prepared for the Massachusetts Historical Society*. Boston: Little, Brown, 1897.

Withington, Mary S. "The Home of Charles Sumner." *Boston Beacon and Dorchester News-Gatherer*. 26 January 1878.

Wittman, Otto J. "The Italian Experience (American Artists in Italy, 1830–1875)." *American Quarterly*. iv(i) (Spring 1952): 3–15.

Wright, Benjamin Fletcher. *American Interpretations of Natural Law: A Study in the History of Political Thought*. New York: Russell and Russell, 1962.

Ziegler, Valarie H. *The Advocates of Peace in Antebellum America*. Bloomington: Indiana University Press, 1992.

INDEX